T0337951

Trading
Price
Action
REVERSALS

Founded in 1807, John Wiley & Sons is the oldest independent publishing company in the United States. With offices in North America, Europe, Australia, and Asia, Wiley is globally committed to developing and marketing print and electronic products and services for our customers' professional and personal knowledge and understanding.

The Wiley Trading series features books by traders who have survived the market's ever changing temperament and have prospered—some by reinventing systems, others by getting back to basics. Whether a novice trader, professional, or somewhere in-between, these books will provide the advice and strategies needed to prosper today and well into the future.

For a list of available titles, please visit our Web site at www.WileyFinance.com.

Trading
Price
Action
REVERSALS

TECHNICAL ANALYSIS of PRICE CHARTS
BAR by BAR FOR THE SERIOUS TRADER

AL BROOKS

WILEY

John Wiley & Sons, Inc.

The first edition of this book, titled *Reading Price Charts Bar by Bar: The Technical Analysis of Price Action for the Serious Trader*, was published in 2009.

Published by John Wiley & Sons, Inc., Hoboken, New Jersey.
Published simultaneously in Canada.

All charts were created with TradeStation. © TradeStation Technologies, Inc. All rights reserved.

For general information on our other products and services or for technical support, please contact our Customer Care Department within the United States at (800) 762-2974, outside the United States at (317) 572-3993 or fax (317) 572-4002.

Wiley also publishes its books in a variety of electronic formats. Some content that appears in print may not be available in electronic books. For more information about Wiley products, visit our web site at www.wiley.com.

Library of Congress Cataloging-in-Publication Data:

Brooks, Al, 1952–
   Trading price action reversals : technical analysis of price charts for the serious trader / Al Brooks.
      p. cm. – (The Wiley trading series)
  "The first edition of this book titled, Reading price charts bar by bar : the technical analysis of price action for the serious trader, was published in 2009"–T.p. verso.
    Includes index.
   ISBN 978-1-118-06661-4 (cloth); ISBN 978-1-118-17228-5 (ebk);
   ISBN 978-1-118-17229-2 (ebk); ISBN 978-1-118-17230-8 (ebk)
  1. Stocks–Prices–Charts, diagrams, etc. I. Brooks, Al, 1952– Reading price charts bar by bar. II. Title.
  HG4638.B757 2012
  332.63'2042–dc23

                                     2011029299

Printed in the United States of America

SKY10091993_112524

I would like to dedicate this book to my daughter, Meegan Brooks, who is adventurous, fearless, focused, and wise. She uses her boldness, common sense, and fiery spirit to make our society a better place. The day Meegan was born 23 years ago was and always will be the happiest day of my life.

Contents

Acknowledgments

My primary goal is to present a series of comprehensive books on price action, and the greatest concern among readers was how difficult my earlier book, *Reading Price Charts Bar by Bar*, was to read. I am deeply appreciative of all of the constructive comments that readers have provided and those from the participants in my daily live webinars. Many of these comments were incredibly insightful and I have incorporated them in this current edition. I am also thankful to all of the traders who have been in my live trading room, because they have given me the opportunity to say things repeatedly until I could clearly articulate what I am seeing and doing. They have also asked many questions that have helped me find the words to communicate more effectively, and I have put those words in these books.

I would like to give a special thank-you to Victor Brancale, who spent long hours proofreading the manuscripts and providing hundreds of very helpful edits and suggestions, and to Robert Gjerde, who built and administers my website and has given me candid feedback on the chat room and the website. Finally, I want to thank Ginger Szala, the Group Editorial Director of *Futures* magazine, for giving me ongoing opportunities to publish articles and speak in webinars, and for regularly giving me very helpful advice on how to become more involved with the trading community.

List of Terms
Used in This Book

All of these terms are defined in a practical way to be helpful to traders and not necessarily in the theoretical way often described by technicians.

always in   If you have to be in the market at all times, either long or short, this is whatever your current position is (always in long or always in short). If at any time you are forced to decide between initiating a long or a short trade and are confident in your choice, then the market is in always-in mode at that moment. Almost all of these trades require a spike in the direction of the trend before traders will have confidence.

barbwire   A trading range of three or more bars that largely overlap and one or more is a doji. It is a type of tight trading range with prominent tails and often relatively large bars.

bar pullback   In an upswing, a bar pullback is a bar with a low below the low of the prior bar. In a downswing, it is a bar with a high above that of the prior bar.

bear reversal   A change in trend from up to down (a bear trend).

blown account   An account that your losses have reduced below the minimum margin requirements set by your broker, and you will not be allowed to place a trade unless you deposit more money.

breakout   The high or low of the current bar extends beyond some prior price of significance such as a swing high or low, the high or low of any prior bar, a trend line, or a trend channel.

breakout bar (or bar breakout)   A bar that creates a breakout. It is usually a strong trend bar.

breakout mode   A setup where a breakout in either direction should have follow-through.

breakout pullback   A small pullback of one to about five bars that occurs within a few bars after a breakout. Since you see it as a pullback, you are expecting the breakout to resume and the pullback is a setup for that resumption. If instead you thought that the breakout would fail, you would not use the term *pullback* and instead would see the pullback as a failed breakout. For example, if there was a five-bar breakout above a bear trend line but you believed that the bear trend would continue, you would be considering shorting this bear flag and not looking to buy a pullback immediately after it broke out to the downside.

breakout test   A breakout pullback that comes close to the original entry price to test a breakeven stop. It may overshoot it or undershoot it by a few ticks. It can occur within a bar or two of entry or after an extended move or even 20 or more bars later.

bull reversal   A change in trend from a downtrend to an uptrend (a bull trend).

buying pressure   Strong bulls are asserting themselves and their buying is creating bull trend bars, bars with tails at the bottoms, and two-bar bull reversals. The effect is cumulative and usually is eventually followed by higher prices.

candle   A chart representation of price action in which the body is the area between the open and the close. If the close is above the open, it is a bull candle and is shown as white. If it is below, it is a bear candle and is black. The lines above and below are called tails (some technicians call them wicks or shadows).

chart type   A line, bar, candle, volume, tick, or other type of chart.

climax   A move that has gone too far too fast and has now reversed direction to either a trading range or an opposite trend. Most climaxes end with trend channel overshoots and reversals, but most of those reversals result in trading ranges and not an opposite trend.

countertrend   A trade or setup that is in the opposite direction from the current trend (the current always-in direction). This is a losing strategy for most traders since the risk is usually at least as large as the reward and the probability is rarely high enough to make the trader's equation favorable.

countertrend scalp   A trade taken in the belief that there is more to go in the trend but that a small pullback is due; you enter countertrend to capture a small profit as that small pullback is forming. This is usually a mistake and should be avoided.

day trade   A trade where the intent is to exit on the day of entry.

directional probability   The probability that the market will move either up or down any number of ticks before it reaches a certain number of ticks in the opposite direction. If you are looking at an equidistant move up and down, it hovers around 50 percent most of the time, which means that there is a 50–50 chance that the market will move up by X ticks before it moves down X ticks, and a 50–50 chance that it will move down X ticks before it moves up X ticks.

doji   A candle with a small body or no body at all. On a 5 minute chart, the body would be only one or two ticks; but on a daily chart, the body might be 10 or more ticks and still appear almost nonexistent. Neither the bulls nor the bears control the bar. All bars are either trend bars or nontrend bars, and those nontrend bars are called dojis.

double bottom   A chart formation in which the low of the current bar is about the same as the low of a prior swing low. That prior low can be just one bar earlier or 20 or more bars earlier. It does not have to be at the low of the day, and it commonly forms in bull flags (a double bottom bull flag).

double bottom bull flag   A pause or bull flag in a bull trend that has two spikes down to around the same price and then reverses back into a bull trend.

double bottom pullback   A buy setup composed of a double bottom followed by a deep pullback that forms a higher low.

double top   A chart formation in which the high of the current bar is about the same as the high of a prior swing high. That prior high can be just one bar earlier or 20 or more bars earlier. It does not have to be at the high of the day, and it commonly forms in bear flags (a double top bear flag).

double top bear flag   A pause or bear flag in a bear trend that has two spikes up to around the same price and then reverses back into a bear trend.

double top pullback   A sell setup composed of a double top followed by a deep pullback that forms a lower high.

early longs   Traders who buy as a bull signal bar is forming rather than waiting for it to close and then entering on a buy stop at one tick above its high.

early shorts   Traders who sell as a bear signal bar is forming rather than waiting for it to close and then entering on a sell stop at one tick below its low.

edge   A setup with a positive trader's equation. The trader has a mathematical advantage if he trades the setup. Edges are always small and fleeting because they need someone on the other side, and the market is filled with smart traders who won't allow an edge to be big and persistent.

EMA   See *exponential moving average (EMA)*.

entry bar   The bar during which a trade is entered.

exponential moving average (EMA)   The charts in these books use a 20-bar exponential moving average, but any moving average can be useful.

fade   To place a trade in the opposite direction of the trend (for example, selling a bull breakout that you expect to fail and reverse downward).

failed failure   A failure that fails, resuming in the direction of the original breakout, and therefore a breakout pullback. Since it is a second signal, it is more reliable. For example, if there is a breakout above a trading range and the bar after the breakout is a bear reversal bar, if the market trades below that bar, the breakout has failed. If the market then trades above the high of a prior bar within the next few bars, the failed breakout has failed and now the breakout is resuming. This means that the failed breakout became a small bull flag and just a pullback from the breakout.

failure (a failed move)   A move where the protective stop is hit before a scalper's profit is secured or before the trader's objective is reached, usually leading to a move in the opposite direction as trapped traders are forced to exit at a loss. Currently, a scalper's target in the Emini of four ticks usually requires a six-tick move, and a target in the QQQ of 10 ticks usually requires a move of 12 cents.

false   Failed, failure.

five-tick failure   A trade in the Emini that reaches five ticks beyond the signal bar and then reverses. For example, a breakout of a bull flag runs five ticks, and once the bar closes, the next bar has a low that is lower. Most limit orders to take a one-point profit would fail to get filled since a move usually has to go one tick beyond the order before it is filled. It is often a setup for a trade in the opposite direction.

flat   Refers to a trader who is not currently holding any positions.

follow-through   After the initial move, like a breakout, it is one or more bars that extend the move. Traders like to see follow-through on the next bar and on the several bars after that, hoping for a trend where they stand to make more profit.

follow-through bar   A bar that creates follow-through after the entry bar; it is usually the next bar but sometimes forms a couple of bars later.

fractal   Every pattern is a fractal of a pattern on a higher time frame chart. This means that every pattern is a micro pattern on a higher time frame and every micro pattern is a standard pattern on a smaller time frame.

gap   A space between any two price bars on the chart. An opening gap is a common occurrence and is present if the open of the first bar of today is beyond the high or low of the prior bar (the last bar of yesterday) or of the entire day. A moving average gap is present when the low of a bar is above a flat or falling moving average, or the high of a bar is below a flat or rising moving average. Traditional gaps (breakout, measuring, and exhaustion) on daily charts have intraday equivalents in the form of various trend bars.

gap bar   See *moving average gap bar*.

gap reversal   A formation in which the current bar extends one tick beyond the prior bar back into the gap. For example, if there is a gap up open and the second bar of the day trades one tick below the low of the first bar, this is a gap reversal.

HFT   See *high-frequency trading (HFT)*.

higher high   A swing high that is higher than a previous swing high.

higher low   A swing low that is higher than a previous swing low.

higher time frame (HTF)   A chart covering the same amount of time as the current chart, but having fewer bars. For example, compared to the day session 5 minute Emini chart on an average day, examples of higher time frame charts include a 15 minute chart, a tick chart with 25,000 ticks per bar, and a volume chart with 100,000 contracts per bar (each of these charts usually has fewer than 30 bars on an average day, compared to the 81 bars on the 5 minute chart).

high-frequency trading (HFT)   Also known as algorithmic trading or black box trading, it is a type of program trading where firms place millions of orders a day in thousands of stocks to scalp profits as small as a penny, and the trading is based on statistical analysis rather than fundamentals.

high/low 1 or 2   Either a high 1 or 2 or a low 1 or 2.

high 1, 2, 3, or 4   A high 1 is a bar with a high above the prior bar in a bull flag or near the bottom of a trading range. If there is then a bar with a lower high (it can occur one or several bars later), the next bar in this correction whose high is above the prior bar's high is a high 2. Third and fourth occurrences are a high 3 and 4. A high 3 is a wedge bull flag variant.

HTF   See *higher time frame (HTF)*.

ii   Consecutive inside bars, where the second is inside the first. At the end of a leg, it is a breakout mode setup and can become a flag or a reversal setup. A less reliable version is a "bodies-only ii," where you ignore the tails. Here, the second body is inside the first body, which is inside the body before it.

iii   Three inside bars in a row, and a somewhat more reliable pattern than an ii.

inside bar   A bar with a high that is at or below the high of the prior bar and a low that is at or above the low of the prior bar.

institution   Also called the smart money, it can be a pension fund, hedge fund, insurance company, bank, broker, large individual trader, or any other entity that trades enough volume to impact the market. Market movement is the cumulative effect of many institutions placing trades, and a single institution alone usually cannot move a major market for very long. Traditional institutions place trades based on fundamentals, and they used to be the sole determinant of the market's direction. However, HFT firms now have a significant influence on the day's movement since their trading currently generates most of the day's volume. HFT firms are a special type of institutional firm and their trading is based on statistics and not fundamentals. Traditional institutions determine the direction and target, but mathematicians determine the path that the market takes to get there.

ioi   Inside-outside-inside—three consecutive bars where the second bar is an outside bar, and the third bar is an inside bar. It is often a breakout mode setup where a trader looks to buy above the inside bar or sell below it.

ledge   A bull ledge is a small trading range with a bottom created by two or more bars with identical lows; a bear ledge is a small trading range with a top created by two or more bars with identical highs.

leg   A small trend that breaks a trend line of any size; the term is used only where there are at least two legs on the chart. It is any smaller trend that is part of a larger trend and it can be a pullback (a countertrend move), a swing in a trend or in a sideways market, or a with-trend move in a trend that occurs between any two pullbacks within the trend.

likely   At least 60 percent certain.

long   A person who buys a position in a market or the actual position itself.

lot   The smallest position size that can be traded in a market. It is a share when referring to stocks and a contract when referring to Eminis or other futures.

lower high   A swing high that is lower than a previous swing high.

lower low   A swing low that is lower than a previous swing low.

low 1, 2, 3, or 4   A low 1 is a bar with a low below the prior bar in a bear flag or near the top of a trading range. If there is then a bar with a higher low (it can occur one or several bars later), the next bar in this correction whose low is below the prior bar's low is a low 2. Third and fourth occurrences are a low 3 and 4. A low 3 is a wedge bear flag variant.

major trend line   Any trend line that contains most of the price action on the screen and is typically drawn using bars that are at least 10 bars apart.

major trend reversal   A reversal from a bull to a bear trend or from a bear trend to a bull trend. The setup must include a test of the old trend extreme after a break of the trend line.

meltdown   A sell-off in a bear spike or a tight bear channel without significant pullbacks and that extends further than the fundamentals would dictate.

melt-up   A rally in a bull spike or a tight bull channel without significant pullbacks and that extends further than the fundamentals would dictate.

micro   Any traditional pattern can form over one to about five bars and still be valid, although easily overlooked. When it forms, it is a micro version of the pattern. Every micro pattern is a traditional pattern on a smaller time frame chart, and every traditional pattern is a micro pattern on a higher time frame chart.

micro channel   A very tight channel where most of the bars have their highs and lows touching the trend line and, often, also the trend channel line. It is the most extreme form of a tight channel, and it has no pullbacks or only one or two small pullbacks.

micro double bottom   Consecutive or nearly consecutive bars with lows that are near the same price.

micro double top   Consecutive or nearly consecutive bars with highs that are near the same price.

micro measuring gap   When the bar before and the bar after a strong trend bar do not overlap, this is a sign of strength and often leads to a measured move. For example, if there is a strong bull trend bar and the low of the bar after it is at or above the high of the bar before it, the midpoint between that low and that high is the micro measuring gap.

micro trend channel line   A trend channel line drawn across the highs or lows of three to five consecutive bars.

micro trend line breakout   A trend line on any time frame that is drawn across from two to about 10 bars where most of the bars touch or are close to the trend line, and then one of the bars has a false breakout through the trend line. This false breakout sets up a with-trend entry. If it fails within a bar or two, then there is usually a countertrend trade.

money stop   A stop based on a fixed dollar amount or number of points, like two points in the Eminis or a dollar in a stock.

moving average   The charts in this book use a 20-bar exponential moving average, but any moving average can be useful.

moving average gap bar (gap bar)   A bar that does not touch the moving average. The space between the bar and the moving average is the gap. The first pullback in a strong trend that results in a moving average gap bar is usually followed by a test of the trend's extreme. For example, when there is a strong bull trend and there is a pullback that finally has a bar with a high below the moving average, this is often a buy setup for a test of the high of the trend.

nesting   Sometimes a pattern has a smaller version of a comparable pattern "nested" within it. For example, it is common for the right shoulder of a head and shoulders top to be either a small head and shoulders top or a double top.

news   Useless information generated by the media for the sole purpose of selling advertising and making money for the media company. It is unrelated to trading, is impossible to evaluate, and should always be ignored.

oio   Outside-inside-outside, an outside bar followed by an inside bar, followed by an outside bar.

oo   Outside-outside, an outside bar followed by a larger outside bar.

opening reversal   A reversal in the first hour or so of the day.

outside bar   A bar with a high that is above or at the high of the prior bar and a low that is below the low of the prior bar, or a bar with a low that is below or at the low of the prior bar and a high that is above the high of the prior bar.

outside down bar   An outside bar with a close below its open.

outside up bar   An outside bar with a close above its open.

overshoot   The market surpasses a prior price of significance like a swing point or a trend line.

pause bar   A bar that does not extend the trend. In a bull trend, a pause bar has a high that is at or below the prior bar, or a small bar with a high that is only a tick or so higher than the previous bar when the previous bar is a strong bull trend bar. It is a type of pullback.

pip   A tick in the foreign exchange (forex) market. However, some data vendors provide quotes with an extra decimal place, which should be ignored.

pressing their longs   In a bull trend, bulls add to their longs as in a bull spike and as the market breaks out to a new high, because they expect another leg up to about a measured move.

pressing their shorts   In a bear trend, bears add to their shorts in a bear spike and as the market breaks out to a new low, because they expect another leg down to about a measured move.

price action   Any change in price on any chart type or time frame.

probability   The chance of success. For example, if a trader looks back at the most recent 100 times a certain setup led to a trade and finds that it led to a profitable trade 60 times, then that would indicate that the setup has about a 60 percent probability of success. There are many variables that can never be fully tested, so probabilities are only approximations and at times can be very misleading.

probably   At least 60 percent certain.

pullback   A temporary pause or countertrend move that is part of a trend, swing, or leg and does not retrace beyond the start of the trend, swing, or leg. It is a small trading range where traders expect the trend to resume soon. For example, a bear pullback is a sideways to upward move in a bear trend, swing, or leg that will be followed by at least a test of the prior low. It can be as small as a one-tick move above the high of the prior bar or it can even be a pause, like an inside bar.

pullback bar   A bar that reverses the prior bar by at least one tick. In an uptrend, it is a bar with a low below that of the prior bar.

reasonable   A setup with a favorable trader's equation.

reversal   A change to an opposite type of behavior. Most technicians use the term to mean a change from a bull trend to a bear trend or from a bear trend to a bull trend. However, trading range behavior is opposite to trending behavior, so when a trend becomes a trading range, this is also a reversal. When a trading range becomes a trend, it is a reversal but is usually called a breakout.

reversal bar   A trend bar in the opposite direction of the trend. When a bear leg is reversing up, a bull reversal bar is a bull trend bar, and the classic description includes a tail at the bottom and a close above the open and near the top. A bear reversal bar is a bear trend bar in a bull leg, and the traditional description includes a tail at the top and a close below the open and near the bottom.

reward   The number of ticks that a trader expects to make from a trade. For example, if the trader exits with a limit order at a profit target, it is the number of ticks between the entry price and the profit target.

risk   The number of ticks from a trader's entry price to a protective stop. It is the minimum that the trader will lose if a trade goes against him (slippage and other factors can make the actual risk greater than the theoretical risk).

risk off   When traders think that the stock market will fall, they become risk averse, sell out of volatile stocks and currencies, and transition into safe-haven investments, like Johnson & Johnson (JNJ), Altria Group (MO), Procter & Gamble (PG), the U.S. dollar, and the Swiss franc.

risk on   When traders think that the stock market is strong, they are willing to take more risks and invest in stocks that tend to rise faster than the overall market, and invest in more volatile currencies, like the Australian dollar or the Swedish krona.

risky   When the trader's equation is unclear or barely favorable for a trade. It can also mean that the probability of success for a trade is 50 percent or less, regardless of the risk and potential reward.

scalp   A trade that is exited with a small profit, usually before there are any pullbacks. In the Emini, when the average range is about 10 to 15 points, a scalp trade is usually any trade where the goal is less than four points. For the SPY or stocks, it might be 10 to 30 cents. For more expensive stocks, it can be $1 to $2. Since the profit is often smaller than the risk, a trader has to win at least 70 percent of the time, which is an unrealistic goal for most traders. Traders should take trades only where the potential reward is at least as great as the risk unless they are extremely skilled.

scalper   A trader who primarily scalps for small profits, usually using a tight stop.

scalper's profit   A typical amount of profit that a scalper would be targeting.

scratch   A trade that is close to breakeven with either a small profit or a loss.

second entry   The second time within a few bars of the first entry where there is an entry bar based on the same logic as the first entry. For example, if a breakout above a wedge bull flag fails and pulls back to a double bottom bull flag, this pullback sets up a second buy signal for the wedge bull flag.

second moving average gap bar setup   If there is a first moving average gap bar and a reversal toward the moving average does not reach the moving average, and instead the move away from the moving average continues, it is the next reversal in the direction of the moving average.

second signal   The second time within a few bars of the first signal where there is a setup based on the same logic as the first signal.

selling pressure   Strong bears are asserting themselves and their selling is creating bear trend bars, bars with tails at the tops, and two-bar bear reversals. The effect is cumulative and usually is eventually followed by lower prices.

setup   A pattern of one or more bars used by traders as the basis to place entry orders. If an entry order is filled, the last bar of the setup becomes the signal bar. Most setups are just a single bar.

shaved body   A candle with no tail at one or both ends. A shaved top has no tail at the top and a shaved bottom has no tail at the bottom.

short   As a verb, to sell a stock or futures contract to initiate a new position (not to exit a prior purchase). As a noun, a person who sells something short, or the actual position itself.

shrinking stairs   A stairs pattern where the most recent breakout is smaller than the previous one. It is a series of three or more trending highs in a bull trend or lows in a bear trend where each breakout to a new extreme is by fewer ticks than the prior breakout, indicating waning momentum. It can be a three-push pattern, but it does not have to resemble a wedge and can be any series of broad swings in a trend.

signal bar   The bar immediately before the bar in which an entry order is filled (the entry bar). It is the final bar of a setup.

smaller time frame (STF)   A chart covering the same amount of time as the current chart, but having more bars. For example, compared to the day session 5 minute Emini chart on an average day, examples of smaller time frame charts include a 1 minute chart, a tick chart with 500 ticks per bar, and a volume chart with 1,000 contracts per bar (each of these charts usually has more than 200 bars on an average day, compared to the 81 bars on the 5 minute chart).

smart traders   Consistently profitable traders who are usually trading large positions and are generally on the right side of the market.

spike and channel   A breakout into a trend in which the follow-through is in the form of a channel where the momentum is less and there is two-sided trading taking place.

stair   A push to a new extreme in a trending trading range trend or a broad channel trend where there is a series of three or more trending swings that resembles a sloping trading range and is roughly contained in a channel. After the breakout, there is a breakout pullback that retraces at least slightly into the prior trading range, which is not a requirement of other trending trading ranges. Two-way trading is taking place but one side is in slightly more control, accounting for the slope.

STF   See *smaller time frame (STF)*.

strong bulls and bears   Institutional traders and their cumulative buying and selling determine the direction of the market.

success   Refers to traders achieving their objective. Their profit target was reached before their protective stop was hit.

swing   A smaller trend that breaks a trend line of any size; the term is used only when there are at least two on the chart. They can occur within a larger trend or in a sideways market.

swing high   A bar that looks like a spike up on the chart and extends up beyond the neighboring bars. Its high is at or above that of the bar before it and that of the bar after it.

swing high/low   Either a swing high or a swing low.

swing low   A bar that looks like a spike down on the chart and extends down beyond the neighboring bars. Its low is at or below that of the bar before it and that of the bar after it.

swing point   Either a swing high or a swing low.

swing trade   For a day trader using a short-term intraday chart like the 5 minute, it is any trade that lasts longer than a scalp and that the trader will hold through one or more pullbacks. For a trader using higher time frame charts, it is a trade that lasts for hours to several days. Typically, at least part of the trade is held without a profit target, since the trader is hoping for an extended move. The potential reward is usually at least as large as the risk. Small swing trades are called scalps by many traders. In the Emini, when the average range is about 10 to 15 points, a swing trade is usually any trade where the goal is four or more points.

test   When the market approaches a prior price of significance and can overshoot or undershoot the target. The term *failed test* is used to mean opposite things by different traders. Most traders believe that if the market then reverses, the test was successful, and if it does not and the move continues beyond the test area, the test failed and a breakout has occurred.

three pushes   Three swing highs where each swing high is usually higher or three swing lows where each swing low is usually lower. It trades the same as a wedge and should be considered a variant. When it is part of a flag, the move can be mostly horizontal and each push does not have to extend beyond the prior one. For example, in a wedge bull flag or any other type of triangle, the second push down can be at, above, or below the first, and the third push down can be at, above, or below either the second or the first, or both.

tick   The smallest unit of price movement. For most stocks, it is one penny; for 10-Year U.S. Treasury Note Futures, it is 1/64th of a point; and for Eminis, it is

0.25 points. On tick charts and on time and sales tables, a tick is every trade that takes place no matter the size and even if there is no price change. If you look at a time and sales table, every trade is counted as one tick when TradeStation charting software creates a tick chart.

tight channel   A channel where the trend line and trend channel line are close together, and the pullbacks are small and last for only one to three bars.

tight trading range   A trading range of two or more bars with lots of overlap in the bars and in which most reversals are too small to trade profitably with stop entries. The bulls and bears are in balance.

time frame   The length of time contained in one bar on the chart (a 5 minute time frame is made of bars that close every five minutes). It can also refer to bars not based on time, such as those based on volume or the number of ticks traded.

tradable   A setup that you believe has a reasonable chance of leading to at least a scalper's profit.

trader's equation   To take a trade, you must believe that the probability of success times the potential reward is greater than the probability of failure times the risk. You set the reward and risk because the potential reward is the distance to your profit target and the risk is the distance to your stop. The difficulty in solving the equation is assigning a value to the probability, which can never be known with certainty. As a guideline, if you are uncertain, assume that you have a 50 percent chance of winning or losing, and if you are confident, assume that you have a 60 percent chance of winning and a 40 percent chance of losing.

trading range   The minimum requirement is a single bar with a range that is largely overlapped by the bar before it. It is sideways movement and neither the bull nor the bears are in control, although one side is often stronger. It is often a pullback in a trend where the pullback has lasted long enough to lose most of its certainty. In other words, traders have become uncertain about the direction of the breakout in the short term, and the market will have repeated breakout attempts up and down that will fail. It will usually ultimately break out in the direction of the trend, and is a pullback on a higher time frame chart.

trailing a stop   As the trade becomes increasingly profitable, traders will often move, or trail, the protective stop to protect more of their open profit. For example, if they are long in a bull trend, every time the market moves to a new high, they might raise the protective stop to just below the most recent higher low.

trap   An entry that immediately reverses to the opposite direction before a scalper's profit target is reached, trapping traders in their new position and ultimately forcing them to cover at a loss. It can also scare traders out of a good trade.

trapped in a trade   A trader with an open loss on a trade that did not result in a scalper's profit, and if there is a pullback beyond the entry or signal bars, the trader will likely exit with a loss.

trapped out of a trade   A pullback that scares a trader into exiting a trade, but then the pullback fails. The move quickly resumes in the direction of the trade, making it difficult emotionally for the trader to get back in at the worse price that is now available. The trader will have to chase the market.

trend   A series of price changes that are either mostly up (a bull trend) or down (a bear trend). There are three loosely defined smaller versions: swings, legs, and pullbacks. A chart will show only one or two major trends. If there are more, one of the other terms is more appropriate.

trend bar   A bar with a body, which means that the close was above or below the open, indicating that there is at least a minor price movement.

trend channel line   A line in the direction of the trend but drawn on the opposite side of the bars compared to a trend line. A bull trend channel line is above the highs and rising to the right, and a bear trend channel line is below the lows and falling to the right.

trend channel line overshoot   One or more bars penetrating a trend channel line.

trend channel line undershoot   A bar approaches a trend channel line but the market reverses away from the line without reaching or penetrating it.

trend from the open   A trend that begins at the first or one of the first bars of the day and extends for many bars without a pullback, and the start of the trend remains as one of the extremes of the day for much if not all of the day.

trending closes   Three or more bars where the closes are trending. In a bull trend, each close is above the prior close, and in a bear trend, each close is lower. If the pattern extends for many bars, there can be one or two bars where the closes are not trending.

trending highs or lows   The same as trending closes except based on the highs or lows of the bars.

trending swings   Three or more swings where the swing highs and lows are both higher than the prior swing highs and lows (trending bull swings), or both lower (trending bear swings).

trending trading ranges   Two or more trading ranges separated by a breakout.

trend line   A line drawn in the direction of the trend; it is sloped up and is below the bars in a bull trend, and it is sloped down and is above the bars in a bear trend. Most often, it is constructed from either swing highs or swing lows but can be based on linear regression or just a best fit (eyeballing).

trend reversal   A trend change from up to down or down to up, or from a trend to a trading range.

20 moving average gap bars   Twenty or more consecutive bars that have not touched the moving average. Once the market finally touches the moving average, it usually creates a setup for a test of the trend's extreme.

undershoot   The market approaches but does not reach a prior price of significance like a swing point or a trend line.

unlikely   At most 40 percent certain.

unreasonable   A setup with an unfavorable trader's equation.

usually   At least 60 percent certain.

vacuum   A buy vacuum occurs when the strong bears believe that the price will soon be higher so they wait to short until it reaches some magnet above the market. The result is that there is a vacuum that sucks the market quickly up to the magnet in the form of one or more bull trend bars. Once there, the strong bears sell aggressively and turn the market down. A sell vacuum occurs when the strong bulls believe that the market will soon be lower so they wait to buy until it falls to some magnet below the market. The result is that there is a vacuum that sucks the market down quickly to the magnet in the form of one or more bear trend bars. Once there, strong bulls buy aggressively and turn the market back up.

wedge   Traditionally, a three-push move with each push extending further and the trend line and trend channel line at least minimally convergent, creating a rising or descending triangle with a wedge shape. For a trader, the wedge shape increases the chances of a successful trade, but any three-push pattern trades like a wedge and can be considered one. A wedge can be a reversal pattern or a pullback in a trend (a bull or bear flag).

wedge flag   A wedge-shaped or three-push pullback in a trend, such as a high 3 in a bull trend (a type of bull flag) or a low 3 in a bear trend (a type of bear flag). Since it is a with-trend setup, enter on the first signal.

wedge reversal   A wedge that is reversing a bull trend into a bear trend or a bear trend into a bull trend. Since it is countertrend, unless it is very strong, it is better to take a second signal. For example, if there is a bear trend and then a descending wedge, wait for a breakout above this potential wedge bottom and then try to buy a pullback to a higher low.

with trend   Refers to a trade or a setup that is in the direction of the prevailing trend. In general, the direction of the most recent 5 minute chart signal should be assumed to be the trend's direction. Also, if most of the past 10 or 20 bars are above the moving average, trend setups and trades are likely on the buy side.

Introduction

There is a reason why there is no other comprehensive book about price action written by a trader. It takes thousands of hours, and the financial reward is meager compared to that from trading. However, with my three girls now away in grad school, I have a void to fill and this has been a very satisfying project. I originally planned on updating the first edition of *Reading Price Charts Bar by Bar* (John Wiley & Sons, 2009), but as I got into it, I decided instead to go into great detail about how I view and trade the markets. I am metaphorically teaching you how to play the violin. Everything you need to know to make a living at it is in these books, but it is up to you to spend the countless hours learning your trade. After a year of answering thousands of questions from traders on my website at www.brookspriceaction.com, I think that I have found ways to express my ideas much more clearly, and these books should be easier to read than that one. The earlier book focused on reading price action, and this series of books is instead centered on how to use price action to trade the markets. Since the book grew to more than four times as many words as the first book, John Wiley & Sons decided to divide it into three separate books. This first book covers price action basics and trends. The second book is on trading ranges, order management, and the mathematics of trading, and the final book is about trend reversals, day trading, daily charts, options, and the best setups for all time frames. Many of the charts are also in *Reading Price Charts Bar by Bar*, but most have been updated and the discussion about the charts has also been largely rewritten. Only about 5 percent of the 120,000 words from that book are present in the 570,000 words in this new series, so readers will find little duplication.

My goals in writing this series of three books are to describe my understanding of why the carefully selected trades offer great risk/reward ratios, and to present ways to profit from the setups. I am presenting material that I hope will be interesting to professional traders and students in business school, but I also hope that even traders starting out will find some useful ideas. Everyone looks at price charts but usually just briefly and with a specific or limited goal. However, every chart has an incredible amount of information that can be used to make profitable trades, but much of it can be used effectively only if traders spend time to carefully understand what each bar on the chart is telling them about what institutional money is doing.

Ninety percent or more of all trading in large markets is done by institutions, which means that the market is simply a collection of institutions. Almost all are profitable over time, and the few that are not soon go out of business. Since institutions are profitable and they are the market, every trade that you take has a profitable trader (a part of the collection of institutions) taking the other side of your trade. No trade can take place without one institution willing to take one side and another willing to take the other. The small-volume trades made by individuals can only take place if an institution is willing to take the same trade. If you want to buy at a certain price, the market will not get to that price unless one or more institutions also want to buy at that price. You cannot sell at any price unless one or more institutions are willing to sell there, because the market can only go to a price where there are institutions willing to buy and others willing to sell. If the Emini is at 1,264 and you are long with a protective sell stop at 1,262, your stop cannot get hit unless there is an institution who is also willing to sell at 1,262. This is true for virtually all trades.

If you trade 200 Emini contracts, then you are trading institutional volume and are effectively an institution, and you will sometimes be able to move the market a tick or two. Most individual traders, however, have no ability to move the market, no matter how stupidly they are willing to trade. The market will not run your stops. The market might test the price where your protective stop is, but it has nothing to do with your stop. It will only test that price if one or more institutions believe that it is financially sound to sell there and other institutions believe that it is profitable to buy there. At every tick, there are institutions buying and other institutions selling, and all have proven systems that will make money by placing those trades. You should always be trading in the direction of the majority of institutional dollars because they control where the market is heading.

At the end of the day when you look at a printout of the day's chart, how can you tell what the institutions did during the day? The answer is simple: whenever the market went up, the bulk of institutional money was buying, and whenever the market went down, more money went into selling. Just look at any segment of the chart where the market went up or down and study every bar, and you will soon notice many repeatable patterns. With time, you will begin to see those patterns unfold in real time, and that will give you confidence to place your trades. Some of the price action is subtle, so be open to every possibility. For example, sometimes when the market is working higher, a bar will trade below the low of the prior bar, yet the trend continues higher. You have to assume that the big money was buying at and below the low of that prior bar, and that is also what many experienced traders were doing. They bought exactly where weak traders let themselves get stopped out with a loss or where other weak traders shorted, believing that the market was beginning to sell off. Once you get comfortable with the idea that strong trends often have pullbacks and big money is buying them rather than selling them, you will be in a position to make some great trades that you previously thought were exactly the wrong thing to do. Don't think too hard about it. If the market is going up, institutions are buying constantly, even at times when you think that you should stop yourself out of your long with a loss. Your job is to follow their behavior and not use too much logic to deny what is happening right in front of you. It does not matter if it seems counterintuitive. All that matters is that the market is going up and therefore institutions are predominantly buying and so should you.

Institutions are generally considered to be smart money, meaning that they are smart enough to make a living by trading and they trade a large volume every day. Television still uses the term *institution* to refer to traditional institutions like mutual funds, banks, brokerage houses, insurance companies, pension funds, and hedge funds; these companies used to account for most of the volume, and they mostly trade on fundamentals. Their trading controls the direction of the market on daily and weekly charts and a lot of the big intraday swings. Until a decade or so ago, most of the trade decisions were made and most trading was done by very smart traders, but it is now increasingly being done by computers. They have programs that can instantly analyze economic data and immediately place trades based on that analysis, without a person ever being involved in the trade. In addition, other firms trade huge volumes by using computer programs that place trades based on the statistical analysis of price action. Computer-generated trading now accounts for as much as 70 percent of the day's volume.

Computers are very good at making decisions, and playing chess and winning at *Jeopardy!* are more difficult than trading stocks. Gary Kasparov for years made the best chess decisions in the world, yet a computer made better decisions in 1997 and beat him. Ken Jennings was heralded as the greatest *Jeopardy!* player of all time, yet a computer destroyed him in 2011. It is only a matter of time before computers are widely accepted as the best decision makers for institutional trading.

Since programs use objective mathematical analysis, there should be a tendency for support and resistance areas to become more clearly defined. For example, measured move projections should become more precise as more of the volume is traded based on precise mathematical logic. Also, there might be a tendency toward more protracted tight channels as programs buy small pullbacks on the daily chart. However, if enough programs exit longs or go short at the same key levels, sell-offs might become larger and faster. Will the changes be dramatic? Probably not, since the same general forces were operating when everything was done manually, but nonetheless there should be some move toward mathematical perfection as more of the emotion is removed from trading. As these other firms contribute more and more to the movement of the market and as traditional institutions increasingly use computers to analyze and place their trades, the term *institution* is becoming vague. It is better for an individual trader to think of an institution as any of the different entities that trade enough volume to be a significant contributor to the price action.

Since these buy and sell programs generate most of the volume, they are the most important contributor to the appearance of every chart and they create most of the trading opportunities for individual investors. Yes, it's nice to know that Cisco Systems (CSCO) had a strong earnings report and is moving up, and if you are an investor who wants to hold stock for many months, then do what the traditional institutions are doing and buy CSCO. However, if you are a day trader, ignore the news and look at the chart, because the programs will create patterns that are purely statistically based and have nothing to do with fundamentals, yet offer great trading opportunities. The traditional institutions placing trades based on fundamentals determine the direction and the approximate target of a stock over the next several months, but, increasingly, firms using statistical analysis to make day trades and other short-term trades determine the path to that target and the ultimate high or low of the move. Even on a macro level, fundamentals are only approximate at best. Look at the crashes in 1987 and 2009. Both had violent sell-offs and rallies, yet the fundamentals did not change violently in the same short period of time. In both cases, the market got sucked slightly below the monthly trend line and reversed sharply up from it. The market fell because of perceived fundamentals, but the extent of the fall was determined by the charts.

There are some large patterns that repeat over and over on all time frames and in all markets, like trends, trading ranges, climaxes, and channels. There are also lots of smaller tradable patterns that are based on just the most recent few bars. These books are a comprehensive guide to help traders understand everything they see on a chart, giving them more opportunities to make profitable trades and to avoid losers.

The most important message that I can deliver is to focus on the absolute best trades, avoid the absolute worst setups, use a profit objective (reward) that is at least as large as your protective stop (risk), and work on increasing the number of shares that you are trading. I freely recognize that every one of my reasons behind each setup is just my opinion, and my reasoning about why a trade works might be completely wrong. However, that is irrelevant. What is important is that reading price action is a very effective way to trade, and I have thought a lot about why certain things happen the way they do. I am comfortable with my explanations and they give me confidence when I place a trade; however, they are irrelevant to my placing trades, so it is not important to me that they are right. Just as I can reverse my opinion about the direction of the market in an instant, I can also reverse my opinion about why a particular pattern works if I come across a reason that is more logical or if I discover a flaw in my logic. I am providing the opinions because they appear to make sense, they might help readers become more comfortable trading certain setups, and they might be intellectually stimulating, but they are not needed for any price action trades.

The books are very detailed and difficult to read and are directed toward serious traders who want to learn as much as they can about reading price charts. However, the concepts are useful to traders at all levels. The books cover many of the standard techniques described by Robert D. Edwards and John Magee (*Technical Analysis of Stock Trends*, AMACOM, 9th ed., 2007) and others, but focus more on individual bars to demonstrate how the information they provide can significantly enhance the risk/reward ratio of trading. Most books point out three or four trades on a chart, which implies that everything else on the chart is incomprehensible, meaningless, or risky. I believe that there is something to be learned from every tick that takes place during the day and that there are far more great trades on every chart than just the few obvious ones; but to see them, you have to understand price action and you cannot dismiss any bars as unimportant. I learned from performing thousands of operations through a microscope that some of the most important things can be very small.

I read charts bar by bar and look for any information that each bar is telling me. They are all important. At the end of every bar, most traders ask themselves, "What just took place?" With most bars, they conclude that there is nothing worth trading at the moment so it is just not worth the effort to try to understand. Instead, they choose to wait for some clearer and usually larger pattern. It is as if they believe that the bar did not exist, or they dismiss it as just institutional program activity that is not tradable by an individual trader. They do not feel like they are part of the market at these times, but these times constitute the vast majority of the day. Yet, if they look at the volume, all of those bars that they are ignoring have as much volume as the bars they are using for the bases for their trades. Clearly, a lot of trading is taking place, but they don't understand how that can be and essentially pretend that it does not exist. But that is denying reality. There is always trading taking place, and as a trader, you owe it to yourself to understand why it's taking place and to figure out a way to make money off of it. Learning what the market is telling you is very time-consuming and difficult, but it gives you the foundation that you need to be a successful trader.

Unlike most books on candle charts where the majority of readers feel compelled to memorize patterns, these three books of mine provide a rationale for why particular patterns are reliable setups for traders. Some of the terms used have specific meaning to market technicians but different meanings to traders, and I am writing this entirely from a trader's perspective. I am certain that many traders already understand everything in these books, but likely wouldn't describe price action in the same way that I do. There are no secrets among successful traders; they all know common setups, and many have their own names for each one. All of them are buying and selling pretty much at the same time, catching the same swings, and they all have their own reasons for getting into a trade. Many trade price action intuitively without ever feeling a need to articulate why a certain setup works. I hope that they enjoy reading my understanding of and perspective on price action and that this gives them some insights that will improve their already successful trading.

The goal for most traders is to maximize trading profits through a style that is compatible with their personalities. Without that compatibility, I believe that it is virtually impossible to trade profitably for the long term. Many traders wonder how long it will take them to be successful and are willing to lose money for some period of time, even a few years. However, it took me over 10 years to be able to trade successfully. Each of us has many considerations and distractions, so the time will vary, but a trader has to work though most obstacles before becoming consistently profitable. I had several major problems that had to be corrected, including raising three wonderful daughters who always filled my mind with thoughts of them and what I needed to be doing as their father. That was solved as they got older and more independent. Then it took me a long time to accept many personality traits as real and unchangeable (or at least I concluded that I was unwilling to change them). And finally there was the issue of confidence. I have always been confident to the point of arrogance in so many things that those who know me would be surprised that this was difficult for me. However, deep inside I believed that I really would never come up with a consistently profitable approach that I would enjoy employing for many years. Instead, I bought many systems, wrote and tested countless indicators and systems, read many books and magazines, went to seminars, hired tutors, and joined chat rooms. I talked with people who presented themselves as successful traders, but I never saw their account statements and suspect that most could teach but few, if any, could trade. Usually in trading, those who know don't talk and those who talk don't know.

This was all extremely helpful because it showed all of the things that I needed to avoid before becoming successful. Any nontrader who looks at a chart will invariably conclude that trading has to be extremely easy, and that is part of the appeal. At the end of the day, anyone can look at any chart and see very clear entry and exit points. However, it is much more difficult to do it in real time. There is a natural tendency to want to buy the exact low and never have the trade come back. If it does, a novice will take the loss to avoid a bigger loss, resulting in a series of losing trades that will ultimately bust the trader's account. Using wide stops solves that to some extent, but invariably traders will soon hit a few big losses that will put them into the red and make them too scared to continue using that approach.

Should you be concerned that making the information in these books available will create lots of great price action traders, all doing the same thing at the same time, thereby removing the late entrants needed to drive the market to your price target? No, because the institutions control the market and they already have the smartest traders in the world and those traders already know everything in these books, at least intuitively. At every moment, there is an extremely smart institutional bull taking the opposite side of the trade being placed by an extremely smart institutional bear. Since the most important players already know price action, having more players know it will not tip the balance one way or the other. I therefore have no concern that what I am writing will stop price action from working. Because of that balance, any edge that anyone has is always going to be extremely small, and any small mistake will result in a loss, no matter how well a person reads a chart. Although it is very difficult to make money as a trader without understanding price action, that knowledge alone is not enough. It takes a long time to learn how to trade *after* a trader learns to read charts, and trading is just as difficult as chart reading. I wrote these books to help people learn to read charts better and to trade better, and if you can do both well, you deserve to be able to take money from the accounts of others and put it into yours.

The reason why the patterns that we all see do unfold as they do is because that is the appearance that occurs in an efficient market with countless traders placing orders for thousands of different reasons, but with the controlling volume being traded based on sound logic. That is just what it looks like, and it has been that way forever. The same patterns unfold in all time frames in all markets around the world, and it would simply be impossible for all of it to be manipulated instantaneously on so many different levels. Price action is a manifestation of human behavior and therefore actually has a genetic basis. Until we evolve, it will likely remain largely unchanged, just as it has been unchanged for the 80 years of charts that I have reviewed. Program trading might have changed the appearance slightly, although I can find no evidence to support that theory. If anything, it would make the charts smoother because it is unemotional and it has greatly increased the volume. Now that most of the volume is being traded automatically by computers and the volume is so huge, irrational and emotional behavior is an insignificant component of the markets and the charts are a purer expression of human tendencies.

Since price action comes from our DNA, it will not change until we evolve. When you look at the two charts in Figure I.1, your first reaction is that they are just a couple of ordinary charts, but look at the dates at the bottom. These weekly Dow Jones Industrial Average charts from the Depression era and from World War II have the same patterns that we see today on all charts, despite most of today's volume being traded by computers.

If everyone suddenly became a price action scalper, the smaller patterns might change a little for a while, but over time, the efficient market will win out and the votes by all traders will get distilled into standard price action patterns because that is the inescapable result of countless people behaving logically. Also, the reality is that it is very difficult to trade well, and although basing trades on price action is a sound approach, it is still very difficult to do successfully in real time.

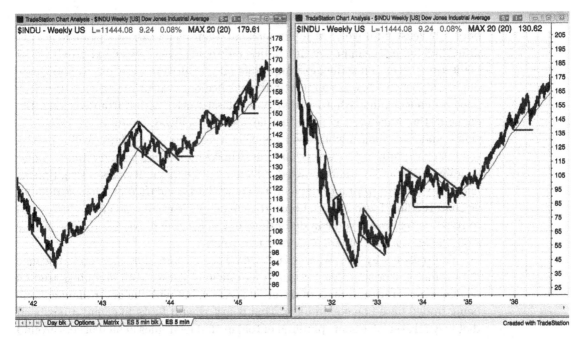

FIGURE I.1 Price Action Has Not Changed over Time

There just won't be enough traders doing it well enough, all at the same time, to have any significant influence over time on the patterns. Just look at Edwards and Magee. The best traders in the world have been using those ideas for decades and they continue to work, again for the same reason—charts look the way they do because that is the unchangeable fingerprint of an efficient market filled with a huge number of smart people using a huge number of approaches and time frames, all trying to make the most money that they can. For example, Tiger Woods is not hiding anything that he does in golf, and anyone is free to copy him. However, very few people can play golf well enough to make a living at it. The same is true of trading. A trader can know just about everything there is to know and still lose money because applying all that knowledge in a way that consistently makes money is very difficult to do.

Why do so many business schools continue to recommend Edwards and Magee when their book is essentially simplistic, largely using trend lines, breakouts, and pullbacks as the basis for trading? It is because it works and it always has and it always will. Now that just about all traders have computers with access to intraday data, many of those techniques can be adapted to day trading. Also, candle charts give additional information about who is controlling the market, which results in a more timely entry with smaller risk. Edwards and Magee's focus is on the overall trend. I use those same basic techniques but pay much closer attention to the individual bars on the chart to improve the risk/reward ratio, and I devote considerable attention to intraday charts.

It seemed obvious to me that if one could simply read the charts well enough to be able to enter at the exact times when the move would take off and not come back, then that trader would have a huge advantage. The trader would have a high winning percentage, and the few losses would be small. I decided that this would be my starting point, and what I discovered was that nothing had to be added. In fact, any additions are distractions that result in lower profitability. This sounds so obvious and easy that it is difficult for most people to believe.

I am a day trader who relies entirely on price action on the intraday Emini S&P 500 Futures charts, and I believe that reading price action well is an invaluable skill for all traders. Beginners often instead have a deep-seated belief that something more is required, that maybe some complex mathematical formula that very few use would give them just the edge that they need. Goldman Sachs is so rich and sophisticated that its traders must have a supercomputer and high-powered software that gives them an advantage that ensures that all the individual traders are doomed to failure. They start looking at all kinds of indicators and playing with the inputs to customize the indicators to make them just right. Every indicator works some of the time, but for me, they obfuscate instead of elucidate. In fact, without even looking at a chart, you can place a buy order and have a 50 percent chance of being right!

I am not dismissing indicators and systems out of ignorance of their subtleties. I have spent over 10,000 hours writing and testing indicators and systems over the years, and that probably is far more experience than most have. This extensive experience with indicators and systems was an essential part of my becoming a successful trader. Indicators work well for many traders, but the best success comes once a trader finds an approach that is compatible with his or her personality. My single biggest problem with indicators and systems was that I never fully trusted them. At every setup, I saw exceptions that needed to be tested. I always wanted every last penny out of the market and was never satisfied with a return from a system if I could incorporate a new twist that would make it better. You can optimize constantly, but, since the market is always changing from strong trends to tight trading ranges and then back again and your optimizations are based on what has recently happened, they will soon fail as the market transitions into a new phase. I am simply too controlling, compulsive, restless, observant, and untrusting to make money in the long term off indicators or automated systems, but I am at the extreme in many ways and most people don't have these same issues.

Many traders, especially beginners, are drawn to indicators (or any other higher power, guru, TV pundit, or newsletter that they want to believe will protect them and show their love and approval of them as human beings by giving them lots of money), hoping that an indicator will show them when to enter a trade. What they don't realize is that the vast majority of indicators are based on simple price action, and when I am placing trades, I simply cannot think fast enough to process what several indicators might be telling me. If there is a bull trend, a pullback, and then a rally to a new high, but the rally has lots of overlapping bars, many bear bodies, a couple of small pullbacks, and prominent tails on the tops of the bars, any experienced trader would see that it is a weak test of the trend high and that this should not be happening if the bull trend was still strong. The market is almost certainly transitioning into a trading range and possibly into a bear trend. Traders don't need an oscillator to tell them this. Also, oscillators tend to make traders look for reversals and focus less on price charts. These can be effective tools on most days when the market has two or three reversals lasting an hour or more. The problem comes when the market is trending strongly. If you focus too much on your indicators, you will see that they are forming divergences all day long and you might find yourself repeatedly entering countertrend and losing money. By the time you come to accept that the market is trending, you will not have enough time left in the day to recoup your losses. Instead, if you were simply looking at a bar or candle chart, you would see that the market is clearly trending and you would not be tempted by indicators to look for trend reversals. The most common successful reversals first break a trend line with strong momentum and then pull back to test the extreme, and if traders focus too much on divergences, they will often overlook this fundamental fact. Placing a trade because of a divergence in the absence of a prior countertrend momentum surge that breaks a trend line is a losing strategy. Wait for the trend line break and then see if the test of the old extreme reverses or if the old trend resumes. You do not need an indicator to tell you that a strong reversal here is a high-probability trade, at least for a scalp, and there will almost certainly be a divergence, so why complicate your thinking by adding the indicator to your calculus?

Some pundits recommend a combination of time frames, indicators, wave counting, and Fibonacci retracements and extensions, but when it comes time to place the trade, they will do it only if there is a good price action setup. Also, when they see a good price action setup, they start looking for indicators that show divergences, different time frames for moving average tests, wave counts, or Fibonacci setups to confirm what is in front of them. In reality, they are price action traders who are trading exclusively off price action on only one chart but don't feel comfortable admitting it. They are complicating their trading to the point that they certainly are missing many, many trades because their overanalysis takes too much time for them to place their orders and they are forced to wait for the next setup. The logic just isn't there for making the simple so complicated. Obviously, adding any information can lead to better decision making and many people might be able to process lots of inputs when deciding whether to place a trade. Ignoring data because of a simplistic ideology alone is foolish. The goal is to make money, and traders should do everything they can to maximize their profits. I simply cannot process multiple indicators and time frames well in the time needed to place my orders accurately, and I find that carefully reading a single chart is far more profitable for me. Also, if I rely on indicators, I find that I get lazy in my price action reading and often miss the obvious. Price action is far more important than any other information, and if you sacrifice some of what it is telling you to gain information from something else, you are likely making a bad decision.

One of the most frustrating things for traders when they are starting out is that everything is so subjective. They want to find a clear set of rules that guarantee a profit, and they hate how a pattern works on one day but fails on another. Markets are very efficient because you have countless very smart people playing a zero-sum game. For a trader to make money, he has to be consistently better than about half of the other traders out there. Since most of the competitors are profitable institutions, a trader has to be very good. Whenever an edge exists, it is quickly discovered and it disappears. Remember, someone has to be taking the opposite side of your trade. It won't take them long to figure out your magical system, and once they do, they will stop giving you money. Part of the appeal of trading is that it is a zero-sum game with very small edges, and it is intellectually satisfying and financially rewarding to be able to spot and capitalize on these small, fleeting opportunities. It can be done, but it is very hard work and it requires relentless discipline. Discipline simply means doing what you do not want to do. We are all intellectually curious and we have a natural tendency to try new or different things, but the very best traders resist the temptation. You have to stick to your rules and avoid emotion, and you have to patiently wait to take only the best trades. This all appears easy to do when you look at a printed chart at the end of the day, but it is very difficult in real time as you wait bar by bar, and sometimes hour by hour. Once a great setup appears, if you are distracted or lulled into complacency, you will miss it and you will then be forced to wait even longer. But if you can develop the patience and the discipline to follow a sound system, the profit potential is huge.

There are countless ways to make money trading stocks and Eminis, but all require movement (well, except for shorting options). If you learn to read the charts, you will catch a great number of these profitable trades every day without ever knowing why some institution started the trend and without ever knowing what any indicator is showing. You don't need these institutions' software or analysts because they will show you what they are doing. All you have to do is piggyback onto their trades and you will make a profit. Price action will tell you what they are doing and allow you an early entry with a tight stop.

I have found that I consistently make far more money by minimizing what I have to consider when placing a trade. All I need is a single chart on my laptop computer with no indicators except a 20-bar exponential moving average (EMA), which does not require too much analysis and clarifies many good setups each day. Some traders might also look at volume because an unusually large volume spike sometimes comes near the end of a bear trend, and the next new swing low or two often provide profitable long scalps. Volume spikes also sometimes occur on daily charts when a sell-off is overdone. However, it is not reliable enough to warrant my attention.

Many traders consider price action only when trading divergences and trend pullbacks. In fact, most traders using indicators won't take a trade unless there is a strong signal bar, and many would enter on a strong signal bar if the context was right, even if there was no divergence. They like to see a strong close on a large reversal bar, but in reality this is a fairly rare occurrence. The most useful tools for understanding price action are trend lines and trend channel lines, prior highs and lows, breakouts and failed breakouts, the sizes of bodies and tails on candles, and relationships between the current bar to the prior several bars. In particular, how the open, high, low, and close of the current bar compare to the action of the prior several bars tells a lot about what will happen next. Charts provide far more information about who is in control of the market than most traders realize. Almost every bar offers important clues as to where the market is going, and a trader who dismisses any activity as noise is passing up many profitable trades each day. Most of the observations in these books are directly related to placing trades, but a few have to do with simple curious price action tendencies without sufficient dependability to be the basis for a trade.

I personally rely mainly on candle charts for my Emini, futures, and stock trading, but most signals are also visible on any type of chart and many are even evident on simple line charts. I focus primarily on 5 minute candle charts to illustrate basic principles but also discuss daily and weekly charts as well. Since I also trade stocks, forex, Treasury note futures, and options, I discuss how price action can be used as the basis for this type of trading.

As a trader, I see everything in shades of gray and am constantly thinking in terms of probabilities. If a pattern is setting up and is not perfect but is reasonably similar to a reliable setup, it will likely behave similarly as well. Close is usually close enough. If something resembles a textbook setup, the trade will likely unfold in a way that is similar to the trade from the textbook setup. This is the art of trading and it takes years to become good at trading in the gray zone. Everyone wants concrete, clear rules or indicators, and chat rooms, newsletters, hotlines, or tutors that will tell them when exactly to get in to minimize risk and maximize profit, but none of it works in the long run. You have to take responsibility for your decisions, but you first have to learn how to make them and that means that you have to get used to operating in the gray fog. Nothing is ever as clear as black and white, and I have been doing this long enough to appreciate that anything, no matter how unlikely, can and will happen. It's like quantum physics. Every conceivable event has a probability, and so do events that you have yet to consider. It is not emotional, and the reasons why something happens are irrelevant. Watching to see if the Federal Reserve cuts rates today is a waste of time because there is both a bullish and bearish interpretation of anything that the Fed does. What is key is to see what the market does, not what the Fed does.

If you think about it, trading is a zero-sum game and it is impossible to have a zero-sum game where rules consistently work. If they worked, everyone would use them and then there would be no one on the other side of the trade. Therefore, the trade could not exist. Guidelines are very helpful but reliable rules cannot exist, and this is usually very troubling to a trader starting out who wants to believe that trading is a game that can be very profitable if only you can come up with just the right set of rules. All rules work some of the time, and usually just often enough to fool you into believing that you just need to tweak them a little to get them to work all of the time. You are trying to create a trading god who will protect you, but you are fooling yourself and looking for an easy solution to a game where only hard solutions work. You are competing against the smartest people in the world, and if you are smart enough to come up with a foolproof rule set, so are they, and then everyone is faced with the zero-sum game dilemma. You cannot make money trading unless you are flexible, because you need to go where the market is going, and the market is extremely flexible. It can bend in every direction and for much longer than most would ever imagine. It can also reverse repeatedly every few bars for a long, long time. Finally, it can and will do everything in between. Never get upset by this, and just accept it as reality and admire it as part of the beauty of the game.

The market gravitates toward uncertainty. During most of the day, every market has a directional probability of 50–50 of an equidistant move up or down. By that I mean that if you don't even look at a chart and you buy any stock and then place a one cancels the other (OCO) order to exit on a profit-taking limit order X cents above your entry or on a protective stop at X cents below your entry, you have about a 50 percent chance of being right. Likewise, if you sell any stock at any point in the day without looking at a chart and then place a profit-taking limit order X cents lower and a protective stop X cents higher, you have about a 50 percent chance of winning and about a 50 percent chance of losing. There is the obvious exception of X being too large relative the price of the stock. You can't have X be $60 in a $50 stock, because you would have a 0 percent chance of losing $60. You also can't have X be $49, because the odds of losing $49 would also be minuscule. But if you pick a value for X that is within reasonable reach on your time frame, this is generally true. When the market is 50–50, it is uncertain and you cannot rationally have an opinion about its direction. This is the hallmark of a trading range, so whenever you are uncertain, assume that the market is in a trading range. There are brief times on a chart when the directional probability is higher. During a strong trend, it might be 60 or even 70 percent, but that cannot last long because it will gravitate toward uncertainty and a 50–50 market where both the bulls and bears feel there is value. When there is a trend and some level of directional certainty, the market will also gravitate toward areas of support and resistance, which are usually some type of measured move away, and those areas are invariably where uncertainty returns and a trading range develops, at least briefly.

Never watch the news during the trading day. If you want to know what a news event means, the chart in front of you will tell you. Reporters believe that the news is the most important thing in the world, and that everything that happens has to be caused by their biggest news story of the day. Since reporters are in the news business, news must be the center of the universe and the cause of everything that happens in the financial markets. When the stock market sold off in mid-March 2011, they attributed it to the earthquake in Japan. It did not matter to them that the market began to sell off three weeks earlier, after a buy climax. I told the members of my chat room in late February that the odds were good that the market was going to have a significant correction when I saw 15 consecutive bull trend bars on the daily chart after a protracted bull run. This was an unusually strong buy climax, and an important statement by the market. I had no idea that an earthquake was going to happen in a few weeks, and did not need to know that, anyway. The chart was telling me what traders were doing; they were getting ready to exit their longs and initiate shorts.

Television experts are also useless. Invariably when the market makes a huge move, the reporter will find some confident, convincing expert who predicted it and interview him or her, leading the viewers to believe that this pundit has an uncanny ability to predict the market, despite the untold reality that this same pundit has been wrong in his last 10 predictions. The pundit then makes some future prediction and naïve viewers will attach significance to it and let it affect their trading. What the viewers may not realize is that some pundits are bullish 100 percent of the time and others are bearish 100 percent of the time, and still others just swing for the fences all the time and make outrageous predictions. The reporter just rushes to the one who is consistent with the day's news, which is totally useless to traders and in fact it is destructive because it can influence their trading and make them question and deviate from their own methods. No one is ever consistently right more than 60 percent of the time on these major predictions, and just because pundits are convincing does not make them reliable. There are equally smart and convincing people who believe the opposite but are not being heard. This is the same as watching a trial and listening to only the defense side of the argument. Hearing only one side is always convincing and always misleading, and rarely better than 50 percent reliable.

Institutional bulls and bears are placing trades all the time, and that is why there is constant uncertainty about the direction of the market. Even in the absence of breaking news, the business channels air interviews all day long and each reporter gets to pick one pundit for her report. What you have to realize is that she has a 50–50 chance of picking the right one in terms of the market's direction over the next hour or so. If you decide to rely on the pundit to make a trading decision and he says that the market will sell off after midday and instead it just keeps going up, are you going to look to short? Should you believe this very convincing head trader at one of Wall Street's top firms? He obviously is making over a million dollars a year and they would not pay him that much unless he was able to correctly and consistently predict the market's direction. In fact, he probably can and he is probably a good stock picker, but he almost certainly is not a day trader. It is foolish to believe that just because he can make 15 percent annually managing money he can correctly predict the market's direction over the next hour or two. Do the math. If he had that ability, he would be making 1 percent two or three times a day and maybe 1,000 percent a year. Since he is not, you know that he does not have that ability. His time frame is months and yours is minutes. Since he is unable to make money by day trading, why would you ever want to make a trade based on someone who is a proven failure as a day trader? He has shown you that he cannot make money by day trading by the simple fact that he is not a successful day trader. That immediately tells you that if he day trades, he loses money because if he was successful at it, that is what he would choose to do and he would make far more than he is currently making. Even if you are holding trades for months at a time in an attempt to duplicate the results of his fund, it is still foolish to take his advice, because he might change his mind next week and you would never know it. Managing a trade once you are in is just as important as placing the trade. If you are following the pundit and hope to make 15 percent a year like he does, you need to follow his management, but you have no ability to do so and you will lose over time employing this strategy. Yes, you will make an occasional great trade, but you can simply do that by randomly buying any stock. The key is whether the approach makes money over 100 trades, not over the first one or two. Follow the advice that you give your kids: don't fool yourself into believing that what you see on television is real, no matter how polished and convincing it appears to be.

As I said, there will be pundits who will see the news as bullish and others who will see it as bearish, and the reporter gets to pick one for her report. Are you going to let a reporter make trading decisions for you? That's insane! If that reporter could trade, she would be a trader and make hundreds of times more money than she is making as a reporter. Why would you ever allow her to influence your decision making? You might do so only out of a lack of confidence in your ability, or perhaps you are searching for a father figure who will love and protect you. If you are prone to be influenced by a reporter's decision, you should not take the trade. The pundit she chooses is not your father, and he will not protect you or your money. Even if the reporter picks a pundit who is correct on the direction, that pundit will not stay with you to manage your trade, and you will likely be stopped out with a loss on a pullback.

Financial news stations do not exist to provide public service. They are in business to make money, and that means they need as large an audience as possible to maximize their advertising income. Yes, they want to be accurate in their reporting, but their primary objective is to make money. They are fully aware that they can maximize their audience size only if they are pleasing to watch. That means that they have to have interesting guests, including some who will make outrageous predictions, others who are professorial and reassuring, and some who are just physically attractive; most of them have to have some entertainment value. Although some guests are great traders, they cannot help you. For example, if they interview one of the world's most successful bond traders, he will usually only speak in general terms about the trend over the next several months, and he will do so only weeks after he has already placed his trades. If you are a day trader, this does not help you, because every bull or bear market on the monthly chart has just about as many up moves on the intraday chart as down moves, and there will be long and short trades every day. His time frame is very different from yours, and his trading has nothing to do with what you are doing. They will also often interview a chartist from a major Wall Street firm, who, while his credentials are good, will be basing his opinion on a weekly chart, but the viewers are looking to take profits within a few days. To the chartist, that bull trend that he is recommending buying will still be intact, even if the market falls 10 percent over the next couple of months. The viewers, however, will take their losses long before that, and will never benefit from the new high that comes three months later. Unless the chartist is addressing your specific goals and time frame, whatever he says is useless. When television interviews a day trader instead, he will talk about the trades that he already took, and the information is too late to help you make money. By the time he is on television, the market might already be going in the opposite direction. If he is talking while still in his day trade, he will continue to manage his trade long after his two-minute interview is over, and he will not manage it while on the air. Even if you enter the trade that he is in, he will not be there when you invariably will have to make an important decision about getting out as the market turns against you, or as the market goes in your direction and you are thinking about taking profits. Watching television for trading advice under any circumstances, even after a very important report, is a sure way to lose money and you should never do it.

Only look at the chart and it will tell you what you need to know. The chart is what will give you money or take money from you, so it is the only thing that you should ever consider when trading. If you are on the floor, you can't even trust what your best friend is doing. He might be offering a lot of orange juice calls but secretly having a broker looking to buy 10 times as many below the market. Your friend is just trying to create a panic to drive the market down so he can load up through a surrogate at a much better price.

Friends and colleagues freely offer opinions for you to ignore. Occasionally traders will tell me that they have a great setup and want to discuss it with me. I invariably get them angry with me when I tell them that I am not interested. They immediately perceive me as selfish, stubborn, and close-minded, and when it comes to trading, I am all of that and probably much more. The skills that make you money are generally seen as flaws to the layperson. Why do I no longer read books or articles about trading, or talk to other traders about their ideas? As I said, the chart tells me all that I need to know and any other information is a distraction. Several people have been offended by my attitude, but I think in part it comes from me turning down what they are presenting as something helpful to me when in reality they are making an offering, hoping that I will reciprocate with some tutoring. They become frustrated and angry when I tell them that I don't want to hear about anyone else's trading techniques. I tell them that I haven't even mastered my own and probably never will, but I am confident that I will make far more money perfecting what I already know than trying to incorporate non-price-action approaches into my trading. I ask them if James Galway offered a beautiful flute to Yo-Yo Ma and insisted that Ma start learning to play the flute because Galway makes so much money by playing his flute, should Ma accept the offer? Clearly not. Ma should continue to play the cello and by doing so he will make far more money than if he also started playing the flute. I am no Galway or Ma, but the concept is the same. Price action is the only instrument that I want to play, and I strongly believe that I will make far more money by mastering it than by incorporating ideas from other successful traders.

The charts, not the experts on television, will tell you exactly how the institutions are interpreting the news.

Yesterday, Costco's earnings were up 32 percent on the quarter and above analysts' expectations (see Figure I.2). COST gapped up on the open, tested the gap on the first bar, and then ran up over a dollar in 20 minutes. It then drifted down to test yesterday's close. It had two rallies that broke bear trend lines, and both failed. This created a double top (bars 2 and 3) bear flag or triple top (bars 1, 2, and 3), and the market then plunged $3, below the prior day's low. If you were unaware of the report, you would have shorted at the failed bear trend line breaks at bars 2 and 3 and you would have sold more below bar 4, which was a pullback that followed the breakout below yesterday's low. You would have reversed to long on the bar 5 big reversal bar, which was the second attempt to reverse the breakout below yesterday's low and a climactic reversal of the breakout of the bottom of the steep bear trend channel line.

FIGURE I.2 Ignore the News

Alternatively, you could have bought the open because of the bullish report, and then worried about why the stock was collapsing instead of soaring the way the TV analysts predicted, and you likely would have sold out your long on the second plunge down to bar 5 with a $2 loss.

Any trend that covers a lot of points in very few bars, meaning that there is some combination of large bars and bars that overlap each other only minimally, will eventually have a pullback. These trends have such strong momentum that the odds favor resumption of the trend after the pullback and then a test of the trend's extreme. Usually the extreme will be exceeded, as long as the pullback does not turn into a new trend in the opposite direction and extend beyond the start of the original trend. In general, the odds that a pullback will get back to the prior trend's extreme fall substantially if the pullback retraces 75 percent or more. For a pullback in a bear trend, at that point, a trader is better off thinking of the pullback as a new bull trend rather than a pullback in an old bear trend. Bar 6 was about a 70 percent pullback and then the market tested the climactic bear low on the open of the next day.

Just because the market gaps up on a news item does not mean that it will continue up, despite how bullish the news is.

As shown in Figure I.3, before the open of bar 1 on both Yahoo! (YHOO) charts (daily on the left, weekly on the right), the news reported that Microsoft was

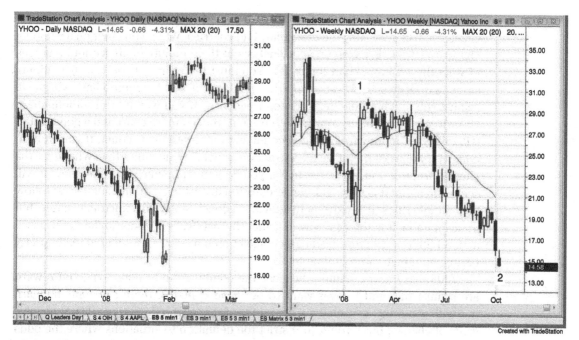

FIGURE I.3 Markets Can Fall on Bullish News

looking to take over Yahoo! at $31 a share, and the market gapped up almost to that price. Many traders assumed that it had to be a done deal because Microsoft is one of the best companies in the world and if it wanted to buy Yahoo!, it certainly could make it happen. Not only that—Microsoft has so much cash that it would likely be willing to sweeten the deal if needed. Well, the CEO of Yahoo! said that his company was worth more like $40 a share, but Microsoft never countered. The deal slowly evaporated, along with Yahoo!'s price. In October, Yahoo! was 20 percent below the price where it was before the deal was announced and 50 percent lower than on the day of the announcement, and it continues to fall. So much for strong fundamentals and a takeover offer from a serious suitor. To a price action trader, a huge up move in a bear market is probably just a bear flag, unless the move is followed by a series of higher lows and higher highs. It could be followed by a bull flag and then more of a rally, but until the bull trend is confirmed, you must be aware that the larger weekly trend is more important.

The only thing that is as it seems is the chart. If you cannot figure out what it is telling you, do not trade. Wait for clarity. It will always come. But once it is there, you must place the trade and assume the risk and follow your plan. Do not dial down to a 1 minute chart and tighten your stop, because you will lose. The problem with the 1 minute chart is that it tempts you by offering lots of entries with smaller bars and therefore smaller risk. However, you will not be able to take them all and you will instead cherry-pick, which will lead to the death of your account because you will invariably pick too many bad cherries. When you enter on a 5 minute chart, your trade is based on your analysis of the 5 minute chart without any idea of what the 1 minute chart looks like. You must therefore rely on your five-minute stops and targets, and just accept the reality that the 1 minute chart will move against you and hit a one-minute stop frequently. If you watch the 1 minute chart, you will not be devoting your full attention to the 5 minute chart and a good trader will take your money from your account and put it into his account. If you want to compete, you must minimize all distractions and all inputs other than what is on the chart in front of you, and trust that if you do you will make a lot of money. It will seem unreal but it is very real. Never question it. Just keep things simple and follow your simple rules. It is extremely difficult to consistently do something simple, but in my opinion, it is the best way to trade. Ultimately, as a trader understands price action better and better, trading becomes much less stressful and actually pretty boring, but much more profitable.

Although I never gamble (because the combination of odds, risk, and reward are against me, and I never want to bet against math), there are some similarities with gambling, especially in the minds of those who don't trade. Gambling is a game of chance, but I prefer to restrict the definition to situations where the odds are slightly against you and you will lose over time. Why this restriction? Because without it, every investment is a gamble since there is always an element of luck and a risk of total loss, even if you buy investment real estate, buy a home, start a business, buy a blue-chip stock, or even buy Treasury bonds (the government might choose to devalue the dollar to reduce the real size of our debt, and in so doing, the purchasing power of the dollars that you will get back from those bonds would be much less than when you originally bought the bonds).

Some traders use simple game theory and increase the size of a trade after one or more losing trades (this is called a martingale approach to trading). Blackjack card counters are very similar to trading range traders. The card counters are trying to determine when the math has gone too far in one direction. In particular, they want to know when the remaining cards in the deck are likely overweighed with face cards. When the count indicates that this is likely, they place a trade (bet) based on the probability that a disproportionate number of face cards will be coming up, increasing the odds of winning. Trading range traders are looking for times when they think the market has gone too far in one direction and then they place a trade in the opposite direction (a fade).

I tried playing poker online a few times without using real money to find similarities to and differences from trading. I discovered early on that there was a deal breaker for me: I was constantly anxious because of the inherent unfairness due to luck, and I never want luck to be a large component of the odds for my success. This is a huge difference and makes me see gambling and trading as fundamentally different, despite public perception. In trading, everyone is dealt the same cards so the game is always fair and, over time, you get rewarded or penalized entirely due to your skill as a trader. Obviously, sometimes you can trade correctly and lose, and this can happen several times in a row due to the probability curve of all possible outcomes. There is a real but microscopic chance that you can trade well and lose 10 or even 100 times or more in a row; but I cannot remember the last time I saw as many as four good signals fail in a row, so this is a chance that I am willing to take. If you trade well, over time you should make money because it is a zero-sum game (except for commissions, which should be small if you choose an appropriate broker). If you are better than most of the other traders, you will win their money.

There are two types of gambling that are different from pure games of chance, and both are similar to trading. In both sports betting and poker, gamblers are trying to take money from other gamblers rather than from the house, and therefore they can create odds in their favor if they are significantly better than their competitors. However, the "commissions" that they pay can be far greater than those that a trader pays, especially with sports betting, where the vig is usually 10 percent, and that is why incredibly successful sports gamblers like Billy Walters are so rare: they have to be at least 10 percent better than the competition just to break even. Successful poker players are more common, as can be seen on all of the poker shows on TV. However, even the best poker players do not make anything comparable to what the best traders make, because the practical limits to their trading size are much smaller.

I personally find trading not to be stressful, because the luck factor is so tiny that it is not worth considering. However, there is one thing that trading and playing poker share, and that is the value of patience. In poker, you stand to make far more money if you patiently wait to bet on only the very best hands, and traders make more when they have the patience to wait for the very best setups. For me, this protracted downtime is much easier in trading because I can see all of the other "cards" during the slow times, and it is intellectually stimulating to look for subtle price action phenomena.

There is an important adage in gambling that is true in all endeavors, and that is that you should not bet until you have a good hand. In trading, that is true as well. Wait for a good setup before placing a trade. If you trade without discipline and without a sound method, then you are relying on luck and hope for your profits, and your trading is unquestionably a form of gambling.

One unfortunate comparison is from nontraders who assume that all day traders, and all market traders for that matter, are addicted gamblers and therefore have a mental illness. I suspect that many are addicted, in the sense that they are doing it more for excitement than for profit. They are willing to make low-probability bets and lose large sums of money because of the huge rush they feel when they occasionally win. However, most successful traders are essentially investors, just like an investor who buys commercial real estate or a small business. The only real differences from any other type of investing are that the time frame is shorter and the leverage is greater.

Unfortunately, it is common for beginners to occasionally gamble, and it invariably costs them money. Every successful trader trades on the basis of rules. Whenever traders deviate from those rules for any reason, they are trading on hope rather than logic and are then gambling. Beginning traders often find themselves gambling right after having a couple of losses. They are eager to be made whole again and are willing to take some chances to make that happen. They will take trades that they normally would not take, because they are eager to get back the money they just lost. Since they are now taking a trade that they believe is a low-probability trade and they are taking it because of anxiety and sadness over their losses, they are now gambling and not trading. After they lose on their gamble, they feel even worse. Not only are they even further down on the day, but they feel especially sad because they are faced with the reality that they did not have the discipline to stick to their system when they know that discipline is one of the critical ingredients to success.

Interestingly, neurofinance researchers have found that brain scan images of traders about to make a trade are indistinguishable from those of drug addicts about to take a hit. They found a snowball effect and an increased desire to continue, regardless of the outcome of their behavior. Unfortunately, when faced with losses, traders assume more risk rather than less, often leading to the death of their accounts. Without knowing the neuroscience, Warren Buffett clearly understood the problem, as seen in his statement, "Once you have ordinary intelligence, what you need is the temperament to control the urges that get other people into trouble in investing." The great traders control their emotions and constantly follow their rules.

One final point about gambling: There is a natural tendency to assume that nothing can last forever and that every behavior regresses toward a mean. If the market has three or four losing trades, surely the odds favor the next one being a winner. It's just like flipping a coin, isn't it? Unfortunately, that is not how markets behave. When a market is trending, most attempts to reverse fail. When it is in a trading range, most attempts to break out fail. This is the opposite of coin flips, where the odds are always 50–50. In trading, the odds are more like 70 percent or better that what just happened will continue to happen again and again. Because of the coin flip logic, most traders at some point begin to consider game theory.

Martingale techniques work well in theory but not in practice because of the conflict between math and emotion. That is the martingale paradox. If you double (or even triple) your position size and reverse at each loss, you will theoretically make money. Although four losers in a row is uncommon on the 5 minute Emini chart if you choose your trades carefully, they will happen, and so will a dozen or more, even though I can't remember ever seeing that. In any case, if you are comfortable trading 10 contracts, but start with just one and plan to double up and reverse with each loss, four consecutive losers would require 16 contracts on your next trade and eight consecutive losers would require 256 contracts! It is unlikely that you would place a trade that is larger than your comfort zone following four or more losers. Anyone willing to trade one contract initially would never be willing to trade 16 or 256 contracts, and anyone willing to trade 256 contracts would never be willing to initiate this strategy with just one. This is the inherent, insurmountable, mathematical problem with this approach.

Since trading is fun and competitive, it is natural for people to compare it to games, and because wagering is involved, gambling is usually the first thing that comes to mind. However, a far more apt analogy is to chess. In chess, you can see exactly what your opponent is doing, unlike in card games where you don't know your opponent's cards. Also, in poker, the cards that you are dealt are yours purely by chance, but in chess, the location of your pieces is entirely due to your decisions. In chess nothing is hidden and it is simply your skill compared to that of your opponent that determines the outcome. Your ability to read what is in front of you and determine what will likely follow is a great asset both to a chess player and to a trader.

Laypeople are also concerned about the possibility of crashes, and because of that risk, they again associate trading with gambling. Crashes are very rare events on daily charts. These nontraders are afraid of their inability to function effectively during extremely emotional events. Although the term *crash* is generally reserved for daily charts and applied to bear markets of about 20 percent or more happening in a short time frame, like in 1927 and 1987, it is more useful to think of it as just another chart pattern because that removes the emotion and helps traders follow their rules. If you remove the time and price axes from a chart and focus simply on the price action, there are market movements that occur frequently on intraday charts that are indistinguishable from the patterns in a classic crash. If you can get past the emotion, you can make money off crashes, because with all charts, they display tradable price action.

Figure I.4 (from TradeStation) shows how markets can crash in any time frame. The one on the left is a daily chart of GE during the 1987 crash, the middle is a 5 minute chart of COST after a very strong earnings report, and the one on the right is a 1 minute Emini chart. Although the term *crash* is used almost exclusively to refer to a 20 percent or more sell-off over a short time on a daily chart and was widely used only twice in the past hundred years, a price action trader looks for shape, and the same crash pattern is common on intraday charts. Since crashes are so common intraday, there is no need to apply the term, because from a trading perspective they are just a bear swing with tradable price action.

FIGURE I.4 Crashes Are Common

Incidentally, the concept that the same patterns appear on all time frames means that the principles of fractal mathematics might be useful in designing trading systems. In other words, every pattern subdivides into standard price action patterns in smaller time frame charts, and trading decisions based on price action analysis therefore work in all time frames.

HOW TO READ THESE BOOKS

I tried to group the material in the three books in a sequence that should be helpful to traders.

Book 1: *Trading Price Action Trends: Technical Analysis of Price Charts Bar by Bar for the Serious Trader*
- *The basics of price action and candles.* The market is either trending or in a trading range. That is true of every time frame down to even an individual bar, which can be a trend bar or a nontrend bar (doji).
- *Trend lines and trend channel lines.* These are basic tools that can be used to highlight the existence of trends and trading ranges.
- *Trends.* These are the most conspicuous and profitable components of every chart.

Book 2: *Trading Price Action Trading Ranges: Technical Analysis of Price Charts Bar by Bar for the Serious Trader*

- *Breakouts.* These are transitions from trading ranges into trends.
- *Gaps.* Breakouts often create several types of intraday gaps that can be helpful to traders, but these gaps are evident only if you use a broad definition.
- *Magnets, support, and resistance.* Once the market breaks out and begins its move, it is often drawn to certain prices, and these magnets often set up reversals.
- *Pullbacks.* These are transitions from trends to temporary trading ranges.
- *Trading ranges.* These are areas of largely sideways price activity, but each leg is a small trend and an entire trading range is usually a pullback in a trend on a higher time frame chart.
- *Order and trade management.* Traders need as many tools as possible and need to understand scalping, swing trading, and scaling into and out of trades, as well as how to enter and exit on stops and limit orders.
- *The mathematics of trading.* There is a mathematical basis for all trading, and when you see why things are unfolding the way they do, trading becomes much less stressful.

Book 3: *Trading Price Action Reversals: Technical Analysis of Price Charts Bar by Bar for the Serious Trader*

- *Trend reversals.* These offer the best risk/reward ratios of any type of trade, but since most fail, traders need to be selective.
- *Day trading.* Now that readers understand price action, they can use it to trade. The chapters on day trading, trading the first hour, and detailed examples show how.
- *Daily, weekly, and monthly charts.* These charts have very reliable price action setups.
- *Options.* Price action can be used effectively in option trading.
- *Best trades.* Some price action setups are especially good, and beginners should focus on these.
- *Guidelines.* There are many important concepts that can help keep traders focused.

If you come across an unfamiliar term, you should be able to find its definition in the List of Terms at the beginning of the book.

Some books show charts that use the time zone of the location of the market, but now that trading is electronic and global, that is no longer relevant. Since I trade in California, the charts are in Pacific standard time (PST). All of the charts were created with TradeStation. Since every chart has dozens of noteworthy price action events that have not yet been covered, I describe many of them immediately after the primary discussion under "Deeper Discussion of This Chart." Even though you might find this incomprehensible when you first read it, you will understand it on a second reading of the books. The more variations of standard patterns that you see, the better you will be able to spot them as they are developing in real time. I also usually point out the major one or two trades on the chart. If you prefer, you can ignore that supplemental discussion on your first read and then look at the charts again after completing the books when the deeper discussion would be understandable. Since many of the setups are excellent examples of important concepts, even though not yet covered, many readers will appreciate having the discussion if they go through the books again.

At the time of publication, I am posting a daily end-of-day analysis of the Emini and providing real-time chart reading during the trading day at www.brookspriceaction.com.

All of the charts in the three books will be in a larger format on John Wiley & Sons' site at www.wiley.com/go/tradingreversals. (See the "About the Website" page at the back of the book.) You will be able to zoom in to see the details, download the charts, or print them. Having a printout of a chart when the description is several pages long will make it easier to follow the commentary.

SIGNS OF STRENGTH: TRENDS, BREAKOUTS, REVERSAL BARS, AND REVERSALS

Here are some characteristics that are commonly found in strong trends:

- There is a big gap opening on the day.
- There are trending highs and lows (swings).
- Most of the bars are trend bars in the direction of the trend.
- There is very little overlap of the bodies of consecutive bars. For example, in a bull spike, many bars have lows that are at or just one tick below the closes of the prior bar. Some bars have lows that are at and not below the close of the prior bar, so traders trying to buy on a limit order at the close of the prior bar do not get their orders filled and they have to buy higher.
- There are bars with no tails or small tails in either direction, indicating urgency. For example, in a bull trend, if a bull trend bar opens on its low tick and trends up, traders were eager to buy it as soon as the prior bar closed. If it closes on or near its high tick, traders continued their strong buying in anticipation of new buyers entering right after the bar closes. They were willing to buy going into the close because they were afraid that if they waited for the bar to close, they might have to buy a tick or two higher.

- Occasionally, there are gaps between the bodies (for example, the open of a bar might be above the close of the prior bar in a bull trend).
- A breakout gap appears in the form of a strong trend bar at the start of the trend.
- Measuring gaps occur where the breakout test does not overlap the breakout point. For example, the pullback from a bull breakout does not drop below the high of the bar where the breakout occurred.
- Micro measuring gaps appear where there is a strong trend bar and a gap between the bar before it and the bar after it. For example, if the low of the bar after a strong bull trend bar in a bull trend is at or above the high of the bar before the trend bar, this is a gap and a breakout test and a sign of strength.
- No big climaxes appear.
- Not many large bars appear (not even large trend bars). Often, the largest trend bars are countertrend, trapping traders into looking for countertrend trades and missing with-trend trades. The countertrend setups almost always look better than the with-trend setups.
- No significant trend channel line overshoots occur, and the minor ones result in only sideways corrections.
- There are sideways corrections after trend line breaks.
- Failed wedges and other failed reversals occur.
- There is a sequence of 20 moving average gap bars (20 or more consecutive bars that do not touch the moving average, discussed in book 2).
- Few if any profitable countertrend trades are found.
- There are small, infrequent, and mostly sideways pullbacks. For example, if the Emini's average range is 12 points, the pullbacks will all likely be less than three or four points, and the market will often go for five or more bars without a pullback.
- There is a sense of urgency. You find yourself waiting through countless bars for a good with-trend pullback and one never comes, yet the market slowly continues to trend.
- The pullbacks have strong setups. For example, the high 1 and high 2 pullbacks in a bull trend have strong bull reversal bars for signal bars.
- In the strongest trends, the pullbacks usually have weak signal bars, making many traders not take them, and forcing traders to chase the market. For example, in a bear trend the signal bars for a low 2 short are often small bull bars in two or three bar bull spikes, and some of the entry bars are outside down bars. It has trending "anything": closes, highs, lows, or bodies.
- Repeated two-legged pullbacks are setting up with trend entries.
- No two consecutive trend bar closes occur on the opposite side of the moving average.

- The trend goes very far and breaks several resistance levels, like the moving average, prior swing highs, and trend lines, and each by many ticks.
- Reversal attempts in the form of spikes against the trend have no follow-through, fail, and become flags in the direction of the trend.

The more of the following characteristics that a bull breakout has, the more likely the breakout will be strong:

- The breakout bar has a large bull trend body and small tails or no tails. The larger the bar, the more likely the breakout will succeed.
- If the volume of the large breakout bar is 10 to 20 times the average volume of recent bars, the chance of follow-through buying and a possible measured move increases.
- The spike goes very far, lasts several bars, and breaks several resistance levels, like the moving average, prior swing highs, and trend lines, and each by many ticks.
- As the first bar of the breakout bar is forming, it spends most of its time near its high and the pullbacks are small (less than a quarter of the height of the growing bar).
- There is a sense of urgency. You feel like you have to buy but you want a pullback, yet it never comes.
- The next two or three bars also have bull bodies that are at least the average size of the recent bull and bear bodies. Even if the bodies are relatively small and the tails are prominent, if the follow-through bar (the bar after the initial breakout bar) is large, the odds of the trend continuing are greater.
- The spike grows to five to 10 bars without pulling back for more than a bar or so.
- One or more bars in the spike have a low that is at or just one tick below the close of the prior bar.
- One or more bars in the spike have an open that is above the close of the prior bar.
- One or more bars in the spike have a close on the bar's high or just one tick below its high.
- The low of the bar after a bull trend bar is at or above the high of the bar before the bull trend bar, creating a micro gap, which is a sign of strength. These gaps sometimes become measuring gaps. Although it is not significant to trading, according to Elliott Wave Theory they probably represent the space between a smaller time frame Elliott Wave 1 high and a Wave 4 pullback, which can touch but not overlap.

- The overall context makes a breakout likely, like the resumption of a trend after a pullback, or a higher low or lower low test of the bear low after a strong break above the bear trend line.
- The market has had several strong bull trend days recently.
- There is growing buying pressure in the trading range, represented by many large bull trend bars, and the bull trend bars are clearly more prominent than the bear trend bars in the range.
- The first pullback occurs only after three or more bars of breaking out.
- The first pullback lasts only one or two bars, and it follows a bar that is not a strong bear reversal bar.
- The first pullback does not reach the breakout point and does not hit a breakeven stop (the entry price).
- The breakout reverses many recent closes and highs. For example, when there is a bear channel and a large bull bar forms, this breakout bar has a high and close that are above the highs and closes of five or even 20 or more bars. A large number of bars reversed by the close of the bull bar is a stronger sign than a similar number of bars reversed by the high.

The more of the following characteristics that a bear breakout has, the more likely the breakout will be strong:

- The breakout bar has a large bear trend body and small tails or no tails. The larger the bar, the more likely the breakout will succeed.
- If the volume of the large breakout bar is 10 to 20 times the average volume of recent bars, the chance of follow-through selling and a possible measured move down increases.
- The spike goes very far, lasts several bars, and breaks several support levels like the moving average, prior swing lows, and trend lines, and each by many ticks.
- As the first bar of the breakout bar is forming, it spends most of its time near its low and the pullbacks are small (less than a quarter of the height of the growing bar).
- There is a sense of urgency. You feel like you have to sell but you want a pullback, yet it never comes.
- The next two or three bars also have bear bodies that are at least the average size of the recent bull and bear bodies. Even if the bodies are relatively small and the tails are prominent, if the follow-through bar (the bar after the initial breakout bar) is large, the odds of the trend continuing are greater.
- The spike grows to five to 10 bars without pulling back for more than a bar or so.

- As a bear breakout goes below a prior significant swing low, the move below the low goes far enough for a scalper to make a profit if he entered on a stop at one tick below that swing low.
- One or more bars in the spike has a high that is at or just one tick above the close of the prior bar.
- One or more bars in the spike has an open that is below the close of the prior bar.
- One or more bars in the spike has a close on its low or just one tick above its low.
- The high of the bar after a bear trend bar is at or below the low of the bar before the bear trend bar, creating a micro gap, which is a sign of strength. These gaps sometimes become measuring gaps. Although it is not significant to trading, they probably represent the space between a smaller time frame Elliott wave 1 low and a wave 4 pullback, which can touch but not overlap.
- The overall context makes a breakout likely, like the resumption of a trend after a pullback, or a lower high or higher high test of the bull high after a strong break below the bull trend line.
- The market has had several strong bear trend days recently.
- There was growing selling pressure in the trading range, represented by many large bear trend bars, and the bear trend bars were clearly more prominent than the bull trend bars in the range.
- The first pullback occurs only after three or more bars of breaking out.
- The first pullback lasts only one or two bars and it follows a bar that is not a strong bull reversal bar.
- The first pullback does not reach the breakout point and does not hit a breakeven stop (the entry price).
- The breakout reverses many recent closes and lows. For example, when there is a bull channel and a large bear bar forms, this breakout bar has a low and close that are below the lows and closes of five or even 20 or more bars. A large number of bars reversed by the close of the bear bar is a stronger sign than a similar number of bars reversed by its low.

The best-known signal bar is the reversal bar and the minimum that a bull reversal bar should have is either a close above its open (a bull body) or a close above its midpoint. The best bull reversal bars have more than one of the following:

- An open near or below the close of the prior bar and a close above the open and above the prior bar's close.
- A lower tail that is about one-third to one-half the height of the bar and a small or nonexistent upper tail.
- Not much overlap with the prior bar or bars.

- The bar after the signal bar is not a doji inside bar and instead is a strong entry bar (a bull trend bar with a relatively large body and small tails).
- A close that reverses (closes above) the closes and highs of more than one bar.

The minimum that a bear reversal bar should have is either a close below its open (a bear body) or a close below its midpoint. The best bear reversal bars have:

- An open near or above the close of the prior bar and a close well below the prior bar's close.
- An upper tail that is about one-third to one-half the height of the bar and a small or nonexistent lower tail.
- Not much overlap with the prior bar or bars.
- The bar after the signal bar is not a doji inside bar and instead is a strong entry bar (a bear trend bar with a relatively large body and small tails).
- A close that reverses (closes below) the closes and extremes of more than one bar.

Here are a number of characteristics that are common in strong bull reversals:

- There is a strong bull reversal bar with a large bull trend body and small tails or no tails.
- The next two or three bars also have bull bodies that are at least the average size of the recent bull and bear bodies.
- The spike grows to five to 10 bars without pulling back for more than a bar or so, and it reverses many bars, swing highs, and bear flags of the prior bear trend.
- One or more bars in the spike have a low that is at or just one tick below the close of the prior bar.
- One or more bars in the spike have an open that is above the close of the prior bar.
- One or more bars in the spike have a close on the high of the bar or just one tick below its high.
- The overall context makes a reversal likely, like a higher low or lower low test of the bear low after a strong break above the bear trend line.
- The first pullback occurs only after three or more bars.
- The first pullback lasts only one or two bars, and it follows a bar that is not a strong bear reversal bar.
- The first pullback does not hit a breakeven stop (the entry price).
- The spike goes very far and breaks several resistance levels like the moving average, prior swing highs, and trend lines, and each by many ticks.

- As the first bar of the reversal is forming, it spends most of its time near its high and the pullbacks are less than a quarter of the height of the growing bar.
- There is a sense of urgency. You feel like you have to buy but you want a pullback, yet it never comes.
- The signal is the second attempt to reverse within the past few bars (a second signal).
- The reversal began as a reversal from an overshoot of a trend channel line from the old trend.
- It is reversing a significant swing high or low (e.g., it breaks below a strong prior swing low and reverses up).
- The high 1 and high 2 pullbacks have strong bull reversal bars for signal bars.
- It has trending "anything": closes, highs, lows, or bodies.
- The pullbacks are small and sideways.
- There were prior breaks of earlier bear trend lines (this isn't the first sign of bullish strength).
- The pullback to test the bear low lacks momentum, as evidenced by its having many overlapping bars with many being bull trend bars.
- The pullback that tests the bear low fails at the moving average or the old bear trend line.
- The breakout reverses many recent closes and highs. For example, when there is a bear channel and a large bull bar forms, this breakout bar has a high and close that are above the highs and closes of five or even 20 or more bars. A large number of bars reversed by the close of the bull bar is a stronger sign than a similar number of bars reversed by only its high.

Here are a number of characteristics that are common in strong bear reversals:

- A strong bear reversal bar with a large bear trend body and small tails or no tails.
- The next two or three bars also have bear bodies that are at least the average size of the recent bull and bear bodies.
- The spike grows to five to 10 bars without pulling back for more than a bar or so, and it reverses many bars, swing lows, and bull flags of the prior bull trend.
- One or more bars in the spike has a high that is at or just one tick above the close of the prior bar.
- One or more bars in the spike has an open that is below the close of the prior bar.
- One or more bars in the spike has a close on its low or just one tick above its low.
- The overall context makes a reversal likely, like a lower high or higher high test of the bull high after a strong break below the bull trend line.

- The first pullback occurs only after three or more bars.
- The first pullback lasts only one or two bars and it follows a bar that is not a strong bull reversal bar.
- The first pullback does not hit a breakeven stop (the entry price).
- The spike goes very far and breaks several support levels like the moving average, prior swing lows, and trend lines, and each by many ticks.
- As the first bar of the reversal is forming, it spends most of its time near its low and the pullbacks are less than a quarter of the height of the growing bar.
- There is a sense of urgency. You feel like you have to sell, but you want a pullback, yet it never comes.
- The signal is the second attempt to reverse within the past few bars (a second signal).
- The reversal began as a reversal from an overshoot of a trend channel line from the old trend.
- It is reversing at a significant swing high or low area (e.g., breaks above a strong prior swing high and reverses down).
- The low 1 and low 2 pullbacks have strong bear reversal bars for signal bars.
- It has trending "anything": closes, highs, lows, or bodies.
- The pullbacks are small and sideways.
- There were prior breaks of earlier bull trend lines (this isn't the first sign of bearish strength).
- The pullback to test the bull high lacks momentum, as evidenced by it having many overlapping bars with many being bear trend bars.
- The pullback that tests the bull high fails at the moving average or the old bull trend line.
- The breakout reverses many recent closes and lows. For example, when there is a bull channel and a large bear bar forms, this breakout bar has a low and close that are below the lows and closes of five or even 20 or more bars. A large number of bars reversed by the close of the bear bar is a stronger sign than a similar number of bars reversed by only its low.

BAR COUNTING BASICS: HIGH 1, HIGH 2, LOW 1, LOW 2

A reliable sign that a pullback in a bull trend or in a trading range has ended is when the current bar's high extends at least one tick above the high of the prior bar. This leads to a useful concept of counting the number of times that this occurs, which is called bar counting. In a sideways or downward move in a bull trend or a trading range, the first bar whose high is above the high of the prior bar is a high 1, and this ends the first leg of the sideways or down move, although this leg may become a small leg in a larger pullback. If the market does not turn into a bull swing and instead continues sideways or down, label the next occurrence of a bar with a high above the high of the prior bar as a high 2, ending the second leg.

A high 2 in a bull trend and a low 2 in a bear trend are often referred to as ABC corrections where the first leg is the A, the change in direction that forms the high 1 or low 1 entry is the B, and the final leg of the pullback is the C. The breakout from the C is a high 2 entry bar in a bull ABC correction and a low 2 entry bar in a bear ABC correction.

If the bull pullback ends after a third leg, the buy setup is a high 3 and is usually a type of wedge bull flag. When a bear rally ends in a third leg, it is a low 3 sell setup and usually a wedge bear flag.

Some bull pullbacks can grow further and form a high 4. When a high 4 forms, it sometimes begins with a high 2 and this high 2 fails to go very far. It is instead followed by another two legs down and a second high 2, and the entire move is simply a high 2 in a higher time frame. At other times, the high 4 is a small spike and channel bear trend where the first or second push down is a bear spike and the next pushes down are in a bear channel. If the high 4 fails to resume the trend and the market falls below its low, it is likely that the market is no longer forming a pullback in a bull trend and instead is in a bear swing. Wait for more price action to unfold before placing a trade.

When a bear trend or a sideways market is correcting sideways or up, the first bar with a low below the low of the prior bar is a low 1, ending the first leg of the correction, which can be as brief as that single bar. Subsequent occurrences are called the low 2, low 3, and low 4 entries. If the low 4 fails (a bar extends above the high of the low 4 signal bar after the low 4 short is triggered), the price action indicates that the bears have lost control and either the market will become two-sided, with bulls and bears alternating control, or the bulls will gain control. In any case, the bears can best demonstrate that they have regained control by breaking a bull trend line with strong momentum.

PART I

Trend Reversals: A Trend Becoming an Opposite Trend

One of the most important skills that a trader can acquire is the ability to reliably determine when a breakout will succeed or reverse. Remember, every trend bar is a breakout, and there are buyers and sellers at the top and bottom of every bull and bear trend bar, no matter how strong the bar appears. A breakout of anything is the same. There are traders placing trades based on the belief that the breakout will succeed, and other traders placing trades in the opposite direction, betting it will fail and the market will reverse. A reversal after a single bar on the 15 minute chart is probably a reversal that took place over many bars on the 1 minute chart, and a reversal that took place over 10 to 20 bars can be a one-bar reversal on a 120 minute chart. The process is the same on all time frames, whether it takes place after a single bar or many bars. If traders develop the skill to know which direction the market will likely go after a breakout attempt develops, they have an edge and will place their trades in that direction.

Reversal setups are common because every trend bar is a breakout and is soon followed by an attempt to make the breakout fail and reverse, as discussed in Chapter 5 of book 2. If the breakout looks stronger than the reversal attempt, the reversal attempt will usually not succeed, and the attempt to reverse will become the start of a flag in the new trend. For example, if there is a bull breakout of a trading range and the bull spike is made of two large bull trend bars with small tails, and the next bar is a bear doji bar, that bear bar is an attempt to have the breakout fail and reverse back down into a bear trend. Since the breakout is much stronger than the reversal attempt, it is more likely that there are more buyers than sellers below the bear bar, and that the entry bar for the short will become a breakout pullback buy signal bar. In other words, instead of the reversal succeeding, it is more likely that it will become the start of a bull flag and be followed by another leg up. If the reversal setup looks much stronger than the breakout, it is more likely that the breakout will fail and that the market will reverse. Chapter 2 in book 2 discusses how to gauge the strength of a breakout. In short, the more signs of strength that are present, the more likely that the breakout will succeed and that the reversal attempt will fail and lead to a breakout pullback setup.

Institutional trading is done by discretionary traders and computers, and computer program trading has become increasingly important. Institutions base their trading on fundamental or technical information, or a combination of both, and both types of trading are done by traders and by computers. In general, most of the discretionary traders base their decisions primarily on fundamental information, and most of the computer trades are based on technical data. Since the majority of the volume is now traded by HFT firms, and most of the trades are based on price action and other technical data, most of the program trading is technically based. In the late twentieth century, a single institution running a large program could move the market, and the program would create a micro channel, which traders saw as a sign that a program was running. Now, most days have a dozen or so micro channels in the Emini, and many have over 100,000 contracts traded. With the Emini currently around 1200, that corresponds to $6 billion, and is larger than a single institution would trade for a single small trade. This means that a single institution cannot move the market very far or for very long, and that all movement on the chart is caused by many institutions trading in the same direction at the same time. Also, HFT computers analyze every tick and are constantly placing trades all day long. When they detect a program, many will scalp in the direction of the program, and they will often account for most of the volume while the micro channel (program) is progressing.

The institutions that are trading largely on technical information cannot move the market in one direction forever because at some point the market will appear as offering value to the institutions trading on fundamentals. If the technical institutions run the price up too high, fundamental institutions and other technical institutions will see the market as being at a great price to sell out of longs and to initiate shorts, and they will overwhelm the bullish technical trading and drive the market down. When the technical trading creates a bear trend, the market at some point will be clearly cheap in the eyes of fundamental and other technical institutions. The buyers will come in and overwhelm the technical institutions responsible for the sell-off and reverse the market up. Trend reversals on all time frames always happen at support and resistance levels, because technical traders and programs look for them as areas where they should stop pressing their bets and begin to take profits, and many will also begin to trade in the opposite direction. Since they are all based on mathematics, computer algorithms, which generate 70 percent of all trading volume and 80 percent of institutional volume, know where they are. Also, institutional fundamental traders pay attention to obvious technical factors. They see major support and resistance on the chart as areas of value and will enter trades in the opposite direction when the market gets there. The programs that trade on value will usually find it around the same areas, because there is almost always significant value by any measure around major support and resistance. Most of the programs make decisions based on price, and there are no secrets. When there is an important price, they all see it, no matter what logic they use. The fundamental traders (people and machines) wait for value and commit heavily when they detect it. They want to buy when they think that the market is cheap and sell when they believe it is expensive. For example, if the market is falling, but it's getting to a price level where the institutions feel like it is getting cheap, they will appear out of nowhere and buy aggressively. This is seen most dramatically and often during opening reversals (the reversals can be up or down and are discussed in the section on trading the open later in this book). The bears will buy back their shorts to take profits and the bulls will buy to establish new longs. No one is good at knowing when the market has gone far enough, but most experienced traders and programs are usually fairly confident in their ability to know when it has gone too far.

Because the institutions are waiting to buy until the market has become clearly oversold, there is an absence of buyers in the area above a possible bottom, and the market is able to accelerate down to the area where they are confident that it is cheap. Some institutions rely on programs to determine when to buy and others are discretionary. Once enough of them buy, the market will usually turn up for at least a couple of legs and about 10 or more bars on whatever time frame chart where this is happening. While it is falling, institutions continue to short all the way down until they determine that it has reached a likely target and it is unlikely to fall any further, at which point they take profits. The more oversold the market becomes, the more of the selling volume is technically based, because fundamental traders and programs will not continue to short when they think that the market is cheap and should soon be bought. The relative absence of buyers as the market gets close to a major support level often leads to an acceleration of the selling into the support, usually resulting in a sell vacuum that sucks the market below the support in a climactic sell-off, at which point the market reverses up sharply. Most support levels will not stop a bear trend (and most resistance levels will not stop a bull trend), but when the market finally reverses up, it will be at an obvious major support level, like a long-term trend line. The bottom of the sell-off and the reversal up is usually on very heavy volume. As the market is falling, it has many rallies up to resistance levels and sell-offs down to support levels along the way, and each reversal takes place when enough institutions determine that it has gone too far and is offering value for a trade in the opposite direction. When enough institutions act around the same level, a major reversal takes place.

There are fundamental and technical ways to determine support. For example, it can be estimated with calculations, like what the S&P 500 price earnings multiple should theoretically be, but these calculations are never sufficiently precise for enough institutions to agree. However, traditional areas of support and resistance are easier to see and therefore more likely to be noticed by many institutions, and they more clearly define where the market should reverse. In both the crashes of 1987 and 2008–2009, the market collapsed down to slightly below the monthly trend line and then reversed up, creating a major bottom. The market will continue up, with many tests down, until it has gone too far, which is always at a significant resistance level. Only then can the institutions be confident that there is clear value in selling out of longs and selling into shorts. The process then reverses down.

The fundamentals (the value in buying or selling) determine the overall direction, but the technicals determine the actual turning points. The market is always probing for value, which is an excess, and is always at support and resistance levels. Reports and news items at any time can alter the fundamentals (the perception of value) enough to make the market trend up or down for minutes to several days. Major reversals lasting for months are based on fundamentals and begin and end at support and resistance levels. This is true of every market and every time frame.

It is important to realize that the news will report the fundamentals as still bullish after the market has begun to turn down from a major top, and still bearish after it has turned up from a major bottom. Just because the news still sees the market as bullish or bearish does not mean that the institutions still do. Trade the charts and not the news. Price is truth and the market always leads the news. In fact, the news is always the most bullish at market tops and most bearish at market bottoms. The reporters get caught up in the euphoria or despair and search for pundits who will explain why the trend is so strong and will continue much longer. They will ignore the smartest traders, and probably do not even know who they are. Those traders are interested in making money, not news, and will not seek out the reporters. When a reporter takes a cab to work and the driver tells him that he just sold all of his stocks and mortgaged his house so that he could buy gold, the reporter gets excited and can't wait to find a bullish pundit to put on the air to confirm the reporter's profound insight in the gold bull market. "Just think, the market is so strong that even my cabbie is buying gold! Everyone will therefore sell all of their other assets and buy more, and the market will have to race higher for many more months!" To me, when even the weakest traders finally enter the market, there is no one left to buy. The market needs a greater fool who is willing to buy higher so that you can sell out with a profit. When there is no one left, the market can only go one way, and it is the opposite of what the news is telling you. It is difficult to resist the endless parade of persuasive professorial pundits on television who are giving erudite arguments about how gold cannot go down and in fact will double again over the next year. However, you have to realize that they are there for their own self-aggrandizement and for entertainment. The network needs the entertainment to attract viewers and advertising dollars. If you want to know what the institutions are really doing, just look at the charts. The institutions are too big to hide and if you understand how to read charts, you will see what they are doing and where the market is heading, and it is usually unrelated to anything that you see on television.

A successful trend reversal is a change from a bull market to a bear market or from a bear market to a bull market, and the single most important thing to remember is that most trend reversal attempts fail. A market has inertia, which means that it has a strong propensity to continue what it has been doing and a strong resistance to change. The result is that there is really no such thing as a trend reversal pattern. When there is a trend, all patterns are continuation patterns, but occasionally one will fail. Most technicians will label that failure as a reversal pattern, but since most of the time it fails as a reversal and the trend continues, it is really more accurately thought of as just a continuation pattern. A trend is like a huge ship that takes a lot of force applied over time to change its direction. There usually has to be some increase in two-sided trading before traders in the other direction can take control, and that two-sided trading is a trading range. Because of this, most reversal patterns are trading ranges, but you should expect the breakout from the trading range to be in the direction of the trend because that is what happens in about 80 percent of cases. Sometimes the breakout will be in the opposite direction or the with-trend breakout will quickly fail and then reverse. When those events happen, most traders will label the trading range as a reversal pattern, like a double top, a head and shoulders, or a final flag. All of the reversal patterns listed in Part I can lead to a trend in the opposite direction, but they can also simply lead to a trading range, which is more likely to be followed by a trend resumption. In this case, the reversal pattern is just a bull flag in a bull trend or a bear flag in a bear trend.

When a trend reverses, the reversal can be sharp and immediate and have a lot of conviction early on, or it can happen slowly over the course of a dozen or more bars. When it happens slowly, the market usually appears to be forming just another flag, but the pullback continues to grow until at some point the with-trend traders give up and there is a breakout in the countertrend direction. For example, assume that there is a bear trend that is beginning to pull back and it forms a low 1 setup, but the market immediately turns up after the signal triggers. It then triggers a low 2 entry and that, too, fails within a bar or so. At this point, assume that either the market breaks out of the top of the bear flag or it has one more push up, triggering a wedge bear flag, the entry fails, and then the market has a breakout to the upside.

A reversal at some point makes the majority of traders believe that the always-in position has reversed, and this almost always requires some kind of breakout. This is discussed in detail in Chapter 15, but it means that if you had to be in the market at all times, either long or short, the always-in position is whatever your current position is. The breakout characteristics are the same as with any breakout, and were discussed in the chapter on breakouts in Part I of book 2. At this point, there is a new trend, and traders reverse their mind-set. When a bull trend reverses to a bear trend, they stop buying above bars on stops and buying below bars on limit orders, and begin selling above bars on limit orders and selling below bars on stops. When a bear trend reverses to a bull trend, they stop selling below bars on stops and selling above bars on limit orders, and begin buying above bars on stops and buying below bars on limit orders. See Part III in the first book for more on trend behavior.

Every trend is contained within a channel, which is bordered by a trend line and a trend channel line, even though the channel may not be readily apparent on a quick look at the chart. The single most important rule in these books is that you should never be thinking about trading against a trend until after there has been a breakout of the channel, which means a break beyond a significant trend line. Also, you should take a reversal trade only if there is a strong signal bar. You need evidence that the other side is strong enough to have a chance of taking control. And even then, you should still be looking for with-trend trades because after this first countertrend surge, the market almost always goes back in the direction of the trend to test the old trend extreme. Only rarely is the trend line break on such strong momentum that the test won't be tradable for at least a scalp. If the market fails again around the price of the old extreme, then it has made two attempts to push through that level and failed, and whenever the market tries twice to do something and fails, it usually tries the opposite. It is after this test of the old extreme that you should look for countertrend swing trades and only if there is a good setup on the reversal away from the old extreme.

It is very important to distinguish a reversal trade from a countertrend scalp. A reversal trade is one where an always-in flip is likely. A countertrend scalp is not a reversal trade; it usually has a bad trader's equation and most often forms within a channel. Channels always look like they are about to reverse, suckering traders into countertrend trades using stop entries. These traders soon get trapped and have to cover with a loss. For example, if there is a bull channel, it will usually have a reasonable-looking bear reversal or inside bar after the breakout to every new high. Beginners will see that there is enough room to the moving average for a short scalp and will short on a stop below the bar. They will lose money on 70 percent or more of their countertrend scalps, and their average loser will be larger than their average winner. They take the shorts because they are eager to trade and most of the buy signals look weak, often forcing traders to buy within a few ticks of the top of the channel. The countertrend setups often have good-looking signal bars, which convince traders that they can finesse a short scalp while waiting for a good-looking buy setup. They see all of the prior bear reversal bars and pullbacks as signs of building selling pressure, and they are right. However, most short scalps will end up being just micro sell vacuums, where the market is getting sucked down to a support level, like around the bottom of the channel, or below a minor higher low. Once there, the strong bulls begin to buy aggressively. Many take profits at the new high, creating the next sell signal, which will fail like all of the earlier ones. High-frequency trading firms pay minuscule commissions and can profitably trade for one or two ticks, but you cannot. Although there are good-looking reversal bars, these are not tradable reversals, and traders should not take them. As long as the signal is not good enough to flip the always-in direction to short, only trade in the direction of the trend. The institutions are buying below the lows of those sell signal bars. If you want to trade while the channel is forming, you either have to buy with limit orders below prior bars, like the institutions, or buy above high 2 signal bars, which is where the bears usually buy back their losing shorts. However, this is difficult for many traders, because they can see that the channel has a lot of two-sided trading and know that buying at the top of a channel, where there is a lot of two-sided trading, is an approach that often has only a marginally positive trader's equation.

A trend reversal, or simply a reversal, is not necessarily an actual trend reversal because the term implies that the market is changing from one behavior to any opposite behavior. It is best thought of as a change from a bull trend to a bear trend or vice versa, and that is the subject of Part I. Trading range behavior is arguably the opposite of trending behavior, so if a trading range breaks out into a trend, that is a reversal of the behavior of the market, but it is more commonly described as a breakout. A pullback is a small trading range and a small trend against the larger trend, and when the pullback ends, that minor trend reverses back into the direction of the major trend. Most trend reversals end up as higher time frame pullbacks in the trend, which means that most end up as large trading ranges; however, some become strong, persistent trends in the opposite direction. Even when the reversal leads to a trading range, the reversal entry will usually go far enough to be a swing trade.

Most trend reversal attempts do not result in a strong, opposite trend and instead lead to trading ranges. Strictly speaking, the behavior has reversed into an opposite type of price action (from one-sided trading to two-sided trading), but the trend has not reversed into an opposite trend. A trader never knows in advance if there will be a reversal into a new trend, and a reversal into a trading range often looks the same as a reversal into a new trend for dozens of bars. Because of this, a trader does not know until much later whether there has been a reversal into the opposite trend or just a transition into a trading range. This is why the probability of most trades, where the reward is many times greater than the risk, is so small at the outset. As the moves becomes more certain, the reward gets smaller, because there are fewer ticks left to the move, and the risk gets larger because the theoretically ideal stop for a swing trade goes beyond the start of the most recent spike (below the most recent higher low in a bull or above the most recent lower high in a bear, which can be far away). From a trader's perspective, it does not matter because traders are going to trade the reversal the same way, whether it evolves into a strong new trend or simply into a couple of large countertrend legs. Yes, they would make more money from a huge swing that does not come back to their breakeven stops, but they can still make a lot of money if the market stalls and simply becomes a large trading range. However, in a trading range, traders will usually make more money if they look for scalps rather than swings. Trading ranges and pullbacks were discussed in book 2. In a true trend reversal, the new trend can go a long way and traders should swing most of their position.

If the market does reverse into an opposite trend, the new trend may be either protracted or limited to a single bar. The market may also simply drift sideways after a bar or two, and then trend again later, either up or down. Many technicians will not use the term *reversal* except in hindsight, after a series of trending highs and lows has formed. However, this is not useful in trading because waiting for that to occur will result in a weaker trader's equation, since a significant pullback (a greater drawdown) in that new trend becomes more likely the longer the trend has been in effect. Once a trader is initiating trades in the opposite direction to the trend, that trader believes that the trend has reversed even though the strict criteria have not yet been met. For example, if traders are buying in a bear trend, they believe that the market will likely not trade even a single tick lower; otherwise they would wait to buy. Since they are buying with the belief that the market will go higher, they believe the trend is now upward and therefore a reversal has taken place, at least on a scale large enough for the trade to be profitable.

Many technicians will not accept this definition, because it does not require some basic components of a trend to exist. Most would agree on two requirements for a trend reversal. The first is an absolute requirement: the move has to break a trend line from the prior trend so that the old trend channel has been broken. The second requirement happens most of the time, but is not required: after the trend line break, the market comes back and successfully tests the extreme of the old trend. Rarely, there can be a climactic reversal that has a protracted initial move and never comes close to testing the old extreme.

The sequence is the same for any reversal. Every trend is in a channel and when there is a move that breaks the trend line, the market has broken out of the channel. This breakout beyond the trend line is followed by a move back in the direction of the trend. The trend traders want this to be a failed reversal attempt and for the old trend to resume. If they are right, the new trend channel will usually be broader and less steep, which indicates some loss of momentum. This is natural as a trend matures. They see this trend line break as simply leading to another flag that will be followed by an extension of the trend.

The countertrend traders want this reversal back in the direction of the old trend, after the breakout, to be a breakout test and then be followed by at least a second leg against the old trend. In a successful breakout, instead of resuming the trend, the test reverses once more and the test becomes a breakout pullback in the new trend, or at least in a larger correction. For example, in the breakout above the bear trend line in a bear trend, at some point the reversal will attempt to fail and then sell off to a lower low, a double bottom, or a higher low, which is the test of the bear low. If that test is successful, that test becomes a breakout pullback in the breakout above the bear trend line and the new bull trend resumes for at least one more leg. When the reversal up results in a reversal into a new trend, the rally that broke above the bear trend line is when the bulls began to take control over the market, even if the pullback from this bull breakout falls to a lower low. Most traders will see the lower low as the start of the bull trend, but the bulls often take control during the spike that breaks above the bear trend line. It does not matter if you say that the bull began at the bottom of the bull spike or at the bottom of the lower low reversal, because you trade the market the same. You look to buy as the market is reversing up from the lower low (or double bottom or higher low). The rally that follows could become a large two-legged correction, the start of a trading range, or a new bull trend. No matter what the end result is, the bulls have a good chance of a profitable trade. If the test is unsuccessful, the market will continue down into a new bear leg and traders have to look for another breakout above the new bear channel and then another test of the new bear low before looking to buy a bottom. The opposite is true when there is a bull trend that has a bear spike below the bull trend line, and then a higher high, double top, or lower high pullback from the breakout. The bears began to take control over the market during the spike. The test of the bull high, even if it exceeds the old high, is still simply a pullback from the initial bear breakout below the bull trend line.

Once there has been a strong countertrend move, the pullback will be a test for both the bulls and the bears. For example, suppose there was a strong downward move in a bull market, and the move broke through a trend line that had held for 20 to 40 bars; it then continued down for 20 bars and carried well below the 20-bar moving average, and even beneath the low of the last higher low of the bull trend; in this case the bears have demonstrated considerable strength. Once this first leg down exhausts itself, bears will begin to take partial profits, and bulls will begin to reinstate their longs. Both will cause the market to move higher, and both bulls and bears will watch this move very carefully. Because the down leg was so strong, both the bulls and the bears believe that its low will likely be tested before the market breaks out into a new high. Therefore, as the market rallies, if there is not strong momentum up, the new bulls will start to take profits and the bears will become aggressive and add to their shorts. Also, the bulls who held through the sell-off will use this rally to begin to exit their longs. They wanted to stay long until they saw strong bears, and since the bears demonstrated impressive strength, these bulls will look for any rally to exit. This represents supply over the market and will work to limit the rally and increase the chances of another leg down. The rally will likely have many bear bars and tails, both of which indicate that the bulls are weak. A sell-off down from this rally would create the first lower high in a potential new bear trend. In any case, the odds are high that there will be a second leg down, since both the bulls and the bears expect it and will be trading accordingly.

There will still be bulls who bought much lower and want to give the bull trend every possible chance to resume. Traders know that most reversal attempts fail, and many who rode the trend up will not exit their longs until after the bears have demonstrated the ability to push the market down hard. Many longs bought puts to protect themselves in case of a severe reversal. The puts allow them to hold on to give the bull trend every possible chance to resume. They know that the puts limit their losses, no matter how far the market might fall, but once they see this impressive selling pressure, they will then look for a rally to finally exit their longs, and will take profits on their puts as the market turns back up. Also, most of their puts expire within a few months, and once expired, the traders no longer have downside protection. This means that they cannot continue to hold on to their positions unless they keep buying more and more puts. If they believe that the market will likely fall further and not rally again for many months, it does not make sense to continue to pay for ongoing put protection. Instead, they will look to sell out of their positions. Their supply will limit the rally, and their selling, added to the shorting by aggressive bears and the profit taking by bulls who saw the sell-off as a buying opportunity, will create a second leg down.

These persistent bulls will each have a price level on the downside that, if reached, will make them want to exit on the next rally. As the market keeps working lower, more and more of these bulls will decide that the bull trend will not resume anytime soon and that the trend might have reversed into a bear trend. These remaining die-hard longs will wait patiently for a pullback in the bear swing to exit their longs, and their positions represent a supply that is overhanging the market. They sell below the most recent swing high because they doubt that the market will be able to get above a prior swing high and are happy to get out at any price above the most recent low. Bears will also look for a pullback from each new low to add to their shorts and place new shorts. The result is a series of lower highs and lower lows, which is the definition of a bear trend.

Typically, the initial move will break the trend line and then form a pullback that tests the end of the old trend, and traders will look to initiate countertrend (actually with-trend, in the direction of the new trend) positions after this test. Most traders will want the leg that breaks the trend line and the one that tests the trend's extreme to have more than just two or three bars. Is five enough? What about 10? It all depends on context. A trend line break that has just one or two exceptionally large bars can be enough to make traders expect at least a second leg. Is a two-bar pullback enough of a test of the old extreme? Most traders prefer to see at least five bars or so, but sometimes the trend line break or the pullback can be only two or three bars long and still convince traders that the trend has reversed. If one of the two legs is just a couple of bars, most traders will not trade the new trend aggressively unless the other leg has more bars. Because of this, the new trend will rarely begin after just a two-bar trend line break and then a two-bar test of the old trend. Even when one does, the odds are high that there will be a larger pullback within the next 10 bars or so.

The test after the trend line break may fall short of the prior extreme or it may exceed it, but not by too much. With any countertrend trade, traders should insist on a strong signal bar, because without it the odds of success are much less. For example, if there is a bear trend and then a sharp move upward that extends well beyond the bear trend line, traders will look to buy on the first pullback, hoping for the first of many higher lows. They will want a strong bull reversal bar or two-bar reversal before taking the trade. However, sometimes the pullback extends below the low of the bear trend, running stops on the new longs. If this lower low reverses back up within a few bars, it can lead to a strong swing up. If, in contrast, the lower low extends too far below the prior low, it is better to assume that the bear trend has begun a new leg down, and then wait for another trend line break, upward momentum surge, and a higher or lower low pullback, before going long again.

Although traders love to buy the first higher low in a new bull trend or sell the first lower high in a new bear trend, if the new trend is good, there will be a series of pullbacks with trending swings (higher highs and higher lows in a bull trend or lower highs and lower lows in a bear trend), and each of these pullbacks can provide an excellent entry. A pullback can be a strong bear spike, but as long as traders think the trend is now upward, they will buy around the close of the strong bear trend bar, expecting no follow-through and looking for the bear reversal to fail. The bulls see the strong bear spike as a brief value opportunity. Beginners unfortunately see it as the start of a new bear trend, ignoring all of the bullishness of the prior bars and focusing on only this one- or two-bar bear spike. They short exactly where the strong bulls are buying. The bulls will expect every attempt by the bears to fail, and therefore look to buy each one. They will buy around the close of every bear trend bar, even if the bar is large and closes on its low. They will buy as the market falls below the low of the prior bar, any prior swing low, and any support level, like a trend line. They also will buy every attempt by the market to go higher, like around the high of a bull trend bar or as the market moves above the high of the prior bar or above a resistance level. This is the exact opposite of what traders do in strong bear markets, when they sell above and below bars, and above and below both resistance and support. They sell above bars (and around every type of resistance), including strong bull trend bars, because they see each move up as an attempt to reverse the trend, and most trend reversal attempts fail. They sell below bars (and around every type of support), because they see each move down as an attempt to resume the bear trend, and expect that most will succeed.

The first pullback after a reversal up into a new bull trend is usually a test of the bear low, but it may not even get very close to the bear low. It, like all subsequent pullbacks in the new bull trend, can also be a test of a breakout of a key point like the most recent signal bar high or entry bar low, a trend line, a prior swing point, a trading range, or a moving average. After the market moves above the high of the first leg up, bulls will move their protective stops up to just below this higher low. They will continue to trail their stops to just below the most recent higher low after every new higher high until they believe that the market is becoming two-sided enough to start having two-legged corrections down. Once they believe that the market will have a second leg down that will likely fall below the low of the first leg down (the most recent higher low), they will look to exit their longs on strength, like around the close of a bull trend bar that is at, above, or slightly below the trend's high, or below the low of the prior bar. It does not make sense for them to exit below the most recent higher low once they believe that the market will get there. Instead, they will exit higher and look to buy again around that higher low. If this bull flag is sideways, it could be a simple high 2, a triangle, or a double bottom; it could also form a lower low and be a traditional ABC correction.

All trends are in channels, and most trends end with a breakout of the trend channel, which may not be obvious on the time frame of the chart in front of you. For example, a bull trend typically ends in one of two ways. First, there can be a breakout above the channel in an attempt to create an even steeper bull trend. This only rarely succeeds and usually fails within one to five bars. The market then reverses back down below the trend channel line and into the channel, and then the minimum target is a poke below the trend line at the bottom of the channel. This will usually have at least a two-legged sideways to down correction and may lead to a trend reversal or a trading range. The pullback from the first leg down usually becomes a lower high, and the second leg down will usually extend to some measured move target, like a leg 1 = leg 2 move or a projection based on the height of the bear spike or of some trading range within the bull channel.

Alternatively, the market can break below the bull trend line without first over-shooting the trend channel line. The breakout can be a sharp spike down or a sideways drift into a trading range. In either case, the pullback that tests the bull high can be either a higher high or a lower high; they occur about equally frequently. Since at least two legs down will happen in about two-thirds of cases, a higher high should be followed by two legs down, and a lower high may be followed by a single leg, since the first leg down already occurred just before the lower high formed. In the other third of cases, the reversal attempt fails, and the bull trend resumes or a trading range forms.

If the market forms a higher high in its test of the old bull high, one of the best trades is to look for a short setup on the first lower high, which is a test of the higher high. In a bear trend where there is an upward momentum surge that breaks above a major bear trend line, traders will buy the first higher low. Their buying lifts the market and reinforces everyone's belief that a new bull trend might be beginning.

An important point is that trends last much longer than most traders would ever imagine. Because of that, most reversal patterns fail and evolve into continuation setups, and most continuation patterns succeed. Traders have to be very careful when trading countertrend based on a reversal pattern, but there are price action setups that greatly increase the chances of a profitable trade.

Since most reversal attempts fail, many traders enter in the opposite direction. For example, if there is a bull trend and it forms a large bear trend bar closing on its low, most traders will expect this reversal attempt to fail, and many will buy at the close of the bear bar. If the next bar has a bull body, they will buy at the close of that bar and above its high. The first target is the high of the bear trend bar, and the next target is a measured move up, equal to the height of the bear trend bar. Some traders will use an initial protective stop that is about the same number of ticks as the bear trend bar is tall, and others will use their usual stop, like two points in the Emini.

If you find yourself drawing many trend channel lines during a trend and seeing lots of wedge reversal setups, then you are too eager to find a reversal and are likely missing many great with-trend trades. Also, since most trend channel line overshoots and reversals are minor in a strong trend and fail, you will be trading loser after loser and wondering why these patterns are failing when they are supposed to be so good. Wait for a strong trend line break before looking for a countertrend trade; look at all those minor trend channel line overshoots as the start of with-trend setups, and enter where the losers are exiting on their protective stops. You will be much happier, more relaxed, and richer, and you will be entertained by how well they work when intuitively they should not.

One of the reasons it is so tempting for a beginner to sell rallies in a strong bull trend is that the market spends so much time near the high of the leg, and one gets impatient waiting for a pullback that never seems to come. Also, there does not seem to be enough room to the top of the screen for the market to go any higher, so it is easy to imagine that it has to go lower. The market is so overdone that there surely has to be an imminent regression to the mean in the form of a reversal that will fall far enough to make at least a scalper's profit. Traders begin to believe that they have to do something in the meantime while they wait for the market to pull back, and as traders, they assume that they must trade. Instead, they should think of themselves as traders who must make a lot of money, not a lot of trades. Since they are afraid to buy at the high and they believe that a pullback is overdue, they short, expecting that they will make money as the market begins to pull back. Most of the time, the market will pull back a little but then reverse back up. It does not fall far enough for them to make a profit on their countertrend short scalps, and they are stopped out with a loss. The bull trend then resumes again in a quick breakout, and they are on the sidelines, watching, feeling sad, and a little bit poorer. Experienced traders take the other side of this trade. Many place limit orders to buy at the low of that weak bear signal bar, and others place stop orders to get long at one tick above the high of the prior bar in the small pullback. When the pullback sets up a long, beginners are still fixated on that top that led to the pullback, and they are afraid that the market might fall further. Or they are still short, hoping for the market to drop just a little more so that they can make a profit on their short scalp. Surely one of their short scalps has to work. They just lost on their last four shorts, and the market has to realize how unfair it has been, and will now make up for it by giving them a profit. They do not accept that it is all math and has nothing to do with fairness or emotion. After several months or years of losing, they decide that when they see a bull trend, they will not take a single short all day. That is the day when they stop losing money. After many months, they decide that when there is a bull trend, they are only going to buy pullbacks and take no other trades. That is the day that they begin to make money.

In a bull trend, buyers continue to buy until they decide that the trader's equation is no longer as favorable as they would like it to be, and at that point they begin to take partial profits. As the market continues to rise, they continue to take more profits and are not eager to buy again until there is a pullback. Also, shorts are being squeezed out of the market as the market continues upward, and they are being forced to buy back their short positions. At some point, they will have covered all that they wish to cover, and their buying will stop. There will also be momentum traders who will continue to buy as long as there is good momentum, but these traders will be quick to take profits once the momentum slows. The market will continue up until it overshoots the directional probability of an equidistant move. The bulls and bears are never sure when that probability is 50 percent, and the trend will continue until the math clearly favors a move down. Neutrality is never clear, and excess is much easier to spot. It will always occur at some magnet area, but since there are so many to choose from, it is difficult to know which will work. Usually, there has to be a confluence of magnets before a pullback will develop. Some firms will be placing trades based on one or more magnets, and other firms will use different ones; but once there is a critical mass of firms expecting a pullback, the market will turn. The critical mass comes when the selling pressure becomes greater than the buying pressure and is due to more dollars being traded by traders expecting a pullback. There will no longer be a shortage of offers, requiring the market to go higher to find traders to take the other side of the bull trades. Instead, traders will be quick to place shorts at the offer. In fact, they will start shorting at the bid and the market will have to go lower to find enough buyers to fill the large number of sell orders. Those sellers will be a combination of bulls selling out of their longs and bears establishing shorts.

So who is buying that last tick at the top of a bull trend or selling the low of a bear trend? Is it the accumulation of countless small traders who are getting caught up in the panic and either are on the wrong side and being forced to liquidate in the face of rapidly growing losses or are flat and impulsively entering late in a rapidly moving trend? If only we could be so influential! That might have been the case long ago, but not in today's market. If there is so much volume at the high and low of the day and the institutions make up most of that volume, why would they buy the high tick of the day if they are so smart? The majority of the day's volume is driven by statistically based mathematical algorithms, and some of those models will continue to buy until there is a clear trend change, and only then will they reverse to the short side. These momentum programs will buy right up to the last tick of a bull trend and short to the very low of a bear trend because the designers of the systems have determined that this approach maximizes their profit. Remember, there is inertia in a trend and trends are very resistant to ending, so betting on them continuing is a good bet. Because they trade such huge volume, there is an ample supply of buying at the high to take the other side of the huge volume of shorts that is coming in at the top (and vice versa at the bottom).

Just because they are very smart and trade huge volume does not mean that they are making a 5 percent profit a day. In fact, the best of them are netting a fraction of a percentage point each day, and some of them have determined that their profit is maximized by continuing to buy, even including the high tick of the day, because they believe that the market might go at least a tick or two higher. Many high-frequency trading (HFT) algorithms are designed to make very small profits on each trade, and if these quant firms have done tests that tell them that they can make a couple more ticks by buying at the high, they will continue to buy. Many firms also have complex strategies involving options and other products, and it is impossible to know what all the factors are at play at the extremes of the day. For example, they might be expecting a reversal down and be entering a delta-neutral spread where they would buy 200 Emini contracts and buy 2,000 SPY at-the-money puts. They lose only if the market goes sideways in a very tight range for several days. If the market goes up, the puts will lose money at a slower rate than the rate at which the Eminis gain in value. If the market falls, the puts will increase in value faster than the long Eminis will fall in value, and their neutral spread becomes increasingly more of a bear play. This will allow them to profit, even though they bought the Eminis at the high of the day. All that you need to know is that there is huge volume at the extremes, and it is coming from institutions, some of which are buying the high while others are selling it.

Incidentally, there is one other common sign of just how active mathematical, computer-generated trading is. Just look at correlated markets, like the Emini and all of the related exchange-traded funds (ETFs) like the SPY, and you will see that they basically move tick for tick. This is also true for other related markets. This could not be taking place so perfectly all day long if it was being done manually. Also, chart patterns would not be as perfect as they are on all time frames, even down to tick charts, unless a huge volume of the trading was computer generated. People simply cannot analyze and place orders that quickly in so many markets simultaneously, so the perfection has to be the result of computer-generated trades, and they must make up the majority of the trading volume.

When there is a strong trend with no significant pullbacks, it is common to start looking for a small reversal because common sense dictates that the market will eventually have to pull back as traders begin to take partial profits and enough countertrend traders take new positions. Regression to a mean logic works everywhere in life and it should in trading as well. And it does, but it usually occurs after the market has reached a far greater extreme than most traders could imagine. A trader will have to decide if it is better to look for a countertrend scalp or to wait for the pullback to end and then enter in the direction of the trend. If the trend is strong, it is usually better to trade countertrend only if there are clear signs of a trend reversal, such as a prior strong trend line breakout and then a test that ends with a strong reversal bar. However, the temptation is great to do something, and many traders will begin to look at smaller time frame charts, like a 1 minute or 100 tick chart. Smaller time frame charts continue to form reversals as the trend progresses, and the vast majority of the reversals fail. A trader can rationalize taking the countertrend trade by thinking that a 1 minute chart has small bars so the risk is only about four ticks, and if this turns out to be the very top of the market, the potential gain is huge. Therefore, taking a few small losses is worth it. Invariably, the few small losses turn into six or seven and their combined effect is a loss that cannot be recovered later in the day. When traders get lucky and pick the exact end of a trend, they will scalp out with a few ticks of profit instead of riding the trade for a long way, as they originally had planned. This is death by mathematics. It's great to feel smart enough to buy the low of a bear trend or short the high of a bull trend, but if you lose in nine out of 10 attempts, you will slowly go broke. In general, buying pullbacks in bull trends and selling rallies in bear trends is a much better approach for most traders. There are far more trades, and the winning percentage is higher.

If you are becoming agitated because you are not in the market during an extended trend and you feel like you need to trade so you begin to look at a 1 minute chart, those 1 minute reversals offer a very profitable way to make money. However, it is by doing the opposite of the obvious. Wait for a 1 minute reversal to trigger a countertrend entry, which you do not take, and then determine where you would place a protective stop if you had taken the trade. Then, place a stop order to enter with trend at that price. You will be stopped into a with-trend position just as the countertrend traders are getting stopped out. No one will be looking to enter countertrend at that point and likely not until the trend has moved far enough to make a profit before the next countertrend setup begins to form. This is a very high-probability with-trend scalp.

The single most reliable countertrend trade is actually a with-trend trade on a larger time frame. A pullback is a small trend against the larger trend, and when you enter against the trend of that pullback, you are entering in the direction of the larger trend. Once the pullback traders have exhausted themselves and the trend traders have again demonstrated their resolve by breaking the trend line that contained the pullback, any small pullback to test this breakout is a great breakout pullback entry. This entry is counter to the trend of the pullback, but in the direction of the major trend, and will usually lead to at least a test of the major trend's extreme. The more momentum that is present in the trend line break, the more likely it is that trade will be profitable. For example, if there is a bull flag, you can buy the bottom of the bull flag, the breakout of the bull flag, or on a small pullback from that breakout for a test of the high of the bull trend.

Momentum in a reversal can be in the form of a few large trend bars or a trending series of average-looking bars. The more signs of strength, the more reliable the reversal will be. These are discussed in more detail in Chapter 2 of book 2 on the strength of breakouts and in Chapter 19 of book 1 on the strength of trends. Ideally, the first leg of the reversal will extend for many bars, break well beyond the moving average, have the majority of the bars be trend bars in the direction of the new trend, and extend beyond swing points in the prior trend (if the prior trend was a bull trend, then it is a sign of strength if the first leg of the new bear trend drops below and closes below one or more of the higher lows of that prior bull trend).

Big traders don't hesitate to enter a trend during its spike phase, because they expect significant follow-through, even if there is a pullback immediately after their entry. If a pullback occurs, they increase the size of their position. For example, if there is a strong bull breakout lasting several bars, more and more institutions become convinced that the market has become always-in long with each new higher tick, and as they believe that the market will go higher, they start buying. This makes the spike grow very quickly. They have many ways to enter, like buying at the market, buying a one- or two-tick pullback, buying above the prior bar on a stop, or buying on a breakout above a prior swing high. It does not matter how they get in, because their focus is to get at least a small position on and then look to buy more as the market moves higher or if it pulls back. Because they will add on as the market goes higher, the spike can extend for many bars. Beginning traders see the growing spike and wonder how anyone could be buying at the top of such a huge move. What they don't understand is that the institutions are so confident that the market will soon be higher that they will buy all of the way up, because they don't want to miss the move while waiting for a pullback to form. Beginners are also afraid that their stops would have to be below the bottom of the spike, or at least below its midpoint, which is far away. The institutions know this, and simply adjust their position size down to a level where their dollars at risk are the same for any other trade. At some point, the early buyers take some profits, and then the market pulls back a little. When it does, the traders who want a larger position quickly buy, thereby keeping the initial pullback small.

Although the best reversals have strong momentum and go a long way, they often are very slow to start and can have several small bars before the sharp moves begin. The result is that most trend reversal setups have a less than 50 percent chance of success. For example, a reversal up in a new bull trend often starts as a low-momentum rally with overlapping bars and pullbacks, making many traders believe that another bear flag is forming. The first pullback is a low 1 short setup. However, traders should not short a low 1 unless the market is in a strong bear spike in a clear bear trend, so this low 1 is likely to fail. Aggressive traders will instead buy at the bottom and below the low 1 signal bar, expecting it to fail. There is often then a low 2 short setup. However, if you believe that the trend has reversed up, this is also likely to fail and again aggressive bulls will buy with limit orders at and below the low of the low 2 signal bar. Once it does fail, traders will see this failed low 2 as a failed bear flag, and it often leads to a strong breakout to the upside. That bear flag becomes the final flag in the bear trend, even though it never broke out to the downside by more than a tick or so. Sometimes the market has one more push up into a wedge bear flag before the upside breakout forms.

You can think of the bear flag as an attempt by the market to trap you out of the long trade that you entered a few bars earlier on the first reversal up so that you will have to chase the move up and add fuel to the new bull trend. One of the failed short entries often quickly becomes a strong outside up bar. This happens so quickly that many bulls who were looking to buy the failed low 1 or low 2 become paralyzed. They were hoping for a quiet buy signal bar with a high near the bottom of the low 2 signal bar, and instead they are being forced into a quick decision. Do they want to buy an outside up bar at what could be the top of a bear flag? Most traders will hesitate and wait for a pullback to buy, but at this point everyone believes that the bears have lost and that the market is going higher. They don't know if there will be a pullback in the next several bars, but they do know that if there is, it will be followed by a new high to the bull leg. When that kind of clear always-in mentality is present, there usually will not be a pullback until the market is much higher. That is why it is important to buy at least a small position. The mathematics of bull spikes is discussed in Part I of book 2 on breakouts and even more so in Chapter 25 in book 2 on the mathematics of trading, but the important thing to remember is that if you are trapped out of the market, enter at least a small position at the market or on a one- or two-tick pullback, and place a very wide stop. The mathematics of this trade is strongly in your favor.

The low 1, low 2, or wedge bear flag will trap weak new bulls out and force them to reenter the new bull trend at a much worse price. Some of the strongest trends come from these traps because they tell traders that the last bear trend trader just got burned and there is no one left from the old trend. Also, they tell us that weak bull traders just got out and now will be chasing the new bull trend, adding orders in the new direction. This gives traders confidence. When this kind of agitated reversal happens after a trend line break and on the test of the trend's extreme, the new trend will usually last for at least 10 bars and it will retrace a good portion of the most recent part of the old trend.

Even if there are no pullback bars on the 5 minute chart, it is common at the very start of a trend to find pullbacks on 1 and 3 minute charts, which also trap traders out. Sometimes traders will enter based on a 5 minute signal and think they are clever by using a stop based on a smaller time frame chart. When the 5 minute signal is strong, this will usually be a mistake. It is better to suffer through a few bars of anxiety than to exit on a smaller time frame chart, because you will get trapped out of too many great trends.

If a trader enters early but the move is hesitant (for example, with overlapping bars) for a few bars, this should not be a concern, especially if those bars are mostly trend bars in the right direction. This is a sign of strength, and everyone is watching and waiting for the momentum to begin before entering. A good price action trader can often get in before that happens and then is able to move her stop to breakeven soon after the momentum starts, allowing her to make a lot of money with minimal risk. If you are confident in your read, take your trade, and don't worry that no one else sees what you see yet. They eventually will. Make sure to swing part or even all of your position even though you sometimes will get stopped out on your breakeven stop once or twice before the trend begins its run.

So what is the best reversal setup? It is the end of a pullback when the short-term countertrend move is ending and reversing back into the direction of the major trend. In other words, the best reversals are a bull flag in a bull trend just as it is breaking out to the upside and a bear flag in a bear trend just as it is reversing back down. Major reversals are less common since most reversal attempts fail and become flags. A reversal trade can be based on a traditional reversal after a trend line break and then a test of the extreme, followed by a very strong countertrend spike that leads to an always-in flip to the opposite trend. If it comes after a trend line break, there is often a second entry. If the trend was strong, it is usually better to wait for that second entry; but if it does not come, the market will likely create a strong enough countertrend spike to make most traders believe that the always-in position has reversed. For example, if there is a bull trend and traders are looking for a reversal but the setup is not particularly strong, they should wait to see if the market will give a second entry in the form of a lower high or a higher high within the next five bars or so. If it does not and it instead sells off for four or five bars, breaks out of a pattern, and then has follow-through on the next bar, this will be enough bear strength to convince most traders that the always-in position has flipped to short. They will sell either at the market or on pullbacks.

Much of this material is in book 2 on trading ranges, but it is relevant here as well because of the widespread misconception that reversal patterns are reliable. Since trends are constantly creating reversal patterns and they all fail except the final one, it is misleading to think of these commonly discussed patterns as reversal patterns. It is far more accurate to think of them as continuation patterns that rarely fail, but when they do, the failure can lead to a reversal. It is a mistake to see every top or bottom as a great reversal setup, because if you take all of those countertrend entries, the majority of your trades will be losers and your occasional wins will not be enough to offset your losses. However, if you are selective and look for other evidence that a trend might reverse, these can be effective setups.

All head and shoulders tops and bottoms are really head and shoulders continuation patterns (flags) because they are trading ranges, and like all trading ranges, they are much more likely to break out in the direction of the trend and only rarely reverse the trend. The same is true for double tops and bottoms. For example, if there is a head and shoulders top in a bull market, a breakout below the neckline will usually fail and the market will most likely then reverse up and have a with-trend breakout to the upside, above the right shoulder. The pattern is a triangle, a triple bottom, or a wedge bull flag, and the three pushes down are the down legs after the left shoulder, the head, and the right shoulder. Other bulls see the move down from the head to the neckline as a bull flag, and the rally that forms the right shoulder as the breakout above the bull flag. The sell-off from the right shoulder to the neckline is then either a lower low or higher low pullback from that breakout, and if the market reverses up, the bulls see the reversal as a buy setup.

Since the right shoulder is a lower high, the bears see it as the first pullback in a new bear trend, and therefore the rally to the right shoulder is a bear flag. If the market trades above the right shoulder, the bear flag will have failed, and the market usually rallies for a measured move up based on either the height of the right shoulder or the entire head and shoulders top. Also, if there is a bear market that is forming a trading range and that trading range assumes the shape of a head and shoulders top, a break below the neckline is a with-trend breakout of a bear flag and is likely to lead to lower prices.

Similarly, head and shoulders bottoms are also with-trend setups. A head and shoulders bottom in a bear trend is usually a triangle or a wedge bear flag and should break out to the downside, below the right shoulder. A head and shoulders bottom in a bull market is a bull flag and should break out to the upside, above the neckline. The right shoulder itself is a smaller bull flag, and if the market trades below it, it has failed, and a sell-off usually ensues.

The vast majority of reversals are related to trading ranges. Since trading ranges are flags and usually break out in the direction of the trend, most reversal patterns do not lead to reversals. Therefore, there are no reliable (high probability) reversal patterns. For example, when there is a bull trend, most double tops, triple tops, head and shoulders tops, and triangle tops break to the upside instead of the downside, and are bull flags and do not lead to reversals. Occasionally, one will instead break to the downside and lead to a reversal. When that happens, traders apply one of the reversal pattern names to refer to the trading range; they select the name that best describes the shape of the range. Many upside breakouts of bull flags soon reverse down and then the market breaks to the downside, creating a reversal. When that happens, the bull flag becomes the final flag in the bull trend (discussed in Chapter 7). Most climactic reversals are usually variations of final flag reversals. The opposite is true in bear trends where most reversal patterns are bear flags and lead to bear breakouts. When one instead leads to a bull breakout (whether or not it first breaks to the downside, reverses up, and becomes the final flag in the bear trend), traders then apply the name of the reversal pattern that best describes the shape of the trading range.

When a reversal is gradual, like when it comes from a trading range, the trading range is traditionally called an area of distribution at the end of a bull trend or an area of accumulation at the end of a bear trend. When there is a trading range top, the bulls are said to be distributing their longs, which simply means that they are selling out to take profits. When there is a trading range bottom, the bulls are said to be accumulating their longs, which means that they are buying as they build a long position. Since short selling has become so common, it is logical to refer to the trading range at the top of a bull trend as an area of distribution by the bulls and an area of accumulation for the bears, who are building a short position. Likewise, when there is a trading range bottom in a bear trend, it is an area of accumulation for the bulls and an area of distribution for the bears who are taking profits on their shorts.

Many days that become reversal days on the daily chart are trending trading range days on the 5 minute chart. For example, if there is a bear trending trading range day and later in the day it breaks back into the upper trading range, which is common, and rallies to the top of that upper trading range and closes near the high of the day, the day will be a bull reversal day on the daily chart (discussed more in Chapter 22 of book 1).

Typically, entries in trend pullbacks look bad but are profitable, and entries in reversals look reasonably good but are losers. If you are looking to buy a reversal in a bear trend or sell a top of a bull trend, make sure that it is perfect. Trends constantly form reversals that somehow don't look quite right. Maybe there is too much overlap with the prior bars or too many dojis, or the reversal bar is too small or pulls back several ticks in the seconds before it closes, or there is no prior break of a significant trend line, or there has been no failed breakout of a trend channel line. These almost perfect reversals sucker you in and trap you, so you should never take a reversal trade unless it is clear and strong. Most of the time, you should wait to buy after there is a higher low in a new bull trend and wait to sell after a lower high in a new bear trend.

Many traders look for countertrend scalps. They become impatient as they wait for a strong reversal that should have at least two legs and they instead take a weak signal. For example, they might buy a bull reversal bar at a swing low in a bear trend. However, if they believe that the trend is still down and they are only looking for a scalp, they need to have a plan to get out if their trade fails. Many traders will allow the market to trigger a low 1 short if they believe that there should be a second leg up. They will hold long and hope for the low 1 short to fail and form a higher low. If the market then does not go up much and instead forms a low 2 short setup, most traders would exit if the low 2 triggers. If the low 2 does not trigger and there is one more small push up, this is a low 3 setup, which is a wedge bear flag. Bulls must exit if it triggers, because it is a strong sell signal in a bear trend. They don't want a trend to attempt to resume twice, and many will correctly reverse to short as the low 2 or 3 triggers. They needed the higher low to hold if the market was going to turn up and if it is now forming a low 2 or 3 short, they don't want to risk to below that higher low. Rather than wait for a protective stop below the higher low to be hit, they will exit their long on the low 2 or 3 short entry because they know that the bears will begin to short aggressively there, and many more shorts will come in below that higher low. They know that in about 80 percent of cases, a low 2 or 3 short in a strong bear trend will hit the stops below the higher low, and they want to minimize their losses. This is one of the reasons why low 2 and 3 shorts are so reliable in strong bear trends and high 2 and 3 longs are reliable in strong bull trends. The trapped countertrend scalpers will take their losses there and not look for another countertrend trade for at least a couple more bars. This makes the market one-sided in favor of the trend traders.

There is a rhythm to the market as it forms alternating trends. One trend will often end with a trend channel line overshoot and reversal followed by a two-legged move that breaks the trend line. The two legs then allow for the drawing of a channel for the new trend. Some trends end with simply a trend line break and then a test, followed by a second leg. Again, these two legs form a new trend channel that may be the start of a new trend or simply a flag in the old trend. If the new trend is weak, it will usually just result in a pullback and then a resumption of the old trend. Traders should always be drawing or at least visualizing trend lines and trend channel lines and watching how the market reacts when it tests these lines.

Major reversals from bear markets are often volatile with large bars and several pushes up and down creating one to several sell climaxes. People think that the worst is over but then realize "Oops, I'm too early," and they are quick to sell out. This can happen several times before the final bottom is in and accounts for why so many major reversals end with large range bars and either a failed flag or a three-push pattern. Climactic reversals with big bars and huge volume are more common at bottoms than at tops. More often, a top comes from a trading range, like a double top or a head and shoulders top, followed by a downside breakout in the form of a strong bear spike. However, tops can be climactic, and bottoms can be trading ranges.

When the market is in a bull trend on the higher time frame charts, the 5 minute chart often has a rally into the close, and the bar of the daily chart has a higher chance of being a bull trend bar. If the market has started to sell off into the closes of recent days, the market might be transitioning into a bear trend or at least into a bigger pullback. Pay attention to what the market does in the final 30 to 60 minutes, because it often is a reflection of the higher time frame trend. That sell-off into the close can be from mutual fund redemptions, from long liquidation by day traders, and obviously from programs, which make up most of the day's volume. The programs are based on math and if the math is indicating that the market should fall into the close, the market might be in the process of transitioning from a trend into a trading range or even a bear trend. Those low closes create weak bars on the higher time frame charts, and traders will see them as a sign of building selling pressure. This will make them hold off buying until the pullbacks are deeper, and it will encourage bears to short more aggressively. This is not good for the bulls. The opposite is true of a bear trend on the 60 minute or daily charts. Strong rallies into the close of the day on the 5 minute chart often mean that the next rally might be large and that it might be the start of a bull reversal.

Significant tops in the S&P are often presaged by a big down day or two in a bellwether stock like Apple (AAPL). If the market leaders are selling off, the market might be topping. Traders usually take profits on their big winners if they expect a bigger correction in the overall market. In a strong stock market, some stocks tend to rise faster than others. At these times, traders look for "risk-on" trades and invest heavily in these stocks (and currencies, like the Australian dollar, the New Zealand dollar, the Canadian dollar, the Swedish krona). Once they believe that the stock market is going to turn down, they sell their risk-on stocks and buy "risk-off" stocks and currencies, like Johnson & Johnson (JNJ), Altria Group (MO), Procter & Gamble (PG), the U.S. dollar, the Swiss franc, and the Japanese yen. They also invest in risk-off currencies, gold, and Treasury notes and bonds when they are afraid of some international event and want to make sure that their money will be safe and readily available whenever they need it. When a strong bull trend begins to top out, the institutions transition from overweighting to regular weighting of their stocks, and this often causes the market leaders to turn down several days before the overall market. For example, if AAPL is up 40 percent over the past year and the S&P is overbought, and then Apple loses 3 percent in one day, it might be a sign that big traders think that the market might turn down in the coming days. There is a natural tendency to take profits where you have them, and if you have a lot in a major tech stock like Apple and you are expecting the overall market to pull back 5 to 10 percent, you might first take profits in the stocks where the profits are the greatest. If many funds do this in one day, Apple can fall 3 percent at the top. This might be a sign that the funds are ready to start taking profits in their other stocks as well. If they do, the overall market might correct. As the overall market falls, traders get margin calls, and they tend to sell out of the stocks where they have the most profits, which are the market leaders. This can cause the stocks that rose the fastest in the bull trend to fall the fastest in the correction.

The mathematics of reversals is similar to that of breakouts. In general, if the setup is strong, you believe that there is at least a 60 percent chance of a minimum of a two-legged move that will last at least 10 bars. In most cases, your profit target will be two or more times greater than your risk, and that great risk/reward ratio, combined with the high probability of success, makes reversal trades so appealing to traders. The trick is to know when a setup is good, and the problem is that trends are constantly creating reversal setups that are almost good enough, but aren't quite right. These weak setups constantly trap overly eager reversal traders, and as they are forced out with losses, they add fuel to the growing trend. However, there are many signs that traders can use to identify reliable setups, and these signs of strength are detailed in the next chapter.

Most initial entries have relatively low probability (about 40 to 50 percent) of success. Some traders prefer a higher probability, and they wait for strong follow-through and a clear always-in flip. The trade-off is a smaller reward for a higher chance of success. Both approaches can be mathematically sound, and traders should choose the approach that best suits their personalities. For example, when the average range in the Emini is about 10 to 15 points, the probability of a four-point swing on a reasonably good-looking reversal (one where the context is good and there is a decent signal bar) is often only about 40 percent (it can be 50 to 60 percent when the setup is very strong). However, the chance of a two-point stop being hit before either the profit target is reached or a reversal signal develops, where the trader can exit with a smaller loss or a small profit, is often only about 30 percent. This makes the trader's equation very favorable for this type of trade. If traders win four points in four out of 10 trades, they have 16 points of profit off of their swing trades. If their other trades consist of maybe three losses of two points or less and three wins of about one to three points, they will end up about breakeven on those trades. This is fairly typical when traders pick appropriate setups. They then have about 16 points of profit on 10 trades, or an average of 1.6 points of profit per trade, which is good for a day trader. Remember, most traders will not take any reversal trade, no matter how minor, unless there is at least a double top or bottom, a micro double top or bottom, or a final flag.

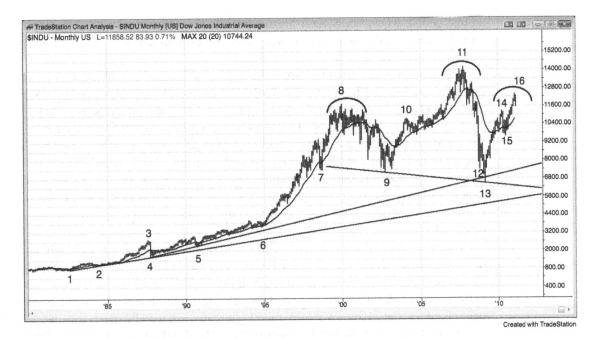

FIGURE PI.1   Dow Jones Industrials Monthly Chart

Most reversal patterns fail at least 80 percent of the time, and the large head and shoulders top on the monthly Dow Jones Industrials chart shown in Figure PI.1 will likely fail as well and become a large wedge bull flag or some other type of bull flag. With the spike down to bar 13 as strong as it was, it will probably get tested by a lower low, where the pattern will probably form a wedge bull flag and be followed by a new high a decade or two later. At the moment, the rally from bar 13 is a rally from the double bottom with bar 9.

Bar 8 is the top of the left shoulder, bar 11 is the head, and the right shoulder is in the process of forming at bar 16, but it may extend higher before the market reverses down, if it reverses down. It might reach a new high and form an expanding triangle top, or it might break out into a new bull leg and then continue up for a measured move based on the height of the trading range. This could be from the bar 9 low to the bar 8 or bar 11 high, or the bar 13 low to the bar 11 high.

Newsletter writers who make their living by selling fear will make a fortune by scaring people into believing that the Dow will fall for a measured move down to below 1,000 without understanding that this is a trading range in a bull trend, and therefore the odds are 80 percent or better that it will break out to the upside before dropping far below bar 13. For a trader, it is far better to bet on the 80 percent, but newsletter writers who make their living by selling fear make more money from being right 20 percent of the time or less. They need catastrophic events to be rare so that people worry about their financial death. If crashes were common, people would learn to trade them and there wouldn't be enough fear for these writers to stay rich.

The market will probably form a dueling lines bottom around the bull trend line drawn below the bars 1, 2, and 4 lows, which it will probably overshoot, and the trend channel line drawn below the bars 9 and 13 lows, which is the neckline of the head and shoulders top. Incidentally, notice how the 2008–2009 crash reversed up after breaking below the bull line drawn from the bar 4 and bar 5 lows, and from below the bars 7 and 9 double bottom. This is what usually happens. The market has been in a trading range since around bar 7, and most attempts to break out of a trading range fail. The market has inertia and tends to continue to do what it has been doing. This also makes most attempts to reverse a trend fail.

Bears see the right shoulder of a head and shoulders top as a lower high and the first pullback in a new bear trend. It is therefore a bear flag. If the market clearly breaks well below the bear flag, whether or not it also breaks below the neckline of the head and shoulders top, and then reverses up and rallies above the top of the right shoulder, the pattern will have failed. The rally will usually reach a measured move target based on the height either of the right shoulder or of the entire head and shoulders top. Some traders see the neckline as a horizontal line drawn across the bottom between the head and the right shoulder (here, the bar 13 low), whereas others see it as the trend channel line drawn across the lows on both sides of the head (bars 9 and 13).

The move down to bar 13 had such strong momentum that it will likely be tested, and since the down move was so strong, the test will probably be a lower low. That should trap bears in and bulls out, and then the odds favor the market reversing up in a wedge bull flag. If that is the case, the most likely course from there would be a breakout above bar 11 and a measured move up, but it might take a decade or two before that happens.

In the days leading up to the bar 13 crash low, a trader familiar with a dueling lines pattern would have seen the potential for a reversal up, especially after the small final flag from several bars earlier, the consecutive sell climaxes, and the large expanding triangle bull flag (bars 7, 8, 9, 11, and 13).

If the market does sell off from a lower high around bar 9, it might find support at the trend line drawn from the bar 1 and bar 4 lows. This is an especially important line because it involves the 1987 crash low, which was the most dramatic stock market event since the Great Depression. An event of that magnitude will make traders respect any technical pattern associated with it.

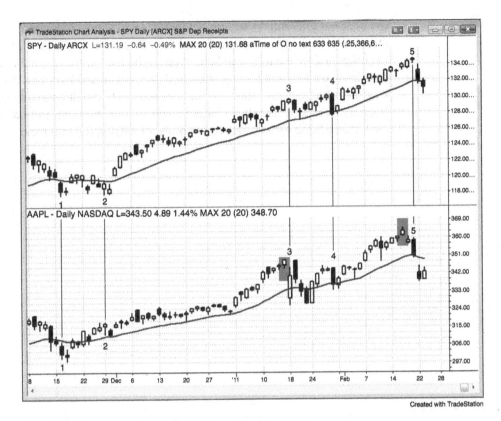

FIGURE PI.2 Market Leaders Often Lead the S&P

Market leaders are called that because they often lead the overall market in time, and not just in price. In Figure PI.2, notice how the daily chart of AAPL in the bottom chart topped out before the SPY at bars 3 and 4. When a market leader begins to turn down and the overall market does not, it is often a sign that the market might be about to correct. Traders are switching from risk-on stocks that go up strongly in a strong stock market to risk-off stocks that will be more stable and fall less, if at all, in a weak stock market. When traders think that a deeper market correction is imminent, they take profits first where they have them the most, which is usually in the market leaders. Even if the small sell-off in AAPL is because they are simply transitioning from overweighting the stock to normal weighting, it can be a sign that they expect trouble ahead in the overall market.

Incidentally, since most reversal attempts fail, many traders look to fade them. When they see a bull trend with a large bear trend bar closing on its low, like bar 4, especially if it is around the moving average, aggressive bulls will buy the close of the bear bar and will try to buy below its low. Their initial stop might be about as many ticks as the bear bar is tall, and their first profit target is often the high of the bear bar, and then a measured move up. If the next bar has a bull body, as was the case here, traders will buy its close and above its high. They wait for bars like this large bear bar, because they see them as brief opportunities to buy at a great price. Bear scalpers also like these large bear bars and use them to take profits, buying back their shorts exactly where the bulls are buying the pullback.

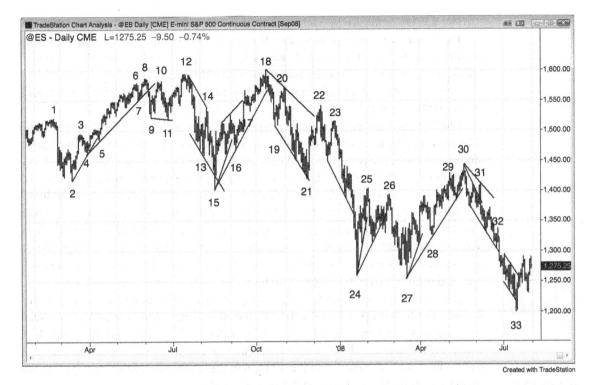

FIGURE PI.3   Reversals in the Daily Emini

When a chart discussion runs for multiple pages, remember that you can go to the Wiley website (www.wiley.com/go/tradingreversals) and either view the chart or print it out, allowing you to read the description in the book without having to repeatedly flip pages back to see the chart.

As shown in Figure PI.3, the daily Emini had many trend changes, all of which followed standard price action principles.

Bar 2 was a final bear flag reversal (discussed in Chapter 7) leading to a strong move up to bar 3, which exceeded the last lower high of the bear trend. Anytime the market goes above a swing high, it is a sign of strength, even if that high was in the prior down move and not part of a series of higher highs in an uptrend.

Bar 4 formed a higher low buy setup, and it allowed for the drawing of a bull trend line. It was also a pullback from the breakout above that last lower high in the bear leg.

Bar 5 pulled back below the trend line and immediately reversed up and set up a failed wedge bear flag buy (the swing high just before bar 2 was the first of the three pushes up). However, this now generated a flatter trend line.

Bar 6 was a small wedge top, and the pullback to bar 7 created a new trend line.

Bar 8 was a reversal down after the bar 6 wedge top, and a wedge reversal usually leads to two legs down. It was a higher high pullback from the downside breakout below the bar 6 signal bar at the top of the wedge.

The bar 9 leg fell sharply below the last higher low (bar 7) of the bull trend, indicating bear strength.

Bar 10 was a strong two-legged rally and a lower high test of the bull high, and it formed a possible double top with bar 8. It was a pullback from the bar 9 bear spike and would likely be followed by a second leg down that would test the bar 9 bear spike low. It could then be followed by a bear channel or a trading range.

Bar 11 reversed back up after falling just a little below bar 9, so this was likely the end of a two-legged correction in the prior bull trend. It formed a double bottom with bar 9. However, this correction broke a major trend line from the bar 2 low, which meant that the market could reverse down after a test of the bar 8 high. Some traders would have used the bull trend line drawn across the bar 4 low to the bar 7 low, and others would have used one drawn from the bar 2 low to bar 7 low.

Bar 12 formed a two-legged higher high after a break below a bull trend line. If this were to lead to a trend reversal, the new bear trend should have at least two legs down. It was also a failed breakout above the bars 8 and 10 double top. Whenever a breakout above a double top fails, it is a three-push top. The first two pushes here were the bar 8 and bar 10 tops in the double top. Additionally, it was a small expanding triangle top (bars 6, 7, 8, 11, and 12).

The first leg down to bar 13 was very strong, dropping well below the bars 8 to 11 bull flag. A strong spike usually leads to a measured move, and here there was a leg 1 = leg 2 move down to bar 15 where leg 2 (bar 14 to bar 15) was just a little larger than leg 1 down to bar 13.

Once the bar 14 lower high formed, it could be used to create a trend line and then a trend channel line.

Bar 15 reversed up from its breakout of the trend channel line, so it should have two legs up and break above the bear trend line, which it did.

Bar 16 broke below the first bull trend line and reversed up, forming a double bottom bull flag with the higher low from six bars earlier.

Bar 17 was a pullback from the breakout above the bull trend channel line and from the breakout above the double top formed by the two swing highs just before bar 16. This double top was seen by some traders as a wedge top, created by the three small pushes up after the bar 15 low.

This rally ended in a small wedge at bar 18, which formed a nominal new high and an expanding triangle top (bars 8, 11, 12, 15, and 18). It was also the top of the bull channel that followed the spike up (the spike just before the bar 17 pullback).

Bar 19 fell below the bull trend line and therefore was a breakout below that trend line. Bar 19 reversed up in an attempt to have the breakout fail. This failed breakout then failed to resume the bull trend, and the rally to bar 20 then became a breakout pullback and a lower high after a break below the bull trend line. Remember, any failed breakout that fails in its attempt to resume the trend becomes a breakout pullback in the new trend.

The bar 20 lower high allowed for the creation of a bear trend line and trend channel line.

Bar 21 fell below a trend channel line and formed a wedge bottom where bar 19 was the first push down. It was also the bottom of a small wedge bear channel following the small two-legged spike down from bar 20. It formed a double bottom with bar 15 and a test of the bottom of the trading range that was formed by the bar 2 and bar 15 lows.

The rally up to bar 22 broke above the last small high of the bear trend, and it broke above a small double top and above the bear trend line. The test of the bar 22 high failed at bar 23 (it did not go above bar 22), so another down leg was likely.

Bar 24 reversed up after falling below a trend channel line and breaking out of the large trading range. This could have set up a lower trading range, and the chart could have become similar to a trending trading range day on a 5 minute chart. It was almost an exact measured move down from the bar 20 high to the bar 21 low. Since this bear spike was down so strongly with large bear trend bars, it was a sell climax and it might have needed to correct for two legs sideways to up. The two-legged correction ended at bar 26. A sell climax does not have to lead to a reversal. It just means that the market went too far too fast and needs to pause as traders decide what to do next.

The rally to bar 25 broke a steep bear trend line and tested the bottom of the upper trading range.

Bar 26 failed to go above the bar 25 first leg up, and this lower high or double top bear flag was likely to lead to a leg down and form either a new low (which it did) or a two-legged pullback bull flag.

Bar 27 was a two-legged lower low following the bar 25 break above the bear trend line. The second leg down began at bar 26. This could have been a setup for a trend reversal or for at least a protracted correction. The breakout down to bar 24 might have been setting up a lower trading range of approximately the same height as the upper trading range between the bar 15 low and the bar 18 high.

Bar 28 was a pullback from the two legs up, but it formed a second higher low, so at least two more legs up were likely. The move from bar 27 to bar 28 covered too few bars and too few points to convince enough traders that the correction was over. It also formed a double bottom bull flag with the slightly lower swing low that formed after the bar 27 low.

Bar 29 was the third push in a small wedge, but the spike up from bar 28 was strong enough to make traders wait before shorting aggressively.

Bar 30 was a breakout pullback to a higher high after that small wedge, and it also was the top of a larger wedge where the first push up was the high before the bar 28 low. It was also the second failed attempt to break back into the upper trading range of the past several months, and whenever the market tries to do something twice and fails both times, it usually tries the opposite. Here, the sell-off led to a breakout below the lower trading range's low at bar 27.

Bar 31 formed a double top bear flag following the break of the bull trend line. Since this was a lower high in a possible resumption of a bear trend, it was a strong short setup.

Bar 32 tested the wedge bear trend channel line, and it was an attempt to form a double bottom bull flag with bar 28 or the higher low just before it. The market was likely to either reverse up or collapse. Traders saw bar 32 as a breakout pullback in the attempt to break below bar 28. They shorted on a stop at one tick below bar 32 and below the swing low of one bar earlier, which was the low of the wedge.

Bar 33 was a reversal up from a bear trend channel line overshoot, and it led to a small rally above the trend line. It was also a large expanding triangle bottom (bars 24, 25, 27, 30, and 33).

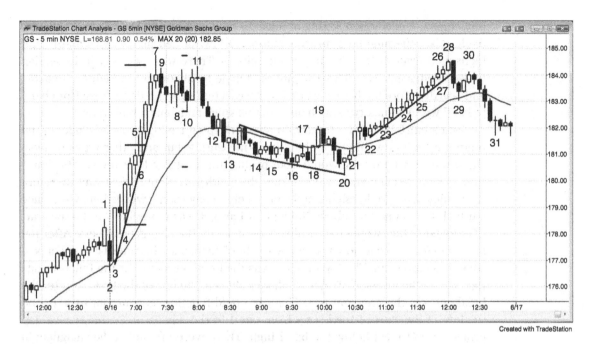

FIGURE PI.4   Consecutive Buy Climaxes and Deep Corrections

A pullback in a bull trend is a smaller bear trend, as was the correction down to bar 16. The rally to bar 19 broke above the bear trend line and alerted traders to a possible major trend reversal up after a test of the bar 16 low. Bar 20 was the signal bar. The term "major" gives the false impression that something exceptional must be happening, but that is usually not the case. It is a relative term that simply means that a trend is trying to reverse. When each leg has 20 or more bars, as was the case here, traders don't usually use the term "major trend reversal" and instead use some other description. Traders use terms to describe what is happening on the chart in front of them. If they instead were trading the 15 minute chart, bar 28 would be a double top major trend down, since it tested the bar 7 bull high after the bar 20 break below the bull trend line.

Consecutive buy climaxes usually are followed by a protracted correction that has at least two legs. As shown in Figure PI.4, bar 7 in Goldman Sachs (GS) was about 10 percent above yesterday's low, capping off a huge two-day bull trend. The spike up from bar 3 to bar 7 was very strong and therefore likely to be tested after any pullback. The bar 3 bull spike bar was a buy climax, as was the three-bar spike up from bar 4. The bull bodies became progressively smaller in the spike, and this was a sign of a loss of momentum.

Instead of correcting, however, the market broke out at bar 6 into an accelerated trend, which ended in a four-bar spike up to bar 7. After a third consecutive buy climax, a correction lasting at least 10 bars and having at least two legs was likely. Also, the nine bars up from the bar 2 low all had higher lows and higher highs, and eight of the nine had higher closes. There was also very little overlap between adjacent bars. This was unsustainable behavior and therefore climactic, and was therefore likely to correct. Bar 3 was a bull spike, and the move from bar 4 to bar 7 was a climax type of channel in this spike and climax bull trend.

Since bar 6 broke the trend into an accelerated trend, it was a breakout and therefore traders would be looking for a measuring gap and other types of measured moves where they would take profits and possibly look for shorts. Bar 6 broke above bar 5, which was the third bar with shrinking bodies, and therefore the bodies had a wedge shape and were likely to have some wedge behavior. Once bar 6 closed many ticks above the high of bar 5, it was more likely to be the start of a breakout that would have follow-through over the next several bars. After the next bar closed and its low was above the bar 5 high, bar 6 became a gap and a possible measuring gap. The top of bar 5 was the breakout point for the failed wedge top, and, in the absence of an immediate pullback, the low of the first bar after the breakout was the breakout test. This gap could function as a measuring gap, and the low of the start of the leg up from bar 4 to the middle of the measuring gap projected up to just below the bar 7 high. There were probably other magnets in this area, with different firms relying on different magnets as signs to take profits or to go short, and the cumulative effect was to begin the correction.

The market broke the steep trend line when it fell to bar 8. Since the correction should last at least 10 bars, it was a mistake to buy either the high 1 at bar 8 or the high 2 at bar 10. Both failed, and the market formed a lower high in the form of a double top bear flag at bar 11. Once the market broke out below bar 10, the double top projected down to around the bar 13 low. The move down to bar 13 was so steep that lower prices were likely.

Bar 16 was arguably an acceptable end of a two-legged correction where the first leg down ended at bar 10. It was also below the target of the moving average and it lasted more than 10 bars. This should have been enough to make many traders start to buy for a test of the bar 7 bull trend high. It was the end of a wedge bull flag where either bar 13 or bar 14 was the first of the three pushes down. Some traders saw bar 13 as the first leg and other traders believed that bar 14 was the first leg.

The bar 17 breakout of the wedge bull flag was weak and could have been a sign that the correction was not over. Bar 18 was an acceptable breakout pullback long setup, but the breakout of the wedge pulled back again to a lower low at bar 20. This was a lower low after a trend line break (the move to bar 19 broke above the bear trend line) and a possible end of a pullback in a larger bull trend. The signal bar had a bull body with a close on its high. The risk/reward ratio was excellent for a long because the bar was only 64 cents high and traders were buying for a test of the high of the day, which was almost $4.00 higher. Because they were buying at the bottom of a trading range, the probability of success was at least 60 percent, meaning that they had a 60 percent chance of making $4.00 while risking only 66 cents. This is 2 cents more than the height of the signal bar since they would buy on a stop at one tick above the bar and their protective stop would be one tick below its low. After the strong bull spike formed at bar 21, the bulls would have moved their stop to one tick below its low, which was just about breakeven. Although you don't have to check other time frames, the first big pullback in a strong trend usually tests the 15 minute moving average. This one was an almost exact test, but that information was not needed to place the trade. As great a price action buy setup as this was, notice how the entry bar was a small bull trend bar. The market had not yet realized how good this was. It is natural to become nervous when you take what you think is a great trade in a major stock, but no one else sees it as great yet. Sometimes this happens and the market can have several small bars, usually with bull bodies, before the bull reversal is perceived as having taken place. That realization occurred during the big bull trend bar, bar 21. It had great momentum and a shaved top and bottom, meaning that the bulls were extremely aggressive and higher prices should follow. The bar 21 bull spike was followed by a strong, tight bull channel up to bar 28, where traders took some profits on the move above the bar 7 high.

A pullback in a bull trend is a smaller bear trend, as was the correction down to bar 16. The rally to bar 19 broke above the bear trend line and alerted traders to a possible major trend reversal up after a test of the bar 16 low. Bar 20 was the signal bar. It does not matter whether you call this a lower low or a double bottom (with bar 16). All that matters is that you see it as a test of a bear low after a break above the bear trend line. That makes it a major trend reversal. The term "major" gives the false impression that something exceptional must be happening, but that is usually not the case. It is a relative term that simply means that a trend is trying to reverse. If the trend is not particularly big, the reversal might not be impressive either. Here, the trend was a bear trend, which was a pullback in a bull trend, and the bull trend that followed was simply a test of the bar 7 bull trend high. Since the pullback down to bar 16 fell well below the bull trend line, the rally to bar 28 was a test of the bull trend high and a setup for a major trend reversal down. When each leg has 20 or more bars, as was the case here, traders don't usually use the term "major trend reversal" and instead use some other description. The rally up to bar 28 had enough bars for traders to see it as a new trend, and the bar 30 lower high was a major trend reversal down after the drop to bar 29 fell below the bull trend line. Traders use terms to describe what is happening on the chart in front of them. If they instead were trading the 15 chart, bar 28 would be a double top major trend down, since it tested the bar 7 bull high after the bar 20 break below the bull trend line, and each leg would be about 10 bars or less on the 15 minute chart, which is not enough for traders to see the legs as new trends.

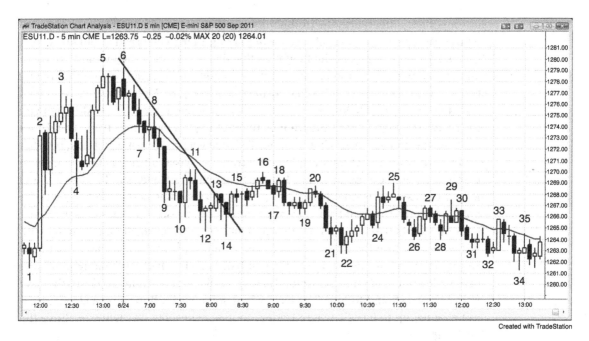

FIGURE PI.5 Uncertainty as a Major Trend Reversal Sets Up

Since markets have inertia and tend to continue what they have been doing, most attempts at reversing a trend fail. Most reasonable major trend reversal setups have only a 40 to 50 percent chance of success, except when the setup is especially strong, where the probability of success can be 60 percent or higher. Since there was not much buying pressure today (see Figure PI.5), the selling pressure was strong all the way down to the bar 22 two-bar reversal, and the rally to bar 16 was not even enough to flip the always-in position to long, the probability that the bar 22 lower low would lead to a successful reversal was about 40 percent. Simply breaking above a bull trend line and then forming a lower low is not enough to have a high probability of success. The bulls tried to form a double bottom higher low at bar 28, but the setup was weak. Bar 28 had a bear close and, although the next bar formed a two-bar reversal, it would have forced bulls to buy at the top of a trading range, which is a low-probability bet (the trading range was both the small one from bar 26 and the large one from bar 10).

Another problem for the bulls was that the bears had a strong case. Bar 2 was a huge bull trend bar with huge volume (98,000 Emini contracts), yet the market could not even get the high of the bar 6 third push up to extend above the bar 5 second push up. The attempt to resume the bull trend on the open failed at yesterday's high, and the market reversed down. Once the market broke to the downside at bar 9, traders were looking for either a bear trending trading range day or a spike and channel bear trend day. In either case, bar 9 was likely to become a measuring gap and lead to a measured move down. The move down to bar 10 had many strong bear trend bars and only three bars with bull bodies, and all three were only one tick tall. Although there were many tails and overlapping bars during the sell-off, the entire move down to bar 10 or bar 14 was strong enough for many traders to see it as a bear spike. This made them think that three pushes down and a spike and channel bear trend day were possible. They sold below the bar 16 gap bar for the second push down. Traders bought as the market fell below bar 14, which is a sign that the bears were not urgently looking to short. Instead of selling at the new low, the bears bought to take profits. The bulls also bought, thinking that bar 22 could be the start of a lower low major trend reversal, since the move to bar 16 broke the bear trend line. The bull bodies and the move above the moving average were also signs of strength.

During the rally to bar 25, the bulls had a good argument for the major trend reversal, and wanted a higher low to follow their bar 22 lower low. The bear argument for a spike and channel bear trend day and a third push down was still intact. Both the bull and bear cases were valid, which usually means that the market is in a trading range, which it was. The bulls were hoping that the trading range would become a base and be followed by an upside breakout, and the bears saw the trading range as a broad bear channel following the spike on the open down to bar 14. The bears shorted again below bar 25, since the rally was still below the bar 16 pullback from the first push down, and it was a double top with bar 20. Bar 25 went one tick above bar 20 and ran some stops, but most bears who were swinging their shorts based on the spike and channel theory would have had their stops above the bar 16 pullback from the first push down. They shorted again below the bar 29 low 2. Bar 29 was also a signal bar for a bear breakout of the triangle where the bar before bar 24 was the first push down and bars 26 and 28 were the next two pushes down.

The bulls saw bar 28 as a double bottom higher low with bar 26, but were concerned that it had a bear body. Although the next bar was a bull trend bar and a two-bar reversal buy setup, it is rarely good to buy at the top of a trading range (bar 27 was the top of the small trading range). Most bulls would have exited below the strong bear reversal bar at bar 29. It was a low 2 sell signal and a failed breakout of the triangle. The bar after bar 31 was a bull doji and followed three bear bars, and therefore was not a good enough reason for the bulls to buy again. The bull inside bar that followed bar 32 was a final flag reversal setup from the two-bar final flag that followed bar 31, but the micro channel down from bar 29 was so tight that the probability of success was not high. Although bar 33 was a strong bull breakout from that micro channel, there was no follow-through, and the bulls sold out of their longs either below the bar 33 bear inside bar or one tick below the doji bar that followed. Bulls will sometimes allow one bar to go against them, but most would not allow two when the original buy signal was weak and the bar 33 bull breakout did not have any follow-through.

Both the bulls and the bears had swing setups with positive trader's equations. The bulls who bought above the bar 22 lower low had about a 40 percent chance of success, with a risk of about two points and a reward of six to 10 points (a measured move up from the breakout above the trading range). The bears who shorted either the bear spike down to bar 14 or below bars 16, 20, or 25 had about a 50 to 60 percent chance of a third push down, with a risk of about a couple of points and a reward of four to six points, and possibly more if there was a bear breakout and measured move down, instead of simply another bear stair.

Because the spike down to bar 14 was weak, many traders anticipated a trading range or a weak bear channel. Instead of swinging up or down, they instead just scalped for two to four points all day long, as many traders do when they expect predominantly two-sided trading.

Most traders will not take any reversal trade, no matter how minor, unless there is at least a double top or bottom, a micro double top or bottom, or a final flag. For example, bars 6, 8, 18, 20, 25, and 29 were double tops or micro double tops, bars 4, 10, 12, 14, 17, 19, 22, 28, and 32 were double bottoms or micro double bottoms, and bars 3, 6, 10, 12, 14, 16, 18, 19, 22, 25, and 32 were final flag reversals (some from one bar final flags).

CHAPTER 1

Example of How to Trade a Reversal

When traders enter a reversal trade, they are expecting the pullback from the trend to be large enough for a swing trade, or even a trend in the opposite direction. The entry, protective stops, and profit taking are then the same as for any other swing or trend trade, and were discussed in the first two books. Since traders are expecting a large move, the probability of success is often 50 percent or less. In general, when risk is held constant, a larger potential reward usually means a smaller probability of success. This is because the edge in trading is always small, and if there was a high probability of success, traders would neutralize it quickly and it would disappear within a few bars, resulting in only a small profit. However, since a trend reversal trade may have a reward that is several times larger than the risk, it can have a profitable trader's equation.

Trading a reversal is much more difficult than it appears when a trader looks at a chart at the end of the day. Once there has been a strong break of the trend line and then a reversal on the test of the trend's extreme, a trader needs a strong signal bar. However, it usually comes in a very emotional market at a time when beginning traders are still thinking that the old trend is in effect. They also probably lost on several earlier countertrend trades in the day and don't want to lose any more money. Their denial causes them to miss the early entry. They then wait to evaluate the strength of the follow-through. It is usually in the form of a large, fast spike made of several strong trend bars, forcing the traders to quickly decide whether to risk much more than they usually do. They often end up choosing to wait for a pullback. Even if they reduce their position size so that the dollar risk is the same as with any other trade, the thought of risking two or three times as many ticks frightens them. Entering on a pullback is difficult because every pullback begins with a minor reversal, and they are afraid that the pullback might be the resumption of the prior trend. They end up waiting until the day is almost over, and then finally decide that the new trend is clear; but now there is no more time left to place a trade. Trends do everything that they can to keep traders out, which is the only way they can keep traders chasing the market all day. When a setup is easy and clear, the move is usually a small, fast scalp. If the move is going to go a long way, it has to be unclear and difficult to take, to keep traders on the sidelines and force them to chase the trend.

Figure 1.1   EXAMPLE OF HOW TO TRADE A REVERSAL   **75**

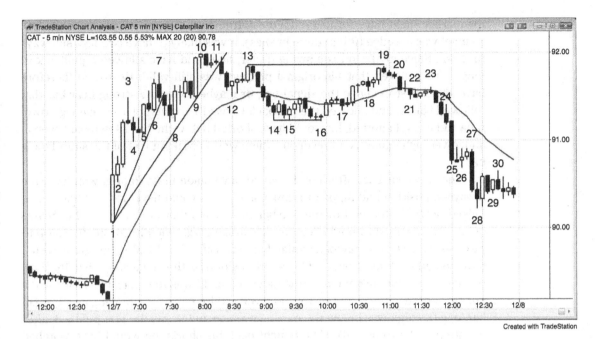

FIGURE 1.1 Trading a Major Reversal

As shown in Figure 1.1, traders had several ways to trade the reversal in Caterpillar Inc. (CAT) today, and one that I think is worthwhile is an approach used by a friend. I had a lengthy discussion with this trader several years ago. He specializes in trading major reversals. He would usually take just one or two trades a day, and he always wanted to see a strong break beyond the trend line before looking for a reversal entry. For example, in a bull trend like this one, he would not have shorted below bar 3 because there was no prior break of a bull trend line. He would also not have shorted below the bar 7 reversal bar, because there was no prior significant break below a bull trend line. The sell-off below bar 3 lasted only one bar and did not even reach the moving average.

The three bear bars starting at bar 7 broke below the bull trend line, which was a sign of selling pressure, but the sell-off was not strong enough to reach the moving average. He would then have studied the rally that would test the bar 7 trend high. It was two-legged, which meant that there was some two-sided trading and therefore the bears showed some strength, and it was the third push up on the day. Since major reversals often occur in the first hour or so, he probably would have shorted below bar 11, which was a second entry short, but he probably would not have been expecting a major reversal. Since the day was a spike and channel bull at that point, the sell-off might have just tested the bar 4 start of the bull channel, where the market might have formed a double bottom and then rallied. Because the bull channel was a wedge (it had three pushes), it was likely to have two legs sideways to down. Since my friend is a swing trader, he would have allowed a pullback as long as he believed that his original premise was still valid. He would therefore have kept his stop above the signal bar, or maybe above the strong bear bar that followed bar 11, and allowed the pullback to bar 13, expecting a second leg down. If he had not yet shorted, he would have shorted below the bar 13 two-bar reversal and lower high major trend reversal, which was a breakout test of the short below bar 11.

The two bear bars after bar 11 would have made most traders wonder if the always-in position had flipped to down, and most would have decided that it was indeed down by the end of the five-bar bear spike that ended at bar 14. At this point, if he decided to hold short, he would have tightened his protective stop to just above the start of that bear spike that began after bar 13. More likely, he would have bought back most or all of his short position on the move above bar 16, since two legs down had taken place (the move to bar 12 was the first), bar 16 formed a double bottom with bars 14 or 15, and it was a third entry for a moving average gap bar long (its high was below the moving average and it was the first pullback after the strong rally to bar 10). If he bought back his shorts, he would have watched the rally from bar 16 to assess its strength relative to the sell-off to bar 16. If it was relatively weak, he would have looked to short again on a test of the bar 10 bull trend high. The test could have been in the form of a lower high, a double top, or a higher high.

The rally from bar 16 to bar 19 had three legs, and was therefore a wedge bear flag. Since it was a rally after a strong break below the bull trend line, it was likely to become part of a larger correction with at least one more leg down. The probability was that the market would form either a trading range or a trend reversal. The rally did not contain two consecutive strong bull trend bars, so the bulls were unable to regain control of the market. Bar 19 formed a double top with bar 13, and since this was now a possible bear trend, that was a double top bear flag, as well as a double top or lower high major trend reversal, when compared to the bar 10 top of the bull trend. Bar 19 was also a bear reversal bar, which is important when looking for a market top. This was the strongest trend reversal setup of the day, because the bear spike down to bar 14 convinced most traders that the always-in position was short and that the bears owned the market as long as the rally could not get above the top of the bear spike that began after bar 13. Many traders believed that as long as the market could not get above bar 13, the bears were still in control and the market might be forming a lower high in a possible new bear trend. Bears had their protective stops just above bar 13, because they wanted either a double top or a lower high, and if they got neither, they would exit and wait for another sell signal. Many bulls who bought between bars 10 and 13 held their longs through the

Figure 1.1   EXAMPLE OF HOW TO TRADE A REVERSAL   **77**

sell-off to bar 16, to see how strong the bears were. They decided that the selling was strong (it broke the trend line and the moving average, and it lasted for many bars) and that the rally to bar 19 was not strong enough for them to expect the bull trend to make a new high without at least more of a correction.

These were the most determined bulls (since they were willing to hold through the protracted sell-off to bar 16), and once they gave up, there was no one left to buy at these prices. The market had to probe lower to find a level where the bulls would return and where the bears would buy back their shorts. There were no consecutive strong bull trend bars or other signs of strong buying in the move up from bar 16, and this made the bears more aggressive and the bulls less willing to buy. Since the bulls were confident that the market would soon be lower, they used the rally to bar 19 to exit their longs around breakeven or with a small loss. The selling by these disappointed bulls, combined with the selling of the aggressive bears who were shorting heavily in an attempt to keep the market from going above bar 13, resulted in the market turning down at bar 19. The bulls were willing to buy again lower, but needed a sign that the market was about to reverse up. The sideways move to bar 23 after seven bars down was not a strong bottom, so most bulls were unwilling to buy unless the price got marked down further. The bears were willing to take profits at any time, but they would buy back their shorts only if there was a sign of a reasonable bottom. With no sign of a bottom, neither the bulls nor the bears were willing to buy. Also, the remaining longs continued to sell out of their positions, adding to the selling pressure. Bears continued to sell when they saw the increasing selling pressure in the move down from bar 23. The result was a strong trend reversal in the form of the bar 19 lower high after the bar 16 break below the bull trend line. As is the case in all strong trends, traders pressed their shorts, adding to their positions as the market quickly fell in the spike down to the bar 25 low and down to the bar 28 low, where they began to take profits. All trend bars are spikes, climaxes, breakouts, and gaps. Bar 25 was a large bear breakout bar and was likely going to be followed by a measured move down, based on the height of the trading range. It was possible that bar 25 itself became a measuring gap, with the middle of the gap being the midpoint between the bar 16 low (the top of the gap) and the 27 high (the bottom of the gap). This could lead to a measured move down today or tomorrow.

The rally to bar 19 was a double top bear flag, a wedge bull flag, and two legs up in a bear trend (the two-legged swing high between bars 15 and 16 was the first), and it had an excellent trader's equation. The risk was to above the bar 19 high, or about 10 cents, and the reward at a minimum was 50 cents lower on a test of the bar 16 low, where the market might have formed a double bottom and possibly a large triangle or bull flag. Since the market was in a bear trend or at least at the top of a trading range, the chance of success was at least 60 percent. A 60 percent chance of success combined with a 10 cent risk and a 50 cent reward makes for a great trade. A trader who took it 10 times would make $3.00 and lose 40 cents, an average of 26 cents per trade.

Traders believed that if the market fell below bar 16, it would probably fall for a measured move down from the double top, which it did. The bar 16 area was the breakout test of the breakout gap, which was the bull spike from bar 1 to bar 3. After the market rallied from this test, bulls did not want it to fall below the test, because they would have seen that as a sign of weakness. Just like the bears did not want the rally to bar 19 to go above the bar 13 lower high, which could have been followed by a measured move up, the bulls did not want the sell-off from bar 19 to fall below the bar 16 higher low, which could have been followed by a measured move down. Since my friend would have seen this move down from bar 19 as a trend trade, he would have traded it like a trend (book 1 discusses how to trade a trend). The initial risk was only 10 cents and the odds were good that the market would have tested the bar 16 low at a minimum, so he would have taken about half off on the test if there was a pause bar. Since there was no pause, there was no significant profit taking, and he probably would not have taken any profits until around bar 28. This was a pause after a sell climax bar that followed a potential final flag (the three bars ending at bar 27). He would have taken maybe half off there with a $1.20 profit and held the remainder until a minute or two before the close, for another $1.30 profit.

Incidentally, remember that both strong bulls and strong bears like to see a large bull trend bar in an overdone bull trend, because it often leads to a two-legged pullback to below the moving average, as it did here at bar 9. The expected correction provided both of them with a temporary trading opportunity, although not a trend reversal trade. Bar 9 was the third consecutive buy climax without much of a pullback (bars 1 to 3 was the first, and bars 5 to 6 was the second). It was more likely to become an exhaustion gap than a measuring gap (it was more likely to be the start of a correction instead of a new leg up). In this scenario, both the strong bulls and the strong bears sold at the close of the bar, above its high, at the close of the next bar or two (especially since the bar after bar 10 had a bear body), and below the low of the prior bar. The bulls were selling out of their longs as they took profits, and the bears were selling to put on shorts. Most bears would have picked a protective stop that was less than the number of ticks in the bar 9 buy climax bull trend bar. The bulls wouldn't look to buy again and the bears would not have taken profits on their shorts until after the two-legged correction was complete, which was in the bar 14 to bar 16 area (the move to bar 12 was the first leg down). The sell-off was strong enough for both to think that the market could have a trend reversal into a bear trend after a lower high or higher high test of the bar 10 bull high.

CHAPTER 2

Signs of Strength in a Reversal

Strong reversals have essentially the same characteristics of any strong move, like a strong breakout or a strong trend. Here are a number of characteristics that are common in strong bull reversals:

- There is a strong bull reversal bar with a large bull trend body and small tails or no tails.
- The next two or three bars also have bull bodies that are at least the average size of the recent bull and bear bodies.
- The spike grows to five to 10 bars without pulling back for more than a bar or so, and it reverses many bars, swing highs, and bear flags of the prior bear trend.
- One or more bars in the spike have a low that is at or just one tick below the close of the prior bar.
- One or more bars in the spike have an open that is above the close of the prior bar.
- One or more bars in the spike have a close on the high of the bar or just one tick below its high.
- The overall context makes a reversal likely, like a higher low or lower low test of the bear low after a strong break above the bear trend line.
- The first or second bar of the breakout has a close that is above the highs of many prior bars.
- The first pullback occurs only after three or more bars.
- The first pullback lasts only one or two bars, and it follows a bar that is not a strong bear reversal bar.
- The first pullback does not hit a breakeven stop (the entry price).

- The spike goes very far and breaks several resistance levels like the moving average, prior swing highs, and trend lines, and each by many ticks.
- As the first bar of the reversal is forming, it spends most of its time near its high and the pullbacks are less than a quarter of the height of the growing bar.
- There is a sense of urgency. You feel like you have to buy but you want a pullback, yet it never comes.
- The signal is the second attempt to reverse within the past few bars (a second signal).
- The reversal began as a reversal from an overshoot of a trend channel line from the old trend.
- It is reversing a significant swing high or low (e.g., it breaks below a strong prior swing low and reverses up).
- The high 1 and high 2 pullbacks have strong bull reversal bars for signal bars.
- It has trending "anything": closes, highs, lows, or bodies.
- The pullbacks are small and sideways.
- There were prior breaks of earlier bear trend lines (this isn't the first sign of bullish strength).
- The pullback to test the bear low lacks momentum, as evidenced by its having many overlapping bars with many being bull trend bars.
- The pullback that tests the bear low fails at the moving average or the old bear trend line.
- The breakout reverses many recent closes and highs. For example, when there is a bear channel and a large bull bar forms, this breakout bar has a high and close that are above the highs and closes of five or even 20 or more bars. A large number of bars reversed by the close of the bull bar is a stronger sign than a similar number of bars reversed by only its high.

Here are a number of characteristics that are common in strong bear reversals:

- There is a strong bear reversal bar with a large bear trend body and small tails or no tails.
- The next two or three bars also have bear bodies that are at least the average size of the recent bull and bear bodies.
- The spike grows to five to 10 bars without pulling back for more than a bar or so, and it reverses many bars, swing lows, and bull flags of the prior bull trend.
- One or more bars in the spike has a high that is at or just one tick above the close of the prior bar.
- One or more bars in the spike has an open that is below the close of the prior bar.
- One or more bars in the spike has a close on its low or just one tick above its low.

- The overall context makes a reversal likely, like a lower high or higher high test of the bull high after a strong break below the bull trend line.
- The first or second bar of the breakout has a close that is below the lows of many prior bars.
- The first pullback occurs only after three or more bars.
- The first pullback lasts only one or two bars and it follows a bar that is not a strong bull reversal bar.
- The first pullback does not hit a breakeven stop (the entry price).
- The spike goes very far and breaks several support levels like the moving average, prior swing lows, and trend lines, and each by many ticks.
- As the first bar of the reversal is forming, it spends most of its time near its low and the pullbacks are less than a quarter of the height of the growing bar.
- There is a sense of urgency. You feel like you have to sell, but you want a pullback, yet it never comes.
- The signal is the second attempt to reverse within the past few bars (a second signal).
- The reversal began as a reversal from an overshoot of a trend channel line from the old trend.
- It is reversing at a significant swing high or low area (e.g., breaks above a strong prior swing high and reverses down).
- The low 1 and low 2 pullbacks have strong bear reversal bars for signal bars.
- It has trending "anything": closes, highs, lows, or bodies.
- The pullbacks are small and sideways.
- There were prior breaks of earlier bull trend lines (this isn't the first sign of bearish strength).
- The pullback to test the bull high lacks momentum, as evidenced by it having many overlapping bars with many being bear trend bars.
- The pullback that tests the bull high fails at the moving average or the old bull trend line.
- The breakout reverses many recent closes and lows. For example, when there is a bull channel and a large bear bar forms, this breakout bar has a low and close that are below the lows and closes of five or even 20 or more bars. A large number of bars reversed by the close of the bear bar is a stronger sign than a similar number of bars reversed by its low.

Some reversals result in trend reversals and others simply in small countertrend swings. Carefully analyzing the price action before and after the reversal helps traders gauge how much if any of their position they should swing and how big a move to anticipate. When there is a strong trend, traders should not be taking countertrend trades until there has been a trend line break or at least a climactic reversal from a trend channel line overshoot. In a trading range market, however, traders can trade reversals in both directions.

There are many characteristics of strong reversals, and the more that are present, the more likely a countertrend trade will be profitable and the more aggressive traders should be in their decision about how much of their position they should swing. The stronger the prior trend line break in a trend reversal, the more likely the reversal will gain more points and last longer and have two or more legs. The strongest trend line breaks have strong momentum and surge well past the moving average and usually beyond swing points in the prior trend.

The stronger the trend, the more likely it will need a strong reversal for a trader to make a profit from a countertrend trade. The characteristics of strong trends were discussed in Chapter 19 of the first book and they are listed at the beginning of this book. For example, if traders are looking to short a very strong bull trend, they will want to see as many signs of a strong reversal as possible. In contrast, if the bull trend has been very two-sided, they will be comfortable shorting a weaker reversal setup. If instead the market is simply rallying to the top of a trading range, they may not even need a reversal bar when they are shorting. Finally, if the market is in a wedge bull flag and they are looking for it to reverse back up into the bull trend, they might even be willing to buy above a bear trend bar.

Incidentally, if the market is a zero-sum game, how can it have 95 percent of the participants be profitable institutions? This is because it is not really a zero-sum game. Our economy grows and therefore creates wealth. The total value of the market is greater than it was 10 years ago, and far greater than 100 years ago. The firms all compete to get as much of that new wealth as possible, and there is enough to make almost all firms profitable in most years. In years when the economy contracts, most firms lose money, but during expansions, they make more than what they lose during the down years.

CHAPTER 3

Major Trend Reversal

Here are many institutions that invest for the long term and view every strong break below the bull trend line as a buying opportunity, because they know that the bears will constantly try to reverse the trend but will fail 80 percent of the time. They will buy even if the bear spike is huge and strong, and goes far below the trend line and the moving average. They hope that their buying will provide the leadership that other traders need to see before they will also buy. At a minimum, they expect the rally to test the breakout point below the market top. Once there, they will decide if the trend has reversed. If so, they will stop buying and instead will exit their new longs as well as all of the other longs that they bought all the way up. Most of their position was profitable because they bought it long ago, far below their last entry. However, since they are buying as the trend continues up, they bought some of their position at the top of the bull and will take a loss when they exit. Once these long-term investing institutions believe that the market is going lower, the trend will reverse, because they were the traders who previously bought every sharp sell-off, and now there is no one left to buy strong bear spikes. They will wait until they believe that the bear trend has reached a long-term value area, which will always be at a long-term support area, like a monthly trend line. Once there, they will buy aggressively again, and they will buy every further attempt by the bears to extend the bear trend. At some point, other institutions will see the support forming and they will also buy. There will soon be a strong bull spike, a pullback that tests the bear low, and then a reversal into a new bull trend.

Every reversal pattern is some kind of trading range, and therefore has two-sided trading until it is clear that the countertrend traders have gained control. The term *major trend reversal* means different things to different traders, and no one can say with certainty that the trend has reversed until the move has gone on for at least enough bars for the always-in position to change direction in the eyes of most traders. However, that alone is not enough for a reversal to be labeled "major." The always-in position changes with every tradable swing on the 5 minute chart for many traders, which means that it changes many times a day on most days, even though the dominant trend usually remains the same. A major trend reversal means that there are two trends on the chart in front of you, with a reversal in between them where either a bull trend has reversed into a bear trend or a bear trend has reversed into a bull trend. This type of reversal is different from the many up and down reversals on the chart that usually move far enough for a trade, but not far enough to change the direction of the major trend. Also, those minor reversals happen whether or not there is an obvious trend on the screen.

The earliest signals for most major trend reversals have a low probability of success, but offer the largest reward, often many times greater than the risk. The market is often mostly sideways at the outset, with many pullbacks, but if the trend is actually reversing, the new trend will soon be obvious. Many traders prefer to wait to enter until the trend is clear. These traders prefer to only take trades with at least a 60 percent chance of success and are willing to make less (they are entering after the move has already begun) on the trade for the increased chance of success. Since both approaches have positive trader's equations when done properly, both are reasonable.

Four things are needed for a major trend reversal:

1. A trend on the chart in front of you.
2. A countertrend move (a reversal) that is strong enough to break the trend line and usually the moving average.
3. A test of the trend's extreme, and then a second reversal (a higher high, a double top, or a lower high at the top of a bull trend, or a lower low, a double bottom, or a higher low at the bottom of a bear trend).
4. The second reversal going far enough for there to be a consensus that the trend has reversed.

First, there has to be a trend on the screen in front of you, and then a countertrend move that is strong enough to break the major trend's trend line, and preferably convincingly beyond the moving average. Next, the trend has to resume and test the old trend's extreme, and then the market has to reverse again. For example, after there is a strong move down below the bull trend line in a bull trend, traders will watch the next rally. If the market turns down again in the area of the old high (from a lower high, double top, or higher high), the test was successful and traders will begin to suspect that the trend is reversing. Finally, the move down has to be strong enough for traders to believe that the market is in a bear trend. If the move down is in the form of a strong bear spike composed of many consecutive large bear trend bars, everyone will see the market as now being in a bear trend. However, the market will instead often be in a broad bear channel for 50 or more bars, without enough clarity to convince traders that the trend has truly reversed to down. They may wonder if it instead has evolved into a large trading range, which will often be the case. In the absence of a very strong bear spike, there will not be strong agreement that the trend has reversed until after dozens of bars and a series of lower highs and lows. At this point, the market can be far below the old bull high and there might not be much more left to the bear trend.

It does not matter that agreement about the reversal often does not come until long after the market has actually reversed, because there will be trades all the way down. If the move down is unclear and two-sided, traders will trade it like any other two-sided market and take trades in both directions. If it is a very strong bear trend, traders will almost exclusively take shorts. If there are trades all the way down, then why should a trader ever think about a major trend reversal? Because the trader's equation is excellent if a trader enters early, just as the market is turning down from its test of the old high. The reward is often many times larger than the risk, and even if the probability is only 40 to 50 percent, the result is a very favorable trader's equation. Most lead to trading ranges, but still profitable trades.

Virtually all major trend reversals begin with either a trend line break or a trend channel line overshoot and reversal, and all of those eventually break the trend line when there is a reversal. For example, if a bull market is ending in a head and shoulders top, the move down from the head usually breaks below the bull trend line for the entire bull trend, and always below the smaller bull trend line along the bottom of the bars that rally up to form the head. The bulls buy when the sell-off from the head reaches the area of the pullback from the left shoulder, trying to create a double bottom bull flag. Many bears, who shorted as the rally to the head moved above the left shoulder, take profits in the same area, in case the market enters a trading range or forms a double bottom bull flag. The bears see the rally that creates the right shoulder as a lower high breakout pullback short setup, and short. The trend line break is what a bear needs to see before feeling confident about taking a countertrend position (a short in a bull trend), because it signifies a break of the trend and the start of a possible major trend reversal. Also, bulls who bought at the prior high (the head), expecting another leg up, and held on to their positions watch the strength of the sell-off from the head. Once they see that it was strong enough to fall below the trend line, they will use the rally to exit their longs with a small loss. The selling by both the bulls and the bears causes the market to drop and form the lower high (the right shoulder). Once the market sells off to the neckline (a roughly horizontal line drawn across the bottom of the pattern, along the lowest points of the sell-offs from the left shoulder, head, and finally right shoulder), both the bulls and the bears will assess the strength of the sell-off. If it is strong, the bears will no longer simply scalp out of their shorts, thinking that the market is still in a trading range. Instead, they will hold on to their shorts and even sell more, expecting a major trend reversal, especially on and after the breakout below the neckline. The bulls will see the strength of the selling and will not be willing to buy until the market stabilizes, which they expect will be at least several bars later, and possibly after a measured move down.

If, in contrast, the sell-off from the head to the neckline is weak, both the bulls and the bears will buy on the test of the neckline. The bulls will buy because they see the entire pattern as a trading range in a bull trend and therefore just a large bull flag. They are buying what they expect is the bottom of the bull flag, where there is an approximate triple bottom (the three reversals up from the neckline). Some bulls will scalp out as the market tests toward the middle or top of the trading range, and others will hold, looking for a bull breakout and a swing up. The bears will buy back their shorts and not look to sell again until they can get a better price. They hope that the bounce stays below the right shoulder, and if it does or if it forms a double top with the right shoulder, they will short again, hoping that the pattern becomes a head and shoulders top with two right shoulders, which is common. If the market breaks above the right shoulder, they will buy back their shorts and not look to sell again for many bars, concluding that the entire pattern evolved into a large bull flag and that the breakout will likely rally for at least a measured move up. The bulls will also buy the breakout above the right shoulder, knowing that the bears will cover their shorts and not look to sell again for many bars. They, like the bears, will expect an approximate measured move up, and will buy more as the new bull leg progresses.

The same is true of a double top or a higher high. Whenever the market returns to the area of a prior high after having a sharp sell-off, the bulls who bought at the old high become disappointed by that sell-off and use the rally to exit their longs. This means that they become sellers (they sell out of their longs), and they won't buy again until prices get marked down considerably. With no one left to buy at the current prices and both the bulls and bears selling, the market falls.

The same happens at a market bottom. Once there is a rally that is strong enough to break above the bear trend line (either the trend line for the entire bear trend or simply the one above the sell-off to the head), the bears who shorted at the bottom as the market broke below the left shoulder, expecting another leg down, will be disappointed by the rally and will expect at least another leg up after a test down. Traders will see the next leg down as a test of the strength of the bear trend. If the bear trend is strong, the market will eventually break below the old low (the head) by many bars and have another leg down. If the trend is reversing, aggressive bulls will buy around the old low, and the bears who shorted at the old low will be disappointed by the strong rally from the head and the weaker move down to test the bear low, and will use this dip to buy back their shorts around breakeven. With both the bulls and the bears buying, and the bears unwilling to sell again around this level, the market will rally. This test can form a perfect double bottom with the old bear low, a higher low, or a lower low. It does not matter, because they are all manifestations of the same process. If it forms a higher low, some traders will see it as a right shoulder of a head and shoulders bottom, and will look for a reasonable left shoulder. If they find one, they will be more confident that this is a trend reversal because they believe that many traders will recognize the pattern and begin to buy. However, whether there is a clear left shoulder is irrelevant to most traders. The important point is that there is the strong break above the bear trend line, followed by a test of the bear low, and then by a reversal up into a bull swing or trend.

Whether a top comes from a higher high, a perfect double top, or a lower high is irrelevant, because they all represent the same behavior. The market is testing the old high to see if there will be mostly buyers and a bull breakout, or mostly sellers and a bear reversal. There are two pushes up to the top: the first is the original bull high, and the second is the test of that high after the market has fallen below the bull trend line. The market does not care how perfect the double top is; regardless of their appearance, all of the tests should be thought of as variations of double tops. The same is true of market bottoms. There is a market low and then a rally that is usually strong enough to break above the bear trend line. That low is the first bottom of the double bottom. After the market breaks above the bear trend line (and therefore out of the bear channel) and sells off again to test the first bottom, when the market reverses up, this low is the second bottom of the double bottom, whether it is above, exactly at, or below the first bottom.

The relationship between traditional double tops and bottoms and their micro versions on higher time frame charts is the same as it is for all micro patterns. For example, if a trader sees a double bottom on a 5 minute chart and then looks at a higher time frame chart, the two bottoms will be just two or three bars apart, creating a micro double bottom. Similarly, if a trader looks at a micro double bottom on the 5 minute chart where the two bottoms are just two or three bars apart, this bottom would be a perfect trend reversal on a small-enough time frame chart, where the rally after the first bottom broke above the bear trend line, and the second bottom is the test. In fact, most tradable reversals on every chart, even small scalps, begin with a micro double bottom or top, and most traders will not place the reversal trade unless one is present. A micro double top is a failed breakout in a bull trend, and therefore either a failed high 1, high 2, or triangle buy signal, and a failed double bottom is a failed low 1, low 2, or triangle sell signal. This means that these reversals are small final flag reversals (discussed in Chapter 7). In fact, a final flag is a variation of a double top or bottom. For example, it there is a two-legged rally on a trading range day and the market then forms an ii pattern, traders will be alert to a possible final flag breakout and reversal down. The spike that formed just before the ii pattern is the first push up, and the small bull breakout is the second. Since that is two pushes up, even though the highs are not at the same level, it is just a variation of a double top.

Traders anticipating a reversal down will short at and above the high of the signal bar for the breakout of what they anticipate will be the final bull flag. When it is a micro pattern, their limit orders to short will be at and just above the high of the signal bar. When it is a larger pattern, it will be a micro pattern on a higher time frame chart, and some traders will have their limit orders at and above that higher time frame signal bar. Other traders, and probably many institutions, will scale into shorts as the market moves out of what they believe will be the final bull flag. They do the opposite at market bottoms with a double bottom or micro double bottom that they expect will become the final flag of the bear leg and lead to a reversal up.

Remember, all trends are in channels, and until there is a *strong* breakout of the channel, the best bet is against any attempt to break out beyond the trend line. Until there is a strong break beyond the trend line, most traders will view any countertrend trade as only a scalp. In the absence of a trend line break, there is still a strong trend in effect and traders should make sure that they take every with-trend entry and do not worry about missing an occasional countertrend scalp. The best odds and the most money are with the with-trend trades. True V bottoms and tops in the absence of trend channel line overshoots and reversals are so rare that they are not worth considering. Traders should focus on common patterns, and if they miss an occasional rare event, there will always be a pullback where they can start trading with the new trend.

The trend line break does not reverse the trend. It is simply the first significant sign that countertrend traders are getting strong enough that you should soon begin to trade in their direction. However, you first should continue to trade with the trend because after the break of the trend line there will be a test of the old trend extreme. The test can slightly overshoot or undershoot the old extreme. You should take a countertrend trade only if a reversal setup develops during this test. If it does, the countertrend move should form at least two legs, and it might even result in a new, opposite trend.

A move above a prior high in a bull trend will generally lead to one of three outcomes: more buying, profit taking, or shorting. When the trend is strong, strong bulls will press their longs by buying the breakout above the old high and there will be a measured move up of some kind. If the market goes up far enough above the breakout to enable a trader to make at least a profitable scalp before there is a pullback, then assume that there was mostly new buying at the high. If it goes sideways, assume that there was profit taking and that the bulls are looking to buy again a little lower. If the market reverses down hard, assume that the strong bears dominated at the new high and that the market will likely trade down for at least a couple of legs and at least 10 bars.

Some traders like to enter on the earliest sign that a trend is reversing, such as when it is breaking out of the channel. However, this is a low-probability style of trading. Yes, the large reward can offset the risk and low probability of success, but most traders end up cherry-picking and invariably talking themselves out of the best cherries. As with all breakouts, it is usually better to wait to see how strong the breakout is. If it is strong, then look to enter on the pullback. This concept applies to reversals from all trends, even small trends, like pullbacks in larger trends, micro channels, channels after spikes, and trends that are in broad channels. If the countertrend breakout is weak, look to enter in the direction of the trend as the reversal attempt fails. If the breakout is very strong and goes for many bars without a pullback, then treat it like any strong breakout and enter the new trend at the market or on a small pullback, as was discussed in Part I of the second book.

In the absence of some rare, dramatic news event, traders don't suddenly switch from extremely bullish to extremely bearish. There is a gradual transition. A trader becomes less bullish, then neutral, and then bearish. Once enough traders make this transition, the market reverses into a deeper correction or into a bear trend. Every firm has its own measure of excess, and at some point, enough firms decide that the trend has gone too far. They believe that there is little risk of missing a great move up if they stop buying above the old high, and they will buy only on pullbacks. If the market hesitates above the old high, the market is becoming two-sided, and the strong bulls are using the new high to take profits.

Profit taking means that traders are still bullish and are looking to buy a pullback. Most new highs are followed by profit taking. Every new high is a potential top, but most reversal attempts fail and become the beginning of bull flags, only to be followed by another new high. If a rally to test the high has several small pullbacks within the leg up, with lots of overlapping bars, several bear bodies, and big tails on the tops of the bars, and most of the bull trend bars are weak, then the market is becoming increasingly two-sided. The bulls are taking profits at the tops of the bars and buying only at the bottoms of the bars, and the bears are beginning to short at the tops of the bars. Similarly, the bulls are taking profits as the market approaches the top of the bull trend and the bears are shorting more. If the market goes above the bull high, it is likely that the profit taking and shorting will be even stronger, and a trading range or reversal will form.

Most traders do not like to reverse, so if they are anticipating a reversal signal, they prefer to exit their longs and then wait for that signal. The loss of these bulls on the final leg up in the trend contributes to the weakness of the rally to the final high. If there is a strong reversal down after the market breaks above the prior high, the strong bears are taking control of the market, at least for the near term.

Once that happens, then the bulls who were hoping to buy a small pullback believe instead that the market will fall further. They therefore wait to buy until there is a much larger pullback, and their absence from buying allows the bears to drive the market down into a deeper correction, lasting 10 or more bars and often having two or more legs.

There is one situation where the breakout in a bull trend is routinely met by aggressive shorts who will usually take over the market. A pullback is a minor trend in the opposite direction, and traders expect it to end soon and for the larger trend to resume. When there is a pullback in a strong bear trend, the market will often have two legs up in the minor bull trend. As the market goes above the high of the first leg up, it is breaking out above a prior swing high in a minor bull trend. However, since most traders will see the move up as a pullback that will end very soon, the dominant traders on the breakout will usually be aggressive sellers, instead of aggressive new buyers, or profit-taking longs, and the minor bull trend will usually reverse back down into the direction of the major bear trend after breaking out above the first or second swing high in the pullback.

The same is true of new lows in a bear trend. When the bear trend is strong, strong bears will press their positions on the breakout to a new low by shorting more, and the market will continue to fall until it reaches some measured move target. As the trend weakens, the price action at a new low will be less clear, which means that the strong bears are using the new low as an area to take profits on their shorts rather than as an area to add to their shorts. As the bear trend further loses strength, eventually the strong bulls will see a new low as a great price to initiate longs and they will be able to create a reversal pattern and then a significant rally.

As a trend matures, it usually transitions into a trading range, but the first trading ranges that form are usually followed by a continuation of the trend. How do the strong bulls and bears act as a trend matures? In a bull trend, when the trend is strong, the pullbacks are small because the strong bulls want to buy more on a pullback. Since they suspect that there may not be a pullback until the market is much higher, they begin to buy in pieces, but relentlessly. They look for any reason to buy and, with so many big traders in the market, there will be some buying for every imaginable reason. They place limit orders to buy a few ticks down and other limit orders to buy a few ticks above the low of the prior bar, at the low of the prior bar, and below the low of the prior bar. They place stop orders to buy above the high of the prior bar and on a breakout above any prior swing high. They also buy on the close of both any bull or bear trend bar. They see the bear trend bar as a brief opportunity to buy at a better price and the bull trend bar as a sign that the market is about to move up quickly.

The strong bears are smart, and they see what is going on. Since they believe, just like the strong bulls, that the market is going to be higher before long, it does not make sense for them to be shorting. They just step aside and wait until they can sell higher. How much higher? Each institution has its own measure of excess, but once the market gets to a price level where enough bear firms believe that it might not go any higher, they will begin to short. If enough of them short around the same price level, more and larger bear trend bars form and bars start to get tails on the tops. These are signs of selling pressure and they tell all traders that the bulls are becoming weaker and the bears are becoming stronger. The strong bulls eventually stop buying above the last swing high and instead begin to take profits as the market goes to a new high. They are still bullish, but are becoming selective and will buy only on pullbacks. As the two-sided trading increases and the sell-offs have more bear trend bars and last for more bars, the strong bulls will want to buy only at the bottom of the developing trading range and will look to take profits at the top. The strong bears begin to short at new highs and are now willing to scale in higher. They might take partial profits near the bottom of the developing trading range if they think that the market might reverse back up and break out to a new high, but they will keep looking to short new highs. At some point, the market becomes a 50–50 market and neither the bulls nor the bears are in control; eventually the bears become dominant, a bear trend begins, and the opposite process unfolds.

A protracted trend will often have an unusually strong breakout, but it can be an exhaustive climax. For example, in a protracted bull trend, all strong bulls and bears love to see a large bull trend bar or two, especially if it is exceptionally big, because they expect it to be a brief, unusually great opportunity. Once the market is close to where the strong bulls and bears want to sell, like near a measured move target or a trend channel line, especially if the move is the second or third consecutive buy climax, they step aside. The absence of selling by the strongest traders results in a vacuum above the market, which creates one or two relatively large bull trend bars. This bull spike is just the sign that the strong traders have been waiting for, and once it is there, they appear as if out of nowhere and begin their selling. The bulls take profits on their longs and the bears initiate new shorts, both betting against the breakout. Both sell aggressively at the close of the bar, above its high, at the close of the next bar (especially if it is a weaker bar), and at the close of the following bar, especially if the bars are starting to have bear bodies. They also short below the low of the prior bar. When they see a strong bear trend bar, they short at its close and below its low. Both the bulls and the bears expect a larger correction, and the bulls will not consider buying again until at least a 10-bar, two-legged correction, and even then only if the sell-off looks weak. The bears expect the same sell-off and will not be eager to take profits too early.

Weak traders see that large bull trend bar in the opposite way. The weak bulls, who had been sitting on the sidelines, hoping for an easy pullback to buy, see the market running away from them and want to make sure they catch this next leg up, especially since the bar is so strong and the day is almost over. The weak bears, who shorted early and maybe scaled in, were terrified by the rapidity with which the bar broke to a new high. They are afraid of relentless follow-through buying, so they buy back their shorts. These weak traders are trading on emotion and are competing against computers, which do not have emotion as one of the variables in their algorithms. Since the computers control the market, the emotions of the weak traders doom them to big losses on big bull trend bars at the end of an overdone bull trend. The market is reversing, not successfully breaking out.

Once a strong bull trend begins to have pullbacks that are relatively large, the pullbacks, which are always small trading ranges, behave more like trading ranges than bull flags. The direction of the breakout becomes less certain, and traders begin to think that a downside breakout is about as likely as an upside breakout. A new high is now a breakout attempt above a trading range, and the odds are that it will fail. Likewise, once a strong bear trend begins to have relatively large pullbacks, those pullbacks behave more like trading ranges than like bear flags; therefore, a new low is an attempt to break below a trading range, and the odds are that it will fail, and that the trading range will continue.

Every trading range is within either a bull trend or a bear trend. Once the two-sided trading is strong enough to create the trading range, the trend is no longer strong, at least while the trading range is in effect. There will always eventually be a breakout from the range, and if it is to the upside and it is very strong, the market is in a strong bull trend. If it is to the downside and strong, the market is in a strong bear trend.

Once the bears are strong enough to push a pullback well below the bull trend line and the moving average, they are confident enough that the market will likely not go much higher and they will aggressively short above the old high. At this point, the bulls will have decided that they should buy only a deep pullback. A new mind-set is now dominant at the new high. It is no longer a place to buy because it no longer represents much strength. Yes, there is profit taking by the bulls, but most big traders now look at the new high as a great opportunity to initiate shorts. The market has reached the tipping point, and most traders have stopped looking to buy small pullbacks and instead are looking to sell rallies. The bears are dominant, and the strong selling will likely lead to a large correction or even a trend reversal. After the next strong push down, the bears will look for a lower high to sell again or to add to their short positions, and the bulls who bought the pullback will become concerned that the trend might have reversed or at least that there will be a much larger pullback. Instead of hoping for a new bull high to take profits on their longs, they will now take profits at a lower high and not look to buy again until after a larger correction. Bulls know that most reversal attempts fail, and many who rode the trend up will not exit their longs until after the bears have demonstrated the ability to push the market down hard. Once these bulls see this impressive selling pressure, they will then look for a rally to finally exit their longs. Their supply will limit the rally, and their selling, added to the shorting by aggressive bears and the profit taking by bulls who saw the sell-off as a buying opportunity, will create a second leg down.

If the market enters a bear trend, the process will reverse. When the bear trend is strong, traders will short below prior lows. As the trend weakens, the bears will take profits at new lows and the market will likely enter a trading range. After a strong rally above the bull trend line and the moving average, the bears will take profits at a new low and strong bulls will aggressively buy and try to take control of the market. The result will be a larger bear rally or possibly a reversal into a bull trend.

A similar situation occurs when there is a pullback that is large enough to make traders wonder if the trend has reversed. For example, if there is a deep, sharp pullback in a bull trend, traders will begin to think the market may have reversed. They are looking at moves below prior swing lows, but this is in the context of a pullback in a bull trend instead of as part of a bear trend. They will watch what happens as the market falls below a prior swing low. Will the market fall far enough for bears, who entered on a sell stop below that swing low, to make a profit? Did the new low find more sellers than buyers? If it did, that is a sign that the bears are strong and that the pullback will probably fall further. The trend might even have reversed to down.

Another possibility on the breakout to a new low is that the market enters a trading range, which is evidence that the shorts took profits and that there was unimpressive buying by the bulls. The final alternative is that the market reverses up after the breakout to a new low. This means that there were strong bulls below that swing low just waiting for the market to test there. This is a sign that the sell-off is more likely just a big pullback in an ongoing bull trend. The shorts from higher up took profits on the breakout to the new low because they believed that the trend was still up. The strong bulls bought aggressively because they believed that the market would not fall further and that it would rally to test the bull high.

Whenever there is any breakout below a swing low, traders will watch carefully for evidence that the bulls have returned or that the bears have taken control. They need to decide what influence is greatest at the new low, and they use the market's behavior to make that decision. If there is a strong breakout, then new selling is dominant. If the market's movement is uncertain, then profit taking by the shorts and weak buying by the bulls is taking place, and the market will likely enter a trading range. If there is a strong reversal up, then aggressive buying by the longs is the most important factor.

Strong trend channel line reversals are from greatly overextended trends and often run far after they reverse through the channel to the opposite side and then break the trend line. The first pullback after the reversal is often shallow because the market is emotional and everyone quickly agrees that the trend has reversed. Because of the confidence, traders will be much more aggressive and will add on during the smallest pause and not take profits, keeping the pullbacks small.

When there is a strong break of a trend line, there will usually be a second leg after a pullback. The pullback often retraces and tests the old trend line, but there are almost always more reliable price action reasons for entering there in your attempt to catch the second leg of the pullback or new trend. The stronger the move through the trend line, the more likely it is that there will be a second leg after a pullback. If the break of the trend line is not even strong enough to reach the moving average, it is usually not strong enough to reverse the trend, so do not begin looking for a trend reversal just yet. The trend is still strong and you should take only with-trend setups, despite the break of the trend line.

Trends end with a reversal, which is a countertrend move that breaks the trend line, and then a test of the final trend extreme. The test may overshoot the old extreme as in the case of a lower low in a new bull trend or a higher high in a new bear trend, or it may undershoot it with a higher low in a new bull trend or a lower high in a new bear trend. Rarely, the test will form a perfect double top or double bottom to the exact tick. Overshoots are, strictly speaking, the final leg of the old trend, because they form the most extreme price in the trend. An undershoot is the pullback from the first leg in the new trend. Tests themselves are frequently made of two legs (for example, like a two-legged rally after a bear breakout).

If the overshoot goes too far and is in too tight a channel, you should not be looking for a reversal. The trend has likely resumed and is not in the process of reversing. Instead, begin the process over and wait for another trend line break and then another test of the trend's extreme before looking for a reversal trade.

The test of the trend extreme is usually in the form of some type of channel, and the strength of the channel is especially important when the market might be in the process of reversing. For example, if there is a strong bull trend and then there is a strong sell-off that breaks well below the bull trend line, traders will study the next rally carefully. They want to see whether that rally will simply be a test of the bull high or instead it will break out strongly above the high and be followed by another strong leg up in the bull trend. One of the most important considerations is the momentum of that test of the bull high. If the rally is in a very tight, steep channel with no pullbacks and very little overlap between consecutive bars, and the rally goes far above the bull high before having any pause or pullback, the momentum is strong and the odds are increased that the bull trend will resume, despite that earlier strong sell-off and breakout below the bull trend line. In contrast, if the rally has many overlapping bars, several large bear trend bars, two or three clear pullbacks, maybe a wedge shape, and a slope that is noticeably less than the slope of the original bull trend and of the sell-off, then the odds are that the test of the bull high will result in either a lower high or a slightly higher high and then another attempt to sell off. The market might be reversing into a bear trend, but at a minimum, a trading range is likely.

Markets have inertia and tend to continue to do what they have been doing. This causes most trend reversals to fail. Also, when one succeeds in reversing the market, a trading range is more likely to form than a trend in the opposite direction, since a trading range represents less change. In a trading range, traders from the old trend are still strong, but are balanced by traders from the opposite trend. This is more likely than the market quickly changing control from one set of trend traders to trend traders in the opposite direction. However, even if a trading range forms, it usually will have large, tradable countertrend swings and it might take dozens of bars before traders know whether the market has reversed into an opposite trend or instead has been forming a large flag in an ongoing trend.

Since the countertrend move after a trend line break usually has at least two legs, if a bull reversal has a higher low for the test of the bear low, it will also be the start of the second leg. However, if it forms a lower low for the test, that low will be the start of the first leg; after that first leg, it is likely that there will be a pullback and then a second leg. Likewise, in a bear reversal, a lower high is the start of the second leg, but a higher high test is the start of the first leg.

Everything is relative to the chart in front of you and looks different on higher and smaller time frame charts. If the legs that break off the trend line and test the trend's extreme have only two bars on a 5 minute chart, traders will not see this as a major trend reversal, although those legs might have about 10 bars on a 1 minute chart and create an excellent major trend reversal setup. Similarly, if a bull trend that has lasted 60 bars has a pullback and a test where the legs have 20 or more bars, they might create a major trend reversal setup on the 15 minute chart, but when the legs have that many bars on the 5 minute chart, traders will not use the term "major trend reversal." They will instead look for other patterns. For example, if the pullback that breaks a bull trend line has 30 bars, traders will see it as a bear trend (all pullbacks in bull trends are smaller bear trends), and will look for a break above the bear trend line and then a major trend line up. If the rally also has about 30 bars, they will see it as a new bull trend, and look for a break below its trend line and a major trend reversal down. They realize that these legs have only 10 bars on the 15 minute chart and form a major trend reversal on that chart, but that is not the chart that they are trading, and they will use terms that are appropriate for the chart in front of them.

An average setup has about a 40 percent chance of leading to a profitable swing, a 30 percent chance of a small loss, and a 30 percent chance of a small profit. Most result in trading ranges instead of opposite trends, but there is still a 70 percent chance of at least a small profit. The best setups have a 60 percent chance of profitable swing trades.

FIGURE 3.1   A Higher High Followed by a Lower High

A major trend reversal is shown in Figure 3.1, and many other examples are mentioned on charts throughout the book.

If a trend reverses down at a higher high after the bull trend line break (a major trend reversal down), there is usually a lower high major trend reversal that will give traders a second chance to get short. AAPL had both a higher high and a lower high trend reversal. A major reversal usually follows a strong break of the trend line, which is evidence that the traders in the opposite direction are getting strong. The weak bear leg to bar 4 barely broke the trend line, and it did not come close to falling below the last higher low in the bull trend (bar 2). It could not even hold below the moving average. However, it continued sideways for many bars, indicating that the bears were strong enough to halt the bull trend for a long time.

Bar 6 was a higher high short setup after this trend line break, but because the move down to bar 4 was not particularly strong, the sell-off down to bar 9 stalled.

Bar 9 became the bottom of a wedge bull flag or a bull channel and a high 4 buy setup, and it formed a double bottom bull flag with bar 5. This led to a rally to bar 10. The move up to bar 10 was a low-momentum, low 4 short setup and a wedge bear flag, with the first push up being the lower high just before the bar 9 low. It was also the right shoulder of a head and shoulders top, but most head and shoulders tops fail and become triangles or wedge bull flags. In this case, however,

Figure 3.1   MAJOR TREND REVERSAL   **97**

it became the first lower high after a trend line break and a lower high test of the bull high.

The bear leg to bar 9 broke well below a longer trend line, the moving average, and the last higher low of the bull trend (bar 5), and it followed a previous sharp attempt at a trend reversal (the sell-off to bar 4). Also, it did not come close to testing the underside of the bull trend line or the bar 8 first pullback in the first leg down. All of these were signs of strength of the trend line break and increased the chances for at least a second leg down or an actual trend reversal. The bulls who bought around the bar 6 top of the bull trend saw the strength of the bears in the sell-off to bar 9 and the weakness of the bulls in the rally to bar 10, and were disappointed by the price action. They used the weak rally to bar 10 as an opportunity to exit their longs with a small loss, and they were not willing to buy again until the market traded lower. The bulls wanted to see signs of strength before buying, but none came, so they sat on the sidelines as the market sold off to bar 11.

Some traders like to see a Fibonacci 61.8 percent retracement on the rally to the lower high. However, a 61.8 percent retracement is never as precise as the number leads one to believe, and probably no more likely than a 60, 63, or 67 percent pull-back, and it has probably lost value now that trading has become so computerized. For example, if a trader is selling a 50 percent pullback in what he believes is a bear swing, he might risk to a new high (above bar 6) to get a test of the bar 9 bottom of the bear spike. His reward equals his risk, and since he sees the rally as a pullback, his short has at least a 60 percent probability of success. If the market retraced higher, there is an argument that a 67 percent retracement is more important than a 61.8 percent retracement. Once a pullback rallies to above 50 percent, the chance of the bear resuming becomes less, let's say 50 percent. Once the probability is 50 percent or less, traders will need more of a reward if they are going to short. Since their stop is above the bar 6 high, they might want a reward that is twice the size of their risk. This means that they might short a 67 percent retracement, because then a test of the bar 9 low would create a reward that is twice as large as their risk.

FIGURE 3.2   A Lower Low Followed by a Higher Low

The Emini had a lower low and then a higher low major trend reversal (see Figure 3.2). The rally to bar 1 broke a bear trend line, and the bar 3 test of the bear low was a lower low. A lower low test usually results in at least two countertrend legs, and that is what happened here (the up moves from bars 3 and 9). Bar 9 was a higher low after the break of yesterday's major bear trend line (broken by the rally to bar 1), and as a higher low, it was the start of the second leg, and the completed second leg can be the end of the move up. A trading range is a more common outcome than a reversal into an opposite trend.

The channel down to bar 7 (from both bar 5 and bar 6) was strong. Many traders preferred to wait to see how strong the breakout was before buying. The two bull bars after bar 7 had relatively big bodies and small tails, and represented a strong breakout in the eyes of many traders. At that point, many traders thought that the market had become always-in long and waited to buy a pullback. The bear bar after bar 8 was an attempt to make the breakout of the high 2 bull flag down to bar 7 fail (the first leg down ended three bars after bar 5). The bears wanted the bar 6 and bar 8 double top to lead to a swing down. The bulls expected the bears to fail and for traders to come in and buy the test of the bar 7 low, creating a higher low after the strong bull spike up to bar 5 (bar 4 and the bar after bar 3 were strong enough to make traders think that at least a second leg up was likely). Bar 9 was a lower low breakout pullback buy setup (and a double bottom bull flag with bar 7), and the bulls bought it aggressively.

The bull trend bar after bar 9 reversed the highs and closes of many prior bars, which is a sign of a strong bull reversal. It closed above the close of every bar since bar 6 and its high was above the high of every bar since the bar after bar 6. The more highs and closes that a strong bull bar reverses, the stronger the bull reversal and the more likely that there will be follow-through buying (higher prices).

The earliest entries in major trend reversals often do not look strong, like at bars 3 and 9. This means that the probability of success is often less than 50 percent. However, the potential reward is at its greatest and the result usually is a positive trader's equation. Traders can wait for a clear always-in long reversal before buying, and this usually increases the probability to 60 percent or higher. At that point, there is less profit remaining and the risk is usually larger (the protective stop is further away), but the trader's equation is usually still positive. For example, the bulls could have waited to buy above the bull trend bar that followed bar 3 for a swing, or on the close of bar 4 for a scalp. They also could have bought on the close of the bull trend bar after bar 9 or on the close of the bull trend bar that followed it.

This is a good example of an average major trend reversal attempt, where the setups and context are acceptable but not strong, and the reversals up led to a trading range and not a bull trend, as is the case about 70 percent of the time. The bar 3 lower low led to a test of the bar 1 high, which was a likely top of an evolving trading range. Some traders took full or partial profits there, while others held, expecting a second leg up, and exited on the failed breakout of the trading range at bar 10 (as the bear bar turned down, or below its low). The bar 3 lower low resulted in a scalper's profit for traders who exited as bar 5 turned down, and a swing profit (a reward that was at least twice as large as the risk) for traders who exited in the reversal down after bar 10. The traders who bought the bar 7 two-legged higher low either had a small loss if they held until their protective stop was hit, or they got out around breakeven if they moved their stop to breakeven after a four-bar rally above the moving average. The traders who bought the bar 9 double bottom higher low (higher than bar 3), which was also a lower low for the reversal up from the small bear trend (bull flag) from bar 5 to bar 7, were able to exit some or all with a reward that was at least twice as large as their risk (a swing profit).

In an average setup like this, the chance of a profitable swing is about 40 percent, and there is about a 30 percent chance of a small profit, and a 30 percent chance of the protective stop being hit (a small loss). The result is still a profitable strategy. In the strongest setups, the chance of a profitable swing is 60 percent or greater, and maybe only a 30 to 40 percent chance of the protective stop being hit and leading to a small loss. Because the trader's equation is so strong, this is an excellent setup for all traders, including beginners.

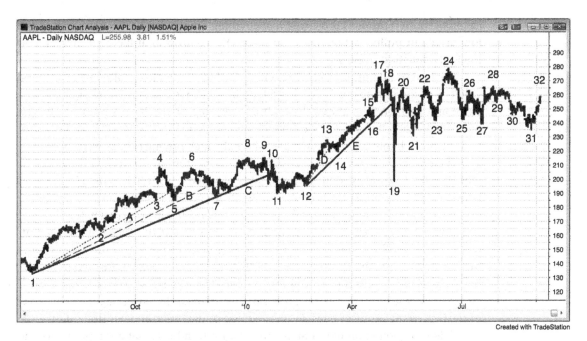

FIGURE 3.3   A Trend Line Break Alone Does Not Make a Reversal

Just because there is a break of a bull trend line and then the market moves to a higher high, it is not always prudent to look for shorts. If there is a trend line break, but the move to a higher high goes five or more bars above the old bull high, traders usually should begin the process from the beginning and wait for another break below a bull trend line and another test of the bull trend high before going short. The daily chart of AAPL shown in Figure 3.3 had a break of the bull trend line (the solid line C) on the move down to bar 11. The market then rallied to a new high at bar 13. However, the move to bar 13 was in a very steep bull channel (the dotted D bull trend line is the bottom of the channel) and therefore traders should have waited before shorting. It is always better not to short the first breakout of a steep bull channel. Wait to see if there is a pullback to a higher high or lower high. The market corrected sideways and formed a double bottom bull flag (a high 2) at bar 14, and there never was a breakout pullback to set up the short. The move to bar 13 was a successful breakout that led to a resumption of the bull trend, and not a failed breakout that led to a reversal process.

The market had been in a bull trading range from bar 3 to bar 11, and the move from bar 12 to bar 13 was a strong spike up that broke above the large bull flag. When the move to the higher high is so steep with so little overlap, the odds favor a successful breakout and about a measured move up instead of a reversal. Once

Figure 3.3   MAJOR TREND REVERSAL   **101**

this happens, the process of looking for a reversal begins again. Wait for a trend line break, like the move down to bar 19, and then for a higher high, double top, or lower high test of the bull high. Although there were several tradable swings after bar 19, bar 19 was a climax reversal up (a spike down and then a spike up), and this is usually followed by a trading range. During the trading range, the bears who created the spike down to the bar 19 low were continuing to short and trying to generate a bear channel, and the bulls who bought the bar 19 low were continuing to buy in an attempt to create follow-through to the upside in the form of a bull channel. Incidentally, the bulls saw bar 19 as simply a large breakout test of the breakout above bars 8 and 9. Since bar 19 fell below the bar 9 breakout point, the breakout gap was negative, but because the market rallied quickly up, it nonetheless was a type of breakout gap.

The move down to bar 5 broke the dotted trend line A, and bar 6 was a reasonable double top short setup.

The move down to bar 7 broke the dashed trend line B. The move up to bar 8 was in a steep channel, so it was better to wait for a breakout below the channel and then wait to see if there was a breakout pullback to short.

Bar 9 was a two-legged move up to a double top and an acceptable short.

Bar 10 was a double top bear flag and another short setup.

Bar 19 was obviously caused by some news event (it was the 2010 Flash Crash), but that is not important. What is always more important is who controls the market during and after the bar. It was in part a breakout test of the middle of the trading range between bars 4 and 12 (a test of the bottom of the channel from bar 11 to 17). Many traders expect a breakout to be tested, and once the market begins to move quickly in that direction, as it did as bar 19 was forming, the strongest bulls began to believe that the market might fall all of the way back to the bottom of that trading range. So, what should they do once they believe that the market is going lower? It does not make sense for them to keep buying when they can soon buy lower. This absence of buying results in the market getting sucked down quickly in a sell vacuum to the level where the bulls believe that it will find support. Even though they thought that there was value as the market was falling (you know this because the market quickly reversed up above most of the entire bar), they believed that it had further to go and waited until it reached support. Since they saw the market as offering tremendous value that they thought would be very brief, they appeared out of nowhere and bought aggressively. The bears saw the same thing and quickly took profits, buying back their shorts. There was no one left to sell and the market rallied strongly. Momentum programs accelerated the fall and the rally back up, because they detect strong momentum and trade relentlessly in its direction until the momentum slows, and then they exit with their profits. Spikes like this are common in trends. However, the test of the bottom of a channel usually leads to a trading range as it did here. Big up + big down = big confusion = trading range.

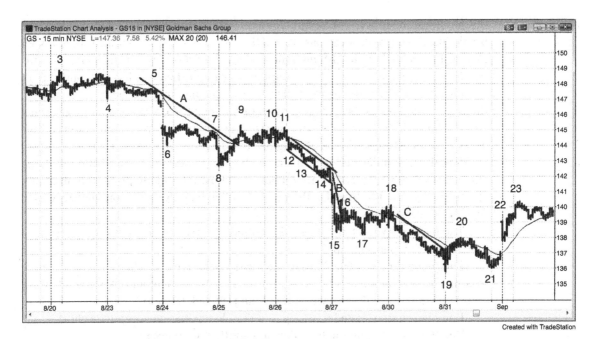

FIGURE 3.4 If a Test Is Too Strong, Wait

If the test of the low has too much momentum, another leg down is more likely than a reversal up. In Figure 3.4, GS broke above the bear trend line A, but the sell-off from bar 11 to test the bar 8 bear low was in a steep bull channel. Rather than buying above bar 13 or bar 14 and looking for a failed breakout and a trend reversal, traders had to consider that GS might be successfully breaking out to the downside. The move down to bar 13 and then to bar 14 was in a steep bear channel, instead of a low-momentum sell-off with pullbacks along the way. When that happens, it is better to wait for a breakout above that bear channel and then see if a breakout pullback forms. If one does, it is a buy setup for a higher low or lower low trend reversal up.

Once the market fell below the bar 14 wedge (bars 12 and 13 were the first two pushes down in this bear channel that followed the spike down to bar 12), it spiked down to bar 15 in about a measured move (using the height of the bars 12 to 14 wedge).

The trading range to bar 18 broke the steep trend line B, but again the market broke to the downside in a steep bear channel instead of a low-momentum test of the bar 17 bear low.

The rally to bar 20 broke bear trend line C and there was a higher low buy setup at bar 21. The move down to 21 had three small legs and many overlapping bars, indicating two-sided trading. This was a lower-momentum move and more likely an attempt at a higher low major trend reversal than a breakout to another bear leg.

Figure 3.5

MAJOR TREND REVERSAL   **103**

FIGURE 3.5 Don't Look for Reversals on Smaller Time Frame Charts

When there is a strong trend, there will be many reversal attempts on the 3 minute chart (see Figure 3.5) and far more on the 1 minute chart. Until there is a clear reversal on the 5 minute chart, if you choose to look at the 1 or 3 minute charts, you should treat each reversal attempt as a with-trend setup, here, a bear flag. Each of the five attempts on this 3 minute chart to reverse attracted eager bulls who thought they were risking little and might be gaining a lot if they were catching the bottom of a climactic V bottom reversal, a very rare event. Rather than joining them, think about where they will have to sell out of their longs, and place an entry sell stop at that very location. You will consistently succeed in transferring money from their accounts into yours, which is the primary objective of trading. For example, as soon as the bulls went long at the bull reversal bar before bar 1 (there was not a prior trend line break in this steep sell-off, so no longs should have been considered), smart traders would have placed orders to go short on a stop at one tick below the signal bar. As with all bear channels, you can also short on a limit order at the high of the prior bar. If you don't get filled on the limit order, make sure to short on a stop below the low of every pullback bar.

The short at bar 4 was below the long entry bar, since the bulls would have tightened their stops once the entry bar closed. The bull entry bar was the bear signal bar. Since this is a trend, they would swing a large part of their positions.

Bar 5 was an ii pattern, which is often a reversal pattern (but it needs an earlier trend line break), and it is commonly the final flag before a two-legged countertrend move, as was the case here. It represents balance between the bulls and the bears, and a breakout is a move outside of the balance. There is often a strong force pulling it back to the pattern, and usually through the other side. Since there was no prior trend line break, the only breakout that was a valid entry was a bear breakout. However, an ii pattern is just wide enough to break a small trend line, so any reversal up within a few bars afterward is a valid long.

Some aggressive traders turn to smaller time frame charts for setups that will allow them to enter in the direction of the trend. For example, if a trader was trading the Emini and saw the sharp sell-off on his 5 minute chart and was looking for a reason to short, he could have looked at the 3 minute chart above. Once he saw five or more consecutive bear bars, he could then place a limit order to short at the high of the prior bar, expecting the first reversal attempt after a strong bear spike to fail. He would have gone short on bar 1 as it moved above the high of the prior bar.

Figure 3.6

MAJOR TREND REVERSAL   **105**

FIGURE 3.6 Smaller Time Frames Are for With-Trend Trading Only

Figure 3.6 is the 1 minute chart of the same bear move shown in Figure 3.5, and the numbered bars are the same as on the prior chart. Bars C, D, and E were valid countertrend setups that followed two legs down and small trend line breaks; each was a tradable long scalp. Although these were possible to trade, it is usually too difficult to read a second chart and place orders this quickly, and you would likely make more money if you just traded the 5 minute trend. It looks very easy on a chart printed at the end of the day, but is much more difficult in real time. If you were to sell based on the 1 minute chart, all five of the numbered bars provided with-trend (on both the 1 and 5 minute trend) short entries that would have allowed for swinging part of the position.

Bar 1 was a small spike top, but since it formed in a bear trend, there was no need for it to be tested. This is unlike the spike bottoms at C and D. Spike bottoms in a bear trend usually get tested, as they did here.

The two-legged sideways move to bar 4 broke the bear trend line that could be drawn across the highs of bars 1 and 2. Why should traders not yet be looking to buy a test of the bar C low? Because the trend line break has to be during a strong move up. The move to bar 4 was so weak that it never even reached the moving average. If it had, it would have set up a 20 gap bar short. The bear trend was too strong for traders to be looking for longs. They should only have been shorting.

Figure 3.7

MAJOR TREND REVERSAL   **107**

FIGURE 3.7 Smaller Time Frame Reversals Are Losers

A 1 minute chart allows for smaller stops, but the reduced risk alone does not make a trade worth taking. Remember the trader's equation. The chance of success also drops, and in fact this more than offsets the reduced risk; the result is a losing strategy.

Figure 3.7 is a 1 minute chart of a strong bull trend on a 5 minute chart (not shown). Trading shorts profitably is difficult (none of the six shorts yielded a four-tick profit). It is far more profitable and less stressful to simply look for with-trend entries on the 5 minute chart and never look at the 1 minute chart. The only valid reason to look at 1 minute short signals is to find long (with-trend) entries. Once a short triggers, look for where the protective stops are and place buy orders there, since the trapped shorts will push the market to your long profit target as they buy back their losers.

FIGURE 3.8 Micro Double Bottoms and Tops

Most tradable reversals begin with at least a micro double bottom or top, a traditional double bottom or top, or a final flag reversal, which can be considered a type of double bottom or top. As shown in Figure 3.8, traders who anticipated a reversal down placed limit orders at and above the signal bar of what they thought would become the final bull flag of the leg, whether the setup was a high 1, high 2, or triangle. When they expected a reversal up from a down leg, they placed limit orders at and below the signal bar of what they believed was likely to be the final flag (a low 1, low 2, or triangle) of the bear leg. Examples of micro double bottoms were bars 1 and 2, 5 and 6, 16 and 17 (15 and 16, but the entry never triggered), and 19 and 20. Micro double tops were at 3 and 4, 10 and 11, and 13 and 14. Bar 8 was a reversal from the bar 7 one-bar final flag, a double top with bar 4, a lower high in a bear channel, and a low 2 in a trading range (bar 6 was the low 1).

The bar 17 low formed a small wedge around a measured move down from the upper trading range on what, at that point, was likely to be a trending trading range day. It was also a two-legged lower low from the breakout below the ii final flag that followed bar 15, and a double top with bar 23.

Intraday reversals often come from larger patterns, and not just micro double bottoms and tops. Bar 22 was a two-legged rally that tested the apex of the triangle (the upper trading range on this trending trading range day was the triangle that

Figure 3.8   MAJOR TREND REVERSAL   **109**

broke out four bars after bar 14). Bar 25 was a sell climax and lower low breakout pullback from the two-legged breakout to bar 22 above the bull flag that ended at bar 17 (the entire move from the open down to bar 17 was a pullback after a big gap up and a huge rally yesterday and was therefore just a large bull flag).

The sell-off to bar 9 was a double bottom bull flag with bar 6. Bar 27 was a double top with bar 24 and the second leg up from the bar 25 low. Bar 27 was the first bar of a micro double top, because the bar after it had a big tail on its bottom, indicating that the market went down, and then up. The top of that doji inside bar formed a micro double top with the high of bar 27, and aggressive bears shorted below its low, which was the entry for the breakout below the micro double top.

As dramatic as the bar 25 sell climax was, it was just a micro double bottom on a higher time frame chart (it was a three-bar-long micro double bottom on the 60 minute chart). Institutions anticipated the bottom and scaled into longs as bar 25 was forming, especially as it broke out below the bar 17 low. They expected the breakout to fail and therefore offer a brief opportunity to buy at a very good price. Since they control the direction of the market, if enough of them expect the bottom, their buying will make it happen. The two-legged rally to bar 22 broke above the bear trend line, and the sell climax to bar 25 was a lower low that became the bottom of a major trend reversal up. The rally lasted two more days.

Just because a market forms a double bottom or top does not mean that a reversal trade should be taken. The decision has to be based on context. For example, the double top at bar 27 followed six bars up and a strong sell climax, so the market could easily have gone sideways.

There were several examples of small final flag reversals that followed low and high 1 setups, resulting in micro double tops and bottoms. The bulls saw the doji bar after bar 1 as a weak low 1 breakout pullback sell signal. They bought at and below its low, expecting a bull opening reversal and low of the day. The doji became the final bear flag in the leg down, and bar 2 formed a double bottom with the bar 1 low.

The bear inside bar after bar 3 was a high 1 buy signal, but many traders thought that if the market could hold below the top of the strong two-bar bear spike at the open, it could form a double top and then have a downside breakout. Bears shorted at the high of the bear inside bar, expecting it to become a failed high 1, which would also be a one-bar final flag and a double top.

The bear inside bar after bar 5 was a breakout pullback sell signal bar. Bulls thought that the test of the moving average would hold and that the inside bar would become a one-bar final bear flag and lead to a double bottom reversal up from the moving average. They bought at the low of the bear signal bar.

CHAPTER 4

Climactic Reversals: A Spike Followed by a Spike in the Opposite Direction

The market is always trying to break out, and then the market tries to make every breakout fail. This is the most fundamental aspect of all trading and is at the heart of everything that we do. Every trend bar is a breakout, which might have follow-through and succeed, or fail and lead to a reversal. Even a climactic reversal like a V bottom is simply a breakout and then a failed breakout. The better traders become at assessing whether a breakout will succeed or fail, the better positioned they are to make a living as a trader. Will the breakout succeed? If yes, then look to trade in that direction. If no (and it becomes a failed breakout, which is a reversal), then look to trade in the opposite direction. All trading comes down to this decision.

Many people restrict the definition of a climax to a sharp move at the end of a trend that is followed by a sharp move in the opposite direction, resulting in a trend reversal. A broader definition is more useful to traders: any type of unsustainable behavior should be considered to be a type of climax, whether or not a reversal follows. Just how small can a climax be? As mentioned in Chapter 2 of book 1, every trend bar is a climax, although most do not result in climactic reversals. Any trend bar or series of trend bars where the bar or bars have relatively large ranges are climaxes, even though most traders would not think of them this way. A climax ends as soon as there is any interruption of the strong trending behavior, such as the formation of a pause bar or a reversal bar. Even a single large trend bar can be a climax. Most climaxes are usually followed by a trading range that lasts one or more bars, instead of by a spike in the opposite direction, and the trend often resumes instead of reverses. A climactic reversal is a climax that is soon followed by a sharp move in the opposite direction, and all are failed breakouts of something. For example, if there is a trading range in a bull market and it has a bear leg down from the top, this leg down is a bear channel and therefore a bull flag. If the market has one or more bull trend bars breaking above the channel, it is a breakout of the bull flag. If the market then reverses down, even if the reversal is from a lower high (the buy climax did not break above the trading range), this is still a climactic reversal. When a market is moving climactically, fundamental traders often refer to the market as being a crowded trade, meaning that they believe that too many people already have a position, so there might not be many traders left to keep pushing the market further in the trend. For example, if the market is moving up parabolically, the fundamental analysts will often say that it is a crowded trade and that they would only look to buy a pullback. Most would not advocate going short, even though they believe that a significant pullback is imminent. Other examples of buy climaxes include the 2006 housing bubble, the tech wreck of 2000, and the tulip mania of 1637. They were all examples of the greater fool theory of investing—buy high with the expectation that someone dumber than you will buy from you even higher, allowing you to exit with a profit. Once there are no fools left, the market can go in only one direction, and it often goes there quickly. China and Brazil might be developing bubbles, because they appear to be growing at an unsustainable pace. Momentum traders might be responsible for much of the growth at this point, meaning that its pace is not sufficiently based on fundamentals. Once profit takers come in, the reversal could be fast and deep. Investors could panic as they attempt to exit with at least minimal profits, and the hope of averting a big loss, as is the case with any climax.

Sometimes when the market is in a strong trend, a bar forms that has an exceptionally large range and body, and it may open near one extreme and close near the other. This can be either a climax or a breakout. For example, suppose the market is selling off and then a bear trend bar forms that opens near its high and closes near its low, and the body and range are the largest of the down move, maybe twice the size of many of the bear trend bars. This bar might represent the last desperate longs who are so eager to get out that they are selling at the market instead of waiting for a pullback. They are finally giving up and want out at any price. Once the last long has exited, there is no one left to short. The institutions are not shorting here because they already shorted much higher. In fact, they are taking profits on their shorts at the bottom of the bar and many are likely going long there. The market can then reverse up sharply within the next couple of bars once traders sense that there is no significant follow-through selling. However, if that large bear trend bar is a breakout of one or more areas of support, it might generate a measured move down before attempting to reverse again.

An important component of a climax is a vacuum effect created by the absence of traders in the opposite direction. For example, if the market is accelerating to the upside toward the top of a bull channel, there will be institutional bears who believe that the market will soon reverse, but that the market will likely first break out above the trend channel line. Why would they choose to short as the market is racing toward the line when they believe that it will soon be above the line? It makes no sense for them to go short when they think that the market will soon be higher and they could short at an even better price. So what do they do? They wait. The same is true for the strong bulls. They are looking to take partial or full profits, but if they believe that the market will soon be a little higher, they will not sell until the market reaches a resistance area that they think the market will likely not exceed, at least for the time being. This means that there are some very strong bears who are not shorting, and some very strong bulls who are not selling out of their longs, and the absence of selling creates a vacuum that sucks the market up higher to a level where the bears feel there is value in shorting and the bulls feel there is value in taking profits. The programs that detect the momentum early on in a bar see this and quickly buy repeatedly until the momentum slows. Because these buy programs will buy up to the final tick and are relatively unopposed, the market races up in a strong bull spike that can last several bars. But what happens once the market reaches a level where the bears feel that there is value and the bulls feel that the market is unlikely to go much higher before a pullback, like several ticks above that trend channel line? These huge institutional bears will begin to short heavily and relentlessly, and the strong bulls will sell out of their longs, because they feel that this price level is a great value. The buy programs will see the loss of momentum and sell out of their longs. Since it is such a great value for shorting and profit taking, it cannot last long, so bulls and bears sell very aggressively on this brief opportunity. Since both the strong bulls and the bears expect lower prices, that's what will follow. With all of the major traders selling and no longer buying the market reverses down, at least for about 10 bars and a couple of legs. At that point, they will decide whether the pullback has ended and the bulls should buy back their longs and the bears should scalp out of their shorts, or they believe that the sell-off has further to go.

The weak traders do the opposite as the market is racing up: the weak bulls who were sitting on the sidelines finally buy, and the weak bears cover their shorts, both unrealistically afraid of another big leg up. Experienced traders can do exactly what the institutions are doing. For example, they can short the close of that strong bull trend bar, above its high, or at the close of the next bar or two. If they do, they should use a stop that is about as many ticks as the bull trend bar is tall. If they wait for a bear reversal bar and short on a stop below its low, they can risk to above the signal bar's high. Alternatively, they could use a wider protective stop to allow for one more minor high, but if they do, they need to reduce the size of their position.

The strong bulls keep buying during the bull spike because they, too, believe that the market will go higher. However, at some point, they know that the market will have gone too far, too fast, and that there will be just a brief window where they can sell out of their longs with a windfall profit. If they wait too long, the pullback might become a reversal and they will lose out on the opportunity to exit at a very high price. They then seize this brief moment to sell out of their longs. Their aggressive profit taking combined with the aggressive selling by institutional shorts makes the market fall very quickly for a bar or two or even longer, and this creates a climactic reversal. The bulls will try to buy back lower, hoping that the reversal will fail, but if they are not able to push the market back up, they will sell out of their longs once again. The bears who sold higher are continuing to sell down here, and both they and the bulls are fighting in a trading range over the direction of the channel that will follow. If the bears win, there will usually be a spike and channel bear trend with the spike being the sharp move down from the climactic top. If the bulls win, there will usually be a spike and channel bull trend with the spike being the sharp move up to the top of the buy climax.

Spikes are tests of the strength of both the trend and countertrend traders. A bull trend is made of a series of higher highs and lows, both of which can be created by spikes. If the market has a spike up in a bull trend and then a selloff in the form of a spike down, the probability is that the market will test and exceed the top of the bull spike, but not come back and test the bottom of the bear spike. The bull spike will be just another leg up in the bull trend and the spike down will usually just evolve into a bull flag and a higher low, and will likely not get tested once the bull trend resumes. The same is true for a bear trend, which is made up of lower highs and lows. The most recent new low, whether or not it is in the form of a spike, will likely get tested and exceeded after any pullback. Any rally, whether it is in the form of a strong bull spike or a quiet move up, will likely evolve into a bear flag and just another lower high, and will usually not get tested. There is a widely held, but incorrect, belief that the strongest rallies occur during bear trends and the strongest selloffs occur during bull trends. While this is not true, it is important to realize that countertrend spikes can be exceptionally strong and make many traders believe that the trend has reversed. All spikes, up and down, in bull or bear trends or in trading ranges, are simply tests of the determination of the countertrend traders and the resolve of the with trend traders. The pullbacks often come close to flipping the always-in position to the opposite direction, but there is inadequate follow-through. Strong traders love these reversal attempts, because they know that most will fail. Whenever the countertrend traders are able to create one, the with trend traders come in and heavily fight the reversal attempt, and usually win. They see these sharp countertrend moves as great opportunities to enter in the direction of the trend at a great price that is likely to exist only briefly, and quickly become simply a spike pullback in the trend.

Every pullback is a small trend, and every trend is just a pullback on a higher time frame chart. This includes the 1987 and 2008–2009 stock market crashes, which were just pullbacks to the monthly bull trend line. Every countertrend spike should be considered to be a vacuum effect pullback, and many pullbacks end with or soon after very strong trend bars that are attempts to reverse the trend. For example, if there is a sharp bear spike in a bull trend on the 5 minute chart and then the market suddenly reverses into a bull leg, there was an area of support at the low, whether or not you saw it in advance. The bulls stepped aside until the market reached a level where they believed that value was great and the opportunity to buy at this great price would be brief. They know that most attempts to reverse fail, and that many reversal attempts have strong bear trend bars. They bet against the follow-through selling that traders would need to see to be confident of an always-in reversal, and they came in and bought aggressively at the close of the bar and as the next bar was forming. Since there was no one left to short, the market raced up for many bars, ending the pullback and resuming the trend. The smart bears were aware of that magnet, and they used it as an opportunity to take profits on their shorts.

The market is always trying to reverse (although most attempts fail), and a successful reversal needs follow-through to convince traders that the always-in direction has flipped. These spikes come close to forming convincing flips, but fail to have enough follow-through. The result is that they make traders wonder if the always-in position will flip, but when the follow-through is inadequate, they decide that the reversal attempt will fail. The bulls then see the spike down as a brief opportunity to buy at a great price. The bears who shorted near the bottom of the bear trend bar and higher also realize that the reversal attempt is failing, and they quickly buy back their shorts and step aside until they see another opportunity to try to take control of the market again. The result is a market bottom on the 5 minute chart. That bottom, like all bottoms, occurs at some higher time frame support level, like a bull trend line, a moving average, or a bear trend channel line along the bottom of a large bull flag. It is important to remember that if the 5 minute reversal was strong, traders would buy based on that reversal, whether or not they saw support on the daily or 60 minute chart. Also, traders would not buy at that low, even if they saw the higher time frame support, unless there was evidence on the 5 minute chart that it was forming a bottom. This means that they do not need to be looking at lots of different charts in search of that support level, because the reversal on the 5 minute chart tells them that it is there. If they are able to follow multiple time frames, they will see support and resistance levels before the market reaches them, and this can alert them to look for a setup on the 5 minute chart when the market reaches the magnet; but if they simply carefully follow the 5 minute chart, it will tell them all that they need to know.

Stock traders routinely buy strong bear spikes in bull trends because they see the spike as a value play. Although they usually look for strong price action before buying, they will often buy a stock that they like at the bottom of a sharp sell-off, especially to the area of the bull trend line or other support area, like a trading range low, even if it has not yet reversed up. They believe that the market is temporarily, incorrectly underpricing the stock because of some news event, and they buy it because they doubt it will remain discounted for long. They don't mind if it falls a little further, because they doubt that they can pick the exact bottom of the pullback; but they want to get in during the sell-off because they believe that the market will quickly correct its mistake and the stock will soon rally.

A climax is simply any market that has gone too far, too fast in the eyes of traders. It is a trend bar or a series of trend bars with little overlap, and it can occur at any time, including as a breakout, at the start of a trend, or after a trend has gone on for many bars. The market pauses after the spike, and then the trend can resume or reverse. When there is a large spike and it is followed either immediately or soon thereafter by a spike in the opposite direction, the market is trying to reverse. When this happens, it creates a climactic reversal, which is a two-bar reversal that may be visible only on a higher or lower time frame chart. For example, if there is a bull trend that has gone on for 20 bars and now has the largest bull trend bar of the entire trend, traders will wonder if it is a climactic end to the trend (a blow off top). If there is then a strong bear trend bar or two on the reversal down, the bear spike forms a two-bar reversal with the final bull trend bar or bars of the climax, whether or not there were several bars separating the final bull trend bar and the first bear trend bar. On a higher time frame chart, traders can see a simple two-bar reversal. This will be a simple reversal bar on an even higher time frame chart. As long as you understand what the market is doing, there is no need to look through several time frames in search of a perfect two-bar reversal setup. You know it exists by what you are seeing on the chart in front of you, and that is all you need to place a trade.

Both bulls and bears will sell when there is a second or third consecutive buy climax without much of a correction between the climaxes, and this selling can lead to a climactic reversal. The bears are selling to initiate shorts for what they believe will be at least a scalp down. The bulls see the final large bull trend bar or two as a great price to take profits, since they believe it is likely at least a temporary end of the trend, and beginning of a deeper pullback, a trading range, or an opposite trend. They expect the market to trend down for about 10 bars and two legs, and are afraid that the bull trend might have ended and the old high might not be exceeded. When there is a second buy climax and then a reversal setup, both bulls and bears wonder if the market is setting up a final flag reversal (with the pullback after the first buy climax being the final flag). When the reversal signal bar forms after a third push up, traders wonder if the market is creating a wedge top. The opposite is true after consecutive sell climaxes where traders look for possible final flag and wedge bottoms.

When the climax is very impressive and the context is right, they will sell out of their entire long positions. If they thought that the market would only fall a few ticks, they would not exit their longs and then try to buy a couple of ticks lower.

They are exiting because they expect that they will be able to buy low enough below their exit price that the additional profit will more than make up for transaction costs. They are also concerned that the market might reverse into a bear trend, or at least into a deep enough pullback so that the market might not make another high for more bars than they would be willing to wait. Because they are not looking to buy until the market trades down significantly, there is an absence of buyers. Also, strong bears will short as the market falls. Because there are more sellers than buyers, the pullback can be sharp and even become a trend reversal. If the market instead continues up after their exit, they will look to buy again higher or on a pullback. If the market begins to turn down, they will look to buy lower if there is a setup, but usually not for about 10 bars. If there is no buy setup after 10 or 20 bars, then the trend has likely reversed to down, and then traders would not be looking to buy. If there is a buy setup after about 10 bars and two legs, the bulls will reinstate their longs and the bears will take profits on their shorts.

Consecutive climaxes increase the chances of a correction. For example, if there is a buy climax (one or a few large bull trend bars) and then only a brief pause or pullback and then a second buy climax, the odds of a significant correction or a reversal are higher. If there is instead just another small pullback and then a third buy climax, the market will usually begin at least a two-legged correction that will last at least 10 bars. The pause can be any bar that is not another big bull trend bar. A doji with a bear or bull body or a bear trend bar, which might be small, are the most common pauses. The pause bar sometimes has a high that is slightly above the high of the second buy climax bar, but still acts as a one-bar final flag and leads to a reversal after the third climax. The third climax is usually only one or two large bull trend bars. The consecutive climaxes indicate that the market might have gone too far, too fast, and bulls might then only be willing to buy much lower. Two consecutive buy climaxes create two pushes up and is effectively a double top, even though the second high is much higher. Three consecutive buy climaxes is a wedge top. The second top can be far above the first and the third can be far above the second, and the pattern can look more like a bull spike than a wedge. However, they have the same implications and can be traded the same. Only very experienced traders should short buy climaxes because it is easy to misread the price action and end up shorting a strong bull where there really is no significant climax or reversal pattern.

If a pullback after a buy climax lasts 10 or more bars and it breaks out of the bottom of a bull channel, it usually has sufficiently worked off the excess so that if there is another buy climax, there is less of a sense of excess and less of a need for a big correction. Some trends have a series of strong breakouts and then trading ranges. Each breakout is a spike and therefore a buy climax, but the trading ranges that follow show that the strong bulls are still buying near the high. This means that the breakout was created more by strong bulls than by weak bears who were buying back their shorts in a panic. The market is now going sideways because the strong bulls believe it will go higher and are not waiting for lower prices, and the strong bears are not shorting aggressively, because they too believe that the market will go higher. It does not make sense for them to begin to establish shorts if they believe that they will be able to do so higher.

The reversal spike can be smaller or larger than the trend spike, and if it is larger, the odds of a reversal are greater. After the initial move of the reversal spike, the market then either pauses or forms a trading range, which can be brief or last for dozens of bars. During this pause, both the bulls and the bears are adding to their positions in an attempt to get follow-through in the form of a channel in their direction. For example, if there is a strong spike up and then a strong move down, both the bulls and the bears are being aggressive. The spike down can be in the same bar as the spike up, and when that happens, there will be a large tail at the top of a large bar. On a smaller time frame, there would be one or more bull trend bars followed by one or more bear trend bars. Alternatively, the spike down can be on the next bar or even several bars later. On a higher time frame, the reversal would simply be a bull trend bar immediately followed by a bear trend bar, creating a two-bar reversal. On an even higher time frame, the reversal would be a single reversal bar. The spike down may have follow-through over the next bar or several bars. Whether or not it does, the market will soon pause or correct some back up. Very often, it will form a trading range that can be brief or last for dozens of bars. The bulls are buying more, trying to push the market up into a bull channel, and the bears are selling in the trading range, hoping for a channel down. At some point, one side will win and the other side will be forced to cover. If the bulls win, the bears will buy back their shorts, adding to the buying pressure and increasing the strength of the rally. If the bears win, the bulls will have to sell out of their longs, and this will enhance the force of the bear channel.

When a climactic reversal occurs in a trend, the reversal usually takes place after a breakout of a trend channel line. A reversal back into a channel often leads to a test of the opposite side of the channel, which offers a good trading opportunity. Because of this, it is important to be looking for channels, and if you see a breakout through the trend channel line and an immediate and strong reversal, be prepared to take the reversal entry. Sometimes the trend will resume within a bar or two and break beyond the channel line again and that second breakout will also fail. When that happens, the reversal trade is even more reliable.

Sometimes a double top bear flag forms within the trading range after a buy climax, providing an additional reason to enter short into a trend reversal trade. If instead there is a double bottom bull flag, it is a buy setup. The opposite is true after a sell climax. If there is a double bottom bull flag after the spike up off the low, it is a buy setup. If the trading range after the reversal up instead forms a double top, it is a sell setup.

The reversal leg that leads to the trading range is often relatively small compared to the prior trend, but it usually breaks the trend line and it can be the first leg of an opposite trend. Despite that, it still can be easy to overlook, so whenever there is a climactic move, it is something that you should try to find. It may have a low-momentum drift toward the old extreme, leading to a failed test (a lower high at a bull top or a higher low at a bottom), or it could continue to a new extreme and there may not be a reversal. If instead it does reverse, the new, opposite trend sometimes becomes very strong very fast and often forms a spike and channel trend pattern.

An inside bar after a breakout bar is often soon followed by a trend bar in the opposite direction, creating a climactic reversal setup. As with all climactic reversal setups, the channel that follows can go either way, and the important thing is to be aware of both possibilities. Once the trend begins, look for with-trend setups.

Sometimes there can be an impressive spike, then a pullback, and then the start of a channel, only for the channel to fail and reverse direction. In hindsight, that pullback was the spike in the opposite direction and it led to a channel in the opposite direction. However, once you recognize it, then you know there is an opposite, new trend and you should try to take every with-trend entry.

Strong climactic reversals without a significant test of the extreme occur only a few times a month on 5 minute charts. These are sometimes called V bottoms and inverted V tops, which are simply two-bar reversals. The up and down spikes can contain many bars, but there is always a higher time frame where the pattern is a simple two-bar reversal. However, as with any type of reversal pattern, most attempts to form a climactic reversal fail, or the market at least tests the spike before reversing. In a bull market, most spike tops get tested, and in a bear market, most V bottoms get tested, no matter how emotional and strong the reversal appears to be. This is because these climaxes are reversal attempts, and traders know that most reversals fail. They are not willing to trust a reversal unless it gets tested.

However, if there is a bull trend and a pullback ends in a strong, emotional spike down, the low of that spike may or may not get tested. Once everyone senses that the pullback has ended and the trend is resuming, traders are eager to buy the trend. There is no hesitancy or uncertainty and there is no need for a test. Here, it is the bottom of a bull flag and not the bottom of a bear trend that is trying to reverse into a bull trend. Similarly, when there is a spike top in a pullback in a bear trend, the top of the spike may or may not get tested. It is just the top of a bear flag and not the top of a bull trend that is in the process of reversing.

Climaxes, parabolas, and V tops and bottoms all have one thing in common, and that is their slope. Instead of it being linear (a straight line), it is curved and increasing. At some point, the market quickly reverses direction, and usually, at the very least, there will be a protracted sideways move and possibly a trend reversal. All of these patterns are simply trend channel line overshoots and reversals and therefore they should be traded as such; giving them special names adds nothing to your trading success. The trend channel line might not be obvious at the moment of the reversal, but once a parabolic move is underway, price action traders are constantly drawing and redrawing trend channel lines and then watching for an overshoot and reversal. The best reversals have large reversal bars and preferably a second entry. The first leg of the reversal will almost always break the trend line, and if it does not, then the reversal is suspect, and a trading range or continuation pattern becomes much more likely. When trading countertrend, it is better to wait for a test of the old trend before trading in the opposite direction. For example, it is a more profitable strategy to buy a higher low after a sell climax than it is to buy the initial reversal up, because too many reversal attempts fail. If a second entry fails, the old trend will likely run for at least two more legs.

Parabolic moves often have three pushes and therefore are wedge tops, which are discussed more in a following chapter. The third push is a strong breakout that runs for several bars to a support or resistance level, which may not be obvious, and then the market stalls and can reverse sharply. The breakout is beyond a two-push pattern where traders were expecting a reversal, like a higher high at the top of a trading range (or a lower low at the bottom). Remember, a higher high is just a two-legged rally, and therefore the reversal down is a low 2 short setup. Only experienced traders should ever attempt to fade a strong trend, even when it might be forming a climactic reversal. Most traders should wait to see if the always-in direction reverses before looking to trade in the opposite direction (for example, after a parabolic bull trend reverses down strongly enough to now be in a bear trend). If the market triggers the climactic reversal short after the second or third buy climax, and then rallies above the high, there is sometimes a violent breakout as traders switch from trading range mode back into bull trend mode, expecting a measured move up. If the market reverses down from a buy climax, the reversal down usually comes from some form of double top that might only be obvious on a smaller time frame chart but can be inferred from the 5 minute chart. The reversal can be sharp, or the market might pull back for several bars and form a flag, which then might break out in the wrong direction (down, instead of up), before the market then moves down as fast as it moved up. Trend lines and trend channel lines should hold and lead to reversals away from the lines, indicating that they were successful in containing the trend. Sometimes one will fail to hold the price action and the market will not stop and reverse on the test of the line. The breaking of a trend line has the opposite implication from the breaking of a trend channel line. The break of a trend line means that a possible trend reversal is underway, but breaking a trend channel line means that the trend has increased in strength and is now steeper. However, most trend channel line breakouts fail within about five bars and the market then reenters the channel and usually pokes through the opposite side of the channel (it breaks through the trend line).

A trend line break is the first step in a trend reversal, and if the break is on strength, the odds of a successful test of the trend's extreme increase. For example, after a bear trend line break, the test of the low would likely form a higher low and then at least a second leg up, or a lower low and then at least a two-legged up move.

Steep trend lines with one- or two-bar false breakouts are reliable with trend patterns, and therefore attract a lot of traders. However, whenever a reliable pattern fails, then there will be an unusually large number of trapped traders. The reverse move will likely be a profitable trade, and it can be sharp and result in a trend reversal. These reversal attempts are common on the 1 minute chart, but it is far better to not trade countertrend off 1 minute charts since most reversals fail. You should almost always trade in the direction of the 5 minute chart.

Whenever a trend channel line fails (the market breaks through it instead of bouncing off it), you should assume that the trend is much stronger than you thought and you should look for with-trend entries. However, be aware that the trend channel line breakout might soon fail and lead to a reversal, so be prepared to exit any breakout pullback quickly if it starts to fail.

Trend channel line overshoots are parabolic moves because for the market to go beyond the trend channel line, the market is accelerating, which means that it is becoming parabolic. It the market reverses, it will usually have at least a 10-bar and two-legged correction. If it reenters the channel, it will usually poke out of the other side of the channel, beyond the trend line, and it may become a trend reversal.

Traditional technical analysis teaches that major reversals come with exceptional volume, especially at market bottoms. That is more often true with stocks, especially those that have smaller volume, but it is not a reliable sign in huge markets. Most major reversals up or down in markets like the SPY or Emini occur in the absence of clearly understandable volume patterns, although sometimes there is huge volume at a climactic market bottom, when there is a sell vacuum into a support level and the bears finally take profits and the bulls finally buy aggressively. When there is a reversal up from a bottom where one or more bars have 10 to 20 times the volume of the most of the bars of recent days, the odds of more follow-through buying are greater. Also, if there is a bull spike with 10 to 20 times the average volume and a range that is five or more times larger than most bars of recent days, the odds are good that there will be higher prices over the next many bars. The market will usually go up for at least a measured move. Much less often, the market instead falls below the bull spike and then has a measured move down.

Climactic tops are rarely as dramatic and rarely have useful volume patterns. Active traders who pay attention to volume will likely miss out on many good trades and make less money than if they simply traded on the price action alone. While it is true that most tradable tops and bottoms where the volume is unusually high will have a volume divergence on the 1 minute chart, most traders will make more money if they ignore it and carefully watch the price action on the 5 minute chart or some other higher time frame chart. The 1 minute volume divergence means that the final low will have less volume than a recent previous attempt to reverse up. There are usually tick and oscillator divergences as well, but experienced traders are aware of this when they see a tradable bottom, and will not feel a need to check for something that they already know is present.

The key to understanding climactic reversals is to realize that they are just failed breakouts. For example, when a bull trend goes on for 40 bars without much of a pullback and then has the biggest bull trend bar of the trend, and it has small tails and a close well above the high of the prior bar, giving it the look of an exceptionally strong breakout, the odds of follow-through buying are less than with all of the other breakouts earlier in the trend. This is because experienced traders will expect a transition into a trading range after a trend goes on for dozens of bars without much of a pullback. They know that the probabilities begin to favor this. If instead the market has the strongest breakout of the trend at this point, the market is trying to convert an overdone bull trend into an even steeper bull trend, and the chance of success is probably less than 30 percent. The bulls and bears look to fade the breakout, expecting it to fail and become an exhaustion gap instead of a measuring gap, and be followed by at least a two-legged, ten-bar correction to the moving average. The bulls sell out of their longs to take windfall profits and the bears short. Beginning traders do the opposite. The ones who are flat and missed the entire rally are afraid that they are now missing the strongest part of the bull trend and buy. The weak bears who have been holding, hoping for a reversal, are terrified and buy back their shorts, Both are doing the exact opposite of what the institutions are doing and are therefore doomed to lose money. The beginners are such a small part of the market that their effect is not significant, although decades ago this type of backwards behavior by beginners and experienced traders was probably an important component of climactic reversals. Today's smart traders don't buy in a panic, and instead fade likely climaxes. Most breakouts fail, and sometimes the strongest breakout attempts are the most likely to fail.

Figure 4.1   CLIMACTIC REVERSALS   **123**

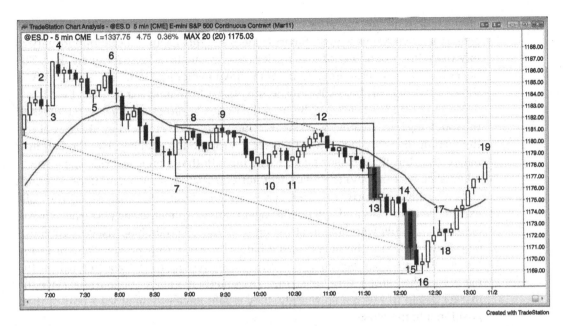

FIGURE 4.1 Late Acceleration Can Be Exhaustion

If a trend suddenly accelerates, it can be a successful breakout, leading to another leg down, or an exhaustive end of the trend. In Figure 4.1, bar 13 and bar 15 on this 5-minute Emini chart had very large ranges and bodies and followed several other bear bars, but signified opposite conditions. Bar 13 was a breakout below a trading range in a possible trend-resumption bear trend day. It became a measuring gap. Strong breakouts usually have at least two legs, as was the case here. The pullback after the second sell climax can be a single bar or several bars, and the low of one or more of those bars can be below the low of the sell climax, as it was here in the bear flag to bar 14.bar 15 was a larger bear trend bar and therefore represented even more intense selling, and the market became almost vertical. The last longs had sold out and there was no one left to sell. It became an exhaustion gap as the market reversed above its high. Consecutive sell climaxes often are followed by at least a 10-bar, two-legged reversal. (I use the phrase "10-bar, two-legged" often, and my intention is to say that the correction will last longer and be more complex than a small pullback. That type of correction usually requires at least 10 bars and two legs.) The strong bull reversal traded back into the trading range, which, like all trading ranges, was a magnet.

All strong bulls and bears love to see an exceptionally large trend bar like bar 15 after a protracted trend, because they expect it to be a brief, unusually great opportunity. A trend bar is a breakout, and since most breakout attempts fail, and this one is after a prior sell climax that did not have much of a correction and after a bull trend that has gone on for dozens of bars without a correction, the odds against a crash are very high. Smart traders see this as an unusual opportunity to buy when the probability of lower prices is very small, at least for many bars. The bears buy back their shorts and the bulls buy new longs. Both buy aggressively at the close of the bar, below its low, at the close of the next bar (especially if it is a less strong trend bar or has a body in the opposite direction), and at the close of the following bar. That bar was bar 16, which had a bull close. They also buy above the high of the prior bar. When they see a strong bull trend bar, like the bar after bar 16, they buy at its close and above its high. Both the bulls and the bears expect a larger correction, and the bears will not consider shorting again until at least a 10-bar, two-legged correction, and even then only if the rally looks weak. The bulls expect the same rally and will not be eager to take profits too early. The aggressive, experienced bulls who bought at the close of bar 15 could have used a protective stop equal to about the height of the bar, which was four points. They probably had at least a 60 percent chance of the market testing to at least the high of the bar before their stops were hit, so this was a mathematically sound trade. Once the market began to reverse up sharply, they would have swung at least part of their position into the close.

Weak traders see bar 15 in an opposite way. The weak bears who had been sitting on the sidelines, hoping for an easy pullback to short, see the market running away from them and they want to make sure they catch this next leg down, especially since bar 15 is such a strong bar. They see the large bear trend bar as a possible crash. They know that the probability is very low, but don't want to risk missing a huge reward, which they believe will more than offset the tiny probability. The weak bulls who bought early and maybe scaled in are terrified by the rapidity with which bar 15 fell and are afraid of relentless follow-through selling, so they sell out of their longs. These weak traders are trading on emotion and are competing against computers, which do not have emotion as one of the variables in their algorithms. Since the computers control the market, the emotions of the weak traders doom them to big losses on bars like bar 15.

Bar 11 was a second-entry buy signal for a lower low major trend reversal. The two-legged rally to bar 9 broke above the bear trend line of the sell-off from bar 6 to bar 7. However, only one bar closed above the moving average, so there was not impressive buying. The five-bar bull spike up to bar 12 might have been the start of a major bull trend reversal, but it failed to have any large bull trend bars and simply tested the bar 9 top of the trading range, where it formed a double top with bar 9. At this point, the market was either undergoing a weak major trend reversal up or testing the top of a trading range in a bear market (a bear flag). The large bar 13 bear trend bar was a breakout of the bear flag and a resumption of the bear trend. The attempt at a major trend reversal failed. The trend line break and the rally off the bar 11 low both lacked consecutive, large bull trend bars, and traders never saw the market as having flipped to always-in long.

Figure 4.2   CLIMACTIC REVERSALS **125**

FIGURE 4.2 Spike Up but Channel Down

Sometimes the market will have a spike up and then a spike down. This is usually followed by a trading range as the bulls and bears fight to form a channel. The bulls are trying to create a channel up, whereas the bears want one down.

As shown in Figure 4.2, the Globex 1 minute Emini spiked up on a 5:30 a.m. PST report, but formed a strong reversal bar down at bar 1. Bar 1 was a three-point-tall bar, which is big on a 1 minute chart and therefore qualifies as a possible spike down. Bar 3 was a two-legged move up, forming a low 2 in the possible new bear trend. Also, bar 2 was an ii variation if you look only at the bodies (the body of bar 2 was inside that of bar 1, which was inside that of the prior bull breakout bar, and an ii pattern indicates indecision), and the move up to bar 3 was a false breakout of the top of the ii pattern. The market went sideways for about 10 bars, which qualifies as a trading range after the down spike. Bar 4 had a minimal break above a minor trend line and then the market resumed its downtrend. Bar 5 was a second-chance entry. It was a pullback from the breakout below bar 2 and a failed micro channel breakout.

As a general rule, big up + big down = confusion = trading range, at least for a while, as was the case after the bar 1 bear reversal bar and buy climax.

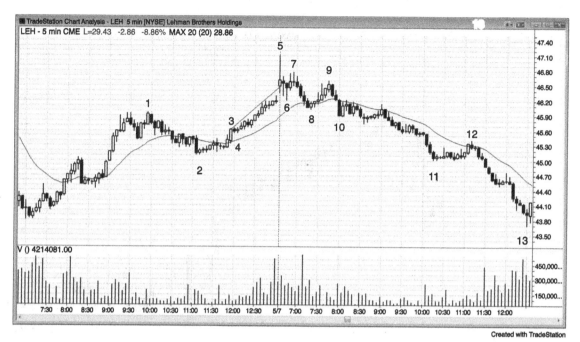

FIGURE 4.3 Spike Up and Down in One Bar

A large bar with a large tail on top is a spike up and a spike down, but in a single bar.

Sometimes the channel can be very tight as it was in Figure 4.3 after the bar 3 spike. There were more than 10 bars in a very tight channel, and this is unsustainable activity. Almost every bar had a higher high, low, and close. However, being in an unsustainable mode is not reason enough to go short, because the market can sustain this unusual behavior longer than you can sustain your account. Whenever the market does something extreme, it will soon be followed by the opposite type of behavior. An extreme trend will be followed by a trading range and sometimes a reversal, and an extreme trading range will be followed by a trend.

The tight channel is basically an upwardly sloping tight trading range, and it had to break out eventually. It broke to the upside on bar 5, and when that failed, it was likely to break to the downside as it ultimately did. The market went sideways for 5 bars and then formed a lower high at bar 7, completing a small trading range after the bar 5 spike down (it spiked up and reversed down in what had to be a spike down on a 1 minute chart). On a higher time frame chart, the sell-off to bar 2 broke below the bull trend line, and the rally to bar 5 was a higher high major trend reversal.

Bar 9 can have been viewed as an expansion of the trading range, a lower high major trend reversal after the bar 8 break below the bull trend line, or a double

Figure 4.3

CLIMACTIC REVERSALS **127**

top bear flag (it was approximately the same level as bar 7, and at least a second attempt to rally to the bar 5 high). The name is irrelevant, but it was a good short setup. The market then trended lower for the rest of the day, and accelerated as it fell.

Bar 10 was a three-bar bear spike and the move down to bar 11 was a channel. Yesterday, bar 3 was a spike followed by a channel that began at bar 4. The start of the channel usually gets tested within a day or two (the bar 4 low was taken out with the bear trend following the climactic top that began with the bar 5 large tail, but the bar 10 high beginning of the channel down was not tested during the following two weeks).

The move to bar 12 barely broke above the bear trend line, but it was a weak move. Therefore, traders should have continued to look only for shorts and not a trend reversal. A break of a trend line alone is not enough reason to look for a reversal. The break has to be strong before traders will believe that the bulls will be able to sustain a strong move up.

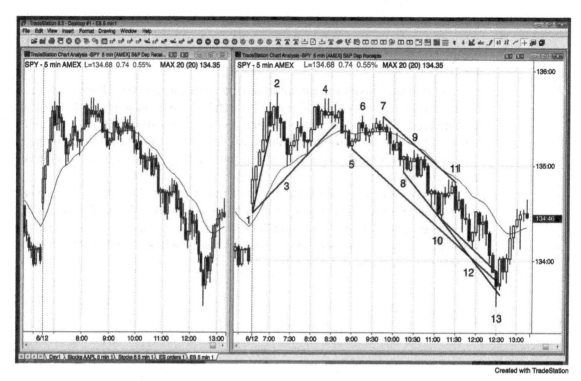

FIGURE 4.4   After a Climax, the Channel Direction Can Be Unclear for a While

After a buy climax (a spike up and then a spike down, sometimes within a single bar), there will often be a bull channel that fails, and then the market will form a bear channel. Both charts in Figure 4.4 show the 5 minute SPY. The run-up to bar 2 was a strong bull spike. After the sharp moving average pullback to bar 3 that broke a trend line, the bull channel began. However, it failed in a two-legged lower high at bar 4. Once the market broke below the bull channel with the bar 5 pullback, which also broke the major bull trend line, it became obvious that this was not a bull spike and channel day and that the market was forming a trading range. This became a triangle top, and then a spike and channel down. Some traders saw the move down to bar 3 as the important bear spike, while others saw the move down to bar 5 as more important. Both spikes were part of the selling pressure that resulted in the bears gaining control over the market.

Bar 8 formed a double bottom bull flag with bar 3, and it was the second long entry for the moving average gap bar. Once the buy failed, it was clear that the bears were in control and that a bear channel was underway, with the push down to bar 5 being the bear spike. At this point, you should try to take all short entries and consider any longs to be scalps until there is a climactic overshoot of the bear

Figure 4.4   CLIMACTIC REVERSALS   **129**

trend channel line and reversal up. In general, it is better to ignore the long setups and just trade with the trend when there is a strong bear trend like this. Bar 13 reversed up from breaking three such lines.

Consecutive climaxes often result in a significant correction, but the odds go down if there is a significant correction after each climax. There was a sell climax down to bar 3 and another down to bar 5, but the rallies to bars 4 and 7 relieved the selling pressure and reduced the need for a sharp reversal up. However, in the bear channel from bar 7 to bar 13, there was no relief from the intense selling that occurred during the climaxes from bar 9 to bar 10 and from bar 11 to bar 12. The four-bear trend bar plunge down to bar 13 was the exhaustive sell climax that showed the capitulation of the weak traders. The third sell climax is usually the most dramatic, and it typically has a large bear spike, which overshoots trend channel lines and creates a parabolic bend to the channel. The parabolic slope indicates that the momentum down was increasing as the market was falling, and a parabolic trend usually is in its last stage. The final weak bulls gave up and sold at any price, and the final weak bears finally joined the other bears by shorting at the market during the free fall. This was the third consecutive sell climax without a significant break, and channels often end with the third push. The tight channel meant that there was urgency, and the momentum increased on the way down. The move to bar 13 collapsed through the trend channel line, which is how many channels end.

So what about the *strong* bulls and bears? They see the climaxes and understand the excess. The strong bears already shorted higher and were not interested in shorting down here. They would short only a significant pullback, maybe near the top of the channel where they originally shorted. With no more strong or weak bears shorting and no more weak bulls exiting, the selling pressure disappeared. The strong bulls saw the collapse and stepped aside. They knew that the market was going lower, so there was no incentive for them to buy until they believed that the market was as low as it would go. They wanted to buy at the best price and that was at the bottom. The different institutions each had their own measures of value and excess, and when enough of them agreed that the market was a good value, there was enough strong buying for a rally. Also, the strong bears understood the excess and took profits. Their buying contributed to the rally. They would have considered shorting again if the market was able to get back to around the start of the channel, which is where they had shorted earlier and made a profit.

The bottom is always at a confluence of magnets. Here, it was just beyond a measured move down from the open of the bull spike at bar 1 to the close of the final bar of the bull spike five bars later. It was also a trend channel line overshoot from a trend channel line drawn across the two swing lows of yesterday (not shown), and the bar 13 two-bar reversal up was also the signal for a large, two-day expanding triangle bottom. Bar 13 also overshot three smaller trend channel lines created by the channel down from bar 7.

FIGURE 4.5   Opposite Trend Bars Create a Climactic Reversal

A trend bar in one direction followed by another in the opposite direction is a climactic reversal, and the channel that follows can be in either direction since there are spikes in both directions. In Figure 4.5, AAPL had several climaxes and reversals on this 5 minute chart.

Bar 3 was a large bear trend bar and therefore a spike, a breakout, and a climax. It was immediately followed by an even larger trend bar in the opposite direction, which was a buy climax. It was tempting to assume that this represented even stronger conviction, but you needed to be patient and let the market show you where it was going. Your job is to follow the institutions and not guess what they might do.

The rally to bar 5 was a higher high breakout pullback from the bar 3 bear breakout, and a pause after the bar 4 bull breakout. Bar 6 was another bear spike and therefore another sell climax. The tight trading range after bar 6 was a pullback from the bar 4 bull breakout, and a possible start of the bear channel following the bar 3 breakout and bar 6 bear spike. During the tight trading range that followed bar 6, the bulls were buying in an attempt to create a bull channel, and the bears were shorting as they tried to create a bear channel. The bears ultimately won. Even though the bar 4 buy climax was a larger and stronger trend bar than were the bar 3 and bar 6 bear spikes, the bears were able to overcome the bulls.

Figure 4.5   CLIMACTIC REVERSALS   **131**

Bar 15 was a bull reversal bar and since it had a fairly large range and a big body, it was a buy climax. It immediately followed a large bear bar, which was a sell climax. Since the channel down had been so steep, it was more likely that the first attempt to break out would fail. Whenever there is a small entry bar in a reversal in a strong trend, the odds favor it becoming just a with-trend flag. Here, the two bars after the bar 15 reversal were small, showing the weakness of the bulls, and they formed a bear flag.

All two-bar reversals are opposite climaxes, albeit usually small. Bar 17 was a small bear climax followed immediately by a bull trend bar, setting up a two-bar reversal. The spike down was the sell climax, and the spike up was the bull breakout. The spike up lasted for three bars. Bar 19 was a bear spike, which was a sell climax and a breakout of the bear flag, which was also a pullback to the moving average. It was reversed by the bar 10 buy climax.

The bull spike from bar 23 to bar 25 or consisting of just bars 24 and 25 was reversed by the smaller bar 29 bear trend bar. That sell climax was followed by a couple of dojis and then a sell-off into the close. The bear channel ended on the next day.

Bar 31 was a buy climax followed by the bar 32 sell climax, which was reversed on the next bar. Bar 33 was another large bull trend bar, and therefore a buy climax, and it broke out above the opening range. It was followed by a four-bar pullback, which contained a bear breakout bar, and then the rally resumed in the form of a bull channel.

The rally to bar 18 broke above the bear channel from bar 5 to bar 17, but stalled at the moving average. The market turned down from the double top at bar 20, but found buyers at the bar 22 low, where the market formed a double bottom bull flag. Was that double bottom higher low a good setup for a major trend reversal? It was not ideal since, although the two-legged rally above the bear trend line to bar 20 had many bull bars, it could not hold above the moving average and was therefore not strong. The two-legged rally from the bar 22 double bottom to bar 28 was surprisingly strong, but many traders saw it as the first rally in a bear trend and therefore possibly just a bear rally instead of a new bull trend. It was strong enough, however, to make traders look to buy a test of the bear low. Traders bought above the bull bar that followed the bar 32 sell-off on the open of the next day, and again above the second bull signal bar that formed two bars later. It created a second signal (a micro double bottom with the bull bar after bar 32), and was therefore more reliable. The result was a major trend reversal from the lower low after the strong bear trend line break (the rally to bar 28). Because it unfolded over so many bars, the pattern was probably easier to see on a higher time frame chart.

FIGURE 4.6 V Tops and Bottoms Are Rare

V bottoms and inverted V tops that reverse the market without first having a significant pullback are rare. Most spikes fail to immediately reverse the market, and instead the end of the spike usually gets tested. In Figure 4.6, the bar 3 wedge bottom led to a rally to the moving average. This was a potential V bottom, but the sell-off to the bar 5 higher low tested the bottom of the spike. Most reversals that are called inverted V tops or V bottoms are actually some other type of bottom, like a final flag reversal or a micro double top or bottom. For example, the reversal up from the bar 3 low was a wedge bottom, and a final flag reversal, based on the two-bar bear flag that followed bar 2. The bar 19 bottom was a micro double bottom, because the bar before bar 19 traded down and then up into its close. Bar 19 traded down again and the bar after it traded up, creating a micro double bottom. The double bottom could easily be seen on the 1 minute chart (not shown) and is easily inferred based on this 5 minute chart.

Bar 20 was the top of a protracted rally off of the bar 19 bear spike and an attempt at a V bottom, but the bar 19 spike low was tested at the close of the day.

The move up to bar 4 was a strong break above the bear trend line, and that made bulls look to buy either a lower low or a higher low test of the bear 3 low. The bulls wanted to see a strong break above the trend line and not just a drift that broke above the trend line by going sideways.

Figure 4.6   CLIMACTIC REVERSALS   **133**

Traders expected that the three consecutive sell climaxes down to bar 3 would be followed by a large correction with at least two legs sideways to up and lasting at least 10 bars. The final climax often has the largest bear trend bar of the entire move, as it did here two bars before bar 3. Strong bears would look to sell only after a significant pullback, whereas strong bulls bought aggressively, and they would have bought more if the market went lower. There was no group of strong traders willing to sell at the bar 3 low after the third sell climax in the tight channel down from the high of the day. Strong bears were buying back their shorts, and strong bulls were aggressively buying new longs.

The two-legged rally to bar 6 broke well above the bull trend line, alerting traders that the next push down could test the bar 3 bear low and then reverse up. Bar 7 was a double bottom major trend reversal. Some traders saw the first bottom as the bar 3 low, whereas others saw the pattern as a double bottom bull flag with the bar 5 low.

Since most reversal attempts fail, including climactic reversals, many traders fade the reversals, expecting the trend to resume at least enough for a trade. For example, as strong as the rally to bar 4 was, many bears saw it as simply a pullback to the moving average and a double top with the pullback from bar 1. They shorted what they saw was a great opportunity to sell at a brief high price, and took profits on bar 5, as evidenced by the tail at its bottom and the small bull body.

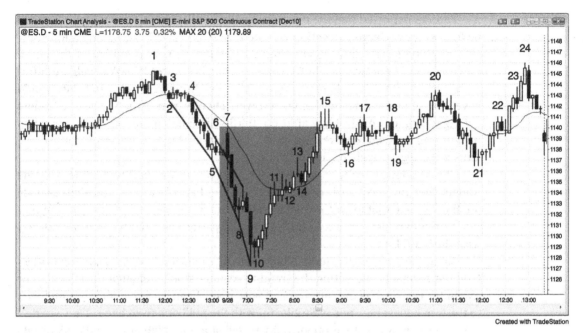

FIGURE 4.7 V Bottoms Are Rare but Strong

A V bottom or an inverted V top without any significant test of the spike occurs only a few times a month on 5 minute charts. Figure 4.7 shows a 5 minute V bottom, which is a sell climax and a climactic reversal. The sell-off on the open down to bar 9 was a parabolic move, which is a type of sell climax. You can see how the slope of the three trend channel lines became increasingly steep (from bar 2 to bar 3, bar 5 to bar 8, and bar 8 to bar 9), which indicated panic. Traders wanted to sell at any price. The bears pressed their shorts, quickly adding to their positions as the market fell in the strong bear spike. However, when there are consecutive sell climaxes, the market soon runs out of traders who are eager or even willing to short without a significant pullback. This lack of selling creates a buy imbalance, and it is usually followed by a rally that lasts at least 10 bars and has at least two legs.

Whenever there is a sell climax or a pair of consecutive sell climaxes as there was here (the bear spikes that ended at bars 8 and 9) and the increased selling comes after the market has already fallen for 10 or more bars, there is a good chance that there will be a strong reversal. The strong bulls stepped aside because they expected the market to trade down to some confluence of magnets; once it got there, they appeared out of nowhere and bought aggressively. The strong bears understood what was going on and they quickly took profits on their shorts once

Figure 4.7   CLIMACTIC REVERSALS   **135**

they saw the exceptionally large bar 9 sell climax bar, and were unwilling to consider shorting again until the market was much higher. The strong bulls and bears were both buying at the close of bar 9 and on the two-bar micro double bottom that followed, and the market could only go up.

When there is a strong spike in a market that appears to be falling too far, too fast, there is a possibility that the sell-off is a sell vacuum down to test a support level, and many traders will watch for a sign of a climactic reversal. There was a strong bear spike down to bar 8 and then a one-bar low 1 sell signal. Experienced bulls and bears were aware that if there was a particularly large bear trend bar within a bar or two, it could have been an exhaustive end to the selling. That low 1 signal bar could have been a one-bar final flag (discussed in Chapter 7). When bar 9 closed and was an especially large bear trend bar, it was a consecutive sell climax and could have led to a final flag reversal and a rally that could reach 10 or more bars and have two or more legs. Many bears buy back their shorts in such a scenario because they are aware that the market might rally sharply. If there is a reasonable sell signal after about 10 bars, they will look to short again. In this case, the market rallied strongly and the bears saw no sign that it would sell off, so they never saw a sensible setup to short.

Aggressive bulls also thought that the market was likely to rally and they, too, bought. Some of the bulls and bears bought on the close of bar 9, risking about the height of bar 9; some chose to risk less, like maybe a couple of points. Other bulls and bears bought during and on the close of the next bar, since it was a small bar and therefore a sign that the selling was abating. Others waited until bar 10 had a strong bull close and bought on the close or above its highs. Finally, the remaining bears bought back their shorts, and the cautious bulls, who wanted to be certain that the market had flipped to always-in long, bought during the five-bar bull spike off the low and during the rally that followed. Many bulls pressed their longs, adding to their positions during the fast, strong bull spike up from the bar 10 low.

When the market is moving quickly and experienced traders' positions have immediate profits that are growing fast, they will often buy more as they try to maximize their profits during this brief, exceptional opportunity. This is the opposite of what they would do when the market is in a tight trading range, like it was during the first 20 bars on the left of the chart. When there is little movement, most traders step aside and are comfortable not trading until a trend begins. However, institutions and high-frequency trading firms continue to trade heavily all day long, including in tight trading ranges.

A perfect V bottom, where the market goes straight down and then up, is extremely rare. Most V bottoms have subtle price action that shows hesitation in the selling, as it did here, alerting traders to a possible reversal. The bar after bar 8 was a one-bar final flag, which alerted traders to a possible reversal up after another one- or two-bar sell climax. Bar 10 formed a micro double bottom with the bar before it, and a micro triple bottom with the bar before it and the low of bar 9. This was a micro three-push down pattern, and a likely triangle on a smaller time frame chart, and it gave the bulls a low risk, high probability entry after the consecutive sell climaxes and one-bar final flag.

Volume for most bars when the market was quiet yesterday was about 5,000 to 10,000 contracts per bar. Bar 9 had 114,000 contracts. This amount of volume was almost entirely institutional. Was it more likely due to shorting by the institutions because they finally decided that the market was going down after it had already gone down for many bars, or was it due to aggressive buying by the bulls and bears because they saw this consecutive sell climax as the end of the selling for the time being? Institutions are smart money, so whenever they all suddenly agree and trade extremely heavily in a protracted bear trend, the odds are very high that the trading is due to aggressive buying by both the bears (taking profits) and the bulls. If institutions are smart, profitable, and responsible for every tick, why would they ever sell the lowest tick in a bear trend? It is because that is what their algorithms have been doing profitably all of the way down, and some are designed to continue to do it until it is clear that the bear trend is no longer in effect. They lose on that final sell, but make enough on all of their earlier trades to offset that loss. Remember, all of their systems lose between 30 and 70 percent of the time, and this is one of those times. There are also HFT firms that will scalp for even a single tick right down to the low tick of a bear trend. The low is always at a support level, and many HFT firms will sell a tick or two above support to try to capture that final tick, if their systems show that this is a profitable strategy. Other institutions are selling as part of a hedge in another market (stocks, options, bonds, currencies, etc.) because they perceive that their risk/reward ratio is better by placing the hedge. The volume is not from small individual traders, because they are responsible for less than 5 percent of the volume at major turning points.

Figure 4.8   CLIMACTIC REVERSALS   **137**

FIGURE 4.8   Spike Pullbacks Are More Common Than Spike Reversals

Spikes are tests of the strength of both the trend and countertrend traders. Up spikes in bull markets and down spikes in bear markets usually get tested, since spike reversals are much less common than simple temporary trend extremes, which usually get tested and exceeded. Down spikes in bull markets and up spikes in bear markets are pullbacks and may or may not get tested. They are already tests, testing the determination of the countertrend and the resolve of the with trend traders. The pullbacks often come close to flipping the always in position to the opposite direction, but there is inadequate follow-through. Strong traders love these reversal attempts, because they know that most will fail. Whenever the countertrend traders are able to create one, the with trend traders come in and heavily fight the reversal attempt, and usually win. They see these sharp countertrend moves as great opportunities to enter in the direction of the trend at a great price that is likely to exist only briefly, and quickly become simply a spike pullback in the trend. In Figure 4.8, the bar 1, bar 3, and bar 6 bear spikes in a bear market and the bar 4 and bar 8 bull spikes were all tested on this 60 minute AAPL chart.

Bar 4 was a bull spike in a bear trend and did not have to be tested, but it was tested about 10 bars later.

Bar 8 was a bull spike in a trading range and a break of a major trend line, so it was likely to be tested.

Bar 7 was a new swing low, but not a spike, so it did not have to be tested.

FIGURE 4.9   Spike Pullbacks Usually Don't Get Tested

A spike *pullback* does not have to get tested since traders agree that the trend is resuming and they are eager to get on board, but a spike *reversal* usually gets tested because it is countertrend and traders are less willing to believe that a reversal will succeed.

Most of the bear spikes in bull trends are caused by profit-taking bulls who are looking to buy again lower, and by aggressive bears who are only looking for a short scalp. When the market makes its sharp move down, like at bar 3, bulls buy aggressively to initiate long positions or to add to their longs, and the bears buy back their profitable scalps. Once the bears are able to get follow-through selling, as they did in the move down to bar 7, they expect that the market is becoming two-sided enough to be transitioning into a trading range or even a major trend reversal. Rather than scalping shorts at the next rally, they will begin to hold some or all of their position for a swing down. The bulls will also expect a deeper selloff and will only buy much lower, and only if there is a clear buy signal. With both sides unwilling to buy until the market falls further than on past pullbacks, the chance of a deeper pullback, a trading range, or even a major trend reversal increase.

Bar 3 in Figure 4.9 was a bear spike in a strong bull trend and was unlikely to be tested. It was simply the first moving average gap bar and it trapped bears. As strong as the selling was, there was not enough follow-through selling to convince traders that the market had reversed into an always-in short direction. The bears who shorted during the spike realized this, quickly bought back their shorts, stepped aside, and waited for another possible opportunity to reverse the market. The bulls bought aggressively, since they realized that the bears had failed and that this markdown was a brief opportunity to buy at a great price. They look forward to bear spikes because they know that most reversal attempts fail and therefore become great buy setups. With no one left willing to sell, the market went up sharply for many bars.

Bar 6 was a bear spike that followed a wedge top, making it likely to be tested since at least two legs down were expected.

Bar 7 was a bear spike in a bear leg and was tested with a higher low that led to a trend resumption of the higher time frame bull trend, based on the wedge bull flag of bars 4, 6, and 7.

Bar 11 was a strong spike down and a possible first leg down of a new bear trend, since it followed the bar 10 higher high. At this point, it was unlikely to be a pullback in a bull trend and therefore was likely to get tested. The market was likely to have at least two legs down after the strong bull trend line break (in the move down to bar 7) and then the higher high.

Bar 13 was the bottom of a two-legged pullback in a large bull trend. This could have led to a new bull high, since it was above the bar 7 low and the market was therefore still making higher lows and highs and might still have been in a bull trend. With the momentum down so strong, it was better to wait for a rally from here and then a higher low before going long. The market broke to the downside with a large gap.

Bars 14 and 15 were bull spikes in a strong bear trend and did not have to be tested.

Bar 17 was a bull spike in a bear trend and therefore did not have to be tested, and it could simply have been another lower high in the bear trend, which has a series of lower highs and lows. However, it followed a small wedge bottom (bar 15 was the pullback from the first push down), which was likely to have at least two legs up, so the move to bar 17 was the first of the two possible legs. Also, the bar 16 low was in the area of the bar 1 tight trading range, which was an area of support, and therefore a possible area where a trading range could reasonably be expected to form. This meant that there was a good chance for a second rally from the bar 18 double bottom. The rally to bar 17 broke the bear trend line (for the trend from bar 12 down to bar 16), making traders wonder if it was going to be followed by a test of the bear low and then either a trading range or a major trend reversal. It turned out to be the start of a large trading range that continued to the end of the chart.

FIGURE 4.10   Test of a Bull Spike

As shown in Figure 4.10, Research in Motion (RIMM) closed yesterday with a strong bull spike, so the odds were excellent that today was going to try to exceed it. Although today's rally was sloppy and did not look particularly bullish, the bears still could not put two consecutive closes below the moving average. This chart was going up, but its strength was deceptive.

Figure 4.11   CLIMACTIC REVERSALS   **141**

FIGURE 4.11 Inverted V Top

As shown in Figure 4.11, this bar 2 climactic opening reversal (inverted V top) in the ProShares UltraShort Financials ETF (SKF) was simply a reversal after breaking out of the top of a small bear trend channel line (dotted line). It was also a second entry after breaking above yesterday's high, and the end of a leg 1 = leg 2 trend resumption that began at yesterday's open. It was the third consecutive buy climax since the open without a significant pullback and a possible one-bar final flag reversal (the bear bar after bar 1 was the one-bar high 1 bull flag). On a higher time frame chart, yesterday's sell-off broke below the bull trend line, and bar 2 was a reversal down from a higher high. It was a measured move up from yesterday's trading range, but this alone is not reason enough to short a bull trend. When a strong trend reaches an area of a measured move, the bulls are taking profits, but bears will short only if there are other factors, like there were here.

Bar 2 was a micro double top with the bull trend bar before it. The market went up on the bull trend bar and then up again on the tail at the top of bar 2. It went down to the bottom of bar 2 and had a third push up to the high of the small doji bar that followed, creating a micro head and shoulders top or triangle, which was likely visible on a smaller time frame chart. The top was also a one-bar final flag reversal from the one-bar final flag that followed bar 1. The bodies of bar 2 and the doji that followed formed an ii with the body of the bull bar before bar 2.

FIGURE 4.12   Climactic Reversal with More Reasons to Reverse

Climactic reversals are more reliable when other factors are involved. As shown in Figure 4.12, the 5 minute Oil Service HOLDRS (OIH) had a climactic opening reversal below yesterday's low and it was also a reversal of three trend channel line overshoots. A trader should have bought above the large two-bar reversal at bar 1, and again at the high 2 first pullback at bar 2, expecting at least two legs up. Always swing part when two legs are likely, because sometimes there will be a new trend rather than just a two-legged pullback.

Bar 1 was a two-bar reversal bottom. The bar before bar 1 was a large bear trend bar, larger than the bear bar before it and with a close well below it. This means that it was a breakout below that bar, and that the smaller bear trend bar was a variant of a one-bar final flag. It was probably a small final flag on a smaller time frame chart.

Figure 4.13   CLIMACTIC REVERSALS   **143**

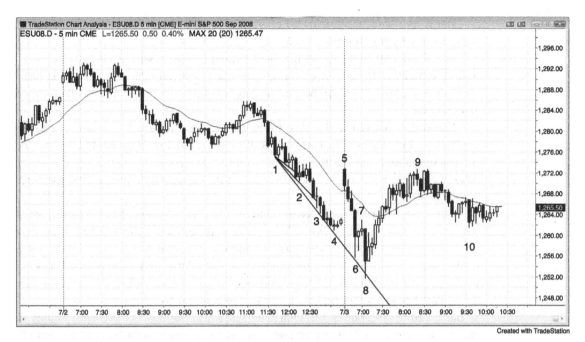

FIGURE 4.13 Don't Buy Tests of a Bear Trend Channel Line

Countertrend traders are always drawing trend channel lines, hoping for an over-shoot and a reversal that will allow for at least a scalp and preferably a two-legged countertrend move. When a channel is steep, it is a losing strategy to buy every reversal from a trend channel line overshoot. Instead wait until there is a strong breakout of the channel, like the big gap up to bar 5 in Figure 4.13, and then look to buy the breakout pullback, like the bar 8 second attempt to reverse yesterday's low.

Bar 2 broke a small trend channel line, but there was no earlier countertrend strength and the setup bar had only a small bull body. Smart traders would have waited for a second entry, especially a higher low, and if one did not develop, they would have viewed this as a with-trend setup, which it turned out to be. Notice how the breakout below bar 2 was in the form of a strong bear trend bar. This is because there were many longs who entered early on this small wedge, and most would not concede that the reversal had failed until there was a move below the bar 2 low of the wedge. That is where their protective stops were. Also, many bears had entry stops there as well because a failed wedge usually runs about the height of the wedge as a minimum, creating a great short entry for the measured move down. When a bear channel is steep like this, smart bears will have limit orders to short at or above the high of the prior bar, exactly where overly eager bulls are buying.

Bar 3 overshot another trend channel line, but there was no entry signal so there were very few trapped bulls.

Bar 5 opened well above the bear channel, but it was a 20 gap bar short and essentially a first moving average gap bar (close enough—its body was large and entirely above the exponential moving average), creating a trend from open move down.

Bar 6 did not reach the trend channel line, so although it tried to reverse yesterday's low, the reversal attempt was suspect. Most traders would have waited for the overshoot, and in its absence would have wanted at least a second entry. Also, the signal bar was a doji with only a tiny body, which meant that the bulls were not strong.

Bar 8 overshot the bear trend channel line, and the signal bar was an inside bar with a good-sized bull body. This setup was also a second attempt to reverse yesterday's low, creating a dependable opening reversal setup for a possible low of the day. It was a reversal up from the bar 7 final flag and a lower low breakout pullback from the bar 5 break above the bear channel. Remember, a bear channel is a bull flag. Some traders reasonably saw it as a major trend reversal after the rally to bar 5 broke well above the bear trend line and the moving average. Finally, it was a consecutive sell climax and its body was the largest bear body of the sell-off, which is common at the end of consecutive sell climaxes.

Figure 4.14

CLIMACTIC REVERSALS **145**

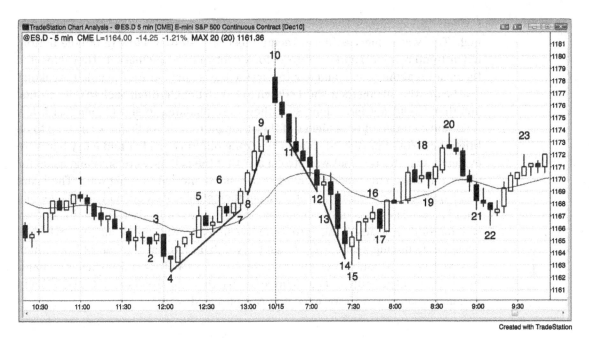

FIGURE 4.14 Increased Slope Usually Means Climactic Emotion

Once the slope increases, the trend is accelerating and probably about to correct. This is because the increased slope indicates increased emotion, and once the emotional traders have exited, there is neither anyone left to exit nor anyone willing to enter the trend until there is a pullback. The move up from bar 8 in Figure 4.15 was steeper than the bull trend before it, and the entire bull trend ended with the gap up bear reversal at bar 10.

The move down from bar 13 was steeper than the bear channel before it, and this sell climax was reversed up at the bar 15 strong bull trend bar, which formed a double bottom with the bar 4 start of the bull spike up to bar 10. These two days had a huge spike up and then a huge spike down and formed a large buy climax. A climax is usually followed by a trading range, as it was here in the two-legged rally to bar 20.

The large bear trend bar before bar 14 was seen at the time as either a breakout that could lead to a measured move down, or an exhaustive sell climax that might lead to a reversal up, lasting about 10 bars and two legs. Since it followed such a steep series of bear bars without a correction, it was likely the end of unsustainable and therefore climactic behavior. Many traders wait to begin buying until they see a large bear trend bar like this. Some buy on the close of the bar, but with the low of yesterday so close, many traders waited to see if the market might fall a little further. Those traders bought as bar 15 was forming, on its close, and above its high. This was a successful sell vacuum test of yesterday's low (a double bottom major trend reversal) and the buyers took control over the market. They expected the bear breakout to fail, and bar 15 was the buy signal bar for the failed breakout. The bears who swung their shorts down to bar 15 bought them back to take profits, and they would not have done so if they were planning to short again just a few ticks and a couple of bars higher. If they thought that the pullback was going to be brief, they would have held short. The strong bull reversal bar and entry bar were evidence that the reversal was strong and that the sellers were stepping aside for about ten bars. This made the market one-sided and led to a big rally. The bears were looking for a reasonable setup to put their shorts back on, and did not get one until bar 20. The bulls understood that the bears were likely to come in, so they sold out of their longs to take profits, and planned to wait for about 10 bars before considering buying again. They bought seven bars later at the bar 22 low, which reversed up in a double bottom with the bar 17 low. It was a higher low major trend reversal (the rally to bar 20 broke above the bear trend down to bar 15) and a triangle (bars 4 and 15 were the first two pushes down).

Figure 4.15   CLIMACTIC REVERSALS   **147**

FIGURE 4.15 Reversals Need Momentum

When a climax pattern fails to form any countertrend momentum, assume that you read the market wrong and are looking to trade in the wrong direction. Wedge reversals are not the same as wedge pullbacks, even though they can look the same. You need to pay attention to the context. If there is a wedge-shaped pullback in a bull trend, you can buy the first signal since you are buying in a bull trend. Unfortunately, when the market is in a bear trend, overly eager bulls treat all wedge bottoms as pullbacks, but most are reversals. When a wedge is a reversal, it is a countertrend trade and you should wait for a higher low before buying, and only after there has been a strong break of a trend line. Trying to scalp longs in a strong bear trend is a losing strategy.

As shown in Figure 4.15, bar 4 completed a three-push down move from bars 2 and 3, and also bounced off a bear trend channel line from bars 1 and 3. However, the market went sideways rather than up. The bulls were not strong so what appeared to be excess bearishness was not an excess at all. Whenever there is a strong bear trend, it is always better to only look for shorts until after there is a higher low, and even if you then buy, you need to be ready to short if the bear trend sets up a low 2.

Bar 8 was a bull reversal bar until the final seconds before it closed, and it quickly sold off into a bear trend bar. What overly eager bulls thought was going to be a bull reversal bar at the bottom of a wedge and two bear trend channel lines turned into a bear breakout of the bear trend channel lines, which meant that everyone now agreed that there was much more to go. This was confirmed by the series of bear trend bars that followed the wedge reversal failure. If you watched the market action, you would have seen the bull reversal bar collapse into a bear trend bar and you then would have shorted it, knowing that there were trapped early-entry longs who had bought what they thought was going to be a strong bull reversal bar off a bear trend channel line (don't front-run the bars; always wait for them to close and the next bar to confirm the reversal). Even without knowing this, shorting one tick below the low of that bear trend channel line breakout is still a smart trade.

Bar 11 was another three-push down pattern, but with all of those dojis and large, overlapping bars, a second signal was needed for any long, and traders should have been looking for a small bar near the high of the barbwire to short (like bar 12, which clearly trapped longs on the breakout from the bull reversal bar entry one bar earlier). Bar 11 was a bad bull reversal bar because there was no prior significant bull strength in the form of a break above the bear trend line, and it had too much overlap with the prior bars, forcing you to be buying near the high of a bear trading range (remember, buy low, sell high!). This had been a very strong bear trend day, and the best traders would not have been looking for wedges. Instead, they would have been looking to short near the moving average. Since there were so few, the bears were very strong and smart shorts would have been selling every failed buy signal as well as low 1 and low 2 entries.

There were consecutive sell climaxes down to bars 2, 3, 6, and 9 and down from bar 12. The move down was not in a tight channel, and each excess was worked off by the market going sideways for about 10 bars. This created a series of trending trading ranges, which is common in strong trends, and it prevented an exhaustive climactic reversal.

Figure 4.16   CLIMACTIC REVERSALS   **149**

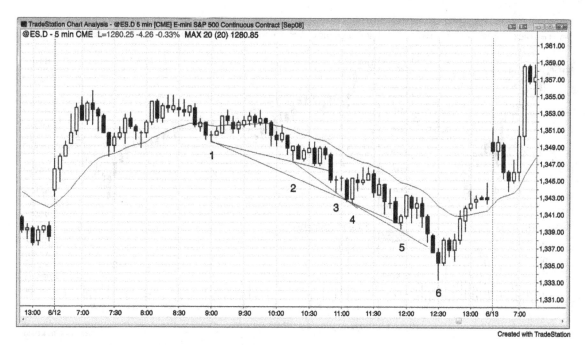

FIGURE 4.16   Too Many Trend Channel Lines

Whenever you find yourself drawing multiple trend channel lines, you are invariably blinded to what is in front of you by your anxiety over what you can't believe is happening (see Figure 4.16). Even though the trend is in a bear channel and channels have a lot of two-sided trading, they can last much longer than what seems possible. Always assume that any channel will last forever, and once it finally does not, then change your mind. The two-sided trading gives the appearance that it will soon reverse, but most reversal attempts of anything fail. The trend is strong and you are missing all of the with-trend shorts because all you are seeing are trend channel lines and potential reversals in what you believe is an overdone sell-off in a trading range day (channels in spike and channel patterns always look that way). Be patient and trade only with the trend until there is a reversal that is so clear and strong that you don't need to draw the line to see the excess, like the large bar 6 that reversed yesterday's low and was a three-push down pattern (bars 4, 5, and 6). Don't trade what you believe should be happening. Only trade what is happening, even if it seems impossible. As discussed in Chapter 15 on channels in the first book, when the market is in a bear channel, smart traders are buying only below bars and not above; they are much more interested in shorting, and look to short above prior bars, not below.

FIGURE 4.17 Volume at Reversals Is Not Particularly Helpful

As shown in the right-hand chart in Figure 4.17, the 5 minute SPY had an exhaustive sell climax at bar 3 and a two-bar reversal at bar 4 that was followed by a strong rally above the moving average.

The chart on the left is a 1 minute chart showing a volume divergence at the low, which is common. The volume at the bar 4 low was less than the volume at the earlier bar 3 low, even though bar 4 was at a lower price. There probably was a tick divergence and divergences on many oscillators as well, but experienced traders do not have to look at anything beyond the 5 minute chart to know that.

Traditional technical analysis teaches that the volume on the bull reversal should be greater than on the final bear bar. Here, on the 5 minute chart, the volume on the bar 4 bull reversal bar was less than that of the two prior bear trend bars. Does that make the reversal less reliable? Not at all. However, it might have been enough to make a trader not buy the bottom. I don't want the distraction and do not look at volume or any indicators when I am trading, because the chart tells me all that I need to know. Incidentally, bar 2 had much larger volume than the bar 4 low, but resulted in a failed reversal that ended with a double top bear flag.

The big tail on the bottom of bar 3 was a sign that buyers were coming in; the market usually only falls for another bar or two before trying to correct. Bar 4 was a strong two-bar reversal and a micro double bottom with the bar 3 low. Bar 3 was a type of final flag, and was probably a final flag on a smaller time frame chart.

CHAPTER 5

Wedges and Other Three-Push Reversal Patterns

W hen the market makes three pushes in one direction and then creates a reversal setup that triggers the reversal trade, the first target is the beginning of the pattern, and the next is a measured move based on the height of the pattern. For example, if there is a wedge top where the third push up ends with a strong bear reversal bar, and the next bar trades below the reversal bar, the first target is a test of the bottom of the wedge (the bottom of the pullback from the first push up), and the next is a measured move down, based on the height from the bottom to the top of the wedge. All three push patterns are manifestations of the same underlying market behavior, regardless of the shape that the pattern takes. It does not matter if it is a wedge, a micro wedge, a parabolic wedge, a wedge with a fourth push, a wedge pullback in a trend or a trading range, a wedge trend reversal pattern, another type of triangle (including an expanding triangle), a triple top or bottom, a double top or bottom pullback, a head and shoulders top or bottom, or a failed breakout below a double top or above a double bottom. At some point, the trend traders give up trying for a strong breakout, and the reversal traders gain control of the market. A third consecutive reversal is usually enough for that to happen.

Three-push patterns often contain large trend bars and create consecutive climaxes. If the pushes are strong one- to three-bar spikes, traders will see them as climaxes. For example, if there is a strong bear spike, and a pullback, and then another strong bear spike, traders will wonder if the pullback is the final flag in the bear trend and if the consecutive sell climaxes will be followed by a bigger pullback. If there is only a small pullback from the second push down instead of a 10-bar rally, and then there is a third strong bear spike, traders will see this as three consecutive sell climaxes. They know that the odds are 60 percent or better that the market will try to have a more complex correction, like two legs up, that lasts for about 10 or more bars. So, if the pattern has a good signal bar, reasonable shape, adequate buying pressure, and is not a tight bear channel, they will consider buying the reversal up from the third push down.

Wedges can be pullbacks or reversals. Wedge pullbacks are discussed in Chapters 18 and 19 in the second book. When they are pullbacks in trends, they are with-trend setups and it is reasonable to enter on the first signal. A wedge reversal is an attempt to reverse a trend and it is therefore a countertrend setup. In general, it is better to wait for a second signal when trading countertrend. For example, if there is a wedge bottom in a bear trend, buy above the signal bar only if the pattern is exceptionally strong. It is usually better to wait to see if the market has a strong bull breakout and then look to buy a pullback, which can be a higher low or even a lower low. If the bull breakout goes straight up for several bars without a pullback, then traders should trade it like any other breakout, as discussed in the second book. Another difference between wedge pullbacks and reversals is their direction. A wedge bull flag points down, whereas a wedge reversal at the top of a bull trend points up. A wedge pullback in a bear trend points up, but a wedge bottom in a bear trend points down. Also, wedge flags are usually smaller patterns, and most last about 10 to 20 bars. Since they are with-trend setups, they don't have to be perfect, and many are subtle and look nothing like a wedge, but have three pullbacks. A reversal usually needs to be at least 20 bars long and have a clear trend channel line to be strong enough to reverse a trend.

Trends often end with a test of the extreme, and the test often has two legs, each reaching a greater extreme (a two-legged higher high in a bull trend or lower low in a bear trend). The first extreme and then those two legs make three pushes, which is a well-recognized reversal setup with many names. Sometimes it takes a wedge shape (an ascending triangle in a bull trend or a descending triangle in a bear trend), but usually it does not. It is not useful for a trader to draw subtle distinctions among the variations because there are enough similarities that they trade the same. For simplicity, think of these three-push patterns as wedges since most of them end in a climactic wedgelike point. Remember, a wedge is simply a trend channel where there are three pushes and often the trend line and trend channel lines converge. A trend line and trend channel line in a three-push pattern can be parallel like a stairs pattern, convergent like a wedge, or divergent like an expanding triangle. It does not matter because they all behave similarly and you trade them the same. They are all climaxes and frequently have a parabolic shape, which at times can be subtle. For example, if there is a bull wedge and the slope of the trend channel line drawn across the tops of the second and third legs is steeper than the line drawn across the highs of the first two legs, the wedge is parabolic. This is climactic behavior (discussed in the last chapter), and if the market reverses down, it will usually do so in about two legs and 10 bars.

When a channel has a wedge shape, it is due to urgency (and if it has a parabolic wedge shape, it is due to extreme urgency), and often leads to a climactic reversal. For example, in a wedge top, the slope of the trend line is greater than the slope of the trend channel line. The trend line is where the with-trend traders enter and the countertrend traders exit, and the opposite happens at the trend channel line. So if the slope of the trend line is greater, that means that the bulls are buying on smaller pullbacks and the bears are exiting on smaller sell-offs. What first distinguishes a wedge from a channel where the lines are parallel is the second pullback. Once the second push up has begun to reverse down, traders can draw a trend channel line and then use it to create a parallel line. When they drag that parallel line to the bottom of the first pullback, they have created a trend line and a trend channel. That tells bulls and bears where support is, and bulls will look to buy there and bears will look to take profits there. However, if the bulls begin to buy above that level and the bears exit their shorts early, the market will turn back up before it reaches the trend line. Both are doing so because they feel a sense of urgency and are afraid that the market will not drop down to that support level. This means that both feel that the trend line needs to be steeper and that the trend up is stronger.

Once the market turns up, traders then redraw the trend line. Instead of using the parallel of the trend channel line, they now can draw a trend line using the bottoms of the first two pullbacks. They now see that it is steeper than the trend channel line above and they begin to believe that the market is forming a wedge, which they know is often a reversal pattern. Traders will draw a parallel of that new steeper trend line and drag it to the top of the second push up, in case the market is forming a steeper parallel channel instead of a wedge. Both the bulls and the bears will watch to see whether the original trend channel line will contain the rally or the new, steeper one will be reached. If the original one contains the rally and the market turns down, traders will think that although there was more urgency in the buying on the second pullback, that urgency did not continue on the third push up. The bulls took profits at the original, shallower trend channel line, which means that they exited earlier than they could have. The bulls were hoping that the market would rally to the steeper trend channel line, but are now disappointed. The bears were so eager to short that, afraid that the market would not reach the steeper, higher trend channel line, they began to short at the original line. Now it is the bears who have a sense of urgency and the bulls who are afraid. Traders will see the turndown from the wedge top and sell, and most will wait for at least two legs down before they look for the next major signal up or down.

Once the market makes its first leg down, it will break below the wedge. At some point, the bears will take profits and the bulls will buy again. The bulls want to cause the wedge top to fail. When the market rallies to test the wedge top, the bears will begin to sell again. If the bulls begin to take profits, they believe that they will be unable to push the market above the old high. Once their profit taking combined with the new selling by the bears reaches a critical mass, it will overwhelm the remaining buyers, and the market will turn down for that second leg. At some point, the bulls will return and the bears will take profits, and both sides will see the two-legged pullback and wonder if the bull trend will resume. At this point, the wedge has played itself out and the market will be looking for the next pattern.

Markets often reverse after a test of the trend's extreme. For example, when a bull trend is at its strongest, bulls will buy above the prior high since they believe that there will be a successful breakout and another leg up. However, as the bull trend weakens and gets more two-sided trading, the strong bulls will see a new high as a place to take profits instead of a good location for more longs, and they will buy only on a pullback. As selling pressure builds, strong bears will dominate at the next new high and will try to turn this higher high into the top of the rally. If they are able to push the market down in a strong bear spike, traders will watch the following rally carefully to see if it reverses down once it gets back up to around the old high. The reversal might come at a lower high, a double top, or a higher high. Most will buy back their shorts if the market rallies to just above their short entry price or above that higher high. However, they are aware of the possibility of a wedge top, and if the breakout above the second high does not look too strong, they will look to short again.

When the up and down swings are especially sharp and when the first or second push down doesn't clearly break below a major bull trend line or hold below the moving average, the bears will see the reversal down as weak. However, those two pushes down represent selling pressure, and they tell everyone that the bears might be able to take control of the market. The bears know that the market might need a third push up to exhaust itself. However, they saw that they were able to turn the market down at the new high on the second push up and they believe that they might be able to do it again. The bulls took profits above the first high and will likely be quicker to take profits as the market goes above the second high. If the bull trend was very strong, the bulls would have bought more on a breakout above the first high. When traders instead see the market sell off, they know that the strong bulls are taking profits instead of buying the breakout, and this tells them that the strong bulls do not believe that the market is going up without more of a pullback.

Both the bulls and the bears know that markets often reverse after a third push up, and they will need a strong breakout well beyond the second high for them to believe that the market is not topping. They view the second high as a large low 2 short setup. If the low 2 fails and the breakout above the low 2 top is strong, the market will likely have at least two more legs up. If it is not strong, the market will probably form a wedge top. The breakout above the second high is often sharp, but it will reverse down quickly if the bulls and the bears think that it is forming a top instead of a new breakout. The sharp poke above the second top might be due more to short covering than to aggressive buying by the strong bulls, and if there is not immediate follow-through, traders will assume that the strong bulls will buy only a deep pullback. If the strong bulls are stepping aside, then the bears will have the confidence to short aggressively. If they can push the market down far and fast enough, the bulls might wait for a more protracted sell-off before looking to buy. This can create a sell vacuum where the market falls quickly until it reaches a price at which traders are willing to buy again (the bulls initiating new longs and the bears taking profits). If the bulls take profits on their new longs on a rally that stalls below the top of the wedge, the market will form a lower high and it will likely fall for at least a second push down. The strong bears will be shorting more at the lower high, exactly where the strong bulls are covering their longs. It will always be at a resistance area where there is a confluence of reasons to sell.

These fast reversals that quickly cover a lot of points represent the urgency that everyone is feeling, and this often makes it difficult for traders to make their trading decisions fast enough to get the best entry. However, if traders understand what the market is doing, they can often get short very early in the reversal down. The move down is often fast and they can move their stops to breakeven after the first strong leg down and the subsequent lower high.

The majority of three-push patterns reverse after overshooting a trend channel line and that alone can be a reason to enter, even if the actual shape is not a wedge. However, the three pushes are often easier to see than is the trend channel line overshoot, and that makes the distinction from other trend channel line failures worthwhile. These patterns rarely have a perfect shape, and often trend lines and trend channel lines have to be manipulated to highlight the pattern. For example, the wedge might be only with the candle bodies, so to draw the trend line and trend channel line in a way to highlight the wedge shape, you have to ignore the tails. Other times, the end point of the wedge won't reach the trend channel line. Be flexible and if there is a three-push pattern at the end of a big move, even if the pattern is not perfect, trade it as if it is a wedge. However, if it overshoots the trend channel line, the odds of success with the countertrend trade are higher. Also, most trend channel line overshoots have a wedge shape, but it is often so stretched out that it is not worth looking at it. The reversal from the overshoot can be reason enough to enter if the pattern is strong.

It is important to remember that a wedge reversal is a countertrend setup. It is therefore usually better to wait for a second entry, like a lower high (less often, a higher high breakout pullback short setup) after a wedge top or a higher low (less often, a lower low) after a wedge bottom. This is unlike trading wedge pullbacks where you are entering in the direction of the larger trend. Then, entering on the first signal is a reliable approach. In general, if you are trading a wedge reversal and it is not as strong as you would like, it is better to wait for a second signal before taking the trade. If the initial breakout is strong, entering on the pullback has a higher chance of success. If there is a wedge reversal in a trading range, it may look and act more like a wedge pullback because there is no trend to reverse. When that is the case, taking the first signal is usually a profitable approach.

If a wedge triggers an entry, but then it fails and the market extends one or more ticks beyond the wedge extreme, it will often run quickly to a measured move based on the height of the wedge. Sometimes, just after failing, it reverses back and creates a second attempt at reversing the trend; when this happens, the new trend is usually protracted (lasting at least 10 bars) and it usually has at least two legs. The new extreme can be thought of as a breakout pullback. For example, if there is a wedge top that begins to reverse down and the downside breakout fails and then the bull trend resumes and reverses down again at a new high, that new high is a higher high pullback from the initial break below the wedge.

When the wedge reversal fails and the market reaches a new extreme, watch to see if the market reverses on this fourth push. Sometimes what appears to be a fourth push is really just a third push in the eyes of most traders. If, after the pullback from the first push, the market creates an especially strong second push, many traders will reset the count and consider it to be the new first push. The result is that many traders won't look for a reversal after the third push and instead will wait for the fourth push before looking for a reversal trade. In hindsight, the decision about whether most traders reset the count is clear, but when you are trading, you cannot always be certain. The stronger the momentum is on the second push, the more likely it is that the market will have reset the count and the more likely it is that there will be a fourth push.

After the first leg of any new trend, the test of the old extreme sometimes assumes a wedge shape, and the wedge pullback from that first leg of the new trend may or may not exceed the extreme of the old trend. In either case, a trader should be looking to enter in the possible new trend as the wedge pullback reverses back in the direction of the new trend (for example, in a new bull trend, the wedge pullback can be a higher low or a lower low).

When there is a trend in the first hour, the market often has a trading range that lasts for several hours, followed by a resumption of the trend into the close. That trading range will often have three pushes, but usually not a wedge shape. For example, in a trend-resumption bear trend day, the trading range might be a bear channel that slopes up slightly, and it might have three pushes but not a wedge shape. It does not matter whether you call it a low 3 short setup or a wedge, but it is important to be aware that the day might have a bear trend resumption into the close and that this three-push, low-momentum rally might be the setup for the short. View this as a type of wedge because it has three pushes, there is often a trend channel line overshoot, it sometimes has the shape of a wedge, and it has the same behavior as a wedge. Remember, if you see everything in shades of gray, you will be a much better trader.

When there are three or more pushes and each breakout is smaller, then this is a shrinking stairs pattern in addition to being a wedge. For example, if there are three pushes up in a bull trend and the second push was 10 ticks above the first and the third was only seven ticks above the second, then this is a shrinking stairs pattern. It is a sign of waning momentum and increases the odds that there will be a two-legged reversal. The bulls are taking profits sooner and the bears are shorting at less of a breakout than last time because they believe the market might not break out as much this time. Sometimes there will be a fourth or fifth step in a strong trend, but since the momentum is waning, countertrend trades can usually be taken. In contrast, if the third step is significantly beyond the second and then reverses, this is likely to become a trend channel line overshoot and reversal setup.

A wedge top fails if, after triggering the entry, the breakout fails to go far and the trend resumes and goes beyond the wedge. For example, if there is a wedge top and the market falls below the signal bar and triggers a short entry, but this is soon followed by a rally that goes above the top of the wedge, then the wedge has failed. When traders are unclear about whether the second push up was strong enough to reset the count, they will watch to see if the breakout is actually the third push of the wedge that began with that second push. When a wedge is very clear and traders were expecting the top to hold, many traders will reverse to long on a stop above the top of the wedge. When a wedge top succeeds, the first target is a test of the bottom of the wedge, and the next target is a measured move down from there. When a wedge top fails, the first target is a measured move up, again using the height of the wedge. Remember, a wedge is an area of two-sided trading, so it acts like a trading range and therefore sets up a breakout mode situation. Whether the breakout is above or below, the target is a measured move equal to about the height of the wedge. As with any breakout, it could fail. For example, if the wedge top triggers, but the market quickly reverses back up and breaks out above the wedge top, the wedge has failed. However, the bull breakout should be viewed like any other breakout. If it is strong, it is likely to be followed by a measured move up. If it is weak, it will likely fail and the market will reverse back down. If that happens, the bull breakout above the wedge becomes simply a higher high pullback from the original breakout below the wedge.

In the Emini, if there is a wedge top and then a brief sell-off, the pullback often tests the top of the wedge to the exact tick, forming a perfect double top. If the market reverses back down, this is a second-entry short opportunity. In the SPY and in many stocks, the pullback will sometimes go above the wedge by a few ticks and traders will not see this as a failure. However, if it races above the wedge by many ticks, this is a sign that traders are buying aggressively and they are looking for a strong leg up and no longer looking for a top. When this is happening, look to buy quickly to catch this fast breakout. Most wedge tops that fail are very steep and tight and occur in strong bull trends. When a bull trend is strong, it will always be forming trend channel line overshoots and three-push patterns, but the pullbacks between the pushes are small and the pushes are very strong. It is a mistake to be looking for reversals in strong trends, because most reversal attempts fail. Instead of seeing everything as a possible wedge top, look to buy the pullback from each new high. Also, wedge tops in strong bull trends often correct in two sideways legs to the moving average, setting up a high 2 buy. This is a reliable entry. A wedge that corrects sideways is a sign that the trend is very strong. The opposite is true for wedge bottoms. As with any breakout, the breakout could fail. For example, if the wedge top triggers, but the market quickly reverses back up and breaks out above the wedge top, the wedge has failed. However, the bull breakout should be viewed like any other breakout. If it is strong, it is likely to be followed by a measured move up. If it is weak, it will likely fail and the market will reverse back down. If that happens, the bull breakout above the wedge becomes simply a higher high pullback from the original breakout below the wedge.

Wedges most often fail when traders are overly eager to enter countertrend, do not wait for a clear trend line break and countertrend strength, and fade the first small three-push pattern that appears. Three pushes alone, especially when small, will rarely reverse a trend in the absence of a prior trend line break or a major trend channel overshoot and reversal. If the channel is tight, even if it has a wedge shape, it is almost always better not to enter on the reversal. Instead, wait for the reversal and see how strong the breakout is. If it is strong, trade it like any other breakout. It is usually best to enter on a breakout pullback, but when the spike is very strong, traders will enter on the closes of the bars and at the market. If the breakout is weak, traders assume that it will fail and they look for the channel to continue. They will then enter in the direction of the wedge channel and not in the countertrend direction. For example, if there is a wedge bottom in a bear trend but the upside breakout is weak, traders will look to short the low 1 or low 2 that is created by the failed upside breakout. These smart traders will enter where the countertrend traders will be taking their losses.

Wedges are often opening reversal patterns. Opening reversals can follow very strong moves in the first hour or so, and sometimes there will be a very steep wedge with only slight pauses after the first two pushes, yet the market will abruptly reverse and trend for the rest of the day. The first pause might be a small final flag, and then there is an even smaller final flag after the second push. Although you should never look for a reversal from such a steep, tight wedge after the first hour or two, they can be reliable opening reversal setups.

A micro wedge is a wedge that is formed by three consecutive bars or three out of four or five consecutive bars. Since the pattern is so small, it usually results in only a minor correction. Usually the bars have tails and a micro trend channel line can be drawn across those tails, and there usually is a clear wedge on a smaller time frame like a 1 minute chart. For example, if the market is selling off and has a bear trend bar with a moderate tail on the bottom, and this is followed by another bear trend bar with a slightly lower low and an obvious tail on the bottom, and then by a third bar with a lower low and a tail, this is a micro wedge reversal pattern. If the bear trend is strong, you should not buy above the high of the third bar, because it will likely lead to a loss. If the micro wedge forms in a trading range day near the bottom of the range and the third bar is a bull reversal bar, this might be a reasonable setup for a buy scalp.

There is a special type of wedge that is really just a three-push pattern and usually does not have a wedge shape, but it is important because it is a reliable breakout setup. If the market is in a trading range and then has a one-tick breakout beyond a minor swing high or low that reverses for maybe three to 20 bars, and then the market again has another one-tick or sometimes a two-tick breakout that once again pulls back, those three pushes set up the pattern. If the market then breaks again beyond that second minor breakout, it usually leads to a significant breakout and an approximate measured move equal to the height of the pattern. It is as if the three pushes constitute a wedge, and then, instead of leading to a reversal, the wedge failed. As is the case with all failed wedges, the market typically breaks out and runs for about the same number of points as there are from the bottom to the top of the wedge. Sometimes the market breaks out after only going beyond a single one-tick failure.

A related pattern is a failed double top or bottom breakout. For example, if there is a double top and then the market breaks above the double top but reverses back down within a few bars, this can function like a wedge top (a wedge is a type of triangle, and some traders would call it a triangle). The first two pushes up are the highs of the double top, and the third push up is the breakout above the double top. If the market reverses down, it will usually go far enough for at least a scalp. A double top is a trading range, and the failed breakout is just a failed breakout of a trading range that is usually followed by just more sideways trading. It usually falls enough for at least a scalp, but sometimes it will be followed by a quick breakout of the opposite side of the trading range and a measured move down based on the height of the trading range. In this case, the bulls who bought the breakout and were stopped out on the reversal will look to buy again only after a substantial pullback.

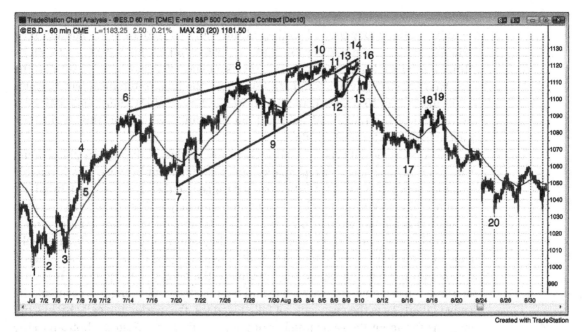

FIGURE 5.1   Wedge Top

As shown in Figure 5.1, the 60 minute Emini had a wedge reversal top and then a smaller wedge pullback to a lower high or double top, followed by two legs down to bar 20.

A wedge does not have to have a perfect shape to be effective. For example, the trend channel line is a best fit line from the bar 6 high to the bar 10 high, and the bar 8 second push up is above the line. After the market reversed down from bar 10 to bar 12, it formed a wedge bear flag that also had an imperfect shape. The three pushes up were the high of bar 11 on the open of the day and then bars 13 and 14. The high was slightly below the bar 10 high. It does not matter if you call this a double top or a lower high. What matters is that you see the large three pushes up and then the reversal down.

This is also a spike and channel bull trend where there was a sharp spike up to bar 4 and then a steep channel to bar 6. The move from the bar 3 low to bar 6 was in such a tight channel that it became a large spike. The bar 7 pullback that led to the channel was tested by the bar 20 sell-off. The bull channel had three pushes and a wedge shape, which is common in spike and channel patterns.

FIGURE 5.2 First-Hour Wedge

If a three-push move is too steep, it is usually not a good reversal pattern except sometimes in the first hour when it can create an opening reversal. As shown in Figure 5.2, the market rallied strongly from bar 11 to bar 12 in three pushes, and although this was a steep channel, it was an acceptable parabolic wedge opening reversal. Bar 12 broke above the bar 8 and bar 10 double top and was followed by a bear inside bar. Bar 12 was both a failed breakout of the double top and a double top with either of those bars. The rally was to a price level where sellers came in several times yesterday, and it was reasonable to think they might return again today around the top of the trading range from yesterday.

In trading range markets, fading breakouts is a good strategy. For the shorts, enter on a stop at one tick below the failure bar near the top of the range, and for longs, buy on a stop at one tick above the failed breakout bar near the low of the range. Breaking out beyond any swing high or low, even if it was part of an earlier and opposite trend, is a sign of strength and a potential trade setup. There were many examples of failed breakouts and reversals over these two days, including failed trend line and failed trend channel line breakouts.

Bars 2, 3, and 6 also represent a shrinking stairs pattern, which often leads to a good reversal. You could also call it a wedge, because of the three pushes up (bars 2 and 3 were the first two, and it was also the third push up from bar 4).

With shrinking stairs, the second breakout is smaller than the first, indicating loss of momentum. Here, bar 3 was 19 cents above bar 2, but bar 6 was only 12 cents above bar 3. Whenever shrinking stairs are present, the trade becomes more likely to be successful and usually signals an imminent two-legged pullback in a strong trend.

Bars 4 and 7 formed a double bottom, and bar 9 was a failed breakout below that double bottom. Bars 4 and 7 were two pushes down, and bar 9 was a third push down and therefore a reversal up, which is a variant of a wedge bottom.

Figure 5.3   WEDGES AND OTHER THREE-PUSH REVERSAL PATTERNS   **163**

FIGURE 5.3 Shrinking Stairs

As shown in Figure 5.3, shrinking stairs, with each breakout extending less than the prior one, signal waning momentum and increase the odds that a profitable countertrend trade is near. After the bar 4 step, the move to bar 5 broke the trend line, setting the stage for a test of the low and a likely two-legged rally (which occurred after the bar 6 lower low and two-bar reversal). The loss of momentum is a sign that the trend is weakening and becoming more two-sided, which increases the chances that it will transition into a trading range, as it did here.

Bars 3 to 5 formed a small wedge bear flag. The first push up was followed by the bar 4 lower low, which is a common wedge variant. The move up to bar 5 had the other two small pushes. Bar 4 was a successful final flag scalp, and the pattern grew into the larger final flag that ended at bar 5 (a wedge), which is a frequent occurrence.

When there is a strong breakout after the pullback from the first push down, it is unclear whether there will be only two more pushes or the momentum is strong enough to restart the count. For example, is bar 3 the third push down, or should you have restarted the count on the strong move down to bar 2? In hindsight, the answer is clear, but when you are trading, you cannot be certain. The stronger the downward momentum is, the more likely it is that the most traders will reset the count and the more likely it is that there will be a fourth push. That fourth push down to bar 4 was really just the third push down in the wedge bottom that began with the spike down to bar 2.

Once bar 6 fell below the bar 4 bottom of the wedge, the wedge bottom failed. Bar 6 should be viewed like any other breakout. It was immediately followed by a bull reversal bar, setting up a two-bar reversal and a failed breakout. Some traders saw this buy setup as a lower low major trend reversal, while others saw it as a lower low pullback from the breakout above the bar 4 wedge bottom. It is also a shrinking stairs buy setup and a failed breakout below a trading range. Finally, it is a small final flag reversal (there was a two-bar bear flag before bar 6). All of these are reasonable reasons for traders to consider buying above the bull bar that followed bar 6.

FIGURE 5.4   Wedge Lower High

The daily SPY topped in March 2000 and then there was a three-push rally to the bar 8 lower high, as shown in Figure 5.4. Bar 8 also formed a double top bear flag with bar 2 (it slightly exceeded the bar 2 high). Bar 8 did not quite reach the dashed bear trend channel line. This wedge bear flag was followed by a huge bull trend. At the time that it formed, it was unclear whether a trend reversal was taking place, but following the three pushes up to bar 1, the market was likely to have at least two pushes down. The move down to bar 3 was the first, and the rally to bar 8 was therefore the pullback, setting up the sell-off to at least one more leg down. Although most trading ranges after bull trends are simply bull flags on higher time frame charts, most trend reversals come from trading ranges. The market usually has to transition into a two-sided market before it changes direction. As the market began to fall from bar 8, it was more likely to find support around the bar 3 low at the bottom of the developing trading range. However, the leg to below bar 3 was so steep that it was clear that there were not many buyers and that the market had to go lower to find traders willing to buy. Strong bulls did not appear until the double bottom pullback and higher low major trend reversal in early 2003.

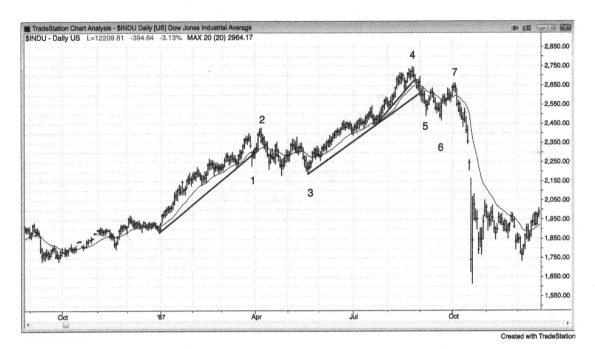

FIGURE 5.5   Wedge Lower High in the Dow

A wedge bear flag lower high in the daily Dow Jones Industrial Average following the break below the bull trend line led to the 1987 crash, as shown in Figure 5.5. The move down to bar 6 was strong and broke well below the trend line and the moving average. Some traders saw the first push up of the wedge bear flag as the rally after bar 5, and the second and third pushes up as any two of the three pushes up to bar 7. Others saw bar 7 as a two-legged lower high major trend reversal and therefore a low 2 short setup, with the first leg up being the rally after bar 5. Still others saw the three small pushes up to bar 7 as a small channel that followed the small spike up from bar 6. Most traders saw all of these factors and attached a different significance to each.

Bar 1 was the first push down of a wedge bull flag. There were two more pushes down and then a small breakout, and this was followed by a higher low breakout pullback to bar 3. Some traders saw bar 3 as a double bottom bull flag with the bottom of the wedge bull flag. Many wedge bull flags are head and shoulders tops that fail, as was the case here.

The rally up before the bar 1 sell-off had four pushes up and was an example of how three pushes alone do not provide a reversal setup. When the three pushes are in a tight bull channel, it is more likely that there will be a fourth or fifth push up than a reversal. The channel up to bar 4 had three pushes in the final segment and

Figure 5.5   WEDGES AND OTHER THREE-PUSH REVERSAL PATTERNS   **167**

again was in a tight bull channel. When the channel is tight, bears should not short the reversal down from the third push up. They should wait to see how strong the bear breakout is.

Bar 1 was a strong bear spike, and many traders then shorted the higher high at bar 2, which they saw as a higher high pullback from the bear breakout down to bar 1. Bar 1 broke the bull trend line, so traders were looking to short a higher high or lower high test of the bull high.

The bar 5 breakout of the bull channel was strong enough to clearly break the bull trend line, so traders were looking to short the breakout pullback. It was a lower high at bar 7, which formed a double top with the small rally after bar 5. Most trading ranges in bull trends become bull flags and are just pullbacks on higher time frame charts. Although the market did not have to reverse up from bar 3, that was the most likely outcome, since bar 3 was at the bottom of a trading range in a bull trend. The market could have continued to fall from the lower high major trend reversal that formed after bar 2 (there was a double top bear flag and lower high), but most major trend reversals are followed by trading ranges and not actual reversals into opposite trends. This entire setup was similar to that at bar 7, which was followed by a big bear trend.

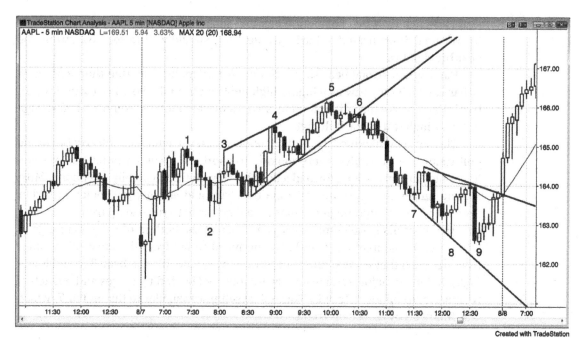

FIGURE 5.6 Reversal Just Shy of Trend Channel Line

When there is urgency on the part of the bears, they will short aggressively just below the trend channel line. They are afraid that the market will not get above the line and they don't want to risk missing the sell-off. In Figure 5.6, bars 3, 4, and 5 formed a wedge top, but bar 5 did not overshoot the trend channel line. Because this was a wedge reversal setup, it was better to wait for a second signal, like a lower high. Bar 5 and the bar after it formed a small bear spike. Bar 6 was a second entry on the failed high 2, and bar 6 was the start of a larger, three-bar bear spike. After a one-bar pullback, there was a five-bar bear spike and a collapse into a strong bear trend. Since the channel up from bar 2 had large swings and therefore had a lot of two-sided trading, this spike and channel bull was not a strong trend. The spike was the low of the day up to bar 1. When there is significant trading range behavior, aggressive traders could short the first entry, which was the two-bar reversal at bar 5. Incidentally, the bar 1 high at the top of the wedge was a micro wedge top, and the sell-off to bar 2 was a double bottom bull flag with the bottom of the wedge, which was the start of the wedge-shaped channel. Bar 2 was also a test of the breakout above the first bar of the day.

Bars 7, 8, and 9 created a three-push long setup with an entry above the bar 9 bull reversal bar, even though the close was midrange. The day was clearly not a trend day, so a weaker reversal bar was reasonable. This pattern had diverging

Figure 5.6   WEDGES AND OTHER THREE-PUSH REVERSAL PATTERNS   **169**

lines, although it was not an expanding triangle since the high after bar 8 was below the high after bar 7. Bar 9 did not overshoot the trend channel line, but it was still a good long setup on a trading range day. If you were concerned that it was risky after the strong sell-off down to bar 7, you could have waited for a higher low before going long. The outside up bar three bars later was a higher low, but when entering on outside bars, you have to be fast because they often reverse up quickly.

The bar before bar 9 was a big bear trend bar and therefore a breakout attempt. However, there was no follow-through selling on the next bar. Instead, it was a small bull bar and therefore a buy setup for a failed breakout. Even though it fell below the bar 8 low, the rally that preceded it had five or six consecutive bull bodies and therefore was a reasonably strong bull breakout attempt. The sell-off was simply a brief, sharp pullback from that bull breakout. A breakout pullback sometimes forms a lower low, as it did here. Never be frightened by a single big bear trend bar. Always view every trend bar as a breakout, and realize that most breakout attempts fail.

FIGURE 5.7   Parabolic Wedge

As shown in Figure 5.7, the Emini reversed down from the bar 5 higher high and formed a trading range, but the market broke out strongly from the range and above the line B top of the bull channel. Remember, every reversal is simply a failed breakout of something. It then reversed down at bar 9, which was the third push up. The slope of the wedge increased and was therefore parabolic (the slope of the trend channel line from bar 5 to bar 9 was steeper than the slope of the line from bar 3 to bar 5). As with any wedge top, two pushes down was likely.

The strong rally to bar 9 broke above the bull channel (dashed line), but then reversed back into the channel on the sell-off to bar 10. Whenever there is a breakout above a bull channel and then a strong reversal back into the channel, there is about a 50 percent chance that the bear swing will continue and break below the bottom of the bull channel, as it did here. When a breakout is going to fail, it usually does so within about five bars of breaking above the channel, as it did here. The bears bought back their shorts and aggressive bulls went long around bar 16, which formed a double bottom with the bar 6 low of the day, and was the first reversal after reaching the target (a poke below the channel).

The bar before bar 8 had a smaller body than the bar before it, which meant that the momentum was waning. Bar 8 had a big body. What did this mean? Bar 8 was an attempt to accelerate the trend again after a pause. Many traders interpreted the large size of bar 8 as indicating climactic behavior, with the pause perhaps being the

Figure 5.7   WEDGES AND OTHER THREE-PUSH REVERSAL PATTERNS   **171**

final flag in the rally, before a two-legged pullback. Traders sold the close of bar 8, above its high, and especially the close of the bar 9 and below its low, because the bear close indicated that the sellers were getting strong. Bulls sold to take profits on their longs and some bears shorted for a scalp, expecting a relatively large (maybe five to 10 bars) pullback after the small buy climax (the small final flag). Other bears shorted for a swing down, based on the parabolic wedge.

Bar 16 was the bottom of a second leg down, where bar 8 was the first. This would be an obvious high 2 pullback on a higher time frame chart. It was also a double bottom test of the low of the day, which occurred at bar 6. The bears were hoping for a reversal day, but the bulls came in and overwhelmed the bears. The rally into the close tested the top of the very strong bull spike that ended at bar 9. Although the rally was not strong and the sell-off to bar 8 was deep, the day was a bull trend day on the daily chart.

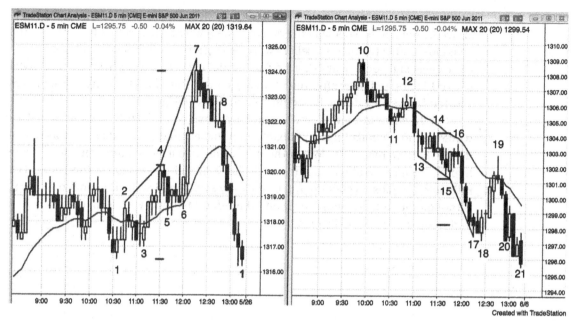

FIGURE 5.8   Bull and Bear Parabolic Wedges

As shown in Figure 5.8, the chart on the left was in a trading range and triggered a low 2 short below bar 4. Most traders would not have shorted this weak setup, because bar 4 was a doji bar and it followed six consecutive bars without a bear body. Bar 6 formed a high 2 buy setup (also a breakout pullback buy setup from the high 1 and failed low 2 that followed bar 5), which led to a strong bull breakout. A rally always reaches some resistance area, like a measured move or a trend line, where traders will take partial or full profits, and aggressive bears will short for a scalp down. This rally overshot a measured move target by a couple of ticks, but there were probably other targets in the area as well. Both the bulls and the bears expected only a pullback, and both planned to buy when the pullback ended (which would always be at a support level, which may not be obvious). The reason moves end at targets is that most trades are being done by computers, and their algorithms are based on math and logic. They only buy at support and sell at resistance. These potential levels are usually visible to experienced traders.

The trend channel line from bar 4 to bar 7 was steeper than the one from bar 2 to bar 4, which means that the move up was parabolic. The bar before bar 7 had a big tail, which usually means that traders who bought the close of that bar were looking for just a scalp up and then a pullback. The high of bar 7 was a second push up. The next bar was a bear inside bar and the signal bar for the short. With that much strength after the failed low 2 at bar 4, most traders correctly assumed that there would be a second push up, which happens in over 60 percent of the cases.

The market pulled back for six bars in a bull flag (here, a bear micro channel), but instead of breaking out to the upside, the flag broke to the downside on the bar after bar 8. This bull flag was then the final flag of the rally, and its downside breakout was a final flag reversal, even though the flag never had an upside breakout. Astute traders were aware of this possibility and shorted below the bear bar that followed bar 7, and on the breakout below bar 8. The traders who took the first entry knew that it had only about a 40 percent chance of success, but they were looking for a reversal down and a reward that was at least twice the size of their risk, and therefore had a positive trader's equation. The traders who shorted on the downside breakout, either as the bar was forming or on its close, or on the close of any of the following bars, had proof that the market was going down, and therefore their shorts had at least a 60 percent chance of success (for them, they wanted a reward that was at least as large as their risk). They traded off a smaller profit for a higher probability, and their trader's equation was also positive.

The chart on the right is a parabolic wedge bottom. Bar 15 was a strong bull reversal bar at a double bottom, and a buy setup for a reversal up from the low 2 final flag that broke out below bar 14. Bar 14 can be viewed as a second entry low 2 short, a breakout pullback from the low 2 short that triggered on the prior bar, or as a triangle short (the three pushes up were the high of the doji that formed two bars after bar 13, the bull inside bar that followed, and the tail at the top of bar 14). The bears saw bar 16 as a pullback from the breakout of the bear triangle. Both bulls and bears sold below bar 16, the bull entry bar after bar 15, and the bar 15 buy signal bar. The bulls were exiting their longs and the bears were initiating shorts. When bulls get stopped out of a bull reversal up from a double bottom, they often expect a breakout and measured move, and don't look to buy again for at least a couple of bars. This allowed the market to fall quickly.

Bar 17 had a tail on the bottom, which alerted traders that the market might have only one more push down before forming a pullback. It also had a close in the middle, which made it a reversal bar, although weak. This was the first attempt to reverse up from a spike, which is a type of micro channel, and first attempts to reverse usually fail. There were more sellers above bar 17 than buyers, as expected. Scalpers shorted the close of bar 17, hoping for one more small push down before a pullback began. Because only a scalp down was likely, shorting the low 1 below the next bar was risky. The market turned up in a small double bottom at bar 18 (bar 17 was the first push down). The low of bar 18 was four ticks below the close of bar 17, so most of those shorts from the close of that bar were trapped and bought back their shorts above bar 18. Bar 18 had a strong bull body and most traders expected a reversal up to around the moving average and maybe to the high of bar 15. Bar 15 was a reasonable buy signal, so some bulls scaled in lower and planned to exit their entire position at their first entry, which was the high of bar 15. The bulls thought that the rally could reach the bar 16 or bar 14 highs. The bar 18 low was at one or more support levels, although none are shown here.

The move down to bar 18 went beyond a reasonable measured move target, which meant that the computers were looking at something else. Most measured move targets do not lead to reversals, but it is still helpful to draw them, because all reversals happen at support and resistance levels. When a reversal happens at one of these levels, and the level is especially obvious, it is a good place for trend traders to take profits and often a reasonable place for countertrend traders to take reversal trades. The final low of the day was also at a support level, whether or not it was obvious. The low of bar 21 was one tick below the earlier low of the day and the close of bar 21 was exactly at the open of the day.

Because the move up was a climactic reversal, it had about a 60 percent chance of having at least two legs up and lasting 10 bars. This means that it had a 40 percent chance of not reaching those goals.

Since bar 18 was a reasonably strong buy signal, most traders entered above its high. This left fewer traders to buy as the market went up. The tail on the top of bar 18 and the doji bar that followed were signs that the market lacked urgency for the bulls, which means that the buy setup was not as strong as it could have been. When the bulls fail to create signs of strength, traders are quicker to take profits. Bar 19 reached 14 ticks above the bar 18 high and had a bear close. This means that many bulls took profits at exactly three points. Instead of finding new buyers as the market rallied, it found profit takers at the moving average, and two ticks below the low 2 short that was triggered two bars after bar 13. The bears saw this as a breakout test that missed the breakeven stops by one tick, and therefore a sign that the bears were aggressively defending their stops. Although the odds still favored a second leg up after a pullback to a higher low, most bulls exited their longs during and below bar 19, and were only looking to buy again on a stop above the high of a bar in the pullback. The higher low never formed and the market fell below the bar 17 bear spike low and closed on the low of the day. The bulls did not get as much profit as they had hoped to make when they took their trade, but this often happens and is not a surprise. Traders always have a plan when they enter a trade, but if the premise changes, they change their plan. Many trades end up with smaller profits or losses than what traders expected when they entered. Good traders just take what the market gives them and then move on to the next trade.

Traders were especially wary of the possibility of a sell-off into the close of the day, because the market had a bear breakout on the daily chart two days earlier after rallying for two years. When a market might be reversing down on the daily chart, many traders look for a sell-off into the close (just like they look for a rally into the close in a bull trend). This made traders unwilling to buy on limit orders as the market traded down below bar 19. They were cautious and only wanted to buy after a reversal bar formed. With so few traders willing to buy on limit orders as the market was selling off into the close on a bear day, the higher low signal bar never formed.

Figure 5.9   WEDGES AND OTHER THREE-PUSH REVERSAL PATTERNS   **175**

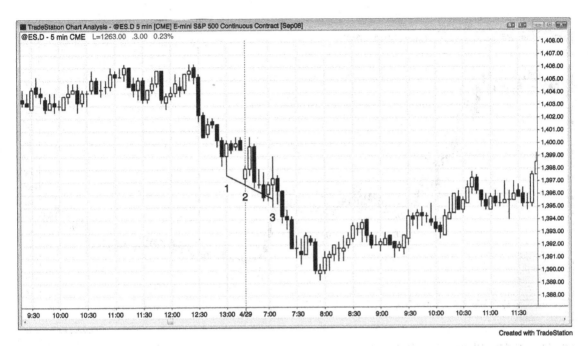

FIGURE 5.9 Failed Wedge

When there is a bottom setup and the market goes sideways instead of up, the market is accepting the lower prices instead of rejecting them and therefore might be in the middle of the move instead of at the bottom. A failed wedge often falls for a measured move.

As shown in Figure 5.9, the market tried to form a wedge reversal, but bar 3 was the fourth consecutive bar that mostly overlapped the prior bar. This was acceptance of the lower price and not rejection, so it made a reversal up unlikely. Also, the channel down was steep, and when this is the case, it is usually safer to wait for a higher low before going long. The bar 3 entry bar was an outside up bar that trapped bulls who overlooked the steepness of the bear trend channel line and only saw the three pushes. Patient traders would not have bought this wedge, because there was no higher low.

When a wedge fails, the move will usually be an approximate measured move equal to the height of the wedge. Here, the move down below bar 3 was about the same number of points as there were from the top of the wedge just after bar 1 to the bottom at the low of bar 3.

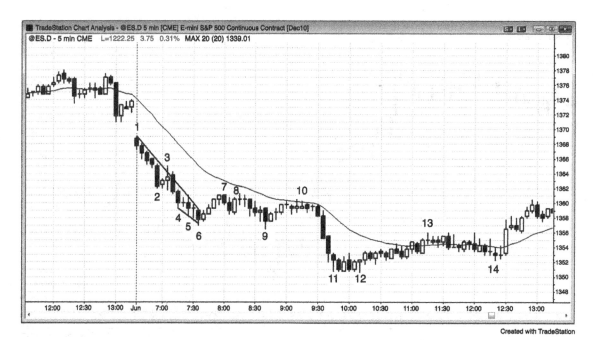

FIGURE 5.10   Wedge That Is Too Tight

A wedge bottom that is in a tight channel in a bear trend and without prior bull strength is not a buy setup. As shown in Figure 5.10, the market was in a bear trend from the open on a gap down day. Overly eager bulls would have rationalized buying the bar 6 wedge reversal by convincing themselves that it was the end of a two-legged move down and there was a trend line break at bar 3. However, bar 3 was a failed trend line break and did not represent the bulls taking control of the market with any momentum. The bar 6 wedge long entry above the inside bar was a successful scalp, but not a setup that would likely turn into anything more. The move down to bar 6 did not have a meaningful trend line break or upward momentum in the middle and therefore looked more like a single leg down made up of two smaller legs in a tight bear channel. There was likely to be a second leg down after a break of the bear trend line. Some traders saw bar 6 as the end of a wedge with its first push down as bar 2, its second push down as bar 4, and the final push down as bar 6. It was also a five-bar-long micro wedge formed by bars 4, 5, and 6. Since a trend channel line can be drawn across the bottoms of the bars, this small pattern can be thought of as a little wedge and therefore should have behaved like one and should have had a correction that reached to about the start of the wedge at the top of the bar that created the first push down.

Figure 5.10　　　　　　　WEDGES AND OTHER THREE-PUSH REVERSAL PATTERNS　　**177**

There was then a low 2 short at bar 8. This little rally did break a trend line, so buyers could look for a scalp up on a failed new low, which occurred at bar 9. However, in the absence of a strong bull reversal bar, this long was likely to fail, which it did at the bar 10 low 2 short, and the market then broke down into the second bear leg that ended at the bar 12 final flag one-tick false breakout. The bar 10 short was a double top with bar 8 and a 20 gap bar short setup, and it resulted in a trend-resumption bear trend down to the low of the day.

FIGURE 5.11 Wedge but Tight Channel

A wedge bottom is not a buy signal when it is in a tight bear channel. As shown in Figure 5.11, bar 9 was a bear trend channel line overshoot reversal and a third push down (a wedge). However, it was not a strong bull signal bar because it was in a tight bear channel, it overlapped the prior bar too much, and it had a weak close (small bull body). There was no clear rejection of excessive selling, and you should never buy the first breakout attempt of a tight bear channel since most fail before going far enough to make a scalp. At best, you should wait for a second entry before buying. Strong traders would short at and above the high of the prior bar in a bear channel, and they would not be looking to buy.

Bar 10 was a one-tick failure for any traders who bought the wedge. It was the third sideways bar, so smart traders were now seeing a trading range in a bear trend, which is usually a continuation pattern. Overlapping bars mean that the market is accepting these lower prices, not rejecting them. You need a sign of rejection before you buy in a bear trend. Basing a trade on a belief that the market is overdue for a correction is a losing approach to trading. Trends can go much further than most traders could ever imagine.

A trader could have shorted the low 1 at bar 11, but this was a trading range and smart traders would not have shorted at its low without a stronger bull trap. It was a second one-tick failed breakout. Also, a wedge usually makes two attempts

Figure 5.11   WEDGES AND OTHER THREE-PUSH REVERSAL PATTERNS   **179**

to rally (two legs up) so they would have shorted only if the wedge failed (i.e., fell below the bar 9 low), or if the second attempt to rally failed.

Bar 12 was a third one-tick failed breakout in a row, but this time it followed two legs up (bars 9 and 11) and was a low 2 short. This was the first trade that smart traders would have taken, because it was a low 2 in a bear flag. What made it especially good was that there were two failed attempts to make the wedge reverse upward (bars 10 and 12) and both failed. These represented the two legs up from the wedge and they were clearly weak. Also, it is very rare to have three one-tick failures in a row, so it was likely that the next move would run.

A trader could also have waited to short below the low of bar 9, because it was only then that the wedge definitively failed. The heavy volume on the breakout (14,000 contracts on the 1 minute chart) confirmed that many smart traders waited until that point to short. A failed wedge bottom often falls for about a measured move, as it did here.

To buy, you first needed a trend line break and it was better to have a reversal bar. Since bar 9 was a weak reversal bar and you would be more inclined to buy after a trend channel line overshoot and reversal, you could have waited for a second long entry. Bar 12 was a second entry, but it was a purchase at the top of a four-bar trading range, and you should never buy above a bear flag in a bear trend. Once that weak second entry failed, the bears took control. That was the trade that you needed to take instead of spending too much energy convincing yourself that the long setups were adequate.

Traders would have recognized this day as a trending trading range day shortly after the breakout from the double top at bar 2. It is usually safe to trade in both directions on this type of bear trend day, but the longs are countertrend so the setups must be strong, like at bar 3 and two bars after bar 4 (second-entry long). The move down to bar 7 was a breakout, but instead of forming much of a third trading range, the market formed a tight bear channel and then broke to the downside again. This became a bear channel down from the spike down to bar 7. Other traders saw the spike as the move from bar 2 to bar 3 and the channel as the move down from bar 5. It does not matter as long as you recognize the day as a bear trend and work hard to stay short.

Incidentally, the three doji bars that formed the swing low before bar 2 created a micro wedge.

FIGURE 5.12 Successive One-Tick Breakouts

One-tick breakouts can be important, especially if there are two in succession, because that creates a three-push pattern. In Figure 5.12, bar 4 was one tick above bar 3, and bar 5 was 1 tick above bar 4. If there was then a pullback or some sideways trading and then the market moved above bar 5, there would likely have been an upside breakout and the micro wedge would have failed to reverse the market.

Bar 2 was a couple of ticks below bar 1, and bar 6 was one tick below bar 2. After several more bars, bar 7 fell below the bar 6 low and led to a downside breakout. When the market breaks out of these micro three-push patterns, there is usually at least a measured move, using the top to the bottom of the trading range for the measurement. Here, the breakout went much further.

Bar 8 was a micro wedge bottom, setting up a one-bar bear flag. It was a sign that the market was pausing; it was not a reversal pattern in a strong bear trend.

CHAPTER 6

Expanding Triangles

An expanding triangle can be either a reversal or a continuation pattern and is made of at least five swings (sometimes seven, and rarely nine), each one greater than the prior one. Part of its strength comes from its trapping traders on each new breakout. Since it is a triangle, it is a trading range, and most breakout attempts in a trading range fail. This tendency results in the expanding triangle. In a bullish reversal (an expanding triangle bottom), it has enough strength to rally above the last higher high, trapping longs in; it then collapses to a third low, trapping longs out and bears in on the lower low, and then reverses up, forcing both sides to chase the market up. The new low is the third push down and can be thought of as a type of three-push pattern, and it can also be thought of as a breakout pullback—the market broke above the last swing high and then pulled back to a lower low. In a bear reversal (an expanding triangle top), it does the opposite. Bears are trapped in by a lower low then are forced out, and bulls get trapped in by a higher high, and both then have to chase the market as it reverses down for the final time. The initial target is a breakout beyond the opposite side of the triangle, where the market often tries to reverse again. If it succeeds, then the reversal fails, and the pattern becomes a continuation pattern in the original trend.

For example, if there is an expanding triangle top (a reversal pattern) in a bull trend, the first objective is a breakout below the pattern; in most cases, that is as far as the trade goes. If the breakout succeeds, the next objective in the reversal down is a measured move that is approximately the same height as the last leg up in the triangle. If the breakout fails and the market reverses up, then the triangle becomes a continuation pattern, which in this case would be an expanding triangle bull flag, since it is a triangle in a bull trend. The initial target would be a new high, and usually that is about as far as the trade goes. If the breakout succeeds, the next target is a measured move up that is about the size of the last leg down in the triangle. If the breakout fails and the market turns down, it is now a larger expanding triangle top with seven legs instead of the original five. At some point, either a breakout succeeds and the market makes an approximate measured move or the triangle evolves into a larger trading range.

The term *triangle* is misleading, because the pattern often does not look anything like a triangle. The salient point is that it is a series of progressively greater higher highs and lower lows that continue to trap breakout traders, and at some point they capitulate and then all of the traders are on the same side, creating a trend. It has three pushes and can be viewed as a variation of a three-push reversal pattern, but with deep pullbacks. For example, in a bull reversal at the bottom of a bear trend, both pullbacks form higher highs; however, in a conventional three-push pattern like a wedge bottom (a contracting triangle that is pointing down), both pullbacks would form lower highs (i.e., not an expanding pattern).

All expanding triangles are variants of major trend reversals, because the final reversal always follows a strong leg. For example, in an expanding triangle bottom, the rally from the final low follows a rally that was strong enough to go above a prior swing high, and that rally always breaks some significant bear trend line. At a minimum, the rally from the second push down breaks above the bear trend line that contained that second leg down, and the third push down is therefore a lower low major trend reversal buy setup. The rally to the first or second leg usually also breaks above some other major bear trend line.

Figure 6.1   EXPANDING TRIANGLES   **183**

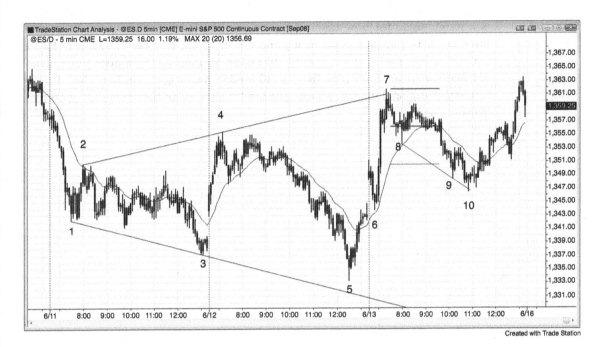

FIGURE 6.1 Expanding Triangle Bottom in the Emini

An expanding triangle bottom in a bear trend often later tries to become an expanding triangle bear flag. In Figure 6.1, the Emini ran up off an opening reversal from the bar 6 gap pullback test of the moving average and yesterday's close. Yesterday's low at bar 5 formed an expanding triangle bottom with bars 1, 2, 3, and 4. This was a reversal pattern, since the trend was down prior to the triangle. The first objective was a new swing high, which was reached at bar 7. Then the market usually tries to form an expanding triangle bear flag, which is a continuation pattern since it is a trading range in a bear trend. It did that at the bar 7 overshoot of the bull trend channel line (the triangle was formed by bars 2, 3, 4, 5, and 7). After a trend channel line fails breakout, especially when there is an expanding triangle, there is usually a two-legged move down. Incidentally, expanding triangles don't have to have a perfect shape and they do not have to touch the trend channel lines (bar 5 fell short).

The rally up to bar 7 was very strong, but the low 2 short at the top of the trading range was worth taking under these circumstances. Bar 8 was the second doji in a row, and dojis represent equilibrium between bears and bulls. Since they are in balance, that balance point is often the midpoint of the move down, and is a rough guide for how much further down the market might go in its search for enough buying power to swing the market back up. The target was hit at bar 9, but the market did not rally until after overshooting the bear trend channel line and reversing up at the bar 10 wedge bull flag signal bar. Bar 10 also tested the original long entry above the bar 6 signal bar to the exact tick (a perfect breakout test).

Figure 6.2   EXPANDING TRIANGLES   **185**

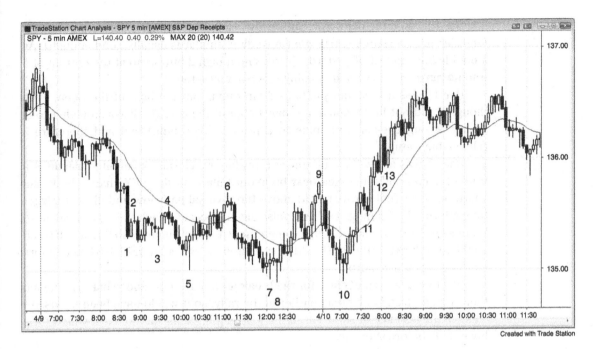

FIGURE 6.2   Expanding Triangle Bottom Reversal

In an expanding triangle reversal pattern, the lows keep getting lower and the highs keep getting higher. Typically, there are five turns before the reversal, but sometimes there are seven, like in the 5 minute SPY chart presented in Figure 6.2. There are usually valid reasons to scalp each leg (for example, each leg is a new swing high or low in a trading range), but once the fifth leg is complete, a larger trend can develop and it is wise to swing part of the position. Also, once the pattern completes, it usually sets up an expanding triangle pattern in the opposite direction. If the first was a reversal pattern, then the next part of this pattern (which will be in the opposite direction), if it develops, will be a continuation pattern and vice versa.

Bar 5 was the fifth leg (bar 1 was the first) and therefore a buy setup for at least two legs up. However, bar 6 was a failed breakout short setup and a small wedge (it was the third of three small pushes in the channel after the spike up from bar 5). This created an expanding triangle bear flag, where the first of the five swings was bar 2.

The seventh leg had a second entry at bar 8. Bar 7 was the first setup at a new low, but it failed, as was expected since the entry was in a barbwire pattern and most traders would have waited for a second signal. Bar 8 was also a high 3 buy setup in the small bear channel after the spike down from bar 6, and the third push down often signals the end of a spike and channel bear trend pattern.

Bar 10 tested the bar 8 low, but its low was one tick higher. It was similar to a ninth leg of an expanding triangle (in trading, similar is usually good enough). As a double bottom test of yesterday's low and a high 2 buy setup at the bottom of a trading range, it was a good opening reversal buy setup.

Bar 11 was a breakout pullback from taking out the high of the open, even though it did not break above the bar 9 high of the triangle. It was a high 1 long after a strong five-bar bull spike in a possible new bull trend and therefore a reliable buy setup.

Bar 12 was a low 2 at the top of a trading range (an expanding triangle is a trading range) and a one-tick bear breakout failure on this SPY chart. The Emini chart, however (not shown), held above the reversal bar's low and did not trigger the pattern. The Emini gives fewer false signals because each tick is equivalent to 2.5 ticks in the SPY. Since the up momentum was strong enough so that a bull trend might be underway, traders should have waited to see if a lower high formed before considering taking shorts.

Bar 13 was a second entry for the breakout failure short above bar 9, but again there was no trend line break earlier in the rally, so it would have been unwise to short in the absence of some earlier bear strength. Bears should have waited for a lower high before shorting.

Instead of breakout failures, bars 12 and 13 were breakout pullbacks in a new bull trend.

Figure 6.3   EXPANDING TRIANGLES   **187**

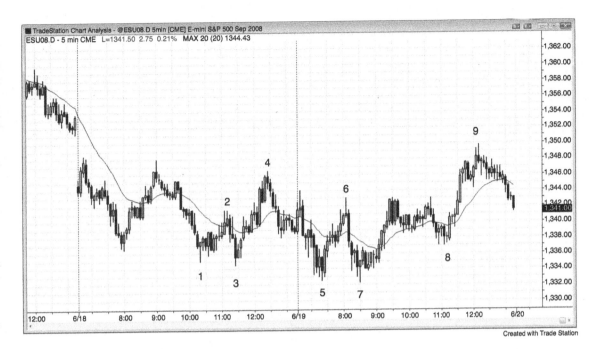

FIGURE 6.3   Second Entry in Expanding Triangle Reversal

As shown in Figure 6.3, bars 1 to 5 created the five legs of the expanding triangle bottom. The entry was one tick above the bar 5 lower low. Bar 6 failed to take out the high of bar 4 before dropping to a new low. Bar 7 was a second-chance entry at the expanding triangle, but with this many bars between bars 5 and 7, the triangle had lost its influence and this had become just a double bottom reversal from a new low on the day.

Bar 8 formed a higher low that was also a double bottom pullback long from the bars 5 and 7 double bottom.

After reaching the target of a new swing high, bar 9 set up an expanding triangle bear flag (bars 2, 3, 4, 7, and 9), and this short had a target of below the bar 7 low. Eventually, however, one of these increasing larger triangles fails and a trend begins. Incidentally, the market gapped below bar 7 on the open of the next day, reaching the target. The proportionality was bad since the spacing between bars 4 and 9 was so much greater than between bars 2 and 4. When the shape is that unconventional, fewer traders will trust it and that weakens the pattern. However, traders still saw bar 9 as the top of a bear trading range, a double top bear flag with yesterday's high, and a test of the gap above yesterday's high, and those are reasons enough to go short.

CHAPTER 7

Final Flags

Once a trend ends, traders can look at the chart and see the final flag in the trend. Final flag reversals are common because every reversal follows some kind of flag and therefore is a type of final flag reversal. If a trader understands what makes a flag likely to be the last one before the trend reverses, he is in a position to anticipate and trade the trend reversal.

Here are several characteristics that are common in final flags:

- The flag occurs in a trend that has gone on for dozens of bars; therefore the trend traders might begin to take profits and the countertrend traders might become more aggressive. Both will believe that the trend is overdone and is therefore prone to have a larger two-legged correction and evolve into a larger trading range or even a reversal.
- The flag is mostly horizontal and has signs of strong two-sided trading, such as several trend bars in the opposite direction, bars with prominent tails, several reversals, and bars that overlap the previous bar by at least 50 percent. Part IV in book 2 on trading ranges gives more signs of two-sided trading.
- A micro trend line breakout pullback is of a one-bar or micro final flag. For example, when there is a break above a bear micro trend line and the market reverses down, that one- or two-bar breakout often becomes the final bear flag in the micro bear trend. If the sell-off fails within a bar or two and then the market reverses back up from a lower low, double bottom, or higher low, this last sell-off is the breakout pullback and the original small breakout becomes the final flag in the micro bear trend. If there is a reversal after breaking out of a final flag, but it only pulls back for a few bars and then the trend resumes,

the pullback has become a breakout pullback in an ongoing trend instead of a reversal, and the final flag has failed to reverse the market.

- Final flags sometimes reverse briefly only to form a larger flag, which can break out or reverse. You will usually be able to make a scalper's profit off the final flag reversal entry before the evolution takes place, and the evolved pattern will typically result in another signal in either direction.
- Sometimes there will be two consecutive horizontal flags with the second one being smaller, and the breakout from the second one can lead to a wedge reversal.
- If the final flag forms after a climax, the failed breakout may not exceed the prior trend extreme. For example, if there is a bear climax and then a horizontal trading range above the low, this could become a final flag with the breakout reversing up after either a higher low or a lower low.
- Sometimes a final flag can be only one or two bars long and develop after a strong spike that is composed of several unusually large trend bars (a potential exhaustive climax). The breakout from that small flag often reverses after a bar or two and usually results in a two-legged pullback that lasts for 10 bars or more. This is a tradable countertrend setup, but it does not reliably lead to a trend reversal. The strong momentum demonstrated by those large trend bars frequently is followed by a test of the trend extreme within 10 to 20 bars. The one-bar final flag can be any type of pause bar. For example, if the market just had two consecutive sell climaxes, and the next bar is a bull doji, even if its low is below the low of the sell climax, the doji can become the final flag in the bear trend. If the next bar or two is a large bear spike and then the market reverses up, the pause bar is a one-bar final flag.
- Tight trading ranges often become final flags. Any sideways trading has a magnetic pull. Since breakouts usually fail, the market usually gets drawn back into the range where both bulls and bears agree that there is value.
- Sometimes there is no breakout, and the final flag just grows into a new trend. This often happens as a reversal after consecutive climaxes.
- Traders see that the market is overdone and expect a correction soon, but think that the breakout will go far enough for one more scalp. They therefore enter on the breakout of the potential final flag, but are looking to exit soon after entering, rather than being willing to hold for a swing. With everyone looking to take small profits, the breakout quickly reverses.

When you look at any chart where there is a trend reversal, you see that the trend was made up of a series of spikes and pullbacks, which are flags. If you study the final flag in that trend, you will discover that it gave clues that the trend was about to end and become either a trading range or an opposite trend. The trading range can have protracted legs and appear to be a trend reversal, but usually becomes just a large pullback on a higher time frame chart. However, those legs are usually big enough for a profitable swing trade. Traders are not certain if the reversal will be a new trend or a large correction, and they trade both the same way. They take partial or full profits after the first or second leg and look to add on during a pullback. If there is a strong move in the direction of the original trend, they might hold on to their position for a test of the old trend's extreme.

Every pullback has two-sided trading, but when the pullback is mostly horizontal, has many bars that largely overlap, has several reversals within the range, and has several bars with bodies in the direction opposite to the trend, then the two-sided trading is especially pronounced. The final flag can be a trading range of any size, including just a single bar, although it usually has at least five to 10 bars. The two-sided trading means that both the bulls and the bears agree that there is value at this level to initiate trades. The bears are shorting aggressively because they believe that the trading range will break to the downside, and the bulls are buying aggressively because they believe that the breakout will be to the upside. Whenever the price drifts to the top of the trading range or breaks out of the top of the range and runs for several bars, the bears see it as an even better value, and they short even more strongly. The bulls see the top of the range as a little expensive, and they buy less. This results in the bears being able to push the price back down. When it gets to the bottom of the range or has a downside breakout, the opposite happens and the bulls think that the value is even better, but the bears think that it is getting too low to short heavily. This makes the market work back up into the middle of the range. The same process takes place in all trading ranges, including bull and bear flags, and the result is that there is a magnetic effect in the middle of these trading ranges, and most breakout attempts do not go far before the market is pulled back into the trading range.

When one develops after a trend has gone on for a few dozen bars, it often becomes the final flag in the trend. After the breakout, the with-trend traders are more interested in taking profits and waiting for a deep correction before entering again, and the countertrend traders will fade the attempt at trend resumption since they expect at least a two-legged correction. For example, if there is a bull trend that has been going on for dozens of bars and it might be ready for a larger correction or even a reversal, traders will watch to see if it forms a bull flag that is mostly horizontal. Since the bull trend is still in effect, traders are willing to buy the breakout, but are looking for only a scalp, not a swing. The bears who were shorting during the flag will buy back their shorts. Their buying contributes to the move up, but they are eager to short again once the market reaches some resistance level, which might be a fixed number of ticks where they think the bulls will scalp out of longs or might be some measured move target. The bulls quickly sell out of their longs for a small profit soon after entering. Aggressive bears see the same thing as the bulls and begin to sell exactly where the bulls are selling. With the bulls and the bears both expecting lower prices, there is no one left to buy and the market reverses down, at least for a scalp. If the move down is strong, the bulls will not be willing to buy and the bears will not be eager to take profits until there are signs that the correction is ending. The reversal can lead to a pullback, a larger correction (like a trading range), or a trend reversal.

As was discussed earlier in Chapter 3 about double bottoms and tops, final flags are caused by the same basic behavior. For example, if there is a potential final flag in a bull trend, there is a push up just before the flag forms. The upside breakout of the flag is a test of that bull high. If more sellers than buyers come in as the market tests up, the market will reverse down from this second push up. Although the underlying force is the same, a final flag looks sufficiently different and has several distinctive properties that warrant its being classified as a separate pattern. The same is true of a final flag in a bear trend, which is just a pair of moves down and then a reversal up. The bear breakout of the final flag is the second move down and a test of the strength of the bear trend that paused to create the final flag.

Many bulls and bears will sell soon after the bull breakout of a bull flag, and if enough do, the market will begin to reverse. If a bear reversal setup develops, traders will become more confident that a bigger correction will follow; more bulls will sell out of their longs, and more bears will begin to short. If the reversal down triggers by moving one tick below the bear reversal bar, the market will get drawn back into that final flag. It may stop there, but the market usually forms at least a two-legged sideways to down correction and often a trend reversal. The trend reversal is more likely if there was a strong bear leg (a sign of selling pressure) in the flag, or earlier, that broke well below the bull trend line. If the original trend lasted for 50 to 100 bars, then the reversal will more likely evolve into a large flag rather than a trend in the opposite direction. Remember, trends have tremendous inertia and tend to resist all reversal attempts. However, each reversal tends to be larger than the one before, and eventually one will succeed in reversing the trend into an opposite trend.

Protracted climaxes often end after breakouts from brief final flags. For example, if there is a strong four-bar bull spike and if the bodies are large and the fourth one is unusually large, it will often lead to brief selling because traders will see the spike as a potential buy climax. Both the bulls and the bears wait for big bars like this. The bulls will use the strength as an opportunity to take partial profits at a very high price, and aggressive bears will sell to initiate short scalps. The result is often a pullback. However, since the bull spike was so strong, there will usually be strong buying at and below the low of the prior bar. The bulls are buying to reestablish their full long positions, and the bears are buying back their short scalps. The result is that the pullback only lasts from one to a few bars and becomes a high 1 or 2 buy setup. Bulls will buy above the high of the prior bar, and many will also buy if the market breaks above the top of the original bull spike.

Since the flag followed a strong bull spike that might have gone too far, too fast, many traders will treat the bull flag breakout as only a scalp. They will quickly take their scalper's profit. Their profit taking, along with shorting by aggressive bears, can quickly turn the market back down after a one- or two-bar breakout of the bull flag. This brief breakout is often made of one or more strong bull trend bars, and therefore is another potential buy climax. If enough traders see this as consecutive buy climaxes (the original bull spike was the first), many will only look to buy again after a pullback forms that has at least two legs and lasts about 10 bars. Many will short, expecting the larger pullback. If the reversal down came at a significant resistance level, many traders will see the move up as simply a buy vacuum test of the resistance level and will be open to the possibility of a trend reversal. They will watch the strength of the move down. If it is slow and weak, traders will expect it to become a pullback and will look for the bull trend to resume before long. If it has many bear bodies, they will not be eager to buy, and the market then has to probe lower to find buyers. Sometimes the market will enter a bear trend, and this can happen even if the original bull spike was very strong and the final flag was only a single bar. Many reversals happen after a second push, which essentially forms a double top. The two tops are often at different prices and form either a higher high or a lower high, but together behave like a double top and should always be considered to be different manifestations of the same price action.

When the market is in a strong spike and it then has a bar with a tail or opposite body, traders often expect one small final push and then a pullback. For example, if there is a strong bear spike with four consecutive large bear trend bars mostly closing near their lows, many traders will short around the close of each bar. If the next bar has a big tail on the bottom or a bull body, the bear trend is intact, but traders believe that a pullback is imminent. Many will short the close of this bar, but will hold only for a scalp, expecting the trade to be the final scalp in the spike. Because they see this as the final scalp, they will then not look to sell again until there is at least a small pullback. With no one willing to continue to sell at the bottom of the spike, the market will move up in search of a price that is high enough for the bears to once again short. Aggressive bulls know this and will buy at the bottom of the spike exactly where they think that the bears will be buying back their final short scalp. With both the bulls and the bears buying, the market moves up. The move up is usually at least enough for the bulls to scalp out of their longs, but it might last for five to 10 bars. Since it is the first pullback in a strong bear spike, there will be sellers above. Both the bulls and the bears will sell as the market moves above the high of the prior bar, and for any other small reason, because both are confident that the probability that the pullback will be brief is high. The selling by both the bulls and the bears results in at least one more push down, and the move down might even become a channel that reaches a measured move, based on the height of the spike. At the other extreme of possibilities, it also might be only a final flag breakout that leads to a reversal up. So how is that five-bar bear spike related to final flags? That tail or bull bar at the bottom of the spike told traders that there would be one more push down before a pullback and that it would go far enough down for a scalp, but that the market would likely reverse up quickly. This means that they saw the tail or the bull body as a micro final flag, and it was certainly a final flag on a smaller time frame chart. Traders don't have to look at smaller time frame charts to verify this, because they know that it has to be the case, or else that tail or bull body would not have formed.

A final bull flag has three ways to break out. First, the breakout can be strong enough to go above the old high of the bull trend and then the market reverses down in a higher high reversal. Alternatively, the breakout can be weaker, and the market can reverse down below the prior high in the form of a lower high reversal. Finally, there might not be much of a breakout at all, or even no upside breakout. For example, the bull flag might form a high 2 or a high 3 buy signal, but the entry bar reverses down after going only a tick or two above the signal bar, or it could simply break to the downside without ever going above the high of the prior bar. If there is a downside breakout of the bull flag, the breakout is usually a spike that is then followed by a bear channel that extends for some type of measured move. If there is no clear breakout and the bull flag just keeps growing into a larger bear channel, at some point traders will give up on the bull flag premise and see the channel as a bear trend. When this happens, there will usually have been at least a one-bar bear spike at the start. When that bear trend bar formed, experienced traders would have wondered if it was strong enough to lead to a bear channel, and many would have been shorting above the highs of the previous bars, just in case a bear trend developed. The bull flag, even though it never broke out to the upside, was the final flag in the bull trend.

With any bull flag, pullback traders buy and look to exit on a test of the trend's extreme (the most recent high). They prefer to take profits above the old high, but watch carefully to see if the market stalls below it. If so, they quickly take profits and will buy again only if there is another pullback. Their selling, and their unwillingness to buy for at least a couple more bars while they wait for a pullback, results in a lower high instead of a higher high. Because scalpers usually take profits at and just above the prior high, most new highs in bull trends find profit takers instead of new buyers. This results in most new highs being followed by pullbacks instead of protracted breakouts and new legs up. However, since most reversal attempts fail, most new highs do not result in reversals into bear trends. The reversal often looks strong, but is usually followed by just another bull flag. Bulls will buy the pullback and bears will take profits on their short scalps, and the market will test the high again. Eventually, one will be the final bull flag and it will be followed by a bigger correction or a reversal, and if there are signs that this will happen, experienced traders will go short.

Similarly, the final flag in a bear trend can also break out to the downside and reverse up from a lower low or a higher low, or it can simply break out to the upside without ever breaking out to the downside. There can be a failed low 2 or low 3 short and then a reversal up in the form of a large bull trend bar. This bull spike becomes the beginning of a new bull swing, and the bear flag will then be seen as the final flag in the bear trend, even though it never had a downside breakout. The bull breakout is the sign that the traders believe that the always-in trade has flipped from short to long.

If there are reasons to believe that a bear swing might be ending and it then begins to form a bear flag, traders might think that the low 1 or low 2 short entries from that bear flag will fail. If they are expecting no significant bear breakout from this bear flag and instead think that the market will trap bears and then break out to the upside, they can fade the low 1 and low 2 setups. For example, if there is a wedge bottom on a trading range day that is beginning to reverse up, traders will expect the low of the wedge to hold. Since they believe that the trend might now be up, they want to buy pullbacks. A pullback can be as small as a single bar. Since there will probably be two legs up, the first leg down should not go far. That low 1 short should fail and become a small higher low pullback in the new bull leg, and these bulls will expect at least a two-legged rally that will last 10 or more bars. The only time that a low 1 short is reliable is in the spike phase of a strong bear trend, and never after a reversal pattern. That low 1 short entry will likely fail to fall below the low of the wedge and will instead form a small higher low in the two-legged correction up. Because of that, traders will place a limit order to buy at the low or one to three ticks below the low of that short signal bar, expecting a small higher low to form instead of a profitable low 1 short. In the Emini, they usually can risk as few as four ticks.

As the reversal up continues, they might think that a low 2 short setup could form. However, since they believe that the trend has reversed into a bull trend, they expect that low 2 to fail as well and be followed by higher prices. They are still in the buy pullbacks mode, and that can include a small pullback like a low 2. Here again, they will place limit orders to buy at or below the low of the low 2 signal bar and risk about four ticks in the Emini. They are expecting this bear flag to fail to break out for more than a few ticks, and instead they look for the market to continue to work up into a bull channel. This is a type of final bear flag because it is the final flag of the bear trend. The bears thought of it as a bear flag, but were able to break it below the bear signal bar by only a tick or two, and then the flag continued to grow up and to the right until traders realized that it was now a bull channel. At some point, when enough traders realize what is happening, the bears cover, and there will usually be an upside breakout and then a measured move up.

Once the bears believe either that the market has reached the top of a trading range or that the bull trend is in the process of reversing down, they will look for high 1 and high 2 signal bars and place limit orders to short at or just above the highs of those bars. They are looking to sell rallies, even very small ones like a high 1 or a high 2. Bulls will look to buy low 1 and low 2 entries at the bottom of a trading range and at the bottom of a bear trend when they feel that the market is in the process of reversing into a bull swing.

If the high 2 is likely to fail, why would it ever trigger in the first place? It triggers because the bears are looking to short above bars, and less so just below the highs of bars. They place limit orders to short at and above the high of the prior bar. With a relative lack of bears willing to short just below the high of the bar, the bulls are unopposed and are able to push the market above the high of the prior bar, hoping that lots of bulls will enter on buy stops. The high of the bar acts as a magnet, and the push above the bar is a micro buy vacuum. The bulls find that there is an overwhelming number of bears waiting to short there, and there are lots of bulls, who bought lower, taking profits there. The result is that the high 2 triggers, but the market immediately turns down. Those bulls who bought over the last several ticks quickly see the lack of a rally above the high of the prior bar. Because the market is not doing what they expected, they exit and will not look to buy again for at least a few bars. Their selling out of their longs contributes to the sell-off.

If a final flag reversal triggers but the reversal fails within a couple of bars, this becomes a *failed* final flag. A failed final flag is a setup for a resumption of the original trend and therefore is a breakout pullback. After the market broke out of the potential final flag, it tried to reverse, but instead just pulled back a little and then the trend resumed instead of reversed. For example, if the market was in a bull trend and had a potential final bull flag that broke to the upside and then began to reverse down, but the short entry bar quickly became a strong bull reversal bar, this is a setup for a breakout pullback long. That bull reversal bar was a pullback from the breakout of the potential final flag, and if the bull trend goes far enough, it will be beyond the magnetic pull of the final flag and traders will look for other patterns. If the rally goes for only a bar or two and reverses down again, it sets up a second entry short from the original potential final flag. If the reversal succeeds, it is a final flag reversal. If it fails and the market again turns up, the market is likely in a bull channel, and channels can last for many bars.

Figure 7.1   FINAL FLAGS   **197**

FIGURE 7.1 Final Flag Reversal

A sell climax that forms after a bear trend has gone on for a long time is often followed by a final flag reversal and at least a two-legged rally. In Figure 7.1, bar 1 ended two legs down from the open and was therefore a possible low of the day. It broke out of a sideways bear flag after a protracted move, so this could have been a final flag and it could have led to a reversal up. Bar 1 was a good reversal bar, triggering the final flag long, causing traders to expect at least two legs up. Some of the best reversals come when the first leg up from the reversal extends beyond the final flag, as it does here. There is then often a sideways flag above the old bear flag, and then the new bull trend continues. Sometimes there is just a brief pullback into the old bear flag and other times there is not even a pause in the new bull leg as it soars higher in a strong spike made of a series of bull trend bars. When you see this type of reversal, it is important to swing some or all of your position because the odds are good that you could receive windfall profits.

The trading range from about 7:30 to about 9:30 a.m. PST had two hours of two-sided, horizontal trading and was a larger final flag. Two-sided trading exerts a magnetic pull that tends to draw the market back to that level after a breakout.

The entry bar after bar 1 closed above the highs of the prior six bars and above the prior seven closes, and therefore reversed many highs and closes. Traders who shorted during those bars either had to cover their shorts or were holding losing positions, which they would soon likely cover with a loss. Also, they would not have been looking to short again for at least several bars, and most would have waited for at least a two-legged rally before considering shorting again. This made the market one-sided, which usually leads to a rally that has at least 10 bars and two legs.

Figure 7.2

FINAL FLAGS **199**

FIGURE 7.2 Tight Trading Range as a Final Flag

A tight trading range after a rally often becomes the final bull flag. In Figure 7.2, the bar 4 breakout above the open was on strength, and led to the formation of a tight trading range. Here, the strong breakout of the flag ended at bar 7, which was a two-legged move up (bar 5 was the first leg), and a wedge top (the first bar of the day was the first push up and bar 4 was the second). Two-legged moves out of flags often set up a major reversal that typically has at least two legs. The move down to bar 10 was in two legs, but it had only a single countertrend bar (bar 9), which meant that it was likely going to be just the first leg of two larger legs. When the two-legged move is in a tight channel, the entire channel usually becomes the first leg. In any case, if short traders were unsure, they could have moved their stops to breakeven after the move down to bar 10 at the moving average.

Bar 9 went above the high of the small bull doji bar to trigger a high 1 buy, but experienced traders expected it to fail after a buy climax and a final flag top. Bar 8 and the two bars that followed became a smaller final flag, with bar 9 being a lower high failed breakout of the three-bar final flag. There was a micro buy vacuum that sucked the market to a tick or two above that high 1 signal bar. Strong bears expected the high 1 to fail and were waiting to see if they would get an opportunity to short at or above the signal bar's high. Many therefore stopped shorting when the market was a tick or two below the high of the bar, and this absence of traders willing to sell sucked the market higher in search of bears. Once the market reached their target (at and just above the high 1 signal bar), the bears aggressively shorted and overwhelmed the bulls, driving the market down. The bulls who bought at and just above the high 1 signal bar's high immediately saw that the market stalled and was reversing, so they sold out of their longs, helping to push the market down. They became convinced that the short-term top was in and would not consider buying again for at least several bars. With no buyers left, the market fell quickly to the support of the moving average and the middle of the final flag (the trading range that began at bar 4), where bears would buy back some of their shorts and bulls would start buying again. Since the sell-off was strong, there were very few buyers, and the market was unable to rally. These buyers quickly became sellers (the bulls sold out of their new longs and the bears shorted once again), and the market fell further in search of a price that was low enough to attract buyers.

Bar 10 and the bar after it formed a two-bar reversal high 2 buy signal at the moving average. Experienced traders would not have bought this high 2 because it followed four strong bear bars (a micro channel). Bar 11 was the signal bar for the failed breakout of the high 2 bull flag. This is a common situation. Some bulls saw the pullback from the bar 7 high to the moving average as a bull flag. However, once the market broke below bar 10, the bulls gave up on that notion and decided that the market was likely to drop for about a measured move and two legs before forming another buy setup. The two-bar bear spike (bar 11 and the next bar) was followed by a bear channel. In hindsight, the bar 4 trading range turned into a final flag in the bull move up from bar 1, but smart traders would have anticipated this possibility and swung part of their shorts. The bar before bar 9 was also a final bull flag, as was the high 2 that triggered two bars after bar 10.

The low 2 lower high at bar 2 was a similar situation. The bears saw it as a bear flag in the sell-off from the open, a possible lower high and start of a bear trend, and at least the top of a possible trading range. Once the short triggered and then the market rallied above the high of bar 2, the bears knew that their premise was wrong. The bear flag failed and the bears expected a rally that would last at least two legs and reach about a measured move up.

Bar 7 was also the third push up on the day where the first bar of the day was a gap spike up, and bar 4 was the second push in the wedge channel that ended at bar 7.

As bar 9 went above the bull bar before it, the market was attempting to create a failed final flag, which is a breakout pullback buy setup. However, since the signal bar for this potential long and two of the prior three bars had prominent tails, shorts would have kept their protective stops above the bar 8 signal bar high until the market move down. Once the strong bar 9 bear trend bar closed, they would have moved their stops to above its high. This was a weak high 1 buy setup and likely to fail, and therefore it was not a buy setup. Most traders would have shorted at or

Figure 7.2   FINAL FLAGS   **201**

above its high, which clearly happened here. They would not have gone long and they would not have exited their shorts.

Bar 12 is an example of a micro final flag. Traders were shorting the closes of the bear bars in the spike down, but the bar before bar 12 had large tails. This alerted traders to the possibility that a small pullback was imminent. Aggressive bears shorted the close of that bar, but were expecting only a scalp and then a pullback. They bought back their profitable scalps on the bar after entry, and their buying created the bar 12 reversal bar. Aggressive bulls understood what was going on, so they bought where they thought that the bears would be buying back their short scalps. The bulls were looking for only a scalp up. Bear swing traders also expected the pullback, so they bought back part of their positions to take profits. All traders with large open profits take partial profits along the way, and they usually do so where they expect a small pullback to form. Their buying contributes to the pullback. When the bulls sold out of their long scalps and the bears shorted at the top of the pullback, the market sold off again, as expected. V bottoms are rare, so everyone was eager to sell, knowing that the probability of at least one more push down was high. Traders sold above the high of the prior bar on limit orders and on stops below the low of the prior bar. There were also reasons to sell on every other time frame and every other type of chart. Other traders shorted the low 2 that triggered four bars after bar 12 (some shorted below the bull bar, while others shorted below the two-bar bear reversal). Early bulls who were unrealistically hoping for a bigger rally sold out of their longs on the low 2 and were not willing to buy again for at least a couple more bars down. With no one looking to buy, the market quickly fell for several bars.

FIGURE 7.3 Triangle as a Final Flag

When the bullish momentum is exceptionally strong, it is better to look only for buy setups and not shorts until after there has been some significant sign of strength by the bears.

As shown in Figure 7.3, the Euro/U.S. Dollar Forex had a final flag short setup at bar 2, but the upward momentum was strong and the flag was only four bars long; it therefore did not break a significant bull trend line. That single bear trend bar was not strong enough to negate that much upward momentum, and it was likely that the market would correct sideways and then rally to a new high. This was likely to fail to reverse the market and instead become just a pullback from the breakout above the bar 1 two-bar reversal. When a final flag setup fails to reverse the market, it becomes a failed final flag, which is a breakout pullback setup. This is what happened here. The bar 1 potential final flag had a reversal signal at the bar 2 two-bar reversal. The reversal entry triggered, but the market did not fall far. Instead, it went sideways and formed another buy setup, and this made buying above bar 3 an entry from a failed final flag setup. The market broke above the bar 1 flag, pulled back, and then broke to the upside again.

Figure 7.3   FINAL FLAGS **203**

The bar 3 two-bar reversal set up a high 2 long and a double bottom with bar 1, and these are reasons enough to buy in a strong bull trend. Conservative traders saw bar 3 as part of a small channel down from bar 2, and they would have bought above the small double top bear flag formed by the bars just before and after the bar 3 two-bar bull reversal. The breakout above bar 3 was weak and the market pulled back to a small higher low. This was a breakout pullback setup, and it turned the pattern into a wedge bull flag where bars 1 and 3 were the first two pushes down, as well as into a triangle (as soon as there was a third push down, the trading range was a triangle). The triangle was horizontal, and it formed after a protracted rally. It could have enough two-sided trading to generate sufficient magnetic pull to draw any breakout back into the trading range. Some traders saw bar 4 as a breakout pullback from the bar 3 bull trend bar and the high 2 entry on the next bar. This bull flag was a potential final flag, and bar 5 was the reversal setup. It was the third push up and a breakout of a one-bar pullback, which was a one-bar final flag. However, the momentum up was still so strong that a sideways correction was more likely than a reversal. The market entered a tight trading range from which it then could have broken out to the upside again or reversed down. If it broke to the upside, the tight trading range could have become the final flag.

FIGURE 7.4   Final Flag, Then a Lower High

Sometimes a final flag breakout reverses at a lower high instead a higher high. In Figure 7.4, the rally up to bar 2 was strong and parabolic and therefore was likely to be followed by at least a two-legged pullback (pullbacks in a bull trend can be sideways or down) that would last at least 10 bars. It formed a horizontal trading range above the moving average from which it broke out at bar 3. However, the breakout failed and the market reversed down in a two-bar reversal. The bar 3 breakout was a lower high instead of a higher high, but it was still the final flag in the bull trend. Traders would have shorted below the two-bar reversal. Bar 3 was also a double top bear flag with the small lower high that followed bar 2. Bar 2 failed to go above the high of the open, and bar 3 was a second failed attempt to break out to a new high of the day. When the market tries to do something twice and fails both times, it usually trends in the opposite direction.

There was a huge two-bar sell spike on the open and then a bull bar. Any trend bar or series of trend bars forms a breakout, a spike, a gap, and a climax. This initial sell climax was followed by a second one at bar 1. Consecutive sell climaxes often lead to protracted corrections and sometimes reversals, as occurred here. The final flag in the sell-off down to bar 1 was that one-bar pause that formed just before bar 1. This bar became a one-bar final flag in the sell-off; even though it was a bull reversal bar and its low was below the low of the huge two-bar bear spike before it, it

Figure 7.4   FINAL FLAGS   **205**

was a pause in the bear trend, and therefore a bear flag. Consecutive sell climaxes in a freely falling market like this often have a one- or two-bar final flag that is followed by a large correction or even a reversal. Traders who knew that consecutive sell climaxes usually lead to big pullbacks were willing to buy the reversal up at the low of the day after they saw that one-bar pause. There was no one left who would sell at the low. The remaining bears would have sold only a pullback and only after at least a 10-bar rally. Bar 1 interrupted the selling and turned it into two separate sell climaxes instead of a single climax. Had it not been there, the selling would have probably continued after bar 1, at least for a bar or two. Many bears would have bought back their shorts on the close of bar 1, expecting a rally to a level where they would consider shorting again. Aggressive bulls would have gone long at the close of bar 1, risking about as many ticks as bar 1 was tall, looking for a test of the bar 1 high and then possibly a measured move up, based on the height of bar 1. Bar 1 had 93,000 contracts, which was about 10 times the average volume of quiet bars over the past couple of days, and was therefore supportive of a spike and climax type of reversal up. Spike and climax variations of spike and channel trends are discussed in book 1. There is a spike down, a pause, and then another sell climax (bar 1), which acts like a one-bar channel in a spike and channel pattern.

The horizontal trading range after bar 1 was also a final flag, although it never broke out to the downside. After a sell climax, the market often forms a bear flag that can be horizontal or in a bull channel, and sometimes it will have a low 1 or a low 2 short setup as it did here, but there is no follow-through and therefore no bear breakout. Instead, the bear flag broke out to the upside, which is a common way for trends to reverse. The doji signal bars were weak signal bars for shorts after consecutive sell climaxes, and aggressive traders would have bought at or below their lows. Since it was the last bear flag, it was a type of final flag. It was also a reversal up from a one-bar final flag, which was the bull reversal bar before the large bar 1 sell climax. The bull trend bar breakout above the bear flag at 8:05 a.m. PST completed the reversal.

Created with TradeStation

FIGURE 7.5   Final Flags Sometimes Reverse without First Breaking Out

Sometimes the final flag does not break out and instead just continues to pull back, eventually becoming a trend in the opposite direction. As shown in Figure 7.5, there was a spike and climax down to bar 14, and bar 14 was a strong bull reversal bar. Some traders saw the spike as starting at bar 6 and ending at bar 9, while others thought that bar 9 and the bear bar before it formed the important spike, or that the two-bar spike that formed two bars after bar 10 was important. All of the bear spikes were important signs of selling pressure, and it does not matter which might have been the spike that mostly contributed to the climactic sell-off to bar 14 (a spike and climax type of spike and channel bear trend). There were then three pushes down in a parabolic move to bar 14 (bars 9 and 11 were the first two legs). This often leads to a protracted rally, but the rally usually begins as a bull channel, as it did here. A bull channel is a bear flag.

Bar 15 was a low 1, and smart traders would have expected that short to fail. In fact, they would have expected the low 2 to fail and a wedge bear flag to fail, and, as with all channels, they would have been buying at or below the low of the prior bar. Institutions would not be selling below the lows of bars in a channel, because that is not what they do. How can I be sure? Because if they did, the market would go down, but since it is going up, they must be buying. At some point, everyone

Figure 7.5   FINAL FLAGS   **207**

realized that this bear flag was never going to break to the downside and the bears eventually bought back their shorts, some after the failed low 2 and others after the failed wedge bear flag. The result was an upside break, which happened here at the bar 19 bull trend bar and again above bar 20.

The bulls saw bars 3, 9, and 11 as forming a wedge bull flag, and when the market fell below bar 11, the wedge failed and the market collapsed. The bear breakout had only one leg because the pattern evolved into a spike and climax bottom.

The four consecutive bull trend bars that started at bar 14 showed buying pressure. The fourth was a breakout above a failed low 1. Bar 17 was a low 2 or low 3 setup, and instead of triggering a short, the market broke to the upside two bars later. Bar 18 was a wedge bear flag setup that triggered by one tick, and then the market reversed up and broke out to the upside on bar 19. Bar 20 was a reversal up from a moving average gap bar short, and it began a spike consisting of three bull trend bars. Unlike the earlier bull breakouts in the growing bear flag, this one had follow-through in the form of consecutive bull trend bars. This convinced most traders that the market was now always-in long, and they were no longer looking for a breakout of a bear flag.

Bar 12 was the start of a bull flag, following the strong move up from the bar 11 low. The bear bar before bar 12 was the first push down, and the two bear bars after bar 12 formed a second push down, setting up a possible high 2 bull flag that could have led to a second leg up. The next bar was a bull bar and therefore a two-bar reversal buy signal, but instead of breaking to the upside for a second leg up, the market broke to the downside with a strong bear trend bar. That bar made the bulls give up on their premise, and they then would not look to buy again for at least several more bars. Bar 13 was a pullback from the bear breakout of the bull flag and it was the start of a plunge down to the bar 14 parabolic wedge reversal (bars 9, 11, and 14 were the three pushes down).

When a bear flag breaks to the upside, like on bar 19, the bulls need a bull trend bar that closes at least several ticks above the top of the flag to make the bears give up on their premise that the rally is only a pullback in a bear. Similarly, when a bull flag breaks out to the downside, traders want to see a strong bear trend bar with a close that is several ticks below the bottom of the flag, like the bear trend bar that formed two bars before bar 13. Traders saw the high 2 bull flag setting up, but one that bear trend bar closed well below the flag, traders assumed that the bull premise was no longer valid and that the market would likely trade down for at least a couple of small legs.

FIGURE 7.6   Bear Breakout of a Bull Final Flag

Sometimes traders want to buy a bull flag, but a buy setup never triggers and the market instead breaks to the downside. As shown in Figure 7.6, there was a strong push up to bar 20 and, as the market began to pull back, traders were looking for a buy setup, since the odds favored at least a test of the high after such a strong bull spike. However, the market never broke above the micro channel down to bar 22, and instead broke to the downside on bar 23. That made the move from bar 20 to bar 22 the final flag of the bull trend, even though it never had a bull breakout. Once the large bar 23 bear trend bar formed, the bulls gave up on their belief that there should be at least one more push up, and instead looked for at least a measured move down, based on the height of the flag. Bears also saw the bear breakout and expected the same thing. Since there was no one to buy for the next several points on the downside, the market fell quickly into the close. As the market fell, the absence of pullbacks triggered momentum sell programs, contributing to the strength of the sell-off.

Once a strong bull spike has a bar with a big tail on the top or a bear body, traders usually can buy the close for one final scalp before the market corrects. The bar before bar 20 had a large tail on the top, and astute traders wondered if it was a sign that the market might soon pull back. Since bar 20 was also the third

Figure 7.6   FINAL FLAGS   **209**

push up from the bar 14 low, traders suspected that it could have been a climactic top. However, if the market had created a reasonable buy setup during the pullback, they would have placed buy stops above the signal bar to make sure to get long. The market never traded above the high of any prior bar, and a bull who wanted to enter on a buy stop above the high of the prior bar never got stopped into a long.

Bars 15, 17, and 20 formed a parabolic wedge top, which is a type of buy climax.

FIGURE 7.7 Small Final Flag and Big Reversal

Small final flags can set up opening reversals. In Figure 7.7, bar 3 was a huge bear trend bar that followed three other strong bear trend bars after the market gapped above the bear trend line. The bar 2 breakout above the bear channel failed.

Bar 4 was the setup for a short off a small bear flag. Given the climactic behavior of the market to this point and yesterday's trend line break, traders were looking for this to be a final flag that would lead to a reversal up after a test of the bar 1 bear low.

Bar 5 was another huge bear trend bar and bar 6 was an ii long entry, with the expectation of a rally that would last at least 10 bars and have at least two legs up. Bar 5 had about 105,000 contracts, which is about 10 times greater than the average volume or recent quiet bars, and therefore was supportive of a possible consecutive sell climax bottom. The second leg ended at bar 9 on the following day. The strength of the downward momentum demonstrated by the large bear trend bars would usually result in traders pushing the market down for a test of the low within a day or two. Although it is not shown, the bar 9 high led to a sell-off later that day that went far below the bar 5 low. Traders look for consecutive sell climaxes as opportunities to buy. Many bears bought back their shorts around the close of bar 5, and aggressive bulls went long. Others bought as bar 6 broke out above the bull ii pattern, expecting the second attempt to reverse up from yesterday's low to be a possible low of the day. They might have risked as many ticks as bar 5 was tall, or maybe two or three points. Their profit targets included the bar 5 high, a test of the moving average, a measured move up based on the height of bar 5, and a new high of the day.

FIGURE 7.8   Two-Bar Final Flag

A one- or two-bar final flag can lead to a big reversal, even after a strong bull spike. This is more likely on the open, when sharp reversals are common. In Figure 7.8, bar 3 was a two-bar pullback after a huge and possibly climactic bull trend bar, and therefore it was a possible final flag.

Bar 4 was an ii setup for a final flag short that was likely to lead to a two-legged, protracted correction, which it did. The bar 3 bull flag turned out to be the final flag, and its breakout failed and reversed down after bar 4. Note that the second bar of the ii pattern had a bear close, which is always desirable when a trader is looking to short.

The strong momentum up to the bar 4 high made traders drive the market up to test the trend extreme later in the day.

Bars 3 to 5 evolved into a larger wedge-shaped bull flag where bar 3 was the first push down and bar 5 was the third. The second push down was three bars before bar 5. This became a final flag when the market reversed down at the bar 6 lower high.

The rally to bar 6 was a wedge bear flag and lower high major trend reversal, where the bar before bar 5 was the first push up.

Bar 7 reversed up from an inside bar, and that bar was the final flag of the sell-off.

FIGURE 7.9   Small Final Flags Commonly Evolve into Larger Final Flags

As shown in Figure 7.9, bar 2 was a successful short scalp from the breakout of the one-bar final flag that preceded it. The pattern then grew into a larger wedge bear flag (another final flag) that ended at bar 3. The first leg up was the top of the first small final flag, which was the bull inside bar before bar 2. The second leg up was the large inside bar after bar 2. There was a small tail on the top of the bull bar, and the next bar had a smaller body. That tail and the smaller bar created the pause from the initial move up from the bar 2 low to the top of the bull bar after bar 2. The final push up was to bar 3. This was probably more clearly a wedge on a smaller time frame chart, but can be inferred from what was present here. Other traders saw this as simply a low 2 short where bar 2 was the low 1 entry bar.

The market reversed up at bar 4 and the pattern grew into a larger wedge bear flag that ended at bar 6. The first push up was to bar 3, and the next two legs up ended at bar 5 (or the swing high after it) and bar 6. Other traders saw bar 5 as the first push up and bar 6 as the third. The small spike and channel up that ended at bar 5 had two small legs, and the rally up to bar 6 after bar 5 had two clearer legs.

The breakout of the bear wedge resulted in a successful scalp, but not a new swing low. This bar 7 higher low major trend reversal was tested by bar 8, which formed a double bottom bull flag and a second entry for the higher low major trend reversal. The rally that followed created a larger bear wedge that ended at bar 9. The first two legs up were the bars 3 and 6 highs. It was irrelevant that a lower

Figure 7.9   FINAL FLAGS   **213**

low developed at bar 4 after the first push up at bar 3, because this was a common wedge variant.

Why the insistence of seeing everything as larger and larger bear flags? Because they were there, and the market was therefore telling traders that it had not reversed into a strong bull trend. The bulls failed in their breakout attempt above the bar 8 double bottom bull flag and head and shoulders bottom. The market reversed down at the bar 9 top of the channel that followed this spike up, and the failure was also from just above the trend channel line from bar 3 to bar 6. This head and shoulders bottom did what most head and shoulders bottoms do. It became a bear flag (this one was slightly sloping up so it was more of a wedge than a triangle) and a continuation pattern, instead of a reversal pattern. The market broke below the bar 4 low on the next day.

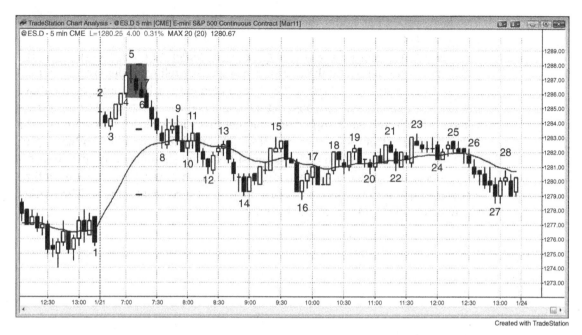

FIGURE 7.10   Final Flags Do Not Have to Break Out in the With-Trend Direction

As shown in Figure 7.10, after the gap up and strong bull spike up to bar 5, traders were uncertain if there was going to be an opening reversal down and a high of the day or a high 1 bull flag and then a bull channel. They watched carefully as the market pulled back from the bar 5 high. From bar 5 to bar 6, traders thought that the market might be forming a bull flag. However, bar 7 was a large bear trend bar that closed on its low and below the bottom of the bar 4 large bull trend bar. Bar 7 closed many ticks below the bar before it and therefore was an attempt to form a breakaway gap. Many traders shorted as soon as it closed and put a stop above its high, expecting that the market was flipping to always-in short and would likely have good follow-through selling. Bar 5 might have been the high of the day, and if the market fell below the bar 3 low of the day, it might have a measured move down. Most traders at this point believed that bar 5 was a good candidate for a high of the day. The follow-through over the next several bars convinced traders that the market was now always-in short. They were looking for a breakout below the bar 3 bottom of the opening range and then about a measured move down. Bar 14 was an exact measured move down from the opening range breakout, and many bears took profits there.

Figure 7.10   FINAL FLAGS   **215**

Since traders saw bar 5 to bar 6 as a bull flag, it was the final flag of the rally, even though there was never an upside breakout.

Bar 16 was a double bottom or slightly lower low major trend reversal, but was followed by a trading range instead of a bull trend. Major trend reversals are more often followed by trading ranges instead of trends in the opposite direction.

FIGURE 7.11 Small Final Flags after Climaxes

The monthly chart of the Dow Jones Industrial Average shown in Figure 7.11 had many one- and two-bar final flags after climaxes. Some led to reversals, like at bars 8, 12, 16, and 19 (the thumbnails show close-ups of bars 12 and 19), whereas others led to pullbacks, like bars 5, 10 (the left-hand thumbnail shows a close-up), 13, and 21. Some ended up as just ordinary flags and not the final flags in the move, like bars 4, 15, and 23, and some triggered but failed to reverse the market and became pullbacks in the trend (bars 13 and 21 are examples of failed final flags, because the market reversed down after the flags, but the reversals failed and the bull trends resumed at bars 14 and 23). Once there is a climax, then a brief flag, and then a breakout of that flag, the breakout is often strong enough to be another climax. Consecutive climaxes are prone to be followed by a reversal that can last about 10 bars and have about two legs. When they occur at a significant support or resistance level, they can lead to strong reversals, like at bar 20. As the market was breaking below bar 19, I told many friends that it could lead to a strong bull reversal because there was a 20-year-long bull trend line just below the bar 18 bear low. There was also the support of the bar 11 low, which led to a double bottom bull flag. Traders are aware of a possible lower high at bar 25, which many would see as the right shoulder of a potential head and shoulders top. I have been telling friends for the past couple of months that bar 24 could be the final flag of the rally. If so, the reversal should last for about 10 bars (10 months) and have at least two legs. It should find support at either the bar 22 high, the bar 23 low, the moving average (not shown), or the bar 20 low.

CHAPTER 8

Double Top and Bottom Pullbacks

If a market forms a double bottom after a sell-off, and before the bull trend takes off, and it then has a higher low pullback that tests just above the double bottom low, this is a double bottom pullback long setup. The double bottom does not have to be exact, and the second bottom is often slightly lower than the first, making the pattern sometimes also a head and shoulders bottom. If the second bottom does not at least reach the first, there is a risk that the bottom is forming only a two-legged sideways to up correction, thereby making it better to look for a scalp long rather than a swing. A double bottom (or top) pullback pattern can be thought of as a three-push bottom (or a triple bottom or triangle) where the third push down did not have strong-enough sellers to create a new low. The pattern always forms at a support level, as does every move up in a bear trend. If the move up from the first of the three bottoms is strong enough, traders will wonder if the trend is evolving into a trading range or even a reversal into a bull trend. In a trading range, every move down is a bull flag and every move up is a bear flag. If the market is in the early stages of a bull trend, then every move down is also a bull flag. Whether the market is entering a trading range or a new bull trend, the sell-off from the first rally is a bull flag, even though it falls to around the level of the first bottom. The rally off the double bottom is a breakout of the bull flag. The pullback (which is the third move down) from the move up off the double bottom is also a bull flag, whether it ends above the double bottom and forms a double bottom pullback (or a triangle), it ends at the level of the double bottom and forms a triple bottom, or it falls below the double bottom and reverses up and forms a failed breakout below a double bottom (basically, a type of final flag reversal). It is also a pullback from that second bull flag, so the rally off the third push down is a breakout pullback from the breakout above the second bull flag. It does not matter where the third push down ends, and it also does not matter if the overall pattern looks like a triple bottom, a triangle, a head and shoulders bottom, a final flag, or a double bottom pullback, because the significance is the same. The third reversal up creates a three-push down reversal pattern, and traders need to be looking for opportunities to get long. When the market forms a double bottom pullback and the shape is good and the bull reversal bars for the three bottoms are strong, especially if the final one is strong, the pattern is one of the most reliable buy setups.

The move up from the second bottom is usually a breakout, even though it may last for only a couple of bars. The pullback is therefore a breakout pullback, which is one of the most reliable setups. It can also be thought of as two failed attempts to exceed the prior extreme (often a low 2), and two failed attempts usually lead to a reversal. Some technicians say that triple bottoms and tops always fail and always become continuation patterns, but they require that the three extremes be identical to the tick. With that strict definition, the pattern is so rare that it is not worth mentioning. Also, it is simply arrogant to tell the market that you will not allow it to do something, and arrogance always costs you money because it is the market and not you that gets to say what can and will happen. Traders will make much more money by using loose definitions. When something resembles a reliable pattern, it will likely trade like the reliable pattern.

This is a reversal pattern and not a continuation pattern, like the double bottom bull flag. Both are long entry setups, but one is the beginning of the trend (a reversal pattern) and the other takes place in an established trend (a continuation pattern), or at least after there has been one strong leg.

Likewise, if there is a double top in a bull trend and there is then a pullback that reaches close to the high, this double top pullback is a good short setup. Again, it does not matter what shape the three-push top takes because the significance is the same. If the signal bar is strong and there is good selling pressure, it is a sell setup, whether it looks like a triple top, a triangle, a head and shoulders top, a final flag, or a double top pullback.

Sometimes there will be both a double top and a double bottom in the same trading range. The result is usually a triangle, which means that the market is in breakout mode. The market tends to move back to the middle of the range and then test either the top or the bottom, and that third push establishes the triangle. If the range is big enough, traders can scalp shorts as the market reverses down and longs as it reverses up. If the setup is good, the probability of success is about 60 percent for a reward that is at least as large as the risk. If the trading range is too tight, traders can choose to either swing a long or short, or wait for the breakout. If the breakout is strong, trade in its direction, because the probability of a reward that is at least as large as the risk is often 70 percent or more. If it fails, trade in the opposite direction.

Figure 8.1   DOUBLE TOP AND BOTTOM PULLBACKS   **219**

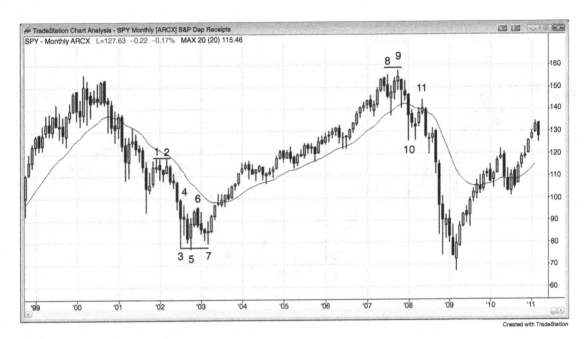

FIGURE 8.1   Double Bottom Pullback in the Monthly SPY

As shown in Figure 8.1, the monthly SPY had a double bottom pullback buy at the bar 7 outside bar as it went one tick above the high of the prior bar. Outside up bars can be reliable entry bars if the bar before was a decent signal bar, as was the case here. Other traders would have bought above the high of the outside up bar, at the close of the bull trend bar that followed bar 7, above the high of that bull trend bar, and at the close of the next bull trend bar, which confirmed the new trend for many traders. Buying above the high of a strong bull trend bar at the start of a move up is a reliable trade, as can be seen by the strong bull trend bar that followed.

Bar 5 was slightly below bar 3, but this is common and actually preferable in double bottom pullback buy patterns. Bar 6 was the breakout from the double bottom, and bar 7 was the pullback that successfully tested the resolve of the breakout traders. Many traders see these as triangles. A breakout pullback is one of the most reliable setups. Breakout pullbacks often are head and shoulders patterns.

Bar 11 was a pullback from the bars 8 and 9 double top. Some traders saw it as a lower high major trend reversal, a low 2 at the moving average, or a pullback from the breakout below the double top.

Bars 1 and 2 formed a double top bear flag (a continuation pattern and not a double top, which is a reversal pattern at the end of a bull trend). A double top in a bear trend is always a low 2 sell setup, because it is two pushes up. The bulls made two attempts to reverse the trend and failed, and will step aside for at least a couple of bars. This creates an absence of buyers and increases the speed and size of the move down, as the market races to a support level where it might find buyers again.

FIGURE 8.2   Bear Flag as a Double Bottom Pullback

Sometimes a bear flag can be a double bottom pullback buy setup. In Figure 8.2, the two-bar reversal at bar 1 was at the end of a large second leg down on the day and therefore a possible reversal setup. However, a two-bar reversal is not enough reason to buy at the bottom of a tight bear channel. Although the move up to bar 2 was small and therefore weak, neither bar 3 nor bar 4 could take out the low and therefore they formed a double bottom bull flag. Some traders saw bar 3 as the end of a wedge bear flag with the first two pushes being four and six bars earlier. This made bar 4 a small breakout pullback buy setup from the small breakout of the bull flag that formed two bars before bar 4. Other traders saw bar 3 as a breakout of the bear flag, but the breakout had no follow-through, which made traders wonder if the flag was a final flag and if the market was going to reverse up.

Bar 6 made an exact test of the bar 3 low and was unable to drop below it (or below the bar 1 low), so this was a broader double bottom bull flag, with bar 3 (or bars 3 and 4) forming the first bottom. This is also referred to as accumulation. The institutions were defending the bar 1 low instead of attempting to run the stops, indicating that they believed that the market was going up.

Bar 5 was a moving average gap bar, which often provides the necessary countertrend momentum to lead to a trend reversal. It broke a major trend line. Bar 6 was a higher low test of the bar 1 trend extreme and a breakout pullback from the bar 5 bull spike. Bar 6 was also a higher low major trend reversal, three pushes down from bar 5, and a one-bar final flag reversal (from 2 bars earlier).

Figure 8.3   DOUBLE TOP AND BOTTOM PULLBACKS   **221**

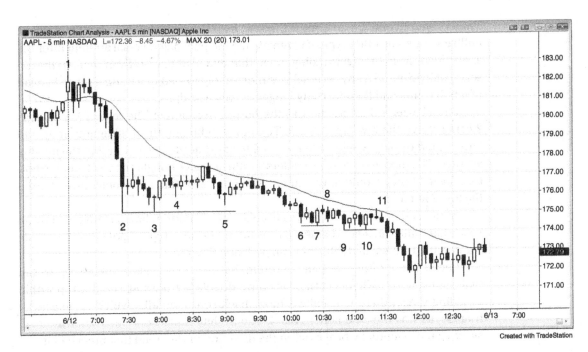

FIGURE 8.3 Weak Double Bottom Pullback

Some double bottom pullbacks just don't look strong, and that usually means that they are part of a bear flag and not a reversal pattern. In Figure 8.3, bar 4 looked like a setup for a double bottom pullback long, but bar 3 was 5 cents above the bar 2 low in a very strong bear trend. This slightly higher low usually negates the pattern and makes a two-legged bear rally much more likely than a new bull trend. Also, the first pullback (whatever minor rally would follow bar 2) in a strong trend almost always sets up a with-trend entry, so it was not wise to be looking for bottoms here. However, the market rallied over $1.00 from the long entry, if a trader took the trade. With the big tails on bars 2, 3, and 4, and with the market still in the first 90 minutes and therefore prone to opening reversals, it was a reasonable trade. The smartest traders would have been shorting the moving average test, which came in the form of a triangle (there were three pushes up, with the first coming two bars after bar 2 and the second forming on the bar before bar 4). If you instead scalped that long, it could have been difficult to quickly switch to a shorting mentality.

Bar 8 was a double bottom pullback setup, with bar 7 being 13 cents below the bar 6 low, but the entry never triggered (the bar after bar 8 was unable to take out the high of bar 8). Again, bottom picking in a strong bear trend without a prior strong trend line break is not a good approach. The market was in a tight bear channel, and channels usually last much longer than what seems reasonable.

Traders should only look to buy if there was first a strong bull breakout and then a pullback, or some other type of reversal, like the final flag reversal attempt after the spike down from the tight trading range that ended at bar 11. Even then, in the absence of a prior rally, any reversal was more likely to lead to a trading range instead of a bull trend, and therefore any long was only a scalp.

Bar 11 was a third attempt at the bottom formation. The low of bar 10 was 2 cents above the low of the bar 9. Traders who bought the double bottom would have exited or they would have reversed to short at the bar 11 low 2 at the moving average. The most experienced traders would not have bought the weak double bottom; instead they would have waited, expecting it to fail, and would have shorted the low 2 at bar 11.

At the end of the day there was a small double bottom bull flag followed by an inside bar. Since an inside bar is a pause and therefore a type of pullback, the inside bar completed a small double bottom pullback buy setup.

Bars 2 and 3 formed a double bottom, but there was also a double top within that trading range. Whenever there is both a double bottom and a double top within a trading range, there is usually a move back to the middle, which establishes a triangle, as was the case here at bar 4. The trading range continued sideways and, as expected, eventually broke out in the direction of the trend that preceded it.

Figure 8.4   DOUBLE TOP AND BOTTOM PULLBACKS   **223**

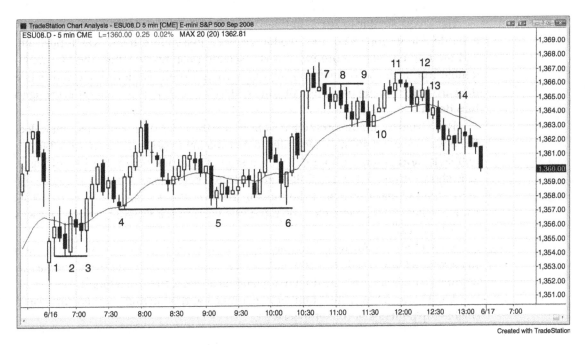

FIGURE 8.4   Double Bottom and Top Pullbacks

As shown in Figure 8.4, the Emini today had both double bottom and top pullback reversals. Bars 1 and 2 formed a double bottom, although at first glance bar 1 might be easy to overlook. The bottom of an entry bar has protective stops below it and it will often be tested, as it was by bar 2, and two moves down to the same level is a double bottom, even if the first one is not a swing low. With the big tail on the bottom of bar 1, there was almost certainly a 1 minute higher low (and in fact there was). Bar 3 was a deep pullback that tested the double bottom, so it was a second attempt to run the stops. It could not even get as close as the first attempt at the bar 2 low before the bears pulled out and the bulls took control. Some traders saw bars 2 and 3 as a double bottom bull flag, while others thought of them as a triple bottom bull flag or a double bottom pullback. It does not matter which feature you think is more important, because they all are buy setups.

Bars 4 and 5 created a double bottom bull flag on this trending trading range day. This double bottom was tested by the bar 6 pullback, forming a large double bottom pullback. You could have called it a triple bottom as well, but that term would not add any trading benefit here so it was not worth using. A trader might also see it as a double bottom major trend reversal from the small bear trend that ended at bar 6 (all bull flags are small bear trends).

Bar 7 was similar to bar 1, in that it was also an entry bar. It and bar 8 formed a subtle double top. Also, the two-bar reversal just before bar 7 was a push up, and the doji bar just before bar 7 was a second push up; together they formed a double top. It does not matter which pattern you think is more important since they are both topping patterns. All you need to know is that the market is trying to turn down.

Bar 8 tried to run the protective stops above the bar 7 short entry bar, but failed. Bar 9 was a second attempt and failed at an even lower price, creating a double top pullback short setup with an entry on a stop at one tick below the low of bar 9. This short formed a five-tick failure and set up a good reversal to a long on a stop above the two-bar reversal at the moving average. Bar 10 was the entry bar. This wedge pullback bull flag tested the top of the bar 4 to bar 6 trading range, and was a breakout test.

Bars 11 and 12 formed a double top bear flag short setup, and alerted traders to look for a later double top pullback short setup. The bar 13 bull trend bar was an attempt to rally and test the double top and an attempt to form a high 2.

Bar 14 was a lower high pullback that failed at the moving average, and was a double top pullback short setup as well.

CHAPTER 9

Failures

A failure is any trade that does not reach its goal, resulting in either a smaller profit or, more commonly, a loss. For a scalper, the goal is a scalper's profit, but if traders were expecting more and the market failed to meet their expectations, even if it provided a scalper's profit, it is still a failure. Every failed bull setup is a sign of weakness by the bulls and strength by the bears and every failed sell setup is a sign of weakness by the bears and strength by the bulls. Since the most common good setups have about a 60 percent success rate, they have about a 40 percent failure rate. When a setup fails, it often creates an excellent setup for a trade in the opposite direction. The traders who were just forced out will be hesitant to reenter in the same direction, making the market one-sided. In addition, as they exit with their losses, they drive the market even further in the opposite direction.

This chapter discusses some of the more common occurrences of patterns that fail and reverse enough for a scalp. When the pattern is large enough and the context is right, they sometimes can even lead to a major trend reversal. It is critical to understand that every pattern fails some of the time, and traders should accept that as a normal occurrence. Look at a failure as a potential opportunity, because, as mentioned, it will often set up a profitable trade in the opposite direction. At other times the failure will result in a second signal in the direction of the original setup.

Here are some of the common failures that often lead to trades in the opposite direction:

- Failed high 1, high 2, low 1, or low 2.
- Failed breakout of anything, like a swing high or low, a trend line, or a trend channel line.

- Failure to break through a magnet, like a measured move target, a prior swing high or low, a trend line, or a trend channel line.
- Failed final flag (the reversal attempt fails and sets up a breakout pullback).
- Failed wedge.
- Failed signal bar or entry bar.
- Failed one-tick breakout.
- Failed reversal, like a failed double bottom or top or a failed head and shoulders pattern.
- Failure to reach a profit target, like a five-, nine-, or 17-tick failure in the Eminis or an 11, 51, 99, or 101 cent failure in a stock.

Some failures are a sign of a strong trend and set up a with-trend trade:

- Failure to fall below the low of the prior bar in a strong bull trend or to rally above the high of the prior bar in a strong bear trend. This indicates urgency and a strong trend.
- Failure of a pullback to reach the moving average. This indicates urgency and a strong trend.
- Failure to reach a magnet, like a measured move target, a prior swing high or low, a trend line, or a trend channel line. This often leads to a pullback and then another attempt to reach the magnet.

If a trade makes a scalper's profit (and therefore the trader exited some or all of the position) and then comes back and takes out the original signal or entry bar stops, there is much less fuel left in the market to drive the market in this new, opposite direction because there are far fewer traders who are trapped in the trade (they already exited with profits). Also, many of the scalpers would exit the balance of their positions at breakeven after taking partial profits, so their stops would be tighter than the original ones beyond the entry or signal bars.

Although a minor reversal might just be a reversal in a trading range that is good for only a scalp, it can sometimes turn into or be a part of a major reversal of a trend. The single most reliable failure is a flag in a trend. As a flag is forming, countertrend traders are hoping for a trend reversal, which is a low-probability bet because markets have inertia and trends resist reversal attempts. For example, if there is a strong bull trend and then a reversal setup, some traders will go short. However, if the trade instead goes sideways to down to the moving average and sets up a high 2 there with a bull signal bar, that bear reversal attempt will likely fail. This is a great buy signal because you are entering in the direction of a larger trend and it is reasonable to expect at least a test of the prior extreme of the trend. Any reversal pattern, including major reversal patterns, can fail and result in the resumption of a trend.

When traders enter a trade, many place a protective stop at one tick beyond the signal bar. After the entry bar closes, if it is strong, many move it to one tick beyond the entry bar. How do you know this? By simply looking at charts. Look at any chart and find possible signal and entry bars and see what happens when a bar reverses beyond them. So much of the time, the reversal will be in the form of a strong trend bar, and most of the time the move will be enough for at least a scalper's profit. This is because once traders get flushed out of a new position with a loss, they become more cautious and want more price action before reentering in the same direction. This leaves the market in the hands of just one side, so the move is usually fast and big enough for a scalp.

Why is a one-tick failed breakout so common, especially in the Eminis? With stocks, failures often come on 1 to 10 cent breakouts, depending on the price of the stock and the personality of the stock. Every stock has distinct characteristics in its trading, presumably because many of the same people trade it every day, so a small group of traders trading sufficient volume can move the market enough to create recurring patterns. If the market is sideways to down in a weak bull trend, many traders will believe that if the current bar extends one tick above the prior bar, traders will buy there on a stop. Most smart traders will expect this. However, if enough other traders with enough volume feel that the correction has not extended deep enough or long enough (for example, if they believe that a two-legged move is likely), those traders might actually go short at the high or at one tick above the prior bar. If their volume overwhelms the new longs and not enough new longs come to the rescue, the market will likely trade down for a tick or two.

At this point, the new longs are feeling nervous. If their entry was at such a great price, why didn't more buyers come in? Also, now that the market is even a tick or two cheaper, this should look like even better value to traders looking to get long. This should quickly drive the price up, but the longer the market stays down even just a couple of ticks, the more new bulls will become concerned that they may be wrong. Some will start selling out at the market, adding to the offers, and others will place sell exit orders at one or two ticks lower, maybe basing these orders on a 1 or 3 minute chart, with the order one tick below the most recent bar. Once these are hit, these new buyers will also become sellers, pushing the price further down. Also, the original shorts will sense that the new longs are trapped, and many will increase their short positions. As price falls three, four, or five ticks, the stopped-out buyers will switch from looking to buy to waiting for more price action to unfold. In the absence of buyers, the price will continue to fall in search of enough bids to satisfy the sellers. At some point, sellers will begin to cover and take profits, slowing the price fall, and buyers will again begin to buy. Once the buying pressure overtakes the selling pressure, the price will then go up again.

A one-tick failed breakout on the 5 minute chart when it occurs in a trading range is often also a one-tick failed breakout on a higher time frame, like a 15 or

60 minute chart. If that is the case, why doesn't the 60 minute chart have a lot of one-tick failed breakouts? That is because many of the one-tick failed breakouts pull back for many bars on the 5 minute chart and then break out again. The result is that even though there was a one-tick failed breakout of the 60 minute chart as the 60 minute bar was forming, by the time the bar closed, the breakout extended to more than one tick.

A one-tick failure is a common source of losses for new traders. They will see what they believe is a good setup—for example, a buy—and they confidently place a buy stop order at one tick above the high of the prior bar. Maybe there is a two-bar reversal just above the moving average, but it overlaps the prior two bars completely and the long entry is at the top of the small trading range. Novice traders will see the strong bull trend bar and buy, but experienced traders know that this type of two-bar reversal is usually a bull trap, and they are likely shorting where the novice traders are buying. As expected, the market ticks up and hits the entry buy stops of the novices, making them long. However, the very next tick is one tick lower, then two, then three, and within 30 seconds they lose two points as they watch their protective stops get hit. They wonder how anyone could be selling exactly where they were buying. It was such a great setup!

These traps are common. Another example is a novice buying in a bear trend before there was a sign of bullish strength, like a prior surge above a bear trend line, or traders buying above a huge doji with a tiny body at the top of barbwire or a bear flag that they misread as a reversal, overcome by their eagerness to get in early in what they perceive as an overdone bear trend.

Another common situation is when there is a huge trend bar with a tiny tail or no tail. If it is a bull trend bar, lots of traders will put their protective stops at one tick below the bar. It is common for the market to work its way down over the next five to 10 bars, hit the stops and trap traders out, and then reverse back up in the direction of the trend bar.

What that novice trader doesn't realize is that lots of big traders view these as great short setups and they are happy to short, knowing that only weak hands would be buying, and as they are flushed out, they will help drive the market down. A one-tick failure is a reliable sign that the market is going the other way, so look for setups that allow you to enter. All of the preceding is true for down markets as well, and all of the one-tick failures can sometimes be two ticks, and even five to 10 ticks in a $200 stock.

Breakout tests often test the entry price to the exact tick, trapping out weak hands who will then have to chase the market and reenter at a much worse price. A breakout test may miss the breakeven stop by one tick and at other times it will go beyond it for a couple of ticks, but in either case, if the market reverses back into the direction of the trend, this failed attempt to reverse the market beyond the original entry price is a reliable with-trend setup. For example, if there is a strong buy setup above a bull reversal bar in the Emini and the market trends up for 10 bars but then later sells off, look to see what happens when the sell-off gets near the high of that original bull signal bar. If there is a bar that turns up at two ticks above the high of the signal bar, then it missed the breakeven stops by a tick. The market failed to flush the bulls out. Traders will then buy above this breakout test bar because they will see the failure to hit the protective stops as a sign that the bulls were aggressively buying around the original entry price, protecting their stops and making a statement that they are strong.

Most days have a lot of trading range price action and offer many entries on failed swing high and low breakouts. When the price goes above a prior swing high and the momentum is not too strong, place an order to short the higher high at one tick below the low of the prior bar on a stop. If the order is not filled by the time the bar closes, move the order up to one tick below the low of the bar that just closed. Continue to do this until the current leg gets so high and has so much momentum that you need more price action before shorting. Wait for another pullback that breaks at least a minor trend line and then look to short a new swing high. You can also fade new swing highs and lows on trend days after a minor trend line break and when there is a strong reversal bar.

Similarly, the first failed breakout below a prior swing low is a lower low buy setup. Place an order to buy at one tick above the high of the prior bar on a stop. If it is not filled, keep lowering the order to one tick above the high of the prior bar, but if the market drops too far or too fast, start the process over; wait for a small rally that breaks a minor trend line and then consider buying a failed breakout to a new low.

In the Emini, a popular trade is a scalp for four ticks when the average daily range is about 10 points. In a trend, there may be a series of successful scalps, but when one hits the limit order and does not get filled, this five-tick failure is a sign of a loss of momentum. These are also common on 1 and 3 minute charts. Since a six-tick breakout is needed to make a four-tick scalp (one tick for the stop entry, four ticks of profit, and usually one more tick to be sure the profit target limit order is filled), a move that goes only five ticks and then reverses often indicates that the trend traders have lost control and a pullback or reversal is imminent. Since many traders also place limit orders to capture two-, three-, or four-point profit targets, if the market reverses at one tick shy of these targets, it is also a sign of weakness. For example, if the market makes a significant intraday low and then rallies 17 ticks above the signal bar high, most traders trying to exit on limit orders with four points of profit will not get filled unless the market goes 18 ticks above the signal bar.

If instead the market hits 17 ticks and then the next bar trades below that bar, the remaining longs who did not exit one tick early will now think about exiting, and this often results in at least a downward scalp. Traders will assume that the bulls were taking their profit at one tick early, which means that the longs were not confident that the market would give them the full four points. This lack of confidence can lead to profit taking by the longs and aggressive shorting by the bears. Bulls could continue to rely on their trailing stops and hope that the market soon fills their four-point limit orders, but most traders would not be willing to risk having a 15-tick open profit turn into a two- or three-tick profit in an attempt to win that extra tick. This is the same as scalping for a one-tick profit while risking 10 or more ticks and is a losing strategy. Once the market hits 17 ticks and pulls back a few ticks, if traders' profit-taking limit orders are not filled, they would most likely lower their profit targets by a couple of ticks and raise their trailing stops to one tick below the low of the prior bar. If neither order is filled and the bar had a weak or bear close, they might just exit at the market. Incidentally, if the market goes 16 ticks above the signal bar high, it has about an 80 percent chance of reaching 17 or 18 ticks. This means that it is usually unwise to exit after 16 ticks unless the market trades below the low of the prior bar, especially if that bar is a short signal.

Most traders handle potential nine-tick failures in a similar way. If traders bought the Emini and were trying to exit with a two-point profit, their limit orders would be nine ticks above the high of the signal bar. The market usually has to go one more tick to fill the order, which is 10 ticks above the signal bar high. If the market hits the order but does not fill it and begins to trade down, they have to decide whether to rely on their initial stop or a trailing stop, like one tick below the low of the most recent bar with a decent-sized bull body. If their limit order is exactly at a resistance level, like a prior swing high, and it does not quickly break above, they might also quickly lower their limit order by a few ticks. Once it hits nine ticks, they should never allow the trade to turn into a loss, because they would then be risking eight or more ticks to make one tick, and this has a terrible trader's equation.

There are comparable failures in other markets that have many scalpers, like the SPY and the QQQ. For both, a common profit target is 10 ticks, which usually requires a 12-tick move beyond the signal bar. If the move reaches only 10 or 11 ticks (or even eight or nine) and then reverses, it usually leads to at least a profitable scalp in the opposite direction, since the scalpers are trapped and will get out on the reversal of the signal or entry bar. This type of failure is common with stocks as well. For example, if a stock reliably reaches more than a dollar on a scalp, but then falls just short on two attempts at the $1.00 target, then this is often a good scalp in the opposite direction.

One of the most common and reliable failures is the first spike through the trend line. Stock traders look for these all the time on daily charts, but it happens on all time frames. For example, if AAPL is in a strong bull market and has a bad earnings report, it might sell off 8 percent in one day and hit the moving average on the daily chart. Instead of looking for shorts, experienced traders will often buy on the close of that spike down or on the open of the next day. They see this just like a shopper sees a sale at the mall. The stock just got marked down 8 percent and the sale won't last long, so they quickly buy it. They know that most attempts to reverse fail and the first attempt almost always is followed by a new high, so they buy it even though they are buying at the bottom of a strong bear spike.

All patterns often fail, no matter how good they look. When they do, there will be trapped traders who will have to exit with a loss, usually at one tick beyond the entry or signal bars. This is an opportunity for smart traders to enter for a low-risk scalp. Place your entry stop order at exactly the same place that these trapped traders are placing their protective stops, and you will get in where they will get out. They won't be eager to enter again in their original direction, which makes the market one-sided in your direction and should lead to at least a scalp and usually a two-legged move.

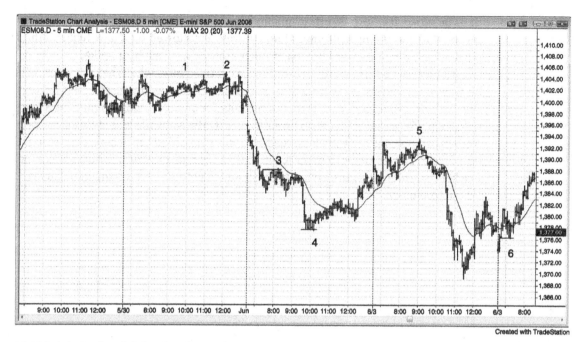

FIGURE 9.1   Small False Breakouts

One- and two-tick false breakouts leading to reversals are common in the 5 minute Emini. Figure 9.1 presents six examples (the label for bar 1 is well above the bar). Once the breakout traders enter on their stop and discover that the market is pulling back by a tick or two instead of immediately continuing in their direction, they start to place protective stops. Countertrend traders smell the blood and will enter just where the trapped traders are taking their losses. Most breakout attempts fail, especially when the market is in a trading range, and the failures are often in the form of one-tick false breakouts. Experienced traders use the breakouts to take profits or to trade in the opposite direction, expecting that most breakouts in a trading range will fail. For example, if a trader bought near the bottom of a trading range, he will likely be scalping for a test of the high of the range and will often have a limit order to sell out of his long and take profits at the top of the range. In a strong trend, they do the opposite. For example, if the market is in a bull trend, traders instead will buy on a stop above the top of the range, since they expect another leg up.

Figure 9.2   FAILURES   **233**

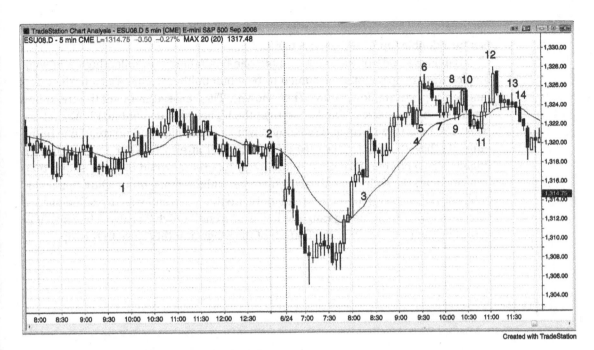

FIGURE 9.2   One-Tick Traps in the Emini

As shown in Figure 9.2, there were many examples of one-tick traps in these two days in the Emini.

Bar 1 was a one-tick failed low 2 and became a breakout pullback entry for the wedge bull flag that began at 8:55 a.m. PST.

Bar 2 was a one-tick failed high 2 in barbwire that trapped traders who thought that they were being conservative by waiting to buy above the large outside bar, only to be trapped buying at the top of a trading range below a flat moving average. This became a double top bear flag.

Bar 3 was a one-tick failed reversal in a runaway bull trend where smart traders were eagerly waiting for any pullback to buy. They were buying below the low of the bar, exactly where weak bears were shorting the reversal down from the breakout above the high of the open.

Bar 4 broke one tick below the small swing low of four bars earlier and set up a high 2 long.

Bar 5 was a large bull trend bar, and there would therefore be stops at one tick below its low. These were run by one tick on bar 7. The bulls were able to hold the market above the bar 4 bottom of the bull spike.

Bar 9 went one tick lower, trapping traders into what they thought was a lower high short, but actually was a sideways bull flag.

Bar 10 ran the breakeven protective stops for the bar 6 shorts by two ticks. It set up a double top bear flag with bar 8.

Bar 14 was one of the most reliable one-tick failures—a failed high 2 in what novice traders erroneously assumed to be a bull pullback. This was a perfect trap and led to a strong down move (not shown). They missed noticing the trend line break by the pullback to bar 11 and then the higher high test at bar 12. Also, there were five bear trend bars and one doji down from the high and no trend line break after the bar 13 high 1. This was a bear channel after a two-bar reversal from a higher high, and therefore it was more likely that there would be more shorts than buyers above the high 2 signal bar. Remember, a high 2 alone is not a buy signal. It is a buy signal at the top of a bull trend, but here the bull trend was over. The market was now either in a trading range or in a bear trend. A high 2 is also a buy signal in a trading range, but only at the bottom of the range, not this close to the top.

Figure 9.3   FAILURES   **235**

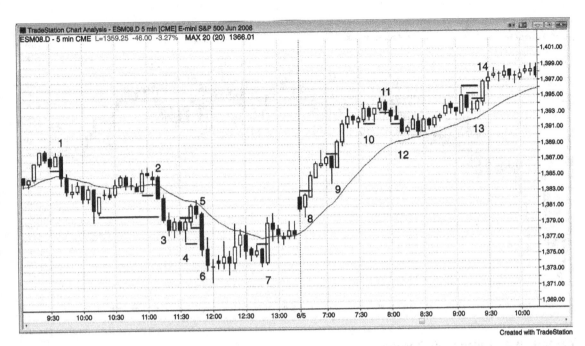

FIGURE 9.3   Breakouts beyond Signal and Entry Bar Protective Stops

Look at what happened in Figure 9.3 as the market broke through the horizontal lines, which were one tick beyond signal and entry bars and were likely places where traders would place their protective stops. Most of the time, there was a trend bar and the move was big enough for a scalper to make a profit. Many of the failures on this chart were for weak setups that smart price action traders would not have taken. However, enough traders took them so that they moved the market in the opposite direction as they were forced out with a loss. For example, traders who went long off the bar 4 reversal bar would have had their stops below either the entry bar or the signal bar. Both were run by the big bar 5 bear trend bar, and smart shorts who had their entry stops at those exact locations made at least a scalper's profit.

As a corollary, if the extreme of the bar is tested but not exceeded, then the stops are tested but not hit, and the trade will often be profitable. If it is a protective stop on a long entry that is missed by one tick, the test effectively forms a double bottom bull flag, with the first bottom being the bottom of the signal or entry bar and the second one being the bar that came back to that level but failed to reach the protective stops.

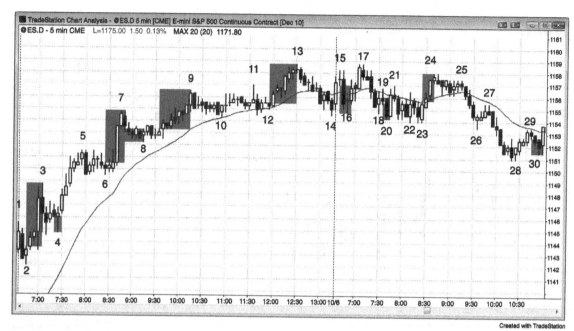

FIGURE 9.4 Failed Profit Targets

When the market hits a profit-taking limit order price and then pulls back, most traders would not have their limit orders filled. When the market then stalls or pulls back for a few ticks, many of these traders will exit at the market because they do not want to risk giving back any more of their open profit. This adds fuel to any correction and is often a sign that the market is trying to reverse.

As shown in Figure 9.4, the market rallied for 21 ticks above bar 2 and then reversed down. Some traders who bought one tick above the bar 2 signal bar had limit orders to exit their longs with five points of profit, 21 ticks above the signal bar high, but most would not have been filled unless the market went one tick higher. Instead, the market reversed, and many of those traders quickly got out of the market as they tried to salvage as much profit as they could before waiting to see if the market would go all the way back to their entry price.

Bar 7 was a 17-tick failure for bulls who had bought one tick above the bar 6 buy signal bar. Many traders who were trying to make a four-point profit saw the market reach their limit order at 17 ticks above the signal bar high and exited once the market fell below the low of that bar. Traders who correctly believed that the trend was strong, and were, instead, swinging their longs and not trying to exit at four points, would rely on a breakeven stop. Once the market moved above the bar 7 high, they would then trail their stops to one tick below bar 8, the most recent higher low.

Figure 9.4   FAILURES   **237**

Bars 4, 8, 20, and 30 were examples of five-tick failures on short trades. Most shorts needed the market to fall six ticks below the bottom of the signal bar for their profit-taking limit order for a four-tick scalp to get filled. Some traders would have had their orders filled, but most would not have been filled.

Bar 9 was a 13-tick failure for longs who bought above bar 8, hoping to make a three-point profit.

Bars 16 and 24 were nine-tick failures for traders who tried to make two points. They would not let those trades turn into a loss and would trail their stops. For example, they would exit the bar 16 signal bar long at one tick below the bar 17 low, or possibly on the bear close of bar 17. They might exit the long from above the bar 23 buy signal at one tick below the bear bar that formed two bars after bar 24.

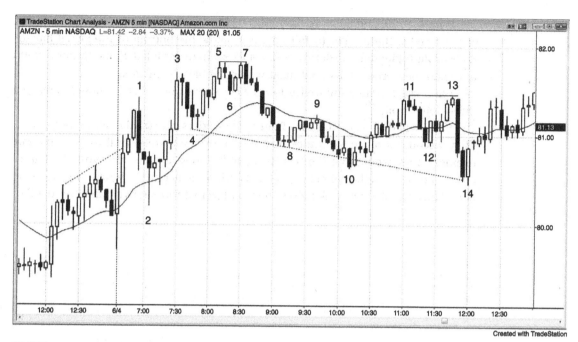

FIGURE 9.5   Trading Range Breakouts Usually Fail

When there is strong two-sided trading, breakouts above swing highs and below swing lows usually fail.

As shown in Figure 9.5, the rally to bar 1 was strong, but since opening reversals are often sharp and it was a higher high (above the swing high near yesterday's close) that broke above a bull trend channel line, it was a reasonable short.

The bar 2 pullback after the bar 1 swing high was deep, and the bars since the open had been large with big tails. There was two-sided volatile trading and until a bull trend clearly developed, traders should have assumed that both bulls and bears were active. Since this had not proven itself yet to be a bull trend day, it should have been traded as a trading range day.

Bar 3 was a higher high since it was a swing high that was above an earlier swing high. The momentum up to bar 3 was too strong to consider a short without a second entry or a strong reversal bar, but if a trader shorted, the move down was 26 cents, so it could have been minimally profitable.

Bar 5 was a higher high and a reasonable short, especially since it had two small legs (there was a bear trend bar in the middle that represented the end of the first leg up from bar 4). The market dropped only 18 cents before going back up. A nimble trader might have taken some off, but most would have just scratched the trade with a 4 cent loss.

Figure 9.5   FAILURES   **239**

Bar 7 was part of this same up move so it was a second-entry (a low 2) short. Bar 7 was a double top with bar 5 to the penny, and essentially a truncated three-push up pattern (bars 3, 5, and 7), so two down legs were likely.

Bar 10 was a lower low and the second leg down in a possible larger bull trend. Its low was above the bar 2 low, so the market might still have been forming large bull trending swings. Two legs down in a bull trend or sideways market, especially two pushes below a flat moving average, are always a good long.

Bar 11 was a higher high because it was above the bar 9 swing high, even though bar 9 was part of the prior down leg. There would still have been traders who would have traded there (there would have been stops on shorts, stops to buy the breakout, and new shorts), because going above any prior swing high is a sign of strength and a potential fade on a trading range day (look for breakouts to fail and signs of strength to lack follow-through).

Bar 13 was one tick below bar 11 and was a double top bear flag and therefore a short setup. It was two legs up from bar 10 and the second leg above a flat moving average (bar 11 was the first).

Bar 14 was a lower low for both the swing lows at bars 10 and 12.

Incidentally, the longs from bars 10 and 14 were both failed overshoots of a bear trend channel line drawn from bars 4 and 8. This increased the chances of successful long trades. Both had two-bar reversal setups. Bar 10 was the bottom of a wedge bull flag, and bar 14 was the bottom of an expanding triangle bull flag.

FIGURE 9.6 Failed Breakouts in AMZN

Amazon (AMZN) had many large one-bar failed breakouts beyond swing highs and lows on the 5 minute chart shown in Figure 9.6. After the climactic run-up on the open and then the large reversal down, the bulls and the bears both demonstrated strength and increased the odds that any move by one side would be reversed by the other throughout the day. This made a trading range likely. All of the labeled bars were failed breakouts. The tight trading range began after bar 3, and turned into a small expanding triangle top that ended at bar 6 and then an expanding triangle bottom that ended at bar 7. The rally from the bottom failed to break out of the top and instead formed a double top with bar 6, and the market sold off into the close.

Figure 9.7

FAILURES **241**

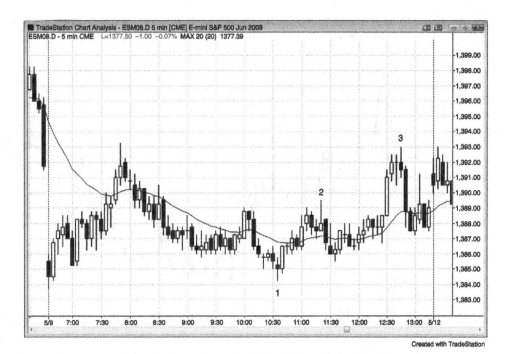

FIGURE 9.7 Trading Range Breakouts Usually Fail

When a day appears to be developing into a trading range day, traders expect breakouts to fail and they look to fade them. As shown in Figure 9.7, by midday it was clear that the day was small and sideways, which greatly increased the chances that breakouts would likely fail. Bars 1, 2, and 3 were second entries on breakout fades. The trend bar leading up to the bar 3 top was large and had big volume, sucking in lots of hopeful bulls who bet that there might finally be a trend. This is always a low-probability bet on a small day, and it is much better to fade the breakouts or look for strong breakout pullbacks. The breakouts to the bar 1 low and the bar 2 high were weak (prominent tails, overlapping bars), so it was likely both times that the breakouts would fail. The breakout that ended in bar 3 never had a breakout pullback to give the bulls a low-risk long, so the only trade was the second-entry short.

Created with TradeStation

FIGURE 9.8 Trapping Traders out of Good Trades

Apple (AAPL) has been one of the best-behaved stocks for day traders, but like many other stocks, it sometimes traps traders out of great trades by running stops at the start of a reversal, as shown in Figure 9.8.

Traders bought the double bottom bull flag at bar 1 by entering either three or six bars later as the market went above the high of the prior bar. There was a rally above the moving average that broke the trend line, and the moving average gap bar short led to the bar 2 test of the bear low. Many bulls had their protective stops below the bar 1 double bottom bull flag. Bar 2 dipped below bar 1 by a tick and trapped the longs out, but it formed a double bottom bull flag with bar 1, which led to a reversal that carried into the next day. The one-tick failed breakout below bar 1 trapped bulls out and bears in. The move down to bar 2 was in a tight bear channel, and it was the third push down and therefore a high 3 buy setup. A high 3 is a more reliable setup in a tight channel than a high 2, because channels often reverse up after a third push down. What made this long especially good was that it trapped new longs out and immediately reversed up on them, so psychologically it would have been difficult for them to buy. They would have chased the market up, entering late, thereby adding fuel to the upswing.

Figure 9.9

FAILURES **243**

FIGURE 9.9 Double Tops and Bottoms in the First Hour

Stocks commonly form double top or bottom flags in the first hour (see Figure 9.9). Most are tradable, but always scalp out part of your position and move your stop to breakeven in case the pattern fails.

Bars 2 and 4 formed a double top bear flag that failed. The market then formed a bars 3 and 5 double bottom bull flag.

You then had to reverse again at the bar 4 and 6 double top bear flag, but you would have netted 70 cents from your long. At this point, you knew that the market was forming a trading range, likely a triangle.

Bar 7 was another failure, but a good long since trading ranges following a strong move (the rally to bar 1) are usually continuation patterns, and bars 3, 5, and 7 all found support at the moving average.

The sell-off to bar 9 was seven bars long with no bullish strength, so it would have been better to wait for a second entry, despite bar 9 being a higher low (compared to bar 7). It was likely to fail to go far.

The breakout pullback at bar 10 was a perfect second entry.

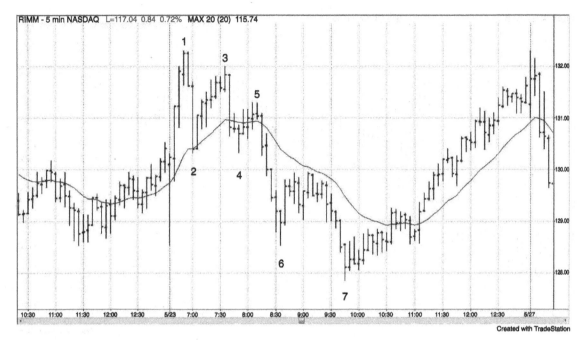

FIGURE 9.10   Failed Double Bottom Bull Flag

As shown in Figure 9.10, bar 4 was a setup for a double bottom bull flag entry, but it failed with the bar 5 low 2, which was a pullback from the strong bear spike down to bar 4. This led to a breakout below the double bottom and then a two-legged move to bar 7. There were several choices for getting short, like below bar 5, one or two ticks below the bar 4 low, on the close of the bar that broke below bar 4, or on the close of the next bar, which was a strong follow-through bar.

Figure 9.11   FAILURES   **245**

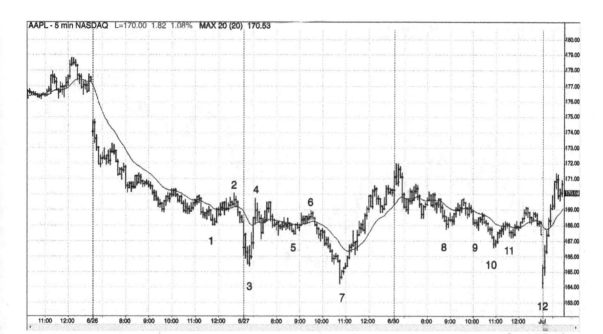

FIGURE 9.11   Most Head and Shoulders Patterns Fail

As shown in Figure 9.11, bars 5 and 11 were right shoulders of head and shoulders bottoms, most of which fail, as they did here (bars 1 and 9 were the left shoulders). The shape alone is not enough reason to place a countertrend trade. You always want to see some earlier countertrend strength prior to the reversal pattern. Even then, there are no guarantees that the trade will be successful. Bar 2 broke a trend line and the rally to bar 4 was strong, although its failure to exceed the bar 2 high was a sign of weakness. Although most smart traders would not have reversed to short at the bar 6 failure after the bar 5 double bottom bull flag and long entry, they would have moved their stops to breakeven, thinking that if the stops were hit but the trade was still good, the stop run would set up a breakout pullback long setup. Here, the stops were hit but the market kept selling off. The one-bar breakout pullback just after the breakout below bar 5 was a great short. Bar 5 was also the third push down in a triangle after the bar 4 spike, and the triangle was also a wedge bull flag.

The bar 11 right shoulder was a buy, but again the breakeven stop would have been hit.

FIGURE 9.12 Two-Legged Test of Trend Extreme

As shown in Figure 9.12, the sell-offs to bar 2 and to bar 6 broke major trend lines, so, in each case, a two-legged test of the prior high should set up a good short. The bar 3 low 2 short was successful, either by shorting below bar 3 or by taking the second entry two bars later.

The bar 8 short was less certain because the test was a large bull trend bar (almost an outside bar, since it had the same low as the prior bar). The traditional way to enter after an outside bar is on a stop at one tick beyond both extremes, getting filled in the direction of the breakout. However, outside bars are basically one-bar trading ranges, and most trading range breakout entries fail. You should only rarely enter on a breakout of an outside bar because the risk is too great (to the opposite side of the bar, which is large). Since this was a two-bar reversal, the safest entry was below the lower of the two bars, which was the large bull trend bar, because very often the market goes below the bear bar, but not below both bars, and that happened here.

If you shorted at the bar 8 breakout of the inside bar, you would have been nervous by the bar's close (a doji bar, indicating no conviction). However, most traders would not have taken that short, because three or more sideways bars, at least one of which is a doji, usually creates too much uncertainty (barbwire). The two small bars before the outside bar were small enough to act like dojis, so it

Figure 9.12   FAILURES   **247**

was best to wait for more price action. However, if you did not short on bar 8, you would have to believe that many did and the doji close of their entry bar made these traders feel uncomfortable with their positions. They would have been quick to exit, thereby becoming trapped. They would likely have bought back their shorts at one tick above the bar 8 entry bar and then be reluctant to sell again until they saw better price action. With the shorts out of the market and with them buying back their positions, going long exactly where they were exiting (bar 9, one tick above the short entry bar) should have been good for a scalp and likely two legs up. A trader could have bought either at one tick above bar 9 or above the bar after bar 9, relying on bar 9 being a bull trend bar and therefore a good long signal bar.

FIGURE 9.13   Five-Tick Failure

Scalping short for four ticks was a successful strategy for almost two hours in Figure 9.13. However, the short from the bar 4 inside bar dropped only five ticks and reversed up. This meant that many shorts did not get filled on their profit-target limit order and that the shorts were quick to exit at breakeven and certainly above bar 5. The market was testing yesterday's low, and it was the second probe below the trend channel line (based on the trend line from bar 1 to bar 3). The bulls were looking for reasons to buy, and the failed short scalp was the final thing that they were hoping to find.

Figure 9.14   FAILURES   **249**

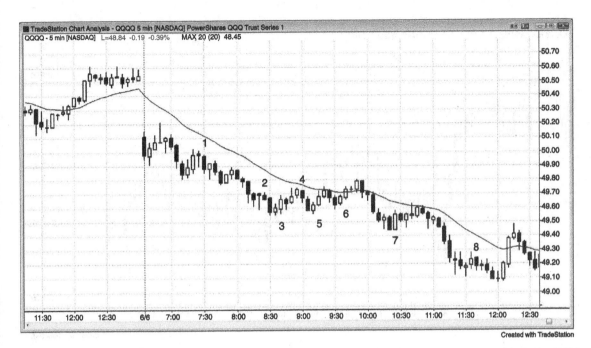

FIGURE 9.14   Failed Signals in QQQ

As shown in Figure 9.14, each of these 5 minute QQQ trades reached between 8 and 11 ticks before failing. The protective stops would get scalpers out at around breakeven in all of them, but it still was a lot of work with little to show for it. Clearly, however, there were many other profitable scalps, but it is tiring to scalp if there are too many unsuccessful trades. This often makes a trader lose focus and then miss profitable trades. On a clear bear trend day, the best approach is to trade only with the trend and look to sell low 2 setups, especially at the moving average. Your winning percentage will be high, allowing you to have a healthy attitude and continue to take entries, preferably swinging at least part of your position.

FIGURE 9.15   Switch to a Smaller Target

AAPL usually yields $1.00 scalps (the moves are usually more than $1.00, allowing a scalper to take partial profits on a $1.00 limit order). As shown in Figure 9.15, however, bar 2 extended only 93 cents above the entry above bar 1, and then set up a low 2 short. This low 2 meant that the market failed twice to reach the target. With the market largely sideways and just missing a $1.00 scalp, traders would likely have reduced their profit target to about 50 cents. They would have been able to take partial profits on this 61 cent drop.

Figure 9.16   FAILURES   **251**

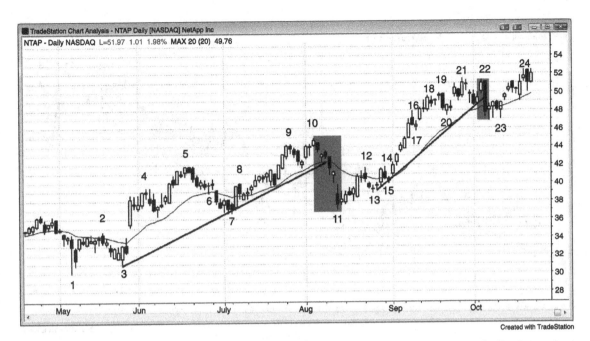

FIGURE 9.16 A Bear Spike Can Be a Buying Opportunity

As shown in Figure 9.16, NetApp Inc. (NTAP) went on sale twice during this bull trend on the daily chart, and traders bought the markdown aggressively. Just because there is a strong spike down below the trend line does not mean that the trend is over. Most reversal attempts look great and most fail. Because of this, experienced traders will buy sharp markdowns aggressively, even at the bottom of a bear spike. Bar 11 was at the bottom of a 16 percent sell-off, but it was still a higher low and a double bottom bull flag with bar 7. Since the channel down lasted so many bars, it was safer to wait to buy the bar 13 higher low or the breakout above the bar 14 low 2 setup, which was a failed double top bear flag.

Bar 22 was a very strong bear trend bar down to the moving average, but the rally up from bar 15 to bar 19 was very strong. The bear trend bar was probably based on some scary news report, but one strong bear trend bar does not create a reversal. Most of the time, it will fail and lead to a new trend high. Bulls thought that a trading range and a new high were more likely than a successful reversal, and they bought the bottom of the bar. Its low also formed a double bottom with bar 20 and was probably going to be the bottom of a trading range or a double bottom bull flag. The bear bar had weak follow-through and went sideways for four overlapping bars, which had prominent tails. This is not how a bear reversal usually looks, and the bears bought back their shorts. Their buying, combined with the bulls buying here, led to the new trend high.

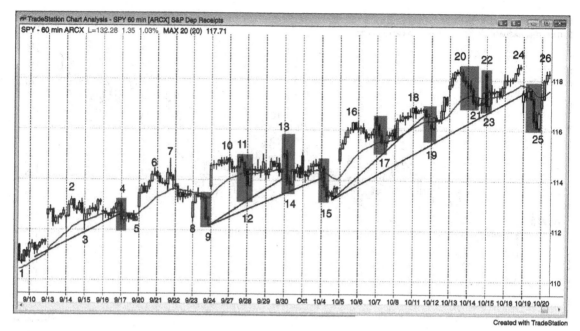

FIGURE 9.17 Most Trend Reversal Attempts Fail

When a bull trend is strong like it was on the 60 minute chart of the SPY shown in Figure 9.17, it has inertia and will resist attempts to end. Overly eager bears looked at strong bear spikes below the moving average and below trend lines as signs that the market was reversing into a bear trend. Bulls saw each bear spike as a buy setup. They knew that a successful reversal requires more than simply a strong bear spike. They believed that each reversal would fail, because most do, and that the market was going higher, so they were eager to buy pullbacks. When the SPY went on sale by just 1 or 2 percent, bulls quickly bought it since they knew that the sale wouldn't last long. Many of the spikes were created by vacuums. The bulls wanted to buy a pullback, so they stopped buying if they thought that the market would go a little lower. This allowed the bears to drive the market down quickly. Once it was low enough and the bulls thought that it wouldn't go lower, they appeared out of nowhere and bought aggressively. They overwhelmed the bears, who then had to buy back their shorts, adding to the rally, and the huge bear spike had no follow-through.

While the spikes were scary as they were forming, if traders understood what was going on, they would be eager to buy at the bottom. If they did not want to have a huge overnight risk, they could buy calls at the bottom of each bear spike and take profits on each new high a few days later.

Figure 9.18   FAILURES   **253**

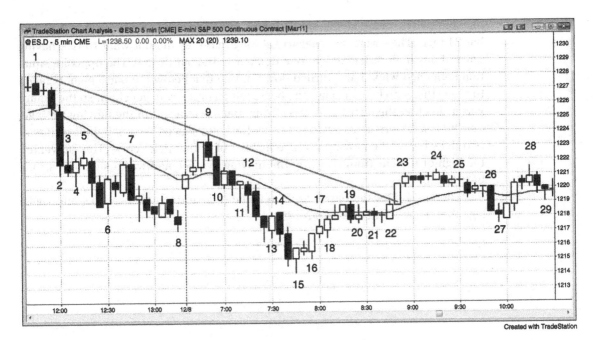

FIGURE 9.18 Failures Can Sometimes Be a Sign of Strength

As shown in Figure 9.18, the lower low major trend reversal up from bar 15 was strong and was likely to have at least two legs up. However, the rally to bar 19 failed to reach the bear trend line. It pushed above the moving average and came close enough to the line to be within its magnetic field. This gave traders confidence to buy the bar 22 high 2 setup because they thought that the market should test above the trend line.

Bar 4 was a bull reversal bar after a strong bear spike. The spike was strong enough to convince traders that the market was always-in short, so traders were looking to sell rallies. Since they did not think that bar 4 was going to lead to a significant reversal, many bears placed limit orders to short at and above its high. Enough traders were so eager to short that they shorted at one tick below its high. The market never made it to above the high of the bull signal bar, which was a sign that the bears were strong. The market sold off below the bar 5 low 2 short signal bar. A similar situation formed at the high of the bar after bar 10, and at bars 11, 13, and 26. Bar 18 was the bullish equivalent. Traders were so eager to get long that they had buy limit orders at and below the low of the bar before bar 18, and the most aggressive bulls with limit orders at one tick above the bar 18 low were likely the only ones who got long. The others had to chase the market higher.

Bar 27 turned up at one tick above the low of bar 21, preventing a perfect double bottom bull flag. This was a sign of eager bulls who placed buy limit orders at one and two ticks above the bar 21 low as the market was trading down from the bar 24 high. They were so eager to get long that they did not want to risk having unfilled buy limit orders at and one tick above the bar 21 low. The opposite situation happened when bar 7 turned down at one tick below the bar 5 high. It failed to reach the bar 5 high because the bears felt an urgency to get short, so the failure was a sign that the bear trend was strong. Bar 7 was a test of the moving average, but the bears were so eager to get short that they placed their sell limit orders at two ticks below the moving average instead of at one tick below. This prevented the high of the bar from reaching the moving average and was a sign of a strong bear trend.

The low 1 after the bar 15 bottom failed to lead to a new bear low and was a sign that the reversal up was strong.

Figure 9.19

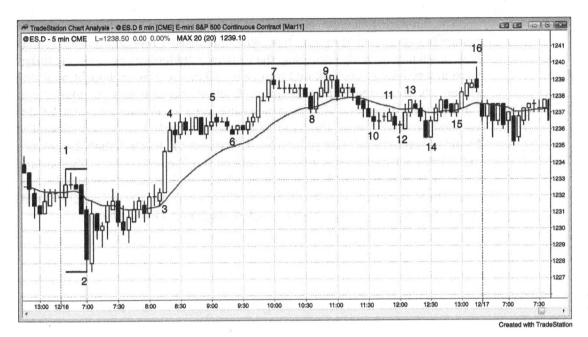

FIGURE 9.19 Just Missing a Target and Then Reaching It

When there is a fairly obvious measured move target and the market comes close enough to be within its magnetic pull, but not close enough for traders to believe that it was adequately tested, the market often pulls back and then makes a more convincing test. As shown in Figure 9.19, today was a trending trading range day in the Emini and the obvious measured move target was a measured move up based on the opening range. Bars 7 and 9 came within three ticks, but most traders would not feel that the test is complete unless the market comes within one tick. The test failed to reach the target, but it was close enough to make traders believe that the magnet was influencing the price action. Traders wanted to see whether the market would fall back after testing it or it would break above and rally to some higher target. The market pulled back to a small expanding triangle bull flag at bar 14 and tested the target to within a tick on the final bar of the day. Incidentally, if the test goes four or more ticks above the measured move target, that usually means that the market is ignoring the target and is heading toward a higher target.

Bar 14 was also the signal bar for a larger wedge bull flag where bar 8 was the first push down and bars 10 or 12 formed the second. Some traders thought the flag ended at bar 12, but the distance between bar 10 and bar 12 was small compared to the distance between bar 8 and bar 10, so many traders were not convinced that the correction was over. This resulted in the lower low final push down to bar 14.

The three-bar bull spike up from bar 14 broke above the high of the prior 60 minute bar (not shown) by one tick. When the market reversed down two bars later in a 5 minute wedge bear flag, the 60 minute traders were wondering if they were in a 60 minute one-tick bull trap. Some 60 minute traders bought on a stop at one tick above the high of the prior 60 minute bar and now the market was turning down. However, most of the time when there is a developing one-tick failed breakout on the 60 minute chart, the market reverses back above the one-tick failed breakout before the 60 minute bar closes. The result is that although the one-tick failed breakout was present for many bars on the 5 minute chart, it disappeared from the 60 minute chart by the time the 60 minute bar closed, as was the case here. The 60 minute bar closed on the bar after bar 15, and the final high of the 60 minute bar was three ticks above the high of the prior 60 minute bar.

CHAPTER 10

Huge Volume Reversals on Daily Charts

When a stock is in a steep bear trend on the daily chart and then has a day with volume that is five to 10 times its recent average, the bulls may have capitulated and a tradable bottom may be present. The huge volume day is very often a gap down day, and if it has a strong bull close, the odds of a profitable long increase. Traders are not necessarily looking for a bull reversal, but after a climactic sell-off, the odds are good that there will be at least a two-legged move to at least the moving average that will allow them to place a profitable trade that will last from days to weeks.

Incidentally, on a 1 minute Emini chart that is in a strong bear trend, if there is a huge volume bar (about 25,000 contracts), it is unlikely to be the end of the bear trend, but often is a sign that a pullback will come soon, usually after one or two lower lows on less volume (volume divergence). You should rarely if ever look at volume on intraday charts because of its unreliable predictive value on the 5 minute chart, which is the chart that you should mainly use for trading.

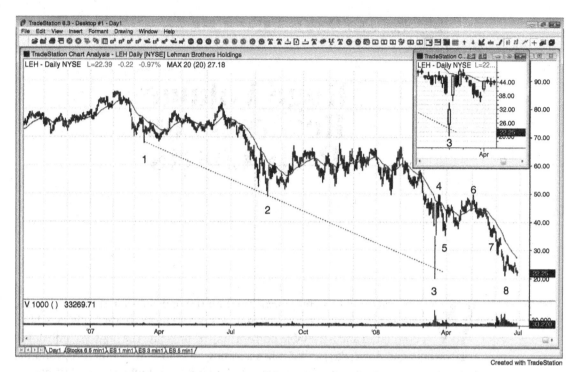

FIGURE 10.1 Huge Volume Reversal

Sometimes markets reverse up on huge volume days. As shown in Figure 10.1, Lehman Brothers (LEH) opened with a huge gap down on bar 3 and then ran below a bear trend channel line (from bars 1 and 2), but rallied strongly into the close. Volume was three times that of the prior day and about 10 times that of the average of the past month. With such a strong bull trend bar (seen more clearly on the candle chart thumbnail), it was safe to buy at the close, but a more cautious trader would have waited until the market took out the high of this possible signal bar. The market gapped up on the next day. A trader could have bought the open, waited for a test down, and then bought a new intraday high, or looked for a sell-off on the 5 minute chart and bought the reversal up after the attempt to close the gap failed. This kind of strength is almost always followed by at least two legs up (the second leg up to bar 6 occurred after the successful bar 5 gap test higher low) and a penetration of the moving average.

Bars 4 and 6 formed a double top bear flag.

Bar 7 attempted to form a double bottom bull flag with bar 5, but instead resulted in a breakout pullback short entry three bars later.

As of the final bar on the chart, the market was testing the bar 3 low in an attempt to defend the stops below it and form a double bottom. Months later, LEH went out of business.

Figure 10.2   HUGE VOLUME REVERSALS ON DAILY CHARTS   **259**

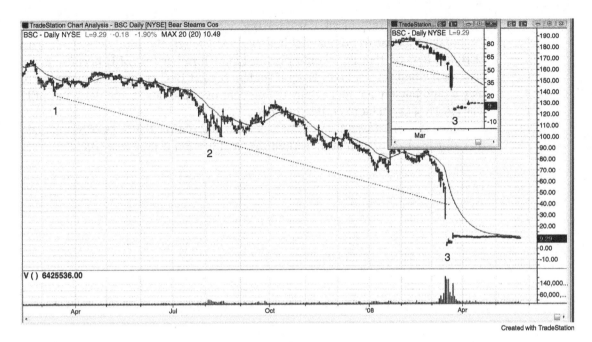

FIGURE 10.2   Huge Volume without a Reversal

Huge volume on a big down day does not guarantee a rally. As shown in Figure 10.2, Bear Stearns (BSC) had a huge bear trend day on a Friday with volume that was about 15 times that of a typical day. The stock had lost about 70 percent of its value over the prior two weeks. However, the volume was only about one and a half times that of the day before and there was only a minimal bull tail. The price action was against the longs since there was no reversal from the break of the bear trend channel. In fact, the huge bear trend bar closed well below the line, confirming the strength of the trend channel line failure to contain the bear trend. The stock lost another 80 percent when it opened on Monday (bar 3), but traded slightly less volume. Traders who bought the Friday close, thinking that a climactic bottom was in and that there was no way that the country's fifth largest investment bank and brokerage could fall any further, were devastated come Monday. Climactic volume in the absence of bullish price action is no reason to fade a strong bear trend.

This chart covers the same time period as the preceding LEH chart. However, the LEH chart did not break the bear trend channel line (bar 3) until Monday and it reversed up on that day on huge volume. Here, on the BSC chart, the huge volume day was a day earlier and it also broke below the bear trend channel line, but the day closed near its low with no bullish price action. It gapped down on bar 3, just like LEH (bar 3 is the Monday for both stocks), but LEH rallied strongly whereas

BSC could barely rally at all. Bar 3 for BSC was still a bull reversal bar following the break of a bear trend channel line, but any traders choosing between buying LEH and BSC on that day would obviously much rather buy LEH because of its very strong bull reversal bar. Even if traders bought BSC at one tick above bar 3, they would have made more than 100 percent over the next three days, but LEH was clearly a much more certain bull bet.

Since this chart was printed, BSC was bought out by JPMorgan Chase (JPM) for a tiny fraction of its market capitalization of just a few months earlier.

Day Trading

If you are not yet consistently profitable, you should not be looking at one- or two-point scalps in the Emini or 10 to 20 cent scalps in stocks as the cornerstone of your trading. In fact, you should avoid scalps until you are an experienced trader, because you need a very high winning percentage to be profitable, and that is difficult for even experienced traders to achieve.

The first consideration in day trading is the selection of the market and type of chart that you want to use. It is best to trade stocks that are popular with institutions, because you want to reduce the chance of manipulation by a specialist or market maker, and you want minimal slippage. There are so many great trades every day on any basket of five to 10 stocks that you won't have to resort to stocks with small volume that might carry additional risks.

The more bars in your day, the more trades you will make, and the risk will be less per trade. However, you might not be able to read the charts fast enough to see the setups, and you might not have time to place your orders without an unacceptable level of mistakes. Also, some of the best trades happen so quickly that you will likely miss many and then be left with all the trades that are less profitable. There is a mathematical sweet spot that you will have to determine based on your personality and trading abilities. Most successful traders can trade a 5 minute candle chart. The price action on a 3 minute chart is very similar and offers more trades and smaller stops, but in general it has a lower winning percentage. If you find that you are missing too many trades, especially the most profitable trades of the day, you should consider moving to a slower time frame, like a 15 minute chart.

You can also use charts based on volume (like each bar representing 25,000 contracts) or ticks (for example, each bar representing 5,000 price changes or ticks) or simple bar charts. Line charts are also tradable, but price action traders are giving up too much information when they cannot see bars or candles.

In general, since your risk per trade is smallest when you day trade, you should be trading your maximum number of contracts. Warren Buffett was quoted as saying, "If it's worth a penny, then it's worth a dime." Once consistently profitable traders have decided that they have a valid entry, they need to be prepared to trade a reasonable number of contracts.

Traders are always thinking about the best way to maximize their profitability, and the two most important considerations are trade selection and position size. A new trader should focus primarily on swinging only the best two to five entries each day, which are usually second entries in the form of reversals at new swing highs and lows on nontrending days (maybe 80 percent of days), and spikes and pullbacks on trend days. Once a trader is consistently profitable, the next goal should be to increase the position size rather than adding lower-probability entries. If a trader consistently nets only one point a day in the Eminis but trades 25 contracts, this comes out to over $1,000 per day. If the trader can get up to 100 contracts, he will make $1,000,000 per year. If he nets four points a day, that is $4,000,000 per year. The Emini and Treasury bond and note markets can easily handle this size of trading. For very liquid stocks with prices over $100, an experienced trader can net 50 cents to a dollar on most days, and these stocks can handle 1,000- to 3,000-share orders with minimal slippage. Exchange-traded funds (ETFs) like the QQQ can handle 10,000-share orders, but the daily range is smaller, and a more realistic daily net profit would be about 10 to 20 cents for a good trader, or a couple of hundred thousand dollars a year.

If a trader was managing a fund of $50,000,000 and trading 1,000 Emini contracts per trade (he might have to split his orders into 200- to 400-lot pieces), and he netted only a point per day, this would generate $10,000,000 for clients before fees. Concentrate on taking the best trades and then increasing your volume.

CHAPTER 11

Key Times of
the Day

The trading day can be divided into three periods, and although the same price action principles apply throughout the day, there are some generalizations about each period that are useful for traders. Any type of price action can happen at any time of the day, but there is a tendency for the first hour or two to be the most likely time of the day to find a trade where you can make two to three times your risk. This is the most important time of the day, and for most traders it is the easiest time to make money (and the easiest to lose money, if a trader is not careful). In general, most traders should work very hard to take trades in the first hour or two because those trades have the best trader's equation combination of reward, risk, and probability. Because of its importance, the chapters in Part III discuss it in detail. There are often reports at 7:00 a.m. PST, and they commonly lead to the trend of the day. Computers have a clear edge in speed of analysis and order placement, and they are your competitors. When your competition has a big advantage, don't compete. Wait for their edge to disappear, and trade when speed is no longer important. Once the always-in direction has been established, then look to take the trend trade. Even though you might miss the first bar or two, if the trend is strong, there will be plenty of points left in the trade.

On the daily chart, there is often a small tail below strong bull trend bars and above strong bear trend bars. These are often caused by opening reversals. For example, if bulls think that the day is likely to be a strong bull trend day and it trades down for the first few bars of the day, the majority of them will believe that this will likely be the low of the day and a great opportunity to buy at a tremendous value that will soon disappear. If they are right, the market will rally, and they will have bought around the low of the day. On the daily chart, there will be a small tail on the bottom of the bull trend bar that resulted from the three-bar sell-off on the open. Because they were ready for that possibility, these smart bulls made a huge reward, risking little, on a trade that probably had at least a 50 percent chance of success (remember, because of the overall character of the market, they believed that the day was likely to rally).

The middle of the day, beginning around 8:30 to 9:30 a.m. PST and ending around 11:00 to 11:30 and sometimes as late as 12:30, is more prone to two-sided trading, like trading ranges or channels. This is the time of the day when tight trading ranges are the most common. This is a terrible environment for entering on stops. In very two-sided markets, when the market goes down a little, buyers come in and take control, so entering on stops as the market is falling is the exact opposite of what the institutions are doing in these tight trading ranges. The buyers are the bears scalping out of their profitable shorts and the bulls buying for scalps up. At the top, the opposite happens and the selling predominates. The bulls sell out of their profitable long scalps, and the bears sell to initiate short scalps. There are swing traders as well, but in general, when the market is in a trading range, whether or not it is tight, most of the volume is scalping and the institutions are buying low and selling high. The best way to make money as a trader is to do what the institutions do, so if you are going to trade in a trading range, look to scalp, and buy low, sell high. Experienced traders will sell on limit orders above weak high 1 and high 2 buy signal bars at the top, and buy on limit orders below weak low 1 and low 2 signal bars at the bottom. Because limit orders trades are more difficult to evaluate accurately, beginners should avoid them. Be very careful about stop entries and only sell on a stop if you are at the top of the range as the market is turning down, and only buy on a stop near the bottom as the market is turning up. The market always races to the top and bottom, suckering hopeful beginners into buying on stops at the top and selling on stops at the bottom. They just look at the strength of the spikes up and down and ignore the trading range of the past 20 bars and end up doing the opposite of the institutions. Because so many of the trade setups are for scalps and most traders cannot make a living by scalping, they should be very selective during this time. Since the high or low of the day forms during the first third of the day in maybe 90 percent of days, the middle third of the day is usually when traders are deciding if the initial trend should resume or reverse. The bulls and the bears are active, each fighting over control and each trying to generate a trend into the close. The market often reverses around 8:30 a.m. PST and then trends for the rest of the middle third of the day. Traders need to be aware that the trend that began at the open might not last all day, and the exact opposite can develop after the first couple of hours.

Beginning traders tend to lose money in the middle third of the day. They often lose more than they have made in the first third of the day, and if that is the case, they should consider not trading in the middle third unless signals are especially strong. Many traders make most of their money in the first couple of hours of the day and then trade much less or not at all during the middle of the day. If a person owns two stores and one makes a lot of money, but the other consistently loses money no matter what the owner does, and often more than what he makes from his good store, should he continue to operate both stores? The answer is obvious. You can look at the first and middle thirds of the day as two stores. There is nothing wrong with closing that losing store. Your goal is to make money, not to trade all day long. If the price action is good all day long and you are not tired, then it is financially wise to trade all day. However, that is usually not the case. The middle third tends to have much more two-sided trading, channels, tight trading ranges, many reversals, trend bars without follow-through, and lots of dojis. Unless traders are very selective with their stop entries or capable of making money by fading moves with limit orders, they should just wait for the price action to become more predictable. It is always better to not take any trades than to take trades where your losses are greater than your wins. Beginners frequently win just often enough to make them continue what they are doing, hoping that all they need is experience. However, no matter how much experience they accumulate, a tight trading range will always be difficult to trade. It is almost always better to wait until the always-in direction is clear, so that the odds of follow-through are high enough to allow for a profitable trade.

The three periods of the day often create a trend resumption pattern. For example, if there is a sell-off for a couple of hours, and then a rally into around 11:30 a.m. PST, the market might sell off again after that, resuming the bear trend of the first third of the day. Sometimes the pattern is clearly up-down-up or down-up-down, but more often it is less obvious, even though the tendency is still there. Because of this, many traders will view any move in the middle third of the day that reverses a move of the first third as simply a potential pullback from the initial trend. They will then look for the original trend to resume around 11:30 a.m., and if there is a sign that this is what's happening, they will take the trade. Even on days when the pattern is not clear, traders know that the market often makes some move around 11:30 a.m. that will often carry into the close of the day as the institutions begin their final trading of the day. The move can be a reversal, but it can also be a breakout. For example, if there was a strong sell-off for the first two hours and then a weak rally into 11:30 a.m., and it appears to be topping out and reversing, the market might instead break out to the upside and lead to a trend reversal day and a rally into the close. Traders aren't married to any particular direction going into 11:30 a.m., but are always ready for a move in either direction as the market enters the final third of the day and the institutions begin their final trades.

The final period of the day runs until the close; it often resumes the trend from earlier in the day, as in a trend resumption day, but it sometimes reverses the trend and forms a reversal day. If there is a strong bull trend on the daily chart, most days will have closes above the opens and the market will usually try to rally in the final 30 to 60 minutes. Bear trends have more days with closes below the opens and often sell off into the close.

There are two very different types of price action that traders should look for in the final 30 to 60 minutes because each offers opportunities if traders are prepared, and each poses problems if they are not. First, the market sometimes will have a relentless trend in the final half hour as risk managers tell their traders that they have to cover their losing positions before the close. Momentum programs detect the strong trend and also trade wth trend relentlessly, as long as the momentum continues. On some days many mutual funds will have similar orders to fill going into the close. Traders who want to enter on pullbacks get trapped out because a pullback never comes. If you see this, enter with the trend on the close of the current bar and put your protective stop beyond the other end of the bar. If the trend continues into the close, you can make a quick windfall profit. It is worth noting that traders often get tired, and since their edge is small, they should refrain from trading if they cannot trade at their best. Traders can get tired, bored, or distracted at any time during the day and should not trade until they are back to normal. The computers don't get tired and trade into the close as well as they did all day long. This is another one of the advantages that they have over individual traders.

When there is a bull trend on the daily chart, there will almost always be more bull trend bars than bear trend bars. The opposite is true when there is a bear trend. For example, if the market is in a strong bear trend and there is a moderate rally going into the last hour, many traders will expect the day to close near its low and for the bar on the daily chart to be a strong bear trend bar with a close near its low. Because of this, experienced traders will be quick to short any rally that begins to reverse down toward the end of the day, expecting a close near the low of the day. Other traders will wait for the sell-off to become clear and then short. The result is often a strong bear trend into the close of a bear trend day when there is a bear trend on the daily chart. The opposite is true of bull trends on the daily chart, where the preponderance of the bars close near their highs and the market often rallies into the close after a sell-off before the final hour.

The other type of close is more difficult for traders because instead of trapping them out of a winning trade, it tends to stop them out with losses. The market will trend into the close but have large bars, big tails, and two or three reversals that run stops but do not hit the original stop beyond the signal bar. If your premise that there is a trend into the close is correct and the market is forming a bar or two with large tails, you can make money if swing the trade and stick to your initial stop until after the pullback, and then tighten your stop to just beyond the pullback.

Whenever a report is released, whether it is a 7 a.m., PST, housing report or an 11:15 a.m. FOMC announcement, slippage is common as you get in or out of your trade, so the risk is often larger and the reward is often smaller. Also, the probability is only 50 percent. The result is a bad trader's equation, and most traders should wait for seconds to minutes until the market becomes orderly before placing a trade.

Figure 11.1   KEY TIMES OF THE DAY   **267**

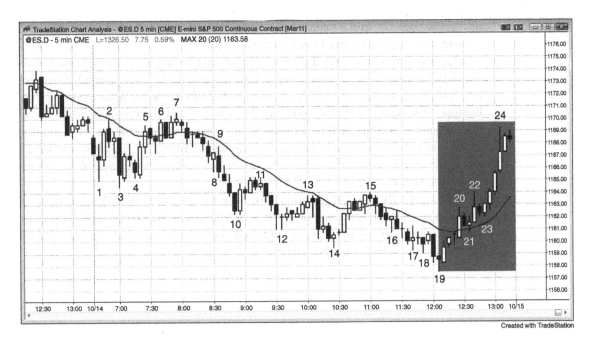

FIGURE 11.1   Risk Managers Contribute to Trends into the Close

As shown in Figure 11.1, the rally into the close was due in part to the risk manager shoulder tap. As the market began to turn up and reached bar 22, all of the traders who shorted after bar 10 were in jeopardy of having losing positions by the close, and all those who shorted after bar 16 were already holding losers. Risk managers at trading firms monitor what positions traders are holding into the close. If a lot of traders are holding shorts that are suddenly becoming losers, they might be emotionally attached to their trades and hope for a late sell-off. Their bonuses depend on their performance, and they might hate to admit that they are suddenly wrong about today's bear trend. The risk manager's job is to be coldly objective, and he will tell the traders to buy back their shorts. If this takes place at enough firms, it can contribute to a relentless uptrend into the close. Traders at home were hoping for a pullback, but it never came. Once they realized what was happening, they could have bought above the brief pullbacks at bars 21 and 23 or bought the close of any bar, and then placed protective stops below the low of their entry bar. Momentum programs detect the relentless buying and begin buying as well, and will continue to buy as long as the momentum up is strong. Mutual and hedge fund purchases going into the close can also contribute. All of these traders are doing the opposite when the market sells off into the close.

The market was in a tight bull channel on the daily chart (not shown). Only two of the past 32 days closed near the low of the day, and 21 of the past 32 days closed above the open. In bull swings on the daily chart, most days had bull bodies, and traders were eager to buy a rally into the close.

The market was in a trading range for the first couple of hours; the range was about half the size of an average daily range, alerting traders to a possible breakout into a trending trading range day. As the market moved down from the bar 7 double top with bar 2, traders became more convinced that the breakout would be to the downside, and the selling increased. The market then formed a lower trading range, but then sold off from the bar 15 moving average gap bar, broke out to the downside, but reversed up to above the open. Remember, most reversal days begin as trending trading range days.

As is often the case, the market went sideways in the middle third of the day, and then the bear trend from bar 7 to bar 10 tried to resume in the final third of the day. However, the downside breakout failed, and the bar 10 to bar 16 trading range became the final flag in the bear trend.

Figure 11.2   KEY TIMES OF THE DAY   **269**

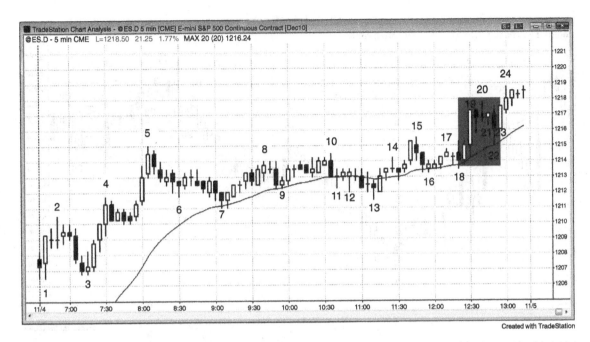

FIGURE 11.2   Trends into the Close Can Be Scary

You can be right about the trend into the close and still lose money when the market has a couple of dojis before the close. As shown in Figure 11.2, the two strong bull trend bars that formed a spike up to bar 19 were likely to have follow-through, but the protective stop on any long needed to be below the spike or at least below the low of the second large bull trend bar. Once the market began forming dojis around bar 20, there was a risk of a sharp pullback. If you bought above bar 16, you could have used a tight stop below bar 20 or a breakeven stop. However, if you bought the close of the bar 19 spike or above the bar 21 doji, you needed to risk to below the low of both bars of the spike or at least to below bar 19. The tails were a warning that the market was two-sided. If you take a trade in this type of market, and only very experienced traders should ever consider staying in when the market enters a tight trading range at the end of the day, you have to trade it for the swing and allow for two-sided movement and use a wide stop.

This was a trend resumption day, where there was a rally for approximately the first third of the day, ending at bar 5, and then a trading range for the middle of the day, and a resumption of the bull trend into the close of the day. The final rally began at 11:15 a.m. PST, although the upside breakout did not come until 12:30 p.m.

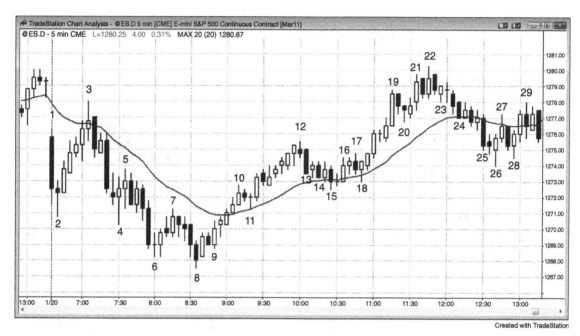

FIGURE 11.3   Midday Reversal

After the trend of the day becomes established within the first hour or so, the market often reverses at the start of the middle third of the day, between about 8:00 a.m. and 9:30 a.m. PST (usually around 8:30 a.m.). Sometimes the market instead enters a trading range for several hours, and then breaks out in either direction at some point in the final hour or two. The breakout can lead to either a trend resumption day or a reversal day. As shown in Figure 11.3, the rally from bar 8 to bar 12 was so strong that the earlier bear trend was unable to reassert itself going into the final third of the day. Instead, the rally from bar 8 to bar 12 resumed upward after the weak attempt at bar 17 to reverse the market down. The bull resumption began with the bar 18 pullback from the bar 12 to bar 15 wedge bull flag to the moving average. The bulls were unable to continue the rally, though, and the market sold off back to the open, creating a doji day on the daily chart.

Bar 3 was a test of the moving average and a double top with bar 1, and therefore a possible high of the day. Traders were looking for a breakout of the bottom of the opening range and then about a measured move down. Instead, the market had a bear spike down to bar 4 and then two more pushes, creating a bear spike and channel trend where the channel was a wedge. Traders saw this as a possible reversal up at the start of the middle third of the day and a potential low of the day. The buy signal was above the two-bar reversal that began with bar 8. Many traders saw the market as having flipped to always-in long on the bar 9 outside up bar, and most traders believed it was long by the end of the bar 10 bull spike.

CHAPTER 12

Markets

P rice action techniques work in all markets, but most day traders prefer markets that have many entries a day on the 5 minute chart and can handle large position sizes without slippage. The 5 minute Standard & Poor's (S&P) Emini futures contract can handle any order size that an individual trader can place; you will never outgrow it. The Russell futures contract, however, is popular with some individual traders because they feel that it trends well intraday and the margin is relatively small for the size of the average swing. Most successful individual traders eventually want to trade more contracts than the Russell can handle without the worry of slippage.

When starting out, you should consider trading the SPY instead of the Emini. If the Emini is trading around 1,100, the SPY will be around 110.00 and an eight-tick scalp for two points in the Emini is a 20 cent scalp in the SPY (each Emini tick is two and a half times larger than an SPY tick). One Emini is equivalent to 500 SPY. If you trade 300 to 500 SPY, you can scale out of your swing position and not incur too much risk. One advantage of the SPY is that the 20 cent scalp size feels so small and comes so quickly that it will be easier to place orders for swing trades than for scalps, which is a better approach when just starting out. You will notice that the SPY often hits a one-tick entry or exit stop when the Emini does not. Because of this, some traders use a two- or three-tick stop in the SPY.

Once you have increased your position size to 1,000 to 1,500 SPY, if you plan to continue to increase your size, switch to the Emini, which can handle huge volume without slippage being a significant problem. When just starting out, you can scalp 100 SPY using a 20 cent profit target and a 20 cent protective stop, which is equivalent to a two-point Emini stop, so your risk is just $20 plus commissions. However, you cannot scalp and make money in the SPY unless your commissions are minimal, like $1.00 for 100 shares. Also, you need an order entry system that allows you to place orders quickly. Otherwise, just swing trade until you are consistently successful, and then look to add some scalping.

Currency futures, foreign exchange (forex), and Treasury bond and note futures can handle huge volume, but give fewer entries than the Eminis on most days. Bonds and notes can have protracted trends intraday, so when a trade sets up, you can often enter and let it swing for hours. The forex market usually doesn't offer many great trades during the Emini day session, and since you don't want any distractions, it is best to avoid it during the day if you are actively trading the Eminis. The DIA and Dow futures are a little thin, so slippage can be a problem for scalpers. Just as the SPY is identical to the Eminis, the QQQ is identical to the NASDAQ futures. The QQQ is also very popular with day traders and can accommodate large orders.

Many stocks trade very well intraday. It is easiest to trade only those with an average daily range of several dollars and an average volume of five million shares or more. You want to be able to scalp 50 cents to a dollar with minimal slippage, and you want the possibility that the swing portion can run several dollars. Currently, Apple (AAPL), International Business Machines (IBM), Google (GOOG), Amazon (AMZN), Goldman Sachs (GS), Oil Service HOLDRS (OIH), UltraShort Oil and Gas ProShares ETF (DUG), Ultra Financials ProShares ETF (UYG), and SPDR Gold Trust (GLD) are all good, but there are many others, and you can add or subtract from your list as needed.

CHAPTER 13

Time Frames and Chart Types

For a scalper, it is easiest to use a 5 minute candle chart for the Emini. However, for intraday swing trading of the Emini or stocks, a simple 5 minute bar chart works well. This is because on a laptop or a single monitor, you can fit six bar charts on your screen, each with a different stock, and each chart will contain a full day's worth of bars. If you use candles, which are wider than bars, your charts will show only about a half day of price action. An important reason for mentioning this is to remind traders that this approach works well with simple bar charts, especially when you are trying to swing trade only the best entries. The advantage of candle charts on the Emini for scalpers is that it is easy to quickly see who owns the bars, especially the setup bar. Also, a lot of high and low 2 variants are not easy to see on bar charts.

Price action trading techniques work in all markets and all time frames, so traders have to make the obvious basic decision of which markets and time frames they should trade. The objective of most traders is to maximize profitability over the long run, and implicit in that is that each trader needs to find an approach that suits his or her personality.

If a 5 minute Emini chart offers a dozen good entries on average every day, and the 3 minute chart offers 20, and the 1 minute offers 30, and the risk (size of the protective stop) is eight ticks on the 5 minute, six ticks on the 3 minute, and four ticks on the 1 minute, why not trade the shorter time frames? More trades, smaller risk, more money—right? Right, if you can read the charts correctly fast enough in real time to be able to place your entry, stop, and profit target orders at the exact prices correctly, and do this constantly for seven hours a day, year in and year out. For many traders, the smaller the time frame, the more good trades they miss, and the lower their winning percentage becomes. They simply cannot scalp with this method fast enough on the 1 and 3 minute charts to be as profitable as they are on the 5 minute chart, so that should be their focus and they should continually work on increasing their position size. The best trades often come as a surprise, and the setups can be hard to trust. Most traders simply cannot process the information fast enough. Invariably, they will cherry-pick and tend not to pick the very best setups, which are the most important ones to their bottom lines. The best trades often set up and trigger so fast that they are easy to miss, and then you are left with all the trades that are less good, including all of the losers.

The average size of a move on a higher time frame chart is greater than that on a smaller time frame chart. However, almost every higher time frame swing starts with a reversal on the 1 and 3 minute charts. It is just hard to know which ones will work, and it can be draining trying to take 30 or more trades a day, hoping for a big move. The very best trades on 1 and 3 minute charts lead to strong entries on 5 and 15 minute charts, and for most traders it is much more profitable to focus on the best 5 minute trades and work on increasing their position size. Once they can trade successfully, they can make an incredible amount of money and have a very high winning percentage, which results in much less stress and a better ability to maintain their performance over time.

Also, as your position size increases, at some point the volume will affect the market on too many trades on a 1 minute chart. As an extreme example, if you had a profit-target limit order to sell 5,000 Emini contracts at two ticks above the market, anyone with a price ladder would see the aberration and you would have a difficult time getting filled on 10 to 15 trades a day. Also, entering that size on a stop would result in a tick or two of slippage, which would ruin the risk/reward ratio of scalping. A trader can trade even 5,000 contracts per trade using price action, but not with the entry and exit scalping techniques needed for most trades. May you someday have the problem of having to rethink your approach because your volume is adversely affecting your fills!

The 1 minute chart can be helpful in two situations. If the 5 minute chart is in a runaway trend and you are flat but want to get in, you can look at a 1 minute chart for high/low 2 pullbacks to enter with the trend. The second situation where 1 minute charts are helpful for experienced traders is in swing trading trending stocks off the 5 minute chart. When stocks are trending, they are very respectful of the moving average and with-trend trades can be made off high/low 1 or 2 setups at the moving average, risking the height of the signal bar. Traders can reduce that risk somewhat by entering on the 1 minute chart on the first reversal after a moving average touch or penetration on the 5 minute chart. If you plot a 5 minute 20 bar moving average on the 1 minute chart, you can quickly see the touches and then place the order. You actually need to plot a 90 bar moving average on the 1 minute chart as a surrogate for the 5 minute 20 bar moving average. Why 90 and not 100 bars? Because the moving average on the 1 minute chart is recalculated at the close of every 1 minute bar, and not just at the close of every fifth bar, so the weighting of the more recent bars tends to make a 100 bar moving average a tiny bit too flat. Also, the first four closes on the 1 minute chart are not part of the 5 minute moving average. To correct for this, use a 90 bar moving average (I use an exponential moving average, but any moving average is fine), which is very close to the 5 minute 20 bar moving average. In actual practice, you will rarely have time to look at a 1 minute stock chart because of your focus on the Emini. However, when a stock is strongly trending, you might occasionally take quick entries off the 1 minute chart.

Implicit in this discussion is that there can be opposite trends on different time frames. For example, if the market has been going up strongly for a couple of weeks, but for the past two days it has been in a trending bear channel and for the past 15 minutes it is in a pullback up to the falling 5 minute moving average, then the 5 minute chart is in a bear trend, the 1 minute chart is in a bull trend, and the two days of downward movement are likely forming a bull flag on the 60 minute chart. It is also possible that the daily chart is bearish and the monthly chart is bullish, both at the same time. It is too confusing to try to reconcile all of this, and it is a waste of time to wait for all time frames to be going in the same direction, because that rarely happens, and even if it does, there is no guarantee of a profitable trade. Just pick one time frame, and trade the price action that is in front of you. If you read correctly and trade well, you will do fine without ever knowing what is going on in all of those other charts.

Many traders use charts where the bars are based on volume and not time. For example, an Emini chart can be constructed where each bar closes as soon as 5,000 or more ticks have occurred, or as soon as 25,000 contracts were traded. It does not matter what type of chart you use as long as you are comfortable with the speed needed to read the chart and place the order. The patterns on all charts are based on human behavior and are therefore the same. Trend lines tend to be more precise on charts based on time than those based on volume, but many traders don't worry about precise trend lines and instead just use approximations.

I have a group of friends who use tick charts based on Fibonacci numbers, and other friends who use time charts based on odd times, like eight or 13 minutes. Everything works some of the time, but it is easier to trade if you pick just one chart. It does not matter if it is a tick chart, a volume chart, or a time chart, and it does not matter how many ticks, shares, or minutes are in each bar. There will be great price action signals on all types of charts all day long. What is far more important is a trader's ability to read real time and manage trades correctly. You can experiment with totally random numbers of ticks, shares, or minutes per bar and you will see that the charts look great and have lots of reasonable signals. I personally like the 5 minute chart because trend lines and trend channel lines are often precise, there are plenty of setups every day, and I can see when the bar is about to close, which allows me to anticipate trades. With tick or volume charts, a flurry of trades over the course of a few seconds can cause the bar to close much sooner than expected, and I find that I end up missing too many of those great signals that are so easy to see on a printout of the chart at the end of the day. Also, the trend lines are less accurate. There is also a tendency for traders who use charts based on ticks or volume to use smaller time frame charts. They do so to minimize their stop sizes, hoping that the reduced risk will result in being profitable. Invariably, they ignore the trade-off of a lower winning percentage and end up losing money.

Figure 13.1   TIME FRAMES AND CHART TYPES   **277**

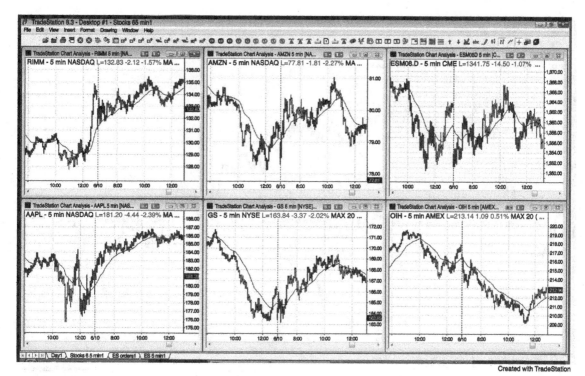

FIGURE 13.1   Swing Trading with Bar Charts

A simple bar chart such as those in Figure 13.1 is all that is necessary to swing trade using price action. When there is a trend, look to enter with trend on a pullback, like a high 2 in a bull trend or a low 2 in a bear trend. Also, after a strong trend line break, look to enter countertrend on a test, like a higher low or lower low in a possible new bull trend, if there is a strong reversal bar.

FIGURE 13.2 Pullbacks on 1 Minute Chart

If the 5 minute chart does not have pullbacks and you are struggling with how to get long, consider looking at the 1 minute chart (see Figure 13.2). The thumbnail of the 5 minute Emini shows that it went 11.75 points up off the open without a pullback. If traders missed the trend from the open long, they would have missed the entire swing because there were no pullbacks. However, if they instead looked at the 1 minute chart, there were three high 1 setups (bars A, B, and C) where they could have entered. Aggressive bulls will buy place limit orders at the low of the prior bar on the 1 minute chart, expecting every reversal attempt to quickly fail. Once long, they will then manage their trades on the 5 minute chart, never look at the 1 minute, and suddenly realize that those are reversals that can be shorted. You looked at the 1 minute for only one reason—to find high 1 and 2 long entries because there were no pullbacks on the 5 minute chart. Trading countertrend on the 1 minute chart will cost you money. In fact, those three long setups are at exactly the price that the 1 minute shorts would have covered, and as they covered, they would become additional buyers and help drive the market up.

Figure 13.3

TIME FRAMES AND CHART TYPES **279**

FIGURE 13.3 Moving Average Pullbacks on 1 Minute Chart

As shown in Figure 13.3, this 1 minute chart of AAPL during a strong bear trend day offered three good shorts at the 90 bar exponential moving average (equivalent to the 5 minute 20 bar ema) with low risk (the height of the bar). The thumbnail shows the strong 5 minute spike and channel bear trend. Most traders should just use one chart and not bother with looking at a 1 minute chart. It is easy to get entranced by all of the little moves on the 1 minute chart and miss the big picture on the 5 minute chart, and then end up making far fewer ticks profit. It is very easy for beginners to over-trade, exit too soon, and not let profits run, and end up losing money, even though they correctly shorted all of the way down.

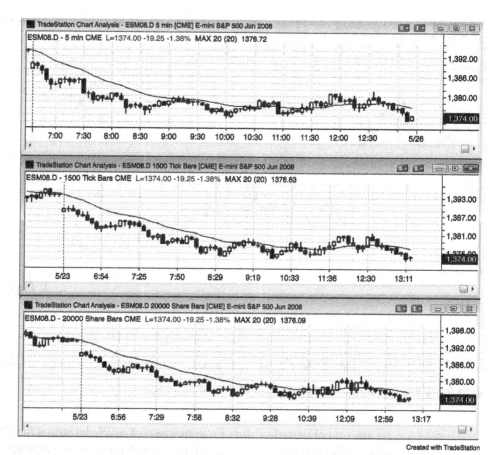

Created with TradeStation

FIGURE 13.4 Volume and Tick Charts Have More Bars in the First Hour or So

The three charts shown in Figure 13.4 were from the same Emini day session. The top was a 5 minute chart, the middle had 1,500 ticks per bar (1,500 trades per bar), and the bottom had 20,000 contracts per bar (each bar closed on the first trade that made the volume 20,000 or more contracts since the start of the bar). They had similar price action and all were tradable, but since the highest volume usually takes place in the first hour or so, the tick and volume charts were skewed, with many more bars per hour earlier in the day and in the final hour.

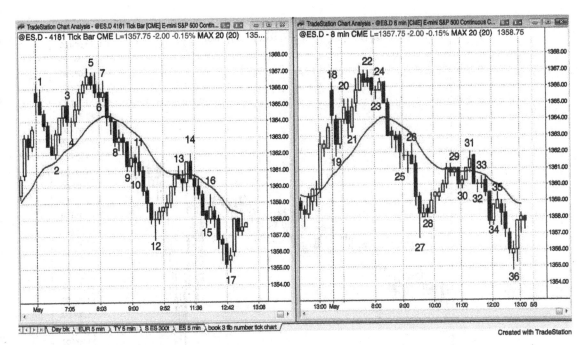

FIGURE 13.5 Price Action Works on Any Time Frame and Any Type of Chart

The chart on the left in Figure 13.5 has a Fibonacci 4,181 ticks per bar, and the chart on the right is an 8 minute bar chart. Both had many reliable setups. Every type of chart gives good signals some of the time, but it is easier to trade if you pick just one chart. It does not matter if it is a tick chart, a volume chart, or a time chart, and it does not matter how many ticks, shares, or minutes are in each bar. You can pick totally random numbers. What is far more important is a trader's ability to read real time and manage trades correctly. What takes place on all of the charts is just an expression of our genes, and it does not matter which portrayal of that expression you use. All charts show the same behavior.

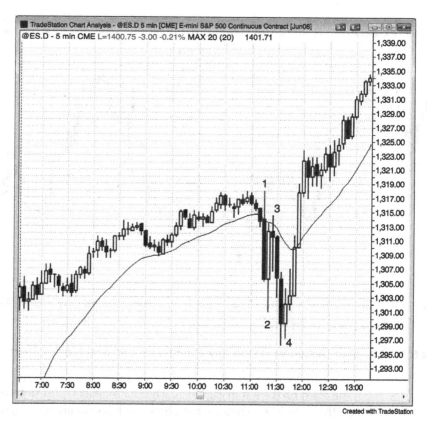

FIGURE 13.6 Big Bars and Reversals during a Report

Reports can lead to very emotional moves with big bars, outside bars, and several reversals. In the seconds to minutes after a report comes out, computerized trading by institutions gives them a clear edge in speed of analysis and order placement. When your competition has a big advantage, don't compete. Wait for their edge to disappear and trade when speed is no longer important, which is usually after the first one to three bars. Despite the emotion that the rapid moves and big bars generate in all traders, price action setups are still very reliable. In general, always swing part of the position with a breakeven stop because sometimes a swing will go much farther than you could ever imagine.

As shown in Figure 13.6, the Federal Open Market Committee (FOMC) report was released at 11:15 a.m. PST (it sometimes comes out several minutes late) and caused emotional trading as evidenced by large bars, outside bars, and several reversals within the next 30 minutes. However, price action traders who remembered the basic rules did well. Bar 2 was a large bull reversal bar, but whenever there is a

Figure 13.6   TIME FRAMES AND CHART TYPES   **283**

lot of overlap with the prior bar, a trading range might be forming and you should never be looking to buy at the top of a range. Instead, look for trapped traders, small bars, and second entries.

Bar 3 was a great short scalp because there were trapped overly eager bulls who mistook the large reversal bar for a sensible long setup.

Bar 4 was the second attempt to reverse the breakout below the low of the day that formed at the open. Second entries are always worth taking, and a bull trend inside bar is as good as you are likely to get on an emotional day. Since this would have resulted in at least two legs up, you needed to swing part of your position. The initial stop was around the middle of the signal bar, and then one tick below the bar 4 entry bar once that bar closed. The stop could then have been trailed below the low of the prior bar and eventually moved to breakeven.

Emotional days often lead to trends that carry much further than you would ever anticipate, and catching one like this is much more profitable than the combined profits from many, many scalps. Here, the bull trend continued for almost 30 points, or about $1,500 per contract.

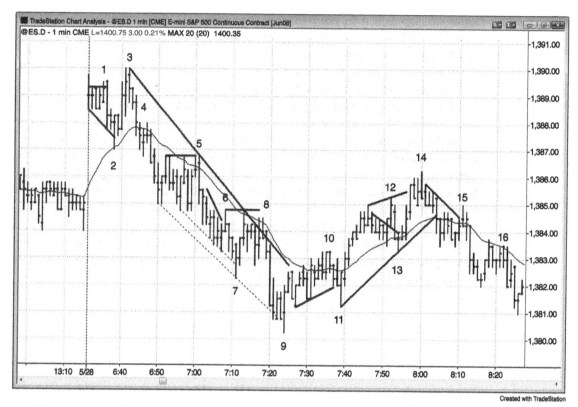

FIGURE 13.7 Scalps in First Hour on 1 Minute Chart

As shown in Figure 13.7, the first couple of hours of the Emini provided many profitable scalps on the 1 minute chart for someone who could read price action and place orders very quickly. It is very difficult to do in actual practice, and most traders would find it too stressful to do correctly, resulting in them losing money.

Bar 1 was a false upside breakout of an iii pattern and a lower high on a gap up day.

Bar 2 set up a high 2 at the moving average, a wedge bull flag, and a trend channel line reversal.

Bar 3 was a short on a failed breakout to a new high on a gap up day that could have led to a test of the gap (the market usually tries to test gaps, so traders should look for opportunities to trade in that direction).

Bar 5 was a low 3 at the moving average. A low 3 is a type of wedge or triangle, and here it was also a triple top bear flag.

Bar 6 was a failed micro trend line breakout and a breakout pullback from the breakout of the bar 5 bear flag.

Figure 13.7   TIME FRAMES AND CHART TYPES   **285**

Bar 7 reversed two bear trend channel lines, but was not a profitable long, leading traders to believe that the bears were strong. Because the channel was steep, this was a wedge reversal and not a wedge bull flag, so it was better to look to buy a higher low after a trend line break or a move above the moving average.

Bar 8 was a failed trend line breakout, a double top pullback, a low 2 short setup, and a five-tick failure long from bar 7. With so many factors favoring the shorts, it was no surprise that the market fell quickly.

Bar 9 was a second attempt to reverse up from the bear trend channel line overshoot and a reversal up after a sell climax at the end of a bear channel. When a bear channel breaks to the downside and reverses up, it usually leads to at least a two-legged rally that goes through the top of the channel.

Bar 10 was a bad short because traders were expecting a higher low and a second leg up. It turned into a five-tick failure at bar 11, which is a reversal pattern. If anything, traders should have bought below bar 10, expecting a second leg up.

Bar 11 was a double bottom bull flag and a higher low that should have led to a second leg up.

Bar 12 was a failed bull flag breakout, but the spike up from bar 11 was strong enough so that traders should have looked to short only a lower high.

Bar 13 was a high 2 at the moving average and a test of the breakout above bar 10.

Bar 14 was a second-entry short in an expanding triangle top, as well as the third push up in this bear rally and therefore a wedge short. It was also a trend channel line reversal and a double top bear flag with bar 5.

Bar 15 was a low 2 at the moving average, a failed trend line breakout (from the bar 14 high), and a lower high after the bar 11 to bar 13 trend line breakout.

Bar 16 was another low 2 short at the moving average and a double top bear flag.

CHAPTER 14

Globex, Premarket, Postmarket, and Overnight Market

The same price action techniques apply in all markets at any time of the day or night. There are so many sophisticated international traders that many markets are traded 24 hours a day. The premarket extremes are often targets that get tested during the day session, but it is not necessary to look at Globex prices when trading the day session since very little is gained and the day session price action will give adequate signals. Many traders use the Globex chart throughout the day when they are day trading, and that is perfectly reasonable. I prefer the day session chart, since trend lines and trend channel lines that extend over two or more days are very reliable on the day session charts, and important to my trading.

When a stock has an earnings report after the close, some traders try to trade them because the big moves appear to offer great profit potential, but these moves are very difficult to scalp and most traders should not attempt it. The moves are frequently too fast to read and allow proper order placement, have big slippage on stop entries, have pullbacks that are large, and have reversals, and the market often suddenly stops moving as soon as you understand what it has been doing.

FIGURE 14.1 Trading after the Close

As shown in Figure 14.1, Dell had an earnings report after the close and appeared to offer some postmarket trading opportunities, but the moves are usually too difficult to trade profitably for most traders. Bar 1 was a high 1 bull inside bar after the upside breakout and set up a long at one penny above its high.

Bar 2 was a long at 1 cent above the high of the outside bar, which also broke below a bull micro trend line and reversed up.

Bar 3 was a high 1 breakout long after a major trend line break.

Bar 4 was a bear reversal bar and a setup for a final flag short following a buy climax after a breakout above a bull channel. Also, the bar 3 flag broke a big bull trend line, indicating that the bears were gaining a little strength. Fade a strong trend only if there was first a trend line break. Also, a countertrend trade in a strong trend needs a 5 minute (not a 3 or 1 minute) reversal bar. The market went sideways in a tight trading range for the rest of the postmarket session.

Figure 14.2   GLOBEX, PREMARKET, POSTMARKET, AND OVERNIGHT MARKET   **289**

FIGURE 14.2   Trading the Premarket

The premarket is tradable, but there are usually not many entries in the hour or two before the New York Stock Exchange opens at 6:30 a.m. PST (see Figure 14.2). There are often reports at 5:30 a.m. that result in quick trends and reversals, though.

Bar 1 was a wedge long and a double bottom, but traders would have had to hold through the bar 2 pullback to make a profit. A wedge bottom (or three pushes down, or any of many other names for this pattern) usually leads to two legs up.

Bar 2 was a higher low and a small trend line reversal.

Bar 3 was a high 2 at the moving average.

A report resulted in a false breakout to the upside and then an outside down bar (bar 4). Traders would have shorted below bar 3, where many longs would have placed their stops.

Bar 5 was a breakout pullback.

Bar 6 was a second entry for a second attempt to reverse up from a new swing low (bar 5 was the first).

FIGURE 14.3   Tick Charts Have More Bars in a Fast Market

As shown in Figure 14.3, the Emini reacted poorly to the 5:30 a.m. PST unemployment report. This is a 100 tick chart where each bar represents 100 trades, independent of the volume of the trades or the time. Note that the 30 bars between bars 1 and 5 all occurred within one minute due to the fast action off the report. These bars were forming so rapidly that it would have been difficult or impossible to trade anything other than market orders. It was theoretically possible to make many profitable scalps based on the price action, but most traders should never attempt to trade this. The only purpose of showing it is to demonstrate that standard patterns were present throughout.

The thumbnail charts are the 1 and 5 minute charts for the same 30 minutes of trading.

Figure 14.4   GLOBEX, PREMARKET, POSTMARKET, AND OVERNIGHT MARKET   **291**

FIGURE 14.4   The Globex and Day Session Often Have Different Setups

As shown in Figure 14.4, the bar chart of the Globex 24-hour session had an expanding triangle ending at the bar 5 high (bars 1 and 3 were the first two pushes up), and the thumbnail shows the day session with the same numbering. A day session trader did not need to see the Globex expanding triangle to go short at bar 5. Bar 5 took out yesterday's high and pulled back to the moving average. The market then bounced to a lower high and had a short setup at the bar 6 double top bear flag (the first top was six bars earlier).

CHAPTER 15

Always In

T his might be the single most important concept in trading. Traders should constantly assess whether the market is trending, and an "always-in" approach can help a trader to make that important determination. If you had to be in the market at all times, either long or short, the always-in position is whatever your current position is. Some variation of this is used by many traders, including institutions. For example, most mutual funds are usually always-in long, and most hedge funds remain close to fully invested, but often have always-in long positions in some markets while simultaneously having always-in short positions in others. Individual traders should consider using an always-in approach if they tend to miss too many big moves.

Determining the always-in direction is different from asking whether the trend is up or down, because most trend traders don't hold a position when the market is unclear. The market, at all times, is either always-in long or always-in short, and there is usually a general consensus about the direction of the trend. Traders who take 20 or more trades a day see the always-in position flipping repeatedly throughout the day, but very few traders could reverse this often, day after day. However, traders who are just looking for the best three to 10 swings a day, and are willing to allow multiple pullbacks without changing their opinion about the direction of the current swing, have an always-in mentality. They can either reverse at each new signal or take profits once a swing begins to weaken and then look for a trade in either direction. Few traders actually stay in the market all day long, reversing at every opposite signal. Most traders need to take breaks during the day and they have a difficult time placing reversal trades. Although they will take many always-in reversal setups, they usually trade each as a swing trade, exiting before looking for a trade in the opposite direction. They focus more on making a profit that is at least as large as the risk, rather than on reversing on the next opposite signal, and use always-in signals as their entry setups. In general, if a signal is clear enough to be an always-in reversal, traders should assume that it is then at least 60 percent certain of reaching a profit target that is at least as large as the risk. Even though the minimum criterion for an always-in signal is that the market is more likely to go in the new direction than in the old one, which implies that all that is needed is 51 percent certainty, most such signals are 60 percent certain or higher. For example, in the Emini, if traders need to use a two-point stop to take a trade, they should use a profit target that is at least two points from their entry, and they will likely have at least a 60 percent chance of success if they read the price action correctly.

If traders look at the chart at this moment and are forced to initiate a position right now, either short or long, and they could decide at least slightly in favor of one direction or the other, then they see an always-in position. This is the direction of at least the short-term trend. If they cannot formulate an opinion, they should look at the moving average and at the move that led to the current state of uncertainty (remember, uncertainty means that the market is in a trading range). If most of the closes of the recent bars are below the moving average, the always-in position is probably short. If they are mostly above, always in is probably long. If the move leading up to the trading range was a rally, the always-in position is probably long. If it was a sell-off, always in is probably short. If you are hoping for a pullback to buy, the always-in position is probably long. If you are hoping for a rally to short, always in is probably short. If you simply cannot decide, then the market is in a trading range and you look to buy low and sell high. Your goal is to get synchronized with what the market is doing. It is like when you were a child and two of your friends were swinging a jump rope and you were about to run in and start jumping the rope. You would watch it intensely to sense the rhythm. Once you were reasonably confident, you began jumping. With trading, once you are reasonably confident of where the market it heading, that is the time to jump in.

Some traders use higher time frame charts to determine the always-in direction. For example, if they trade the 5 minute chart, and the 60 minute chart is in a bull trend and above the moving average, they will look only for buy setups on the 5 minute chart. Others use indicators on higher time frame charts in the same way. For example, if the 60 minute stochastic is rising, they will look only to buy pullbacks on the 5 minute chart. Some traders don't feel comfortable evaluating 10 to 20 reversals a day on the 5 minute chart and instead prefer a higher time frame chart where there might be only three to five decisions a day. This is an effective approach, but since the bars are larger, stops have to be larger as well, and that means that position sizes should be smaller.

Even before the market opens, traders have a bias that the final always-in position from yesterday might still be controlling the market. However, once there are two consecutive reasonably strong trend bars in the same direction, they probably create the new always-in direction. It is uncertain until there is a breakout and then follow-through, but it is a starting point. If the context is right, it can lead to a trade, like entering on the first pullback. With a lot of experience, a trader could theoretically stay in the market all day, reversing at each reasonable signal.

The market is always trying to reverse, and often comes very close, but lacks that last bit of follow-through that traders need to become confident that the reversal was successful. These near flips are great opportunities for the with-trend traders. For example, if there is a bull trend that forms a strong bear breakout bar, many bulls will buy the close of the bar, expecting that there will be no follow-through selling. They correctly believe that most reversal attempts fail and that this will be a brief opportunity to buy at a great price. Other bulls will wait to see what the close of the next bar looks like. If it is not a bear close, they will buy the close, and other bulls will buy above its high, and above the high of the strong bear bar where bears might have their protective stops. When the bears don't get the immediate follow-through that they need, they will buy back their shorts. With both the bulls and the bears buying, the market goes up for at least several bars. The bears will not be willing to short until another reasonable setup occurs, and that often will occur after a new trend high. When beginning traders see that strong bear spike, they become scared. They think that the market is breaking out and that they need to short immediately. All they see is the very strong bear bar and suddenly ignore the strong bull trend that preceded it. They end up shorting within a tick or two of the low of the failed breakout attempt, and get stopped out as the market works back higher. Often, the rally looks weak, so they do not buy. They keep looking to sell a low 1 or low 2 short, expecting follow-through after that strong bear spike, but the low 1 fails, and their stop gets hit. Then the low 2 fails, and they lose for a third consecutive time. This is because they do not understand what it means when a market is always-in long. It means that the bull trend is still in effect, and although it almost flipped to always-in short, it did not. Until it does, the only direction for trades is long. It is a costly mistake to keep betting that reversals will be successful, because 80 percent of them are not.

Always in is a swing approach to trading. For it to be effective, traders should look for only the most significant three to as many as 10 swings a day and not keep reversing at every minor signal (many days have 20 or more reversals, but most are too small to be traded profitably). Also, most traders exit some or all of their position once the trade has moved in their direction for a distance equal to about two or three times their initial risk, and they do not worry about staying in the market at every moment. When institutions begin to take profits, the result is a pullback to a level where these institutions will reenter in the direction of the trend, resulting in a resumption of the trend. When a strong trend transitions into a trading range, the always-in position often remains unchanged. If traders are going to trade in the trading range, they should scalp most or all of their trades. However, if the always-in position does not change, they should consider taking scalps only in the direction of the trend. For example, if there is a strong bear trend that is starting to correct up, but there is no strong bull spike and the market is staying below the moving average, the always-in position will remain down. Even though the market is in a trading range, traders should look for scalps only in the direction of the trend, which means that they should look for shorts. If there is a strong buy setup, it will probably flip the always-in position to long, at least for enough bars to buy for a scalp. However, any buy setup that is not strong enough to flip the always-in direction to up is generally not worth trading.

Since this is a swing approach, traders should not use it when the market is in a tight trading range. In fact, most traders should not trade then, and should instead wait for the breakout or failed breakout. Either can lead to an always-in swing trade. If experienced, profitable traders want to trade in a tight trading range, they should either take the always-in trade that was present prior to the formation of the tight trading range and hold for a swing profit, or simply trade scalps with limit order entries, fading the extremes of the range and the breakouts above and below the prior bars.

On trading range days, always-in reversals are often unclear until the market gets near the opposite end of the range. For example, it often is not clearly long until there is a bull spike that surges to the top of the range, and it is often not clearly short until there is a strong bear spike that races to the bottom of the range. However, buying near the top of the range and shorting near the bottom is the exact opposite of what traders should be doing. Always in is a swing concept that applies to trends, and is dangerous within trading ranges, where it is better to scalp and buy low and sell high. For example, as the market is moving toward the top of the range, there will be breakouts above swing highs within the range that might make some traders see the market as flipping to always-in long, but usually the swing high is not important enough and the breakout and follow-through are not strong enough to convince everyone that the market has flipped. If you are looking at the move up and are wondering if it has truly flipped into an always-in long move, then you are uncertain. Since uncertainty is the hallmark of a trading range, you have your answer. Trends create a sense of sustained urgency. You are certain that the market has more to go and you are desperately hoping for a pullback so you can buy lower. Traders realize that if the move up is a new bull trend and not just a brief spike up in a trading range, the move will have a series of strong bull bars and won't pause after going above each swing high. A consensus forms only if the market breaks strongly above the entire range and has follow-through, not if there is simply a sharp move within the range toward the top or bottom. Beginners are afraid that there might not be much left to the move, but experienced traders know that a strong successful breakout from a trading range will usually reach a measured move target at a minimum and provide plenty of room for a profit.

On trading range days, the strongest bear spikes often form near the low of the day because of a sell vacuum. The strong bulls expect a test of the low of the trading range, so they stop buying as the market approaches the low. This creates an imbalance and the market falls quickly in a bear spike. Also, momentum programs will sense the acceleration and they will also quickly short until the momentum slows or reverses. If traders looked at only the current leg down, they would see a strong bear spike and assume that the always-in trade had just become strongly short. However, if they stepped back and looked at the entire chart, they would be suspicious of a possible sell vacuum. Instead of looking for shorts, they would look to buy the failed breakout attempt.

So what does a trader need to see to be able to choose an always-in direction? Almost all always-in trades require a spike before traders will have confidence. Traders want to see a breakout that is strong enough for them to expect follow-through. The signs of strength of breakouts were discussed in the second book. There usually has to have been at least two consecutive strong bull trend bars before most traders will believe that the always-in direction is long, and at least two consecutive strong bear trend bars before they will think that always in is short. During the first hour, before a clear trend is established, two consecutive bull trend bars will make traders look for buy scalps, and two consecutive bear trend bars will make them look for sell scalps. This is discussed in Chapter 19 on trading the open.

If the context is right, even a single trend bar with an average range can be enough to make traders believe that the always-in position has flipped to the opposite direction. Usually, however, at least two or more consecutive trend bars are needed before enough traders believe that the direction has reversed for there to be significant follow-through. Just like a countertrend trader might be willing to hold a position through one pullback but not two (for example, when buying a bottom, the bulls will exit and sometimes reverse to short if a low 2 triggers), always-in traders will generally prefer to see a second consecutive strong trend bar before they feel that the always-in position has reversed.

Since a second trend bar is usually needed for traders to believe that the always-in position has reversed, the close of that trend bar is important. For example, if there is a bear breakout bar, then traders will carefully watch the close of the next bar. The bears will want a bear close and the bulls will want a bull body. The market has inertia, so most attempts to change what it is doing will fail. This means that many traders will buy the close of the bear breakout bar, expecting that the follow-through bar will have a bull close and the bears will give up. If the breakout is not too strong and there is a good reason to believe that the breakout should fail (like a breakout attempt at the bottom of a bull flag), this can be a good trade; but because the decision is difficult, only experienced traders should consider it. The bulls want to buy pullbacks, so they look for bear spikes to fade. They see a bear spike as a commitment by the bears who are on the wrong side of the market, and will therefore have to buy back their shorts with losses. Also, those bears will not look to sell again for at least a bar or two, so there will be fewer bears coming into the market. This increases the chances that the bulls who bought that bear spike will make a profit. Similarly, when the market is always-in short, bears look at bull spikes at the top of small legs as great opportunities to short. They assume that the bulls will be trapped and will soon have to become sellers as they exit their longs with losses.

If the follow-through bar is strong, traders can enter on the close of the bar or on a small pullback. For example, if there is a strong bull breakout and the next bar is a strong bull trend bar, many traders will buy on the close of that follow-through bar or on a one- or two-tick pullback. If the follow-through bar is weak, like a doji, it is usually better to look to buy pullbacks rather than the close of the bar. If the follow-through bar goes only a few ticks beyond the breakout bar, odds favor a failed breakout. If it goes many ticks beyond, the odds favor the bar becoming a strong trend bar once it closes. Most traders will see the market as having a clear always-in direction. Sometimes the market goes only a few bars beyond the break-out bar and then quietly reverses in a channel against the direction of the breakout without ever clearly confirming that the breakout has failed and that the always-in direction has flipped. In this case, the always-in position is probably unchanged for most traders, but they will have protective stops to get them out if the pullback grows too far. The market is likely entering a trading range, so they will convert to a trading range mode of trading, which means scalping and not allowing their winners to turn into losers. For example, if there is a bull breakout followed by a few weak bars of follow-through, and then the market begins to form a weak bear channel without ever having a bear spike, the market can remain always-in long. However, bulls should have protective stops, just in case the bear channel falls a long way without ever having a clear bear reversal. If bulls bought early on and had a large open profit, they could have their stops at breakeven. If they bought late, they should probably exit below the signal bar. In general, if the follow-through is weak, traders should not buy near the high, and should instead wait to buy a pull-back. If they did buy near the top, they could only do so because they sensed urgency. If there is no immediate follow-through to prove that the urgency is present, they should exit and look to buy on a pullback.

As a guideline, the minimum requirement for an always-in flip to short is usually that the follow-through bar not have a bull close. If it is a small bear bar or a doji bar, this is confirmation that the bears are in control for most traders, but it is a sign that the new bear trend is not strong. It is better to look to sell rallies and low 1 and low 2 setups than it is to sell the closes of the bars. If the follow-through bar has a strong bull body or is a bull reversal bar, this can be a buy signal for a failed breakout. If it has a small bull body, most traders will wait for more evidence before shorting, but believe that the chance of a new trend is much less. The opposite is true when the market is breaking out into a possible always-in bull. The minimum requirement for the follow-through bar is usually that it does not have a bear close. If the follow-through bar is not impressive, then look to buy pullbacks instead of buying the close of the bar. If the follow-through bar has a bear close, the breakout might be a bull trap, and this is often a signal bar for a failed breakout short. However, occasionally the market might have flipped into a bull trend, but traders will need more confirmation before drawing that conclusion.

Once traders are confident that the breakout has follow-through, they will then look for a measured move. For example, if there is a strong bull spike lasting three bars and breaking above a trading range, many traders will believe that there will probably be a measured move up based on the height of the spike or the height of the trading range, and many will immediately buy at least a small position at the market. Since they are confident, then they are at least 60 percent certain about the directional probability (discussed in book 2) of an equidistant move, and whenever that is the case, the math favors taking a trade. As the spike continues, the risk remains constant, and the directional probability of an equidistant move will stay at 60 percent or better, but the reward grows and this makes the trade even better mathematically. If they buy at the top of a strong three-bar spike in Goldman Sachs (GS) and the spike is $1.00 tall, there is at least a 60 percent chance that the market will go up for a measured move of $1.00 before it falls $1.00 to the bottom of the spike. If the spike grows to $1.50 over the next couple of bars, they are still risking to the bottom of the spike (they would probably have tightened their stop at this point), and now the measured move target is $1.50 above the current bar and $2.00 above their entry. They now have at least a 60 percent chance of making $2.00 before losing no more than $1.00, which means that their trade is very strong. If the spike continues to grow, the probability will remain good and the reward will continue to grow. As traders tighten their stops, the risk shrinks and the trade becomes even better mathematically. In general, whenever the market is clearly always in and traders are assessing a trade using the trader's equation, they should assume that the probability is at least 60 percent.

The market usually enters always-in mode at some point in the first hour, and many traders like to take an always-in trade at that point. Some take profits once the market moves in their direction for a distance that is one or two times greater than their risk. For example, if they bought an always-in entry in Apple (AAPL) and their initial protective stop was a dollar below their entry price, they would try to exit some or all of their trade after a dollar or two of profit. Others prefer to hold their position until there is a clear reversal and the market has flipped to always in, but in the opposite direction. Then they would reverse their position and truly stay always in the market. Since most traders do not have the ability to flip on every minor reversal, they instead look for only the very strongest two to five reversals of the day. Sometimes there will be a pullback that just keeps growing, but does not clearly create an always-in reversal. For example, if the market had a strong bull spike and the market was clearly always-in long, but then there was a low-momentum pullback that went on for hours, traders need to reassess their premise. They should keep a worst-case scenario protective stop in the market just in case the pullback continues to grow to the point that the market falls below their entry price. It will sometimes do that without ever having a clear bear spike and an always-in sell signal. If they had an open profit of several Emini points, they would probably not want the market to come back to their entry price, and they might choose to use a breakeven stop. If they get stopped out, they could wait and look for an always-in trade in either direction. If the market pulls back within minutes of their entry before they had any meaningful profit, their protective stop should be below the bull spike, even though it might be far away. If it is far, their position size has to be small enough to keep their risk within their normal limits.

Once you believe that the market has become always in, it is usually best to enter at least a small position at the market or on a tiny pullback. This is especially true when the always-in direction is clear and strong. When the momentum is low and there is not that sense of urgency, some traders prefer to enter on a larger pullback. However, they risk missing the move since many great always-in trades begin with low momentum, but they just keep going without a pullback until after many bars and many points. In general, whenever the market is always-in long, traders will look at every attempt by the bears to turn the market down as a buying opportunity, because they know that most attempts to reverse a trend will fail. They will buy at and around the close of any bear trend bar, at and below the low of the prior bar or any prior swing low, and below all support levels, like bull trend lines. When the market is always-in short, traders will see every attempt by the bulls to reverse the market up as a selling opportunity, because they correctly assume that most such attempts will fail. They will short around the high of any bull trend bar, the high of the prior bar, any prior swing high, and any resistance level, like a bear trend line.

Since you are swinging during always-in trading, you have to allow pullbacks, which are inevitable. Most pullbacks are not reversal entries, so you cannot allow yourself to be constantly worrying about every move that is against your position. In general, if there is a pullback that would have hit a breakeven stop and then the market resumes in your direction for several bars, it should not come back to your entry price again. Therefore, in most cases, you could then move your stop to breakeven. If it is hit by that second pullback and you are not certain of the market's direction, just remain flat until you feel comfortable with another always-in setup. Remember, uncertainty is a hallmark of a trading range and always in is an approach for trends.

If you believe that there is an always-in direction, you should not take countertrend trades. This is because they almost certainly would have to be scalps, which means that the risk would probably be about twice the reward and the chance of success would have to be an unrealistic 70 percent or greater. If you think that there is going to be a pullback, it is far better mathematically to wait to enter in the direction of the trend at the end of the pullback than it is to bet that the pullback will be large enough and mathematically certain enough for you to make a profitable countertrend scalp.

I have a friend who patiently waits for an always-in setup in the first couple of hours every day, and when he finds one, he expects a trend to last for at least a couple of hours and cover at least a third of an average daily range. Once he sees his always-in setup, he enters the market and then places a bracket order where the stop is beyond the signal bar and his profit-taking limit order is at some measured move target or support or resistance area that is at least twice as far away as his stop. Since he is taking an always-in entry, the probability of at least an equidistant move is 60 percent or better. If he is risking two points in the Emini, then he has at least a 60 percent chance of making two points before his protective stop is hit. However, when he is risking two points, his profit target is always four points or more, and with an always-in entry, his probability of success is likely at least 50 percent. Although the probability is never known with certainty, it is likely over 60 percent with many of his entries. However, he, like many traders, does not want to trade in the middle of the day when minor reversals are common. So what does he do while he is waiting for his trade to work? He goes on errands or out for exercise. He comes back a couple of hours later, and at that point, he looks for an always-in trade into the close of the day.

What constitutes a strong always-in market? Since always in can occur only when there is trend or at least a potential trend, look for the signs of strength in trends and reversals. There is a list of them at the beginning of this book (Introduction). The more that are present, the more likely you will make a profit. An obvious one is a strong spike, especially if it lasts for several bars. For example, if there is a strong reversal up on the open and the spike at this point is made of three reasonably sized bull trend bars, traders are buying at the market and on tiny pullbacks. They do not want to wait for a pullback, because they are more confident that the market will be higher at some point over the next several bars than they are that there will be a pullback. This urgency is a perfect always-in situation, and if you are not long, you should consider buying at least a small position at the market or on a limit order located a few ticks below the high of the bar. You can see where your stop would have to be, which might be at the low of the entry bar of the reversal. If that means you have to risk eight points and you normally risk only two, then take only a quarter of your normal position size. The most important consideration for you is that you must get long, even if it is a tiny position, because you are confident that the market is going higher. If you believe that the day is becoming a strong bull trend day, try to hold at least some of your position until the close of the day, unless a clear and strong bear reversal develops.

For stocks, breakeven stops have less chance of being hit, so it is more profitable to look to swing trade. Typically, look to scalp out a third to a half after about a 0.5 to 1 percent move or about twice the size of your initial risk, and then swing the balance. If the market appears to be reversing against your trade but has not yet reversed, like at a test of a high of the day, take off another quarter to a third, but always try to let at least a quarter run until your breakeven stop is hit, until there is a clear and strong opposite signal, or until the close. Trends often go much further than you could ever imagine.

Hold the position through repeated pullbacks until you exit at your target price, until there is a clear reversal setup, or until the protective stop is hit. Sometimes a pullback is violent, but not enough to trigger an always-in reversal, so stick with your original plan and don't be upset by a single large trend bar against your position. If your stop is hit, stay out of the market until there is another clear and strong setup in either direction. If there is a clear and strong setup, repeat the process. If your trading size is two contracts and you are long one when a reversal pattern triggers, sell three. One gets you out of your remaining long position and the other two start the process in this new, opposite direction. Scalp the first for one to two times the size of your risk and swing the second.

The key to this approach is to enter or reverse only when there is a clear and strong setup. If not, rely on your breakeven stop, even though you may give back all of the gains on your swing portion. If you watch a small basket of stocks, almost every day at least one will set up with a reliable entry that will allow you to put on a swing trade.

At any moment during the day you might decide that there is clearly a trend or that there has been a clear reversal. You need one or both for any always-in trade. One side is in control of the swing and there is likely more to go in that direction. Think about where the protective stop would be and calculate the number of ticks that you would be required to risk if you were to enter at the market. As a general rule, the trend will likely continue about the same number of ticks and the odds of success are better than 50–50, since you believe that there is a trend. If you are confident that the market is always in, the probability is likely 60 percent or more. After the trend continues, you are usually able to trail the protective stop and reduce your risk. Also, your original profit goal can increase if the market has trended a long way since your entry, and the new protective stop location leads to a new profit projection. This results in a revised evaluation with a profit potential that is greater than your risk with the probability of success still greater than 50–50.

The improving math that is inherent in swing trading during trends is the reason that it is one of the best ways to trade, especially for beginners.

Experienced traders can use the always-in approach to scale into positions in the direction of the trend, but this requires confidence in your assessment of the strength of the trend. For example, if traders feel that there is a strong bull trend, then they might use limit orders to scale into longs based on the recent average daily range. If they are trading the Emini and the recent average daily range has been about 12 to 15 points and the largest pullback in the past couple of hours has only been two points, they might buy a small position on a one-point pullback and buy more at one and two points lower (10 to 20 percent of the average daily range) and then maybe use a stop on the entire position another couple of points down. If the earlier pullbacks were three points, they might instead place a limit order to buy three points down and buy more two or three points lower and use a two-point stop on the entire position. If at any time the market flipped to always-in short, they would exit the position and look to get short. Scaling in is discussed in book 2.

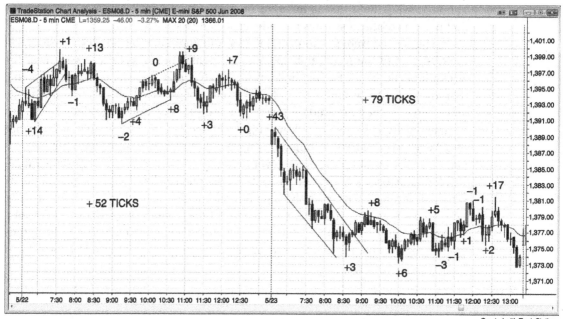

FIGURE 15.1 Always-In Swing Trading

Always-in trading can be a profitable swing trading approach during both trend days and trading range days, if the trading range days have large enough swings. As shown in Figure 15.1, the first day was a trading range day, and the always-in approach could have netted 52 ticks, or about $600 per contract. The second day began as a trend from the open bear and then entered a trading range. An always-in trader could have netted 79 ticks or about $950 per contract. A trader who traded two lots, scalping one and swinging one, could have had 10 successful scalps each day, yielding an additional $450 per contract per day. It sounds and looks easy, but is very difficult to do.

Figure 15.2   ALWAYS IN   **305**

FIGURE 15.2   Higher Time Frame Charts

A 5 minute chart, such as the one on the right in Figure 15.2, has 81 bars and more than 20 reversals on most days. Traders who are uncomfortable making that many decisions about the always-in direction can reduce the number of decisions by reducing the number of bars on the chart. The bar numbering on all three charts is the same. The chart on the upper left is a 15 minute chart and the one on the bottom left has 10,000 ticks per bar. Both of these higher time frame charts had far fewer reversals, yet had several good signals, which were enough for a trader to make a living. Since the bars are bigger, stops have to be larger to give the trade a chance to work. To keep the total dollars at risk the same as with a trade on the 5 minute chart, the position size has to be smaller.

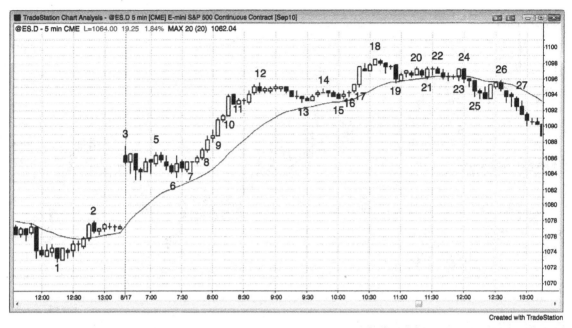

FIGURE 15.3 Gap Up, Then Pullback

As shown in Figure 15.3, the market had a large gap up, but a strong bear rever-sal bar followed, so the day might have become a trend from the open bear day. This is a reliable always-in short setup. However, traders know that large bull trend days can develop whenever there is a large gap up and that the market often trades sideways to down for an hour before there is a bull breakout. Because of this, even though they shorted, they were willing to reverse to long. Bar 4 was a bear trend bar, but it had a large tail and no follow-through over the next couple of bars. Also, the second bar of the day was a strong bull bar instead of a strong bear bar, which traders would have wanted to see for their entry bar. This was not behaving like a strong bear trend. Many would have exited above the inside bar after bar 4 and waited for a second signal, but technically the market was still always-in short be-cause there had not been a clear buy signal. There was a small two-legged move up to bar 5, and the market might have been trying to form a double top with either the first or the second bar of the day. It did not matter which you chose to consider as the first top, because the implication was the same. Some traders thought of the first top as the first bar and others attached more significance to the second bar. The bar after bar 5 was a bear inside bar and a second sell sig-nal, but the market again failed to create a strong bear trend bar over the next couple of bars. Again, the bears would have seen this as a problem. At this point, the market had been in a tiny range for over 30 minutes, and when that happens, especially when there is a large gap opening, the market is in breakout mode.

Figure 15.3   ALWAYS IN   **307**

Traders would have placed buy stops at one tick above the high of the range and would go short on a stop at one tick below the low of the range. This was a reliable breakout mode situation.

Bar 7 was a bull ii pattern after the bar 5 double top and after the bars 4 and 6 double bottom. An ii pattern is a pause, which is a type of pullback, so this was an even smaller breakout mode setup since the market was setting up both a double top pullback and a double bottom pullback entry. Although some traders would have entered on the breakout of the ii pattern, most would have waited for the breakout of the opening range.

The bar before bar 8 was a strong bull trend bar that closed above the bar 5 high, and many traders went long above that swing high. Bar 8 was an even larger bull trend bar and a breakout of the opening range. At this point, traders saw the bull breakout of a breakout mode setup on a strong gap up day and believed that the market was now in a bull trend. Since they didn't know if there would be a pullback anytime soon and they were confident that the market would likely be higher before long, they were buying at the market, which was exactly what the institutions were doing and therefore the correct thing to do. The odds were good that the range would be at least equal to the recent average daily range, and that increase in range would very likely be due to higher prices. Beginners are often frightened by the rapidity of a breakout and the size of the stop required, but they should learn to enter at least a small position at the market and hold until there is a strong sell setup, like the bar 18 final flag reversal. If they bought around the close of bar 8, their theoretical protective stop was below bar 7, the most recent higher low. If this is three times larger than they are comfortable using, they should buy just one third size. Alternatively, they could risk to just below the bar 8 low, since a strong breakout should have immediate follow-through. They would have a higher chance of being stopped out, but if the market hit their stop and turned back up, they could buy again for the swing.

Bars 9 and 10 were also large bull trend bars, but as such they were buy climaxes, and consecutive buy climaxes are usually soon followed by a larger sideways to down correction. The bars became small and the market entered a tight trading range for the next couple of hours, but it never pulled back to the moving average. It tried to on the pullbacks to bars 13 and 15, but the bulls were so aggressive that they had buy limit orders several ticks above the moving average. They were so afraid that the market might not touch the moving average that they placed their buy orders above it. This is a sign of a very strong bull market. However, whenever there is a long sideways correction in a strong bull trend, it will break the bull trend line and it might become a final flag, as it did here. This made the bulls ready to quickly take profits. Bars 11, 13, and 15 were three pushes down in a tight trading range and can be viewed as a triangle or a wedge bull flag.

Consecutive bear trend bars breaking below a trading range will not necessarily convince traders that the always-in direction has flipped to short. The two bear trend bars that broke below the tight trading range that followed bar 12 were small, and there was no prior bear strength. Traders did not short and instead were looking to buy a 20 gap bar pullback to the moving average. The three bear trend bars that broke below the bar 14 lower high did not create an impressive bear spike, and the bulls were still looking to buy the first pullback to the moving average. There was no significant selling pressure leading up to this and no significant bear strength. Traders believed that the always-in direction was still long, and they bought the two-legged sideways correction to bar 15.

Bar 17 was another strong bull breakout and therefore also a spike and a climax, but since it might have been a breakout of a final flag, it could have failed and been followed by a trend reversal. Bulls and bears look for large bull trend bars in a trend that has gone on for 20 or more bars, especially if the move up is out of a potential final flag, as it was here. Traders saw the large trend bar as climactic, and suspected that a correction might soon begin. Because of this, traders began to sell. The bulls sold out of their longs to take profits, and the bears sold to initiate new shorts. They sold on the close of the bar, above its high, on any small bar that followed (especially if it had a bear close), and below the low of the prior bar. Both the bulls and the bears expected at least a two-legged correction that would last at least 10 bars and possibly test the bottom of the bar 15 bottom of the potential final flag. If the move down was very strong, both would have waited to buy. If it was a simple two-legged correction and the market looked poised to rally, both would have bought. The bulls would have reinstated their longs, and the bears would have bought back their profitable shorts. Here, the series of bear bars down from bar 14 were likely to be followed by lower prices, and therefore there was no significant buying into the close.

Bar 18 was the third push up on the day (bars 3 and 12 were the first two pushes) and a possible final flag reversal, both from the large trading range between bar 11 and bar 16, which was a triangle, and from the two small bars that followed the bar 17 buy climax. It was also the third push up, where bars 14 and 17 were the first two pushes. The market often pulls back around 10:30 to 11:00 a.m. PST, with the pullback ending around 11:30 a.m. Also, the market had not touched the moving average all day, although it came close at bar 15. The next pullback was likely to be deeper, since subsequent pullbacks often are, especially after 11:00 a.m. PST or so, and a deeper pullback would have been so close to the moving average that it would almost certainly have to penetrate it, at least by a little. This combination of factors made experienced traders wonder if the strong bull trend was transitioning into a trading range. There was also a chance that the pullback could become a large, deep pullback, or even a bear trend, since the triangle to bar 15 broke the steep trend line from the bull trend between bars 6 and 12, and bar 18 was a possible higher high trend reversal. Many took their final profits below the two-bar reversal at the bar 18 high, and looked for at least a two-legged, 10 bar correction that touched the moving average before considering getting long again into the close of the day.

Figure 15.3   ALWAYS IN   **309**

Bar 19 was a strong bear spike, which alerted traders to a possible bear channel after a pullback. Some traders would have reversed to short on the final flag top, but since the market had not yet touched the moving average all day, there would have been 20 gap bar longs coming in at the moving average. Because of this, the always-in position was probably still long. Bulls assumed that there would likely not be a bear bar for the next bar, so they bought at the close of the bar. Most attempts to flip the always-in position fail, especially in a strong trend.

Bar 23 was a double bottom long entry at the moving average, but became the first bar of a two-bar reversal down. The always-in position flipped to short for most traders once the market traded below the bar 24 low. This was a bull trap and a small final flag top (the breakout from a final flag can be a lower high). The bar after bar 25 was a first moving average gap bar long setup, but the trend was now down. There was a strong bull trend bar, but instead of a failed breakout below the top trading range, it failed to have follow-through and was followed by a breakout pullback short entry at the moving average either on bar 26 as it went outside down or below its low (shorting below a bear bar that is a moving average test below the moving average is a reliable trade).

By bar 27, the market was clearly always-in short, and traders were shorting at the market for the trend into the close. Risk managers were walking the floors and telling their traders that they had to dump their longs. The traders hated that because they were clinging to the hope that the bull trend would resume and bail them out, but their boss would not allow them to wait. They and the risk managers get paid for performance, and the traders can be emotionally attached to their losing longs, but the risk manager's job is to be unemotional and to accept losses when doing so makes sense. The boss always wins, and the result was a bear trend into the close. The trend is enhanced by momentum sell programs that detect the strong trend and sell into it, as long as the momentum down continues.

In the rally from bar 6 to bar 12, the biggest pullback was only about a couple of points. Experienced traders might have placed limit orders to scale in on any one- or two-point pullback and add on at one to two points lower, and might have risked two to three points below their final entry. If the market flipped to always-in short, they would have exited their longs and looked to go short. If they bought one contract on a one-point pullback and added one more one point lower, they would have been long two contracts at bar 13. They could have placed their protective stops two to three points lower or maybe a couple of points below the moving average. Since this was a bull trend, they expected at least a test of the high, and they could have taken a one-point profit on their first contract as the market went to a new high and then either placed a limit order to exit the other contract at about four points (about twice their initial risk on that entry) or exited once the market stalled around bar 18 where the market might have been setting up a final flag reversal from the bar 12 to bar 16 potential final flag.

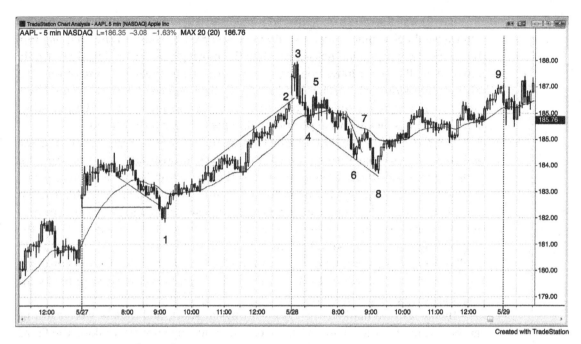

FIGURE 15.4 Look for Early Swing Setups

Traders should look for always-in trades early in the day because they often result in profitable swing trades. Also, sometimes just a single strong trend bar is all that is required to make most traders believe that the market has established an always-in direction. In Figure 15.4, the bar 3 strong bear outside down bar that reversed down from the breakout above the bull channel probably made most traders believe that there would be follow-through and that the always-in position was now short. This large bear bar following the strong bull trend bar was a reasonable candidate for a high of the day and a trend from the open bear setup.

AAPL had a gap test at bar 1, which was a strong reversal bar that reversed up after hitting a new low on the day and after breaking below a bear trend channel line. This was a great entry for a swing long that would have netted almost $4.00 by the close. The gap up was the spike and bar 1 was the pullback that led to the channel that topped out at bar 3. Some traders assumed that the always-in position had flipped to long above bar 1, and others came to that conclusion during either of the two bull trend bars that followed. The five-bar bull spike erased the five-bar bear spike that led to the bar 1 low. This was a climactic reversal, and the odds favored at least a second leg up.

The four-bar bull spike to bar 7 was strong, but the four-bar bear spike down to bar 6 had been stronger. Most traders still believed that the always-in position

Figure 15.4 ALWAYS IN **311**

was still short and they wanted to see a higher low or lower low pullback before looking for longs.

Bar 8 was a reversal up in a wedge bull flag and a higher high above bar 1. If you simply exited your short instead of reversing to long, the trade would have netted about $2.40. Many traders believed that the always-in position reversed to up when the market went above bar 8, and more became convinced in the bull trend bar that followed. The prior bull strength on the move up to bar 7 was a sign of buying pressure, and it gave the bulls confidence that the buying might even be stronger on this second attempt to reverse the market up.

When the market needs one more bar to flip the always-in direction, traders often fade the move, expecting that bar to not materialize. For example, if bar 5 was a strong bull trend bar, many traders would have changed their always-in short position to long (most saw the market always-in short after the five bars down from bar 3). Because they know that most attempts to flip the direction fail, they would have shorted the close of the bull trend bar before bar 5, expecting bar 5 to not be a strong bull bar and for the bear swing to resume.

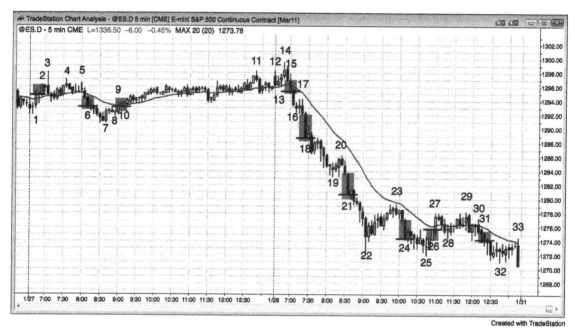

FIGURE 15.5 Follow-Through Is Often Likely

Whenever traders are confident of the direction over the next several bars, there is an opportunity for a trade. Each gray rectangle in Figure 15.5 is an area where traders believed that there would have been follow-through. The small horizontal line within each box was at the price where most traders shared that belief, although many traders were confident earlier. When a trend is strong, as it was in the sell-off from bar 14, there usually are several consecutive breakouts where traders develop renewed confidence.

Although some traders are strict always-in traders and stay in the market, long or short, for the entire day, most take profits along the way and exit whenever they believe that the market has lost its direction. Traders will generally exit a trade on a signal in the opposite direction, even if that signal is not strong enough for them to reverse direction. Remember, it takes less to convince traders that it is time to exit a long than it does for them to take a short. The bulls who bought at the close of bar 1 or one tick above its high were concerned by the large bar 3 bear reversal bar, especially since opening reversals can have protracted follow-through. Bar 3 alone was not likely to be enough for most traders to see the market as always-in short, but many would have exited their longs or reversed to short below the bar 4 small wedge bear flag lower high. Others would have exited their longs or reversed to short below the bar 5 second-entry breakout pullback from that bear flag.

Figure 15.5

ALWAYS IN **313**

Most traders would have seen the market as always-in short by the close of the bear bar that broke below bar 5, one tick below its low, or the close of bar 6.

The strong reversal up from a new low of the day at bar 7 was a concern for the bears because it was another opening reversal and a possible low of the day. There was a two-bar spike down from bar 3, and bar 7 was the third push down in a possible spike and wedge channel, where the bar after bar 3 was the first push down and bar 6 was the second. Some bears would have exited above bar 7, and most would have gotten out above the bar 8 higher low. Bar 7 was a breakout above the micro channel from bar 5, and bar 8 was the breakout pullback buy signal. Many traders saw the market as flipping to always-in long above bar 8, and most were convinced when the market reversed above the bull ii pattern at bar 10, which was also a failed low 2 short. They believed that the bear flag failed and that the market would go up for at least a measured move based on the height of the bar 7 to bar 9 bear flag.

In the free fall from bar 14, there were several other areas where traders developed renewed confidence that the market was going to fall more over the following bars, like on the close of bar 18, one tick below the inside bar that followed it, and one tick below the bar 18 low. Even though the inside bar after bar 18 had a bull body, traders still felt that the trend was down and that the bar was likely a low 1 short setup. This was also the case at bars 21 and 24. The trader's equation is excellent for shorting, even if the probability only feels like it is 50 percent. It is actually at least 60 percent, but traders often are frightened and are in denial, and conclude that the probability of an equidistant move is only 50 percent. This gives them a plausible, but incorrect, reason to not take the trade. They should short an "I don't care" size position at the market and use whatever size protective stop is appropriate, like above the high of the most recent big bear trend bar, and then hold through pullbacks until there is a clear buy setup, like the bar 25 lower low major trend reversal. If the risk is four times bigger than normal, trade no more than one quarter normal size. If they are still afraid, trade just 10 percent normal size. It is important to get short when the institutions are shorting so aggressively, because run-away trends have the strongest trader's equations.

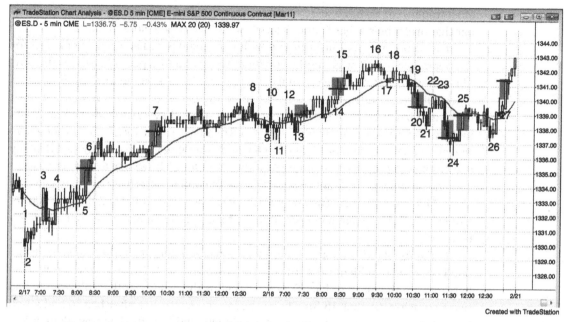

FIGURE 15.6 Always-In Setups

As shown in Figure 15.6, there were several areas where traders were confident of the direction over at least the next several bars, and each was a reasonable entry for an always-in trade. Aggressive traders would have entered earlier and taken more reversal trades, but the highlighted areas were where the majority of traders were confident of the always-in direction.

The traders who bought on the close of bar 14 or above the doji high 1 that followed it would have been concerned about the second-entry short at the bar 16 higher high. This was also a potential top of the channel that followed the bar 14 spike, and the entire move from bar 11 to bar 16 might have been a higher high after the potential bar 7 to bar 12 final flag. Most bulls would have exited below bar 16, and aggressive traders would have shorted, thinking that this was a reasonable always-in flip. More conservative traders who look for only three to five reversals a day would have waited for the strong bear close on bar 19 or bar 20 before seeing the market as always-in short.

When traders are confident, they should assume that they are at least 60 percent certain. If their risk is about two points, then they need a profit target that is at least two points to have a favorable trader's equation. This means that they could have looked for entries around each of these areas and, after entering, placed a bracket order for their exit. Their stop could be two points away from their entry price, and their profit-taking limit order could also be two points away. If the

Figure 15.6

ALWAYS IN   **315**

market approaches their profit target but then reverses, as it did on the rally after the bar 7 close, they could tighten their stop. In this case, they would have exited below the two-bar reversal at around breakeven. Some traders won't adjust their stop and will hold until their premise is clearly no longer valid, allowing pullbacks along the way. Other traders will try for three- or four-point profit targets when they think that the signal is strong enough, like buying the close of either bar 5 or bar 6, buying above the bar 13 breakout pullback (from the bars 9 and 11 high 2 bull flag), shorting below the bar 16 small wedge top, shorting the close of bar 20, shorting below the bars 22 and 23 small low 2 breakout pullback, or buying above the bar 26 breakout pullback. Some traders would see those as the strongest setups, and therefore maybe 70 percent certain of reaching a two-point profit target before hitting a two-point scalp. They would then just go for the two points, knowing that the math was very strong.

Since most traders saw the market as always-in long by bar 6, they expected that attempts to reverse it to short would fail. They then looked to buy the closes of strong bear trend bars, like the one that formed four bars after bar 6 and the one that tested the moving average two bars before bar 7.

CHAPTER 16

Extreme Scalping

T here are high-frequency trading firms that make tens of millions of trades a day on a basket of 4,000 stocks, and they scalp for just a penny profit on each trade. That form of scalping is as extreme as it gets, but it is something that average traders without supercomputers located right next to the exchanges cannot hope to do. I have a friend who is an extreme scalper in the Emini, placing about 25 trades a day and scalping for two ticks per trade. I could never get him to tell me whether he used a protective stop or how big a loss he would allow. He also would never clearly answer my questioning about scaling in. Some traders are resistant to telling too much about what they do. I am not sure if it is because of the unrealistic fear that the world would copy them and their system would no longer work, or if they would be embarrassed to have people realize that they take lots of trades but still net only a couple of points a day. However, he did say that he trades about a hundred contracts per trade. A mutual friend told me that he had been to his $2 million house, and I believe that he is making over a million dollars a year.

Although I think this is possible for the very few people who have a personality that would allow them to do it, it would be virtually impossible for most traders, so most people should never attempt it. In general, since scalping usually requires the risk to be greater than the reward, the winning percentage has to be at least 70 percent to be consistently profitable. That is not realistic for most traders, even for very successful traders. However, there are some people who can make a living scalping. Most traders, however, should only take trades where the reward is at least as large as the risk, because the required winning percentage of at least 60 percent is much more realistically achievable. Even better, traders should focus on trades where the reward is at least twice the risk because then they will make money even if they win only about half the time.

Even though traders should focus on swings, they might be surprised to learn that there are far more scalp setups on a 5 minute chart than they would ever imagine. However, just because the setups exist is not an adequate reason to take the trades. In fact, virtually no one should attempt to take the 30 to 40 scalps that are present on a 5 minute chart of an average day because it is so difficult to read the chart accurately enough to quickly be able to trade profitably this way. About a third of the setups are for stop entries and about two-thirds are for limit order entries. This is true of all markets and all time frames; about half of the bars have reasonable scalp setups. Showing an example of extreme scalping is a good way to demonstrate just how much subtle price action information is in front of you all day long, and it might help you increase your focus. Some traders might be able to do this for an hour or two at a time, but most should look for two- to four-point swings instead.

There are many times when scalpers can make money by either buying or selling at the current price, as long as they manage their trades properly. This is true of all trading, and beginners might find it surprising. For example, if there is a big bull trend bar in an established bull trend in the Emini and it is likely to have follow-through, traders could buy around the close of the bar and risk about three points to allow for a possible pullback. If the market goes right to his target, they could exit with a profit. If instead it pulls back for five to 10 bars but does not hit their stops, they could wait through the pullback for the trend to resume, and then take profits at their original target. Many experienced traders would scale in during the pullback and on the breakout of the bull flag. Some would hold their entire position until the market reaches their original target, where they would take profits. Others might choose to exit at the original entry and get out at breakeven on the first entry and with a profit on the later entries.

Bears could have shorted at exactly the same price that the bulls bought, expecting the large bar to represent exhaustion. If the market sold off over the next few bars, the bears would exit with a profit. If instead the market went up for another bar or two, they might scale in and sell more, maybe risking as many ticks as there were in that large bull trend bar. For example, if the bar was 12 ticks tall, they might add to their short at four or eight ticks higher, and risk 12 ticks from their original entry for the entire position. If the market turned down after they scaled in, they could exit the entire position at the original target or at the original entry. If they exited at the original entry, they would make a profit on their late entries and would get out at breakeven on their first entry. Both the bull and the bear scalpers could therefore make a scalper's profit by entering at exactly the same time, but in opposite directions. The key is money management.

Figure 16.1   EXTREME SCALPING   **319**

FIGURE 16.1   Extreme Scalping

The 5 minute Emini chart shown in Figure 16.1 illustrates extreme scalping. There are 81 bars in a day, and every third one is numbered in the chart. If a trader wanted to scalp 1 point using a two-point stop, there were at least 40 opportunities to do so today. Remember, a trader entering on a stop usually needs a six-tick move beyond the signal bar to be able to scalp four ticks with a profit-taking limit order.

Bar 1 was a bull reversal bar and a possible failed breakout below a bear flag from yesterday's close. However, it had a two-tick tail at the top and its high was only four ticks below yesterday's close and the moving average, so there might not have been enough room for a buy scalp. Traders who bought above bar 1 saw the weak close on the entry bar, and many would have exited around breakeven.

Bar 2 was a doji, and it could not close above bar 1. This was a sign of weakness for the bulls and a sign of strength for the bears. This one-bar rally could have developed into a breakout pullback, and it could have been followed by another leg down. A trader could have placed an order to go short at one tick below bar 2.

Bar 3 did not fill the short order, but it had a bear close and the bar failed to go above bar 2. It therefore formed a double top with bar 2, just below the moving average, and could have led to a leg down. A trader could have shorted the close of the bar and exited above its high or reversed to long there, or shorted on a sell stop at one tick below its low. This would also have been shorting at one tick below the bar 2 long entry bar. Many of those longs would likely have been exiting at this exact location (below the entry bar), adding to the down move. If triggered, this would have created a breakout pullback and likely led to a swing down. Traders could have considered scalping one or two points, swinging the entire position (they would have netted six ticks), or scalping part (maybe half) and swinging part, hoping for three or four points on their swing portion.

The bar 4 entry bar was a strong bear trend bar and likely to form a new low of the day at a minimum. The market tried to break out above bar 1 but failed and was now trying to break out below its low. Since the market was below the moving average and it gapped down out of a bear flag from yesterday, the bears were strong and could create a good swing down for a measured move. Bar 2 could have ended up as the high of the day, and the day could have become a strong bear trend day. With this bear strength, traders could have shorted more on the bear close below the bar 2 long entry bar, or on a stop below the low of bar 4, or on the breakout below bar 1 to a new low of the day.

Bar 5 expanded into a large bear trend bar on the breakout below bar 1. This could have been either a sign of increased strength by the bears or of climactic selling. Since the bar poked below a bear trend channel line, if the market had reversed up from there it could have had at least two legs up. Also, since that would have been the second attempt to reverse up from below yesterday's low and it also would have been a wedge reversal, it could have formed the low of the day. Traders could have shorted the close of the bar, but if they did, they had to be prepared to exit around breakeven if the market paused down here, and they had to be prepared to reverse to long. There was a gap down on the open and then a pullback to the moving average and now a sell climax. This could have been a spike and climax bottom, and since the high or low of the day forms in the first 90 minutes or so in about 90 percent of days, traders had to look at every possible early reversal as a possible extreme of the day.

The low of bar 6 was only five ticks below the close of bar 5, so those bears who shorted below bar 5 came up one tick short of being able to scalp out one point. At this juncture, they were nervous. They might have exited above this bar, and some might even have reversed to long. Since the bar was a bear trend bar, the bears were still in control, and most traders would have held short. The bar 6 low was also an exact measured move down from the high and low of bar 1, and a perfect breakout test of a strong move up from two days ago (not shown).

Bar 7 was a bull two-bar reversal. This was a problem for the bears. Most would have tried to exit at breakeven, but would have been willing to take a one- or two-tick loss. Some traders would have bought the bull close for a possible low of the day and a likely two-legs-up rally. Other traders would have entered long on lower time frame charts and on reversals on other types of charts, like volume or tick charts. Since about half of the range of bar 6 was overlapped by both the bar before

Figure 16.1   EXTREME SCALPING   **321**

and the bar after, a small trading range was forming. Countertrend trades usually have pullbacks, so if traders bought above bar 7, they needed to hold their longs during the expected pullback and hope that it formed a higher low.

Bar 8 closed on its high, so the bulls bought into the close of the bar, indicating that they were eager to get long. However, the selling down to bar 6 was strong, so the first attempt to reverse up was likely to fail and probably to be followed by an attempt to drive the market down. An alternative was to buy this strong close. If traders believed that a second leg up was likely and they were expecting pullbacks along the way, they could have looked to buy at or one or two ticks below the low of any of the next few bars, expecting a failed low 1 and a higher low.

Bar 9 was a bear reversal bar, and it was unable to close above the high of bar 8, which was a strong bull bar. There was no follow-through buying. Maybe the bulls were weak and the bar 8 reversal up would fail and become a breakout pullback on the breakout below bar 1 and therefore a low 1 short. Since the market was correcting from a wedge bottom, a second leg up was likely, so rather than shorting at one tick below bar 9, those already long would have held with stops below the bar 5 signal bar. Because it was only one tick above the low of the day, they would probably have put their stops one tick lower at just below the low of the day. Some bulls who hadn't yet bought would have waited to buy a higher low, if one formed. Aggressive bulls would have bought on limit orders at the low of bar 9, thinking that the market would probably have to dip one tick below its low for those long limit orders to get filled, and if the market reversed up from there, the bears would be trapped short on a one-tick failure and they would be very eager to get out and help drive the market up. Other bulls would have placed limit orders to go long at one, two, or three ticks below the low of bar 9. All of these orders would have given support to the market. If the market dipped one tick below bar 9 and then bounced up two or three ticks within the next few seconds, some bulls who had limit orders to buy at one or two ticks lower would have moved their long limit orders up by a tick or two because they would have become more eager to get in when they saw the market failing to sell off. Bar 9 was a bad low 1 short setup, and therefore a higher low was likely. The market had a strong bear spike, which is needed for a low 1, but it was not clearly in a bear trend, which is also needed before shorting a low 1. Also, a trader should not short a low 1 after a sell climax, and this was possibly one.

The bears saw bar 10 as a double top in a bear trend and hoped that it would have resulted in a move similar to the move that followed the bars 2 and 3 double top. However, they were concerned about that wedge bottom and would have exited any new shorts quickly if the market did not fall sharply, as it did earlier in the day.

Bar 11 fell two ticks below bar 9 and then rallied up sharply. The bulls who tried to buy at the low of bar 9 and at one tick below it were happy to be long, and those who wanted to buy at two or three ticks below bar 9 were afraid that they had missed their chance. They were changing their limit orders to market orders, which caused bar 11 to move up quickly. Also, those bears who shorted below bar 9 were afraid that the low 1 would fail and that the wedge would have a second leg up, so they were now covering at the market or above the highs of 1, 2, or 3 minute bars, or above bars on volume or tick charts. Bar 11 closed above the closes of the past six bars (a sign of strength), and it was essentially an outside up bar at the start of a possible new bull trend. Some bulls would have bought this strong close, given that it followed strength in bars 7 and 8 and the trend might have reversed up. It failed to have a high above the high of the prior bar, but with a low below the prior bar and a high at the high of that bar, it was close enough for the market to react to it as if it was an outside bar. At this point, it was a triple top with the two prior bars, and if the market failed to reverse down and instead went one tick higher, the pattern would have become a failed top and would likely be followed by more buying. Bar 11 also broke below the trend line from bars 6 and 7 and below the trend channel line from bars 9 and 10, and this created a small dueling lines long setup. Bars 9, 10, and 11 formed a small expanding triangle that should have acted as a bull flag instead of a reversal pattern because a second leg up was likely.

Bar 12 broke out above the triple top and above the high of the bar 11 outside up bar. Even though it was a small bar, it reached two ticks above the triple top. If it reversed down after just a one-tick breakout, traders would have viewed that as a possible bull trap and they would have looked to exit longs. Bears would also have shorted it as a two-legged bear rally. Some bears would have placed orders to go short at one tick below this bar, in case it became a low 2 short. However, with its high so close to the moving average, they would have felt more confident about their shorts if the market first touched the moving average. Many would not have looked to short until after the moving average was touched, because until it was touched, they would have worried that the market might just go sideways until it was tested. When the market gets within a tick or so of a magnet, traders do not feel confident about the test unless the market gets that extra tick and actually touches the magnet. Until that happens, they usually will not aggressively trade it as a completed pullback. Some bulls would have added to longs above this bar, thinking that it was a failed chance for the bears to take control, which made the market more likely to go up. The high of bar 12 was two ticks below the low of bar 3 and missed the breakeven stops on those shorts by one tick. If the market sold off here, this would have created a perfect breakout test (perfect because it tested those stops as closely as it could without actually hitting them). If instead the market went one tick higher, this breakout test would have failed; those remaining shorts would have covered, and their buying would have propelled the market upward. Longs knew this and would have placed buy stops to add to their longs at exactly that price to profit from that short covering.

Figure 16.1   EXTREME SCALPING   **323**

Bar 13 was a strong bull breakout bar, with the market breaking and closing well above the moving average, the bear trend line, and the high of the strong bar 5 bear trend bar. The bear flag failed and broke to the upside, and traders would have looked for about a measured move up. If it was a successful bear flag, they would have expected a test of the low of the day. Once it failed, they would have looked for it to go up for about the same number of points. Bulls would have bought this close for a test of the high of the day. The day's range had been only five points, which was about half of the recent average daily range, so the market could have formed a measured move up or down. At this point, since the bears had just covered, they would have been unlikely to go short until at least two more attempts up and that would have left the bulls in control for the next few bars. If there was to be a measured move, up was more likely than down at this point.

Bar 14 was a bear reversal bar that could have formed a lower high, a failed breakout, and a low 2 short. However, for the reasons just stated, it was more likely that the market would have at least two attempts up after the bar 13 breakout, so if this short triggered, it would be more likely to fail, and the failure would create a breakout pullback long. The bulls would therefore have been trying to buy any move below its low. If there was going to be just a one-tick move below its low, forming a one-tick bear trap, aggressive bulls would have wanted to buy that move. To do so, they would have put their limit orders to go long at the low of bar 14. This is because there probably would not be enough bears shorting below bar 14 to fill all of those long limit orders placed by aggressive bulls. Since the bulls were in control, there would probably have been more traders looking to buy than looking to sell. Alternatively, the bulls could have placed a market if touched buy order below the bar or simply bought at the market as soon as the market dipped below bar 14. Other bulls would have placed limit orders to go long at two and three ticks below.

Others would have wanted to buy two- and three-point pullbacks and would have placed limit orders to go long at seven ticks and 11 ticks below the bar 14 high. If the market pulled back exactly two points, most traders trying to buy the end of that pullback would have only been able to get long at seven ticks down and not at the exact low, because there would likely have been far more contracts being bid than being offered at the low tick, and those bulls would instead have had to buy one tick higher.

Finally, some bulls would have seen every bear setup as a bull setup and would have assumed that there would have been trapped eager bears who shorted into the bear close. Those bears would have had to buy back their shorts at some point, and many would have had their buy stops at one tick above this bear reversal bar. Smart bulls knew this and were always trying to go long exactly at the price where trapped bears would have been buying back their shorts. These longs would therefore have placed buy stops at one tick above bar 14.

Bar 15 took out the high of the bar 14 bear reversal bar, but pulled back on the close. It was possible that the bars 14 and 15 double bottom could fail to be a bull flag and lead to a sell-off, just like what happened with the bars 2 and 3 double bottom. Also, the high of the bar formed a double top with the high of the open, so the day could have turned into a double top bear flag and could have a measured move below the low of the day. The highs of bars 13, 14, and 15 created a micro wedge. If it triggered, by the market moving below the bar 15 low, there could have been a two-legged sideways to down correction. If the market instead broke to the upside, the move up would have been a breakout to a new high of the day and above a micro wedge, and there would have been more bears covering their shorts and new bulls scalping the breakout.

Bar 16 was a big range breakout bar that broke a trend channel line. It could have been a buy climax and it could have been followed by at least a two-legged sideways to down correction that could have lasted an hour or more. Whenever there is a large bull trend bar after a bull trend has gone on for a while, the odds favor it representing exhaustion, with the last weak bulls buying, the last weak shorts covering, and the strong bulls and bears waiting for the close of a large bull trend bar like this to sell (the bulls selling their longs to take profits, and the bears initiating new shorts). The remaining shorts would have exited only on a pullback, and the strong bulls would have bought again only after a pullback. This would be similar to the sell climax that bar 5 represented. The high of bar 16 was just five ticks below yesterday's high, which is always a resistance area, and therefore traders looking to buy above the high of this bar for a scalp would have been concerned that the market would have to go above that resistance for them to make their one-point profit. Some bulls would have bought the close of this bar because they could have exited with a one-point profit on an exact test of yesterday's high. An exact test was more likely than a breakout above the high, but a lower high was even more likely, especially after a trend channel line overshoot. Some new bulls would have been quick to exit their longs on any hesitation or pullback because they wouldn't want to lose even one tick when they bought a possible buy climax in an area of resistance. Others would have used a wider stop and added on as the market went against them. These traders would have ultimately been successful. Aggressive bears would have shorted the close of bar 16, or at or above its high, and would have scaled in higher, risking about as many ticks as there were in bar 16. Since it was two points tall, they might have risked two points to make one point, and they would have tried to sell more at one point above the close or high of bar 16. They were unable to scale in higher, but were able to scalp out with a one-point profit on the bar 26 strong bear trend bar. Their profit taking contributed to the reversal up after bar 26. Remember, all traders look at every tick as both a buy and a sell setup, and constantly assess the trader's equation for both possible trades. There are many times every day where both bulls and bears can enter for

Figure 16.1   EXTREME SCALPING   **325**

a scalp and both make money, if they manage their trades correctly. The close of bar 16 is an example.

Bar 17 reversed down after moving three ticks above bar 16. Those late bulls were quick to exit, and aggressive bears were beginning to short. Bar 17 became a strong bear reversal bar, and bears would have looked to short at its close and at one tick below its low. Other bears would have already shorted on smaller time frame charts. This was one bear setup that the bulls wouldn't buy. Once the market fell below the bar 17 low, the bulls saw that as a failed breakout above the bull trend channel line, and they and the bears expected a two-legged correction that would last an hour or more. Bulls would not have looked to buy aggressively until the correction was complete. Since traders were looking for a two-legged correction, bears would have started placing limit orders to short a lower high. The move up to bar 17 was a strong bull spike, so bulls were hoping for a bull channel and a measured move up that would have about as many points as the spike from the low of bar 6 or bar 11 to the bar 17 high.

Bar 18 did not trigger a short and became a bull inside bar. Since traders were expecting a two-legged correction, smart bulls wouldn't have been looking to buy above its high, and aggressive bears would have had limit orders to go short at its high and one and two ticks higher with a stop above the bar 17 bear reversal bar high.

Bar 19 did not fill those short limit orders at the bar 18 high, and it also did not trigger the sell stops below the bars 17 and 18 low. Instead, there was now an ii pattern. Bulls, however, still wouldn't buy, and bears were getting eager to short.

Bar 20 was now an iii setup and it had a bear close, which favored the bears. Smart money was still looking to short below bar 17 (which was below the iii), and on a lower high.

Bar 21 might have been the bull trap that everyone was expecting. It was the second leg up (bar 18 was the first) and it extended one tick above bar 18, where other mistaken bulls also likely went long. There were not any trapped bears, because the most conservative bears would have entered on a stop below bar 17 and that had not yet happened. The only bears in the market now were the smart, aggressive ones who were hoping for a lower high bull trap. They wanted trapped bulls in the market because if the market went down, these bulls would have to sell out of their longs, and this would add to the selling. Also, after there were trapped bulls, bulls would have wanted to wait for more price action before looking to buy again. Smart bulls were already waiting for a two-legged correction, so there was no serious buying here. Weak bulls mistakenly bought the iii pattern. Smart bears were shorting at 1, 2, and 3 ticks above the iii pattern with a protective stop above the high of bar 17. Bears would have looked to short below this bar and especially below bar 17, which was a strong bear reversal bar. Most bears would have waited to short below bar 17 because they would see that as a confirmation of the top.

However, smart bears were only looking for a scalp since the move up had been strong, and the day's range was still smaller than average. At this point, if the range was to expand, up was much more likely than down. Also, everyone believed that the buy climax was most likely a pause that would be followed by at least one more leg up. This sideways to down correction had the potential to create a final flag and then a swing down, but that would happen only after an upside breakout.

Bar 22 turned bar 21 into a lower high final flag short (the iii descending triangle was the final flag), but the bar was not able to extend below the iii pattern and bring in additional shorts who were looking to enter on a stop below the flag and below bar 17. Also, the bar closed in its middle, which means that traders bought into the close of the bar, which was the opposite of what should have happened if the bears were in control.

The sideways correction was continuing at bar 25 and the market was forming a tight trading range, which is a breakout setup. The bears would have preferred that the market fell below bar 17 within a bar or two of its formation, which would have indicated that there was an urgency to sell. The market was correcting sideways instead of down, and this is a sign of bull strength. Also, the market was now only two ticks above the moving average, and since the market might have found support there and because the correction was 10 bars long, bulls would have begun to look to reestablish their longs. This was a problem for the bears. They were originally expecting a high percentage bear scalp and now the chance of success had become less. They would have been quick to cover if a bear breakout stalled. Bar 25 touched the bar 17 and 21 bear trend line and created a descending triangle, which is a bull flag when it occurs in a bull trend. However, bars 21 through 25 were also in a small channel if you use the bodies of the bars. A channel often has three pushes and then tries to reverse, just like a wedge. Bars 22 and 24 were two pushes down, so there might have been only one more push down and therefore a downside breakout of the triangle might fail.

Bar 26 was a bear breakout that closed on its low and below the moving average. The new bears were hoping that the market would fill their profit-taking limit orders just a couple of ticks lower. However, the bear trend bar closed only one tick below the moving average, and a strong breakout would have closed several ticks below, just as the bar 13 bull breakout closed several ticks above the moving average. It was also an exact test of the breakout above the high of the open. Even the aggressive bears who shorted the close of the bar 21 bull trend bar had not yet been able to scalp out one point; and if the market reversed up here, they would have had a five-tick failure and would have bought back their shorts. The bears who shorted the close of bar 16 or above its high bought back their shorts here. The bulls saw bar 26 as an attempt by the bears to flip the market to always-in short, but they knew that most reversal attempts fail. They believed that the bears needed the next bar to be a strong bear trend bar to convince traders that the market had

Figure 16.1   EXTREME SCALPING   **327**

reversed its always-in position. Since the bull trend was so strong, they doubted that the bears would succeed, and were not even confident that the bears would be able to push the market below the low of the bar 26 bear trend bar. Because of this, they bought on the close of the bear trend bar, and they would have bought more below its low. Other bulls would have had limit orders to buy seven ticks below the bar 17 high because they were trying to buy two- and three-point pullbacks in a bull trend.

Bar 27 was a bull inside bar and could have been setting up a high 2 long at the moving average. It would have been a two-legged correction that lasted about 10 bars, which was about long enough for the bulls. The bulls wanted a channel up after the spike up to the bar 17 high, and this pullback to the moving average could have been the beginning. It would also have been a breakout test of the bar 2 high. It could also have been seen as a breakout pullback and bears would have shorted below its low, which would also have been the low of the bar 26 bear breakout bar. The bears wanted a bear body to increase the chances of the always-in direction flipping to short. Once traders saw the bull close, they assumed that the bears failed and that the always-in direction remained up, and they bought the close and above the bar.

Bar 28 was a second bull inside bar and formed an ii pattern. At this point, traders were wondering if the trading range was continuing, if the breakout was pausing before more selling came in, or if the breakout had failed and the bulls would take control again.

Bar 29 was a bull breakout of the ii pattern and a successful test of the moving average and of the breakout of the opening range. However, it was only a one-tick breakout and a small bear trend bar, and it could easily have set up a short as a pullback from the bar 26 bear breakout. Bears would have placed orders to short below its low. However, all of the bears who had been shorting for the past hour were now concerned that the market had an opportunity to give them a scalper's profit and it failed. They would not have held on to their shorts much longer. They would have had buy stops above the bar 26 bear trend bar high; the bars 23, 24, 25 triple top; the bar 21 lower high; the bar 17 bull climax high; and yesterday's high. Since all of these stops were within a tick or two of each other, the stops could have been quickly hit in a cascade of stop running, resulting in the bears giving up and the bulls taking control of the market.

Bar 30 took out the high of bar 29 and broke above the bear trend line by a tick, but failed to break above the bar 26 short entry bar. This was two legs up, and the bears would have allowed that as an acceptable pullback from the bear breakout, but they would have been concerned that their shorts were not behaving well. They would have been quick to buy back their shorts. The bulls knew that the correction had two legs and had now lasted about 10 bars, so their minimum criteria had been met and they were getting ready to buy aggressively, hoping for a measured move up to the 1,127.50 area. This was far enough up for them to be swinging some or all of their new positions. They would have seen each of those bear stops as buy setups and would have been buying at the exact same prices at which the bears were covering their shorts. With both bulls and bears buying at the same prices as the market went up, the market should have accelerated upward. Some bulls also viewed this trading range as a wedge bull flag with bar 17 as the first push down, bar 20 as the second, and bar 26 as the third. They also saw the third push down as being composed of a smaller wedge, with bars 22, 24, and 26 forming the three pushes down.

Bars 32 and 33 were small dojis and were a sign that traders were deciding to run those buy stops. At this point, bears were beginning to cover at the market because they knew that their shorts were only countertrend scalps. They were likely happy to get out at breakeven or even with a one- or two-tick loss. The market was holding above the moving average, and after a big spike up, that was bullish.

Bar 34 was a bull trend bar, but it closed a couple of ticks off its high. The market found sellers at the bar 17 high and in the area of the high of yesterday.

Bar 35 gave the bulls a scalper's profit, but formed a bear reversal bar with a one-tick new high of the day. Some traders would have shorted the close of the bar, and others would have shorted at one tick below its low. Aggressive bulls would not have been bothered by the pullback, hoping that it would become a breakout pullback and lead to a move above yesterday's high. They would have stayed long as long as the market held above the moving average, above the bar 26 higher low, or above the bar 34 bull trend bar low.

The bears who shorted on bar 36 were worried that the bar closed at their entry price and that they could not push the market below the bar 34 bull entry bar. They would have covered their shorts at the close of the bar and above its high. Some bulls would have gone long above its high, but most would not have because it would have been buying near the high of the day when the day had been in a trading range for a couple of hours. Buying the high of the day is a good strategy only in strong bull trends, and that was not the current price action.

Bar 37 was a bull trend bar, but it is bad to buy above three large bars that mostly overlap. The three bars create a trading range, and it is risky to buy at the top of a trading range since most breakouts fail. If anything, it was better to short up there.

Bar 38 reversed down at five ticks above the bar 36 long signal bar and one tick above the high of yesterday. Many bulls who were long from earlier in the day likely had limit orders to take profits at yesterday's high, and aggressive bears would have shorted there as well. The bar 37 longs would likely have moved their stops to around breakeven after the five-tick move up, and the market fell through those stops. Bar 38 became a large bear reversal bar, but since it overlapped the prior four bars by so much, it was forming more of a trading range than a reversal. This was the second attempt to reverse the high of the open, so some traders would

Figure 16.1

EXTREME SCALPING **329**

have placed stops to go short at one tick below this bear reversal bar. Others would have looked to short a lower high. The move up to the bar 38 high can be seen as a two-legged higher high after a bull trend line break, and therefore it was a possible trend reversal. Because of this, bulls might have waited for a two-legged correction before buying again.

Bar 39 was a doji inside bar. Bears would still have tried to short below the bar 38 low, and now other bears would have placed limit orders to short a lower high. They would have had limit orders to go short at the bar 39 high and at one or two ticks higher. Overly eager bulls would have seen this as a high 2 buy setup (bar 37 being the high 1) and would have gone long exactly where aggressive bears were shorting. The market was now in the middle third of the day and was more likely to have trading ranges, so bulls had to be patient, and they had to avoid buying at the high unless the market became very strong again.

Bar 41 again lacked strength, and those early bulls who bought bar 40 would have been quick to take a two-tick loss if the market fell below the low of this bar. Bears would have shorted there for a possible lower high, but they would not have been enthusiastic, because the market was starting to form overlapping small bars with tails (which is barbwire behavior), and breakout entries would have been more likely to fail. It is usually better to buy breakouts near the bottom of barbwire and short breakouts near the top.

Bar 42 would have made some of those high 2 longs cover, and the rest would have covered below bar 38 and the signal bar low.

Bar 43 would have made traders wonder if the market was setting up a wedge bull flag. A small, sideways head and shoulders top often becomes a triangle or a wedge bull flag, and bars 35 and 40 were shoulders. Since traders were looking for a wedge bull flag, they were trying to find three pushes down and a high 3 long setup. Bars 36 and 38 were the first two. Bar 42 could have been the start of the third push down, and if there was a reversal up from there, the wedge bull flag (and the failed head and shoulders top) would have triggered.

Bar 44 broke out below the bar 36 low by one tick and tested the breakout above bar 27 and the moving average. It could be a signal bar although it had a bear body (signal bars often look bad in trading ranges). Traders really need a good signal bar only when looking to trade countertrend in a strong trend, and signal bars often look weak most of the rest of the time. Aggressive bulls had limit orders in to buy at the low of bar 36, expecting that any break below it would fail within a few ticks. Other bulls would have bought the high 3 above this bar because it would have been a wedge bull flag. This would also have been a five-tick bear trap if the market went above the high of bar 44, forcing trapped bears to buy back their shorts.

Bar 45 triggered the buying, even though it went only one tick above the bar 44 high. The market often lacks momentum in the middle third of the day even though the actual shape of the price action is usually reliable. Other traders would have bought above bar 45 because they saw it as a two-bar reversal. Also, many traders prefer to buy above bull bars because the bull close means that the market has already moved at least a little in their direction.

Bar 49 gave the bulls a one-point scalp, but many bulls kept buying every signal, scalping part and swinging the rest. The strong parabolic surge up to the bar 17 high could have been a spike, and the two-sided trading since then was finding support at the moving average and could have been forming a channel. The swing longs kept buying and were trailing their protective stops below the most recent swing low, which was bar 44.

There were many more similar trades over the remainder of the day, but this illustrates the point that if traders have the ability to focus intensely and read clearly, they can take dozens of scalps all day long. However, extreme scalping would be a losing strategy for most traders, and they should not attempt it, and they should never be using a risk that is greater than their reward. Instead, they should restrict themselves to any of the many other approaches that are far more likely to be successful and easier to execute. This chapter is here simply to illustrate that there is much more happening on every chart than what might appear to be the case, and how traders need to be thinking constantly throughout the day. There were many setups today where a trader could go for a reward that was at least as large as his risk, but he should be thinking about every setup that he sees. This chart illustrates just how many decisions that a trader can make during the day. Most experienced traders would take only a fraction of these trades.

The First Hour (The Opening Range)

I once had many online discussions with a trader who traded 100 Treasury bond futures contracts at a time, but he disappeared every day by 7:30 to 8:00 a.m. PST. He said that he studied his results and discovered that he made 85 percent of his profits in the first hour and decided that he just drained himself emotionally during the rest of the day, and sometimes this carried over into the next day. Because of this, he stopped trading after the first hour or so several years ago and was doing very well trading just the first hour.

Here are some of the characteristics of the first hour:

- What is referred to as the first hour is rarely an hour. It is the time before the first good swing begins and can be 15 minutes or two hours; it is often called the opening range.
- It is the easiest time to make money. Experienced scalpers know that reversals are common. These traders can often make many carefully selected scalps, betting that breakout attempts will usually fail, as is typical of breakout attempts at any time of the day. They look to buy low and sell high. In general, they avoid doji signal bars, but will often short below either a bull or a bear trend bar after a move up, or buy above a bull or a bear trend bar after a move down. Consecutive trend bars in the same direction often indicate the direction of their next scalp. Two consecutive, strong bull trend bars will usually make scalpers look to buy, and consecutive bear trend bars will bias them in favor of shorts.

- It is the easiest time to lose money. Beginners see large trend bars and are afraid of missing a huge breakout. They buy late, at the top of strong bull spikes, and short late, at the bottom of strong bear spikes, only to take repeated losses. There are more variables to consider, and the setups come faster. Because they often confuse swing and scalp setups, they end up managing their trades wrong. They should never scalp, especially in the first hour.
- When the bars are big, traders should use wider stops and trade smaller size.
- Yesterday's always-in direction going into the close often carries over into the open of today.
- Reversals are common, abrupt, and often large. If you can't read the price action fast enough, wait until the market slows down and the always-in direction becomes clear.
- The first bar of the day is the high or low of the day only about 20 percent of the time, so don't feel a need to enter on the second bar. In fact, there is no need to rush to take any trade, because before long the always-in direction will be clear, and the probability of a successful trade will be higher.
- Either the high or low of the day usually forms within the first hour, so swing traders patiently wait for a setup that can be one of the extremes of the day. The setup for the high or low of the day often has only a 40 percent probability of success. Since the reward can be many times larger than the risk, the trader's equation can still be excellent for a swing trade. Most traders should focus on a logical reversal in the opening range for their most important trade of the day. The trade often looks bad for five or more bars, but then suddenly breaks out and the always-in direction becomes clear to most traders. On most days, a trader will have to take more than one reversal before catching a successful swing, but even the ones that don't go far usually make a small profit or have only a small loss. This creates a favorable trader's equation for this particular type of relatively low-probability trade.
- The high of the day usually begins with some type of double top, although it is rarely exact. The low of the day usually begins with an imperfect double bottom of some type.
- Once the always-in direction becomes clear, traders can enter at the market or on any small pullback for a swing. Experienced scalpers look for pullbacks to scalp in the direction of the trend.
- Trading in the minutes after a report is dominated by computer programs, many of which get a nearly instantaneous numerical version of the report and use the data to generate trades. Other programs trade off statistics and not fundamentals. It is very difficult to compete in an environment where your opponent has the edge of being much faster at making decisions and placing trades. It is better to wait for a bar or two before entering.
- Gap openings are present on most days (see Chapter 20 on gap openings).

- The open often foretells the type of day. If the first bar is a doji or the first several bars overlap and have prominent tails, the day is more likely to have lots of two-sided trading.

There are often reports at 7:00 a.m. PST. Even if a report is not listed on the Internet, the market usually behaves as if there was a report. Computers have a clear edge in speed of analysis and order placement, and they are your competitors. When your competition has a big advantage, don't compete. Wait for their edge to disappear and trade when speed is no longer important.

The first hour or, more accurately, the opening range is the time when the market is setting up the first trend of the day, and it ends once that trend begins. It often lasts for a couple of hours and sometimes is as short as 15 minutes. It is the easiest time to make money, but is the easiest time to lose money as well. This is because many traders cannot process all of the variables fast enough, and the information is limited, since there are not many bars yet in the day. They have to decide on whether to treat a trade as a swing, a scalp, or both, and have to base the decision on the three trader's equation variables of probability, risk, and reward, in an environment when there are usually economic reports, where reversals and therefore decisions come often, and where the bars are often unusually large and therefore require them to adjust their risk to much larger than normal, as opposed to other times during the day when risk is a variable that is usually fixed at a certain size and does not usually require much thought. Get the picture? A trader has more to think about and less time to do the thinking. Computers have a clear edge in speed of analysis and order placement, and they are your competitors. When your competition has a big advantage, don't compete. If you are thinking, "Boy, I wish that I had the speed advantage that the firms using computers for program trading have," then you realize that you are at a disadvantage. Wait for their edge to disappear and trade when speed is no longer important.

Trading is difficult enough and the edge is always small, and the added complexity of the first hour can push traders beyond their ability to trade effectively. If there are too many variables to consider to trade profitably, traders can increase their chances of success by reducing the number of variables. For example, they can decide to look only for high-probability scalps or for only likely swing setups, or they can wait until there is a clear always-in trade and then swing, or take scalps in that direction, entering on pullbacks. They can also trade half to a quarter of their normal size and use a protective stop that is beyond the signal bar, which often requires a stop that is two or more times larger than their usual size.

One of the biggest causes of losses is a trader's inability to distinguish between swing and scalp setups. From the trader's equation, readers know that scalpers generally have to win on 60 percent or more of their trades, since the risk usually has to be about the size of the reward. Scalp setups are much more common than swing setups, but most scalp setups do not have a 60 percent probability of success and should be avoided. However, reversals are common in the first hour, and traders often do not have enough time to adequately assess the trader's equation. If their default is to take every reversal and then do the math after they are in, they will lose over time. The high or low of the day often follows a setup that has less than a 50 percent chance of success, and is therefore a terrible setup for a scalp, but it can still be a great setup for a swing.

Experienced traders can usually find four or more scalps in the first hour and even make a living off those trades. For example, if they average two profitable scalps a day of two points each and trade 25 Emini contracts, they could make a million dollars a year. Since most traders cannot process the risk, reward, and probability reliably when they have to do it quickly and with only five or 10 bars of information, they should not scalp in the first hour when reversals come quickly and abruptly. Instead, they should wait patiently for a setup that is likely to lead to an always-in swing, or wait until the swing has begun and the market has a clear always-in direction, and then take a swing trade. They will then have a reward that is larger than their risk (it may be two or three times as large), and since the always-in direction is clear, they'll have a 60 percent or better chance of the market going at least as many ticks in their direction as they have at risk from their stop, at which point they can move their stop to breakeven.

Many experienced traders look for a strong trend bar or consecutive trend bars in the first hour, and then will scalp a pullback. For example, if there are two consecutive strong bull trend bars and then a doji bar, they might place limit orders to buy at or below the low of the doji bar. Since they see it as a weak reversal signal, especially after such a strong bull spike, they expect it to fail. This means that the bears who sold below the bar will have to buy back their shorts and probably won't want to sell again for at least a bar or two. This removes bears from the market and turns some bears into buyers, which gives the bull scalpers a good chance to make a profit. The protective stop size and target size depend on how large the bars are. If the Emini has had an average daily range of about 15 points and the bull trend bars are about two points tall, traders might risk about two points to make two points, if they believe that there is a 60 percent chance of success, which there often is in these circumstances. Other bulls might scale in lower and risk to below the bottom of the bull spike. Only very experienced traders should be fading breakouts of bars in the first hour, because the moves can be fast and go very far, and traders have to be very confident of their read and their ability to manage their trades in a fast, volatile market.

The moves in the first hour can be fast, and traders often get caught up in the excitement of big trend bars and enter late. They know that a trend will soon begin and are fearful of missing it, and instead get caught in a reversal. Since the market is searching for direction in the first hour, reversals are common. Traders might take a trade and think that they will swing it, only to discover that it reverses on the next bar. They then have to decide whether to exit or to rely on a stop beyond the signal bar. Invariably, as they are making that decision, they realize that the reversal trade is better than the trade they took, and they struggle with trying to figure out how to minimize their loss and get into a trade in the other direction. They hold too long, hoping for a pullback, and then exit with a larger loss than they planned on taking. Not only that; they are upset by the large loss and need to recover before taking the next trade. Once they are ready to trade again, the market has moved so far in the new direction that they are afraid to take the trade, even though the trend looks strong. At the end of the day, they print the chart out and cannot believe how clear the setups actually were. But hindsight is very different from real time.

Traders can also lose money on scalps that should be swings. If they lost several times earlier in the week on what they thought were good swing trades, they will be wary of swing trading on the open today. Assume that several times this week the market went far enough for a scalper's profit, but quickly reversed and stopped them out with a loss. Today, they decide to scalp every trade in the first hour. They lose on the first two scalps, but when they were stopped out on the second trade, the bar that hit the stop reversed into an outside bar and led to a very strong trend in the direction of the trade that they no longer held. Since they decided that they wanted to trade only scalps on reversals, they are on the sidelines as the market trends relentlessly, bar after bar. The trend runs for eight points before there is a pullback, and they suddenly realize that this one swing trade offered as much profit as four successful scalps.

After several days of losing when they tried to scalp because they took low-probability setups, and having given up on trying to swing because they got stopped out so often (only to miss a big trend after they gave up), they are confused and upset. They feel like they did everything right but still lost, and that trading is so unfair: "Why can other people do so well in the first hour, yet I lose no matter what I do?" It is because they are trying to do too much. They are buying at the top and selling at the bottom of the developing range, hoping for a successful breakout, denying the reality that most breakout attempts fail. They then do not take the best swing setup, because it looks weak and it looks like it will probably fail, just like the past five reversals in the past hour. When traders feel this way, they should take a break from trading the opening range until the always-in position is clear. Yes, they will be entering after the trend has already gone a couple of points and they stand to make less, but the chance of success is much greater. It is far better to win a little, but win frequently, than it is to lose several times a day while hoping to finally figure out how to trade the first hour profitably.

Traders who can scalp successfully often have to make adjustments in the first hour. In general, scalpers usually have to risk about as much as their reward, but since it is always best to begin by looking at what risk is required, they can set a reasonable reward after determining their risk. For example, if the bars in the Emini are usually about two points tall, but they are about four points tall today, a trader might have to risk about four points. The market is moving quickly and it is difficult to spend time doing exact math while trying to read the charts and to place orders. Scalpers should just quickly cut the position size in half or by two-thirds. It doesn't matter what they do. What matters is that they do it quickly, stop thinking about it, and concentrate on what is much more important: reading correctly and placing orders. If they are unwilling to use a larger stop when it is necessary, they should not take the trade. Also, once traders are in the trade and the market pulls back further than they think it should have (but does not hit their stop), and then the move resumes but looks weaker than they think it should, they have to be willing to get out at a smaller profit target. For example, the large bars might force them to risk four points instead of two on an Emini trade, but once the move has gone their way, it looks weak. If they believe that their premise is no longer valid, they have to be able to change their goal, and it is often worth exiting with just a point or two profit and then waiting for more information.

Only experienced traders, who can handle changing position, stop, and profit target sizes quickly, should attempt it. Because scalping usually requires a risk that is as large as the reward, and therefore a high winning percentage, most traders should avoid scalps, especially in the first hour. Most traders have a better chance of being profitable in the long run if they can wait for a clearly always-in market and then take a swing trade. This means that the probability of an equidistant move is 60 percent or more. They can then use a profit target that is at least as large as the risk, and preferably twice the size of the risk, and have a favorable trader's equation.

Because the first hour has many reversals, it is better to look to buy low and sell high until the market becomes clearly always-in long or short. Unfortunately, many traders do the opposite. They see large trend bars up or down and are afraid that they are missing a breakout, which almost always fails. They have to learn to wait for a confirmed breakout and a clear always-in market. Then they should switch to a swing approach and become willing to buy near the top when the market is always-in long, or sell near the bottom when it is always-in short. If traders cannot quickly distinguish swing setups from scalp setups, they should not make rash decisions. Instead, they should wait patiently for a clear always-in signal and then begin trading. Most traders cannot successfully scalp in the first hour, and certainly are unable to scalp initially and then switch to swing trading when the time is right. They should instead wait patiently for swing setups.

Since the first hour or two frequently provides setups that result in great swing trades, traders must be ready to take them. Although there is a tendency to think that the patterns are different in the first hour, the reality is that from a price action perspective, they are not. The setups are the same as during any other time of the day and on any time frame. What is different is that the volatility is often greater and therefore the patterns run further, and the reversals are often unexpectedly abrupt. It is common for reversals to look weak and have two or three weak doji bars before the trend breaks out. Realize that this is common and, if you entered and see this weakness, don't scratch out. Rely on your read because you will likely be right, and you stand to make a large swing profit.

One other difference about the open is that many trades set up based on yesterday's price action. There will often be a channel that develops in the final couple of hours of yesterday followed by either a breakout or a market gap well beyond that flag on today's open. In either case, watch for reversals and continuations. Remember, a channel is just a flag, so a bull channel is a bear flag and a bear channel is a bull flag. Also, if the market ended clearly always-in long or short, traders should assume that the trend will continue on the open until they see evidence to the contrary.

A final important difference is that the high or low of the day occurs in the first hour or so on most days, and it is beneficial to try to swing part of any trade that might be the high or low of the day. If you are in a trade with such potential and the market moves strongly in your direction, use a breakeven stop to allow yourself to collect the windfall profits that often happen off the open.

Although any reversal in the first hour or so can create the high or low of the day, the probability of any one particular reversal doing so is usually not more than 50 percent. If a trader instead waits for clear follow-through and a clear always-in move after the reversal, the probability that the reversal will be the high or low of the day is often more than 60 percent. The traders who wait for the always-in confirmation pay for that increased probability with smaller profits, but traders who prefer to take only high-probability trades are happy with the trade-off. Since the high or low of the day setup is often only 40 to 50 percent certain, it is usually a bad scalp setup, even though it has a strong trader's equation for a swing trade. The trend, as it begins, often starts slowly and does not look like a trend at all, but usually within five bars or so has a breakout into a clear always-in market. Most of the time, the setup for a bull trend day is part of a double bottom of some type, even though it is usually so imperfect that it does not look like a double bottom. Likewise, the setup for a bear trend day is usually part of an imperfect double top. For example, if there is a series of strong bull trend bars off the open and then a partial pullback that gets tested five to 10 bars later, this forms a double bottom flag entry and has a good chance of leading to a new high of the day. The breakout then might run for a measured move up and lead to a bull trend.

Traders often enter on the second bar of the day as it breaks beyond the high or low of the first bar, but the probability of a successful scalp is often under 50 percent, depending on the situation. That means that the trader's equation makes sense only for a swing, but traders often mistakenly treat the trade like a scalp, which is a losing approach when the probability is about 50 percent and the risk is as large as the reward. They convince themselves that they will swing and hold through pullbacks, but within a bar or two, they grab a small profit and feel relieved. They really intended to scalp but did not realize it, and they will wonder at the end of the month why they lost money. It is because they took a trade that had a losing trader's equation. Some reversals in the first hour have a 70 percent chance of reaching a scalper's target, but only a 40 percent chance of reaching a swing target. Traders have to know in advance how they plan to manage the trade before they take it, because changing goals after entering is a losing strategy. You can't have one premise and then manage the trade as if it was based on a different premise, but it is common for traders to confuse scalps and swings in the first hour when everything happens so quickly and the bars are large and have big pullbacks within the bars as they are forming.

The first bar of the day has about a 20 percent chance of being either the high or low of the day (except on days where there is a large gap opening, when the probability can be 50 percent or more if the bar is a strong trend bar). Also, the bar is often large, frequently about 20 percent of an average day's ultimate range. For example, if the average range in the Emini has been about 10 points and the first bar of today is two points tall, a trader who buys as the second bar breaks above the first bar has about a 20 percent chance of making eight points while risking a little more than two points. This is a losing trader's equation. If traders are very good at subjectively evaluating all of the variables and selecting trades with a higher probability, they can have a mathematical edge, but these high-probability trades based on the first bar of the day happen only about once a month. Even if traders take profits once the reward is twice the size of the risk, they will be successful only a couple of times a month, so looking for a swing entry on the second bar of the day is rarely worthwhile. However, since a reliable swing in the first hour, where the reward is twice the size of the risk, occurs on most days, if there is a strong reversal setup early on, traders should consider swinging the trade. Once the trend reaches about twice the size of their stop, they can move their stop to breakeven and swing part of the trade until there is an always-in reversal.

Sometimes the market trends for the first bar or two of the day and that first bar ends up as one of the extremes of the day. When the market trends from the open, it is important to enter early, but not necessarily on the second bar. This pattern is most common with gap openings, large or small. When you enter a trade where you might be at the start of a huge trend, it is particularly important to try to swing some contracts. If the pattern is very strong, you could swing most of your contracts and then quickly move your stop to breakeven.

However, if the strong opening is reversed (a breakout to a new extreme of the day in the opposite direction), then the day might trend in the opposite direction or it could turn into a trading range day. A strong trend off the open, even if it is reversed, still means that there were traders willing to trade aggressively in that direction, and they will be quick to trade again in that direction later in the day if the reversal falters.

If you think that a reversal down is not the high of the day, you should never be more than 30 percent certain, because you would then be at least 70 percent certain that it is not, and the market is never that certain when the opening range is forming. In fact, rarely is anything that certain at any time of the day. That edge is simply too large, and traders would quickly neutralize it long before it got that certain. Don't get too committed to an opinion, especially in the first hour, because even the strongest moves can reverse sharply on the next bar. However, although a reversal in the first couple of hours might have only a 30 to 40 percent chance of becoming the high or low of the day, if there is good follow-through, the odds can quickly increase to 50 to 60 percent.

Even though most early reversals are good for scalps and not swings, when one is particularly strong, a trader should try to swing at least half of the position. As mentioned earlier, there is a tendency for the first hour or two to be the most likely time of the day to find a trade where a trader can make two to three times the risk. In general, most traders should work very hard to take potential swing trades in the first hour or two because those trades have the best trader's equation combination of reward, risk, and probability.

Why does the market make a big move over the first several bars and then reverse? Why doesn't it simply open at the low or high of the day? The location of the open of the day is not set by any firm or group of firms; instead, it represents a brief equilibrium between buyers and sellers at the instant of the open, and it is usually determined by the premarket activity. For example, the Emini is basically a 24-hour market and trades actively, uninterrupted, for hours leading up to the open of the New York Stock Exchange. If the institutions have a large amount of buying planned for the day, why would the market ever open a stock above yesterday's close and then sell off before rallying to a new high? If you were an institutional trader and had a lot of buy orders to fill today, you would love the market to open above where you wanted to buy and then have a sharp move down into your buy zone where you could aggressively buy along with all the other institutions that likely also have lots of similar buy orders from their clients; you would then hope to see a small sell climax that will form a convincing low of the day. The lack of buying by the bullish institutions creates a sell vacuum that can quickly suck the market down into their buy zone, which is always at an area of support, where they will buy aggressively and relentlessly, often creating the low of the day.

If the reversal back up from that sell climax on the open is strong enough, very few traders will be looking to short, because there will be a general feeling that the upward momentum is sufficiently strong to warrant at least a second leg up before the low is tested, if it gets tested. Would there be anything that you, if you were an institutional trader, could do to make this happen? Yes! You could buy into the close of the premarket to push the price up and fill some of your orders. Not as much volume is needed in stocks to move the price before the 6:30 a.m. PST open. Then, once the market opens, you could liquidate some or all of your longs and even do some shorting. Since you want to buy lower, you will not start buying until the market falls to an area that you consider represents value, which will be at a support area. This is a vacuum effect. The buyers are there, but they will step aside if they think that the price will be lower in a few minutes. Why buy now if you can buy for less in a few minutes? This absence of buying despite the existence of very strong bulls allows the price to get sucked down quickly. Once it is in their buy zone, they see value and doubt the market will fall further. They appear as if out of nowhere and buy relentlessly, causing a very sharp bull reversal. The shorts will also see the support, and if they believe that the leg down is likely over, they, too, will become buyers as they take profits on their shorts.

Price action is very important. A trader wants to see how the market responds once it gets down to some key support price, like the moving average, or a prior swing high or low, or the low of yesterday, or a trend line or trend channel line. Most of the trading is done by computers, which use algorithms to calculate where these support levels are. If enough firms are relying on the same support levels, the buying will overwhelm the selling and the market will reverse up. It is impossible to know in advance how strong the buying will be, but since the support is always based on mathematics, an experienced trader can usually anticipate areas where reversals might occur and be ready to place trades. If the downward momentum begins to wane and the market starts to reverse up from the key price, institutions will liquidate any shorts and aggressively buy to fill their orders. Since most firms will have similar orders, the market will start to rally. If a firm believes that the low of the day might be in, it will continue to buy as the market rallies and will aggressively buy any pullbacks. Since its order size is huge, it doesn't want to buy all at once and risk causing a spike up and then a buy climax. Instead, it would rather just keep buying in an orderly fashion all day long until all of its orders get filled. As they get filled, the relentless buying causes the market to go up more, which attracts momentum traders who will also buy throughout the day, adding to the buying pressure.

Is this what actually happens? Traders at institutions know if this is what they do, but no one ever knows for certain why the market reverses on any given day. The reversal is due to countless reasons, but those reasons are irrelevant. All that matters is price action. Reversals often happen seconds after a report is released, but an individual trader is unlikely to understand how the market will respond to a report by simply watching CNBC. The market can rally or sell off in response to either a bullish or a bearish report, and a trader is simply not qualified to reliably interpret a report in the absence of price action. The best way to know how the market will respond is simply to watch it respond and place your trades as the price action unfolds. Very often, the bar before the report is a great setup that gets triggered on the report. If you feel compelled to trade on the release of the report, place your order and then your stop and trust your read. Since slippage can be significant on a report, it is almost always better to wait until after the report is released. If you enter on the report, you might find that you got a few ticks of slippage on the entry, and then the market violently reverses and you get additional slippage on your exit. What you thought was a trade with a risk of eight ticks ends up as a trade where you lost 16 or more ticks. If you trade thinner markets, your slippage could be much worse and you could be so far down in the first hour that you will not get back to breakeven by the close.

When the market rallies sharply on a 7:00 a.m. PST report, it is usually because the institutions were already planning on buying, but were hoping to buy lower. When the report appeared sufficiently bullish for them to believe that they would not be able to fill their orders lower, they bought on the report. If they have enough buying to do, they will continue to buy all day, and the day will become a bull trend day. If, on the other hand, their initial buying is overwhelmed by other institutions who were hoping for a rally that would allow them to short at a higher price, the upside breakout will fail and the market will trend down. These bears were invisible because they were waiting for a rally to short and their power became evident only once they began to aggressively short the rally and turn the market back down. Obviously, countless other factors are always in play, and there are huge momentum traders who have no opinion about a report and simply trade heavily in the direction of the move as it is unfolding. However, the institutional bias going into the report is an important component. The institutions already knew what they wanted to do before the report was released, although all would have contingencies if the report was a complete surprise.

About 70 percent of all trading is automated, and this computer-generated buying and selling will become increasingly important. Dow Jones & Company now has a news service called Lexicon that transmits machine-readable financial news to its subscribers. Lexicon scans all of the Dow Jones stories about stocks and converts the information into a form that the algorithms can use to make decisions to buy and sell stocks in a fraction of a second. Some of the algorithms are based on the fundamental components in the report. How many new jobs were created last month? What was the core consumer price index (CPI)? What was the bid-to-cover ratio in the bond auction? Other algorithms operate on a longer time frame and analyze stock performance and earnings statements, in addition to the news feeds, to make trading decisions. Still other algorithms are purely statistical, like if the Emini rallied 10 ticks without at most a one-tick pullback, then buy at the market and exit with a two-tick profit. Another firm might find a statistical reason to short that rally for a three-tick profit. It is impossible to know what any firm is doing, but if someone can think of an idea and it can be tested and found to be mathematically sound, their computers are probably trading it. Some firms might have algorithms that are hybrids of the fundamental and statistical approaches. Maybe if the economic number is favorable, the programs will buy immediately, but if they have statistical evidence that tells them that the Emini will then reverse to a new low after rallying three points on this particular economic number, the program might take profits and even reverse for a scalp.

Some programs use differential evolution optimizing software to generate data that is used to generate other data. They can continue to refine the data until it reaches some level of mathematical certainty, and then the result is used to automatically buy or sell stocks. Some orders are so huge that they take time to place, and algorithmic trading software breaks the orders into small pieces to conceal the trading from traders who would try to capitalize on the incipient trend. Predatory trading algorithms try to unravel what the algorithm trading programs are trying to hide. Everyone is looking for an edge, and more and more firms are using computers to find the edges and place the trades.

Since computers can analyze the data and place trades far faster than a trader can, and the computers are running programs that have a mathematical edge, it is a losing proposition to try to compete with them at the moment a report is released. These are very high-powered computers and are located very close to the exchanges, and can trade huge volumes in a fraction of a second. The result is price movement that is often too fast to read. In fact, the price movement can be so fast that your computer at home may be several seconds behind what is actually taking place. Too often the moves are very large in the first second or two, only to reverse a few seconds later, and then maybe reverse again. Traders simply cannot make decisions and place orders fast enough to trade this situation profitably. It is better to wait to see if a clear always-in move comes from the report and then trade in that direction. When your opponents have an edge over you—in this case, speed—it is better to wait for their edge to disappear before trading again. Most traders should not trade in the seconds after a report but should wait for the price action to return to normal, which often takes one to about 10 minutes.

No one knows in advance whether the sum total of all the buy orders at all of the major institutions would be enough to overwhelm the institutions that were looking to short, or whether the shorts represented vastly more dollars and would be able to drive the market down. On most days, the action is two-sided for a while as the bulls continue to buy and the bears continue to sell. The market probes up and down in buy and sell vacuums, looking for one side to take control over the market when the market reaches an extreme. When it is low enough, strong bulls, who have been waiting for the market to reach a level that they see as value, will buy aggressively. The market then races up to an area where the bulls no longer feel that the price represents good value, and they stop buying and begin to take profits. The strong bears, who have been waiting for higher prices to sell, appear out of nowhere and short aggressively. At some point, one side decides that they are unwilling to continue trading aggressively at the current price, and this creates an imbalance that allows the other side to begin to move the market in their direction. The losing side begins to cover, and this adds to the trend. The winning side sees the market moving their way and they add to their positions, creating a stronger trend. At some point, they will begin to take profits and this will result in a pullback. Once the market comes back far enough to represent value to these firms, they will once again begin to add to their positions and the result will usually be a test of the trend's extreme.

Sharp reversals are common on economic reports, and the reversals may not make sense to you, but that is irrelevant. How can a bullish report lead to a rally and then seconds later be followed by a new low of the day? If the market was so bearish a couple of minutes ago, how can it be so bullish now? Don't give it any thought. Instead, just look for standard price action setups and trade them mindlessly without giving any consideration to the reasons why the reversal is taking place. All that you need to know is that it is in fact taking place and you must enter. You don't need to understand it, but it is important to realize that it can happen quickly and you might not react fast enough to avoid losing money.

Although the 5 minute chart is the easiest to read and the most reliable, the 3 minute chart trades well, particularly in the first hour. However, it is prone to more losers, and if you like the highest winning percentage and don't want the negative emotion that comes from losing, you should stick to trading the 5 minute chart and work on increasing your position size.

As a trader, it is best to keep your analysis simple, especially in the first hour when the market is moving quickly. The vast majority of opens are related to the price action of the final hour or so of the prior day and take the form of a breakout, a failed breakout, a breakout pullback, or a trend from the open, and any of these can move very fast.

One of the most difficult aspects of day trading is maintaining focus. Most traders simply cannot stay intensely connected to the market for the entire session, and they succumb to boredom and distractions and often suspect that this is a major obstacle to them becoming consistently profitable. And they are right. The first hour provides you with a great opportunity to remedy this problem. Even if you think that watching every tick or at least every 5 minute bar is impossible for you for an entire day, you might believe that you can do it for an hour. This has to become one of your primary goals because it is a great way to make money. The volume is huge and there are several trades every day in that first hour. If you simply trade the first hour and increase your position size once you become consistently profitable, you might discover that the intensity is needed for only that hour. Then, for the rest of the day, just look for two or three major reversals, which you can almost always anticipate 10 or more minutes in advance, especially if you are waiting for second entries (once you see the first one, get ready to take the second, which will usually follow within a few bars). Once you can trade the first hour well, look to trade the first two hours, which usually provide the best trading of the day and can very often give you all of the profit that you expect from the entire day.

When trading around holidays like Christmas week and the week of the Fourth of July, the first hour is often very important because often that is the only time when the market behaves like a normal day. It then frequently enters a tight trading range for the rest of the day. If you want to trade around holidays, you have to be particularly alert to setups in the first hour.

When trading the 5 minute chart, it is easy to not be thinking about the many institutional traders who are also paying attention to 15 minute charts. The first 15 minute bar closes at the close of the third 5 minute bar and therefore activity around this third bar will influence the appearance of the first 15 minute bar. For example, if the first two bars of the day move in one direction and then the third bar is a smaller pause bar, the breakout of the bar will determine whether there is a 15 minute breakout or there could be a failure. Therefore, trading the breakout of the third bar of the day often leads to a big move. Do not place a trade on the third bar alone on most days, but be aware of its extra significance. If it is an important bar, there will usually be other price action to support the trade, and that additional information should be the basis for the trade.

Similar logic can also be used for the last 5 minute bar of the 30 and 60 minute charts (for example, the 60 minute chart is made of 12 bars on the 5 minute chart, so the final one closes when the 60 minute bar closes), but focusing on such longer time frames and their infrequent entries increases the chances of missing one or more profitable 5 minute trades and therefore is not worthwhile.

Barbwire represents two-sided trading, and when it develops in the first hour, it often will be followed by a day where bulls and bears alternate control of the market. If there is a trend after the barbwire, there will usually be a tradable countertrend setup at some point.

The first bar of the day often shows what the day will be like. If it is a doji in the middle of a tight trading range from the final hour of yesterday and the moving average is flat, the odds favor a trading range day. If the bar is a trend bar but has prominent tails, it is a one-bar trading range. Since most trading range breakouts fail, the market will probably not be able to move above or below the bar for more than a bar or two before there is a reversal. Some traders fade the breakouts of the first bar if it has prominent tails, and they will scale in once or twice. For example, whether the market gaps up or down or has a bull or bear body, if the tails are fairly prominent, many traders will short above the bar and buy below the bar for a scalp, since they know that reversals usually dominate the first hour and that the breakout of a trading range, even if the trading range is a single bar, is likely to fail. Therefore, they bet that it will fail and trade in the opposite direction. Since they see that bar as a one-bar trading range, they are in trading range mode, which means that they will usually scalp most or all of their position.

The next several bars can also show the bias of the day. If dojis continue and there are five reversals in the first hour, the odds of a trading range day go up. If there is a large gap opening and the market trends for the first four bars, the odds of a trend day are good. Traders will be ready for a trend from the first bar trend, and those first bars might be the spike of a spike and channel trend day. However, they will be ready if the first pullback becomes a small final flag. This can lead to a spike in the opposite direction, a breakout of the opposite end of the opening range, and then a trend in the opposite direction.

The strongest swing trades in the first couple of hours come from a confluence of patterns, but the patterns are sometimes subtle and traders should look for them before the open and think about what might happen. Always consider both the bull and bear case for everything, because there is smart money on both sides. As always, traders are looking for breakouts and failed breakouts. For example, was there an 18-bar long bear flag at the end of yesterday that pulled back to the bear trend line, and if so, did today open just below the bear flag and below the moving average, creating a breakout of the flag, but then rally for two bars to the moving average where it formed a bear reversal bar? If so, this is an opening reversal down at the moving average and a breakout pullback short, after a test of the bear trend line, with a good signal bar, creating a high probability swing (and scalp) short. The more factors that are present, the higher the probability, and when there is a swing setup with a high probability, the setup is very strong. Alternatively, did yesterday end with a bull breakout from a 25-bar long trading range in a three day weak bull trend that had a wedge shape, and was the market near the top of a two week long trading range, and did the breakout have two legs up and did the market close at the trend channel line above the three day wedge rally? Is so, did today open a few ticks below the close of yesterday, trade up, and then reverse down into a strong bear reversal bar, creating a second entry sell signal on the failed breakout above yesterday's high and the trading range (a likely final flag) and above the top of the wedge bull channel? If so, this is a high probability swing (and scalp) short.

FIGURE PIII.1 Failed Early Reversal

The market often abruptly reverses after the first few bars, but always be prepared for the reversal to fail and set up a breakout pullback. As shown in Figure PIII.1, bar 1 was the third bar of the day and it was a small bull reversal bar. It reversed up from the moving average and a swing low from yesterday. This was a great opening reversal long entry, and it also prevented the first 15 minute bar from being a strong bear trend bar.

The market had four consecutive bull trend bars starting at bar 1. After the second one, some bulls started placing buy limit orders at the low of the prior bar, expecting the first attempt to reverse down to fail. They were filled on the small bear bar that formed three bars after bar 2.

The next day, bar 3 also reversed a swing low from the day before and led to a scalper's profit, but the bull entry bar reversed down in a two-bar reversal for a short entry. Note that bar 3 was a bear trend bar and not a strong reversal bar, so this was not a good countertrend long setup. The bulls were hoping for a wedge reversal, where the first two pushes occurred in the final couple of hours of yesterday. However, bar 3 and the bar before it were small trading range bars. The bars were too small and lacked sufficient bullish strength to have much chance of reversing that strong sell-off. The bulls tried to create that strength on the bar after bar 3, but the bears quickly reversed the market down with an even larger bear trend bar.

The break below the bar 3 low was also a break below the first 15 minute bar of the day on a day with a large gap down, increasing the odds of a tradable downswing.

Notice that yesterday's close was just below its open and well below the high of the day. This created a reversal bar on the daily chart, even though it had a small bull body. Some traders who trade off of the daily chart would then have placed sell stops to go short if today fell below yesterday's low. Because there were so many traders willing to sell down there, the market gapped down today and traded below yesterday's low on the first bar, triggering the sell signal on the daily chart. The breakout attempted to fail at bar 3, but the reversal up failed and created a double top bear flag and breakout pullback short, with an entry below the bar 4 two-bar reversal.

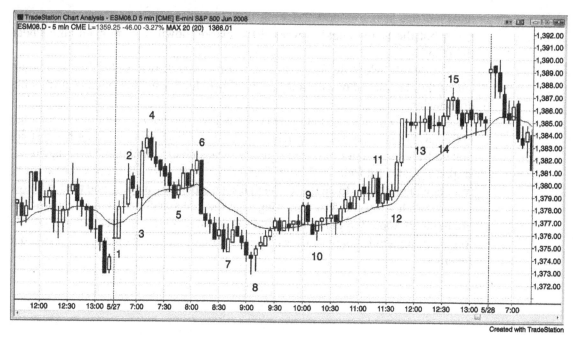

FIGURE PIII.2   The First Few Bars Can Set the Tone

As shown in Figure PIII.2, the price action in the first several bars often foreshadows what happens later. The rally from the open to the bar before bar 4 had several large bull bars and only two small bear bars, showing that the bulls were willing to be aggressive. This was something to remember later in the day in case another buy setup appeared. Keeping that in mind, traders should have been more willing to swing part of their longs because the trend was more likely to resume.

The high of the day usually comes from some kind of double top that rarely looks like a double top. Here, bar 6 was the end of a second test up and therefore was the signal for a double top short. Bar 4 became the possible high of the day. Bar 8 was a double bottom with the closing low of yesterday, and it formed the low of today. Even though the probability of a successful swing on an opening reversal might be only 40 percent, many of the trades result in a small profit or a small loss. These small trades usually balance out, and the 40 percent that reach four or more points become the source of a trader's profit. Trading these opening moves should be a cornerstone for most traders as they try to build a business in day trading.

Experienced scalpers expect most breakout attempts to fail, and look to buy low and sell high in the first hour or two. Possible scalps included: selling above the first bar, which was a doji bar, and scaling in higher (exiting the first entry at breakeven and the second and third entries with a profit); buying above the bar 1 bull trend bar; shorting below the bear inside bar that followed bar 2 (a failed breakout above the trading range of yesterday); buying on bar 3 as it broke above the high of the prior bar (since the spike up to bar 2 was strong and was likely to be followed by a second leg up); shorting below the two-bar reversal that followed the bar 3 breakout to a new high of the day (a low 2 short); and shorting below the bar 6 bull trend bar, since it was a two-legged breakout of the bear micro channel down to bar 5 and the bottom of the strong bear micro channel down to bar 5 was likely to be tested.

Bar 8 was a successful second attempt to reverse the breakout to a new low of the day and a double bottom with the close of yesterday, so it was likely to lead to a rally that had at least two legs. In fact, the two-legged rally only had a small sideways pause and therefore the move up was mostly in a channel. When a rally is mostly in a channel, even if there is a pause and a small second leg, most traders will see the entire channel as the first leg and expect a more obvious second leg to follow. The move up to bar 11 was just an extension of that channel with no significant pullback, and therefore many traders would have considered the rally from bar 8 to bar 11 to be just one leg. However, as with most channels, there were many overlapping bars, prominent tails, and bear trend bars. A bull channel is a bear flag, so traders were looking for a downside breakout, which could have led to a pullback that was large enough to make traders believe that the first leg up was clearly over. They then needed to decide whether a second leg up was still likely or the correction had lasted long enough for the bears to feel that the market would not go much higher, thereby convincing them that this was a good price level to again aggressively short. Instead of breaking to the downside, the market broke strongly to the upside and the bears who had been shorting for the past couple of hours had to quickly buy back their shorts. The bulls saw how strong the bull spike was, and they bought at the market all of the way up because when a spike is this strong, the odds favor higher prices.

Bar 12 was a high 2 buy for a second larger leg up, which also had two smaller legs.

FIGURE PIII.3   Don't Scalp Stocks with Small Ranges

Traders should not often scalp stocks with average daily ranges under a dollar, but price action entries still work. As shown in Figure PIII.3, Intel (INTC) had two large bear trend bars in the first 15 minutes and then formed a double top bear flag (bars 3 and 5). This is a reliable pattern that often leads to a bear trend day, and here it led to a spike and climax bear trend. Yesterday's bull trend was so strong that today's two-legged selling reversed back up at bar 6, likely at the moving average on the 15 or 60 minute charts, but it was good for at least a 10 cent scalp.

Whenever the moving average is as steeply up as it was yesterday, any strong sell-off below it will almost always be followed by a tradable rally back up. Bar 6 was the signal for a double bottom bull flag with yesterday's 11:35 pullback from a strong spike up. It then formed an even stronger bull spike into the close and the entire move up became a spike and climax bull trend. Since the second spike is comparable to the channel in a traditional spike and channel bull trend, its bottom usually gets tested, as it did here.

FIGURE PIII.4   Early Barbwire Often Leads to a Trading Range Day

Barbwire type (tight trading range with big tails and big bars) of trading with prominent tails, overlapping bars, and many reversals for the first 90 minutes of the day
is a sign of intense two-sided trading and uncertainty, and the day usually becomes
a trading range day. As shown in Figure PIII.4, today was a trending trading range
day, but since the market closed at the top of the upper trading range, it was also a
bull reversal day.

When barbwire develops at the open, it is usually followed by tradable swings
in both directions at some point in the day. By the third bar of the day, barbwire was
likely because about half of its range was overlapped by the prior bar and it closed
in its middle, meaning that the following bar would also likely overlap about half of
its range. The barbwire continued right through the entire weak rally to bar 2. It was
followed by a break of the bear trend line, a lower high, and then a second entry
to the lower high at bar 4, which formed a double top with bar 3. The breakout
to the downside over the next several bars made a trending trading range likely,
especially since the range to that point was only slightly more than half of that of
recent days and was likely to increase in a channel down after the spike. Traders
were looking for a downside breakout and then a measured move down for their
swing shorts. The downside breakout made the market always-in short, and follow-
through selling was likely. The channel down to the bar before bar 6 was likely the

start of a trading range. Bar 9 was the first of a two-bar bull spike after the higher low, and once that spike completed, most always-in traders would have concluded that the market was then always-in up.

The rally to bar 7 broke the bull trend line and was followed by a lower low and a two-bar reversal buy entry at bar 8, and then the bar 9 higher low rally into the close.

The two consecutive bull trend bars at bar 1 were enough for some bull scalpers to place buy limit orders at the low of bar 1 and protective stops below the bull bar before it. They got long on the bear bar that followed and could have scalped out with one or two points of profit over the next couple of bars.

CHAPTER 17

Patterns Related to the Premarket

When looking at tick or volume charts of the Globex Emini, the open is not easy to spot because it is just part of the 24-hour trading day and appears indistinguishable from the rest of the chart. In fact, the bar that contains the open of the day session will almost always contain ticks from before that open. There is a tendency for the Globex highs and lows to get tested in the day session, and there are patterns in the Globex that get completed during the first many bars of the day session. The first hour or so usually moves quickly, and the day session alone provides great price action. Since most traders are not capable of trading two charts well, especially in a fast market like after the open, just choose either the Globex or day session 5 minute chart. It is a matter of personal preference. Some successful traders watch the Globex all day, but I prefer to watch the day session. Other traders watch the Globex chart for an hour or so and then switch to the day session chart. Most trades that set up on the Globex chart will have price action reasons for traders who watch only the day session to take the same entry. You should be willing to miss an occasional trade rather than risk losing money while being confused as you quickly try to analyze two charts while you place entry, stop, and profit-target orders.

When the market has a large gap on the day session and moves to close it in the first 30 minutes or so, the moving average on the Globex is often in the opposite direction to that in the day session during this time. For example, if there is a large gap down, the moving average for the day session will be down, but if there was a lower low on the Globex and the market had been rallying for the 30 minutes before the open, the Globex moving average can be rising and the

Globex prices can be above the moving average. If you look at only the day session and see a large gap and the market is trending strongly to close it off the open, look at the momentum and not the moving average, since the momentum is a reflection of the actual price action that is taking place. Traders who watch only the day session have to be aware that the moving average is often unreliable for the first hour or so.

Figure 17.1   PATTERNS RELATED TO THE PREMARKET   **355**

FIGURE 17.1   The Globex and Day Session Usually Give Related Signals

As shown in Figure 17.1, the Globex and day session charts usually give signals at the same time, but often from different patterns. Bar 1 on both the Globex chart on the left and on the day session chart on the right is the 6:35 a.m. PST bar. The Globex had a final flag reversal buy signal, and the day session had a bear trend bar reversal that was a breakout pullback above the two-legged up move into yesterday's close. Remember that if the first bar of the day is a trend bar, it is usually a setup for a scalp. If it fails, especially with an opposite trend bar, it is a setup in the opposite direction.

In the Globex session, bar 1 was below a falling moving average, but bar 1 was above the moving average in the day session. It can take an hour or two before the moving average is the same in both sessions, and it can provide different and equally valid setups in each. However, nothing is gained by most traders who watch both charts, and doing so usually increases the chances that a trader will not be quick enough to take all of the available trades and will make mistakes in order placement.

FIGURE 17.2   The Moving Average Is Different on the Globex

Sometimes the moving average on the day session is not helpful in the first 30 minutes when there is a large gap. In Figure 17.2, the day session on the right gapped down and the market could not push above the falling moving average for more than 90 minutes. However, the rally in the Globex (it trades almost 24 hours a day) on the left began 30 minutes before the open, and the market was above the rising moving average from 6:30 a.m. PST onward and appeared more bullish. The 7:20 a.m. barbwire setup at bar 1 was above the moving average and therefore bullish in the Globex, but below the moving average on the day session. However, the upward momentum was strong in both, and traders should have been looking for buy setups.

CHAPTER 18

Patterns Related to Yesterday: Breakouts, Breakout Pullbacks, and Failed Breakouts

M any trades in the first hour are related to patterns from the prior day, so try to anticipate setups before the market opens. Look at the final hour or two of yesterday to see if there was a strong trend (an always-in direction that might carry over to today), a trading range, a channel, or any kind of pattern that could lead to a breakout on today's open. Although some days open within a quiet trading range from the final hour or two of the prior day and the moving average is flat, on most days there is some kind of breakout on the open. When you are uncertain what the breakout is, simply look at the moving average and use that as a proxy. If the first bar is entirely above the moving average, think of the open as a gap up. If the first bar is entirely below the moving average, assume that the market is gapping down. There is usually a gap between the close of the final bar of yesterday and the open of the first bar of today, and that alone is a breakout. Look for breakouts of anything, including a channel or flag into yesterday's close. It can be a one-bar final flag or a three-hour channel. Look for a breakout below any swing high or low, especially the high or low of yesterday.

Once today opens and you see a breakout, you have to evaluate how likely it is to have follow-through. If there is a large gap down and the first bar is a strong bear trend bar with an open near its high and a close near its low, today might be a trend from the open bear. If instead it is a strong bull reversal bar, the breakout might fail and the day might become a trend from the open bull. If that bear breakout has follow-through for a few bars and then there is a strong bull reversal, this could set up a failed breakout and a possible low of the day. If the rally lasts only a bar or two and then there is another strong bear trend bar, the failed breakout might be failing. If so, shorting below that bear bar is a breakout pullback entry. The market broke out and then it failed, but the failure turned into a pullback in the bear trend instead of a reversal.

The opposite is true when there is a bull breakout on the open. Look for follow-through or a reversal into a failed breakout short entry. Does the reversal down continue with two or three or more large bear trend bars, making a bear trend day likely? Or is there a bull reversal bar within a bar or two, resulting in a failure of that failed breakout? If so, the pattern is evolving into a breakout pullback buy setup. You need to evaluate every open this way. Look for the breakout, and then look for a possible reversal into a failed breakout setup. Finally, if there is a failed breakout, look to see if it has follow-through or if it is failing. If it is failing, it is setting up a breakout pullback trade and a resumption of the breakout.

Figure 18.1   PATTERNS RELATED TO YESTERDAY   **359**

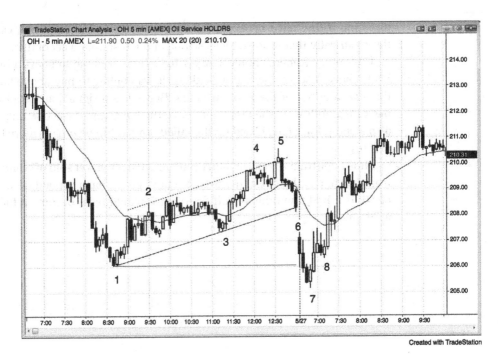

FIGURE 18.1   A Bull Channel Is a Bear Flag

A bull channel from yesterday is a bear flag, and the market often breaks below it on the open (see Figure 18.1). Yesterday, the Oil Service HOLDRS (OIH) 5 minute chart had a nearly four-hour, two-legged rally that broke the major bear trend line (not shown) after the strong move down to bar 1, and the rally overshot a bear trend channel line twice and reversed down both times (bars 4 and 5). This was evidence that the bulls were losing control. The length of the rally was evidence of bullish strength.

The sell-off from bar 5 into the close flipped the market to always-in short, and traders assumed that this trend would carry into today's open. Today, the market gapped down, had a strong bear trend bar, and quickly traded below yesterday's low, where it formed a strong two-bar bull reversal. This large bear flag failed breakout occurred over two days and provided an excellent long entry at one tick above the high of bar 7. This was a final flag reversal from the bear flag that began at bar 1, and a lower low major trend reversal. Opening reversals that reverse the high or low of the prior day often form the high or low of the day, so traders should swing some or most of their contracts. Here, a breakeven stop would have allowed a trader to make as much as $5.00 on a swing to a new swing high above bar 5.

When the open forms a breakout of a pattern from the prior day's close, traders should enter on a failed breakout setup, like bar 7, and then enter in the opposite direction if the failed breakout fails and becomes a breakout pullback. Here, the three-bar rally that followed was strong enough so that a second leg up was likely and therefore traders should not yet have been looking to short a breakout pullback. Since a second leg up was likely, it was better to buy above bar 8 or below the low of either of the prior two bars. Bar 8 was a signal bar for a breakout pullback long, following the breakout above the bar 6 top of the opening range. It was also a setup for a long based on the failed double top bear flag where bar 6 was the first top.

It is important to realize that, even though the market sold off sharply yesterday from bar 5 into the close, the market could easily have gapped up on the open at bar 6. If it had, then the sell-off from bar 5 would have become a failed breakout attempt.

Figure 18.2   PATTERNS RELATED TO YESTERDAY   **361**

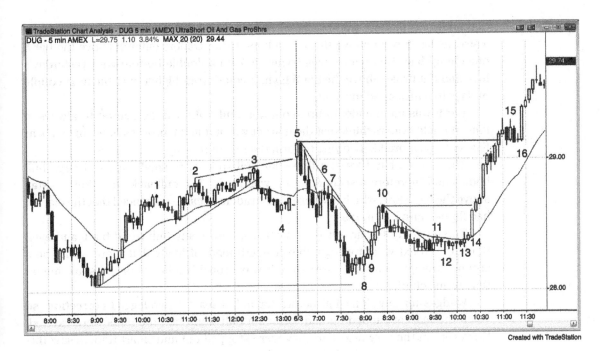

FIGURE 18.2 Failed Breakout Early in the Day

Always be ready for a failed breakout, no matter how strong the first bar is and even if there are trapped traders from yesterday's close (see Figure 18.2).

The UltraShort Oil and Gas ProShares (DUG) closed yesterday with a four-hour bull channel, which is a bear flag, and it broke to the downside going into the close. The bull channel was made of a spike and channel bull trend, and the sell-off to bar 4 set up a possible double bottom bull flag. The sell-off down to bar 4 broke below the bull channel, and today's open broke out of the top of the channel. Although the first bar of the day was a strong bull reversal bar and could have been the beginning of a trend from the open bull, it was followed by a strong bear trend bar and created a two-bar reversal and a setup for a failed breakout short and a higher high major trend reversal. The result was a failed breakout above the bar 3 wedge top and expanding triangle top (bars 2 and 3 were the first two pushes), and a trend from the open bear.

Yesterday's spike and channel bull trend ended in a wedge channel and was therefore likely to have at least a two-legged correction, but the pullback from the breakout to bar 4 was a higher high up to bar 5. When there is a strong reversal setup like a second entry for a wedge or an expanding triangle, the market usually corrects for at least 10 bars and two legs, which happened here. The market fell for an approximate measured move and tested just above yesterday's low. The two bull bodies at the low were a sign of buying pressure, and some bulls entered on a stop as bar 8 went above those bull bars. Other traders entered above the bar 8 outside up bar. The market was trying to form a double bottom with yesterday's low, and if it broke above the bar 5 high, it could work higher over the next couple of days to a measured move up.

Bar 9 was an outside up breakout bar, and it flipped the market to always-in long. It made traders think that the market was not in the process of forming a bear flag and was more likely trying to form the low of the day.

The rally to bar 10 was a three-bar bull spike with small tails and large bull bodies and therefore a second leg up was likely. The pullback was likely to stay above the bar 9 low, which is where most traders became convinced that the market had flipped into bull mode.

The move up to bar 3 was very strong, with many bull trend bars, and even though it ended with a wedge, this strength made it likely that there would be a second attempt up after a correction. It was probably a bull spike on some higher time frame chart.

Wedges usually don't fail before having at least a two-legged correction, so when the market gapped up and formed a bull trend bar, the bulls were excited. However, on the very next bar, they were stopped out and smart traders saw this as a consecutive, opposite failure and shorted.

Bar 6 was a failed trend line break in a steep bear trend, so it was a micro trend line low 1 short. This was a low 1 short in a strong bear spike in a possible new bear swing and therefore a reasonable trade.

Bar 7 set up a bear low 2 short setup, and was a small double top with bar 6.

Bar 8 was the deep correction that price action traders were looking for after the strong move up to bar 3. It was also two legs down on the day and a test of yesterday's low. Some traders saw the move down to bar 8 as a two-legged correction where the first leg down was to bar 4 and the pullback was to a higher high.

Bar 9 was another chance to buy since it was a failed low 2, which usually results in at least two more legs up. This was a great trade because it trapped bulls out of a strong up move and they would then have to chase the market up. An outside up failed low 1 or low 2 trap like this is common at the start of a strong trend and is a sign that the trend will likely go far.

Bar 10 was a strong up leg that broke the trend line and broke above the moving average and had many bull trend bars, so a higher low was likely to follow. Bar 10 was also a moving average gap bar, but at this point you would be looking to buy a pullback and you would short only a great setup and then only for a scalp. The trend was up since bar 9 until proven otherwise.

Bar 11 was a failed breakout from a bear micro channel, and bar 12 became a lower low breakout pullback buy setup.

The market formed two small bear trend bars en route to bar 13, and this is effectively a two-legged correction from the bar 12 reversal up. You could have bought on bar 13, above the second bear trend bar, or on bar 14, after the inside bar that acted as a breakout pullback. This was a higher low major trend reversal.

There was no pullback when the market broke above bar 10, indicating that the bulls were strong. You could have looked for a high 2 on the 1 minute chart to go long or waited for a 5 minute pause or pullback.

Bar 15 was not a good high 1 long because the move up was no longer a strong bull spike. It followed a small spike and climax bull move that reversed down from a small trend channel line overshoot (dashed line), and it was likely to correct sideways to down for at least a couple of legs. Also, the signal bar was a strong bear trend bar, which was a sign of more two-sided trading. The first sign of the two-sided trading was the bear trend bar from four bars earlier, and the five bars before bar 15 had some overlap and prominent tails.

Bar 16 was a high 2 long on the breakout above the small inside bar, which allowed for a tight stop.

FIGURE 18.3   First-Hour Double Top

As shown in Figure 18.3, in the first hour, the market often forms a double top or bottom that becomes an extreme of the day or of at least the next few hours. AAPL closed yesterday with a tight trading range, which could have been a setup for a final flag. On bar 3, the first bar of the day, AAPL quickly broke below the bull flag from yesterday's close and then broke out of the top, forming a small wedge bull flag breakout. However, this breakout also failed, and it reversed back down on the next bar. Although this two-bar reversal at bar 4 was a decent final flag short entry, the momentum up was strong and the original failed breakout through the downside meant that it might have been better to wait for more price action before shorting. At this point, a failed flag breakout after a failed downside breakout and a reversal of yesterday's high made the bear case more likely.

Bar 5 came at the end of a barbwire pattern that trapped bulls into buying a high 2, and was a great short entry at one tick below the low of the high 2 signal bar (the prior bar). This bar trapped the bulls long and it then forced them out. The market could have found support at the moving average and within the bull flag between bars 2 and 3, so traders were cautious about their shorts. Any area of overlapping bars, especially when they are large and when the tight trading range has multiple reversals, is an area of strong two-sided trading. Bulls will short

Figure 18.3

PATTERNS RELATED TO YESTERDAY   **365**

below and not buy above, and bears will short above and not below. The result is that breakouts tend to get pulled back into the range, as they were after the bear breakouts at bars 3, 9, and 11 and the bull breakouts at bars 4 and 7.

Bar 6 was a signal to reverse to long, because it was a failed breakout, a second leg down to the moving average in a bull trend (most bars were above a rising moving average), a two-bar reversal, and a bull bar on a pullback to the moving average.

Note that the sell-off to bar 6 broke a trend line, indicating that the bears were willing to become aggressive, so traders were prepared for a failed test of the bar 4 top of the bull trend.

Bar 7 was a reversal bar that failed in its breakout to a new high. It was the second failed attempt to break out above yesterday's high (bar 4 was the first), and it created a wedge top and a higher high major trend reversal. Since the range of the day so far had been only about half of that of a typical recent day, there was a good chance that a breakout in either direction would double the range and likely have at least two legs (the trend traders would probably be confident enough to make at least a second push down after any pullback). Bar 7 was the second failed attempt to break out above yesterday's high, and when the market tries to do something twice and fails, it usually tries to go in the opposite direction. The bar 7 double top (and third push up in the bull trend) was the top of the day.

Many traders would have thought that the market became always-in short on the two strong bear trend bars that broke below the four-bar bull flag that followed bar 7. Some traders would have wanted more evidence.

Bar 9 broke below the bar 6 swing low, but not the low of the day. Since the range was still small and the market twice failed to get follow-through on the breakout above yesterday's high, the odds were very high that there would be at least one more push down to test the low of the day, which was a magnet and in very close proximity. The market was now within its magnetic field.

Bar 10 completed a barbwire pattern, but since everyone was confident of a second leg down and a test to a new low of the day, it offered a great low 2 short below the small inside bar. It was also a breakout pullback entry from the breakout below bar 6. Finally, since it was such a large breakout bar and it closed on its low, the traders who wanted more evidence that the market was in fact now always-in short were satisfied. There was a lot of confidence that the market would work lower, maybe to around a measured move down.

The barbwire pullback to bar 10 broke a minor bear trend line (not shown), so it might have been the correction that ended the first leg down, but the momentum down had been so strong that the bulls were not confident enough to buy aggressively yet. They needed more price action.

The break to the bar 11 new low of the day was essentially straight down, and therefore likely not the end of the move (traders will look for a second leg down to at least test the bar 11 low). Since it was a failed breakout of a bear trend channel line (the line began on the bar before bar 8), two legs up were likely first.

Bar 12 was a small double bottom pullback long setup after the small bar 11 double bottom, but in the absence of a prior good trend line break or a strong reversal bar, it would only be a scalp. Also, since a second leg down was likely and there was no evidence that the always-in trade had reversed back up, it would have been much wiser to focus on getting short again or adding to shorts than allowing yourself to be distracted by a small bull scalp after seven sideways bars with big tails.

Bar 13 was another low 2 opportunity for the bears, but the rally to the moving average broke a good bear trend line. This was a signal to both the bulls and the bears that the next reversal up from a new swing low had a good chance of having two legs up, if the reversal was strong enough. The low 2 short was a second entry, and it had a bear signal bar at the moving average, which increased the chance of success.

Bar 14 was another low 2 short and followed a reasonably strong two-bar bear spike down from bar 13.

Bar 15 was a two-bar reversal up from a break to a new low. It had a strong bull reversal bar off the new low after overshooting two bear trend channel lines. It was the second leg down (the channel after a small spike, which was the first leg down) from the first trend line breakout pullback to bar 13 and a breakout test of the bar 1 lowest high of yesterday. Some traders saw it as a double bottom buy setup, and others saw it as a higher low after a strong rally to bar 7. It was the second leg down from the high of the day and the bottom of a large wedge bull flag where bars 3 and 11 were the first two pushes down. All of these were signs of strength and increased the odds that the rally would have two legs. The second leg ended at bar 16, which broke above the high of the first leg and reversed. It failed to break above the bar 14 high, forming a double top bear flag with bar 14. It was also the bottom of a parabolic channel that followed the bear spike down from bar 13. Other traders saw the two bear trend bars before the bar 8 low as the more important spike, and their channel down began at bar 10. Some traders saw bar 10 as a spike and the move down from bar 13 as the channel. Some traders thought that the bear trend bar after bar 4 or the bar 5 bear trend bar were important spikes. They saw bar 7 as a higher high breakout pullback. The reality was that each of those bear trend bars represented selling pressure, which is cumulative. Once it reached enough critical mass to overwhelm the bulls, the market went down.

Incidentally, when there is a strong move up that ends in three pushes and then sells off with less momentum (shallower slope, smaller trend bars, more tails), the odds are good that the high of the three pushes will be exceeded before long because this bottom is likely a higher time frame higher low. The market fulfilled its objective on the open of the next day. If the market continues up, the next target would be a measured move up from the double bottom.

Figure 18.4   PATTERNS RELATED TO YESTERDAY   **367**

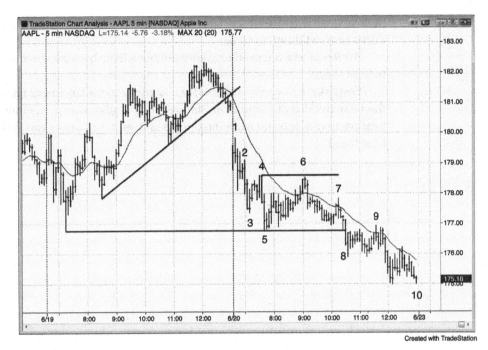

FIGURE 18.4 Breakout from Yesterday's Pattern

As shown in Figure 18.4, the first bar of the day is often a breakout of a channel from yesterday. Yesterday was a bull trending trading range day and a spike and channel bull trend that had three pushes up. The market broke below the channel on the close, and it broke further below on the gap opening. Bar 1 was a breakout pullback short, and it could have been the start of a bear trend from the open.

Bar 3 tried to form a failed breakout opening reversal, but the move down was steep and in a channel. This made bar 3 a risky buy, despite the small three pushes down on the day. When the move down is in a tight channel, it is safer to wait to buy until there is a breakout and then a pullback.

Bar 5 was a lower low breakout pullback, and it tried to form a double bottom with yesterday's low (to the penny). It led to a small wedge rally that formed a double top bear flag at bar 6.

A double top bear flag is a common setup after an initial down move off the open, especially in stocks, and is often followed by a protracted bear trend that is frequently a trending trading range bear. The bar 6 signal bar was a moving average gap bar.

Bar 7 was a breakout pullback short even though the breakout of the low of the day had not yet developed. Close enough. It was also a failed double bottom pullback and a successful double top pullback setup, and a failed breakout of the micro channel down from bar 6.

Bar 9 was a two-legged breakout pullback from breaking below yesterday's and today's lows.

Yesterday's daylong bull trend was actually just a large bear flag, and today was the bear trend that came from its breakout. Today was a trending trading range bear trend day, a trend from the open bear trend day, and a gap spike and channel bear trend.

Figure 18.5   PATTERNS RELATED TO YESTERDAY   **369**

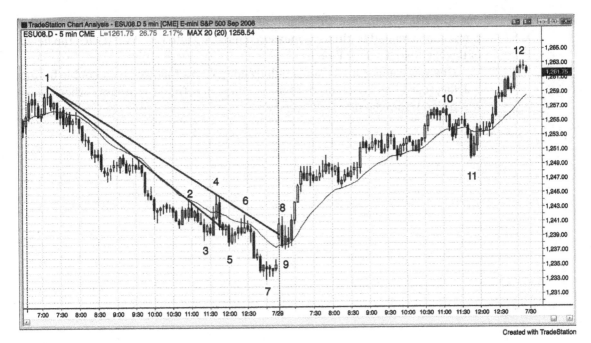

FIGURE 18.5   A Bear Channel Is a Bull Flag

A bear channel is a bull flag, and a breakout above it on the open is often followed by a breakout pullback buy signal. As shown in Figure 18.5, yesterday was a strong bear trend day, but bar 4 broke above a major trend line, indicating that the market might try to reverse after a test of the bar 3 low (usually a two-legged drop). Instead, the market sold off in two legs into the close.

Bar 8 broke above the new, flatter major trend line generated by the bar 4 rally and then had a small two-legged breakout pullback at the moving average at bar 9 (two bear trend bars separated by a bull trend bar). This breakout pullback, which was a higher low major trend reversal, led to a trend from the open bull trend day. When the first 5 to 10 bars form a sideways range, many institutions enter on the breakout of the range, and this breakout often leads to a trend day. There is less risk entering earlier, like above the moving average test bar in this case.

Bar 10 was the third push up (three trending trading ranges), so a two-legged pullback was expected. However, the channel up to bar 10 was tight, so the breakout and two-legged sell-off below the channel were likely to be followed by a test of the high.

Bar 11 tested the low of the prior trading range and was an 11:45 a.m. PST sharp move down to trap bulls out of the market. It formed a moving average gap bar long that was also a high 2, and this final bull leg broke out of the top of the third trading range and extended to almost a measured move up into the close (twice the height of the bar 10 to bar 11 sell-off).

This was a spike and channel bull trend that was followed by a double bottom bull flag (bar 11 and the bottom of the trading range from two hours earlier), and it was a trend from the open bull trend day.

Figure 18.6

PATTERNS RELATED TO YESTERDAY   **371**

FIGURE 18.6   Yesterday's Patterns Are Important

Patterns from the prior day almost always influence the first hour. Looking at Figure 18.6, don't worry about the tiny bars in this chart and instead focus on the concepts.

Bar 1 was a sharp pullback to test yesterday's strong close, and it quickly reversed up, creating a buy entry at one tick above the high of the bar 1 pullback and again above the high of the first bar of the day.

Bar 4 was a breakout pullback short setup. The open generated a lower low after the bar 3 lower high, major trend reversal and bar 4 set up a low 2 short.

Bar 5 was an opening reversal that followed the lower low major trend reversal test of the bear low that formed yesterday after the bear trend line break. Today opened up and traded down to test that lower low. The breakout pullback entry above bar 5 was effectively a high 2 since bar 5 was the second leg down (yesterday's close was the first leg) and a small double bottom with both the final bar of yesterday and with the low that formed earlier that day.

The small bar 6 lower high and then trend line break resulted in a breakout pullback short. The first bar of the day tested below the trend line and reversed up, but the move up failed at bar 6.

Bar 7 was a wedge long setup (a failed breakout below the bear trend channel line and below yesterday's low), and the wedge followed a break of a major bear trend line. It was a reversal up from the breakout below the small trend channel line.

Bar 8 was a breakout pullback from the break above the trend line going into yesterday's close. That bear channel was a bear flag, so bar 8 was a setup for a breakout pullback long. It was also the end of a large two-legged pullback after the strong rally on yesterday's open. The easiest entry after the bar 8 breakout pullback higher low was the high 2 at bar 9.

CHAPTER 19

Opening Patterns
and Reversals

Institutional traders have orders to fill before the day opens, and they want to fill them at the best possible price. For example, if they have mostly buy orders and the market opens with a large gap down, they will buy immediately if they feel that the lower open represents a great value that won't last long. If they believe that the market will trade down a little, then they will wait to buy lower. If the market instead opens with a gap up, they might decide that the market should pull back. If that is their belief, there is no incentive for them to buy now because they expect that they will soon be able to buy lower. This creates a sell vacuum, and the market can move down quickly since the institutional bulls are simply waiting to buy at a more favorable price. Invariably, they will wait until the market reaches a support level like the moving average, a trend line, a measured move, or a swing high or low. If enough institutions have order imbalances to the buy side and if they all begin their buying at around the same level, the sharp sell-off can reverse up strongly. The sell-off wasn't as much due to strong bears as it was due to strong bulls who were simply waiting for the market to fall to a support level, whereupon they bought relentlessly and overwhelmed the bears. This is the vacuum effect; the market got sucked down quickly to a level where there were lots of strong buyers waiting.

The opposite happens on days when the institutions have a lot of sell orders going into the open. There will often be a buy vacuum that sucks the market up quickly and then suddenly the bears appear and drive the market down hard. They were bearish from the open, but if they believed that the market was going to trade up to some resistance level, they would refrain from shorting until the market reached the point where they thought that it would not go higher. It does not make sense for them to short if they think the market will go a little higher. At that point, they begin shorting and they overwhelm the bulls. The result is an opening reversal down.

These sharp reversals up and down are opening reversals and often become either the high or the low of the day. If traders understand what is going on and do not get tricked into believing that all sharp moves are just spikes that will be followed by channels, they will be ready to swing trade on the reversal and sometimes can hold part of their position for most of the day.

Although most days have an opening reversal or trend from the open where there is a 50 to 60 percent chance of making at least twice the size of the risk, beginners struggle to determine which of the often several setups is that best one. The exact probabilities of any setup cannot be known with a high degree of certainty because there are so many variables, and this is especially true of setups in the opening range, but the ones that I am using are reasonable guidelines. On most days, there are several reasonable reversals in the opening range, but they have only about a 30 percent chance of leading to a swing trade where the reward is at least twice as large as the risk (although many have about a 60 percent chance of making a reward that is as large as the risk). Also, the earliest is sometimes the best one, but the several reversals that follow often pull back beyond the entry price and scare beginners out of their positions. Beginners can either take one that they feel is strong and then simply rely on their protective stops and allow for pullbacks, waiting for the ultimate breakout, or they can scalp for a reward that is equal to their risk and then trade in the opposite direction if the next reversal setup looks good. Most traders have a better chance of becoming profitable if they take what they believe is a good setup, rely on their protective stops, and allow the pullbacks, exiting only if a strong signal in the opposite direction forms.

The first bar of the day has about a 20 percent chance of being either the high or the low of the day for all markets. If it is a strong trend bar without big tails, it has a 30 percent chance. Either the high or the low forms within the first five bars or so in 50 percent of days, and it forms within the first hour or two in 90 percent of days. Even though most reversals do not lead to a profit that is at least twice as large as the risk, if a trader held them for a swing, most would end up as scalps. The profits from the winning trades are usually at least as large as the losses from the losing trades, and the occasional big winner makes this approach worthwhile. Alternatively, a trader can simply look to scalp for a reward that is at least as large as the risk. The high of the day usually comes from some kind of double top, even though the two highs are often not at the same price, and the low of the day usually comes from a double bottom. In general, if the day is having reversals, a trader should wait until there is a double top or bottom before looking for a swing trade. Once one forms, it has about a 40 to 50 percent chance of leading to a swing, depending on the context and the setup, and an extreme of the day.

Most traders should work hard to become experts at spotting and trading the best opening reversals, and make these swing trades the cornerstone of their trading. For example, when the average range in the Emini is about 10 to 15 points, the probability of a four-point swing on a reasonably good-looking opening reversal (one where the context is good and there is a decent signal bar) is often only about 40 percent (it can be 50 to 60 percent when the setup is very strong). However, the chance of a two-point stop being hit before either the profit target is reached or a reversal signal develops, where the trader can exit with a smaller loss or a small profit, is often only about 30 percent. This makes the trader's equation very favorable for this type of trade. If traders win four points in four out of 10 trades, they have 16 points of profit off of their swing trades. If they then have maybe three losses of two points or less and three wins of about one to three points, they will end up about breakeven on those trades. This is fairly typical when a trader picks appropriate setups. The trader then has about 16 points of profit on 10 trades, and averages 1.6 points of profit per trade, which is good for a day trader.

When there is not a reversal, the spike in fact can be followed by a channel and the day can become a spike and channel trend day. If there is a reversal, but it lasts for only a few bars and then reverses back in the direction of the spike, the reversal attempt has failed and has become a breakout pullback setup that will usually be followed by some type of channel. For example, if the market rallies up strongly on the first three bars of the day but then has a bear reversal bar, many traders will reverse to short below that bar. However, if the spike is strong and the reversal bar is weak, more traders will assume that the reversal attempt will fail. They will place buy stop orders above the high of the prior bar in any pullback, including the high of the bear reversal bar if there is no pullback. If the market trades up, the small sell-off becomes a breakout pullback and the reversal attempt will have failed. Some bulls will place buy limit orders at and below the reversal bar if they are especially confident of the strength of the up move.

The open always leads to a breakout or a reversal, and sometimes to both. Other than gap openings, common patterns on the open are the same as patterns occurring at any other time of the day and include:

- Trends from the open, which were discussed in Part I in the first book.
- Breakouts and reversals, which are failed breakouts. Look for reversals at support or resistance areas like the moving average, trend lines, trend channel lines, swing highs and lows (especially the high and low of yesterday), breakout areas, trading range tops and bottoms, and measured move targets.
- Breakout pullbacks (a failed breakout that failed to reverse the market).

On most days, either the high or low of the day is formed within the first hour or so. Once one of the day's extremes is formed, the market reverses toward what will become the other extreme of the day. Obviously, there is no reversal on a trend from the open day, but the market still works toward the other extreme, which will usually be near the close of the day. The opening reversal is often recognizable and can be a great trading opportunity for a swing trade. The first move on the open is often fast and covers many points, and it is hard to believe that it could suddenly reverse direction, but this is a common occurrence. The turn is usually at some key point like a test of the high or low of yesterday, a swing high or low of yesterday or today, a breakout of a trading range of yesterday or today, a trend line or trend channel line, a moving average, or any of the above on a different time frame chart or on the Globex chart. Even if the best setup is on a 60 minute or daily chart, there will almost always be a price action reason to take the trade based entirely on the 5 minute day session chart, so traders adept at chart reading only need to watch the one chart that they are using for trading.

The initial price action often reveals the character of the day. If the first bar is a doji bar in the middle of yesterday's closing range, then the bar is a one-bar trading range, and the odds of a trading range day are increased. If the first hour has many overlapping bars with big tails and multiple reversals, the odds of a trading range day are also increased. In contrast, if there is a gap up or down and then a three- or four-bar bear spike within the first hour and the trend bars are large with little overlap and only small tails, the odds of a bear trend day increase. Traders often look for a pair of consecutive bull trend bars in the first hour or so. If they are present, traders would see them as a sign that the market is always-in long, at least for a scalp. This means that they think that the market might be in the early stages of a bull trend. Until there is enough follow-through for traders to believe that a measured move of some kind is likely, many traders will scalp most or all of their position. This leads to the many reversals that are common in the first hour or so. If instead there were consecutive strong bear trend bars, they would assume that the market was always-in short and that the day was trying to become a bear trend day. For example, if there have been consecutive strong bear trend bars and then a bar trades above the high of the prior bar, many traders will short below the low of that pullback bar for a scalp. If the context is right, they might think that the pullback is the start of a large trend and they will swing most or all of their trade.

The opening range often gives clues to how the day will unfold, provides support and resistance for the rest of the day, and leads to measured move projections. There are almost always several choices for the top and bottom of the opening range, so there will rarely ever be perfect agreement as to the exact bars that contain it or the length of time that it takes to form. In general, it is the height of either the trading range, if there is one, or the largest leg of the first 30 to 90 minutes. Sometimes the leg will have two or three smaller legs within it, and sometimes there will be a pullback and then a brief higher high or low or lower high or low.

If there is that new extreme, some traders will use that to enlarge the opening range, and others will continue to use the original range and will view the new extreme as a meaningless overshoot.

It is helpful to classify the size of the opening range into three categories. If the range is only about 25 percent of the size of the range of recent days, traders will enter on a breakout of the range in either direction. A couple of times a month, this will become a trend from the open day with small pullbacks and relentless progression.

If the opening range is about a third to a half the size of the range of recent days, traders will assume that the range will grow to about the size of an average day. The day will usually have some trading range activity and then break out up or down. About two-thirds of the time it will become a trend day, which will usually be a trending trading range day, although any type of trend day is possible. The breakout will typically reach about a measured move based on the height of the opening range. It will usually come back and test the breakout point later in the day, and it often then breaks back into the earlier range. If the reversal back into the opening range is strong and the market closes at the opposite side of that earlier range, the day becomes a reversal day. This is in fact the most common way that reversal days form. In the other third of cases, the day just trades a little beyond the opening range, then reverses and breaks out of the opposite side of the range, and then trades back into the range. When this happens, the day usually becomes a small trading range day, but sometimes that second breakout can lead to a trending trading range day in the opposite direction.

The third possibility is when the opening move is large. This is usually due to a strong spike and the day often becomes a spike and channel trend day, but sometimes it leads to a climactic reversal, usually after a small final flag.

An important point to recognize is that if the market makes a strong move on the open and then reverses, that initial strong move indicates strength, and it may return later in the day. For example, if the market sells off strongly for the first four bars of the day and then reverses up into a strong bull trend, you should remember the initial bear trend and not assume that the bulls will control the market until the close. That initial downside strength indicates that bears were willing to aggressively short the market earlier in the day and may look for another opportunity later in the day, despite the bull trend. So if there is a strong correction in the bull trend, do not ignore the possibility that it could be another trend change taking place, this time back to a bear trend.

The patterns in the first hour are the same as those later in the day, but the reversals are often more violent and the trends tend to last longer. An important key to maximizing trading profits is to swing part of any position that could be a high or a low of the day. If the trade looks particularly strong, swing all of the position and take partial profits on a third to a half after the trade has run one to two times your initial risk. If you bought what you think could be the low of the day and your initial stop was below the signal bar, which was about three points below your entry price, take about a quarter to half off at around two to four points and maybe another quarter to half off at four to six points. Alternatively, instead of using fixed limit orders, take some off at the first pause after two points of profit and some more off at the first pause after four points. Hold the remaining contracts until there is a clear and strong opposite signal or until your breakeven stop is hit. Look to add to your position at every with-trend setup, like a two-legged pullback to the moving average in a strong trend. For these additional contracts, scalp most or all of the position, but continue to swing some contracts.

Some reversals start quietly, trend only slightly for many bars, and appear to be just another flag in the old trend, but then the market forcefully breaks into an opposite trend. For example, a bear flag can break out to the upside and the market could reverse into a bull trend. Other reversals have strong momentum from the entry bar. Be open to all possibilities and try to take every signal, especially if it is strong. One of the difficulties is that reversals often are sharp and traders might not have enough time to convince themselves that a reversal setup could actually lead to a reversal. However, if there is a strong trend bar for the signal bar, the chances of success are good and you must take the trade. If you feel like you need more time to assess the setup, at least take a half or a quarter position because the trade might suddenly move very far very fast and you need to be involved, even if in only a small way. Then look to add on at the first pullback.

Unlike a double bottom pullback that is a reversal pattern, a double bottom bull flag is a continuation pattern that develops after the bull trend has already begun. Functionally, it is the same as a double bottom pullback, since both are buy setups.

The same is true for a double top bear flag, which is a continuation pattern in an ongoing bear trend and not a reversal pattern, like the double top pullback. Both, however, are short setups. After a strong down move and a pullback, the bear trend resumes, and then the market pulls back again to about the same level as the first pullback. This trading range is a double top bear flag, and it is a short entry setup. More often than not, the second pullback will be slightly below the first, as would be expected in a bear trend (each swing high tends to be below the prior one). The entry is on a stop at one tick below the setup bar.

Sometimes the market forms a trading range in the first three to 10 bars or so, with two or more reversals. If the range is small compared to the average daily range, a breakout is likely. After the first bar, if there is both a reversal up and a reversal down, some traders will enter a breakout of this small range, looking for a measured move. Traders could enter on a breakout from the range, but the risk is smaller if they are able to fade small bars at the top or bottom of the range, or wait until after the breakout and enter on a failed breakout or a breakout pullback, just as they would with any trading range.

Figure 19.1   OPENING PATTERNS AND REVERSALS   **379**

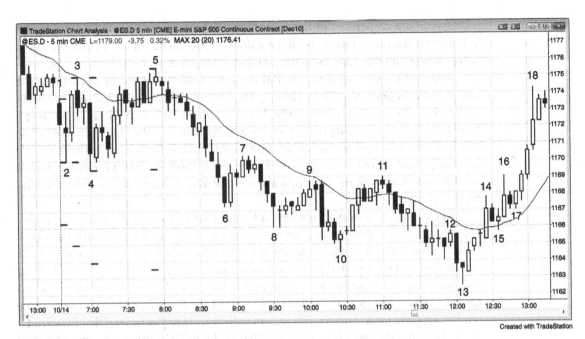

FIGURE 19.1   Measured Move after Breakout of Small Opening Range

When the opening range is about half the size of the range of recent days, the market usually has a breakout of the opening range and an attempt to approximately double it. Sometimes there are many choices for the opening range. Which one is right? They all usually are because different traders will make decisions based on different ones, but on the day shown in Figure 19.1 none led to a precise guide for profit taking or reversals. Most support levels, like measured move projections, do not lead to reversals, because the market has inertia and therefore a strong tendency to continue to do what it has been doing. This means that most reversal attempts fail. However, when the market finally reverses, it is always at a support level. If there is a strong reversal setup at a support level, it is more likely to lead to a profitable trade. By bar 5, the range of the day was still only about half the average range of recent days, so the odds favored a significant increase in the range. With each new reversal, the opening range expanded, but the sell-off down to bar 6 was strong, so the breakout was likely to lead to an approximate measured move down.

The day became a trending trading range day and broke back into the upper range at the end of the day, which is common. Here, the day closed near the top of the upper range and became a reversal day. Most reversal days begin as trending trading range days. If traders understand this, they can look to swing part of their trade off the reversal up from the bottom of the lower range.

Only about 25 percent of reversals in the first hour or so result in swings, so it is better to scalp until there is either a double bottom or top or a clear always-in setup, where the odds are good for a swing. Today was an ordinary day where the first many setups were only scalps. Bar 3 was a double top with bar 1 and therefore had about a 50 percent chance of being the high of the day. It was also a breakout pullback to the moving average. Bar 4 was a double bottom with bar 2 and had a 50 percent chance of being the low of the day. Neither was the high or low of today. The high or low occurs within the first couple of hours in 90 percent of the days, and it usually comes from some type of double top or bottom. Bar 5 formed a double top with bar 3, a small wedge top, and a moving average gap bar, and it became the high of the day.

When retail investors controlled a bigger part of the daily volume, they contributed more to opening gaps and reversals by placing orders before the open, based on the daily chart. For example, if there was a bull reversal bar, traders would see that after the close and place orders before the open to buy above the high of that bar. They were so afraid of missing the buy that they were willing to buy on the open, even if they bought above the high of the bar. This often resulted in the market gapping up to find enough sellers willing to take the other side of the trade. Once these overly eager buyers were filled at the inflated price, the market would trade down to where the institutions thought there was value. They then bought heavily, reversing the market up to a new high, creating the opening bull reversal. The small, brief sell-off on the open creates a tail on the bottom of the bull trend bar on the daily chart, which is common on bull trend days. The opposite happened after bear days where desperate longs were so eager to exit on the open that they were willing to sell the first trade of the day. The market often had to gap down to find enough buyers. Once their sell orders were filled, the market traded up to where institutions felt there was value in selling, and this reversed the market back down to a new low of the day, often creating a bear trend day.

Figure 19.2   OPENING PATTERNS AND REVERSALS   **381**

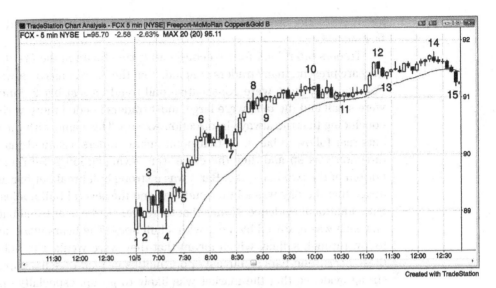

FIGURE 19.2   The Size of the Opening Range Is Important

As shown in Figure 19.2, the size of the opening range often gives a clue to what will happen later in the day. The opening range on this 5 minute chart of Freeport-McMoRan (FCX) was about a quarter of the average daily range of recent days. After several bars, when traders saw that the range might be small, most would have ignored the first bar and then looked for a spike up and a spike down. As soon as the market traded below bar 3, it became a spike up (a reversal down). Once the market traded above bar 4, it became a spike down (a reversal up). At that point, many traders treated those two spikes as a breakout mode setup and placed buy stops at one tick above the top spike and sell stops at one tick below the bottom spike. Once one order is filled, the other becomes the initial protective stop. If after entering, the market reverses direction, a trader will often double the size of the protective stop and plan to reverse the position if the stop is hit.

Traders can often enter before the breakout. Here, for example, there was a large gap up open (the steep moving average shows this) and a bull trend bar for the first bar, so there was a good chance of a bull trend day. Once bar 4 reversed up from a one-tick breakout below the bar 2 ii pattern, many traders went long above the bar 4 double bottom bull flag signal bar (remember, the low of the day often comes from a double bottom of some type). Others bought as soon as bar 5 went above the small bear inside bar, and others bought on the breakout above bar 3.

When the opening range is small like this, the pullbacks within that range are small; and when the day breaks out and trends, the pullbacks often remain small, as they did here. There is usually a pullback in the final couple of hours that is about twice the size of the earlier pullbacks, and that happened on the sell-off from bar 14.

Traders often look for two consecutive trend bars in the first hour, and when they are present, many traders conclude that the market has an always-in position. For example, there were consecutive bull trend bars at bar 2. Since their bodies were small and the tails were large, most traders needed more verification before concluding that the always-in direction was up. This came with the two bull trend bars that followed bar 4. At that point, many traders assumed that the always-in direction was up and they therefore were swinging longs with a stop below the bottom of the two-bar spike. Bar 5 was a strong bull breakout bar and further evidence that the day was a bull trend day, and the several bull bodies that followed gave additional evidence. Notice that there were three bear trend bars before bar 4 and each was followed by a bar with a bull body. The bears were unable to create follow-through selling, which meant that they were weak. The bulls saw each of those bear trend bars as buying opportunities instead of sell setups, and this was strong evidence that the market was likely to go up, especially on a day with a large gap up.

Figure 19.3   OPENING PATTERNS AND REVERSALS   **383**

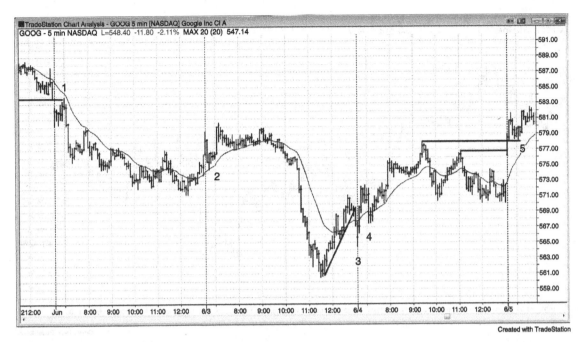

FIGURE 19.3 Breakout Pullbacks on the Open

As shown in Figure 19.3, Google (GOOG) had several breakout pullbacks on the opens of these four days. Bar 1 was a low 2 short at the steep moving average and closed the gap below yesterday's low by 6 cents, setting up a reversal down that formed the high of the day.

Bar 2 was a moving average pullback after breaking above a swing high from yesterday. The bull ii pattern was the setup for the long. The bar after the bar 2 bull bar formed a double top with the first bar of the day, and this was the high of the day.

Bar 3 was a reversal up (a failed breakout) from breaking the bull trend line from the rally into the prior day's close. Bar 4 was a higher low and an approximate double bottom with bar 3.

Bar 5 was a high 2 double bottom bull flag (the first bottom was two bars earlier) that also was the first pullback after the breakout above yesterday's high. This could have turned into a trend from the open day.

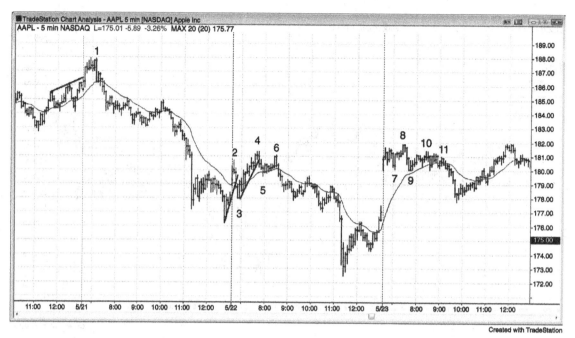

FIGURE 19.4   Early Failed Breakouts

As shown in Figure 19.4, Apple (AAPL) had several failed breakouts on the open during these three days, and they led to opening reversals. Bar 1 was a second entry (low 2) for an opening reversal off a trend channel line overshoot.

Bar 2 was a reversal down from a breakout (a failed breakout) above the trading range in the final hour of the prior day and of the bear trend line (not shown) going into the close of the prior day. The market then reversed up from the moving average, forming the bar 3 higher low, which was also a breakout pullback.

Bar 4 was a reversal down from a higher high on a day that was not yet a bull trend day, and therefore a good short. It also had a wedge shape and was the top of a channel after the gap spike up on the open.

Bar 6 was a lower high final flag reversal down after the bar 5 break below the bull channel. Traders expected a test of the bar 3 bottom of the channel.

Bar 7 was a high 2 breakout pullback in a day with a large gap up, but the market reversed back down at the bar 8 higher high and final flag breakout. Since this was not a bull trend day at this point, this was a good short.

Bar 9 was a new low, but it came with strong momentum, making a second leg down likely. The gap up was a bull spike, and the move from bar 8 to bar 9 was a bear spike. This was a climactic reversal setup and was followed by a trading range, as is often the case. During the trading range, both the bulls and the bears

Figure 19.4   OPENING PATTERNS AND REVERSALS   **385**

were adding to their positions in an attempt to get follow-through in the form of a channel. The bears won and the bulls had to sell out of their longs, adding to the selling pressure.

Bar 10 was a low 2 and a two-legged lower high.

Bar 11 was a second entry into the short based on a failed high 2 after the bar 10 lower high. The bulls made two attempts to reverse the bearish implications of the lower high and they failed twice. When the market tries to do something twice and it fails both times, it usually will go in the opposite direction.

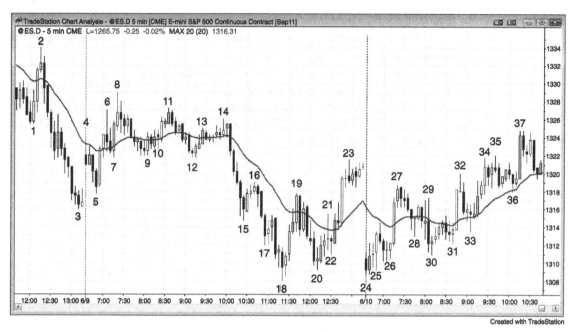

FIGURE 19.5 Both a Gap Down and a Gap Up Can Lead to an Opening Rally

As shown in Figure 19.5, bar 4 was a strong bear reversal bar and a moving average test in a strong bear trend, setting up a breakout pullback short for the breakout below bar 1. The gap up to the moving average was the pullback.

The move from bar 2 to bar 3 was a spike and channel bear trend, and bar 4 was a test near the top of the channel. The test is often followed by trading range price action. Also, the gap up broke above the steep bear trend line of the final hour of yesterday, and bulls were looking for a breakout pullback long setup. When there are reasonable arguments for both the bulls and the bears, there is uncertainty, and uncertainty usually means that the market is at the start of a trading range, as it was here.

Bar 5 was not a reversal bar, but was a breakout pullback from the break above yesterday's bear channel, and a high 2 variant (bar 4 was a bear bar, there was then a bull bar, and then a second small leg formed down to bar 5). This was a possible higher low after a climactic close, and after a climax (the strong bear into the close had virtually no pullbacks, and since it was likely not sustainable, it was therefore climactic) there is often a two-legged countertrend move. The bull trend bar that followed bar 5 was a two-bar reversal with both bar 5 and the bear bar before it, and with the move down from bar 4. Remember, a sharp move down followed by a sharp move up, like that bull trend bar, is a sell climax, which is a two-bar

Figure 19.5   OPENING PATTERNS AND REVERSALS   **387**

reversal on a higher time frame chart and a bull reversal bar on an even higher time frame chart.

Bar 8 was a wedge top and a two-legged move up from the bar 5 higher low.

The day was a trending trading range day, and the rally up from bar 20 tested the bottom of the earlier upper trading range.

Bar 24 was a double bottom bull flag. The first bottom was bar 20 or the inside signal bar following the bar 18 low. It was also a reversal up from a test of yesterday's low and a failed breakout of the large two-legged bear flag from bar 18 to bar 23.

Bar 25 was a strong outside up bar in the first 30 minutes of the day, so traders thought that the always-in position might have become long. They wanted any pullback to stay above the bar 25 low, and when bar 26 turned up, they thought that the low of the day could be in.

Bar 26 was a higher low and led to a breakout from an ii setup. The second bar of the ii pattern had a strong bull close, which increased the chances of a move up. It was also a failed low 2 in a bear flag, which trapped bears who saw the big gap down and shorted the second entry (low 2 gap pullback). This was a small final bear flag. It was a second attempt to reverse the attempt to move below yesterday's low and a second attempt to reverse back up after gapping below yesterday's two-legged bear flag.

FIGURE 19.6 Two-Legged Pullback after Gap Opening

A large gap down often has a two-legged pullback to the moving average and then a breakout into a bear trend, as seen in Figure 19.6.

Bars 2 and 3 formed a double top bear flag on a big gap down day (the gap was the flagpole), and a triangle with bar 1 (three tops and a contracting pattern is a triangle).

Bar 3 was the first bar of a two-bar reversal, and a low 2 short setup. It was safer to short below the bear bar that followed bar 3 rather than shorting below the bar 3 bull trend bar, because there was too much risk that the market might go sideways and then make another attempt to break out above the bars 1 and 2 double top. Shorting below a bear bar at the top of a trading range is more reliable than shorting below a bull trend bar.

Although most traders think of the opening range as lasting only an hour or two, the market often begins a trend around 8:30 a.m. PST, as it did here. Whether the bar 3 double top should be considered to be an opening reversal or just a double top is irrelevant. What is important is that a trend often begins or reverses around 8:30 a.m.

Figure 19.7   OPENING PATTERNS AND REVERSALS   **389**

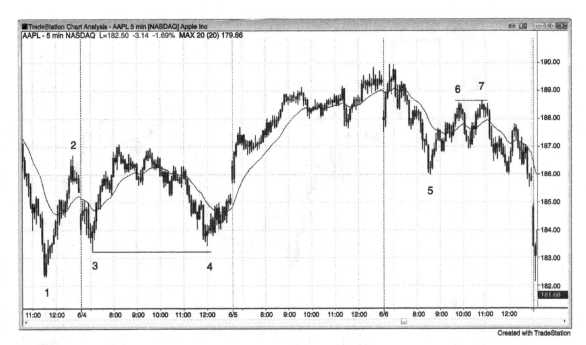

FIGURE 19.7 Double Bottom and Top Flags

As shown in Figure 19.7, double bottom bull flags and double top bear flags are common. Bars 3 and 4 formed a large double bottom bull flag after the rally to bar 2. Bars 6 and 7 formed a double top bear flag after the strong move down to bar 5.

FIGURE 19.8 Two Failed Attempts and Then a Reversal

When the market tries to break out to the upside twice and fails, it usually will then try to break out of the bottom. As shown in Figure 19.8, GOOG went sideways in a small trading range into a 7:00 a.m. PST report and was therefore in breakout mode. Since there were three tops in a convergent trading range, it was a triangle. A trader could have entered on a stop below the trading range low, but it was less risky to short the low 2 below bar 5. This was a low 2 because bars 3 and 5 were two legs up. Since the day was in a trading range at this point, both a high 2 and a low 2 could coexist, as they did here. The high 2 long failed and became a low 2 short. Since the trading range was below the moving average, it was a bear flag and therefore likely to have a downside breakout.

Bar 2 was the second consecutive bear trend bar, and both bars had large bodies and small tails. This led traders to think that the always-in direction was down and that any pullback would set up a short that was likely good for at least a scalp. The low 2 short entry below bar 5 was the first opportunity, and it is clear from the large bear entry bar and follow-through bar that most traders believed that the sell-off was going to extend far enough for a swing, and not just become a scalp and a reversal up. Bar 5 was a double top with bar 3 and led to a swing short.

It does not matter whether a trader calls the double bottom an opening reversal or thinks that it occurred too late in the day to be thought of as part of the opening range. However, the trader needs to be aware that the market often reverses around 8:30 a.m. PST, and be prepared to take the trade.

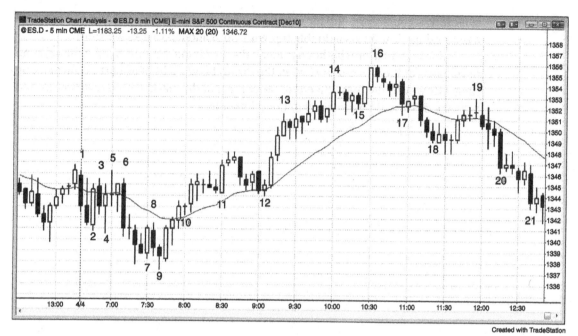

FIGURE 19.9 Barbwire on the Open

As shown in Figure 19.9, some days open with a flat moving average, big overlapping bars, and just no safe setups (no small bars near the top or bottom where a fade trade could be placed). This is barbwire and should be traded like all barbwire; it requires patience. Wait for one side to be trapped with a trend bar breakout and then look to fade the breakout. Because breakouts from barbwire usually fail, barbwire is often a final flag. Here, the breakout fell below the low of yesterday. The market often reverses a breakout of the high or low of the prior day. This tendency increased the odds that the barbwire would become a final flag. The pattern had three pushes up and was sideways. Some traders saw it as a triangle, which is easier to visualize if you use only the bodies of the bars.

Bar 7 was a reversal up after a breakout of the bottom of the barbwire, but it followed four bear trend bars. That was enough bear strength for traders to wait for a second buy signal. Even though some traders saw it as a high 2 where the high 1 was the high of bar 6, bar 6 was a strong outside down bar, and most traders considered it to be the start of the down move. It was the bar when traders thought that the market might be breaking out of a trading range and into a trend, and they expected at least a second leg down after the outside down bull trap bar. This made most traders see bar 7 as a high 1 since the down move began at the top of bar 6 and not at the top of bar 5.

Figure 19.9   OPENING PATTERNS AND REVERSALS   **393**

Bar 7 broke a micro trend line and then bar 9 was a lower low breakout pullback buy setup. Its close was above its midpoint, which is the minimum requirement for a reversal bar. At this point, the price action was mostly two-sided with many reversals and prominent tails, so a second-entry long at a new low of the day did not even need a reversal bar.

The long above bar 9 was a second reversal attempt of the earlier low of the day and of yesterday's low. The market then trended up through the other side of the opening range and gave a high 2 breakout pullback long at bar 12. Bar 12 was a bull reversal bar at the moving average, which was a strong buy signal at the end of a bull flag. The market became always-in long for many traders on the strong bull trend bar that followed bar 9, and other traders became convinced that it was always-in long on the strong bull trend bar breakout above bar 10 and again on the bar 11 strong bull trend bar that broke out of a high 2 buy setup.

CHAPTER 20

Gap Openings: Reversals and Continuations

A gap opening on any time frame means that once the bar in question closes, it does not overlap the bar before it. On most days, there are gap openings on the 5 minute chart. They can be thought of as simple breakouts since the market broke out of the final bar of the prior day. They should be traded like any other breakout except traders know that large gaps increase the chance that the day will become a trend day. The larger the gap, the more likely the day will be a trend day and the more likely the gap will function as a spike and be followed by a trending channel in the same direction. For example, a large gap up has perhaps a 50 percent chance of being followed by a bull channel, a 20 percent chance of being followed by a trading range, and a 30 percent chance of being followed by a bear trend. These probabilities are only guidelines because using computer testing to find exact numbers is subject to too many variables. How big does a gap have to be to be thought of as large? How much of a rally after the gap up constitutes a channel instead of just a slightly upward-sloping trading range? How much of a sell-off constitutes a reversal compared to just a deep pullback? As another guideline, if the gap is the largest gap of the past five days or so, or if it is larger than about half of the average daily range, it can be considered to be a large gap.

A large gap opening on the 5 minute chart from yesterday's close represents extreme behavior and often results in a trend day in either direction. It does not matter whether there is also a gap on the daily chart, since the trading will be the same. The only thing that matters is how the market responds to this relatively extreme behavior—will it accept it or reject it? The larger a gap is, the more likely it will be the start of a trend day away from yesterday's close. The size, direction, and number of trend bars in the first few bars of the day often reveal the direction of the trend day that is likely to follow. Sometimes the market will trend from the opening bar or two, but more commonly it will test in the wrong direction and then reverse into a trend that will last all day. Whenever you see a large gap opening, it is wise to assume that there will be a strong trend. However, sometimes it might take an hour to begin, and the trend often begins with a two-legged countertrend move, like a two-legged pullback to the moving average or a double bottom or top. Sometimes it has a third push and forms a wedge flag. Make sure to swing part of every trade, even if you get stopped out of your swing portion on a few trades. One good swing trade can be as profitable as 10 scalps, so don't give up until it is clear that the day will not trend.

The gap should be looked at as if it is one huge, invisible trend bar. For example, if there is a large gap up and it is followed by a minor pullback and then a channel type of rally for the rest of the day, this is likely a gap spike and channel bull trend, with the gap being the spike. For the Emini, you can look at the S&P cash index and see that the first bar of the day is a large trend bar, and it corresponds to the gap on the Emini.

Trade the open like any other open and look for a trend from the open, a failed breakout (a reversal), or a breakout pullback. The only difference from other days is that you should look to swing more aggressively; and if the day begins to trend, look for pullbacks where you can add onto your position. You should always look to take partial profits along the way, which can be scalps, but as long as the trend is strong, keep looking to take more entries in the direction of the trend.

Just because there is an increased chance of a trend day does not mean that there will be a trend day. Most big gap days have some trading range behavior for the first five to 10 bars as the bulls and bears fight over the direction of the trend, and some continue as trading range days all day long. Be open to all possibilities, and don't get locked into a belief. Your job is to follow the market. You have no ability to influence it and certainly zero chance of telepathically making it go in the direction that you want. If you are wrong, get out and stop hoping that the market will do the low-probability thing and suddenly go your way. If there is a big gap but the price action is unclear, assume that the market is forming a trading range and look to buy low and sell high. There might be several scalps before there is a setup that has a good chance of leading to a swing.

Figure 20.1

GAP OPENINGS: REVERSALS AND CONTINUATIONS   **397**

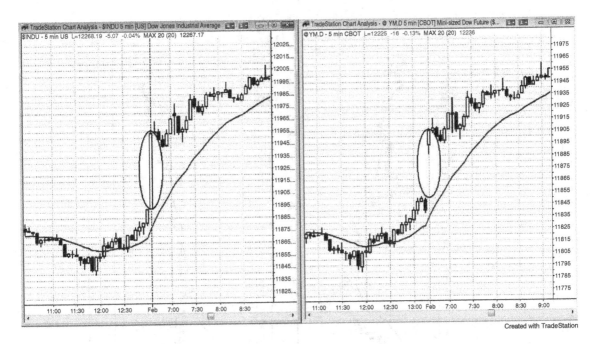

FIGURE 20.1   A Gap Is Just a Spike

As shown in Figure 20.1, a gap opening on a 5 minute chart is just another form of a breakout and a spike. The Dow Futures contract gapped up on the open on the chart on the right, but that gap on the Dow Jones Industrial Average cash index on the left was just a large bull trend bar.

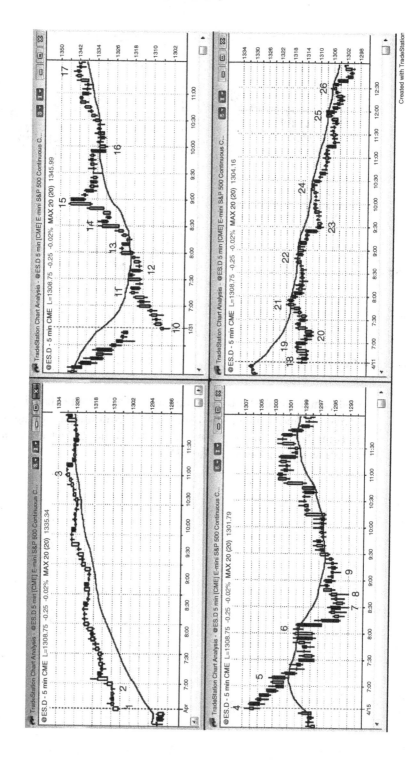

FIGURE 20.2 A Gap Can Lead to a Trend Up or Down

Figure 20.2   GAP OPENINGS: REVERSALS AND CONTINUATIONS   **399**

A big gap opening increases the odds that the day will be a trend day (the trend can be up or down), but it still can become a trading range day. As shown in the lower right-hand chart in Figure 20.2, the sideways move from bar 18 to bar 22 is an example of several hours of sideways movement after a large gap.

The larger the gap, the more likely the day will be a trend day in the direction of the gap. For example, bar 1 in the upper left-hand chart was a large gap up and the day became a bull trend day.

The two charts on the left show large gap up openings; the upper became a bull trend and the lower became a bear trend. The two charts on the right were gap down openings; the upper chart became a bull trend and the lower chart became a bear trend.

Bar 1 was bull trend bar on a large gap up day. The day became a trend from the open, gap spike and channel bull trend.

Bar 4 was a doji, but it had a bull body. The market trended down for a couple of hours. The price action down to the bar 7 low of the day had prominent tails, overlapping bars, and several bull trend bars, all indicating two-sided price action. The bulls were able to consistently create some buying pressure and controlled the market in the second half of the day.

Bar 10 was a bull trend bar on a large gap down day, and the day became a trend from the open bull trend day.

Bar 18 was a doji bar on a large gap down day. The market continued the sideways price action until the market broke to the downside on the bar 23 bear spike. The opening doji was a sign of two-sided trading, which continued for several hours. After the bear spike, the day became a bear trend day, and the shorts overwhelmed the longs on moving average tests at bars 24, 25, and 26. Although the shorts were strong at the bars 21 and 22 moving average tests, they were not yet strong enough to break the market out of the trading range and into a bear trend.

When there is a large gap up or down and no strong reversal, the trader's equation can be strong for the with-trend traders. For example, when the market had the large gap up at bar 1 and it then went sideways, the odds of a bull trend day went up, maybe to 60 percent or higher. Traders expected the range to reach about average for recent days, which was about 20 points. The odds of the market going 20 points higher before closing the gap were probably 60 percent or better, and therefore traders who bought during those first several bars were risking about 10 points to make about 15 to 20 points, and they had a 60 percent chance of success, which is a great trade. They probably could have risked to a move below the middle of the gap, so their risk might have been six points instead of 10. In any case, this excellent math is why large gap openings can offer great trades.

Putting It All Together

Price action is simply a manifestation of human nature and therefore is genetically based. It does not matter what market, time frame, or type of chart a trader studies, because they all are a representation of the behavior of our species. This Part IV gives detailed examples of price action trading on multiple time frames and in different markets, including the options market. It also discusses the best trades that traders should try to trade, especially beginners who are starting out and not yet profitable. Finally, it provides general guidelines that traders should consider as they decide which trades to take and how to manage their trades.

CHAPTER 21

Detailed Day Trading Examples

T his chapter provides many detailed examples of reasonable day trades that incorporate the fundamental ideas from all three books.

FIGURE 21.1 T-Note 10,000-Share Chart

Figure 21.1 is a 10-Year U.S. Treasury Note Futures chart based on 10,000 shares per bar. Each bar closed as soon as the volume in the bar passed 10,000 contracts. Since the final trade in each bar can have any number of contracts, most of the bars have more than 10,000 contracts instead of exactly 10,000 contracts. The bars are not based on time, so some bars might take a few seconds to form, while others may take more than 10 minutes to surpass 10,000 contracts.

Bars 3, 4, and 5 were shorts on tests of the moving average in a bear trend.

Bar 6 was a second-entry bear trend channel line overshoot and reversal up, but the signal bar was weak (a small doji). However, the rally from the bar 6 wedge reversal broke the trend line, setting up a long on a test of the low.

Bar 7 was a two-legged higher low, but it was a doji, which is a sign of two-sided trading and not of strong buying, and it followed two strong bear trend bars. Although this was a minimally acceptable buy setup, it would have been better to wait for a stronger signal. If you took it, you would have exited below bar 8 because that was a low 2 short setup at the moving average and it had a bear body. That is a strong sell signal, and countertrend traders should have exited and possibly even reversed on any second attempt by the bears to resume the trend. Countertrend traders trying to buy in a bear trend should always exit on a low 2 signal, unless the trend has clearly already reversed and the low 2 setup is likely to fail. Bar 11 is an example of this.

Figure 21.1   DETAILED DAY TRADING EXAMPLES   **405**

Bar 9 was a lower low major trend reversal and breakout pullback from the breakout of the wedge bottom that ended at bar 6, and a buy setup for a possible strong trend reversal. It was also a bear trend channel overshoot and reversal, and it was a bull reversal bar and a two-bar reversal. The trading range from bar 6 to bar 9 was a tight channel and became the final flag of the bear trend. Also, it was a reversal from a larger wedge channel following the spike down to bar 2. The channel of a spike and channel bear often ends with three pushes and it did here (bars 2, 6, and 9).

Bar 10 was a breakout above an inside bar that ended the first tiny pullback (bear trend bar), so traders could have gone long above it or added to their longs from above bar 9. After the spike and channel bear (bar 2 ended the spike) and the three pushes down (bars 2, 6, and 9 ended them), it was likely that a protracted two-legged up move would develop, so the bar 10 pause was likely to just be part of the first leg up and not the start of the second leg up. After a bear channel that lasted 20 or 30 bars, the correction was likely to have at least half as many bars as a general rule. If the correction is too small, bears will be hesitant to short and bulls would continue to buy because they would suspect that the correction needed more bars for clarity. Both needed to see if the market was reversing, and the four-bar bull spike up from bar 10 was strong evidence that it was. The bear spike and channel formation was likely to retrace to around the bar 3 start of the channel, which it did. Longs often take profits there. This is the area where some started to scale in, and once the market gets back to their very first entry, they often exit their entire position. They got out of their original longs that they established between bars 2 and 3 at about breakeven, and they made a profit on all of their lower entries. Bears often short aggressively again because they know that the market started down from this area earlier in the day, and it could do the same again. The day was over and there was not enough time left for the bears to make a profit, so they therefore chose to not short into the close.

Bar 11 was a high 2 buy setup (the high 1 was two bars earlier) after a strong bull spike. Traders were expecting at least two legs up, and this two-legged pullback was so small compared to the size of the spike that it might not have signified the end of the first leg up. Traders believed that one of three things was happening: the pullback was so small that it was just part of a complex first leg; the first leg was over and the second leg up was beginning; or the first leg was over and there would be a deeper pullback and then a move above the top of this leg. All three possibilities meant that the market was going higher and this was therefore a great buying opportunity. Yes, bar 11 was an entry bar from a two-bar reversal top, which was the second entry for a moving average gap bar short in a bear trend. This might have led to a test of the bear low. However, the spike up flipped the market to always-in long in the minds of most traders, so the chance of the short going very far was small. Most traders saw the reversal as much stronger than the short setup.

FIGURE 21.2 Strong Open in the EUR/USD

As shown in Figure 21.2, the 5 minute EUR/USD (forex) reversed down at bar 2 after a new high. This bull leg had strong momentum, as evidenced by eight bars in a row without a bear trend bar, so the odds were high that any pullback would test the bar 2 high before it fell below the bar 1 bottom of the bull spike. Bar 3 was a moving average gap bar that also was a breakout test of the bar 1 beginning of the rally. It and the two bars before it formed a micro wedge, which should have led to at least a bounce up. It was also a wedge bull flag after the strong bull spike. The first leg down was three bars before bar 2, the second push down was two bars after bar 2, and the third was bar 3.

The market formed a triangle, which ended up as a tight trading range. Triangles have at least three pushes in one direction, and bars 2, 4, and either 6 or 8 formed three pushes up, while bar 1 or 3 along with bars 5 and 7 formed three pushes down. When there are multiple possibilities, some traders will place more importance on one whereas other traders will feel more strongly about others. Whenever there is confusion, the market is in a trading range and therefore in breakout mode, and most traders should wait for the breakout instead of trading within a tight trading range.

Bar 8 was a failed upside breakout attempt (one tick below the bar 4 high) that reversed through the bottom of the range in a bear outside bar. It formed a double top bear flag with bar 4 or bar 6.

Figure 21.2   DETAILED DAY TRADING EXAMPLES   **407**

Bar 9 was a breakout pullback small bar above the middle of the outside bar, offering a low-risk short.

Bar 10 was another breakout pullback short.

Bar 11 was a low 2 short at the moving average with a bear signal bar and a second attempt to break out below the bar 3 spike low.

Bar 12 was another low 2 short at the moving average. Always keep placing your orders. A bear might become complacent because of the bull doji higher low, but you still need to be thinking that the market is in a bear swing, and if it falls below this bar, it will form a low 2 short.

Bar 13 was an ii setup for a long after a trend channel line overshoot and sell climax bar. This was a parabolic wedge bottom, which means that the move accelerated down to the final low and then reversed up. There were three pushes down from bar 10, and the slope of the trend line from the first two pushes (the swing lows after bars 10 and 11) was flatter than that of the trend line created by the second and third pushes (the swing low after bar 11 and the final low just before bar 13).

The market had been trending down for about 20 bars and suddenly had the largest bear trend bar (two bars before bar 13) and largest two-bar bear spike of the bear trend. This spike had a good chance of representing exhaustion, and it might have been the last weak bulls exiting and the last weak bears shorting. The strong bulls were buying in here and would scale in lower instead of panicking out, and the strong bears would have shorted only after a big pullback. This created a good chance of at least a two-legged rally lasting at least 10 bars. The strong bull inside bar was a sign that the buyers were taking control, and it was a good signal bar.

Bar 15 was three pushes up and the first moving average gap bar. The two-bar bull spike from bar 13 was the spike up. Spike and wedge patterns usually have two more pushes up before a correction down, as this one did.

Bar 16 was an ii setup for a higher low long, since traders were expecting at least two legs up from the trend channel overshoot and reversal off the bar 13 low entry. It formed a double bottom bull flag with the bar 14 bottom of the wedge channel up to bar 15. The large bear trend bar trapped bears into shorts and trapped weak bulls out of longs.

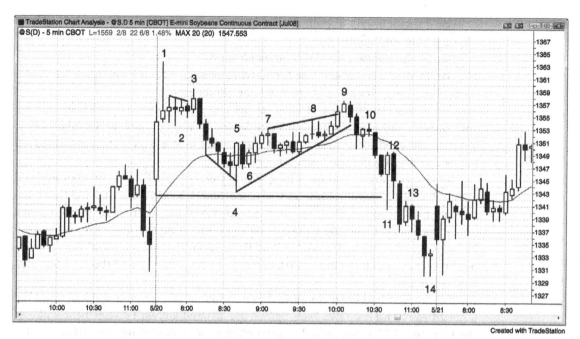

FIGURE 21.3   Soybeans Buy Climax on the Open

As shown in Figure 21.3, the 5 minute chart of soybeans had a buy climax on the open and then a small final flag, and later a wedge bear flag and a large second leg down.

Bar 2 was a doji trading range after the bar 1 spike up and therefore a bad buy setup. There was too much risk of more sideways to down price action. Aggressive traders placed limit orders to short at the high of the prior bar and were filled on bar 3, expecting the high 1 to fail. Bar 3 was a low 2 short, a lower high, and a final flag short. Traders were looking for more of a correction after the bar 1 buy climax and a possible opening reversal and high of the day.

Bar 4 overshot a bear trend channel line and reversed up from a double bottom with the first bar of the day. This could have been the low of the day. The entry was above the bar 6 ii bar, which had a bull close and a close above the moving average.

Bar 9 was a lower high wedge bear flag and a double top bear flag with bar 3. It was a four-legged move up from the bar 4 low, making it a low 4 variation. The market could have been forming a large two-legged move down from bar 1, and traders would have shorted below bar 9 or below the bear bar after it. You can see how the bar after that was a large bear trend bar, indicating that many traders shorted below the bear bar after bar 9.

Figure 21.3

DETAILED DAY TRADING EXAMPLES **409**

Bar 10 was a breakout pullback from the trend line breakout.

Bar 11 was a huge bull reversal bar following a new low on the day and was a two-bar reversal. However, bar 12 could not trade above it. This made bar 12 a great short signal bar because the trapped longs who entered early in bar 11 would have exited below the bar 12 bear trend bar. It was also a breakout pullback short setup. Bar 13 was a breakout pullback short entry.

FIGURE 21.4   Crude Oil Wedge Top

As shown in Figure 21.4, the 5 minute chart of crude oil had a wedge top and then a lower high. Bar 1 was a high 1 breakout pullback from the breakout of the earlier trading range. It was a two-bar reversal and the first pullback after a strong two-bar bull spike, which broke out of a trading range and turned the market into always-in long.

Bar 3 was a good high 2 long above the bull trend bar, despite the barbwire and the second buy climax, because the top at bar 2 was not strong enough to indicate that the bears were in control.

Bar 5 was a wedge top and the top of the channel that followed the bar 2 bull spike. The two-sided trading since bar 2 continued with prominent tails, overlapping bars, pullbacks, and bear bodies, so the odds of a test of the bar 3 channel low were good.

The move down to bar 6 broke the trend line and broke slightly below the bar 3 higher low of the bull trend, indicating strong bears.

Bar 7 was a two-legged breakout test of the bar 5 signal bar low, a lower high after a break below the bull trend line and therefore a possible major trend reversal, a two-bar reversal short setup, a sharp rejection of the poke above the moving average, and a wedge bear flag. The first push up in the wedge bear flag lower high was the small bull bar that formed four bars before bar 6, and the second push up was the bar after bar 6.

Figure 21.5

DETAILED DAY TRADING EXAMPLES   **411**

FIGURE 21.5   Scalps on a 1 Minute Chart

Figure 21.5 is a 1 minute chart showing many price action scalps in the first 90 minutes. The next chart is a close-up of this area. It is virtually impossible for most traders to read a chart correctly fast enough to catch most of these trades, but the chart illustrates that price action analysis works even on the 1 minute level.

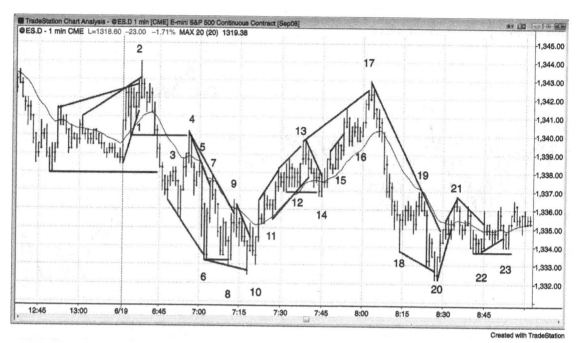

FIGURE 21.6   Scalps on the Open on a 1 Minute Chart

Figure 21.6 is a close-up of the 1 minute Emini's first 90 minutes, highlighting price action scalp setups. The numbering is the same as on the prior chart.

Bar 1 was a high 2 long (there were two pushes down).

Bar 2 was a wedge short and a final flag.

Bar 3 was a breakout pullback short and a low 1 after a bear spike.

Bar 4 was a breakout test short, a lower high, and a low 2 where bar 3 was the low 1.

Bar 5 was a lower high and a low 2 short below the moving average.

Bar 6 was a wedge long, a two-bar reversal, and an expanding triangle bottom.

Bar 7 was a failed trend line breakout short and a double top bear flag with bar 5.

Bar 8 was a two-legged lower low after the bar 7 break of a trend line, and a lower low on a trading range day.

Bar 10 was a wedge reversal second entry and a higher low. The higher low might have meant that a bull trend was forming.

Bar 11 was the first pullback after a trend line break. It was a high 2 long where the high 1 was three bars earlier.

Bar 12 was another bull high 2.

Bar 13 was a wedge short, a final flag, and a possible double top bear flag (with bar 4).

Figure 21.6

DETAILED DAY TRADING EXAMPLES **413**

Bar 14 was a failed bull trend line break, a failed break below the trading range, a double bottom bull flag, and a possible start of a second leg up.

Bar 15 was a high 2. There was a bull flag breakout pullback entry two bars earlier.

Bar 16 was a high 2 in a bull trend.

Bar 17 was a wedge and a failed test of the high of the day (a double top), and therefore a possible lower high.

Bar 19 was a bear low 2 at the moving average, a wedge bear flag, a five-tick failure for traders who bought bar 18, and the first pullback after a bear spike that flipped the market to always-in short.

Bar 20 was two pushes to a new low of the day (bar 18 was the first) in a trading range day (even though there was a strong bear leg from the bar 17 high, it was not a bear day at this point). It was also a reversal up after a one-tick new low of the day (a one-tick failed breakout and a double bottom). It was also a wedge and a two-bar reversal up after a breakout of a two-bar final flag.

Bar 21 was a second leg up, a wedge bear flag (the ii pattern before bar 20 was the first push up), and a possible double top bear flag (with bar 19).

Bar 22 was a two-legged pullback to a higher low after a trend line break (bars 17 to 19) and a double bottom (bars 10 and 20) pullback long.

Bar 23 was a failed trend line break and a double bottom (bar 23 was one tick higher than bar 22) bull flag.

CHAPTER 22

Daily, Weekly, and Monthly Charts

Although daily, weekly, and monthly charts can generate intraday signals, they occur so infrequently that they become a distraction for a day trader and should be ignored. The most common signals are those based on yesterday's high and low, and you can see them on a 5 minute chart. However, there are frequently price action entries on these longer time frames, but because the signal bars are so large, far fewer contracts can be traded if the risk is to be the same as for a day trade. Also, overnight risk may mean that you should reduce your contracts even further or consider trading option strategies that have a limited risk, like outright purchases or spreads. A day trader should trade these charts only if they do not occupy his thoughts during the trading day, because it is easy to miss a few day trades using large volume while nursing a trade of far fewer contracts or shares based on the daily chart, and these misses can more than offset any gain from the daily signal.

Although all stocks form standard price action patterns, stocks of very small companies that have little institutional ownership have a significant risk of unusually big moves up and down. They tend to be more volatile, and in stock market terminology, these stocks are called high-beta stocks. For example, you would not expect Wal-Mart (WMT) to jump 1,000 percent in a month, but when a small drug company gets its one drug approved by the Food and Drug Administration (FDA) or is suddenly a takeover candidate, this is exactly what can happen. Some traders like the huge, fast moves, but most traders prefer to avoid the risk of sudden, huge moves in both directions and bad fills on their trades. Traders who trade these special situations have to watch the stocks very closely, which makes it difficult for them to trade other stocks at the same time. Since the risk is so great, they can only trade a small portion of their portfolio this way and this erases most of the gain derived from the big moves. When you add the stress of the unpredictability, most traders should not bother with these stocks.

When trading counter to a strong trend, the goal should be a scalp of 1 or 2 percent, since most countertrend trades just result in pullbacks that become with-trend entries. Gaps complicate the entries and, in general, the risk is less if the market opens within yesterday's range and then trades through the entry stop at one tick beyond that range. If you cannot watch the stock intraday and there is a gap open, it is probably best to pass on the trade. If you can watch the stock and there is a gap opening, watch for a gap pullback and then enter on the failed pullback into the gap, as the market resumes its move away from yesterday's range. In other words, if you were looking to buy but today gapped up, look for a sell-off on the open today and then buy an opening reversal back up, placing your protective stop below the low of today. If the entry fails and your stop is hit, look elsewhere or give it only one more try if there is a second buy setup. Don't spend too much time on a stock that is not doing what you wanted it to do, because you will lose money. There is a natural tendency to want to make back your money on the same stock after a loss, but this is a sign of your emotional weakness. If you feel a need to prove that you were right and are in fact a great chart reader, you might be right about that, but you are not a great trader. Great traders accept their losses and move on.

Pullbacks on daily charts rarely have classic reversal bars, leaving traders with more uncertainty than when trading 5 minute charts. Uncertainty means risk, and when there is more risk, position sizes need to be smaller, and a trader will have to consider taking a partial position and adding to the position as the price action unfolds. In a bull pullback, additions can be made at a lower price if the market sells off a little more, but the bears have not yet demonstrated that they are in control. Additions can also be made at a higher price after the trend has resumed and a small pullback forms a higher low above your original entry.

When you scan your daily charts at the end of the day, you will frequently see setups to consider for the next day. Once the setup triggers, there will often be an intraday trend that will provide you with many good 5 minute with-trend entries. If the stock is not one that you normally trade intraday but its volume is about five million shares or more, it is worth considering adding it to your basket of day trading stocks for a day or two. Sometimes, however, even with very liquid stocks such as the Oil Service HOLDRS (OIH), your broker might not have an inventory available for selling short, and you might only be able to trade buy setups. If you really want to short, you can buy puts instead, even for a day trade.

Since round numbers are magnets, they can set up trades. For example, if Freeport-McMoRan (FCX) is up 20 percent over the past few months and is now trading at 93, many traders will assume that it will reach 100. Because of this, bears will not short aggressively, because they believe that they soon will be able to short at a better price, and bulls will buy aggressively because they believe that FCX will go above the magnet. This absence of bears creates a vacuum effect that often results in the stock quickly moving up to the magnet. It will typically go 5 to 10 percent above the magnet before it pulls back, and it usually pulls back below the round number at least once before it decides what it will do next. Bulls can buy as it rallies into the magnetic field of the round number and take profits just above it, and bears can wait to short until the market is above and then take profits on the test back down. Bulls will usually buy again there for a scalp.

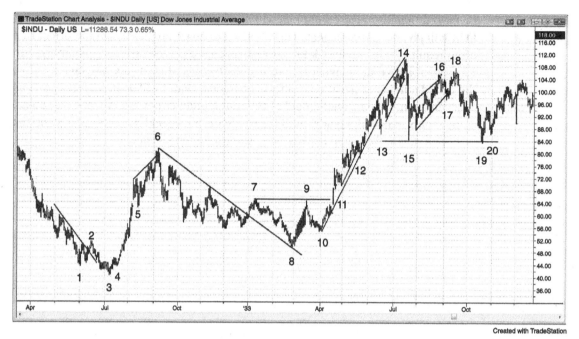

FIGURE 22.1   Price Action Has Not Changed over Time

Price action is the cumulative result of a large number of traders acting independently for countless reasons to make as much money as they can. Because of that, its fingerprint has remained unchanged and will always provide a reliable tool for making money for those who can read it. Figure 22.1 is a daily chart of the Dow Jones Industrial Average in 1932 and 1933, and it looks like any stock trading today on any time frame.

Bar 2 was a low 2 that broke a trend line.

Bar 3 was a small final flag reversal and a lower low test of the bar 1 low after a trend line break (a trend line break and then a test can be a major trend reversal).

Bar 4 was a breakout pullback and a small higher low.

Bar 5 was the first pullback in a strong bull spike and a high 2.

Bar 6 was a wedge channel after the bull spike and led to two large legs down, ending at bar 8.

Bar 7 was a trend line break and a two-legged pullback. It was the breakout of a large wedge bull flag that had its first push down at bar 5.

Bar 8 was a lower low major trend reversal and breakout pullback, a larger wedge bull flag, and a breakout test of bar 2.

Bar 10 was a higher low and a pullback from the bar 9 breakout above the bear channel from bar 7 to bar 8. A bear channel is a bull flag.

Figure 22.1   DAILY, WEEKLY, AND MONTHLY CHARTS   **419**

Bar 11 was a small high 2 breakout pullback after the breakout above the failed bars 7 and 9 double top bear flag.

Bars 12 and 13 were reversals up after minor trend line breaks.

Bar 14 was a wedge and a small final flag reversal.

Bar 15 was a strong-momentum countertrend move that would likely be tested after a rally tested the bar 14 high. It formed a double bottom bull flag with bar 13, but it was strong enough down so that the market might have flipped to always-in short. Traders would have looked to short a lower high and would not have looked to buy here if the long would have made it more difficult for them to get short on the lower high. Sometimes when traders scalp a long when they are looking to short a lower high, they cannot change their mind-set to short as the short is setting up.

Bar 16 was a wedge lower high, and bar 17 was a failed breakout of the wedge.

Bar 18 was the lower high test of the bar 14 bull trend extreme and was a low 2 entry for a short on the wedge higher high breakout pullback. There was a failed breakout below the wedge, and the rally to bar 18 was a higher high breakout pullback from the wedge. Other traders saw it as simply a better wedge than the one that ended at bar 16. Bar 18 was also a breakout test of the bar 14 signal bar low.

Bar 19 was the test of the bar 15 low and was a double bottom bull flag.

Bar 20 was a higher low pullback in the reversal up.

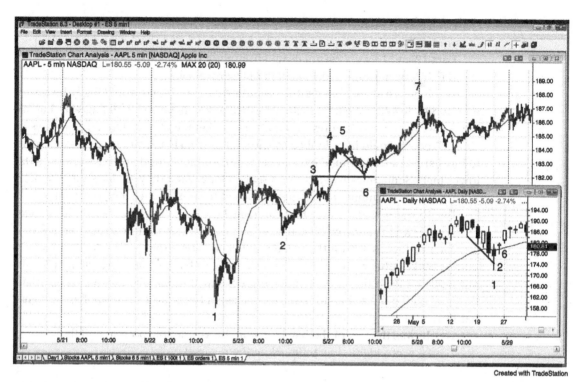

FIGURE 22.2 Gap Pullbacks

As shown in Figure 22.2, when there is a buy setup on the daily chart and the market gaps above yesterday's high, traders will often wait to buy a pullback on the 5 minute chart. AAPL was in a strong bull trend on the daily chart (thumbnail) and had a first moving average pullback at bar 1, which was a bear trend channel overshoot (the numbering is the same on both charts). Bar 2 on the daily chart had a strong intraday reversal up and closed near its high. It was reasonable to want to buy at one tick above the high of bar 2 on the daily chart, which was the high of bar 3 on the 5 minute chart. However, the next day gapped above the day 2 high. Rather than risk a possible reversal down day, it would have been prudent to watch for a reversal up after a pullback test of the gap on the 5 minute chart.

Bar 6 on the 5 minute chart closed the gap and was a moving average gap bar and a bear trend channel overshoot and reversal up. This was a great long entry with a protective stop below bar 6. This 62 cent risk led to a several-dollar gain.

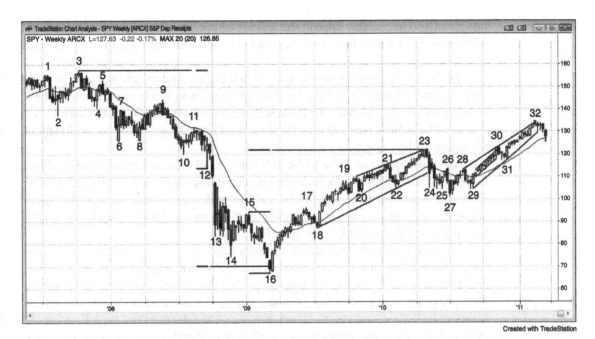

FIGURE 22.3 The Weekly SPY

As shown in Figure 22.3, the weekly chart of the SPY looks like it is in a bear rally because the move up from bar 16 to bar 32 has a shallower slope than the sell-off down to bar 16. Also, the market is not holding above the resistance created by the lows of bars 6, 8, and 10 at the bottom of the upper trading range. However, the rally has retraced so much of the bear trend down to bar 16 that the bear trend does not have much influence left, and the market has therefore become a large trading range. If it is a bear rally, then it should eventually test the bar 16 low. The bulls want the market to continue to go above the swing highs in the bear trend down from bar 3 and eventually to break out to a new all-time high. The bears want the market to fail in an expanding triangle formed by bars 21, 22, 23, 27, and 32, and then break below the bar 27 bottom of the triangle and subsequently to a new bear low below bar 16. Since the rally has been so big, the chart has become more of a large trading range and it has lost the certainty that comes from a trend. Uncertainty is the hallmark of a trading range; once a market appears uncertain, it is usually in a trading range, as is the case here.

On the move down from bar 3, the market began forming lower highs at bars 5, 9, and 11 and lower lows at bars 6, 8, 10, and 12. Since there was yet to be a strong bear breakout, the odds favored this sell-off as being a test of the bottom of the trading range or a possible large bull flag. Some traders believed that the bear spike down to bar 6 might have turned the market to always-in short, but the bear spike down to bar 13 flipped the always-in position to short for any traders who were still in doubt.

Bar 14 was the third bar of a second sell climax and an attempt at a two-bar reversal from a final flag, but the market fell once again in a spike and climax bear down from bar 15. This was the third sell climax and a wedge bottom (bars 13, 14, and 16). The bottom was just past the measured move target based on the height of the upper trading range.

The move up to bar 17 had 12 bull bodies, small tails, and only a couple of bull bodies and was strong enough to be considered a spike by most traders. After the three sell climaxes at the bar 16 low and this spike up, traders thought that there should be at least a second leg up and possibly a measured move up based on the bar 16 low and the top of the bar 15 or bar 17 high.

Bar 23 was just slightly above the measured move target and the top of the trend channel line, and it was a two-bar reversal down in the area of the bars 6, 8, and 10 bottom of the upper trading range. The first target was a break below the channel, which occurred at bar 24. A second leg down ended at the bar 27 two-bar reversal. Bar 29 formed a higher low breakout pullback after the bar 28 breakout of the two-legged bull flag down from bar 23. It was also the right shoulder of a head and shoulders bottom bull flag where the left shoulder formed between bar 24 and bar 25. The trading range between bar 21 and bar 28 was also a head and shoulders top, where bar 21 was the left shoulder, bar 23 was the head, and the bars 26 and 28 double top was the right shoulder. As happens in 80 percent of topping patterns, the market broke to the upside and the bears learned once again that most tops are just bull flags.

The move from bar 29 to bar 32 was in a fairly tight bull channel and could easily be followed by higher prices. However, since the entire chart is a large trading range, big rallies are usually followed by big sell-offs, and the market might soon begin to correct down to the bar 27 bottom of the expanding triangle, or even to the area of the bar 16 bear low.

Bar 16 was a measured move down. Most institutions take trades that they believe will work, which means that the probability is at least 60 percent. They therefore need at least a measured move to have a positive trader's equation (the measured move is where the reward becomes as large as the risk, and the trader's equation begins to become reasonably profitable). The result is that trades often hit a target exactly and then reverse or at least pause, because many firms will take partial or full profits there. Most targets, like all support and resistance, soon fail, because the measured move is the minimum needed, and many firms will feel that the market is strong enough to go well beyond.

Figure 22.4

DAILY, WEEKLY, AND MONTHLY CHARTS   **423**

FIGURE 22.4 Monthly Gold Wedge Channel

As shown in Figure 22.4, the monthly gold chart is in a wedge channel after the bull spike from bar 7 to bar 8. Some traders will see the current move as the third push up where bars 11 and 13 were the first two pushes. Others see bar 8 or 9 as the first push.

Whenever five to 10 bars are close to a trend line, the odds are good that the market will soon fall below the trend line. This makes the bull trend line up from bar 10 vulnerable to a downside breakout. Since the market is just above the trend channel line and the measured move target, the odds favor a two-legged sell-off starting very soon. At a minimum, the market should correct to just below the bar 8 high, and it might correct to the bar 10 bottom of the wedge. Less likely, there will be an upside breakout of the wedge top and a measured move up.

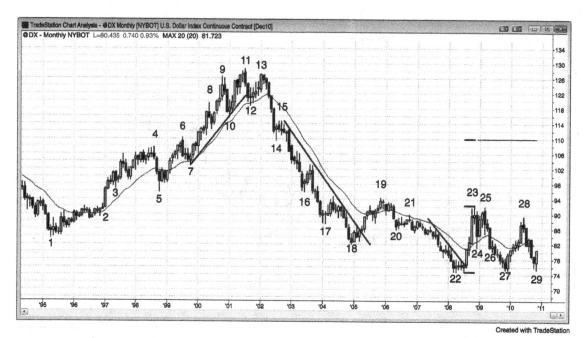

FIGURE 22.5   Monthly Dollar Index Futures

As shown in Figure 22.5, the monthly dollar futures had several trades that qualify as best trades. The dollar, along with the Swiss franc and Japanese yen, are risk-off currencies, and traders tend to buy them when they think that the stock market will fall.

The dollar had a bull spike up as it broke above the top of the bear flag at bar 2, converting the market to always-in long. It then formed a channel, followed by the bar 5 test of the bottom of the bar 3 start of the channel. This created a double bottom bull flag at bar 5 and was followed by a breakout pullback buy setup at bar 7. The market topped out at the bar 11 higher high. Some traders saw the move from bar 3 to bar 11 as a broad channel, and others saw the channel as starting at bars 5 or 7. All traders suspected that bar 11 or bar 13 could be the start of the correction down to the bottom of the channel, because the market was becoming two-sided with several reversals and prominent bear bodies. These represented accumulating selling pressure.

The move down to bar 10 was a strong bear trend bar, and it broke below a steep bull trend line up from bar 7 (not shown). This was a strong enough move to make many bulls take profits on the rally to the new high at bar 11. Bears started shorting at that higher high and even more aggressively at the bar 13 lower high major trend reversal. The move down to bar 12 had two strong bear trend bars and

Figure 22.5   DAILY, WEEKLY, AND MONTHLY CHARTS   **425**

broke below the bull trend line. The market should have had at least two legs down, but instead it had a bear spike down to bar 14 and then a channel down to bar 18. The move down to bar 14 convinced most traders that the market had flipped to always-in short and therefore should be followed by more selling.

The bear channel continued down to bar 18, which was the fifth bar in a sell climax at the end of a big bear trend. Traders expected a rally, at least to the moving average. It was also a double bottom with bar 1.

There was a 20 gap bar short at the moving average, but since the spike up was strong, it was better to wait for a second signal. The second signal came with the bar 19 moving average gap bar, which formed a double top bear flag with the high of the small rally after bar 17.

The spike down to bar 20 was followed by a parabolic and therefore climactic channel down to bar 22, where the market formed a lower low major trend reversal. There, the market went sideways in a variation of an iii pattern (bodies only). It had a failed low 1 short that reversed up in a small double bottom, and the bull spike up to bar 23 was exceptionally strong. This probably flipped the market to always-in long and would have made the bulls try to keep the market above the bottom of the spike. They bought aggressively near the low and they also did at bars 27 and 29, creating a double bottom bull flag. Bar 27 was a double bottom major trend reversal, and bar 29 was a reversal up from the third push down in a triangle, which could ultimately have a breakout up or down.

The wedge bull flag (bars 24, 26, 27) was followed by another rally and then a double bottom at bar 29. This was a good risk/reward setup for a long, since a trader would be buying at the bottom of a trading range. The probability of an equidistant move up was probably 60 percent, since the market was at the bottom of a trading range. The risk was about $5.00 with a 60 percent chance of a test of the bar 28 top of the trading range. A trader would be risking $5.00 to make $10.00 with a probability of 60 percent, which is very good. The average profit per trade would be about $4.00. Since this was also a double bottom bull flag, the odds were probably better than 60 percent. The target would be a measured move up out of this trading range, and it would test to around the bar 15 top of the bear channel.

It is important to realize that this means that there was about a 40 percent chance that the market would fall below the bar 22 low, so traders would need to exit if that happened. If it did, the next target would be a measured move down, based on the height of the bar 27 to 28 or bar 22 to 23 legs down.

Even if the market does go up, the odds favor that it will stall around the bar 11 high and form a larger trading range.

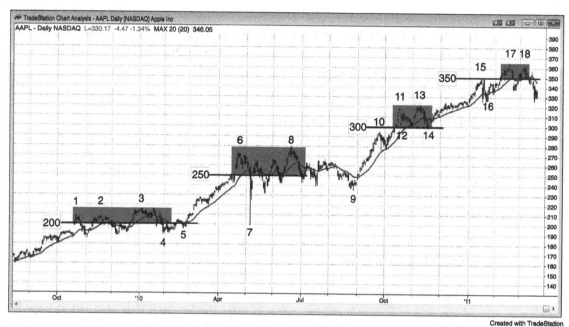

FIGURE 22.6 Round Numbers Can Be Support and Resistance

As shown in Figure 22.6, this daily chart illustrates how AAPL, which was in a strong bull trend, stalled below significant round numbers, which are often magnets that draw the market to them. Once enough traders became convinced that the magnet would be reached, the bears stopped shorting, and the market rallied in a buy vacuum to above the target. For example, the bears believed that the market would get above $300 and probably at least 5 to 10 percent above, because that is what the market usually does once it is in the magnetic pull of a round number. Since the bears expected the market to reach around $315 (5 percent above the round number), they stepped aside. It did not make sense for them to short before the market got there when they believed that the market would be higher within a few bars. Their absence caused the market to go up quickly, since the bulls had to push the market up higher to find enough traders to take the opposite side of their longs.

Once the market gets 5 to 10 percent above the target, bulls begin to take profits and bears begin to short for a test back down to the round number, which usually gets penetrated at least once. The pullback to the bar 12 low missed $300 by a penny (the bar 12 low was $300.01) and the market rallied sharply into the close of that day. Double top shorts around bar 13 succeeded in driving AAPL below $300, but the buyers came back and formed the bar 14 double bottom.

Figure 22.7   DAILY, WEEKLY, AND MONTHLY CHARTS   **427**

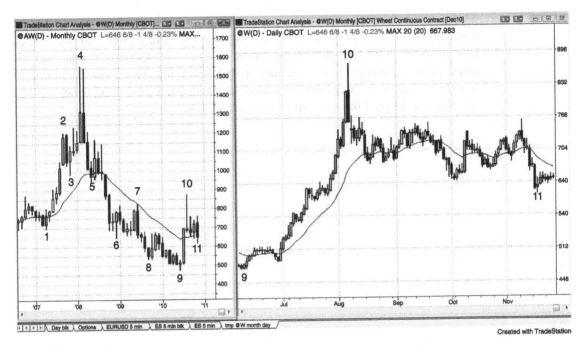

FIGURE 22.7   The Daily and Monthly Charts Can Be in Opposite Trends

As shown in Figure 22.7, wheat had a sharp rally on the daily chart on the right, but it was just a bear market rally on the monthly chart on the left, where bar 10 formed a moving average gap bar in the bear trend, a double top bear flag with bar 7, and a breakout test of the bars 3 and 5 bottom of the upper trading range (a head and shoulders top). The numbering is the same for both charts.

On the day before the bar 10 bear reversal bar formed on the daily chart, a television pundit said that wheat was going much higher and that he was buying it at the market and on pullbacks. When a trend forms large bull trend bars after a long bull spike (10 to 20 bars), there is a great risk of a protracted two-legged pullback because most strong bulls would only buy a significant pullback and most strong bears would short at the market and scale in higher. The television pundit might ultimately be right about wheat going a lot higher, but he was tying up too much of his capital by buying at the top of a parabolic spike and climax. Instead, he should have been doing what the institutions were doing. The bears were shorting and the bulls were waiting for a two-legged pullback before buying.

On the day before bar 10, the news was obviously very bullish for wheat, but that is irrelevant. The chart told traders that strong bears and bulls were expecting a large correction. The spike and parabolic climax told traders that the weak bulls and bears were doing the wrong thing and that the strong bulls and bears were betting on the pullback. The best way to make money trading is by doing what the smart money is doing and not listening to experts on television. The smart money is so huge that those smart traders cannot hide what they are doing. However, you must be able to read the chart to understand what is going on.

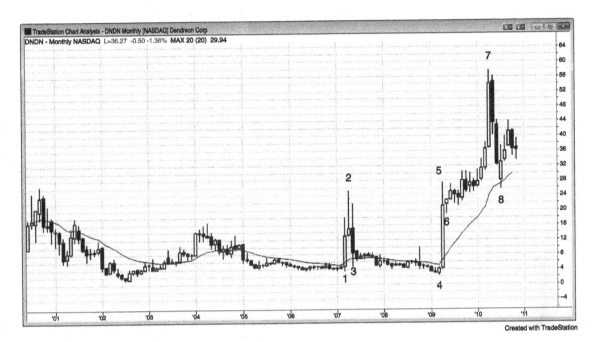

FIGURE 22.8   News Can Move a Stock

As shown in Figure 22.8, Dendreon Corporation (DNDN) had sharp moves up and down due to news releases about its prostate cancer drug. It jumped 800 percent in the two months that ended at bar 2 and gave back 90 percent of that gain over the next couple of months. It then jumped 2,000 percent up to bar 7 and then fell 50 percent in the next three months. With the risk of huge moves up and down, traders can only trade small volume, and this reduced position size offsets any gain that they would get from the large swings. When you add the stress due to the unpredictability, it is almost impossible for most traders to trade anything else when they are in a market like this, and it is likely that they would make more money by avoiding these special situations. They are fun to watch, but your goal is to make a lot of money, not to get an emotional rush or a meaningless sense of power after making a little money from a small position after a rare big move.

CHAPTER 23

Options

I once talked with a woman trader who was a small business owner and managed a stock portfolio for herself and her husband. One day, she awoke to find her portfolio was down $500,000 since the day before. On that day she became a day trader, deciding to never again carry trades home overnight. She was a good chart reader, but was no longer willing to have any overnight exposure that could result in a huge loss. As an alternative, she could have switched to option trading for trades that she wanted to hold for several days to several weeks. She was a strong trader and could have continued to trade a substantial part of her portfolio with options instead of restricting herself to day trading. I haven't talked with her in years, but I am confident that she is doing well whether or not she strictly day trades, but she might be doing better if she incorporated options into her strategies.

Because the bid-ask spread is often wide for options, traders should usually only consider option trades on higher time frame charts. Any setup with a significantly positive trader's equation is reasonable. Here are some examples of situations when traders should can consider call or put purchases based on 60 minute or daily charts:

- Buying calls on a pullback to the moving average in a bull trend.
- Buying puts on a rally to the moving average in a bear trend.
- Buying calls at the bottom of a trading range.
- Buying puts at the top of a trading range.
- Buying calls at a new low in a bear stairs pattern.
- Buying puts at a new high in a bull stairs pattern.
- Buying calls during a bull spike in a strong bull breakout.

- Buying puts during a bear spike in a strong bear breakout.
- Buying calls below a weak low 1 or low 2 at the bottom of a trading range.
- Buying puts above a weak high 1 or high 2 at the top of a trading range.

You can also trade options based on a smaller time frame like a 5 minute chart:

- If you are a new trader and your account is limited or you want to be certain of your risk, you can buy SPY puts or calls instead of trading the SPY or Emini. The bid-ask spread is usually just one tick for the front month, at-the-money (ATM) options on the SPY, and many big cap stocks. This allows traders to place trades on the 5 minute chart and still have a favorable trader's equation.
- On rare occasions when the intraday price movement is so huge that you are unwilling to trust your quotes or your fills on the underlying (like the Emini, stocks, bonds, currencies, or whatever market you are trading), then you can buy puts and calls with limit orders for day trades based on 5 minute charts.

There are many other situations in which trading options is worthwhile, and there are many other useful option strategies, but the aforementioned are the easiest for a day trader and the least distracting. If traders are able to handle other types of option trading, they should trade them, but most active day traders cannot take those trades without interfering with their day trading earning potential. Risk reversals, cashless collars, and ratio spreads in general offer excellent trader's equations, but are probably too distracting for a day trader. The orders are relatively complicated to place and they require a lot of concentration to do them correctly. You have many strike prices and expirations to consider; the bid-ask spreads are often wide and therefore the trades feel a little expensive; and, you should use limit orders, but they often do not get filled quickly. You then have to manage the trades and often will want to make adjustments as the trades evolve. Forex traders will hedge their stock portfolios with currency trades, when they think that the stock market will fall, by buying risk-off currencies like the Swiss franc or the U.S. dollar and shorting risk-on currencies like the Swedish krona to get the same hedge. This avoids the cost of options, but requires a comfort with the foreign exchange (forex) market, where a lot of action takes place overnight. All of this is very distracting for a day trader, and most choose either to focus on day trading or to add only simple put or call purchases to their trading.

It is easiest to mostly buy puts or calls and sometimes spreads and look to hold the trades for one to several days. You can consider allowing one new extreme against your position, and you can be willing to add on because your risk is exactly known and limited with these strategies. At a possible major trend reversal top, you could also simply sell short a small stock position, but you might tend to watch it too much during the day, and this would cause you to miss day trades and ultimately negate any gains from the stock trade.

Options contain a time value that melts away every day, reducing the value of your put or call. If you buy a spread, you lose on the bid and on the ask on both strikes, both when you enter and when you exit the spread, and you have double the commissions. Because of these costs, traders have to restrict themselves to trading only the very best option setups. Also, they should add options to their day trading only if it truly results in an increase in their bottom line, which will not be the case for most traders. Trading anything profitably is difficult for all traders, and most profitable traders usually choose to focus on either options, futures, or stocks and not divide their attention among all three. However, be aware that options traders consider stock positions an integral component of their trading, and most hold their positions for days to weeks and not minutes to hours, like day traders.

There is one other rare occasion in which intraday options can be preferable to futures and stocks. That is when the market is in a huge free fall and it is close to limit down. If a reliable reversal pattern sets up, you might think that the risk of buying the Emini is small, even on a small position, but it can be substantial even with a reputable broker. How can that be? Because the system can get overloaded and your orders might not get processed or reported back to you for 30 minutes or more. If you just bought what you thought was a bottom and then the market fell through your protective stop, you might still see your stop order on your computer screen as a working, unfilled order, even though the market has fallen well below it. So what do you do? You don't know if the order got filled, and when you call your broker to find out, you are on hold for 30 minutes. Then after about 30 minutes, your computer screen will show that your order got filled with some slippage when it was supposed to have been filled. You cannot afford to live with this kind of uncertainty for such a long time on a huge bear day when your broker's order systems are not working correctly. You could easily lose 10 points in the Emini since the broker is never responsible for your order getting filled. An alternative is to buy calls, so that you will be certain of your risk if the market goes into a free fall after you are in the market. You could try to limit any potential loss with a stop on your call, but even if the market falls far below your stop without it being filled, at least you know that your risk is not catastrophic even if the stop order was never processed (assuming that your position size was reasonable). How can the market fall through your protective stop and not trigger it? The stop is based on the last trade, and if no trades took place in your particular option, the bid and ask might fall too far below your stop, but your stop would not get filled and your option would be worth much less than you thought. It is important to understand that protective stops in options often offer no protection, and if the market is moving quickly against you, you should try to exit on a limit order as soon as you can.

You can also consider day trading SPY options instead of the SPY or the Emini, especially when you are starting out and if you are afraid of a huge loss. For example, if you buy a one-month-out, at-the-money (ATM) call in the SPY, it might cost about $250, which is the most that you could lose even if the SPY falls to zero (obviously this assumes that you bought the call and did not make a mistake, like instead shorting a naked put or call). Even if the SPY fell 1 percent over the next hour, you could probably get out of your call with under a $100 loss. If you bought the call during a pullback in a bull trend, the odds are good that you would be able to exit with a 10 to 20 cent profit, which translates into a $10 to $20 profit. This would require about a 25 to 45 cent move in the SPY. If the SPY instead fell 50 cents, you could get out of your call with maybe a 30 cent loss, which is $30. Buying puts or calls gives beginning traders more certainty about the most they have at risk, and this might make it easier for them to think about how to trade without constantly worrying about the dollars.

If you take only a couple of day trades a day in the futures or stock markets, then you can be more active in the options market, especially if you also actively swing trade stocks. The opportunities could fill another book, but a few points are worth making here. For example, if you are long a stock that is basing on the daily chart and you are willing to add on lower, you could sell a put at one strike below the market. You collect the premium if your stock goes up or even drops a little, and if instead it goes down below the strike of the put, the buyer of that put will put the stock to you (you will be forced to buy it at the strike price) and you will therefore be adding to your long stock position at that lower price.

Another common use of options for traders who are long stock is to sell out-of-the-money (OTM) calls to collect premium. This covered call writing can add about a 10 percent return to your portfolio every year, but it will occasionally take you out of a stock that is exploding upward.

If you are expecting a big move in a stock or a futures contract but you don't know the direction, you can buy a straddle (buy both a put and a call), but then you suffer time decay, commissions, and bid-ask spreads on both legs. Straddles are rarely worthwhile. An alternative for futures traders is to combine the futures and options in a delta-neutral position, meaning that it has an equal chance of going up or down. For example, in the Emini, one long contract is equal to buying 500 SPY or 10 at-the-money calls. If you buy one Emini contract (or 500 SPY) and 10 ATM puts (alternatively, you could short one Emini or 500 SPY and buy 10 ATM calls), this is a delta-neutral position at the moment that you placed the trade. If the market moves up or down, the delta changes. If the market goes up, your Emini will make more than your puts will lose; if the market goes down, your puts will gain more than your Emini will lose. You lose money only if the market goes sideways for several days, because your option will decay. There is a lot of fine-tuning that you can do to increase your return as the market moves, but Emini day traders are too busy to add this to their trading.

Option traders often talk about catalysts, which are upcoming news events that can lead to big moves in a stock. The most common one is an upcoming earnings report, and less common ones include anticipated information about new products or possible takeovers. Because there is uncertainty and the potential for a big move up or down is large, the premium is usually greatly inflated. As soon as the news is announced, the premium gets crushed, so much so that you can see the big move in the direction that you expected and still lose money! For example, suppose you thought that Amazon (AMZN)'s earnings were going to be strong so you bought a call for $5.00 on the day before, and the earnings were strong and AMZN went up 5 percent on the open; however, your call might open at only $4.00. You would be right about the strong earnings and the strong open, but the premium was so inflated that AMZN probably had to go up 10 percent for your call to increase in value. Because of this rapid loss of the greatly inflated premium, traders need to be careful when buying options before catalysts. If the volatility is too high, they are expensive and require a huge move to be profitable. One way to reduce the effect is to buy a spread so that your short option's loss of premium will largely offset the loss on your long option, but spreads are usually worth buying only if you plan to hold the position for a week or more, because they usually will be profitable only if there is a big move, or if there is a smaller move and expiration is approaching.

Many index options traders pay attention to the Chicago Board Options Exchange Market Volatility Index (VIX), which tends to move in the opposite direction to the indexes and in general rises greatly when the market falls in a panic and traders are buying a huge number of puts to hedge their longs. Other traders are obviously buying puts as a bet that the bear trend will continue. However, after the market starts to turn up again, there can also be an increase in put buying, but for a different reason. Instead of speculators betting on a fall or scared longs hedging, it is often due to confident longs who are protecting their new longs. When this is the case, that put buying implies that the downside risk is much less. These new longs are willing to hold on to their stock positions during a sell-off because they bought the puts as protection, so if the market falls, they will hold on to their stock and futures positions instead of selling in a panic and driving the market down further. In other words, this put buying is a sign that the downside risk has shrunk and bulls are becoming confident. However, it is impossible to know whether the overall put purchases in the market are for speculation on further declines or for protection of new longs. Relying on the opinions of pundits on television is never a good basis for taking positions. If they could make a lot of money trading, most of them would not be wasting time pontificating on CNBC.

Many hedge funds buy stock and hedge by also buying puts, either in the specific stocks in their portfolios or in the overall market, like SPY puts. Hedge funds are rarely perfectly hedged and most adjust the amount of put protection based on the overall market. Some use the volatility index to make adjustments in their puts. For example, if the volatility index rises 20 percent due to a 10 percent drop in the stock market over the past few weeks, they will buy back some or all of their puts, because the puts would have served their purpose. They initially bought the puts when the market was higher, as protection against a sell-off in their stock portfolio. If the market sells off and their stocks decrease in value, their puts will increase in value. They will take profits on their puts and either become less hedged while they wait for the market to rally again, or they will buy new puts to roll their hedge forward into a further out contract, and usually a lower strike price. If the market rallies strongly and they are relatively less hedged, they will buy more puts to increase their downside protection.

If you are trading options on the daily or 60 minute charts and are confident that the move will begin within the next day or two, it is best to just buy an option instead of a spread. However, if you think that the move might take a week or more to begin, you can reduce the effect of time decay by purchasing a spread. You reduce your total profitability because the value of the short option increases as the market goes your way, but the overall risk/reward ratio improves. In general, choose the strike for the short option near a support or resistance area. For example, if the SPY is at 105 and has a strong buy signal, but there is resistance around 108, you could buy the one-month-out ATM 105 call and finance it in part by shorting the OTM 108 call. The net cost of the long call less the premium you collected on the short call might be about $1.20. Since 108 is resistance and resistance acts as a magnet, the market should get drawn to the 108 area. Both calls will increase in value, but the long ATM 105 call will increase in value faster and more than make up for the loss on the short 108 call. If the market rallies in a very strong bull spike and you think that it will easily break through the 108 resistance area, you can buy back the short 108 call for a loss and hold the long 105 call, which has more than enough profit to offset the loss on the short call. If the rally to 108 is weak and you think that the market might sell off, you should exit your spread with a profit. It is usually not worth holding the spread to expiration, even though that it when the maximum profit is realized. Your premise has changed so you need to reevaluate your position, and this is always a consideration when trading options. If the SPY is at 108 at expiration, the short 108 call will expire worthless and the long 105 call will be worth $3.00, so your total net profit might be about $1.80. However, if the market is at 108 with two weeks to go before expiration and your net open profit is $1.50, it is probably better to simply exit because it is not worth risking turning your $1.50 profit into a loss by sitting through a sell-off below 105 before expiration. As the market rallied to 108, your risk/reward situation changed, and it is no longer as good as it was when you put the trade on. It is better to take your profit and look for the next trade.

A trader can either buy or sell a spread. For example, if the SPY is at 130 and a trader thinks that it will go up, he could buy a call spread by buying the ATM 130 call and selling an OTM call at a higher strike price, like a 133 call. He could also make a bullish bet by shorting a put spread, like selling an ATM 130 put and buying an OTM 125 put. In general, most traders prefer buying spreads to selling them because they prefer to be long and not short the ATM option. If they are short the ATM option and the underlying goes even a little against them, they are at risk of having additional, unwanted work. For example, if they shorted that put spread and the SPY fell to 129 and stayed there as expiration approached, they might be put the stock, which means that the broker will automatically sell them the stock at 130; then they would have to decide what to do with the stock and the remaining long OTM put.

Buying a spread is usually best when you plan to hold the trade for several weeks, especially if you can hold the position into the final week. This is because the short strike is always more OTM; the more a position is OTM, the faster it will lose premium through time decay, and that decay accelerates rapidly in the final week. However, you can also purchase a spread with the intention of holding it for just a few days if you are expecting a huge move beyond your short strike within that time. Buy the spread for a trade that you expect to hold for less than a week only if you think that the market will go beyond your short strike during that week. Otherwise, just buy a simple call or put. For example, say the SPY is at 134 and you think that it will fall to 130 over the next week. Either you could buy a put, like the ATM 134 put, or you might want to consider a spread, like a long 134 put and a short 132 or 131 put.

Since options lose money every day even if the market remains unchanged, you should hold your position only if you believe that your premise is still valid. Otherwise, get out, even at a loss. How do you know if your premise is still valid? Look at the market as it is at this moment and imagine that you are not holding the position. Next, ask yourself if you would put on that exact position. If you would not, then your premise is invalid and you should exit immediately.

A common mistake that a beginner makes is to hold a winning option position too long. For example, if the trader buys a call at the bottom of a trading range with a goal of a test up to the middle of the range over the next week, but the market races to the target in just one day, it is usually better to take most or all of the profits at that point. Yes, the strong momentum might be the start of a bull trend, but it is more likely that the trading range will continue, and either the market will soon go sideways and erode the premium through time decay or the market will pull back and the profit will disappear. Option profits disappear quickly, so it is very important to take them once you have them.

Just because a stock is well-known, do not assume that its options are heavily traded. If they are not, the bid-ask spread can be unacceptably large. For example, the bid for an ATM call might be $1.20 and the ask might be $1.80. This means that you would probably have to pay $1.80 for the call, and if you immediately sold it you would receive $1.20, instantly losing 60 cents, or a third of your investment! In general, if the open interest is less than 1,000 or the recent daily volume is less than 300 options for the strike that you are considering, you usually should not place the trade. You should rarely, if ever, trade thinly traded options. However, if you do, you should always enter and exit with limit orders. Even then, your limit order might sit there for hours while you are waiting for it to get filled, and you will sometimes end up giving in and exiting at the market, greatly reducing your profit potential. One of the nice things about active option markets like the SPY is that the bid-ask spread for the front month is usually only a penny for ATM and near-the-money options, so you can place market orders and get excellent fills.

A large bid-ask spread alone should not be a deterrent to buying an option, because the spread is proportional to the price of the stock. When AAPL is trading at $300, the bid-ask spread on an ATM call might be 20 cents, which might seem like a lot to a beginner. However, traders would not hesitate to buy an option on a stock trading at $30 if the bid-ask spread on the option was 2 cents. They might buy 10 calls of the $30 stock for every one AAPL call. This is a mathematically appropriate way to trade.

Spreads can be useful if you are entering during a strong spike on the daily chart and the market has a way to go before it reaches its target. For example, if the SPY is at 118 and falling sharply well below the moving average in a new bear trend, and you believe that it will hit 115 within the next few days, you might be hesitant to buy a put, because the market might suddenly reverse up to the moving average before falling to the target. As an alternative, you can buy a 118 put and short a 115 put. If the market falls nonstop over the next couple of days to the 115 support area, you could exit your put spread for maybe a $1.50 profit. If instead it rallied to 120 at the moving average, your spread might have an open loss of a dollar. If you believed that your premise was still intact, you could leg out of your spread by buying back your short put for a profit of maybe 50 cents, but holding your long put. If you are right and the market then falls to your 115 target over the next week, you might make an additional $2.00 on the long put for a total profit of about $2.50 on the trade. It takes experience to be able to leg out of a spread when the market is going against you, but if you are confident about your chart reading, this can be a good approach.

Incidentally, short options at support and resistance levels increase the strength of those levels, since options tend to expire near the strike price with the biggest open interest. The more volume traded at any option strike price increases the magnetic effect of that price, which increases the support and resistance at that price. If the volume is large enough, it can affect the market around expiration. The volume can get huge if there is an obvious support or resistance level, because that strike price will generate lots of option activity. In fact, the SPY and the QQQ often expire close to the put and call strike price with the largest open interest. The short side of the options is usually taken by institutions, who are the smart money traders, and they will do whatever they can in the options market and in related markets to make their short options expire worthless so they get to keep the entire premium that they collected.

The VIX is a measure of the volatility of the S&P 500 index options, and although buying a call or the SPY or the Emini is usually a good trade during a strong bull spike when you believe that follow-through is likely, there is a risk associated with the VIX. Incidentally, every 16 points in the VIX corresponds to a 1 percent expected average daily range in the S&P 500 index (so a VIX of 32 means that the average daily range of the SPY and Emini is about 2 percent). If the spike is strong enough, the VIX might also spike up and the cost of your call would be elevated at the time of your purchase. If over the next couple of hours the market enters a quiet bull channel, the VIX might fall enough so that the value of your call will not increase. Because of this, if you want to buy a call during a bull spike or a put during a bear spike, if you are not buying early on in the spike, it is better to wait for a pullback to reduce the risk of buying during a brief spike up in the VIX, which would cause a brief overpricing of all options.

A dramatic increase in option volatility usually causes a disproportionate increase in price of the OTM options. This is called skew, and skewed pricing can be upsetting to beginning spread traders, because it results in smaller profits than what seems fair or logical. If a trader bought a 133/128 put spread in the SPY during a trading range in a bull market when the SPY was around 133, paying $3.50 for the 133 put and receiving $2.00 for the short 128 put, and the SPY fell $4.00 over the next two weeks on some world crisis, the trader might assume that the spread would increase by $4.00 as well. However, since so many traders are buying OTM puts to protect their longs as the market is falling sharply, their price increases disproportionately to the ATM puts, and the spread might increase to only about $2.50, or a $1.00 profit. As the market falls sharply, the volatility increases sharply, which has a greater effect on OTM puts (and calls, as well). However, the market might have to fall about 5 percent below the lower strike price, maybe down to 123, for the spread to have close to a $5.00 profit in the weeks before expiration. Spreads get close to their profit potential only if the market falls far below the lower strike price, or during the last week before expiration. Traders should generally buy spreads only if they are expecting a move to near their short leg at some point over the next few weeks, or if they are willing to hold the spread and exit within a week or so of expiration. The put spread will have the full $5.00 profit at expiration if the SPY is less than 128, the lower strike price, at expiration, but most traders exit before then.

Because of the skewing of OTM options during big spikes on the daily chart, traders should consider outright option purchases if they are expecting a move up or down over the next week or so. If they are planning to exit several weeks before expiration, they should consider not buying a spread. For example, if the market just had a strong 3 percent drop on the daily chart and now has pulled back to a possible lower high, and traders expect a strong second leg down to begin within the next few days, they are probably better off just buying an outright put instead of a spread. If they were willing to buy two put spreads for a total cost of $3.00, they might instead consider buying a single ATM put for about $3.50. If they get the sharp sell-off during the next week or so that they are expecting, their put might be worth $7.50 if the market quickly falls to 128. This is still less than the $5.00 they might have hoped to make (the difference between the 133 in the SPY when they bought the put and the current price of 128), but much more than the $2.00 they would have made on the two put spreads. If their put quickly increases in value by $3.00 or $4.00 within a few days, they should sell out of the position, because the market will probably pull back and enter a trading range. If they continue to hold the put, the $4.00 profit might quickly become a $2.00 profit. The rally might convince them that their premise is no longer valid, and they will then exit with that $2.00 profit, wishing that they hadn't been so greedy. The options market often offers traders unexpected gifts, but rarely as much as a beginner might think is logical. When it does, it is almost always better to take the gift and then look for the next trade.

Figure 23.1   OPTIONS   **441**

FIGURE 23.1 Buy Calls during Bull Spikes

When a stock is in a strong bull spike, traders can buy calls or call spread. Many traders who buy calls in strong bulls prefer OTM strikes because the time decay is slightly less. As shown in Figure 23.1, this daily chart of AAPL had several bull spikes composed of a series of bull trend bars with small tails and bars with little overlap. The momentum was strong, which made the odds favor higher prices. If traders wanted to participate in the up move but limit their risk, they could buy calls or call spreads. They could take partial profits after a few days and then exit the remainder of the position at the first sign of a reversal or on a pullback to near their entry price.

When the market is trending up and traders want to buy it, but would like to buy it a little lower, they will often sell a put just below the market. For example, during any of the shaded bull legs, a trader could have sold a one month out put that was about 2 percent OTM for $8. If the market fell and they were put the stock, they got in 2 percent below the current price and they would be happy. If the market instead continued up, they got to keep the $8, which is about a 2 percent profit in one month. Other traders would simply sell an ATM put. For example, when the market was at 260 and rising sharply, they could have sold a one month out 260 put for about $12. If they were put the stock, they would get to keep the $12. This means that their net cost to buy the stock was 248, even if it never fell much below 260, and simply continued higher.

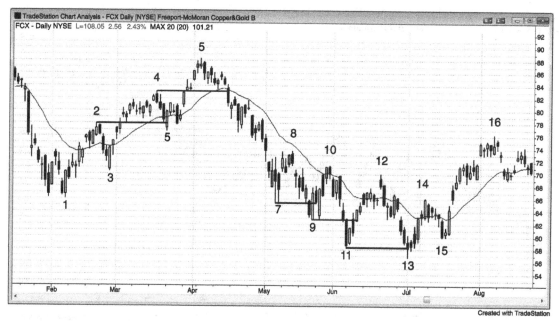

FIGURE 23.2   Fade Stair Breakouts with Options

When a market is in a stairs pattern, you can fade each new breakout with options, expecting a pullback into the prior stair. As shown in Figure 23.2, after the rally to bar 4, the daily chart of FCX had a pullback to below the bar 2 high, which means that the bulls were not too strong. Traders who correctly assumed that a breakout above bar 4 would be followed by a pullback to below the bar 4 high could have bought puts at the bar 5 doji or before the close of the next day once it was clear that the day was likely to be a strong bear trend day.

When the market turned up at bar 9 and rallied several dollars above the bar 7 low, traders could have bought calls on or just before the close of bar 11, expecting a rally of at least a couple of dollars above the bar 9 low. They could have bought calls again on the close of bar 13 when they saw the big tail at the bottom of the bar.

Bar 12 was a bear reversal bar and a potential final flag reversal, a moving average gap bar, a double top with bar 10, and a weak high 1 or high 2 breakout at the top of a possible trading range. It was reasonable to buy puts at the end of the day. Since the market was in a broad bear channel down from bar 5, many traders bought puts on each rally above the midpoint of the prior leg down and near the moving average. Many waited until near the close of the day, to be confident that the day would be a bear trend day, like during bars 8, 10, 12, and the bar after bar 14. They took profits below the most recent swing low, and the profit taking by all bears, combined by the buying by the bulls, resulted in the reversal up after each new low. Bears were buying back their shorts at new lows, not pressing their bets by shorting more on the breakout. This is a sign that the bear trend is transitioning into a two-sided market (a trading range).

Figure 23.3

OPTIONS **443**

FIGURE 23.3 Fade Trading Range Extremes with Options

When the market is in a trading range, traders can buy puts and exit previously purchased calls near the top of the range and then buy calls and exit puts near the bottom of the range. As shown in Figure 23.3, after the reversal up from the bar 5 low, Morgan Stanley (MS) reversed down after bar 9, which was the second attempt to break out above the bar 2 high. Since there was a spike up to bar 6 and then a pullback to bar 7, the three pushes up to bar 9 (bar 6 was the first push) were likely to function as a channel and be followed by a test of the bar 7 bottom of the channel. Traders could have bought puts near the close of the bear bar that formed three bars after bar 9.

Bar 11 was a bull reversal bar and a double bottom bull flag with bar 7, as well as the bottom of a channel after the bear spike to bar 10. Traders could have exited their puts and bought calls going into the close of the bar.

The bar after bar 13 had a bear body, and traders could have exited their calls and bought puts at the top of the range, especially since this was a wedge bear flag. The two bars after bar 10 formed the first push up, and bar 12 was the second.

The move down to bar 15 followed a very strong spike, and even though bar 15 formed a double bottom with bar 11, the market might have needed more of a base before it could rally much. Traders who did buy calls here should have taken profits on the reversal at the bar 16 top of the wedge bear flag.

Bar 17 was a bull reversal bar and the third push down from the bar 9 high. Many traders saw this as a potential bull triangle after the strong move from bar 5 to bar 9, and this was a call-buying opportunity. It was also a reversal up from a low 2 at the bottom of a trading range (bars 7, 11, and 15 established the bottom of the range). A low 2 short signal at the bottom of a trading range usually fails and leads to a reversal up, as do most attempts to break out of a trading range.

When professional options traders believe that the market will rally, they will sometimes put on a risk reversal, which is beyond the scope of this book. For example, the market rallied strongly from the bar 5 low and then entered a trading range. Many traders would rightfully have concluded that the market had a good chance of testing the top of the trading range again, and it might even break to a new high. After the double bottom at bar 15, an options trader saw that there was strong buying around 24.00, and he would be happy to be able to buy there. Since he believed that the market would work higher, he could have bought a call at any point as the market rallied up from the bar 15 bottom of the triangle (with bars 7 and 11). If he bought the one month out November 26 OTM call for 1.50, he might have been able to completely cover the cost of that purchase by selling an OTM 24 put, which would have given him about a 1.50 credit. The net cost of his long 26 call and his short 24 put was zero, and this strategy is called a risk reversal. If the market fell below 24, the stock would have been put to him at 24, the price where he was hoping to be able to buy. He would then be long the stock and still long a call. If the market fell sharply, he would lose the 1.50 he spent for the call and as many dollars as the stock fell below his 24 entry price. However, he believed that this was unlikely, and in this situation, had possibly a 70 percent chance of making money. The market dipped below 24, and on a one-bar small dip like that with several weeks to expiration, it would have been unlikely that he would have been put the stock. If he had been, then he would be long the stock and the call, and he could have taken profits on both around the bar 18 test of the top of the trading range. If he was not put the stock, he could have closed out his risk reversal with a big profit on both his long call and his short put, which would have fallen close to zero (he received 1.50 when he sold it and could now buy it back for about 10 cents). A risk reversal is similar to holding the belief that the market might form a lower low major trend reversal. The trader believes that the market is reversing up and is comfortable buying (being put the stock) if the market falls to a lower low.

Figure 23.4

OPTIONS **445**

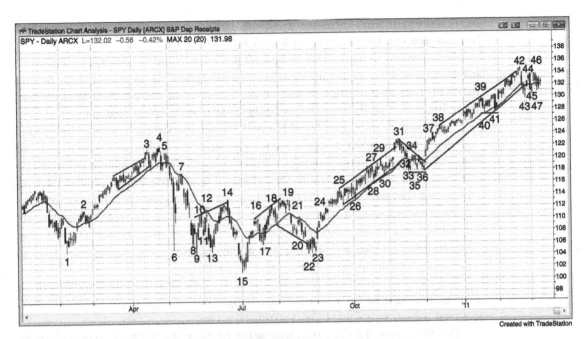

FIGURE 23.4 The SPY Is a Good Market for Options

As shown in Figure 23.4, the daily chart of the SPY regularly offers opportunities to buy options.

The two-legged higher high up to the bar 4 bear reversal bar was a good put-buying setup for a test of the moving average. The market was forming a small double top with bar 3, so the odds were good that the bull trend was evolving into a trading range, in which case a test of the bottom of the range and the moving average was likely. Traders could have bought puts before the close, once they saw that the bar was likely to be a strong bear bar. Bar 3 was a buy climax and a breakout of a bull channel, and it was followed by a strong bear bar. This showed that the bears were willing to be aggressive. On the two-legged higher high up to bar 4, it was reasonable to think that the market would test the moving average again.

When bar 6 closed, many traders assumed its low was likely to get tested. Higher volatility increases option premiums, so put premiums were greatly inflated because the bar was so huge. Traders could have bought a put spread, buying the one-month-out ATM 113 put and shorting a put about four strikes lower. If the short put is too far below, its value is too small to be worth shorting. If the market quickly fell below 109, traders could have exited the spread with a profit. However, if they held and saw the rally to the moving average at bar 7, they could have bought back the short 109 puts, which would be worth much less, and continued to hold the 113 puts, even though they, too, were worth much less. However, the puts would have quickly increased in value over the next several bars, and traders could then have made a profit on both sides of the spread. This is called legging out of the spread, because you exit the two parts or legs at different times.

Bar 7 was a moving average test after the huge bar 6 bear spike. The odds favored a sell-off to at least the middle of the bear spike. Traders could have bought puts at the moving average or just before the close of the bar 7 strong bear bar, when they saw that the bar was probably going to be a strong bear bar.

Bar 9 was a strong bull trend bar and the second strong bull trend bar within three bars and therefore a sign of buying pressure. The big tail at the bottom of bar 6 was also a sign of strong buying at this price level. The odds were good for a test of the moving average, so traders could have bought calls going into the close of bar 9, once they saw that it was probably going to be a strong bull reversal bar.

Bar 13 was a second attempt to reverse up from below the huge bear spike and the bottom of a triangle, where bars 6 and 9 formed the first two legs down. It was also a bull reversal bar and another sign of buying pressure in the 105 area. Traders could have bought calls going into the close of the bar.

Bar 14 was a strong bear reversal bar, a moving average gap bar, and the top of a wedge bear flag, so traders could have bought puts going into the close once they saw that the bar was going to be a strong bear bar.

Bar 15 was a riskier call purchase setup because the momentum down was so strong, but it was the third push down from the bar 4 high, where bar 6 was the first and bars 8 through 13 formed the second. Once traders saw how strong the bull spike up to bar 16 was, they could have bought calls on the close of the strong bar 17 bull reversal bar for a second leg up after the large wedge bottom and strong bull spike.

The market was stalling during the five bars before bar 19, and the doji close was enough reason to buy puts at the top of the wedge (bars 16, 18, and 19) and the double top with bar 14.

Bar 21 was a two-legged pullback to the moving average after a strong bear spike, so traders could have bought puts on the close when they saw that there were two doji bars that failed to close above the moving average.

Bar 23 was the third bull bar in the past five bars, which was a sign of buying pressure. The market was trying to form a higher low after the rally to bar 19. This was also a spike and channel bear from bar 19 and a wedge bull flag with the low after bar 18 and then with bar 20. Traders could have bought calls on the bull close or on the close of the following day, which was a large bull trend bar with tiny tails and a close well above the moving average. This was part of a strong bull spike after a significant bottom and was likely to be followed by higher prices. If they were planning on holding for more than a couple of weeks, many would have bought call spreads instead of calls, to lessen the effect of time decay.

Bar 31 was a bear reversal bar after an upside breakout above a protracted bull channel, and at a minimum, the market should have tested the moving average and poked below the bottom of the channel. This was a good opportunity to buy puts.

Figure 23.4

OPTIONS **447**

In fact, traders could have bought puts on the open when the market was above the high of the prior bar. Why was that a good trade? When the market breaks above a lengthy bull channel, it usually reverses to the bottom of the channel and the reversal generally comes within five bars. Therefore, buying puts above the third bar had limited risk.

There was a very unusual feature to this channel. Only once in the past 10 years did the market not touch the moving average for this many consecutive bars (bars 26, 28, and 30 did not touch it), and that one occurrence was followed by a test of the moving average after about as many bars. Extreme behavior offers a regression to the mean trade. If the market is doing something that it has not done in years, it will likely stop doing that very soon, and option traders can place a bet in the opposite direction. Whenever you see something that appears unusual, look back or test prior data to get a sense of how unusual it is. If you tested back over the past 10 or 20 years, you would find that more than 95 percent of the time when there were 30 or more consecutive gap bars, the market came back and touched the moving average within 10 bars. Traders who saw this started taking profits on longs and buying puts above the high of the prior bar for a bet on a test of the moving average. The odds were excellent that the market was going to touch the moving average soon, so buying puts here was a good trade, and traders could have taken profits on the bar 32 test of the moving average. For example, once the market formed a one-bar pullback before bar 31, traders would have bought puts on any move above its high, which happened on the next bar. The market sold off from the gap up open of bar 31. After a tight bull channel has gone on for a long time, bears begin to enter the market at the top of the channel above swing highs and above the highs of prior bars. When something rarely happens, it is unsustainable and therefore climactic and the ensuing pullback is usually deeper and lasts longer than what most traders expect, so the odds were that the bar 31 high would hold for at least several weeks and for at least a two-legged sideways to down correction. The size of the correction should be comparable in the number of bars and points to the prior legs on the chart, because the market tends to keep doing what it has been doing (inertia).

Similar strong, tight bull channels formed in the move up to bar 3, and from bar 36 to bar 39. Traders bought puts above the highs of prior bars and on the closes of strong bull trend bars, which were possible exhaustive buy climaxes, and on small bars that followed these big bull trend bars, expecting a test down for one to three days. Put buyers made from 50 cents to a dollar on these scalps on the daily chart.

Another example of extreme behavior came at bar 42. Although this SPY chart has a couple of small bear bars in the move up from bar 41, the Emini chart did not. Instead, it had 15 consecutive bull trend bars, which is something that had not occurred in many years. This means that it is extreme, and therefore climactic. Smart bears began to scale into put positions in the several bars before bar 42, expecting at least a 10-bar, two-legged correction that would likely fall below the moving average.

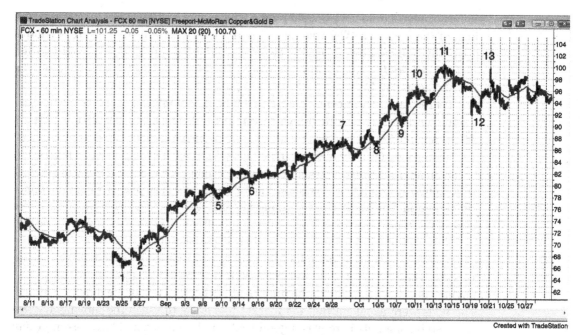

FIGURE 23.5   Buy Calls on Pullbacks to the Moving Average in a Bull Trend

When the market is in a strong bull trend, as it was on the 60 minute FCX chart shown in Figure 23.5, traders could buy calls on each poke below the moving average. About 80 percent of attempts to end a strong trend fail, so the odds were good that the calls would be profitable over the following days. Traders planning on holding for more than a week or two would have bought call spreads to reduce the effect of time decay.

After the three pushes up to bar 11 (bar 10 was the second push), the odds of a two-legged correction were good, so traders should not have bought calls during the leg down that followed.

Because bar 11 was the third push up in an overdone bull, it could have been followed by either a trend reversal or at least a trading range. Many traders who were long would have wanted to hold onto their stock, but protect themselves against a big sell-off. One strategy, which is beyond this book, is a cashless collar (traders "collar up"). A bull could have bought a one month out OTM 90 put for 2.00 and financed it by selling an OTM 105 call, also for 2.00. His net cost for the protection below 90 is zero ("cashless"). If the market rallied 5 percent, his stock would be called away, but he would make that additional 5 percent profit. Instead of collaring up, many traders would simply have sold a call (a buy write, or a covered call), instead of also buying the put, because the puts are disproportionately expensive and you have to give up too much upside to find a call equal in price to the put (the call is usually much closer to the money than the put).

Figure 23.6

OPTIONS **449**

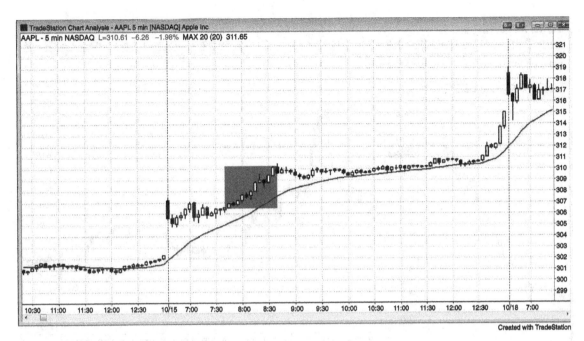

FIGURE 23.6 Buying Calls for a Day Trade

If you don't follow a stock closely but notice a strong bull spike after a big gap up on the 5 minute chart (see Figure 23.6), you can buy calls and hold them until the close. You can use an alert to tell you if the market dropped back below the price of the underlying at the time that you bought the calls and then exit with a limit order with a small profit. Otherwise, exit the calls just before the close.

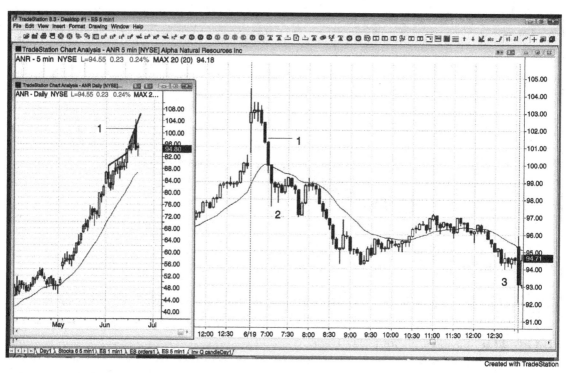

FIGURE 23.7 Day Trade Runaway Trends with Options

Runaway markets often offer profitable fades using options, and this type of trading doesn't cause too much distraction for day traders because the risk is limited. As shown in Figure 23.7, Alpha Natural Resources Inc. (ANR) was in a strong bull trend on the daily chart (insert) and broke out of the top of a wedge four days ago. Yesterday, it gapped above another trend channel line and above 100, a psychologically important number and therefore a magnet. As soon as the 5 minute chart started to come down, a test of 100 was likely. The one-month-out July 100 puts could have been bought for $7.20, and a reasonable worst-case exit would have been a trade above the top of the trading range at the open, risking maybe a dollar or so on the puts. At bar 2, those puts were worth $8.80. This first pause was a great place to take partial profits, because there could have been an opening reversal back up after testing below the moving average and below 100. However, the bear spike off the open was so strong that there was likely to be at least a channel down for a second leg. If traders moved their stop to around $7.30, it would never have been hit. The puts were worth over $10.00 by the close. Instead of placing a stop in the market, they could have their software alert them if ANR traded above maybe 102; if it did, they could have tried to exit the puts with a limit order. The problem with the protective stop is that if the market rallied strongly and no trades took place on the 100 puts, the stop would never have triggered even though the bid and ask were far above the stop.

On the daily chart, the day turned into an outside down day. In strong bull trends, there is usually not much follow-through on the next day (here, there was a small doji day), because the large outside down bar will likely be the start of a small trading range. However, a test of the rising daily moving average was likely in the near term. When a trader makes windfall profits off options, it is best to close the position and then look for other opportunities tomorrow. There was likely little left to be gained from this position, and holding it into the next day would have been a distraction from day trading.

FIGURE 23.8 In Volatile Intraday Moves, Consider Options

The Dow Jones Industrial Average was down 700 points today (September 29, 2008, shown in Figure 23.8) on the House of Representatives' failure to pass a $700 billion Wall Street bailout bill. Because the Dow fell 430 points in just 10 minutes, the risk of order systems getting overloaded and locked up was real. As an alternative to Eminis and stocks, you could have purchased calls if you wanted to trade countertrend. For example, a SPY November 114 call could have been bought for about $6.00 at the close of bar 1 and then sold near the moving average for an 80 cent gain (that is a profit of $80 per contract, since each stock option represents 100 shares of stock).

If you bought the possible bar 3 double bottom bull flag (not ideal because you want a bull signal bar when trading against a strong bear trend), you could have bought the calls for $6.80. I tried to buy the QLD, which is an exchange-traded find (ETF) with twice the leverage of the QQQ, from one broker, but immediately canceled my order based on the bear signal bar. However, the broker's online order system did not let me cancel the order and it did not tell me if it was filled. I placed a stop order just in case, but now I had two orders that I did not know whether they were filled. I immediately hedged with another broker (all traders should have at least two brokers for this very important rare reason), and my hedge was twice the size, even though I did not know if the original long or the stop got filled. I kept

Figure 23.8   OPTIONS   **453**

checking, and 40 minutes later the first broker gave me my fill on my original trade and on my stop. I lost only 4 cents! For the hedge, I could have used a number of different instruments. I bought the QID, which is an ETF that is the inverse of the QQQ and twice the leverage, to offset my QLD. At the new low of the day, which was a lower low after a trend line break (the sideways action to bar 3 qualifies as a break of the bear trend), there was a bull inside bar. I exited my hedge with $1.40 profit and bought SPY calls for $5.80. I exited the calls on the test of the moving average with a 50 cent profit.

This is not how I like to trade, even though everything turned out well. My mistake was assuming that today's technology was good enough so that order systems would no longer lock up. It made much more sense to just trade calls, like at the bar 4 low, so that my risk would have been defined even if the order system locked up.

One final point about buying calls on huge days like this: The CBOE Volatility Index (VIX) hit 50 today, which is extremely unusual. Every 16 points in the VIX means that the S&P will have an average daily range of about 1 percent. A VIX of 50 means that the average daily range is about 3 percent, or over 3 points when the SPY is around 115. That means it is not sustainable. If you buy calls, their premiums will shrink rapidly, which makes them not great overnight trades. For example, the SPY was up $3.00 the next day, but the calls were up only about $0.50 due to the dramatic contraction in volatility. At-the-money calls normally move about $0.50 for every $1.00 move in the underlying, so clearly the risk/reward ratio is poor when buying options when the VIX is high.

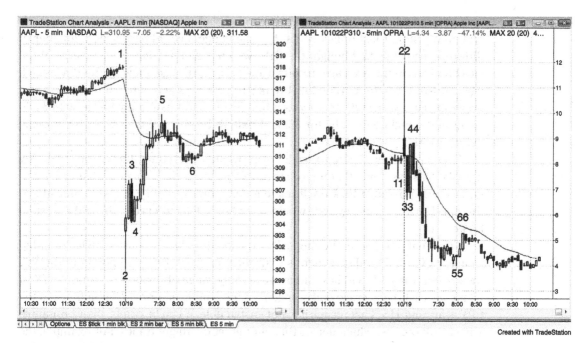

FIGURE 23.9 AAPL Dropped on Earnings but Puts Did Not Rise

As shown in Figure 23.9, AAPL was up 40 percent in the past two months and earnings came out after the close yesterday. A trader who bought an OTM 310 put on the close yesterday for about $8.00 expected a windfall profit on the open when AAPL opened down $14.00. Instead, the put was only briefly profitable and it quickly fell to well below the purchase price even though AAPL remained down for hours. Premium is often so inflated before a catalyst that only a huge move will lead to a profitable trade. Traders need to be very careful when buying options before a catalyst and should not buy them when the volatility is too high, meaning that the options are too expensive.

Bar 2 in AAPL on the chart on the left corresponds to bar 22 on the chart on the right of the OTM one-month-out November 310 put.

At bar 5, AAPL was still down about $5.00, about 1.6 percent, yet at the same time the put at bar 55 was down $4.00 when put buyers were hoping that it would be up at least a dollar to $9.00 or more. This was because the puts were very expensive ahead of earnings, and once the earnings came out last night, the uncertainty evaporated and the premium got crushed.

CHAPTER 24

The Best Trades: Putting It All Together

The market is linear—it can only go up or down. When you plot it on a conventional chart with time on the horizontal axis, you add a second dimension, but the market itself is only price, which means that it has only one dimension. You can make bull and bear bodies have different colors, incorporate volume into the widths of the bodies, or add all kinds of indicators, increasing the number of dimensions, but the market itself is one-dimensional. The recurring theme of these books is that the market is basically simple. It moves up or down because it is constantly searching for the best price, which changes constantly because of unending changes in countless fundamentals. The fundamentals are anything that traders feel are important, and include data on every stock, the overall market, politics, natural and manmade events from earthquakes to wars, and international factors. This results in the market always trying to break out from a trading range (its current area of agreement on the value of the market) into a trend, as it searches for the appropriate instantaneous value for the market. If the breakout is to the upside, the bulls are momentarily successfully asserting their opinion that the market is too cheap. If there is instead a downside breakout, then the bears at least briefly are winning their argument that the market is too expensive. Every breakout attempt is met by traders holding the opposite belief, and they will try to make the breakout fail and the market reverse. This is true on every time frame and on every bar and series of bars. The trading range can be a single bar or a hundred bars, and the breakout can last one bar or many bars. The key to trading is developing the ability to assess whether the bulls or bears are stronger. When a trader believes that the odds favor one side over the other, he has an edge. The "odds" refers to the trader's equation. An edge (positive trader's equation) exists if the probability of a trade reaching his profit target before hitting his protective stop is greater than the probability of the market hitting his stop before reaching his target. Having an edge gives him an opportunity to make money by placing a trade.

Every type of market does something to make trading difficult. The market is filled with very smart people who are trying as hard to take money from your account as you are trying to take money from theirs, so nothing is ever easy. This even includes making profits in a strong trend. When the market is trending strongly with large trend bars, the risk is great because the protective stop often belongs beyond the start of the spike. Also, the spike grows quickly, and many traders are so shocked by the size and speed of the breakout that they are unable to quickly reduce their position size and increase their stop size, and instead watch the trend move rapidly as they hope for a pullback. Swing traders are often uncomfortable entering on the spike because they prefer trades where the reward is two or more times the size of the risk. They are willing to miss a high-probability trade where the reward is only equal to the size of the risk.

Once the trend enters its channel phase, it always looks like it is reversing. For example, in a bull trend, there will be many reversal attempts, but almost all quickly evolve into bull flags. Most bull channels will have weak buy signal bars and the signals will force those bulls who prefer stop entries to buy at the top of the weak channel. This is a low-probability long trade, even though the market is continuing up. Swing traders who are comfortable taking low-probability buy setups near the top of weak bull channels love this kind of price action, because they can make many times what they are risking and this more than makes up for the relatively low probability of success. However, it is difficult for most traders to buy low-probability setups near the top of a weak bull channel. Traders who only want to take high-probability trades often sit back and watch the trend grind higher for many bars, because there may not be a high-probability entry for 20 or more bars. The result is that they see the market going up and want to be long, but miss the entire trend. They only want a high-probability trade, like a high 2 pullback to the moving average. If they do not get an acceptable pullback, they will continue to wait and miss the trend. This is acceptable because traders should always stay in their comfort zone. If they are only comfortable taking high-probability stop entries, then they are correct in waiting. The channel will not last forever, and they will soon find acceptable setups. Experienced traders buy on limit orders around and below the lows of prior bars, and they will sometimes take some short scalps during the bull channel. Both can be high-probability trades, including the shorts, if there is a strong bear reversal bar at a resistance level, and some reason to think that a pullback is imminent.

Once the channel phase ends, the market enters a trading range, where there are many strong bull spikes that race to the top and strong bear spikes that race to the bottom. Traders often focus on the strong spike and assume that the breakout will succeed. They end up buying high and selling low, which is the exact opposite of what profitable traders do. Also, the reversals down from the top and up from the bottom usually have weak signal bars, and traders find it hard to take the entries that they have to take if they expect to make money in a trading range. Within a trading range, the probability for most trades hovers around 50 percent, and only occasionally gets to around 60 percent. This means that there are few high-probability setups. Also, lots of low-probability events happen, like reversals that don't look good but still lead to big swings, and no follow-through after strong spikes.

All of this makes it sound impossible to make money as a trader, but if you go back to each relevant section, you will remember that there are profitable ways to trade the market, no matter how it is behaving. Your edge is always going to be small, but if you are a careful, unemotional, and objective reader of the chart in front of you, and only look to take the best trades, you are in a position to make a living as a trader.

There are traders trading for every reason and on all time frames at every second on every chart. What generalities can be made about how discretionary traders, whether institutional or individual, will trade a bull trend? A bull trend begins with a breakout, which is a spike up, and can contain one or many bull trend bars. If the breakout fails, the market will fall back into the trading range, and traders will fade the breakout (it will be a final flag reversal) and continue to trade the trading range. When a breakout is strong and successful, most discretionary traders will buy with a sense of urgency. They will buy at the market, on small pullbacks, at the close of the bar, and above each prior bar. Once the market transitions into a channel, they will buy below the low of the prior bar, like below low 1 and low 2 signal bars, expecting reversal attempts to fail (in a trend, most reversal attempts fail), and above the high of the prior bar, like above high 1, high 2, and triangle buy setups. They will then buy pullbacks from the breakouts of these small bull flags. They will even buy the first breakout of a bear micro channel in a strong bull trend, knowing that there might not be a breakout pullback setup until after the market has rallied many bars. Early on, when the trend is strong, they will buy on new breakouts above prior swing highs, but as the two-sided trading (selling pressure) increases, as seen by more and larger bear trend bars and more bars with tails on their top, traders will begin to sell above prior swing highs. Most will be selling to take profits on their longs, but as the slope of the channel becomes flatter and the pullbacks become deeper, more traders will start to short above swing highs, looking for scalps. When the two-sided trading increases to the point that the bears are about as strong as the bulls, traders will see the market as having entered a trading range. This means that they are much less certain that the trend will resume on each rally attempt (they no longer are looking for pullbacks in a strong bull trend, where the breakout usually quickly tests the old high). They will buy low, sell high, and most will scalp. They will look for high 1 and high 2 buy setups near the top of the range, and will short above the signal bars, instead of buying up there. At first, they will only look for scalps, like pullbacks to the moving average, the bottom of the trading range, or the bottom of the bull channel. Once they see increasing selling pressure, they will begin to swing some and eventually all of their shorts, and will only look to buy deep pullbacks, lasting 10 or more bars and having two or more legs. After there has been one or more pullbacks where the selling was strong enough to break below the trend line and below the moving average, some bears will look to short the test of the bull trend high, expecting a major trend reversal. They will short a reversal setup at a lower high, a double top, or a higher high, even though they realize that the chance of a swing down might be 40 percent or less. As long as the reward is much larger than the risk, they have a positive trader's equation, even though the chance of success is relatively low. Bulls will buy reasonable setups at the bottom of the trading range, like on larger high 2 buy setups, wedge bull flags, higher time frame trend lines, and measured move targets. Traders realize that a trading range is simply a pullback on a higher time frame chart. When the spike and channel are steep on a 5 minute chart, they together form a simple spike on a higher time frame chart, like a 15 or 60 minute chart. The trading range on the 5 minute chart is usually just a pullback on a 15 or 60 minute chart. When bulls buy near the bottom of a 5 minute trading range, many will hold for a swing up, a breakout to a new high, and a measured move up, even though the probability may be less than 50 percent. This relatively low-probability swing long has a positive trader's equation because the reward is much larger than the risk.

While in the trading range phase, signals are often unclear, and there is a sense of uncertainty. Most of the signals will be micro double bottoms and tops, and small final flag reversals. This is lower probability trading, and traders have to be careful and quick to take profits (scalp). They must force themselves to buy low and sell high, not buy strong bull spikes near the top of the range and short strong bear spikes near the bottom. Invariably, the spikes look strong, but don't overlook all of the bars before them—in a trading range, most breakout attempts fail. Once the market has entered a trading range, if a leg is in a strong micro channel, lasting four or more bars, don't enter on the breakout. Wait to see if the breakout is strong. If so, enter on the pullback from the breakout. If there is a bear micro channel down to the bottom of the range, wait for the bull breakout and look to buy the pullback, whether it forms a higher low, a micro double bottom, or a lower low. If there is a bull micro channel up to the top of the range, wait to sell a lower high, micro double top, or higher high pullback. As with all trades, always make sure that there is an appropriate signal bar.

If the market enters a tight trading range, wait for the breakout, because tight trading ranges trump everything, including every logical reason to take a trade. Using stop entries in a tight trading range is a losing strategy, but the setups always look worthwhile. Instead, patiently wait for the breakout and then decide if it is likely to succeed or fail.

If there is a successful breakout of the top of the entire trading range, the process starts all over again. Traders will see the breakout as a spike and they will look for at least a measured move up. If there is an upside breakout, but it fails and the market reverses, traders will view the trading range as the final flag in the bull trend. If there is then a breakout below the trading range, traders will evaluate the strength of the breakout, and if it is strong, they will repeat the entire process in the opposite direction. The downside breakout from the trading range can occur without first having a failed upside breakout. Instead of a final flag reversal, the trading range can be some other kind of reversal setup, like a double top, a triple top, a head and shoulders top, or a triangle. All that matters is that there is a strong downside breakout, and traders will then expect pullbacks and a bear channel to follow the bear breakout, and then the market to evolve into a trading range, which can be then followed by a bull or bear breakout. Examples of best trades include:

- Opening reversals where the setup is strong:
  - Swing for a reward that is at least twice the risk: the probability of success is 50 to 60 percent.
  - Scalp for a reward that is at least as large as the risk: the probability is about 60 to 70 percent.
- Strong reversals, where the reward is at least twice the risk and the probability is 50 to 60 percent:
  - Major trend reversal: Following a strong break of the trend line, look for a weak trend resumption to fail on a test of the trend's extreme; the reversal signal bar should be strong. After a bear trend, look to buy a higher low, double bottom, or lower low. After a bull trend, look to short a higher high, double top, or lower high.
  - Strong final flag reversal after a swing up or down in a trading range or weak channel.
  - Buying a third or fourth push down in a bear stairs pattern for a test of the low of the prior push down.
  - Selling a third or fourth push up in a bull stairs pattern for a test of the high of the prior push up.
  - Trading when the channel in a spike and channel day or the breakout in a trending trading range day reaches a measured move target and the move is weakening.
- Buying a high 2 pullback to the moving average in a bull trend.
- Selling a low 2 pullback to the moving average in a bear trend.
- Buying a wedge bull flag pullback in a bull trend.
- Selling a wedge bear flag pullback in a bear trend.

- Buying a breakout pullback after a breakout from a bull flag in a bull trend.
- Selling a breakout pullback after a breakout from a bear flag in a bear trend.
- Buying a high 1 pullback in a strong bull spike in a bull trend, but not after a strong buy climax.
- Selling a low 1 pullback in a strong bear spike in a bear trend, but not after a strong sell climax.
- Shorting at the top of a trading range, especially if it is a second entry.
- Buying at the bottom of a trading range, especially if it is a second entry.

Entering using limit orders requires more experience reading charts, because the traders are entering in a market that is going in the opposite direction to their trade. Traders should only use limit orders to trade in the direction of the trend. For example, if a trader is thinking about using a limit order to buy at the low of the prior bar, he should only do so if the market is always-in long, or he thinks that it is likely to immediately switch to always-in long. He should never buy with the intention of scalping the long and then shorting once the low 2 sell setup forms if he believes that the market is still always-in short and is likely to have only one more small push up. The probability of success is simply too low when using limit orders to trade countertrend. The low probability results in a losing trader's equation and you will lose money, unless you are an exceptional profitable and experienced scalper. Surprises in trends are usually in the direction of the trend, so when you think that the low 1 in a bear trend is weak and that the market should have one more push up, the odds are too great that it will not. However, experienced traders can reliably use limit or market orders with these potential best trade setups:

- Buying a bull spike in a strong bull breakout at the market or on a limit order at or below the low of the prior bar (entering in spikes requires a wider stop and the spike happens quickly; this combination is difficult for many traders).
- Selling a bear spike in a strong bear breakout at the market or on a limit order at or above the high of the prior bar (entering in spikes requires a wider stop and the spike happens quickly; this combination is difficult for many traders).
- Buying at or below a low 1 or 2 weak signal bar on a limit order in a possible new bull trend after a strong reversal up or at the bottom of a trading range.
- Shorting at or above a high 1 or 2 weak signal bar on a limit order in a possible new bear trend after a strong reversal down or at the top of a trading range.
- Buying at or below the prior bar on a limit order in a quiet bull flag at the moving average.
- Shorting at or above the prior bar on a limit order in a quiet bear flag at the moving average.
- Buying below a bull bar that breaks above a bull flag, anticipating a breakout pullback.

- Selling above a bear bar that breaks below a bear flag, anticipating a breakout pullback.
- When trying for a swing in a bull trend, buying or buying more on a breakout test, which is an attempt to run breakeven stops from an earlier long entry.
- When trying for a swing in a bear trend, selling or selling more on a breakout test, which is an attempt to hit breakeven stops from an earlier short entry.
- Buying a pullback in a strong bull trend at a fixed number of ticks down equal to or slightly less than the average prior pullbacks.
- Selling a pullback in a strong bear trend at a fixed number of ticks up equal to or slightly less than the average prior pullbacks.
- When a bear trend is about to break into a bull trend and needs one more bull trend bar to confirm the always-in reversal, and the breakout does not look strong, sell the close of the bull breakout bar, expecting the follow-through bar not to confirm the always-in flip and the bear trend to resume.
- When a bull trend is about to break into a bear trend and needs one more bear trend bar to confirm the always-in reversal, and the breakout does not look strong, buy the close of the bear breakout bar, expecting the follow-through bar not to confirm the always-in flip and the bull trend to resume.

Here are some guidelines that beginners should consider following until they are consistently profitable (at that point, they can expand their repertoire):

- Take a trade only where you are going for a reward that is at least as large as your risk. When starting out, focus on trades where the reward is at least twice as large as the risk.
- Take trades only if you think they probably will work. Don't even worry about how far the move might go. You have to simply ask yourself if the setup looks good. If so, you should assume that the probability is at least 60 percent (the directional probability of an equidistant move was discussed in Chapter 25 on mathematics in the second book). With the potential reward at least as large as the risk, this creates a positive trader's equation.
- Enter only on stops.
- Always have a protective stop in the market, because belief and hope will not protect against a premise that is failing.
- Have a profit-taking limit order in the market so that you will not get greedy and watch your profit disappear as you hope for more.
- Buy only above bull bars and short below bear bars.
- Trade only a small position size. If you think that you can trade 300 shares, you should trade only 100 shares so that you are in "I don't care" mode. This will allow you to be more objective and less easily swayed by emotions.
- Look for only three to five reasonable trades a day. If in doubt, stay out.

- Look for simple strategies. If something is not clear, wait.
- The best choices for a trader starting out are trends that develop in the opening range, strong trend reversals, and pullbacks in strong trends.

Most traders starting out will experiment with scalping for a profit target that is about as large as the risk, or swinging for a target that is at least twice as large as the risk, or a combination of the two, because they want to see if they can be successful and if one style better suits their personalities. There is no one right way, since all three have positive trader's equations when traded properly. The single best trade is a high-probability swing, because it gives traders flexibility, creating a bigger margin for error. The high probability allows scalpers to take partial or full profits and enables swing traders to make larger profits, giving all traders a good chance of making money, even if they take profits too early or too late. There are usually two or three a day. Most are either always-in reversals or pullbacks in strong trends.

If you are willing to take low-probability trades where the reward is at least twice the risk, you need to take every reasonable setup, because the math is against you if you cherry-pick. The trader's equation for these trades is positive for a basket of them, but the odds are that any one trade will lose (the probability is less than 50 percent, so most will lose). There will usually be only one or two choices a day where the reward is several times as large as the risk, but the signal is not strong (so the probability is low), and if you are patient, you will be able to anticipate them. Remember, the probability is low because the setup looks bad. If the setup is strong, then the probability might be 60 percent or greater. When that is the case, each trade has a positive trader's equation and cherry-picking is mathematically acceptable. Until a trader is reasonably successful, when he takes reversal trades, he should only trade them if the setups are especially strong (like a 60 percent probability). Every one of these reversals is likely to result in an always-in flip. However, it is important to realize that not all always-in reversals happen as reversals trades. Many often come as strong breakouts that have follow-through.

The mathematics of every trade is critical, and not thinking about it is the main reason people lose money. They see a strong bull reversal bar and quickly enter one tick above its high, ignoring that it is the fourth large overlapping bar in a tight trading range. They see four consecutive, large, bear trend bars creating a strong bear spike, and they short on the close of the fourth bar, ignoring that the spike is a simple bear leg that is testing the bottom of a trading range. They see a bull spike that is soon followed by a low 2 signal bar. They short below it, expecting a reversal, but not realizing that the market is more likely in the early stages of a strong bull channel. The market can change quickly when a person is considering a trade, and traders often struggle to give adequate attention to the strength of the signal and entry bars, the placement of their orders, the overall risk, where they should take profits, whether they are up or down on the day, and all sorts of personal issues. They often cannot process anything else, and that can leave them ignoring the most important consideration—does their plan have a positive trader's equation? Is the probability of success times the reward greater than the probability of failure times the risk? There is a natural tendency to assume that if most of what they are studying looks good that the trade should work, which is a proxy for thinking about the specific math, but it is always better to make sure that your plan is logical. For example, I saw a video on YouTube where the trader carefully explained that he always traded a second Emini contract, scalping it at a one tick profit, so that it would cover his commissions. He had a website and claimed that he was a profitable trader, and he might well have been, but it was not because of this second contract. He was risking to his protective stop, about eight ticks away, on both contracts. That means that he was risking eight ticks to make one tick on his second contract. This requires the market to move three ticks beyond the signal bar before hitting his protective stop in 90 percent of his trades just to break even on that second contract. Since it is very unlikely that this happens, then his second contract is losing money on average, even if it makes money on it 80 percent of the time! He might make enough on his first contract to more than overcome his losing strategy on the second contract, resulting in him being profitable at the end of the month, but he would be more so if he understood the math. If a trader has any strategy, he has to consider the math. If the market is moving too fast for a trader to consider the math of the current setup, he should not take the trade. Instead, he should wait to enter later, and only if he can convince himself that his strategy has a positive trader's equation.

Any kind of trade can be a best trade in the right circumstances, and some of the best traders have personal preferences. Paul Tudor Jones reportedly likes to trade reversals, Richard Dennis was a well-known breakout trader, Paul Rotter is a scalper, John Henry traded a basket of markets using an always-in approach, and just about all traders like to trade pullbacks. I prefer high-percentage trades, and my most common trades are pullback entries and trading range fades. I especially like breakouts because when they are strong the probability of follow-through is often more than 70 percent. I look less often for reversal trades, because most reversal attempts fail, but I will take a strong reversal setup.

After reading three books and 570,000 words, where does a trader begin? Book 1 dealt with trends, which is when the market is largely one-sided. Book 2 discussed trading ranges, where the trading is two-sided, and breakouts, which are transitions from trading ranges into trends. Book 3 has handled reversals, where a trend transitions into an opposite trend, or at least into a trading range. There is far more information than anyone can process all at once, and it is best for traders to pick one or a few approaches starting out. Some trades are illustrated in this chapter, and a trader who is interested in a particular setup can find more information about it in the relevant chapter of the appropriate book. As traders become more skilled and learn more about their personality, they will discover that they are more comfortable and successful with particular patterns and market conditions. Rather than fighting the market or their emotions, they should try to stay in their comfort zone and not worry about all of the other great trades that they are missing. If they followed dozens of markets and time frames and tried to catch the hundreds of set-ups that they would see every day, they would still end up trading between five and 20 setups a day and ignoring the rest. Since the 5 minute chart of any major market has between five and 10 best trades a day, traders stand a better chance of consistently making money in the long term if they just focus on a single market and time frame, like 5 minutes, work hard to spot those best trades as they are unfolding, and then carefully place their orders and manage their trades. Then they should gradually increase their volume, which will put them in a great position to make more money than they ever imagined, and all from a single chart. Trading is as simple as that; but as simple as it is, it is always extremely difficult to do in real time because it is a zero-sum game with edges that are always small, and the competition is the best in the world.

The market either is certain that the price is wrong and is moving in a trend in search of an area of agreement (a trading range), or it is in an area of agreement, waiting for a disagreement (a breakout) to develop. As a trend progresses, it pauses and breaks out again. At some point, traders believe that it has gone too far and they start to fade the breakouts, expecting them to fail and a trading range to develop. This creates double tops and final bull flags in bull trends and double bottoms and final bear flags in bear trends. The final bull flags are usually high 1 or high 2 setups, or triangles, and the final bear flags are low 1 or low 2 setups, or triangles. With time, disagreement sets in while in the trading range, and the market breaks out again in search of a new area of agreement. The breakout sometimes fails, and the market then searches in the opposite direction in the form of an opposite trend. This same process happens all day long in every market and on every time frame. The math favors the breakout in about half of the cases, and the failed breakout and reversal in the other half. The key to trading is being able to assess if one side has enough of an edge to create a positive trader's equation.

Making money always has to be a trader's primary objective, and the long, boring stretches, interrupted by brief moments of anxiety and uncertainty, are inescapable components of the job. If traders wait several hours and there is no setup, they will tend to become complacent. Once the trade begins to set up, they will sometimes not be mentally ready to take the trade. However, that is a challenge that they must learn to overcome. They are trading to make money, and they must learn to perform when the time is right. Firefighters wait for days, never knowing when the alarm will sound, but when it does, they have to act immediately and perfectly. They are professionals and get paid to do their job correctly. Traders also wait for events that come only occasionally, but they have to learn to be professionals and respond quickly and precisely when the time comes. If they can learn to be comfortable in this environment, they are in a good position to make a living as a trader.

A friend once told me that he lost money for many years and never made money until he stopped taking countertrend scalps. He now makes over a million dollars a year. He discovered the importance of taking the best trades, and that made all the difference. Other than when traders are taking a strong reversal setup, they should look to buy only when the market is mostly above the moving average and sell when most of the recent bars are below the moving average. If the market seems to be going both above and below, they should wait until it clearly is mostly on one side or the other. They should avoid countertrend scalps (and all scalps where the risk is greater than the potential reward), which always look so good and are profitable often enough to make traders believe that they just need more practice, but have a negative trader's equation and will slowly make a trader's account disappear. Countertrend scalps are most tempting in weak channels, where the with-trend setups just don't look strong enough, there are great-looking reversal bars at every new extreme, and traders are becoming anxious because they have not taken a trade in so long. For example, if there is a weak bear channel, there will usually be a bull reversal bar soon after each breakout to a new low. However, they are caused by profit-taking bear scalpers who are looking to short again just a few ticks above the high of the bar. An impatient trader who buys above the bull reversal bar on a stop will consistently lose money, because he will lose on 70 percent of his trades and his average loss will be larger than his average win. Always patiently wait for with-trend setups, and if there are none that you like, don't trade, and never take a tempting countertrend scalp. Once the market has clearly transitioned into a trading range, traders can then trade in both directions. However, most beginners start to trade countertrend while the market is still in a channel, long before it evolves into a trading range. If a trader cannot confidently make the distinction, he should only trade with trend.

Another common mistake is to look at 1 minute charts or other smaller time frame charts, like tick and volume charts where there are one or more bars every one or two minutes. The trades are very easy to spot at the end of the day and, because the bars are smaller, the risk is less per trade; but most are hard to trade in real time. The best ones happen fast and are easy to miss, and most traders then end up taking the ones that aren't very good. The market is always trying to reverse, and reversals occur on the 1 minute chart every three to 10 bars. However, most do not go far enough for a profitable scalp and instead become flags in the larger trend. A trader who just shorted a 1 minute top in a 5 minute bull trend will invariably lose and end up missing the 5 minute buy signal that the failed 1 minute top will create. If your goal is to make money (and that should be your goal), take only the best trades and avoid 1 minute charts. If, however, this is just an exciting hobby for you, remember that hobbies cost money and there may be another one out there for you that is just as much fun and much less expensive.

When thinking about taking a trade, a trader has to decide whether to buy or sell, enter on a stop or with a limit order, swing or scalp, trade his usual position size or smaller, and use his usual protective stops and profit targets or ones that are larger or smaller. This generates far more trader's equations than he could possibly evaluate in the limited time available. Once he makes all of these decisions, he then has to correctly place his orders and manage his trades. This is virtually impossible to do when a trader is starting out, so he should therefore look for ways to reduce the number of decisions that he has to make.

Most traders should keep things simple and try to do the same thing on every trade until they are consistently profitable. Stop entries are better than limit entries for a trader starting out. For example, if the market is in a bull trend and he is deciding to either buy on a stop above the high of the prior bar or with a limit order at the low of the prior bar, he should choose a stop entry, because the market is going his way when he enters and the odds that it will continue are higher. If he buys using a limit order, there is too much risk that the pullback will fall so far that he will get upset and exit with a loss just before the trend resumes. He should also begin by trading the same position size, the same size protective stop, and the same size profit target on every trade. He should either swing or scalp, but always use a profit target that is at least as large as his protective stop. He should not change his plan once he is in the trade, like converting a swing to a scalp, a scalp to a swing, or, worse, a scalp to one that is smaller than the size of his risk. If he finds himself changing his plan after he enters, he should just place his bracket orders, walk away, and come back in an hour. If he is worried about money as soon as he places his trade, he needs to trade a much smaller position size. If he has been trading 500 SPY shares, he should trade only 100, so that he is in "I don't care" mode. It is better for a trader to win on 60 percent of his trades using 100 shares than losing on 80 percent using 500 shares because of anxiety that prevents him from following his plan. If he is always eager to place trades, but constantly wants confirmation, resulting in him only buying at the top of a strong bull spike or selling at the bottom of a strong bear spike just before a reversal, then he needs to work on patience. He should avoid entering on breakouts and only enter on pullbacks. To improve his patience, he could try limiting himself to three trades a day. Once he has taken them, he would have to wait until the next day before placing another trade. It takes a long time to become patient and able to not take trades while watching a lot of great ones go without you. When he has any doubt about a setup, he should assume that the confusion is his radar telling him that the market is in or about to enter a trading range, at which point he should only buy low and sell high. A beginner who is looking to take his first trade should consider looking for swing trades either in trends that start in the opening range or in strong trend reversals at any time of the day. The potential reward should be at least twice as large as the risk. Although the forex market is essentially a 24-hour market and has no real open, it otherwise behaves like stocks and futures and should be traded in the same way. If a trader picks setups with strong signal bars and where the context is good, especially if it is a second signal, the probability of success is often 60 percent, creating a strong trader's equation. The trades that do not reach the profit target are either small losses or wins that approximately offset one another, so the overall risk is acceptable. Traders usually can learn to anticipate a setup many bars before it actually triggers, which enables them to be prepared emotionally when the setup is about to trigger. With experience, they can take more trades every day and begin to look for setups where the probability of success is at least 60 percent and the reward is at least as large as the risk (instead of at least twice as large, as is the case for swing trades). There are usually between five and 10 setups like this every day on a 5 minute chart, and since the reward is relatively small compared to the risk, these are scalps (a swing has a profit target that is at least twice as large as the risk). A high 2 pullback to the moving average in a bull trend where there is a strong bull signal bar is an example. A low 2 pullback to the moving average in a bear trend where there is a bear signal bar is another. After traders gain more experience, they can begin to enter during strong spikes. Consistently profitable traders can add any other setup with a positive trader's equation, even if it is not a best trade, including some scalps where the potential reward is less than the risk and the probability is 80 percent, and swing setups where the potential reward is much larger than the risk but the probability is only about 40 percent. They can begin to fade the tops and bottoms of trading ranges (especially on second signals), where they have a reasonable expectation that the always-in trade is about to flip into their direction. Trading breakouts is a good strategy, but is difficult to do for traders starting out, and most traders should instead wait to enter on pullbacks.

Traders often struggle as they decide what their initial stop should be. If the context is good, then the probability of an equidistant move up in a bull (or down in a bear) is 60 percent, as long as the risk is not too big or too small (like using a two-tick stop when the bars are 50 ticks tall). All trades where a trader chooses a risk that is not too big will have a positive trader's equation. If the bars are unusually large, like 50 ticks tall, a trader can use an eight-tick protective stop and reward, or a 19-tick stop and reward, and have a positive trader's equation. It does not matter what the trader chooses, as long as the reward is at least as large as the risk, and the risk is not too big or too small. Most traders instinctively know what too big is, like having a protective stop that is larger than the tallest bar on the chart, and what too small is, like using a stop that is smaller than normal when the bars are much bigger than normal. Just use something in between, like your usual stop, or 50 to 100 percent larger. Knowing this takes some stress out of the decision making. Just quickly pick a stop size that seems reasonable. If the bars are very large, you can use your normal stop, like maybe eight ticks in the Emini, or one that is two to three times bigger, as long as you use a reward that is at least as big.

Any trade with a positive trader's equation is a mathematically sound trade. For example, if a trader has a 50 percent chance of making $2.00 in AAPL before losing $1.00, the trade has a positive trader's equation and is a good trade. If the trader has a 60 percent chance of making $1.00 before losing $1.00, or a 40 percent chance of making $3.00 before losing $1.00, it also is a good trade. These are all trades that experienced traders take every day and make consistent profits by doing so. Among the good trades, there are trades that are especially good because the setup is unusually strong due to a confluence of supporting factors and a strong signal bar, and because the trader's equation is very positive. The very best trades have either a 60 to 70 percent chance of making a reward that is at least as large as the risk or a 50 to 60 percent chance of making two or more times the risk. These are the trades that beginners should primarily take, because trading is difficult and these trades have the biggest margin for error and offer the best chance of generating profits. For example, suppose there is a bull trend that has a strong sell-off to well below the moving average, then a wedge-shaped rally to a marginal higher high; the rally has several prominent bear bodies in it, indicating strong selling pressure, and there is a strong bear reversal bar that pokes above a longer-term bear trend line. Traders shorting below that bear reversal bar probably have about a 70 percent chance of making two to four times their risk. A strong reversal setup comparable to this forms several times a week in every major market, and there are reversals almost every day that are almost as good.

A trend reversal can be trickier for beginners because most reversals fail, and beginners tend to be overly eager and enter on weak setups. For a major trend reversal, there has to be a strong break of a major trend line, with the first reversal leg showing a lot of momentum and having a strong reversal bar. Smart traders will then wait for a test of the trend's extreme and enter on a successful test (a lower high, double top, or higher high in a market top, or a higher low, double bottom, or lower low in a market bottom). They want the signal bar to be a strong reversal bar. If the setup does not have every one of these components, they should not take the trade. The stop management is the same as for the trend trades described earlier. A major reversal has a potential reward that is many times as large as the risk. Those with a chance of success of better than 60 percent form only a few times a week, but other best trade reversals where the probability is 50 to 60 percent and the reward is at least twice the risk occur just about every day in every market. There will usually be a pullback before the target is hit, and many traders have a hard time holding on to a trade that had a scalper's profit and now is back to their entry price. However, if the original premise is still valid, that is the better choice.

There are also strong setups in the opening range on most days. For example, if the market gaps up on the open, rallies for a few bars, pulls back to the moving average, forms a double bottom with the first bar of the day, and has a strong bull reversal bar, there is probably at least a 60 percent chance that a long above that signal bar will lead to a profit that is several times the risk over the course of the next few hours. There is a reasonable swing setup that begins during the opening range on more than 80 percent of the days. A trader will often have to take several signals before one finally evolves into a trend, but the trades that do not are usually small profits and losses that offset each other. Most reversals in the opening range have only a 30 percent chance of generating a reward that is two or more times greater than the risk. However, there is usually at least one where the probability is about 60 percent, and traders should work hard to learn to spot that best setup. When they find one, they have to hold through pullbacks, since reversals are common in the opening range, even after a strong signal triggers. It sometimes takes a while before the trend breaks out. Alternatively, they can trade all of the reasonable reversal setups and scalp for a reward that is at least as large as the risk. Even though the probability of making twice as much as the risk may be only 50 percent on a strong setup, the probability of making as much as they are risking is often 60 percent or more, creating a positive trader's equation. The setups were described earlier in this book in Part III on trading the open, and the math is discussed in the second book.

If traders are comfortable trading in a fast market and increasing their risk, they can enter with the trend during strong spikes. For example, they could sell the close of the second, third, or fourth bar of a strong bear spike, and use a wide stop to possibly even above the top of the spike. However, they would rarely have to risk that much. If they used a wide stop, they would have to reduce their position size, but would still have at least a 60 percent chance of making as many ticks as they had to risk. If the spike was very strong and the context was right, they might be able to risk less than half of the height of the spike and still have a 70 percent chance of making at least twice as much as they had to risk. The difficulty is that the spike happens so quickly that beginners are usually not able to make the adjustments needed in the time that the market is giving them. They have to increase their risk and reward and have to emotionally adjust to a large, fast move, and this is usually more than most beginners can process. The key to any of these best trades is the ability to recognize them as they are forming, and that takes practice. However, if traders learn to recognize just one and carefully wait for it every day, they are putting themselves in a good position to make money.

Another example of a best trade occurs after a strong spike ends. For example, say a market just had a four-bar bear spike that broke far below a trading range where the bars in the spike had small tails and bear bodies of moderate size (not so big as to be climactic), and the market is now forming a low 2 pullback to the moving average with a bear reversal bar for the signal bar. This setup has at least a 70 percent chance of making a profit that is at least as large as the risk.

Some of the best trades are on strong trend days when most of the bars are on one side of the moving average, and there are only a couple of moving average pullbacks during the day. These strongest trend days happen only a couple of times a month, but there are reliable trends almost every day. Entering on those pullbacks, especially if they are high 2, wedge, or triangle buy setups at the moving average in a bull trend, or low 2, wedge, or triangle short setups at the moving average in a bear trend, are probably the single most reliable day trades that a trader can make. If traders follow a basket of about five stocks with large volume (over about five million shares traded each day) and an average daily range of two dollars or more, then they should be able to make one or two trades every day where they can net about one-third of the average daily range on the scalp portion of their trade and usually more on the swing portion, while risking about half of the reward. After entering, they should place a protective stop beyond the signal bar (they rarely will have to risk more than one dollar and usually under 60 cents) until the entry bar closes, and then once there is a trend bar in their direction, they should move the stop to just beyond the entry bar. For example, if the stock has an average daily range of three dollars, once the stock moves about 60 to 80 cents in their direction, they should move the stop to breakeven, or maybe a few pennies worse. If they bought at $120.10 and the stock hit $120.80, they should move their stop to around $120.07. After they exit half or so of the trade on a limit order at one dollar of profit, they should rely on their breakeven stop. They should trail this protective stop beyond swing lows on the 5 minute chart, and take a little more off at two dollars' profit. They should consider letting the final portion run until the stop is hit or a clear and strong opposite signal develops.

If buying a pullback in a bull is such a great trade, why is it so challenging to make money as a trader? It is because there are problems with every setup, and it is often difficult to believe that a setup is really as good as it is until a bar or two after it triggers and you are on the sidelines, watching regretfully. Every pullback starts as a reversal, and when it is time to buy that bull flag, you might still be haunted by that bear reversal and be too afraid to buy. Sometimes as a trend is starting out, it is still within a larger trading range. Since it is best to buy low and sell high in a trading range, traders will hesitate to buy a high 2 at the top of a bull leg because it is at the top of a trading range and has not yet broken out. However, if the overall context is good and the rally and setup are strong, it is the right thing to do. Similarly, shorting a low 2 at the bottom of a trading range is the correct trade when the market is likely beginning a bear trend. If traders are not certain, they should wait until they are more confident, but as long as they believe that the trader's equation is strongly in their favor, they must learn to take the trade. Yes, they will often lose, but the math is on their side. Remember, a great baseball hitter fails 70 percent of the time, but still makes millions of dollars from that other 30 percent. An experienced trader can win 60 percent or more of the time and have an average win that is larger than the risk, and sometimes two or more times larger. Be patient, but when the setup that you have waited for finally arrives, learn to take the trade and trust the math.

The sine qua non of trading pullbacks is that the trader believes that the chart is in a strong trend or swing. Since most traders will not recognize that a day is trending on a 5 minute chart until after the first hour or two, these trades will usually not be in the first hour. The easiest setup to recognize is a two-legged pullback to the moving average. The pullback to the moving average usually looks like it could never lead to much of a with-trend move, but invariably the move will take out the old trend extreme and run much further than you would ever imagine. It is important to swing part of every with-trend entry on a strong trend day, even though that means that sometimes your breakeven stop will be hit on the swing portion of your trade. However, the big runs will more than make up for this. At every new setup, you can either simply add back your scalp portion or instead place a full position on top of your current open swing position. Once you scalp out of part, your swing portion is then twice the size of your normal swing (or three or four times, if you keep adding on at every new signal). Most traders would find it easier just to add their scalp contracts back or to simply stick with their original position and scale out at different profit levels. Otherwise, you will end up with too many contracts to be comfortable, and discomfort makes it hard to follow your rules.

The market has inertia, and as such, when it is trending, about 80 percent of attempted trend reversals fail to reverse the trend and become flags (continuation patterns). Remember, a pullback in a trend is a failed attempt at a trend reversal. Therefore, trading pullbacks is a reliable approach to trading, and it is the approach used most by the majority of successful traders. Some pullbacks are large and extend for a couple of days and the entry can appear to be a reversal entry, but if you look at a higher time frame chart or if you compress the bars on your current chart to see more days, you will see that it is just a pullback.

Without exception, all strong trends eventually have larger pullbacks that evolve into trading ranges. Many traders wait for the pullback to become a clear trading range before beginning to trade the market as a trading range. If traders are particularly good at reading price action, they will sometimes begin at the earliest stage of trading range formation, which is at the end of the most recent trend leg. For example, they could short a minor new high in a weak bull channel that has been accumulating a lot of selling pressure, where the market is also at one or more resistance areas, like a measured move target. When shorting as a trend is temporarily exhausting itself, a trader is expecting a larger pullback or a trading range. Trading range traders are scalpers, and in the Emini, when the average daily range has been about 10 to 15 points, they are looking for two to three points of profit. Trend reversal traders are looking for a large correction, or even a reversal into a bear trend, and are planning to swing their trade for at least four points in the Eminis.

If the chart starts near the lower left-hand corner and ends near the upper right-hand corner and there have not been any bear legs that have dropped below the midpoint of the screen, or if there have been a number of swings with lots of bull trend bars and only small pullbacks, traders should buy every high 2 where the setup bar touches or penetrates the moving average, especially if the signal bar has a bull close above the moving average. Once long and once the entry bar closes, if the entry bar is a strong bull trend bar, they should move the stop from one tick below the signal bar to one tick below the entry bar. They should consider scalping out of half at a reward that is equal to the risk (they can adjust this with experience) and then move the stop to breakeven or maybe a tick or two worse. Add on at every new opportunity. Most markets are in a strong trend maybe 20 percent of the time or less.

When the market is clearly bullish, buying near the high (buying a pullback near the high) and exiting higher is an effective strategy, since the market often goes a long way before there is much of a pullback. When it is in a trading range, buying near the high is usually a mistake, and traders should instead try to buy near the low. When traders cannot tell if the market is in a trend or in a trading range, they should look to enter on pullbacks from strong spikes, which is an approach that works well in both trends and trading ranges and is why it is the best approach for most traders. If the market is forming a bull flag after a rally, look to buy. If it is forming a bear flag after a sell-off, look to sell.

It is natural to get confident after some success, and most traders will start looking to add more setups to their arsenal. Also, they hate sitting for an hour or two waiting for the best setups when they see lots of profitable scalps unfolding in front of them. The absolute worst thing to do is to start trading in tight trading ranges. These often occur in the middle of the day after you have been watching for an entry for a couple of hours. They are usually in the middle of the range near a relatively flat moving average, and they always look so simple. However, they will damage your account and your psyche. Unfortunately, everyone thinks that they can figure them out, and they trade them and wonder at the end of the month why they are down a couple of thousand dollars.

Notice how buying bull breakouts of trading ranges on stops and shorting bear breakouts of trading ranges on stops are not in the list of best trades. In fact, the exact opposites are there. Beginners should not use stops to enter on a breakout of a trading range, since most breakout attempts fail, no matter how good they look. Remember from book 2 that a trading range will regularly have a strong bull spike that races up to the top and looks certain to break out, or a strong bear spike at the bottom that appears to be the start of a strong downside breakout, but both fail and soon reverse. In a trading range, look to buy low and sell high, not buy high and hope for higher, or sell low and hope for lower. If beginners want to trade a breakout, they should wait until after there is a clear and strong breakout and then look to enter on pullbacks. With experience, they can enter on the closes of the bars in the spike and before the close, as the spike is growing.

Selling at the top of a trading range and buying at the bottom of a trading range is a reasonable approach, especially when a trader is entering on a second signal. This is a more difficult trade for beginners because it appears to be going against a trend. The market usually races to the top and to the bottom of trading ranges, giving the appearance of an impending breakout, but most fail. It is particularly good when the setup follows a strong move in this direction. For example, if there was a strong bull spike to the top of the trading range and the market then forms a low-momentum wedge bull flag to the bottom third of the range, buying a strong reversal up or buying a breakout pullback from the bull flag is usually a good trade. Uncertainty, which means relatively low probability, is the hallmark of a trading range. The market spends most of its time in the middle of the range where the probability of most trades is about 50 percent, and when it is at the top or bottom, it usually gets there in a strong spike that looks certain to lead to a successful breakout. Experienced traders understand that the spikes are simply tests and that 80 percent fail, and even though each leg is strong, the probability is 60 to 80 percent that the market will soon reverse and test the opposite end of the range. The difficulty that these setups pose for beginners is that the bull spikes to the top and the bear spikes to the bottom look so strong that it is hard to imagine that they could fail. But almost all do, and that strong momentum traps traders into the wrong direction and out of taking trades in the right direction. Remember, there is something difficult about every trade, but traders who understand the difficulty can see the opportunity that it presents.

When the market is not clearly trending, look to short a low 2 on a rally to around the level of the prior swing high, and buy a high 2 near the prior swing low (buy low and sell high). These days will have several swings lasting five to 10 or more bars and then the trend line breaks, leading to an opposite swing. If the momentum on the move to the prior extreme was strong, wait for a second entry, which usually comes within five bars or so.

Among the best trade setups, beginners should focus on entries that use stops so that the market is going in their direction when they enter. Also, they should only buy above a bull signal bar and sell below a bear signal bar. How do you know if a trade has a 60 percent probability of success? If you believe that the setup looks good and has a good chance of working, you should assume you could not have that belief unless the probability is at least 60 percent. When you feel especially confident about a setup, then you can use 70 percent for the probability in the trader's equation. Any trade in the three books can be a best trade if the circumstances are right, but many setups should be traded only by traders who are consistently profitable and very experienced in reading charts. Most traders should stick to the best trade setups. Remember, a 60 percent chance of success means a 40 percent chance of failure, and someone shooting at you with only a 40 percent chance of hitting you is still a source of great danger. Always recognize that the 40 percent is very real and dangerous, and always use a protective stop.

A best trade setup that has a 50 to 60 percent chance of success and a reward that is twice the risk happens in most markets at least once a day. Another good option is to take a trade where the chance of success is 60 to 70 percent and the reward is about the same as the risk. On the 5 minute Emini chart, there are usually several of these on most days, but most traders have a difficult time convincing themselves that the probability of success is 60 percent; therefore these trades are for more experienced traders. Also, there are usually just a few strong setups a day, so traders will not feel the constant pressure to make decisions that they would if they were trying to place 15 or more trades a day. This gives them a better chance of being objective and of reading the price action to the best of their ability.

Traders need to find a style of trading that is compatible with their personality, because if they plan to trade for a living, they need to be comfortable and happy with their job. Because everyone sees a dozen or more trades on a printout of the chart at the end of the day, there is a tendency to think that scalping is a great strategy. However, very few traders can take all of those trades in real time, and the best ones often happen too quickly to catch. Traders are then left with taking the easy ones, and so many fail that they lose money. This makes scalping for a reward that is less than the risk a bad strategy for virtually all traders. One of the great problems with scalping is that it is fairly easy to win on 60 percent of trades. This gives traders hope that they are very close to making a fortune. However, they actually have to win on about 80 percent of their tiny scalps to make a living at it, and as close as they think they are to that winning percentage, they will never get there. Another problem with small scalps is that beginners will often be wrong about what they think is an 80 percent setup. Many of their trades will actually be only 60 percent certain at best, although they seemed much more certain at the time that they took them. Beginning traders will probably think that they just need a little more experience to increase their winning percentage to 80 percent, where they know that the math would then be on their side. The reality is that they will never become that good because very few of even the best traders ever get there. That is the simple truth. Also, they will never become good enough to place 20 to 40 trades a day, which requires incredible focus and an exceptional ability to read charts quickly for hours at a time. Even if they could trade well enough to win with lots of small scalps for 10 days in a row, that is more likely to be the result of a statistical aberration than an ability to sustain that level of success for years. The result is that they will win most of the time, but their losses will be larger than their wins and their accounts will slowly disappear.

At the other extreme from scalping is swing trading for a profit that is at least twice as large as the risk and looking for only one or two good trades a day. Most of these setups are only 40 to 50 percent certain, but that is enough to have a favorable trader's equation. When one looks like it has a 50 to 60 percent chance of success, it is a best trade. On most days, there are usually a couple of setups, but sometimes there are five or more. This is the most reliable strategy, but most traders are uncomfortable sitting in front of a screen for hours at a time, waiting for a great trade to set up. Also, since it might set up and trigger in a one- or two-minute window, it is easy to miss it when it happens. Another approach that focuses on major swings is to try to be always in the market, looking for one to five reversals a day and trying to stay in the market in either direction for the entire day. However, most traders need to take breaks during the day and they have a difficult time placing reversal trades. Although they will take many always-in reversal setups, they usually trade each as a swing trade, and focus more on making a profit that is at least as large as the risk, rather than on reversing on the next opposite signal. Remember, if a signal is convincing enough to be an always-in reversal setup, it probably has at least a 60 percent chance of success, on average. This means that a trader taking these signals and using a profit target that is at least as large as the stop has a positive trader's equation.

The middle ground is what is probably best for most day traders, and is what most experienced day traders choose. They take about five to 10 trades a day and trade only when the reward is at least as large as the risk and the probability is at least 60 percent. Aggressive, experienced traders who are trying to catch these tradable swings look for micro double tops to short and micro double bottoms to buy. They do not think about the actual percentage, and instead simply decide if the trade looks good. If a trader thinks that a setup is strong and will likely yield a reward that is at least as large as the risk, then it has a probability of success of at least 60 percent (as explained in Chapter 25 of book 2). This allows the trader to have a stop that is the same size as the profit target and still have a favorable trader's equation. Although this is the style that most successful traders adopt, most beginners should instead look for strong swing trades, even though the chance of success is often only 50 to 60 percent. This is because when the reward is two or more times the size of the risk, the trader's equation is even stronger, despite the smaller probability of success. In the Emini, when the average daily range is about 10 to 15 points, look for trades with a good chance of a four-point (twice the size of the initial risk) or more swing, and exit some or all at four points. With experience, traders can scalp out part for two to four points and then swing the balance. If they focus on these setups, they are giving themselves a reasonable chance to become profitable. If they find that they often exit too soon, they should consider placing one cancels the other (OCO) orders (one to take profit at two to four points, the other to get stopped out with a loss of two points or less); they should then walk away and come back in an hour. They might be surprised that they have suddenly become successful. Once the trend is established, look for additional entries in the direction of the trend, scalping most for two points while risking about two points and, if the trend is very strong, swinging some. As simple as this sounds, trading is never easy, because you are competing against very smart people in a zero-sum game, and what looks so obvious at the end of the day is usually not very obvious at all in real time. It takes a long time to learn to trade profitably, and even once you do, you have to stay sharp and maintain your discipline every day. It is challenging, but that is part of the appeal. If you become successful, the financial rewards can be huge.

You have to consider the trader's equation and take a trade only if you believe that the chance of success times the potential reward is significantly greater than the chance of failure times the risk. You determine the reward by your profit-taking limit order and you determine the risk by where you place your stop, although slippage can make the risk worse than what your stop might indicate. The difficult part of the equation is the probability, which can never be known with precision. You usually have very little time to make your determination. Since trading can be easier if you have only two choices, in general, if you are not certain, assume that there is a 50 percent chance that your limit order will be filled before your stop is hit. If you are confident about the trade, assume that the odds are 60–40 in your favor, although they are often higher.

This math has important implications. For example, say you are trading AAPL on a 5 minute chart and are risking $1.00 to make 50 cents, and your chance of success is 60 percent; if you take this type of trade 10 times, you will probably win six times and make $3.00 and you will lose four times and lose $4.00, which means that you are losing 10 cents per trade, plus commissions. This is the scalper's dilemma and is the reason that you should avoid scalps where the risk is more than the reward. With experience you might be able to find scalps with an 80 percent chance of success and be able to use an 80 cent stop and a 40 cent profit target. If you can, then you will average only 16 cents per trade, which is a weak strategy; however, most traders cannot do that and should restrict themselves to trades in which the reward is at least as large as the risk. For example, if you know that you have to risk $1.00 in an AAPL trade, do not take the trade unless you believe that you have at least a 60 percent chance of making $1.00. Whenever you use a swing target, you have to allow for pullbacks, because you will usually need more bars before the target is reached, and when you are waiting for more bars, the chance of a pullback goes up.

Channels are hard to trade, and since the market spends most of its time in channels, the market is difficult to trade during most of the bars of the day. For example, if a trader is entering on stops, a bull channel is always forcing traders to buy at the top. Just after the bull spike ends and the channel begins, there are often one or more good high 1 or high 2 buy signals. However, later in the channel, if the channel is weak, it is better to not buy above bars. A bull channel is a weak bull trend, especially when the slope is shallow, and the trader's equation is rarely better than marginal when buying at the top of a weak bull trend. How to trade channels was discussed in the first book. They rarely offer best trades for most traders, especially when the channel is tight. If the channel has broad swings, it will usually create pullbacks that qualify as best trade setups. When it is tight, most traders should wait for the bear breakout of the bull channel, and then assess the strength of the breakout. If the breakout is strong and the market flips to always-in short, then look for short setups. If the market is in its bear spike phase, the probability of successful shorts during the spike is usually 60 percent or better, and these are often best trades. The first pullback after a strong bear spike usually becomes a reliable low 1 or low 2 short setup, especially if the signal bar is a strong bear bar at the moving average. These, too, are usually best trades. Once the trend slows down and enters a bear channel, especially if it is tight and shallow, most traders do not have enough experience to find best trades, and they should wait for the process to reverse, and then look for longs.

If you trade a 5 minute chart, there is at least a 90 percent chance that there will be at least one trade every day where the reward can be at least twice the risk and the chance of success is at least 50 percent. These trades are always easy to spot on a printout at the end of the day, but as they are happening they rarely look as good as you would like. The key to making money for most traders is to work very hard at spotting those trades as they are setting up, and to restrict themselves to only those trades, at least until they are consistently profitable. It can be very difficult to sit for several hours and not place a trade, but your goal should be to make money. If you are not currently achieving that goal, you should give serious thought to reducing the number of trades that you are taking and to just trying for one to three trades a day. Also, those trades should be the very best trades, like a two-legged pullback in a strong trend, a strong opening reversal, a trend reversal after a very strong trend line break, or entering on a very strong spike. With all swing trades, traders have to sit through pullbacks and not be too eager to stop themselves out. As long as the original premise remains valid, stay with the trade. Once the trend resumes after a test of the entry price (this will often run the breakeven stops of traders who tightened their protective stops too soon), then tighten the stop to breakeven.

When you read charts bar by bar, you will find an incredible number of setups, but just because there is a setup does not mean that you should place a trade. There are setups that form on every couple of bars of every chart on every market on every time frame. For example, on the 5 minute Emini chart, there are often 15 trades where a stop entry order would result in a two-point profit and another 20 to 30 where a limit order would result in a two-point profit, but the majority of these happen too quickly or are unclear as they are setting up, and most traders cannot expect to make a living by trying to trade all of them. A trader should not try to take 40 trades a day. However, beginners with a little practice usually can find three to five best trades a day. Even then, they do not have to take all of them, and should not worry about missing lots of great swings that they see after the fact. Great traders don't take most of the setups that they see during the day. They understand that it is not the number of trades that determines profitability. It is simply a matter of taking trades with a positive trader's equation, and you can take few or many.

One or more of the setups in this chapter occur every day on the 5 minute Emini chart and on the 5 minute chart of just about every market. If traders have the patience to wait possibly hours for one to develop and they restrict themselves to only the trades in this chapter, they would be very successful. However, learning to limit themselves to the very best trades is perhaps the most difficult part of trading. If they are not making money yet, it is something that they seriously need to consider trying. One important component to making money is avoiding bad trades that invariably erase much more than what a trader has earned from good trades. The single most important trade to avoid until one is a skilled, profitable trader is any setup in a tight trading range, especially when it is in the middle of the day's range, near a flat moving average, and the day is not a clear and strong trend day.

The first thing that traders should do when trying a new approach is to print out weeks of charts of the time frame and market they plan to trade and see if their setups appear to be valid. When they begin to trade, they should trade only one futures contract or 100 shares of stock, no matter how large their account is. If they have some experience and are determined to trade larger size, once they decide how large a position they can trade, they should trade only about a quarter of that size. If they think they can trade 10 Emini contracts, they should trade only two or three. They need to be able to not care about losses so that they can remain objective and continue to trade after a couple of consecutive losses. It is unlikely that they will be able to do that if they are trading their maximum size. Only after consistently making a profit for several weeks to months should they begin to increase their position size. However, most traders take many years to become consistently profitable.

The most difficult part of trading is deciding whether a setup is good enough to warrant placing a trade. It is especially difficult to do in real time when you always feel like you need one more bar to be sure, but once that bar forms, you've missed the best entry. It takes many years of practice to be able to look at a chart and instantly see what is happening, and even then nothing is ever perfectly clear. However, some things are easier to recognize than others, and a beginner is wise to focus on just a couple of setups that are easy to anticipate. Fortunately, there are many setups that are easy to spot and have excellent odds for success.

Once you are consistently netting a couple of points every day in the Emini or 50 cents or a dollar in AAPL, you should focus on increasing your volume rather than adding lots of new setups. These are the very best setups, and if you trade 25 Emini contracts and net just two points a day, you will make $500,000 a year. If you trade 100 contracts and net four points, you will make $4 million a year. Many stocks, like AAPL, GS, RIMM, and QQQ, can handle 3,000 or more shares without significant slippage most of the time. If you average 50 cents a day on 3,000 shares of just one stock, that is about $300,000 a year.

One of the most difficult things for beginners is waiting for hours for a trade to set up, and when it finally does, it is so easy to deny how good it really is. For example, if the market has been trading down for 40 bars, rallies to above the moving average, and then sells off to a lower low but forms a strong bull reversal bar, it can be hard to believe that the market might rally for the next 20 bars, but it can. If you cannot pull the trigger, greatly reduce your position size to the point that you really don't care if you lose (the "I don't care" size). As a trader, you must take trades if you are to make money. Keep the math simple and if you think that a trade will probably work, assume that the probability is 60 percent, although it might actually be 80 percent. Then, as long as your reward is as large as your risk, you will have a positive trader's equation. If you are uncertain, assume that the probability is 50 percent, but then use a reward that is at least twice as large as your risk.

If a trader looked at all of his trades over the past year, he might find that one particular setup contributed more to his profits than any other. Why not simply wait to trade only that one pattern? In fact, why not wait for only a perfect version of that setup? It is because you might only take one trade a week, and you stand to make far more money by trading as many good setups from reliable patterns that you can find. No one pattern is best. They all can be the best when the conditions are right. As long as a trade has a strong trader's equation, a trader will make more money trading it than by waiting patiently for the absolute perfect trade that might come only once a week. You make money by trading, not by waiting. The very best trade is a swing setup where the probability is at least 60 percent, because you will have a lot of flexibility in how you manage the trade and can make money by scalping, swinging, or doing some of both.

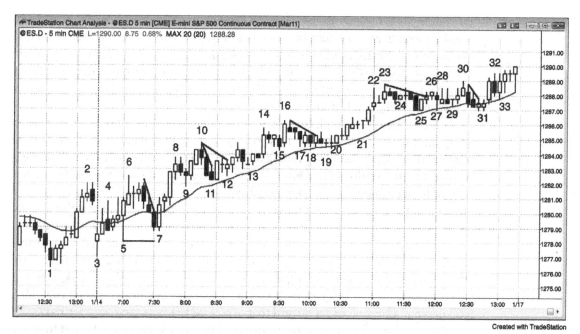

FIGURE 24.1   Best Trades in a Strong Bull Trend

Once a trader believes that the market is always-in long, the best trade is almost always buying a pullback, especially near the moving average and when the signal bar has a bull body. As shown in Figure 24.1, yesterday ended with a strong rally, and the market was always-in long at the close. The two consecutive bull trend bars on the open were enough to make traders suspect that the always-in position was still long. The four-bar bull spike up to bar 6 was further evidence of buying pressure. Bar 7 was a two-bar reversal buy setup because it was a high 2 down from bar 6 and a double bottom bull flag with bar 5. The bar 7 low was three ticks above the bar 5 low, which was a sign of urgency on the part of the bulls. They were so eager to get long that they were afraid that the market might not get all the way to the bottom of bar 5, so they bought several ticks above. This was also a breakout test of the bar 3 high (even though bar 7 fell one tick below the bar 3 high). The four consecutive bull trend bars up from bar 7 probably convinced most traders that the market was always-in long, and therefore they were looking to buy pullbacks, especially two-legged pullbacks to the moving average where the signal bar had a bull body, like at bars 7, 12, 20, 25, and 31. Bar 31 was a larger high 2 since it was the bottom of the second leg down from bar 23. Bar 25 signaled the end of the first leg down. By bar 24, the market had entered a tight trading range. At that point, most traders should have either taken any buy signal and been waiting patiently or been waiting with no position. The probability of an upside breakout

Figure 24.1　　　　　　　　THE BEST TRADES: PUTTING IT ALL TOGETHER　　**481**

falls to 55 percent or less once a tight trading range forms, even if the trend before it was strong.

There are often many ways to interpret a signal, and different traders will see it in different ways. For example, the bar 12 buy signal was a triangle breakout buy setup, where bars 9 and 11 were the first two pushes down. It was also a breakout pullback from the bar 11 two-bar reversal high 1 (bar 11 was the first of the two bars), which was also a double bottom with bar 9. Some traders saw it as a high 2 at the moving average, where the bar 11 two-bar reversal was the high 1. Bar 12 was a micro double bottom with the bull trend bar from two bars earlier. Most tradable bottoms come from some form of micro double bottom (or a simple double bottom, like the two-bar reversal at bar 7 with bar 5), just as most tradable tops come from some form of micro double top, like bar 6 with the bear bar three bars later, the bar 10 final flag and bar 8, the bar 16 final flag and bar 14, and the bar 23 double top with bar 22 (and final flag). In a strong bull trend like this, however, most traders should ignore these countertrend scalps and only look to buy.

Notice how the only bar below the moving average was the first bar of the day, and after the bar 5 bull spike, only two bars were able to close below the moving average, and they were quickly reversed up on the next bar. This is a sign of strength. At the end of the day, it is easy to see that this was a bull trend day (a trend from the open bull, a spike and channel bull, and a trending trading range bull). This was not so obvious as the day was unfolding because trend days always look like they are setting up reversals. However, each pullback becomes just another bull flag. Traders must constantly look for signs of strength, and if those signs are present, as they were today, they must try very hard to buy pullbacks because these are the best trades. The probability of success is 60 percent or higher, and the potential reward is at least as large as the risk. If traders held the trades as swings, the reward ended up being several times as large as the risk.

The market probably became always-in long as it traded above the strong bar 5 reversal bar. If a trader bought above bar 5, his initial stop was below bar 5, giving him a *planned risk* of 14 ticks. Once the market traded above the strong bar 7 two-bar reversal, he would tighten his stop to one tick below the bar 7 low, which was 11 ticks below his entry. At this point, the trader knew that the *actual risk* to stay in the trade was only 11 ticks. Since he thought that the market was always-in long, he believed that the probability of an equidistant move was at least 60 percent. When the probability was 60 percent, the minimum profit that he needed to create a positive trader's equation had to be at least as big as his actual risk of 11 ticks. This means that his strategy would be profitable as long as he took profits at 12 ticks above the bar 5 signal bar high, which meant that the rally had to reach at least 13 ticks above bar 5. This happened during bar 10 (it reached 15 ticks above bar 5), and this profit taking was part of the reason why bar 10 had a bear body. Many traders would have swung part or all of the trade for a larger profit.

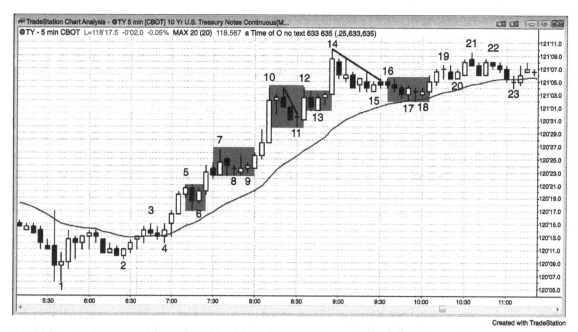

FIGURE 24.2   Best Trades in the 10-Year U.S. Treasury Note Futures

The 10-Year U.S. Treasury Note Futures market is one of the best markets for entering on stops when there is a pullback in a clear always-in trend. As shown in Figure 24.2, some traders saw the market as becoming always-in long on the two-bar bull spike that began at bar 1, and others saw it as flipping to long on the failed low 2 at bar 4, especially after the four bull trend bars up from bar 2. When the market broke out strongly to the upside from bar 4 to bar 5, it was clearly always-in long. At that point, traders were buying pullbacks. Bar 6 was a high 1 long buy setup. Some traders are hesitant to buy high 1 setups because the pullback often grows into a high 2 or a wedge bull flag. If traders do not want to buy the high 1 setup and also do not want to risk missing a strong trend, they can put a buy stop above the trend high. Here, as the bar 6 high 1 was setting up, cautious bulls could have placed a buy stop at one tick above the bar 5 high. This would have ensured that they would get long if the high 1 at bar 6 resulted in trend resumption instead of being followed by a more complex pullback.

Bars 9 and 11 were high 2 buy setups. Bar 9 was also a micro double bottom with bar 8, a pullback from the bar 8 high 1 or high 2 (some traders saw the bear bar before bar 7 as a high 1 pullback), and a triangle breakout setup (the three pushes down were the bear bar before bar 7, bar 8, and bar 9). Bar 12 was a large bull trend bar with a small tail on top and no tail on the bottom. This indicated that the bulls were strong. Bar 13 was then a reliable breakout pullback buy setup.

Figure 24.2   THE BEST TRADES: PUTTING IT ALL TOGETHER   **483**

Bar 14 was a large bull trend bar after a protracted move and after a small trading range (bar 10 to bar 13), which could have been a final flag. After a final flag, traders usually wait for at least a 10-bar, two-legged pullback to the moving average before buying again. The move down to bar 15 formed a wedge bull flag, but since it was a micro channel, most traders saw it as just one leg and were hesitant to buy. Most breakouts above bull micro channels are followed by pullbacks, so the strongest bulls waited to see whether the pullback would find support at the moving average or the move below bar 16 would lead to another leg down. The latter was less likely since the bull trend was so strong, the market was just above the moving average, and the market was still always-in long. The bull ii pattern at bar 18 was an excellent buy setup, since it was a micro channel breakout pullback, it was at the moving average, it had a bull signal bar, it formed a micro double bottom with the bull bar two bars earlier, and it was a 20 gap bar buy setup.

Experienced traders saw bar 14 as the second, third, or fourth buy climax and expected a trading range to follow. Although shorting here is not a best trade for most traders, very experienced traders would have shorted on the close of bar 14, at the close of the bear bar that followed, below that bear bar, or below the doji bar that followed, expecting at least a two-legged pullback to the moving average. Some of these traders might have shorted using a small position either because they were willing to scale in higher or because if they were stopped out, they would become even more confident of the next signal, which they would have traded with their usual size. Once bar 14 closed, some traders immediately placed limit orders to short at that closing price. Most of those orders would not have been filled, because the high of the bear bar that followed never went above the close of bar 14. This was a sign of urgency by the sellers, and it gave the bear scalpers more confidence to short the close of the bear inside bar or below it, expecting at least a test of the moving average. The next bar also failed to get above the bar 14 close, and its tail at the top created a small double top with the bar 14 high.

One of the reasons why many traders like to buy pullbacks is because the risk is smaller. Rather than having to risk to below the bottom of the bull spike, the trader can risk to the bottom of the pullback. There is usually less profit remaining, but that is the trade-off for the reduced risk. For example, a trader could have bought at the close of bar 10, but his theoretical protective stop would have been below the bar 8 bottom of the bull spike. If he instead waited to buy a pullback, like above bar 11, his stop would have been below the low of bar 11 and he would be risking much less.

The market is always trying to keep the probability around 50 percent, because then the bulls and bears are balanced. There always has to be an institution willing to take the other side of your trade, and it does not want to give you a 60 percent chance of success. However, it is unable to contain the probabilities perfectly, and they often reach 60 percent, giving traders a strong trader's equation.

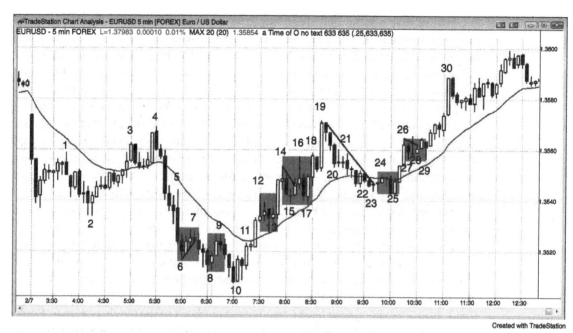

FIGURE 24.3 Best Trades on a EUR/USD Chart

As shown in Figure 24.3, the 5 minute EUR/USD forex chart, once the market is clearly always-in long or short, traders look to enter on pullbacks. The first two bars of the day were big bear trend bars below the moving average and made the market always-in short. Bar 4 was a wedge (with bars 1 and 3) lower high, and a second entry for a moving average gap bar short in the bear trend, which at this point had evolved into a trading range (bar 3 was the first bar with a gap above the moving average in the bear trend). Bar 5 was a large bear trend bar that was an outside down bar and a failed attempt to form a double bottom, so most traders saw the market as always-in short. Shorting below the bar 7 low 1 setup and below the bar 9 double top bear flag (double top with bar 7), which was also a breakout pullback short from the breakout below the bar 7 bear flag, were both reasonable trades. The reversal up at the bar 10 two-bar reversal was an example of a setup with about a 60 percent chance of making a swing profit, and therefore was a great setup for all traders, including beginners. Bar 4 was a gap bar in a bear trend, and that often leads to a test of the bear low (bar 2, as this point) and then a rally that has about ten bars and two legs as minimum objectives. The bear spike down to bar 6 was too strong for traders to buy. Bar 8 was a reasonable buy, since it was a second reversal attempt from the breakout below bar 2, an expanding triangle bottom (the third bar of the day was the first push down and bar 2 was the second), a final flag reversal from the bar 7 bear flag, and a strong bull reversal bar. Expanding triangle bottoms

Figure 24.3   THE BEST TRADES: PUTTING IT ALL TOGETHER   **485**

are always major trend reversal setups. However, since the legs up to bar 4 and down to bar 6 were so large, most traders would not call this a major trend reversal and instead would refer to it in other terms (although it was almost certainly a great looking major trend reversal on the 15 minute chart). Bar 10 was the second entry in an already strong pattern. Traders bought above the bar 10 high, which was the second bar of the two-bar reversal, and their initial protective stop was below its low. They took partial or full profits once the market reached twice the risk, and let the remainder of their position swing up, trailing stops below the most recent higher low. Some would have exited below the bar 19 double top (with bar 4), and wedge (bars 12, 14, and 19, and bars 14, 16, and 19), and others would have held, keeping their stops below bar 17.

The market was clearly always-in long by bar 12, and traders expected at least one more leg up and possibly a measured move up based on the height of the strong bull spike from bar 10 to bar 12. Bulls could have bought either the bar 13 high 1 or the breakout above bar 12.

Bar 15 was another high 1, but at this point the bull spike was not as strong, since it already had one high 1 buy setup, and the market was potentially near the top of a trading range. Bar 17 was a safer buy setup since it was a high 2 at the moving average and the signal bar was a strong bull trend bar (a two-bar reversal with the bar before it).

The pullback to the moving average at bar 22 was a bear micro channel, so the first breakout above the channel was likely to have a breakout pullback before the market rallied very far. Bar 25 was the breakout pullback buy setup.

Bar 25 was a two-bar reversal, and it formed a double bottom with bar 23. Some traders might call it a micro double bottom, since it included only four or five bars. It was also a pullback from the bar 24 breakout of the bear micro channel from bar 19 to bar 23, and an approximate double bottom with bar 17, and the first moving average gap bar in the larger bull trend, which is often a buy signal. Since the channel down was tight, waiting for the second entry above the bar 25 two-bar reversal was a higher-probability approach.

The bull spike up to bar 26 was made of three consecutive strong bull trend bars, so higher prices were likely to follow. The worst-case protective stop on any long was below the bar 25 bottom of the spike, but most traders would have exited sooner, like below the bar 26 low or the bar 25 signal bar high. The market triggered a high 1 long above bar 27 and then a high 2 long above bar 28. The market was still clearly always-in long, so traders should not have been too eager to exit on the pullbacks. Bar 29 was a wedge bull flag buy setup (bars 27, 28, and 29 were the three pushes down); it was also a double bottom with bar 27, a breakout pullback buy setup from the breakout above the bar 28 high 2 bull flag, and a failed lower high (the bar before was a small lower high and a failed high 2 buy setup).

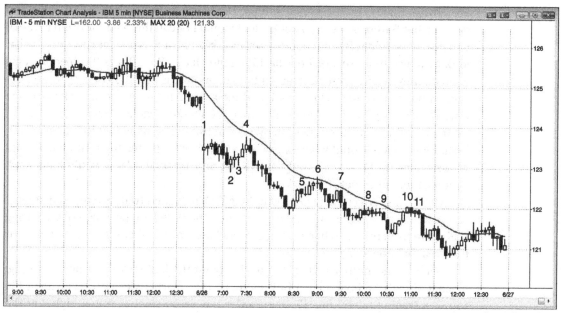

FIGURE 24.4   Best Trades in IBM

As shown in Figure 24.4, the best trades on this 5 minute chart of IBM include the bar 2 opening reversal and gap spike and channel bottom, the bar 4 double top at the moving average, the bar 6 low 2 at the moving average after a strong bear spike, the bar 7 low 2 and micro channel failed breakout, the bar 9 small triangle or sideways wedge bear flag, and the bar 11 low 2 at the moving average.

There were several moving average pullbacks in a strong bear trend. After the breakout below bar 2, traders would have assumed that today was a trending trading range day or possibly even a stronger trend from the open day. By bar 6, traders were shorting two-legged moves to the moving average and every low 2 that they saw.

Bar 6 was a low 2 short at the moving average (bar 5 was a small bear bar, ending the first leg up). It was a micro double top with the high of two bars earlier, and a one-bar final flag reversal from the inside bar just before it.

Bar 7 was a reversal down from the test of the breakeven stops below bar 6. It was also a pullback from the breakout below the bear flag that ended at bar 6.

Bar 9 was a low 2 short, and bar 11 was a low 2 short at the moving average, as well as a micro double top with bar 10. Neither looked good, but you must trust that a low 2 short at the moving average has a very high probability of success during a strong bear trend day.

Figure 24.4

THE BEST TRADES: PUTTING IT ALL TOGETHER **487**

The two-bar bull spike before bar 5 was very strong, and most beginners saw it as the start of a sharp bull reversal. In the move up to bar 6, there were seven bars, and only one had a bear body. It is easy to focus on this strength and deny what took place before it. This sharp rally was the first pullback to the moving average in over 20 bars, and experienced traders saw it as a sell signal. Beginners only saw the strength and looked to buy the higher low that followed, expecting a trend reversal or at least a second leg up. They dismissed the three strong bear trend bars down from bar 6 as just a sharp test of the breakout above the low of the day, and bought for the next leg up. Experienced traders saw this as simply an attempt to reverse a strong trend, and therefore most likely just a bear flag. They shorted the two-legged sideways correction at bar 7, correctly anticipating that the bear trend would resume.

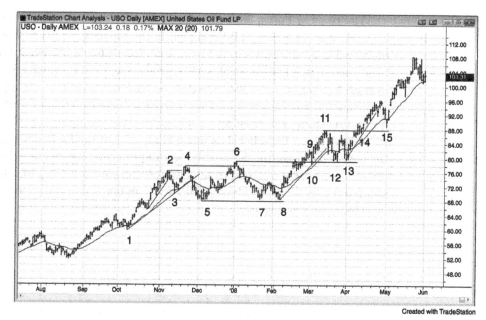

FIGURE 24.5 Best Trades in USO

As shown in Figure 24.5, the best trade setups today on the daily United States Oil Fund LP (USO) include the bar 1 wedge bull flag; the bar 3 high 1 test of the moving average; the bar 5 second entry in a large high 2 (bar 3 was the first push down); the bar 6 expanding triangle and higher high major trend reversal; the bar 8 double bottom (with bar 5) and the micro channel breakout pullback (the rally from bar 7 broke above the micro channel); the bar 10 failed micro channel breakout; the bar 12 second-entry moving average gap bar, double bottom (with bar 10), high 2, and breakout test of bar 6; the bar 13 double bottom and high 2; and the bar 15 high 2 at the moving average and breakout test of bar 11.

The market was clearly in a bull trend, so the best trade was likely to be any high 2, especially near the moving average, like at bars 1, 5, and 12. Bar 1 was a high 2 at the moving average, and some traders saw it as a small wedge bull flag. Bar 5 was the second leg down in a larger high 2 buy setup where bar 3 was the first leg down.

Aggressive traders saw the small sideways move to the moving average around bar 1 as a quiet bull flag and not a reversal pattern. They therefore would have placed limit orders to buy at or below the low of the prior bars rather than waiting for the market to resume the bull trend.

Bar 6 was a higher high major trend reversal and expanding triangle top, and a reasonable short. However, most major trend reversals do not lead to trends in the

Figure 24.5

THE BEST TRADES: PUTTING IT ALL TOGETHER **489**

opposite direction. Instead, they more often evolve into trading ranges, but usually have enough room for a small swing trade (a reward that is at least twice as large as the risk).

Bars 8 and 13 were two-legged pullbacks below the moving average (gap bars).

Bar 8 was the second test of the bar 5 trading range low, and bar 13 was the second test of the bar 6 trading range high breakout; both formed double bottom bull flags.

Bar 10 set up a second long entry on a breakout pullback (and a failed expanding triangle top from bars 2, 3, 4, 5, 6, 8, and 9).

Note that even though this was a clear bull trend, bar 6 was a good short because there was a trend line break down to bar 5. Bar 6 was a two-legged, wedge-shaped rally to a new high and the top of an expanding triangle (bars 2, 3, 4, 5, and 6).

Bar 15 was a breakout test of bar 11. Many with-trend setups will look terrible, but you have to trust your read and place your orders, or else you will be trapped out of great trades like so many other weak hands.

In a strong bull trend, you do not need strong setups to buy. You can buy at the market anywhere and make money, but setups allow you to use tighter stops.

Some traders move their protective stop to breakeven once the trade reaches about halfway to their profit target. For example, if a trader bought above bar 8, expecting an upside breakout of the trading range and then a measured move up, he might move his stop to breakeven once the market reached the bar 9 area, where the market was more than half of the way to his target and there had been several closes above the top of the trading range. If his protective stop gets hit, he should never get upset because it is doing exactly what it is supposed to be doing, which is limiting his losses, which come in at least 40 percent of his trades.

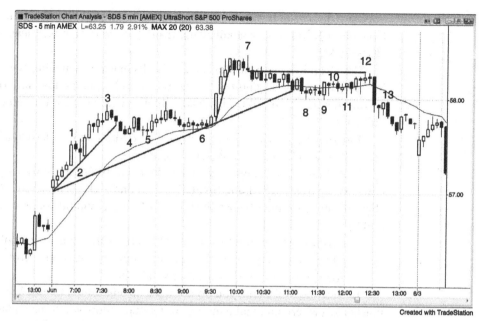

FIGURE 24.6 Best Trades in the UltraShort S&P 500 ProShares (SDS)

As shown in Figure 24.6, the best trade setups on the 5 minute SDS chart today include the bar 2 first pullback in a trend from the open bull, the bar 5 high 2, and the bar 6 wedge bull flag or triangle second entry at the moving average.

This was a trend from the open day. There was strong up momentum with the first major leg ending at bar 3. When there is a strong bull trend, look to buy a high 2. Bars 5 and 6 were great high 2 long entries, and bar 6 was also a moving average pullback. The bar 6 high 2 was for the micro double bottom that formed two and four bars earlier, and for the large two-legged move down from bar 3, where bar 4 was the high 1 buy setup.

Bar 7 was the second leg up and a failed flag breakout (a final flag reversal) that drifted down and broke the major trend line of the day.

When the market enters a tight trading range or a tight channel, most traders should stop trading. Some experienced traders will buy at the low of the prior bar and short at the high of the prior bar, and buy small bull bars at the bottom and short small bear bars near the top like after bar 12.

Since there was no clear rally in the move down to bar 8 and the bears had been in control for over an hour, it was reasonable to look for a second leg down. Bar 10 was a small leg up and bar 12 was a second leg up, and it had a low 2 on its rise from bar 11. Also, bar 12 was a small bar that gapped above the moving average. It was also a small, almost horizontal wedge top where bar 10 was the first push up

Figure 24.6

THE BEST TRADES: PUTTING IT ALL TOGETHER   **491**

and two bars after bar 11 was the second. It was also a low 4 setup, a lower high major trend reversal, and a test of the bar 7 low.

Bar 13 was a breakout pullback of the bar 9 breakout and a failed bull reversal bar, trapping longs.

Just before bar 7, the market entered a tight trading range and it continued until just after bar 12. This is the worst environment for stop entries because that is the exact opposite of what the institutions are doing, and your job is to copy them, whenever you can. As a beginner, you cannot enter with limit orders and scale in, so you have to wait. They are buying below bars and that is why the market goes up after falling below the low of the prior bar. You also know that they are selling above the high of the prior bar because the market then goes down on the next bar or two. Since beginners should only be entering on stops, they should never trade once they see any sign that the market is entering a tight trading range, because entering on stops will result in repeated losses. If you are a beginner and decide to take no more than three trades a day, what are you thinking during the bars after bar 7? Are you telling yourself that this is exactly what you have been waiting for all day . . . a nice, quiet market that is no longer scary? Or, are you thinking that the probability is so low that you would be foolish to waste one of your three trades here? Since clearly this is a terrible environment for entering on stops, a best trade will virtually never develop until after a breakout, and you will lose money by taking trades as you hope that your trade will result in a successful breakout, even though the prior 5 to 10 signals did not. Never trade in a tight trading range until you are consistently profitable, and even then it is better to wait. You could trade like an institution and enter with limit orders, scaling into shorts above and longs below as the market goes against you, but that is emotionally draining. The drawdowns get uncomfortably large and you will end up making mistakes, like exiting with a big loss just before the market reverses and goes your way. It is far better to enter on stops and wait for an environment where the probability is often 60 percent, and not trade in a tight trading range.

FIGURE 24.7 Best Trades in an AAPL Bear Trend

As shown in Figure 24.7, the best trade setups on this 5 minute chart of AAPL include the 20 gap bar short at bar 1 and below the bar 2 two-bar reversal, and the bar 7 double bottom.

AAPL was in a trend from the open bear. Bar 2 was a two-bar reversal setup for a 20 gap bar short. The bar 2 entry price was $169.88, and the initial stop was above the entry bar at $170.38. The entry bar was an outside down bar, and traders put their protective stops above its high as soon as they entered, probably before the bar closed. This was reasonable because it defined their risk, and they would not have wanted to be short if the market immediately reversed above the high of the bar. If it was not an outside bar, they would have placed their stops above the signal bar. The initial risk here was 50 cents.

Aggressive traders would have placed limit orders at the bar 3 and 4 highs, expecting any move up to fail and become a breakout pullback short setup for the bar 3 breakout of the bear flag. They saw this as a quiet bear flag and not a bull reversal, and expected more selling, so shorting above the high of any bar was a reasonable trade.

Bar 5 was a bad high 1 since the market was in a strong bear trend, and traders would not have exited their shorts and would not have reversed to long. The market ran 7 cents above the bar, but traders would not yet have moved their protective

Figure 24.7   THE BEST TRADES: PUTTING IT ALL TOGETHER   **493**

stops down because the largest open profit was only 38 cents, and they would have wanted to give the trade time to work. Typically, traders should not move their stops to breakeven on a trade like this until there has been about 60 to 80 cents of open profit.

On bar 6, traders would have been able to exit half of their shares with $1.00 profit using a limit order (the bottom of bar 6 was $1.07 below their entry price). As you can see by the outside up nature of the bar, lots of traders likely covered part or all of their shorts here. At this point, they would have moved their protective stop to breakeven or maybe a few pennies worse ($170.91 was reasonable, since AAPL rarely runs stops by more than a penny) and would not have exited unless there was a clear and strong reversal, which was unlikely on such a strong bear trend day. They expected pullbacks that scare weak shorts out. For example, the rally to bar 9 hit breakeven stops to the penny ($170.88) and then reversed back down.

If traders were stopped out, they could have shorted again on bar 10, off the bar 9 moving average test and breakout test. Bar 10 showed that the breakout test accomplished its goal of scaring traders out, because clearly lots of shorts came in. If traders let themselves be stopped out, they would now be short again, but at 41 cents worse!

FIGURE 24.8 Best Trades in a Strong GS Bear Trend

As shown in Figure 24.8, the best trade setups on this 5 minute chart of Goldman Sachs Group (GS) include the micro channel failed breakout that formed two bars after bar 1, the breakout pullback short (here, a low 2) below the bar after bar 3, and the second-entry long above the bar 5 bull reversal bar after the spike and channel down from the 11:10 a.m. PST bear spike.

A small pullback trend is the strongest type of bear trend and, since there was no prior bull strength, traders should only have considered shorting all day, unless there was some sign of a setup for a bounce into the close. Traders could have shorted any small pullback until the potential bottom at bar 5. By bar 1, the biggest prior pullback was a little more than a dollar, so traders could have placed limit orders to short at one dollar above the most recent low. They would have needed to determine where their protective stops needed to be in order to calculate a minimum reasonable profit goal. Since this is often difficult, they needed to think about a worst-case situation. For example, if the market traded above the fourth bar of the day, then the bear case would have been much weaker. Therefore, they could have used protective stops just above its high at around $179.50. Since they would have been shorting at around $177, they would have been risking about $2.50 on their trade. If they normally don't risk more than $500 on a trade, then they could only have traded 200 shares. Since this was a trend, they had to assume that there

Figure 24.8   THE BEST TRADES: PUTTING IT ALL TOGETHER   **495**

would be at least a 60 percent chance of a new low, or about a $1.00 profit, but they should take only trades where the potential reward is at least as large as the risk. This means that they should have been trying to take maybe half off (100 shares) at $2.50 below their entry price, or around $174.50. They would have been filled on the bear trend bar that formed two bars before bar 2. At that point, they could move their stop to breakeven and hold until the always-in position reversed to long, until their stop was hit, until any reasonable reversal up in the final hour or so, or until the close of the day. If they exited above bar 5, they would have made $900 on their second 100 shares. If they exited when the market became always-in up on the bull spike up to $170, they would have made $700, and if they held until the close, they would also have made about $700 on those second 100 shares.

This was a perfect example of reversal entries to be avoided. Every day, you should be examining the chart throughout the day, and especially in the first couple of hours, to determine whether the day is a trend day (the major types were described in the first book of this series). If it is, you should not be trading countertrend. A trend from the open day like this is the easiest trend day to see. You would have suspected it by the third bar of the day (a large bear trend bar, dropping far from the open), and you would have been very confident by the time the market broke below bar 1.

The bar 1 rally was a big bull trend bar that broke a micro trend line and was therefore likely to fail. An eager trader might then have bought above the bar 2, bar 3, and bar 4 reversal bars, thinking that the bulls showed adequate strength during that trend line break. However, the market had been below the moving average since the third bar of the day, and traders should remember that on small pullback bear trend days like this, the first rally to the moving average usually fails and then the market tests the low. Don't convince yourself that the market has gone too far and is due for a rally. By definition, you are thinking countertrend and looking for countertrend scalps on a strong trend day. You are afraid to sell near the low and instead are hoping for a trend reversal, which is a low-probability bet. Do the math. Most countertrend scalps will fail, and the amount you lose on each one will be too great to make up with the eventual winner or two.

However, since GS did not have a tradable low 2 short at the moving average all day, experienced traders would have been shorting even the tiniest pullbacks, relying on the typical pullback sequence (described in the second book in the series) to bail them out if a pullback went further up than they thought was likely. Every type of first pullback is usually followed by a test of the trend's extreme (here, the low of the day).

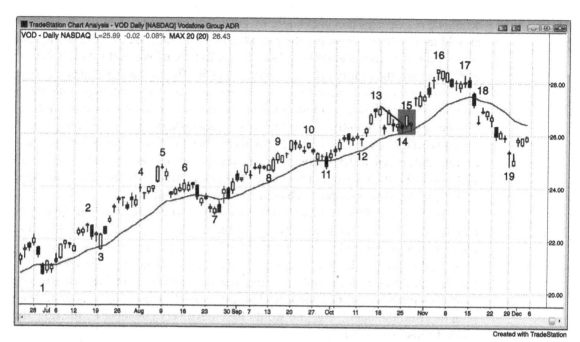

FIGURE 24.9 Best Trades on the Daily Chart of VOD

As shown in Figure 24.9, the best trade setups on this daily chart of England-based Vodafone Group (VOD), one the world's largest communications services companies, include the bar 3 high 1 at the moving average, the bar 7 wedge bull flag and second entry of a moving average gap bar, the bar 8 small triangle, the bar 11 wedge bull flag to the moving average, the bar 12 high 2, the bar 14 wedge bull flag, and the breakout pullback on a long at the low of bar 15.

When there is a strong bull trend and a breakout of a bull flag and the breakout bar has a bull body, buying below its low is a reliable strategy. This is because the pullback usually becomes a breakout pullback long setup and you are buying at a lower price. VOD was in a strong bull trend on the daily chart. Bar 15 was a bull trend bar breakout of a wedge bull flag at the moving average, so the odds were high that any pullback would be brief and become the signal bar for a breakout pullback buy setup. Traders could have bought on a limit order at the low of bar 15. Traders who waited with the plan of buying above the pullback bar were disappointed to see the large gap up on the next day. If they still wanted to go long, they had to do such at a worse price.

Although the market fell from bar 5 to below the trend line (not shown) along the bottom of the channel up from bar 3, the two-bar sell-off did not even touch the moving average. This made bar 6 a bad candidate for a major trend reversal lower high, and it was more likely that the market was simply creating a pullback. It ended at the bar 7 high 2, wedge bull flag, and moving average gap bar.

Figure 24.10

THE BEST TRADES: PUTTING IT ALL TOGETHER **497**

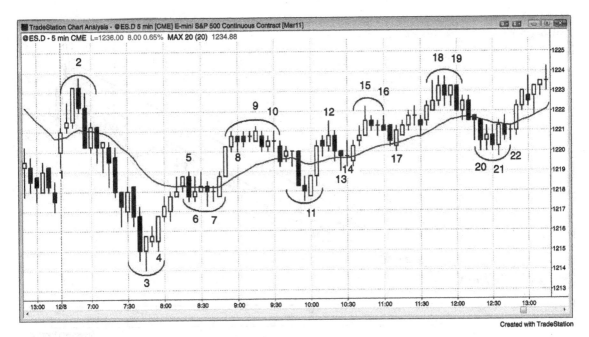

FIGURE 24.10 Look to Buy Low, Sell High Most of the Time

In general, always look to buy low and sell high, except in a strong trend where you buy high and exit higher in a bull trend or sell low and exit lower in a bear trend. However, if you short what you think is a minor top, like below bar 15 or 16 in the Emini chart shown in Figure 24.10, and the market then forms a high 2 as it did at bar 17, exit or even reverse to long. This is especially true if the high 2 signal bar is a bull bar that is testing the moving average. Likewise, if you buy at the bottom of a bear leg and the market then forms a reasonable low 2 with a bear signal bar testing the bottom of the moving average, exit and consider reversing to short.

When the average daily range in the Emini is about 10 to 15 points, traders usually have to risk about two points on a trade. They should look for trades where the reward is at least as large as the risk and the chance of success is at least 60 percent. There are usually five or more such setups on most days, like shorting the bar 1 opening reversal in this chart, buying above the bar 3 low, buying high 2 pullbacks (bar 7, the bar after bar 14, and bar 17), and the bar 22 micro channel breakout pullback. Remember, if traders think that a setup is probably good, they should assume that this means that the chance of success is at least 60 percent. If the reward is at least as large as the risk, this creates a positive trader's equation.

Note that most minor reversals come from micro double tops and bottoms and small final flags. Scalpers like to see these setups before placing their trades.

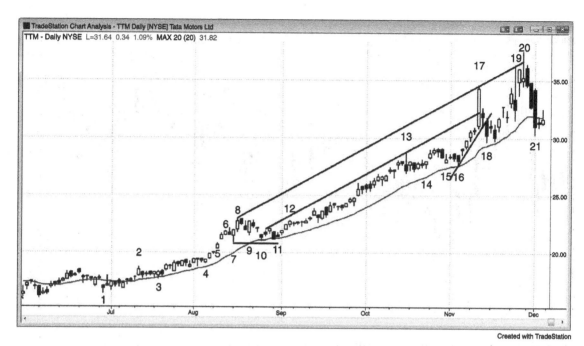

FIGURE 24.11   The Reward Should Always Be at Least as Large as the Risk

A best trade is one where there is at least a 60 percent chance of success and the potential reward is at least as large as the risk. As shown in Figure 24.11, the best trade setups on this daily chart of Tata Motors Ltd (TTM), the carmaker in India, were the bar 3 and bar 4 high 2 setups, any of the three bars in the bull spike from bar 5 to bar 6, the bar 10 high 2, the 11 wedge bull flag, the high 1 after the bar 12 breakout, the bar 14 breakout pullback and the high 2 entry on the bar before it, the bar 16 high 2, and the bar 20 higher high reversal.

A wedge bull flag pullback to the moving average in a strong trend is a reliable buy setup. TTM was in a strong bull trend from bar 1 and rose almost 40 percent in less than two months to bar 8. The market had a high 2 pullback to the moving average at bar 10, which was a reasonable buy, and it evolved into a wedge bull flag buy setup at the bar 11 inside bar, also at the moving average. Bar 11 was a pullback from the breakout of the bull flag that ended at bar 10, and it was therefore also a breakout pullback buy setup. If traders bought above bar 10, they could have exited at breakeven on the sell-off three bars later, or they could have relied on their protective stop below the signal bar, which would not have been hit. They could also have placed their stop a little below the bar 7 low.

Bar 7 was the first pullback in a strong bull spike in a bull trend, and it did not follow a buy climax. This was an ideal high 1 long buy setup, which was also

Figure 24.11   THE BEST TRADES: PUTTING IT ALL TOGETHER   **499**

a micro channel failed breakout buy setup. It was a breakout pullback buy setup, since it was the first pullback after the breakout above the tight trading range that ended with the bar 5 breakout.

The huge bull trend bar at bar 17 was a buy climax. Whenever there is a trend of 10 or 20 or more bars and it then has a huge bull trend bar, the bar often represents exhaustion. It formed due to some of the last shorts exiting and the late bulls buying. Both of these groups were weak traders. The strong bulls at this point would only buy a pullback and the strong bears would be shorting, and they would short more higher. The bar 17 breakout went far above the trend channel line of the past couple of months, and it led to the drawing of a higher trend channel line. The market tried to break above that line on bars 19 and 20 and both times found strong selling, as seen by the large tails on the tops of both bars, the bear body on bar 19, and the close well below the midpoint of bar 20. When the market tries to do something twice and fails both times, it usually then tries to go in the opposite direction. The bear bars starting at bar 18 and the large tails on the tops of bars 19 and 20 represented accumulating selling pressure, and the large size of the bars from bar 17 onward indicated that the bulls were trying exceptionally hard to convert the trend into an even stronger bull trend. Their efforts led to their exhaustion and the selling pressure wore them down. The market was likely to have at least a two-legged correction and a possible trend reversal.

The sell-off to bar 18 broke below a bull trend line, and all of the selling pressure made a sell-off likely, so shorting below the strong bear bar after bar 20 was a high-probability trade. This was a large bear trend bar that closed on its low and formed a large two-bar reversal with bar 20. The size of the bear body and the tiny tails indicated that the selling was very strong.

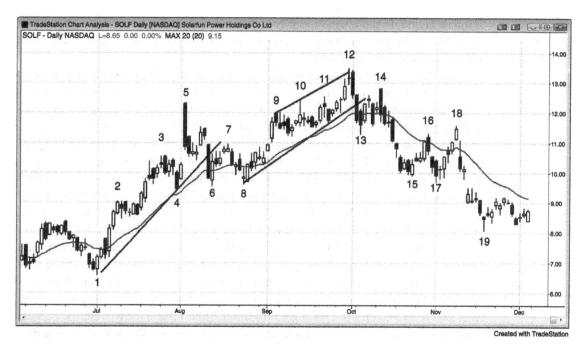

FIGURE 24.12 Best Trades in SOLF

As shown in Figure 24.12, the best trade setups on the daily chart of Solarfun Power Holdings Company Ltd (SOLF), the Chinese manufacturer of photoelectric cells that are used in solar panels, include the bar 4 high 2 at the moving average, the bar 5 huge reversal down from the third push up, the bar 7 low 2 after two strong pushes down, the bar 8 double bottom bull flag, the small high 2 after bar 9 and again after bar 10, the bar 12 higher high, and the bar 14 two-legged lower high.

A higher high reversal is usually followed by a lower high short setup. SOLF had a strong move down from the bar 5 high. There was a second large bear trend bar just before bar 6 and several other bear trend bars around bars 3 and 4. These represented selling pressure, which is cumulative and at some point can lead to a trend reversal. However, the bears were unable to string together consecutive bear trend bars after the trend line break, so the always-in position was still long.

The sell-off to bar 8 strongly broke the bull trend line, but the sharp rally to bar 9 broke above the bar 7 right shoulder of the head and shoulders top and was therefore likely to have follow-through. After the spike up to bar 9, the market had a channel up to bar 12, which formed a higher high above bar 12. After strong selling down from bar 5, bears were looking to short and bulls were looking to take profits. Some traders saw bar 12 as the third push up in the channel where either bar 9 or bar 10 formed the first push and either bar 10 or bar 11 formed the second push.

Figure 24.12   THE BEST TRADES: PUTTING IT ALL TOGETHER   **501**

The bar 12 signal bar was a doji, so some traders may have waited for more bear strength to appear.

The strong bear trend bar after bar 12 was a sign of strong selling and gave the bears the confidence to sell aggressively on the next couple of bars. This three-bar bear spike was made of bars with large bear bodies, and the spike broke the bull trend line. Traders believed that more selling was likely, and since the market was now always-in short, they were looking to short rallies.

The market formed a two-legged lower high at bar 14 that tested the bar 12 low, and the market sold off from the first tick of the bar. Traders were very confident that the market was going down. Some traders shorted as the market went below the low of the bar before it and became an outside down bar, while other traders shorted the breakout below the bar 13 spike, expecting at least a measured move down.

The bear spike down to bar 15 was also strong, but some shorts were trapped out by the sharp rally to bar 18, just above the bar 16 high. Some traders bought above the bar 15 bull trend bar because it was a double bottom bull flag with bar 8, a two-bar reversal, and a one-bar final flag reversal from two bars earlier. However, the bears returned on the bar after bar 18, which had a large bear body. It is easy to get trapped out of a great trade, but it is important to try hard to avoid getting trapped out. Do not tighten your stops too early, and try to hold some of your position with a breakeven stop until the market clearly becomes always-in long. The rally to bar 18 was not enough to flip the always-in position, so swing traders should have stayed short.

The sell-off from bar 5 to bar 8 was strong enough to make traders wonder if the market was evolving from a bull trend into a trading range. The rally to bar 12 had many pullbacks, bear bodies, and bars with tails on the top, which are signs of selling pressure, indicating a change into a two-sided market. This looked more like a bull leg in a trading range than a bull trend. Traders were beginning to sell above swing highs, like when bar 10 moved above bar 9, or when bar 11 moved above bar 10. Bar 12 was a signal bar for a higher high (above bar 5) major trend reversal, but most traders assumed that a trading range and a test of the bar 8 bottom of the range was more likely than a bear trend, as is always the case (most trading range breakout attempts fail). Although there was some profit taking in that area between bars 15 and 17, bars 16 and 18 formed a double top bear flag and led to a breakout below the range. Many traders took partial profits in the bar 15 area and moved their protective stops to breakeven, hoping for a bigger swing down, but knowing that the probability was less than 50 percent. However, they sometimes make a windfall profit, as they did here.

FIGURE 24.13 Best Trades in CX

As shown in Figure 24.13, the best trade setups on this daily chart of Cemex (CX), the large cement producer in Mexico, include the bar 2 final flag reversal and micro double top with bar 1, shorting during any of the three following bars during the bear spike, the bar 4 wedge bear flag pullback to the moving average, buying above the small bull inside bar after the bar 5 sell climax (failed bear breakout) and double bottom, shorting below the bar 7 low 2 and micro double top or as it went below the low of the bar before it (since that was a low 2 sell signal bar), buying the bar 8 triple bottom and bull reversal bar, shorting the bar 10 double top bear flag (with bar 9) at the moving average (which was also a bear reversal bar low 2 at the moving average in a bear trend), shorting the bar 12 micro channel failed breakout and breakout pullback from the breakout below the triple bottom buying the bar 14 micro double bottom bull flag, and failed low 2 after the strong bar 13 bull reversal bar and big two-legged move down (an approximate leg 1 = leg 2 move, where leg 1 was the spike from bar 2 to bar 3, and leg 2 was the bear channel from bar 9 to bar 13, which had three pushes; bar 7 was a smaller bear spike and it shared the same bear channel), and shorting below the bar 15 moving average gap bar, buying above the bar 16 higher low, shorting the bar 17 low 2 (there were two pushes up from bar 16, and bar 15 was the first push up of a larger low 2) and wedge bear flag (the bar after bar 13 was the first push up), buying the bar 19 higher low major

Figure 24.13   THE BEST TRADES: PUTTING IT ALL TOGETHER   **503**

trend reversal, buying the bar 21 high 2 (it was a micro double bottom with the bull inside bar after bar 20), and buying the bar 25 triangle (or wedge bull flag) at the moving average where many bars had bull bodies (buying pressure).

When there is a strong bear spike and traders expect more selling, the market is always-in down and traders will look for shorts. CX had a strong bear spike down to bar 3. Traders were expecting lower prices and were looking to short rallies. They shorted the small two-legged rally to the moving average at bar 4. Some traders shorted with limit orders at the moving average because this was the first pullback to the moving average after a strong bear spike. Other traders shorted on stops below bar 4. Bar 4 traded below the bar before it and was a first-entry short, and the traders who shorted below bar 4 were taking the second entry.

The larger two-legged rally at bar 7 was a low 2 short setup. Aggressive bears shorted on limit orders above the high of the prior bar and above bar 4, and others shorted as the bar fell below the low of the prior bar and generated a second-entry short signal (bar 6 was the first signal). Many traders prefer to short below strong bear trend bars and shorted below bar 7. There were so many traders looking to short there that the market gapped down the next day.

There was a strong bear spike down to bar 11, and bar 12 broke above the micro channel. Bears shorted below bar 12, expecting the first micro channel breakout attempt to fail.

Although the sideways move to bar 17 broke above a steep bear trend line, the move down to bar 13 was so far below the bar 8 low that traders began the process of looking for a bottom all over again. They needed another rally to break above a bear trend line and then another test of the trend's low before they would be willing to think that the market was reversing and not just forming another bear rally. The two-legged move up to bar 17 was strong enough to break well above the moving average and was therefore a sign of buying pressure. Traders shorted below the bar 17 bear reversal bar because they saw it as the end of a large two-legged rally and therefore a low 2 short setup. It was also a moving average gap bar short in a bear trend that had yet to clearly flip into an always-in bull trend.

The bar 19 outside doji bar was not a strong higher low buy signal bar, but some traders bought above it and above the strong bull trend bar that followed it, which broke above a bear trend line. It was a breakout test of the longs above bar 14, and it ran the breakeven stops on those longs. A breakout test that runs breakeven stops and then reverses back up in the direction of the new trend is a good risk/reward setup. The risk is to the bottom of the signal bar, and the reward is that of a new bull trend, which is many times larger.

The bull spike up to bar 20 broke strongly above the moving average and above a long bear trend line. Some traders saw this as a break above the neckline of a sloping head and shoulders bottom. Most traders saw the bull spike from bar 19 to 20 as strong enough so that it should be followed by higher prices. This means that they saw the market as always-in long. They bought above the bar 21 high 2 setup and again above the bar 24 high 2. It was safer to buy above the bull bars at the bar 25 wedge bull flag pullback to the moving average.

Other traders interpreted the move down to bar 23 as a bear micro channel, but since it was still above the moving average and in a strong bull trend, they believed that it was likely to become part of a bull flag. Therefore, rather than looking for the breakout to fail and then shorting below it, it made more sense to assume that the breakout would fail but the failure would not go far and instead would become a breakout pullback buy signal. Remember, when a failed breakout of a bear micro channel fails, it becomes a breakout pullback long entry. Bar 24 was the breakout pullback, but it had a bear body, so most traders would not have bought above its high. However, the pullback became a two-legged pullback to bar 25, which was also a double bottom bull flag.

Figure 24.14   THE BEST TRADES: PUTTING IT ALL TOGETHER   **505**

FIGURE 24.14 Best Trades in GOOG

As shown in Figure 24.14, the best trade setups on this 5 minute chart of Google (GOOG) include the bar 2 and bar 3 low 2 pullbacks to the moving average; buying the bar 4 final flag and wedge bottom reversal; shorting the bar 7 moving average gap bar, low 2, and double top; buying the bar 9 major trend reversal lower low; and buying the bar 10 higher low and stop-running breakout test.

When there is a strong break above the bear trend line, traders will look to buy a test of the bear low, as long as the test does not fall too far below. GOOG had a strong rally to bar 7, composed of bull trend bars with small tails. It broke above the bear trend line and above the moving average, and there had been several strong bull trend bars in the move down after the bear spike down from bar 1. Those large bull trend bars with small tails signify that the bulls are willing to buy. That buying pressure is cumulative and, at some point, it can wear down the bears enough so that the bulls can take control of the market.

Aggressive traders would have shorted on a limit order at the high of the bear bar after bar 5. There were three consecutive overlapping bars, and any longs were being forced to buy at the top of this trading range. That is an especially bad idea, given that it was right at the bottom of the moving average in a bear day. Since it was likely to fail as a buy, astute traders instead shorted just where the weak bulls were buying.

The sell-off from bar 7 had many overlapping bars and several bull bars, which indicated that there was two-sided trading. The bears were not in total control. As soon as the market fell below the bar 4 bear low, buyers came in on bar 8. They were not able to reverse the market, and the market fell again below the bear low. Bar 8 was the first break above the bear channel down from bar 7 and therefore not likely to have follow-through. However, on the bar 9 second attempt to reverse the trend, the bulls were able to own the next three bars. Bar 9 was a breakout pullback from the bar 8 breakout above the bear micro channel, and a bear channel is a bull flag.

When the bears tried to turn the rally from bar 9 into a three-bar bear flag, the bulls overwhelmed them at the bar 10 higher low. Bar 10 reversed back up at 8 cents (8 cents is tiny for a $500 stock) above the signal bar for the bar 9 long and was an excellent breakout test, allowing traders to add on above its high. It also trapped longs out, and they would now chase the market higher. The bulls saw bar 9 as likely leading to at least two legs up, and they therefore placed limit orders to buy at or below the low of the prior bar during the next several bars. They expected any low 1 short to fail and to become a higher low. Their buy limit orders would have been filled on bar 10. Their protective stops would have been below the bar 9 low.

The bears had good shorts earlier in the day. The market gapped down and formed a low 2 short just below the moving average at bar 1. Aggressive bears would have shorted during the formation of the two large bear trend bars down from bar 1, on their closes, and at one tick below their lows.

The bear spike was so strong that there was likely to have been follow-through selling, most likely in the form of a bear channel, and the day would probably become a spike and channel bear trend day. The bears would have looked to sell rallies, which would be at the top of the developing bear channel. Bar 2 was a low 2 short at the moving average and a test of the breakout below the first bar of the day.

Bar 3 was another low 2 short at the moving average, despite the strong bull trend bars in this bear flag.

Bar 4 was a reversal up from a two-bar final bear flag and the third push down in the bear channel, which often leads to at least a two-legged reversal. At a minimum, this wedge bottom was likely to behave like a bear stairs pattern and test the low of the prior push down (the swing low at the bottom of the sell-off from bar 2). It was also a second attempt to reverse up where the first was two bars earlier. Although a doji signal bar is not ideal, the sell-off had many bull trend bars, so not as much

Figure 24.14 THE BEST TRADES: PUTTING IT ALL TOGETHER **507**

force was needed to turn the market up. The bear trend was not all that strong and had a lot of two-sided trading within it.

When buying a low in a bear trend, it is usually good to scalp at least a part of the trade so traders would have exited some on the test of the moving average, which was also just above the prior swing low. They then could have moved their protective stops to breakeven. Most traders would have exited once the market fell below the two bear trend bars that began with bar 5, but some would have kept their stops below the bar 4 bear low. This was not yet a strong bottom because the rally to bar 5 barely broke above the trend line, and therefore the market was still always-in short. It was prudent for bulls to be cautious and get out early.

Bar 7 was an acceptable moving average gap short, a double top bear flag with bar 3, and two legs up in a bear trend. However, it would have been risky to short below a bull trend bar, especially following a three-bar bull spike. It would have been better to look to buy a higher low or lower low test of the bear low.

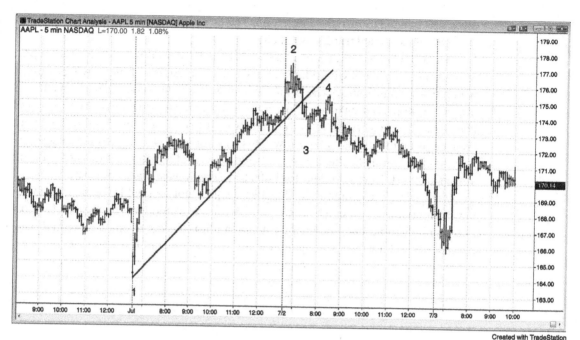

FIGURE 24.15 A Lower High in AAPL

As shown in Figure 24.15, the best trade setup on this 5 minute chart of Apple (AAPL) was the bar 4 lower high major trend reversal and breakout test after the bear spike down to bar 3. Aggressive traders could have bought during any of the bull trend bars in the bull spike up from bar 1, but since their protective stops would have been further away, traders needed to trade smaller positions.

Once the market breaks below a steep channel after a spike and channel top, traders will often look to short a lower high. The move down to bar 3 had strong momentum and broke well below the bull trend line. Traders suspected that the always-in position had flipped to short and were looking for a lower high sell. The two-legged lower high rally to bar 4 was a test of the breakout below the bar 2 two-bar reversal, and it was a low-risk sell signal for at least a second leg down and possibly a trend reversal.

Figure 24.16   THE BEST TRADES: PUTTING IT ALL TOGETHER   **509**

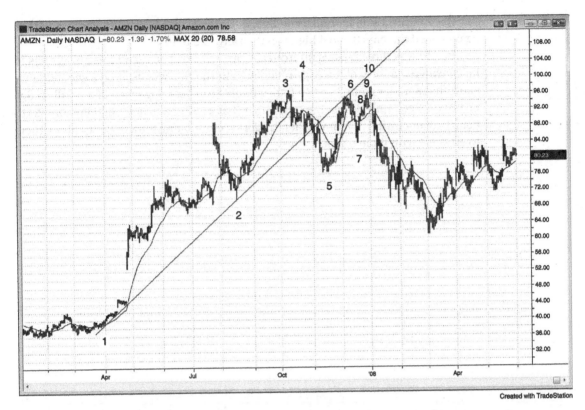

FIGURE 24.16 Best Trades in AMZN

As shown in Figure 24.16, the best trade setup on this daily chart of Amazon (AMZN) was the bar 10 two-legged lower high major trend reversal, which had several other supportive features that are described in the next paragraphs. Other good trades included the wedge bull flag, moving average gap bar, double bottom bull flag at bar 2, and the bar 3 final flag and wedge top. Some traders saw the first push up as the bull trend high before the bar 2 sell-off. Other traders saw that as the second push up and the June high as the first push up.

After a strong break below a bull trend line, traders will look to short a lower high. The AMZN daily chart had a two-legged pullback to a lower high at bar 10. Some traders saw it as a double top with the bar 3 or bar 4 high and certainly with the bar 6 high. It formed a double top bear flag with bar 6 and was therefore a second-entry short signal. Bar 6 was the first, but the move up to bar 6 had too much momentum to have much likelihood of being the start of the bear trend. Other traders ignored bar 4 as an outlier and saw the move up to bar 10 as a form of a large wedge top where the high before bar 2 was the first push, bar 3 was the second, and bar 10 was the third.

Bar 7 broke a smaller bull trend line, indicating more bearish strength, and then again tested the bars 3 and 4 highs on the rally to bar 10.

Bar 10 was three pushes up from a sharp rally off bar 7, and this always has to be considered a form of a wedge reversal pattern. This was as good a second-entry short that a trader could hope to find: a double top bear flag made of a small wedge in a two-legged rally to test the trend high (bar 4) after a major trend line break (to bar 5), all occurring at a time when traders were looking for a setup to allow them to go short with limited risk.

Figure 24.17   THE BEST TRADES: PUTTING IT ALL TOGETHER   **511**

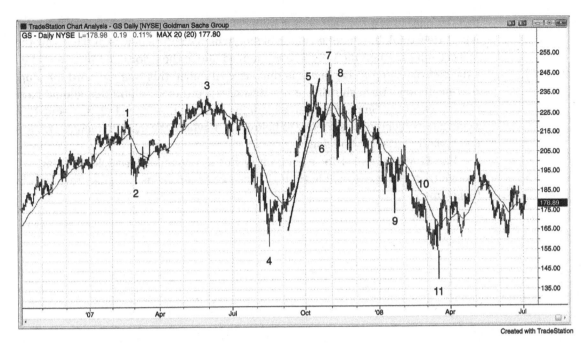

FIGURE 24.17 Best Trades on Daily Chart of GS

As shown in Figure 24.17, the best trade setups on this daily chart of Goldman Sachs Group (GS) include the bar 3 higher high major trend reversal and small wedge top, the higher low and small double bottom bull flag after the bar 4 sell climax, the bar 7 higher high (above bar 5 and bar 3), final flag, and expanding triangle top (it was the second entry for a large expanding triangle where bar 1 was the first push and bar 3 was the second, and it was the first entry for a small expanding triangle where the pause before bar 5 was the first push and bar 5 was the second), the bar 8 lower high, the low 2 and wedge bear flag after bar 9, the bar 10 low 2 near the moving average, and the bar 11 island bottom and expanding triangle bull flag (bar 2 was the first push down and bar 4 was the second; remember, expanding triangle bull flags often follow expanding triangle tops).

Although a strong rally can be part of a bull trend, it can also simply be a test of the top of a trading range, created by a sell vacuum. The bears expected the market to move above the bar 3 high, so they waited to short until it got there. They were bearish all the way up from bar 4, but it did not make sense for them to short until they got the expected breakout above the bar 3 high. If they believe that the market is going higher, it is foolish for them to short until it reaches a level where they think it will not go much higher, which was at a new high. They saw the market sell off when the rally to bar 3 moved above the prior bar 1 high, and they expected the same to happen this time as well. Since this was the third push up, they might have been shorting at the start of a protracted sell-off that should have at least two legs. Since it was an expanding triangle top (bars 1, 2, 3, 4, and 7), a reasonable objective was a move to below bar 4, where the market might then form an expanding triangle bull flag.

Bar 11 was a signal for a long entry in the expanding triangle bull flag. Although that was a reasonable trade, it was not as strong as the other reversals in this chapter.

Figure 24.18   THE BEST TRADES: PUTTING IT ALL TOGETHER   **513**

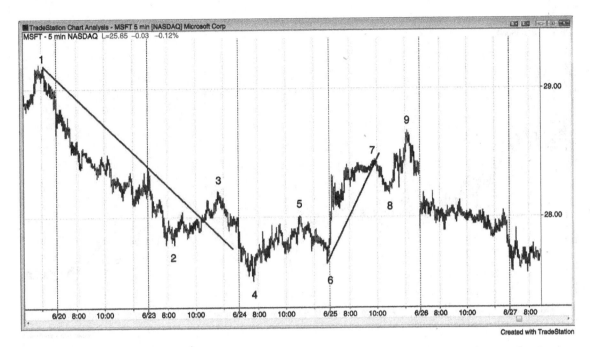

FIGURE 24.18   Best Trades in MSFT

As shown in Figure 24.18, the best trade setups on this 5 minute chart of Microsoft (MSFT) include the bar 3 wedge bear flag; the bar 4 lower low major trend reversal and small wedge bottom; the bar 5 small and large low 2; the bar 6 higher low major trend reversal, wedge bull flag, and double bottom bull flag; and the bar 9 two-legged higher high major trend reversal, small spike and channel top, and wedge bear flag (bars 3, 7, and 9).

Although the rally to bar 3 broke well above the bear trend line, the sell-off down to bar 4 then went far enough below bar 2 so that traders needed a higher low before thinking that a trend reversal might be underway. Bar 6 was a higher low and a two-bar reversal, and alert traders bought on the first bar of the next day as it traded above the two-bar reversal.

The rally to bar 9 was a two-legged higher high after the move down to bar 8 broke below the bull trend line. It was also three pushes up from the bar 4 low, with bars 5 and 7 being the first two pushes. Some traders saw the rally as a large wedge bear flag where bar 3 ended the first push and bar 7 was the second.

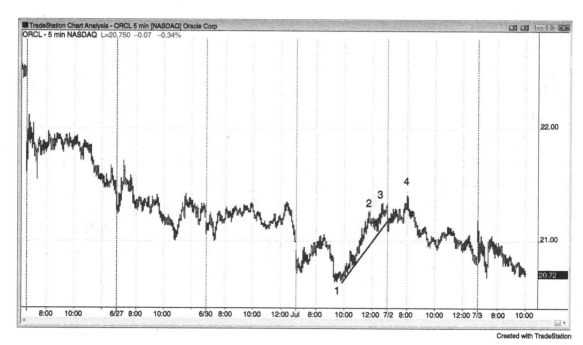

FIGURE 24.19 Best Trades in ORCL

As shown in Figure 24.19, the best trade setups on this 5 minute chart of Oracle (ORCL) include the bar 1 lower low major trend reversal (the rally off the prior low broke above a steep bear trend line) and the bar 4 two-legged higher high major trend reversal and small wedge top.

A sharp rally to the top of a trading range is usually due to a buy vacuum instead of a new trend. The market has inertia, and when it is in a trading range, most attempts to break out fail. The bears expected a test of the top of Oracle's 5 minute trading range of the past couple of days, so there was no reason to short until the market reached that area. This made the market one-sided in the rally up to bar 2, but once the market reached the top of the trading range, the bears appeared as if out of nowhere. They now doubted the market would go much higher without a pullback, and they shorted relentlessly. The three-push rally to bar 4 was an excellent setup to short below the two-bar reversal.

Figure 24.20   THE BEST TRADES: PUTTING IT ALL TOGETHER   **515**

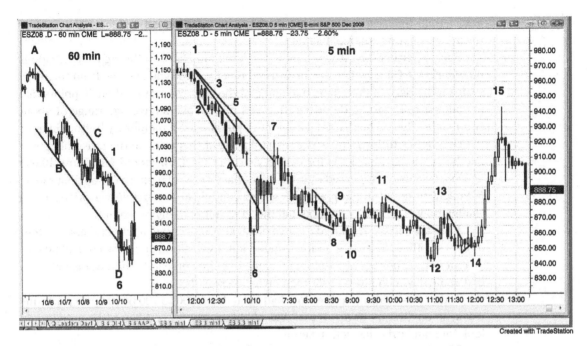

FIGURE 24.20 Emini Opening Reversal

The best trade setups on the 5 minute Emini chart on the right in Figure 24.20 include the bar 6 opening reversal, the bar 7 final flag top and wedge top (the high of the bar before bar 6 was the first leg up, even though it was a bear bar), the bar 8 wedge bull flag and higher low, the bar 10 breakout pullback from the bar 9 breakout above the bear micro channel, the bar 11 low 2 and double top (with the top of the wedge down to bar 8), the bar 12 large two-legged (bar 10 was the first push down) higher low major trend reversal (bar 12 was reversing up from the small bear trend down to bar 10 and from the large bear trend that ended at bar 6), and the bar 14 higher low major trend reversal and second entry breakout pullback buy signal (it was also the right shoulder of a head and shoulders bottom, where bar 10 was the left shoulder).

Although most academics and television pundits argue that all moves in the overall market are based on the composite fundamentals of the individual stocks, politics often creates huge moves. An obvious example is the incredible bull market that took place when the Republicans took control of Congress in 1994, often referred to as the Clinton super bull market. The crash of 2008 is another example. Was this bear trend and panic sell-off caused by the subprime mess, or was it the direct result of the country realizing that Barack Obama was going to win the White House? Although you have to trade the charts based on what they show, it is intellectually interesting to try to understand how politics can influence the market, regardless of your political leanings.

Such a perfect day! If you look at the 5 minute chart on the right, the shape is unremarkable for a higher low bear trend reversal, but you can see from the price scale on the right of that chart that some of the bars were more than 30 points tall, in contrast to a normal day when the bars might have an average range of about two points. This is the market's attempt to put at least a temporary bottom in after the Dow Jones Industrial Average lost 20 percent this week in the crash of 2008. I had been telling my friends for over a year that the Dow would fall below 10,000 in 2008, because it appeared that we might have entered a multiyear trading range. We might have put in a top and the selling could lead to much lower prices, but a trading range is a more common and therefore more likely outcome.

Even though the Dow had a range of 1,000 points today, it was still just another day at the office for a price action trader. I cut my position size down to just 20 percent of normal because I had to risk about 10 points on each Emini trade, yet I still ended the day with more profit than on an average day.

Today was Friday and the Dow had been down 200 to 700 points every day this week, so an attempt at a reversal was likely. However, you had to be patient and look for standard price action setups.

The chart on the left is a 60 minute chart, and bar D (it is also bar 6 on the 5 minute chart on the right) fell through the trend channel line built off bars A and C (it is also bar 1 on the 5 minute chart), and then reversed up.

On the 5 minute chart, bar 6 formed a huge doji bar after the market fell below the bar 2 to bar 4 trend channel line. Dojis are not great signal bars, but the market was reversing trend channel line breakouts on both the 5 and 60 minute charts and the Dow was down 700 points, so a tradable rally was likely.

Bar 7 broke above the bear trend line but formed a final flag top and two legs up, so a pullback was likely. However, the move up from the bar 6 low was violent, so it was likely that there would be a second leg up after a test of the bear trend low. It was prudent to just patiently wait for a higher low (with that much upward momentum, a lower low was not likely).

Bar 10 was a possible bottom since it was a lower low breakout pullback from the bar 9 breakout of the wedge. However, the move down from bar 7 lasted more than an hour or so and was very deep, so a second leg down was likely before the final bottom was in.

The move up to bar 11 broke another bear trend line, so the bulls were gaining strength.

Bar 12 was a lower low compared to bar 10 and therefore a possible higher low on the day, but the move down to bar 12 had too much momentum, so a test was likely.

Figure 24.20   THE BEST TRADES: PUTTING IT ALL TOGETHER   **517**

The bull leg to bar 13 had several bull trend bars and broke another bull trend line.

Bar 14 was a good-sized bull reversal bar and a micro trend line pullback, as well as a higher low compared to bar 12, so this could have been the final low, which it was. This turned bar 12 into the first strong higher low after bar 6 and an excellent test of that bear low. This was the trade of the day and the one that you needed to be waiting for all day after the strong move up to bar 7. There were many other trades today, but this one was easy to anticipate and it unfolded perfectly. There were trend channel line overshoots on the 5 and 60 minute charts, a huge move up to bar 7 making a higher low likely, a two-legged pullback to bar 12 forming a possible 60 minute higher low, followed by a 5 minute higher low at bar 14 that confirmed the bar 12 higher low. You did not need the 60 minute chart to make this trade, and I did not use it. I am including it to show that there were longer time frame forces at work here as well and it is clear from the volume that institutions were paying attention to them.

Bar 15 reversed down after a new high on the day.

The reversal up at the bar 10 two-bar reversal was an example of a setup with about a 60 percent chance of making a swing profit, and therefore was a great setup for all traders, including beginners. Bar 4 was a gap bar in a bear trend, and that often leads to a test of the bear low (bar 2, as this point) and then a rally that has about ten bars and two legs as minimum objectives. The bear spike down to bar 6 was too strong for traders to buy. Bar 8 was a reasonable buy, since it was a second reversal attempt from the breakout below bar 2, an expanding triangle bottom (the third bar of the day was the first push down and bar 2 was the second), a final flag reversal from the bar 7 bear flag, and a strong bull reversal bar. Expanding triangle bottoms are always major trend reversal setups. However, since the legs up to bar 4 and down to bar 6 were so large, most traders would not call this a major trend reversal and instead would refer to it in other terms (although it was almost certainly a great looking major trend reversal on the 15 minute chart). Bar 10 was the second entry in an already strong pattern. Traders bought above the bar 10 high, which was the second bar of the two-bar reversal, and their initial protective stop was below its low. They took partial or full profits once the market reached twice the risk, and let the remainder of their position swing up, trailing stops below the most recent higher low. Some would have exited below the bar 19 double top (with bar 4), and wedge (bars 12, 14, and 19, and bars 14, 16, and 19), and others would have held, keeping their stops below bar 17.

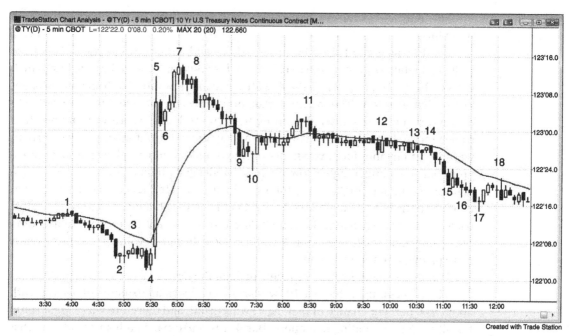

FIGURE 24.21   Treasury Note Final Flag

As shown in Figure 24.21, the best trade setups on this 5 minute 10-Year U.S. Treasury Note Futures chart include the final flag reversals at bars 4, 7, and 10; the small low 2 at bar 3; the high 1 at bar 6; and the wedge bear flag second entry at bar 11.

Final flags often provide high-probability reversal trades.

Bar 4 was a two-bar reversal after a horizontal bear flag that had only a single bear body. The bull bodies in the bear flag were a sign of buying pressure.

Although the huge bar 5 bull trend bar was climactic, the bar 6 high 1 was a reasonable buy setup for at least a scalp up after such strong momentum. Also, there were trapped bears who shorted below the bear inside bar, and they would have covered above bar 6.

Bar 7 was the first bar of a two-bar reversal where the second bar was a strong bear trend bar. The reversal occurred just above the bar 5 high, so the bulls apparently were eager to take profits, and the bears were just waiting for the market to get above bar 5 before shorting. This was a good final flag short setup, especially since the bar before bar 7 was another large bull trend bar and therefore a second buy climax. Consecutive buy climaxes are usually followed by at least a two-legged correction.

Bar 10 was a relatively large doji reversal bar and a signal bar for the reversal up from the ii final flag breakout (ii patterns often become final flags). It was also a wedge bull flag where bar 6 was the first push down and bar 9 was the second.

Bar 11 was the second signal for a reversal down from the horizontal final bull flag that followed the small spike up from bar 10. It was also a wedge bear flag where the bull inside bar after bar 9 was the first push up and the rally from bar 10 was the second. Finally, it was a moving average gap bar short after the strong trend down to bar 10.

Bars 12 and 13 were setups for two-bar reversals up, but they never triggered. The market never traded above the signal bars. Bar 12 was seen by some traders as a setup for a final flag buy where the tight trading range leading up to bar 12 was the potential final flag in the sell-off from bar 12.

FIGURE 24.22   Best Trades in the Emini with Two-Sided Trading

The best trade setups on the 5 minute Emini chart shown in Figure 24.22 include the two-bar reversal up from the low of the prior day that formed three bars after bar 1, the double top at bar 3, the wedge bear flag at bar 7, and the bar 9 small final flag and reversal up in a trending trading range day and stairs pattern.

When a day is not a trend day, it is a trading range day, or at least it will have a lot of two-sided trading.

Bar 2 took out the high of the open, so smart traders would have been looking for a second-entry short, which came at the bar 3 double top. The initial swing of the day often begins with a double top or bottom. The range was about half of an average daily range, so the day was likely to have a breakout and become a trending trading range day up or down, and then later have a pullback to test the breakout of the initial range.

The bear spike to bar 4 turned the market into an always-in bear day, so traders were looking to short rallies and expected a downside breakout and then about a measured move down. The bull channel to bar 6 was a three-push rally and had many overlapping bars and several minor reversal attempts. It was much weaker than the sell-off to bar 4. Once traders decided that there was not going to be a strong bull breakout above the channel, they believed that the channel was a bear flag and would be followed by a bear trend. Bar 6 missed the breakeven stops

Figure 24.22   THE BEST TRADES: PUTTING IT ALL TOGETHER   **521**

below bar 3 by a tick, which was a sign of strength by the bears. They successfully defended their stops by aggressively shorting more at bar 6.

Aggressive traders would have placed limit orders to go short at or above the doji bar that followed the bar 6 two-bar reversal. They saw this as a weak high 1 buy setup that was likely to fail.

Bar 9 was a strong bull reversal bar, but since it overlapped so much of the prior bar, it functioned as a two-bar reversal. Since its high was at the high of the prior bar, it did not matter if a trader saw it as a two-bar reversal or as a bull reversal bar. In either case, it was a strong reversal setup on a trending trading range day and was in the area of a measured move down, and it followed the bar 8 final flag. It was also the third push down on the day. All of these factors led traders to believe that the market would have at least a two-legged rally that would test the bar 4 low. Buying as bar 9 moved above the bull reversal bar before it was an entry that had about a 60 percent chance of leading to a profitable swing trade, and therefore was a strong setup for all traders, including beginners. The bull reversal bar was a strong signal bar for the reversal up from the low 2 final flag that triggered below bar 8, and for the large parabolic wedge bottom (the first push down ended three bars after bar 1 and the second push down ended at bar 4). Although bar 9 was a bear bar, it did not hit the protective stop below the bull signal bar. Other traders bought above bar 9, since it was a second-entry buy signal as a micro double bottom with the bull signal bar. It was likely to go up for at least a measured move based on the height of the micro double bottom (about twice the height of the move up from the bottom of the bull bar to the top of bar 9), and since there was a large bottoming pattern, it was likely to go up much further, like for at least ten bars and two legs.

Note that there were several minor reversals and that most reversals come from double tops and bottoms, micro double tops and bottoms, and final flags, as is always the case. Many traders will not take a reversal trade unless one of these is present.

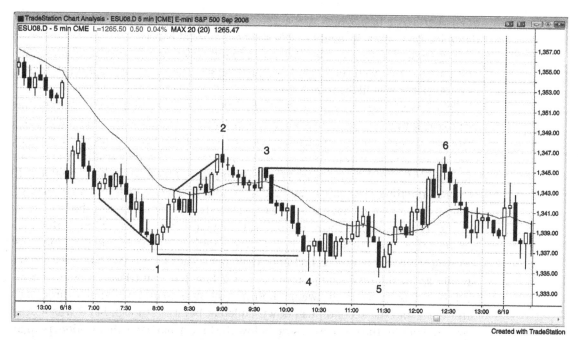

FIGURE 24.23 Several Best Trades in the Emini with No Clear Trend

As shown in Figure 24.23, the best trades on this 5 minute Emini chart include the bar 1 two-bar reversal after the gap spike and channel bottom; the bar 2 reversal at a new high of the day and spike and channel top; the bar 3 micro channel failed breakout (a low 1); the bar 5 third push down on the day, lower low, and final flag breakout and reversal up at the bottom of a trading range; and the bar 6 double top, spike and channel top, low 4, and top of a trading range.

On a day that is not a clear trend day, traders should look to fade new extremes, especially second entries and wedges.

Bar 1 was a wedge reversal with a strong reversal bar.

Bar 2 was a wedge top, a double top, and a second-entry moving average gap bar short.

Bar 3 was a signal bar for the breakout test, which hit the breakeven stops of the shorts below bar 2.

Bar 4 was a doji in a steep decline. Since it might have just turned into a one- or two-bar bear flag, traders waited for a second entry to buy. Aggressive traders would have bought on a limit order at or below the low of the bar after bar 4,

Figure 24.23
THE BEST TRADES: PUTTING IT ALL TOGETHER   **523**

expecting an attempt at a second leg up. They saw this as a weak low 1 short setup and therefore likely to fail.

Bar 5 was a reversal up from the second attempt to break out to a new low below low 1. The inside bar that formed the signal bar had a bull close.

Bar 6 was a low 4 short that reversed after breaking out above the bar 3 swing high.

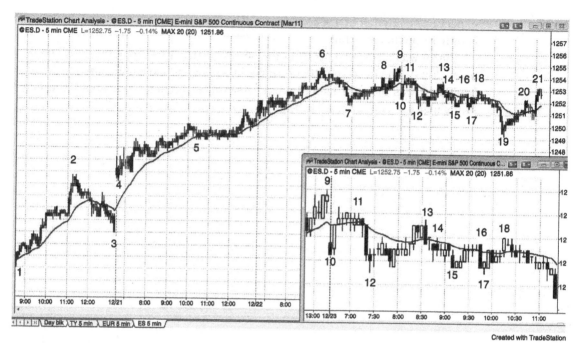

FIGURE 24.24 With a 50 Percent Chance of Success, the Reward Must Be Twice as Large as the Risk

Even though selling in the middle of a trading range might have only about a 50 percent chance of success, if the reward is twice the size of the risk, it can be a best trade. As shown in Figure 24.24, the 5 minute Emini, which had been in a strong bull trend for several weeks, had a moving average gap bar at bar 7. This often leads to the final test of the bull high before a deeper correction that has at least a couple of legs. The small gap opening down to bar 10 was immediately followed by a rally to just above the moving average. The bears were looking for a second leg down, but were unsure if the one-bar drop to bar 10 was enough to constitute a first leg. When a move is unclear, there are usually not enough traders who believe that it will succeed, and therefore not enough traders are willing to bet on it. The result is that there is no follow-through until there is more clarity. The two-legged move to bar 12 led to a two-legged rally to bar 13, which some traders saw as a small wedge bear flag. Others saw it as the right shoulder of a head and shoulders top where bar 6 was the left shoulder. Some also saw it as a double top bear flag with bar 11. It was a high that was below the bar 9 high and below the high around bar 11, and it could have been the start of a larger second leg down.

Since shorting below bar 11 was in the middle of a two-day trading range, the directional probability of an equidistant move was about 50 percent. There was

Figure 24.24   THE BEST TRADES: PUTTING IT ALL TOGETHER   **525**

about a 50 percent chance of a one-point move up before a one-point move down, and a 50 percent chance of a one-point move down before a one-point move up. The same was true for two, three, or four points. In general, when the market is in a trading range and it is up for five to 10 bars, traders should only look for shorts. Bar 11 was the eighth bar since the opening low, and the bar that followed it marked the third time that the market had fallen below the low of the prior bar. Traders could have shorted here or even on the first or second attempt down, hoping that enough traders saw this as a potential lower high so that there would be more selling. Since it was not convincing, the move down did not begin until after a clearer lower high at bar 13.

So why was shorting around bar 11 a best trade when there was only a 50 percent chance of success and it was in the middle of a trading range in a bull trend? Remember that the trader's equation has three variables and that you have to consider reward and risk in addition to probability. Since the average daily range in the Emini had been over 10 points for the past month or so and today's range was only two points, and there were only a handful of days in the past couple of years when the range was under five or six points, the odds were high that today's range was going to double or triple before the close. The problem was that traders did not know if the breakout would be up or down, or both. Since the market was up for eight bars in a trading range, the odds favored a move down in the near term. Traders could simply have shorted and put a protective stop above the bar 11 signal bar, placed a one cancels the other (OCO) limit order four points below the entry, and then patiently waited. Since there was so much uncertainty, they could take this trade only if they were willing to sit through pullbacks, which were inevitable in a trading range. The actual risk was only four ticks, so traders were risking four ticks to make 16 ticks and they had about a 50 percent chance of success. This made this an excellent trade even though it might not have appeared so at the time.

Once there was a large bear breakout bar and then the immediate follow-through at bar 12, the market was always-in short for most traders, and they would assume that it would stay that way unless there was an always-in buy signal or until the market went above the top of the bear spike that had begun with the small bear bar after bar 11. Bar 13 tested the high of that bar to the tick, and the market eventually sold off to bar 19. The bar 19 low was 17 ticks below the bar 11 signal bar, and bar 19 had a bull body. This was a possible 17 tick failure, meaning that many bears were taking profits on their shorts at 16 ticks below the signal bar instead of 17 ticks below. They were getting out one tick shy of a four-point move, which was a sign that the bears were weak. The market hit the limit order for the shorts to exit with a four-tick profit, and the bar turned into a bull reversal bar. Most bears would have exited above the bar 19 bull reversal bar because of the 17 tick failure, taking 11 ticks' profit instead of hoping for the market to go back down and give them the 16 ticks that they had originally planned to make.

This was the week before Christmas, and the average daily range around the holidays is usually less. There were several days in the past couple of weeks when the range was under seven points. Also, since the initial risk was only four ticks instead of the usually seven or eight ticks, many traders assumed that the smaller risk and the smaller recent average range meant that the chance of making four points might also be smaller. Many of these traders bet on the 17 tick failure and placed their limit orders at 15 ticks below their entry price instead of six ticks below. Whenever a move has an increased chance of coming up short, many traders will use a limit order that is one tick less than usual, knowing that the market often hits the obvious target price, but reverses instead of filling the profit-taking limit orders. Other traders would have instead placed profit-taking limit orders at three points below their entry price, and they obviously would have made their three points.

CHAPTER 25

Trading Guidelines

Why guidelines and not rules? Because "rules" imply absolutes and easy trading if only you follow them. However, trading is subjective, your edge is always going to be small, and it is very difficult to get to the point where you are consistently successful. If there were clear, objective rules and they consistently resulted in profitable trades, everyone would soon discover them. There would quickly be no one left to take the opposite side of the trade, and the rules would then stop working.

Here are 78 suggested guidelines.

1. Reading these 570,000 words is like reading a detailed manual on how to do anything, such as playing golf or a violin. It takes a lot of hard work to turn the information into the ability to make a living as a trader, but it is impossible without understanding how markets work. Like being a professional golfer or violinist, no matter how good you get, you always want to be better, so the challenge and satisfaction last long after you become consistently profitable.

2. Everything that you see is in a gray fog. Nothing is perfectly clear. Close is close enough. If something looks like a reliable pattern, it will likely trade like a reliable pattern.

3. There is no easy set of reliable rules to make money as a trader, and everything is subjective. This is a zero-sum game with very smart players, so when an edge exists, it is small and fleeting. For a trader to make money, he has to be consistently better than half of the other traders out there (or more accurately, trade a positive trader's equation more than half of the time). Since most of the

competitors are profitable institutions, a trader has to be very good. However, edges appear constantly, and if you learn to spot them and understand how to trade them, you are in a position to make money.

4. The edge can never get very large because institutions would take advantage of it as it was growing. A trade cannot have a high probability of making a big reward relative to the risk.

5. Reading charts well is difficult, but it is only half of what you need to know to make money. You also need to learn to trade, which is just as difficult. Trading successfully always has been and will always continue to be hard to do, no matter what method you use. If there were an easy way to make money, everyone would do it and then there would be no trapped traders to drive the market to your target. Read a book that teaches you how to play the violin and then go out to see if the world will give you money to hear you play. Just because you understand how to do something does not mean that you can do it effectively, especially if it is difficult to do.

6. A trader needs a mathematical advantage to make money. At every moment, there is always a mathematical edge for both a long and a short trade, but the edges are usually not clear. When they are relatively clear, they are fleeting and small. However, those are the times when traders need to place their trades.

7. The ability to spot trades that have a positive trader's equation is the key to success. That can mean buying above a bar on a stop, selling above a bar with a limit order, buying below a bar with a limit order, or selling below a bar on a stop.

8. The single most important determination that a trader makes, and he makes this after the close of every bar, is whether there will be more buyers or sellers above and below the prior bar. This is particularly true with breakouts and failed breakouts, because the move that follows usually determines the always-in direction and therefore lasts for many points and is not just a scalp.

9. Every time you buy above the high of the prior bar on a stop, someone else is shorting there with a limit order. When you sell one tick below the low of the prior bar, there is a strong bull who is taking the other side of your trade. Always remember that nothing is certain, and the edge is always small because there are smart people who believe the exact opposite of what you do.

10. Every bar, even a strong trend bar, is a signal bar for both directions, and the market can begin a trend up or down on the next bar. Be open to all possibilities, including the exact opposite of what you expect, and when the surprise happens, don't question or deny it. Just read it and trade it.

11. Every time you look to enter a setup, make sure to consider what the market is telling you if instead it breaks out of the opposite end of the signal bar.

Sometimes that buy setup that you see might in fact also be a great sell setup because it will trap longs who will cover below the low of the signal or entry bars.

12. Understanding trend bars that create breakouts is one of the most important skills that a trader can acquire. Traders need to be able to assess whether a breakout is likely to succeed, or it will be met with profit taking and a pullback, or it will be followed by a reversal.

13. Look for signs of strength and weakness and weigh them to determine if they give you an edge. If you see the market doing something, assess how strong the setup is. Did it fail to take an opportunity to do something strong? If so, the setup is weaker.

14. Whenever you are positive that your setup is good, don't take the trade. You are missing something. You don't see what the person who is taking the other side of your trade is seeing, and that person is just as smart as you are. Be humble. If you are too confident, your arrogance will make you lose because you will be using unrealistically high probabilities in your evaluation of the trader's equation.

15. Much of life is not what it seems. In fact, the famous mathematician Charles Lutwidge Dodgson was not what he seemed to be and is better known as Lewis Carroll. We work in an Alice in Wonderland world where nothing is really as it seems. Up is not always up and down is not always down. Just look at most strong breakouts of trading ranges—they usually fail, and up is really the start of down and down is really just part of up. Also, 60 percent is 60 percent in only 90 percent of the cases and can be 90 percent sometimes and 10 percent at other times. If a good setup is 60 percent, how can you win 80 percent or more of the time? Well, in a pullback in a strong trend just above support, a setup might work 60 percent of the time, but if you can scale in as the market goes lower, especially if your subsequent entries are larger, you might find that you win in 80 percent or more of those 60 percent setups. Also, if you use a very wide stop and are willing to sit through a large drawdown for a couple of hours, that 60 percent chance of making two points before losing two points in the Emini might be a 90 percent chance of making four points before losing eight points. If you are flexible and comfortable with constantly changing probabilities and many probabilities coexisting, your chance of success is much greater.

16. The single most important thing that you can do all day is talk yourself out of bad trades. For example, if it is a trading range day, don't look to buy after a strong bull trend bar or a high 1 near the top of the range, and don't look to short after a strong bear trend bar or low 1 near the bottom of the range.

17. The market constantly exhibits inertia and tends to continue what it has just been doing. If it is in a trend, 80 percent of the attempts to reverse it will fail

and lead to a flag and then a resumption of the trend. If it is in a trading range, 80 percent of the attempts to break out into a trend will fail.

18. If ever you feel twisted inside because a pullback is going too far, you are likely mistakenly seeing a pullback when in fact the trend has reversed.

19. If you think the market rationally should be going up, but instead it is offering you a strong sell setup, take it. Trade the trade that you have and not the one that you want or expect, because "the market can stay irrational much longer than you can stay solvent" (a quote attributed to John Maynard Keynes).

20. Price is truth. Never argue with what the market is telling you. For a day trader, fundamentals are almost entirely useless. The market will tell you where it is going and it cannot hide what it is doing. Neither you nor the experts on television can know how the market will react to the fundamentals, although those experts often speak with certainty. Since the market is rarely more than 60 percent certain of anything, whenever pundits speak with certainty, they are ignoring math and therefore the most basic characteristic of the market. If you follow someone who is indifferent to or ignorant of how markets work, you will lose money.

21. Everything makes sense. If you know how to read price action, nothing will surprise you, because you will understand what the market is doing. Beginners can see it on a printout at the end of the day. The goal is to learn how to read fast enough so that you can understand what is happening in real time.

22. "It's not fair!" If that is how you are feeling, take a break from trading. You are absolutely right—it *is* not fair, but that is because it is all based on mathematics, and fairness is never one of the variables. If you are concerned about fairness, you are not synchronized with the market. Computer programs control all market activity, and they have no concept of fairness; they never get tired, they don't remember what their last trade was, and they are relentlessly objective. Since they are making money, you need to try to emulate their qualities. They cannot hide what they are doing, and your job is to see what they are doing and then copy them. Yes, you will enter after their first entry, but they will continue to enter after you do, and they are the force that will drive the market far enough to give you your profit.

23. Price action is based on human behavior and therefore has a genetic basis. This is why it works in all markets in all countries and on all time frames and it has always worked and always will inescapably reflect human behavior, at least until we evolve into a new species.

24. Always have a protective stop in the market because it protects you from the greatest danger you will ever face as a trader. That danger is not the market, which could not care less whether you win or lose, never knows that you exist,

and is never out to get you. It is yourself, and all of your inadequacies as a trader, including denial, arrogance, and a lack of discipline.

25. Thinking is very difficult. Losers prefer instead to look with religious zeal for a savior who will protect them from losing money. Saviors can be confident, impressive experts with outstanding credentials on TV, famous writers of newsletters, chat room leaders, indicators, or any other external idol into which traders infuse the power to protect them and take them to the Promised Land. Instead, they will all slowly suck the last dollar from your account. You will not make money until you do your own analysis and ignore all external influences that promise you success, but in fact exist only to make money for themselves and not you. The experts on TV hope to establish credibility that they can use to sell their services or get a promotion, the TV station makes money off commercials, the chat room and newsletter people sell their services, and the software company that gives you indicators does so for a fee. No one is going to help you in the long run, so never fool yourself into believing that you can make money with the help of all of those nice people.

26. Those who talk don't know and those who know don't talk. Don't watch TV or read any news.

27. If you find that you did not take a couple of Emini trades in a row and they worked, you are likely trading too large a position size. Switch to trading 100 to 300 shares of SPY and swing for at least 20 to 50 cents. Even though you won't get rich, at least you will make some money and build your confidence. If you think that you can comfortably trade three Emini contracts per trade, then you should trade just one. This will make it much easier for you to take every signal. If you trade three Eminis, you will let many good signals go because you really are comfortable trading only three contracts in the rare case of a perfect signal. You need to be trading a size where you are comfortable with any decent signal and remain comfortable if you lose two or three times in a row. One indicator of this comfort is your ability to take the next trade after those losses. If you feel too uncomfortable and are really waiting for perfection, you are still trading too much volume. Once you start cherry-picking, you are on the path to a blown account. Your emotions are a burden and give an edge to your opponents, as is the case in any competition.

28. "I don't care!" That is the most useful mantra. I don't care if I lose on this trade, because I am trading a small enough size that a loss will not upset me and cloud my judgment. I don't care what the experts are saying on TV or in the *Wall Street Journal*. I don't care what is happening on the 3 and 1 minute charts or on volume or tick charts, and I don't care about missing all of the wonderful signals that those charts are generating, because if the trades really are good, they will lead to 5 minute signals as well. I don't care that the market is way

overdone and is due for a correction. I don't care about indicators, especially squiggly lines that show divergences in a huge trend (meanwhile, there has been no trend line break), but I do care about the one chart in front of me and what it is telling me. I also care about following my rules and not allowing any outside influence talk me out of doing what my rules are telling me.

29. If you are afraid of taking a great trade because your stop would have to be too far, reduce your position size to maybe a quarter of normal so that your total dollar risk is no larger than for your usual trades. You need to get into the "I don't care" mode to be able to take these trades. By cutting your position size, you can focus on the quality of the setup instead of being preoccupied with the dollars that you can lose if the trade fails. However, first spot a good setup before adopting the "I don't care" mind-set, because you don't want to be so apathetic about the dollars that you begin to take weak setups and then go on to lose money.

30. The market is never certain when it has gone far enough, but it is always certain when it has gone too far. Most reversals require excess before traders believe that the reversal will work. Market inertia can be stopped only by excess.

31. It is difficult to reverse a position. For most traders, it is far better to exit, even with a loss, and then look for another setup in the new direction.

32. There are no reliable countertrend patterns so, unless you are a consistently profitable trader, never trade countertrend unless there first has been a strong break of a significant trend line, and the signal is a reasonable setup for an always-in reversal. When you are shorting below that great bear reversal bar in a strong bull trend, far smarter traders are buying with limit orders at the low of your signal bar. When you are buying on a stop above a bull reversal bar in a strong bear trend, smarter traders are shorting exactly where you are buying. Since 80 percent of reversals fail, who do you think is making the money?

33. Any reversal setup is a good reason to take partial or full profits, but the setup has to be strong if you are considering a countertrend trade. Since 80 percent of reversals fail, it is far better to view each top as the start of a bull flag and each bottom as the start of a bear flag.

34. Too early is always worse than too late. Since most reversals and breakouts fail, an early entry will likely fail. Since most trends go a long way, entering late is usually still a good trade.

35. All patterns fail and the failures often fail, and when they do, they create a breakout pullback in the original direction and have a high probability of success.

36. When you see that one side is suddenly trapped, the reliability of a scalp in the opposite direction goes up. Trapped traders will be forced out as you are

getting in, and they will likely wait for more price action before entering again in their original direction, so the only traders left will be in your direction.

37. Seeing traders getting trapped out of a trade on a stop run is as reliable a signal as seeing them getting trapped in a trade. If the market suddenly runs stops and then resumes its trend, this is a reliable setup for at least a scalper's profit.

38. Wait. If the market has not given any signals for 30 to 60 minutes and you find yourself checking your e-mail or talking on the phone with your daughter away at college, and suddenly the market makes a large bull trend bar that breaks out of a trading range, wait. You've lost touch with the market and it is trying to trap you in. Never make a quick decision to place a trade, especially on a sudden, large trend bar. If it turns into a great trade and you miss it, you will still be ahead overall because the odds are against you when you take trades under these circumstances. Yes, some will be winners, but if you review all of the times that you took these trades, you will discover that you lost money.

39. You don't have to trade. You goal as a trader is to make money, not to make trades, so take a trade only when it will help you achieve your goal. There will be many other signals all day long, so wait for a good one, and don't be upset when you miss good trades. Many beginners want excitement and tend to overtrade. Many great traders find trading to be lonely and boring, but very profitable. Everyone wants to trade, but you should want to make money more than you want to trade. You should take only trades that are likely to make money, not simply relieve your tension from not having placed a trade in an hour or two.

40. Simple is better. You don't need indicators, and you should look at only one chart. If you can't make money off a single chart with no indicators, adding more things to analyze will just make it more difficult. Also, trade only the very best setups until you are consistently profitable. The single biggest problem with using two charts is that there is a natural tendency to take only signals that occur simultaneously on both charts, which rarely happens. You end up rejecting most of the day's great signals because the second chart does not have a signal or the signal occurred two ticks earlier. For example, if you see a great high 2 pullback to the exponential moving average in a bull trend on the 5 minute chart and then look at the 2 or 3 minute chart and see that it gave an entry two ticks earlier, you might not take the 5 minute entry because you will be afraid that the move will stop at the 2 minute scalper's target and never reach the 5 minute target.

41. Decide whether this is a hobby or a job. If it is a hobby, find another one because this one will be too expensive and it is dangerously addictive. All great traders are likely trading addicts, but most trading addicts will likely end up broke.

42. Begin trading using a 5 minute chart, entering on a pullback and using a stop order for your entry. When the market is in a bull trend, look to buy above a bull bar at the moving average. When it is in a bear trend, look to short below a bear bar at the moving average. Take some or all off on a limit order at a profit target around the prior extreme of the trend, and then move the protective stop to breakeven on any remaining contracts.

43. When starting out, you should consider trading the SPY instead of the Emini. One Emini is virtually identical to 500 SPY shares, and trading 200 to 500 SPY shares would allow you to scale out as you swing part of your trade, yet not incur much risk. Once you reach 1,000 to 1,500 SPY shares, if you are thinking that you will continue to increase your position size, then switch to the Emini. At that size, you can scale out of the Emini and you can increase your position size tremendously without slippage being a significant issue.

44. Buy low and sell high, except in a clear and strong trend (see Part I in book 1 on trends). In a bull trend, buy high 2 setups even if they are at the high of the day; in a bear trend, sell low 2 setups. However, the market is in a trading range for the vast majority of the time. For example, if the market has been going up for a few bars and there is now a buy signal near the top of this leg up, ask yourself if you believe that the market is in one of the established clear and strong bull trend patterns described in these books. If you cannot convince yourself that it is, don't buy high, even if the momentum looks great, since the odds are great that you will be trapped. Remember Warren Buffett's version of the old saw, "Be afraid when others are greedy and be greedy when others are afraid."

45. The two most important feelings for the media and for beginners are fear and greed. Profitable traders feel neither. For them, the two most important feelings are uncertainty (confusion) and urgency, and they use both to make money. Every bar and every segment of every market is either a trend or a trading range. When a trader is certain, the market is in a strong trend. When he feels a sense of urgency, like he wants to buy as the market is going up (or short as it is going down) but is desperate for a pullback, the market is in a strong trend. He will buy at least a small position at the market instead of waiting for a pullback.

46. When a trader is uncertain or confused, the market is in a trading range and he should only buy low and sell high. If he wants to take many trades, only scalp. Uncertainty means that the market has a lot of two-sided trading and therefore might be forming a trading range. Since most breakout attempts fail, it is better to only look to short if you are uncertain and the market is up for five to 10 bars, and only look for longs when it is down for five to 10 bars.

47. When there is a trading range, buy low means that if the market is near the bottom of the range and you are short, you can buy back your short for a profit, and if there is a strong buy signal, you can buy to initiate a long. Likewise, when

the market is toward the top of the range, you sell high. This selling can be to take your profit on your long, or, if there is a good short setup, you can sell to initiate a short position.

48. Good fill, bad trade. Always be suspicious if the market lets you in or out at a price that is better than you anticipated. The corollary of bad fill, good trade is not as reliable.

49. The first hour or two is usually the easiest time to make money, because the swings tend to be large and there are not many doji bars. The first hour is the easiest time to lose money as well, because you are overly confident about how easy it might be, and you don't follow your rules carefully. The first hour usually has many reversals, so patiently wait for a swing setup, which will generally have less than a 50 percent chance of success but a potential reward that is at least twice as large as the risk. Experienced traders can scalp. If you don't follow your rules and are in the red, you've missed the easiest time of the day to make money, which means that you will be unhappy all day as you hope to get back to breakeven in trading that is much slower and less profitable.

50. If you are down on the day and you are now in the second half of the day, it can feel like you are swimming in quicksand—the harder you try to get out, the deeper you sink. Even great traders simply fail to connect emotionally with the flow of the market some days and they will occasionally lose, even though a printout of the 5 minute chart at the end of the day will be shockingly clear. The smartest thing to do is just make sure that you follow your rules into the close, and you will likely win back some of your losses. The worst thing to do is to modify your trading style, which is probably why you are down on the day. Don't increase your position size and start trading lower-probability setups. If you have an approach that makes you money, stick with it and you will earn back your loss tomorrow. Using a different approach will only cost you more.

51. Beginners should avoid trading in the middle of the day when the market is in the middle of a day's range, especially if the moving average is relatively flat and the trading range is tight and has prominent tails (barbwire). When you are about to take any trade, always ask yourself if the setup is one of the best of the day. Is this the one that the institutions have been waiting for all day? If the answer is no and you are not a consistently profitable trader, then you should not take the trade, either.

52. A tight trading range is the worst environment for entering on stops. The institutions are doing the opposite, and you will consistently lose if you insist on trading, hoping that a trend is about to begin.

53. A tight trading range trumps everything. That means that it is more important than every good reason that you have to buy or sell. Unless you are a great

trader, once you sense that a tight trading range might be forming, force your-self to not take any trades, even if you don't trade for hours.

54. Every bar and every series of bars is either a trend or a trading range. Pick one. Decide on the always-in direction and trade only in that direction until it changes. Throughout the day and especially around 8:30 a.m. PST, you need to be deciding whether the day resembles any trend pattern described in these books. If it does and you are looking to take any trade, you must take every with-trend trade. Never consider taking a countertrend trade if you haven't been taking all of the with-trend trades.

55. The best signal bars are trend bars in the direction of your trade. Doji bars are one-bar trading ranges and therefore usually terrible signal bars. You will usually lose if you buy above a trading range or sell below one.

56. Most countertrend setups fail, and most with-trend setups succeed. Do the math and decide which you should be trading. Trends constantly form great-looking countertrend setups and lousy-looking with-trend setups. If you trade countertrend, you are gambling and, although you will often win and have fun, the math is against you and you will slowly but surely go broke. Countertrend setups in strong trends almost always fail and become great with-trend setups, especially on the 1 minute chart.

57. You will not make consistent money until you stop trading countertrend scalps. You will win often enough to keep you trying to improve your technique, but over time your account will slowly disappear. Remember, your risk will likely have to be as large as your profit target, so it will usually take six winners just to get back to breakeven after four losses, and this is a very depressing prospect. Realistically, you should scalp only if you can win 60 percent of the time, and most traders should avoid any trade where the potential reward is not at least as large as the risk. Beginners should scalp only with the trend, if at all.

58. Until you are consistently profitable, take only trades where your potential re-ward is at least as large as your risk. If you need to risk two points in the Emini, do not take your profit until you have at least two points. Most traders should not scalp for a reward that is smaller than the risk, because they will lose money even if they win on 60 percent of their trades. Remember the trader's equa-tion. The chance of winning times your potential reward has to be significantly greater than the chance of losing times your risk. You cannot risk two points to make one point and hope to make a profit unless you are right at least 80 percent of the time, and very few traders are that good.

59. The trader's equation has three variables, and any setup with a positive result is a good trade. This can be a trade with a high probability of success and a reward only equal to the risk, one with a low probability of success and a huge reward relative to risk, or anything in between.

60. Experienced traders can scale into (or out of) trades to improve their trader's equation. For example, the initial entry might have a relatively low probability of success, but subsequent entries might have significantly higher probabilities, improving the trader's equation for the entire position.

61. You will not make money until you start trading with-trend pullbacks.

62. You will not make money trading reversals until you wait for a break of a significant trend line and then for a strong reversal bar on a test of the trend's extreme.

63. You will not make money unless you know what you are doing. Print out the 5 minute Emini chart every day (and stock charts, if you trade stocks) and write on the chart every setup that you see. When you see several price action features, write them all on the chart. Do this every day for years until you can look at any part of any chart and instantly understand what is happening.

64. You will not make money in the long term until you know enough about your personality to find a trading style that is compatible. You need to be able to follow your rules comfortably, allowing you to enter and exit trades with minimal or no uncertainty or anxiety. Once you have mastered a method of trading, if you feel stress while trading, then you haven't yet found either your style or yourself.

65. You will not make money if you lose your discipline and take risky trades in the final couple of hours that you would never take in the first couple of hours. You will invariably give back those earnings from earlier in the day that fooled you into thinking that you are a better trader than you really are.

66. You are competing against computers. They have the edge of speed, so it is usually best not to trade during a report, because that is when their speed edge is greatest. They also have the edge of not being emotional, so don't trade when you are upset or distracted. Third, they have the edge of never getting tired, so don't trade when you are worn out, which often happens at the end of the day.

67. Always look for two legs. Also, when the market tries to do something twice and fails both times, that is a reliable signal that it will likely succeed in doing the opposite.

68. Never cherry-pick, because you will invariably pick enough rotten cherries to end up a loser. The good trades catch you by surprise and are easy to miss, and you are then left with the not-so-good trades and the bad trades. Either swing trade and look to take only the best two or three of the best setups of the day or scalp and take every valid setup. The latter, however, is the more difficult alternative and is only for people with very unusual personalities (even more unusual than the rest of us traders!).

69. Finding winners is easy, but avoiding losers is hard. The key to success is avoiding the losers. There can be far more winners each day than losers, but a few losers can ruin your day, so learn to spot them in advance and avoid them. Most occur: in the middle of the range with weak setup bars, like small dojis with closes in the middle; when you are entering a possible reversal too early (remember, when in doubt, wait for the second entry); when you are in denial of a trend and think that it has gone too far so you start taking 1 or 3 minute reversal entries, which turn into great with-trend setups when they fail (as they invariably will); or, when a very credible, well-credentialed technical analyst from a top firm proclaims on TV that the bottom is in, and you then only see buy setups, which invariably fail because the expert in fact is an idiot who cannot trade (if he could, he would be trading and not proclaiming).

70. If you are in a trade and it is not doing what you expected, should you get out? Look at the market and pretend that you are flat. If you think that you would put that trade on at this moment, stay in your position. If not, get out.

71. Do not scalp when you should swing, and do not swing when you should scalp. Until you are consistently profitable, you should keep your trading as simple as possible and swing just one to three trades a day, and do not scalp. To scalp successfully, you usually have to risk about as much as you stand to gain, and that requires that you win on more than 60 percent of your trades. You cannot hope to do that until you are a consistently profitable trader.

72. If you find that you frequently take swing trades, but quickly convert them to scalps, you will probably lose money. When you take a swing trade, you are willing to accept a lower probability of success, but to make money on a scalp, you need a very high probability of success. Similarly, if you take scalps, but consistently exit early with a profit that is smaller than your risk, you will lose money. If you cannot stop yourself from following your plan, simply rely on your bracket orders and walk away for about an hour after you enter.

73. If you lost money last month, do not trade any reversals. If seven of the past 10 bars are mostly above the moving average, do not look to short. Instead, only look to buy. If seven of the past 10 bars are mostly below the moving average, do not look to buy. Instead, only look to short.

74. Beginners should take only the best trades. It is difficult to watch a screen for two or three hours at a time and not place a trade, but this is the best way for beginners to make money.

75. Discipline is the most important characteristic of winning traders. Trading is easy to understand, but difficult to do. It is very difficult to follow simple rules, and even occasional self-indulgences can mean the difference between success and failure. Anyone can be as mentally tough as Tiger Woods for one shot, but

few can be that tough for an entire round, and then be that way for a round every day of their lives. Everyone knows what mental toughness and discipline are and can be mentally tough and disciplined in some activities every day, but few truly appreciate just how extreme and unrelenting you have to be to be a great trader. Develop the discipline to take only the best trades. If you cannot do it for an entire day, force yourself to do it for the first hour of every day, and as you increase your position size, you might find that this is all you need to be a successful trader.

76. The second most important trait of great traders is the ability to do nothing for hours at a time. Don't succumb to boredom and let it convince you that it's been too long since the last trade.

77. Work on increasing your position size rather than on the number of trades or the variety of setups that you use. You only need to make two points in the Eminis a day to do well (50 contracts at two points a day is seven figures a year).

78. If you perfect the skills of trading, you can make more money than you could ever have imagined possible, and you will have the ability to live your dreams.

About the Author

Al Brooks is a technical analysis contributor to *Futures* magazine and an independent day trader. Called the trader's trader, he has a devoted following, and provides live market commentary and daily chart analysis updates on his website at www.brookspriceaction.com. After changing careers from ophthalmology to trading 25 years ago, he discovered consistent trading success once he developed his unique approach to reading price charts bar by bar. He graduated from the University of Chicago Pritzker School of Medicine and received his BS in mathematics from Trinity College.

About the Website

This book includes a companion website, which can be found at:

www.wiley.com/go/tradingreversals

All of the charts provided in the book are included on the website for your convenience. The password to enter this site is: Brooks3.

Index